Lecture Notes in Computer Science 3779

Commenced Publication in 1973
Founding and Former Series Editors:
Gerhard Goos, Juris Hartmanis, and Jan van Leeuwen

Hai Jin   Daniel Reed   Wenbin Jiang (Eds.)

Network and Parallel Computing

IFIP International Conference, NPC 2005
Beijing, China, November 30 - December 3, 2005
Proceedings

 Springer

Volume Editors

Hai Jin
Huazhong University of Science and Technology
Cluster and Grid Computing Lab
Wuhan 430074, P.R. China
E-mail: hjin@hust.edu.cn

Daniel Reed
University of North Carolina at Chapel Hill
Institute for Renaissance Computing
CB 3175, Sitterson Hall, Chapel Hill, NC 27599-3175, USA
E-mail: dan_reed@unc.edu

Wenbin Jiang
Huazhong University of Science and Technology
Cluster and Grid Computing Lab
Wuhan 430074, P.R. China
E-mail: wenbinjiang@hust.edu.cn

Library of Congress Control Number: 2005935533

CR Subject Classification (1998): C.2, F.2, D.2, H.4, H.5, D.4, K.6

ISSN   0302-9743
ISBN-10   3-540-29810-X Springer Berlin Heidelberg New York
ISBN-13   978-3-540-29810-6 Springer Berlin Heidelberg New York

Springer is a part of Springer Science+Business Media

springeronline.com

© IFIP International Federation for Information Processing 2005
Printed in Germany

Typesetting: Camera-ready by author, data conversion by Scientific Publishing Services, Chennai, India
Printed on acid-free paper   SPIN: 11577188   06/3142   5 4 3 2 1 0

Preface

These proceedings contain the papers presented at the 2005 IFIP International Conference on Network and Parallel Computing (NPC 2005), held in Beijing, China, between November 30 and December 3, 2005. The goal of the conference was to establish an international forum for engineers and scientists to present their ideas and experiences in network and parallel computing.

A total of 320 submissions were received in response to our Call for Papers. These papers were from the following countries or regions: Australia, Canada, China, France, Germany, Hong Kong, India, Iran, Italy, Japan, Korea, Luxemburg, Nepal, Netherlands, Taiwan, United Arab Emirates, and United States. Each submission was sent to at least three reviewers. Each paper was judged according to its originality, innovation, readability, and relevance to the expected audience. Based on the reviews received, a total of 68 papers were retained for inclusion in the proceedings. Among the 68 papers, 48 were accepted as full papers for presentation at the conference. We also accepted 20 papers as short papers for a possible brief presentation at the conference, followed by discussion during a poster session. Thus, only 21% of the total submissions could be included in the final program.

The IFIP NPC conference emerged from initial email exchanges between Kemal Ebcioğlu, Guojie Li, and Guang R. Gao in the year 2002, with a vision toward establishing a new, truly international conference for fostering research and collaboration in parallel computing. We are happy to see that the NPC conference, with its eminent team of organizers, and its high-quality technical program, is well on its way to becoming a flagship conference of IFIP.

We wish to thank the contributions of the other members of the Organizing Committee. We thank the Publicity Chair, Cho-Li Wang, for his hard work to publicize NPC 2005 under a very tight schedule.

We are deeply grateful to the Program Committee members. The large number of submissions received and the diversified topics made this review process a particularly challenging one.

July 2005   Hai Jin
                                                                        Daniel Reed

Conference Committees

General Co-chairs

Jean-Luc Gaudiot (University of California, Irvine, USA)
Lionel Ni (Hong Kong University of Science and Technology, Hong Kong, China)

Steering Committee Chair

Kemal Ebcioğlu (IBM T.J. Watson Research Center, USA)

Program Co-chairs

Daniel Reed (University of North Carolina, USA)
Hai Jin (Huazhong University of Science and Technology, China)

Steering Committee Members

Jack Dongarra (University of Tennessee, USA)
Guangrong Gao (University of Delaware, USA)
Jean-Luc Gaudiot (University of California, Irvine, USA)
Guojie Li (Institute of Computing Technology, CAS, China)
Yoichi Muraoka (Waseda University, Japan)
Daniel Reed (University of North Carolina, USA)

Program Committee Members

Ishfaq Ahmad (University of Texas at Arlington, USA)
Makoto Amamiya (Kyushu University, Japan)
David A. Bader (Georgia Institute of Technology, USA)
Luc Bouge (IRISA/ENS Cachan, France)
Pascal Bouvry (University of Luxembourg, Luxembourg)
Wentong Cai (Nanyang Technological University, Singapore)
Jiannong Cao (Hong Kong Polytechnic University, Hong Kong, China)
Xueqi Cheng (Institute of Computing Technology, CAS, China)
Jong-Deok Choi (IBM T. J. Watson Research Center, USA)
Toni Cortes (Universitat Politècnica de Catalunya, Spain)
Chen Ding (University of Rochester, USA)
Jianping Fan (Institute of Computing Technology, CAS, China)
Xiaobing Feng (Institute of Computing Technology, CAS, China)
Guangrong Gao (University of Delaware, USA)

Minyi Guo (University of Aizu, Japan)
Yanbo Han (Institute of Computing Technology, CAS, China)
Anura Jayasumana (Colorado State Univeristy, USA)
Chris R. Jesshope (Universiteit van Amsterdam, Netherlands)
Jin Suk Kim (University of Seoul, Korea)
Chung-Ta King (National Tsing Hua University, Taiwan, China)
Ricky Kwok (The University of Hong Kong, Hong Kong)
Kuan-Ching Li (Providence University, Taiwan, China)
Chuang Lin (Tsinghua University, China)
Geyong Min (University of Bradford, UK)
Soo-Mook Moon (Seoul National University, Korea)
John Morrison (University College Cork, Ireland)
Yi Pan (Georgia State University, USA)
Wolfgang Rehm (Chemnitz University of Technology , Germany)
Sartaj Sahni (University of Florida, USA)
Simon See (Sun Microsystems Inc., USA)
Selvakennedy Selvadurai (University of Sydney, Australia)
Franciszek Seredynski (Polish Academy of Sciences, Poland)
Hong Shen (Japan Advanced Institute of Science and Technology, Japan)
Xiaowei Shen (IBM T. J. Watson Research Center, USA)
Ninghui Sun (Institute of Computing Technology, CAS, China)
El-Ghazali Talbi (University of Lille, France)
Domenico Talia (University of Calabria, Italy)
David Taniar (Monash University, Australia)
Mitchell D. Theys (University of Illinois at Chicago, USA)
Cho-Li Wang (The University of Hong Kong, Hong Kong)
Weng-Fai Wong (National University of Singapore, Singapore)
Chao-Tung Yang (Tunghai University, Taiwan, China)
Laurence T. Yang (St. Francis Xavier University, Canada)
Qing Yang (University of Rhode Island, USA)
Lixin Zhang (IBM Austin Research Laboratory, USA)
Xiaodong Zhang (The College of William and Mary, USA)
Weimin Zheng (Tsinghua University, China)

Publicity Chair

Cho-Li Wang (The University of Hong Kong, Hong Kong, China)

Publication Chair

Wenbin Jiang (Huazhong University of Science and Technology, China)

Local Arrangements Chair

Wen Gao (Institute of Computing Technology, CAS, China)

Table of Contents

Special Session on Grid and System Software

Session 1: Grid Computing

Session 2: Peer-to-Peer Computing

Session 3: Web Techniques

Session 4: Cluster Computing

Session 5: Parallel Programming and Environment

Session 6: Network Architecture

Session 7: Network Security

Session 8: Network Storage

Session 9: Multimedia Service

Session 10: Ubiquitous Computing

TeraGrid: A Foundation for US Cyberinfrastructure

Charles E. Catlett

Senior Fellow, Computation Institute of Argonne
National Laboratory and University of Chicago
cec@uchicago.edu

Abstract. TeraGrid is a collaboration of partners providing a high-performance, nationally distributed capability infrastructure for computational science. The TeraGrid team has utilized multiple surveys of user requirements to develop five-year roadmaps describing new capabilities and services, organized into several new initiatives: *Deep*, *Wide*, and *Open*. TeraGrid is managed by the University of Chicago and includes resources at eight partner sites (Argonne National Laboratory, Indiana University, National Center for Supercomputing Applications, Oak Ridge National Laboratory, Pittsburgh Supercomputing Center, Purdue University, San Diego Supercomputer Center, and Texas Advanced Computing Center).

TeraGrid *Deep* aims to assist scientists with applications that require the combination of multiple leadership class systems- including TeraGrid storage, computing, instruments, visualization, etc. – working in concert. A team of roughly 15 staff is providing hands-on assistance to application teams pursuing TeraGrid Deep projects.

TeraGrid *Wide* is a set of partnerships with peer Grid projects and prototype "science gateways" that are aimed at making TeraGrid resources available to, and tailored to, entire communities of users. Science gateways are driving policy, process, and technology standards to enable web portals, desktop applications, campus clusters, and other grid infrastructure projects to seamlessly use TeraGrid resources. Initial TeraGrid science gateway projects include community portals and desktop tools supporting life sciences and biomedicine, high-energy physics, neutron science, astronomy, nanotechnology, atmospheric and climate sciences, and environmental and emergency decision-support.

TeraGrid *Open* involves the rapid evolution of the TeraGrid software and services toward interoperability with peer Grids and campus resources. Currently TeraGrid is partnering with the Open Science Grid as well as partners in Europe (e.g. UK eScience, DEISA) and Asia-Pacific (e.g. Naregi, K*Grid).

H. Jin, D. Reed, and W. Jiang (Eds.): NPC 2005, LNCS 3779, p. 1, 2005.
© IFIP International Federation for Information Processing 2005

Globus Toolkit Version 4:
Software for Service-Oriented Systems

Ian Foster

Math & Computer Science Division, Argonne
National Lab, Argonne, IL 60439, U.S.A.
Department of Computer Science, University of Chicago, Chicago, IL 60637, U.S.A.

Abstract. The Globus Toolkit (GT) has been developed since the late 1990s to support the development of service-oriented distributed computing applications and infrastructures. Core GT components address, within a common framework, basic issues relating to security, resource access, resource management, data movement, resource discovery, and so forth. These components enable a broader "Globus ecosystem" of tools and components that build on, or interoperate with, core GT functionality to provide a wide range of useful application-level functions. These tools have in turn been used to develop a wide range of both "Grid" infrastructures and distributed applications. I summarize here the principal characteristics of the latest release, the Web services-based GT4, which provides significant improvements over previous releases in terms of robustness, performance, usability, documentation, standards compliance, and functionality.

1 Introduction

Globus is:

- A *community* of users and developers who collaborate on the use and development of open source software, and associated documentation, for distributed computing and resource federation.
- The *software* itself—the **Globus Toolkit**: a set of libraries and programs that address common problems that occur when building distributed system services and applications.
- The *infrastructure* that supports this community—code repositories, email lists, problem tracking system, and so forth: all accessible at **globus.org**.

The **software** itself provides a variety of components and capabilities, including the following:

- A set of *service implementations* focused on infrastructure management.
- Tools for building *new Web services*, in Java, C, and Python.
- A powerful standards-based *security infrastructure*.
- Both *client APIs* (in different languages) and *command line programs* for accessing these various services and capabilities.

H. Jin, D. Reed, and W. Jiang (Eds.): NPC 2005, LNCS 3779, pp. 2–13, 2005.

– Detailed *documentation* on these various components, their interfaces, and how they can be used to build applications.

These components in turn enable a rich **ecosystem** of components and tools that build on, or interoperate with, GT components—and a wide variety of **applications** in many domains. From our experiences and the experiences of others in developing and using these tools and applications, we identify commonly used design patterns or **solutions**, knowledge of which can facilitate the construction of new applications.

In this article, I review briefly the current status of Globus, focusing in particular on those aspects of the GT4 release that should be of interest to those wishing to work with the software. I provide references to research articles for those desiring more details on the underlying concepts and mechanisms.

2 Motivation and Concepts

Globus software is designed to enable applications that federate distributed resources, whether computers, storage, data, services, networks, or sensors. Initially, work on Globus was motivated by the demands of "virtual organizations" in science. More recently, commercial applications have become increasingly important. Commerce and science often, but not always, have similar concerns.

Federation is typically motivated by a need to access resources or services that cannot easily be replicated locally. For example:

– A scientist (or business analyst) needs to access data located in different databases across a scientific collaboration (or enterprise).
– A business (or physics community) needs to allocate computing, storage, and network resources dynamically to support a time-varying e-commerce (or physics data analysis) workload.
– An engineer needs to design and operate experiments on remote equipment, linking and comparing numerical and physical simulations.
– An astronomy experiment needs to replicate a terabyte of data a day to partner sites around the world.

We find that while every application has unique requirements, a small set of functions frequently recur: for example, we often need to discover available resources, configure a computing resource to run an application, move data reliably from one site to another, monitor system components, control who can do what, and manage user credentials. Good-quality implementations of these functions can reduce development costs. Furthermore, if these implementations are widely adopted and/or implement standards, they can enhance interoperability. Globus software addresses both goals, using an open source model to encourage both contributions and adoption.

GT4 makes extensive use of *Web services mechanisms* to define its interfaces and structure its components. Web services provide flexible, extensible, and widely adopted XML-based mechanisms for describing, discovering, and invoking network services; in addition, its document-oriented protocols are well suited to the loosely coupled interactions that many argue are preferable for robust distributed systems. These mechanisms facilitate the development of service-oriented architectures—

systems and applications structured as communicating services, in which service interfaces are described, operations invoked, access secured, etc., all in uniform ways.

While end-user *applications* are typically concerned with domain-specific operations such as pricing a portfolio or analyzing a gene sequence, computing ultimately requires the manipulation and management of *infrastructure*: physical devices such as computers, storage systems, and instrumentation. Thus, GT4 provides a set of *Grid infrastructure services* [12] that implement interfaces for managing computational, storage, and other resources. In many Globus deployments (e.g., TeraGrid, Open Science Grid, LHC Computing Grid, China Grid, APgrid), these services are deployed to support a range of different application communities, each of which then executes their own application-specific code that relies on those services.

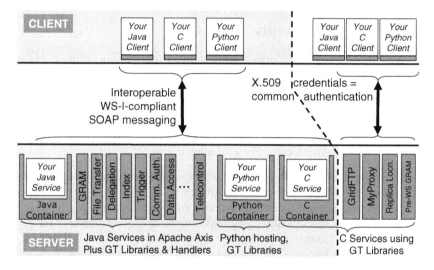

Fig. 1. GT4 architecture schematic, showing many (but not all) components. Shared boxes denote GT4 code; white boxes represent user code.

3 Globus Architecture

Figure 1 illustrates various aspects of GT4 architecture. I note first of all the following three sets of components:

- A set of *service implementations* (the bottom half of the figure) implement useful infrastructure services. These services address such concerns as execution management (GRAM), data access and movement (GridFTP [2], RFT, OGSA-DAI [4]), replica management (RLS [6], DRS), monitoring and discovery (Index, Trigger, WebMDS), credential management (MyProxy [16], Delegation, SimpleCA), and instrument management (GTCP). Most are Java Web services but some (bottom right) are implemented in other languages and use other protocols.
- Three *containers* can be used to host user-developed services written in Java, Python, and C, respectively. These containers provide implementations of security,

management, discovery, state management, and other mechanisms frequently required when building services. They extend open source service hosting environments with support for a range of useful Web service (WS) specifications, including WS Resource Framework (WSRF), WS-Notification, and WS-Security.

– A set of *client libraries* allow client programs in Java, C, and Python to invoke operations on both GT4 and user-developed services. In many cases, multiple interfaces provide different levels of control: for example, in the case of GridFTP, there is not only a simple command-line client (globus-url-copy) but also control and data channel libraries for use in programs—and the XIO library allowing for the integration of alternative transports.

It is important to note that GT4 is more than just a set of useful services. The use of uniform abstractions and mechanisms means that clients can interact with different services in similar ways, which facilitates the construction of complex, interoperable systems and encourages code reuse. This uniformity occurs at several levels:

– WS-I-compliant *SOAP messaging* among Web services and their clients.
– A common *security and messaging infrastructure* enables interoperability among different applications and services.
– A powerful and extensible *authorization framework* supports a range of different authorization mechanisms.
– The fact that all containers and most services implement common mechanisms for state representation, access, and subscription facilitates *discovery and monitoring*.

4   Globus Software Details: How Do I ...?

Figure 2 provides another perspective on GT4 structure, showing the major components provided for basic runtime (on the right) and then (from left to right) security, execution management, data management, and information services. I introduce these components by showing how they are used to perform various tasks.

4.1   How Do I Manage Execution?

Let's say we want to run a task on a computer, or deploy and manage a service that provides some capability to a community. In both cases, we need to acquire access to a computer, configure that computer to meet our needs, stage an executable, initiate execution of a program, and monitor and manage the resulting computation.

The GT4 Grid Resource Allocation and Management (**GRAM**) service addresses these issues, providing a Web services interface for initiating, monitoring, and managing the execution of arbitrary computations on remote computers. Its interface allows a client to express such things as the type and quantity of resources desired, data to be staged to and from the execution site, the executable and its arguments, credentials to be used, and job persistence requirements. Other operations enable clients to monitor the status of both the computational resource and individual tasks, to subscribe to notifications concerning their status, and control a task's execution.

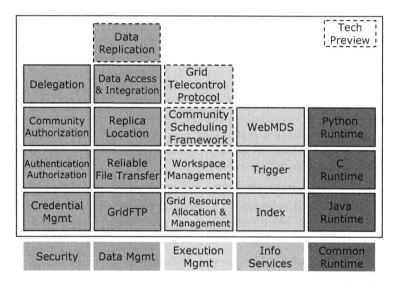

Fig. 2. Primary GT4 components (dashed lines represent "tech previews")

A GRAM service can be used for many different purposes. The following are some examples:

- The GriPhyN Virtual Data System (VDS), Ninf-G, and Nimrod-G are all tools that use GRAM interfaces to dispatch (potentially large numbers of) individual tasks to computational clusters. For example, Rodriguez et al.'s GADU service [17] routinely uses VDS to dispatch several million BLAST and BLOCKS runs as it updates its proteomics knowledge base.
- Various applications use GRAM as a service deployment and management service, using a GRAM request first to start the service and then to control its resource consumption and provide for restart in the event of resource or service failure.
- The MPICH-G2 implementation [15] of the Message Passing Interface uses GRAM to coschedule subtasks across multiple computers. Dong et al. [8] have used MPICH-G2 to conduct a complete simulation of the human arterial tree.

The following execution management components are also provided within GT4 as "tech previews," meaning that they are less thoroughly tested than other components and more likely to change in the future:

- A Workspace Management Service (**WMS**) provides for the dynamic allocation of Unix accounts as a simple form of sandbox. (A variant of this service that provides for the dynamic allocation of virtual machines exists in prototype form.)
- The Grid TeleControl Protocol (**GTCP**) service is for managing instrumentation; it has been used for earthquake engineering facilities and microscopes.

4.2 How Do I Access and Move Data?

Globus applications often need to manage, provide access to, and/or integrate large quantities of data at one or many sites. This "data" problem is broad and complex, and no single piece of software can "solve" it in any comprehensive sense. However, several GT4 components implement useful mechanisms that can be used individually and in conjunction with other components to develop interesting solutions. (A recent article [3] reports on these tools and on various success stories.)

- The Globus implementation of the **GridFTP** specification provides libraries and tools for reliable, secure, high-performance memory-to-memory and disk-to-disk data movement. It has achieved 27 Gbit/s end-to-end over wide area networks, and can interoperate with conventional FTP clients and servers. GridFTP provides the substrate on which are built a wide variety of higher-level tools and applications.
- The Reliable File Transfer (**RFT**) service provides for the reliable management of multiple GridFTP transfers. It has been used, for example, to orchestrate the transfer of one million files from one astronomy archive to another.
- The Replica Location Service (**RLS**) is a scalable system for maintaining and providing access to information about the location of replicated files and datasets. The LIGO experiment uses it to manage more than 40 million file replicas.
- The Data Replication Service (**DRS**: a tech preview) combines RLS and GridFTP to provide for the management of data replication.
- The Globus Data Access and Integration (**OGSA-DAI**) tools developed by the UK eScience program provides access to relational and XML data.

4.3 How Do I Monitor and Discover Services and Resources?

Monitoring and discovery are two vital functions in a distributed system, particularly when that system spans multiple locations, as in that context no one person is likely to have detailed knowledge of all components. Monitoring allows us to detect and diagnose the many problems that can arise in such contexts, while discovery allows us to identify resources or services with desired properties. Both tasks require the ability to collect information from multiple, perhaps distributed, information sources.

In recognition of the importance of these functions, monitoring and discovery mechanisms are built in to GT4 at a fundamental level, as follows (see Figure 3).

- GT4 provides standardized mechanisms for associating XML-based *resource properties* with network entities and for accessing those properties via either pull (query) or push (subscription). These mechanisms—basically implementations of the WSRF and WS-Notification specifications—are built into every GT4 service and container, and can also be incorporated easily into any user-developed service. Services can be configure to register with their container, and containers with other containers, thus enabling the creation of hierarchical (or other) organizations.
- GT4 provides two *aggregator services* that collect recent state information from registered information sources. As not all information sources support WSRF/WS-notification interfaces, these aggregators can be configured to collect data from any information source, whether XML-based or otherwise. The two aggregators implement a registry (**Index**) and event-driven data filter (**Trigger**), respectively.
- GT4 provides a range of browser-based interfaces, command line tools, and Web service interfaces that allow users to query and access the collected information. In particular, the **WebMDS** service can be configured via XSLT transformations to create specialized views of Index data.

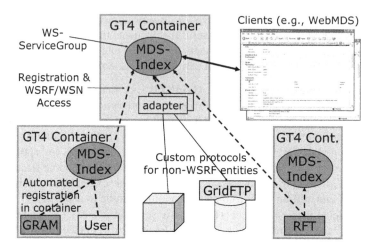

Fig. 3. GT4 monitoring and discovery infrastructure

These different mechanisms provide a powerful framework for monitoring diverse collections of distributed components and for obtaining information about components for purposes of discovery. For example, the Earth System Grid (ESG) [5] uses these mechanisms to monitor the status of the various services that it uses to distribute and provide access to more than 100 TB of climate model data.

4.4   How Do I Control Who Can Do What?

Security concerns are particularly important and challenging when resources and/or users span multiple locations. A range of players may want to exert control over who can do what, including the owners of individual resources, the users who initiate computations, and the "virtual organizations" established to manage resource sharing. "Exerting control" may include variously enforcing policy and auditing behavior. When designing mechanisms to address these requirements, we must work not only to protect communications but also to limit the impact of breakins at end systems. A complete security "solution" must always be a system that combines components concerned with establishing identity, applying policy, tracking actions, etc., to meet specific security goals. GT4 and related tools provide powerful building blocks that can be used to construct a range of such systems.

At the lowest level, GT4's highly standards-based security components implement credential formats and protocols that address message protection, authentication, delegation, and authorization. As shown in Figure 4, support is provided for (a) WS-Security-compliant message-level security with X.509 credentials (slow) and (b) with usernames/passwords (insecure, but WS-I Base Security Profile compliant) and for (c) transport-level security with X.509 credentials (fast and thus the default).

In GT4's default configuration, each user and resource is assumed to have a X.509 public key credential. Protocols are implemented that allow two entities to validate each other's credentials, to use those credentials to establish a secure channel for

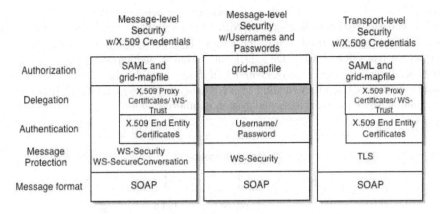

	Message-level Security w/X.509 Credentials	Message-level Security w/Usernames and Passwords	Transport-level Security w/X.509 Credentials
Authorization	SAML and grid-mapfile	grid-mapfile	SAML and grid-mapfile
Delegation	X.509 Proxy Certificates/ WS-Trust		X.509 Proxy Certificates/ WS-Trust
Authentication	X.509 End Entity Certificates	Username/ Password	X.509 End Entity Certificates
Message Protection	WS-Security WS-SecureConversation	WS-Security	TLS
Message format	SOAP	SOAP	SOAP

Fig. 4. GT4 security protocols (see text for details). From [19].

purposes of message protection, and to create and transport delegated credentials that allow a remote component to act on a user's behalf for a limited period of time.

Authorization call outs associated with GT4 services can be used to determine whether specific requests should be allowed. In particular, the *authorization framework* component allows chains of authorization modules with well-defined interfaces to be associated with various entities, e.g. services, in the container. It also provides multiple different authorization module implementations, ranging from traditional Globus gridmap-based authorization to a module that uses the SAML protocol to query an external service for an authorization decision.

Supporting tools, some in GT4 and some available from other sources, support the generation, storage, and retrieval of the credentials that GT4 uses for authentication, and address related issues concerning group membership, authorization policy enforcement, and the like. These tools can be configured so that users need never manage their own X.509 credentials.

4.5 How Do I Build New Services?

A wide range of enabling software is included in GT4 to support the development of components that implement Web services interfaces. This software deals with such issues as message handling, resource management, and security, thus allowing the developer to focus their attention on implementing application logic. GT4 also packages additional GT4-specific components to provide *GT4 Web services containers* for deploying and managing services written in Java, C, and Python. As illustrated in Figure 5, these containers can host a variety of different services:

- Implementations of basic WS specifications such as *WSDL, SOAP, and WS-Security* support services that make use of these specifications to implement basic Web services functionality.
- Implementations of other specifications, notably *WS-Addressing, WSRF, and WS-Notification*, support services that want to expose and manage state associated with services, back-end resources, or application activities [11]. (For example, GT4

GRAM and RFT services use these mechanisms to manage state associated with tens of thousands of computational activities and file transfers, respectively.)

- The Java container is used to host the various *GT4 Java Web services* mentioned earlier, such as GRAM, RFT, DRS, Delegation, Index, and Trigger.
- Enhanced *registry and management capabilities*, notably the representation of information about services running in a container as WS-Resources, facilitate the creation of distributed registries and system monitoring tools.

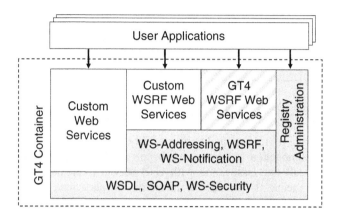

Fig. 5. Capabilities of a GT4 container

In general, the Java container provides the most advanced programming environment, the C container the highest performance [14], and (Python enthusiasts would argue) the Python container the nicest language. If developing new services in Java using GT4, see the tutorial text [18] and its accompanying Web site.

Numerous projects are developing exciting services and applications based on GT4 containers. For example, the Belfast eScience Center has 1.5 million lines of GT4 Java code (converted from GT3, a process that required "relatively few changes in service code" [13]), implementing a range of applications including a digital video management system for the BBC, and the China Grid Support Package provides a rich set of services for eScience and education built on the GT4 Java container.

4.6 How Do I Do More Complicated Things?

GT4 services and libraries do not provide complete solutions to many distributed computing problems: to do anything more complex than submit a job or move a file, you must use GT4 software in conjunction with other tools and/or your own code—or access a (GT-based) service that provides the capabilities that you require [10].

In analyzing how people use Globus software, we find that the same patterns tend to reoccur across different projects and application domains. Thus, we have launched an effort to document these **solutions** [1] and how they can be implemented using components of the Globus ecosystem.

5 Processes, Results, and Evaluation

The Globus Alliance's **software engineering processes** have improved steadily over the past five years. These improvements have been made possible by both increased software engineering resources (i.e., dedicated engineers) and more aggressive users available for further testing. These processes now include:

– Extensive *unit test suites* and the use of *test coverage tools* to evaluate coverage.
– Frequent *automated execution of build and test suites* on more than 20 platforms, via both local systems and the NMI GRIDS Center's distributed build/test facility.
– Extensive *performance test suites* used to evaluate various aspects of component performance, including latency, throughput, scalability, and reliability.
– A cross-GT *documentation plan,* managed by a dedicated documentation specialist, to ensure complete coverage and uniform style for all components.
– A well-defined *community testing process,* which in the case of GT4 included a six-month alpha and beta-testing program with close to 200 participants.
– An *issue tracking system* based on bugzilla, used to track both error reports and feature requests, and the work associated with those issues.

GT4 **performance** is summarized in a recent report [9]. This report also provides pointers to more detailed documentation, including reports on the performance of different Web services containers, including GT4's Java, C, and Python [14]; the GT4 implementation of GridFTP [2]; and the GT4 replica location service [7].

The UK eScience program has released an **external evaluation** of GT4 [13]. This detailed report speaks favorably of the overall quality, usability, and performance of the GT4 code and its documentation. It notes, for example, that "GT4 installation was straightforward," "GT4 services demonstrated significant improvements in performance and reliability over their GT3 versions," and "GT4 package descriptions were of a high quality, well structured, and accurate."

6 Contributing

A large and diverse Globus community is working hard to improve the scope and quality of the Globus software. I hope that you, the reader, will feel inspired to contribute also. There are several ways in which you can do so.

Use the software and report your experiences. Simply using the software and reporting back on your experiences, positive or negative, can be immensely helpful. Reports of problems encountered, particularly when well documented, help guide bug fixes and/or prioritize work on new features. Reports of successful deployments and applications can help justify continued support for the development of the software.

Develop documentation and examples. Despite considerable progress, we remain in desperate need of code examples and associated documentation that can help other users to start work with Globus software or related tools. Take the time to document your successful application, and you will be repaid in gratitude from other users.

Contribute to the development of the software. The list of new features wanted by users is always far greater than Globus developers can handle. You can contribute bug fixes, test cases, new modules, or even entirely new components.

7 Futures

We are entering an exciting time for Globus, due to the confluence of the following factors:

- The completion of GT4 means that Globus now has a solid Web services base on which to build additional services and capabilities.
- Sustained funding for eScience support will allow us to accelerate efforts aimed at meeting demands for ever-greater scalability, functionality, usability, and so forth.
- The creation of organizations dedicated to the support needs of industry means that commercial adoption (and contributions) will accelerate.
- A rapidly growing user community is increasing the quantity and quality of user feedback, code contributions, and components within the larger Globus ecosystem.
- Revisions to the Globus infrastructure and governance processes will make it easier for us to engage additional contributors to the software and documentation.

Acknowledgements

I report here on the work of many talented colleagues and collaborators (see www.globus.org). The core team is based primarily at Argonne National Lab, U. Chicago, the USC Information Sciences Institute, U. Edinburgh, the Royal Institute of Technology, the National Center for Supercomputing Applications, and Univa Corporation. Many others in both academia and industry have contributed to code, documentation, and testing, or made our work worthwhile by using the code.

Work on Globus has been supported in part by the Mathematical, Information, and Computational Sciences Division subprogram of the Office of Advanced Scientific Computing Research, U.S. Department of Energy, under Contract W-31-109-Eng-38, by the National Science Foundation (NSF) under its NSF Middleware Initiative and other programs, and by IBM, DARPA, NASA, Microsoft, the UK Engineering and Physical Sciences Research Council and Department of Trade and Industry, and the Swedish Research Council.

Foster is also co-founder and Chief Open Source Strategist at Univa Corporation.

References

1. Grid Solutions, 2005. www.globus.org/solutions.
2. Allcock, B., Bresnahan, J., Kettimuthu, R., Link, M., Dumitrescu, C., Raicu, I. and Foster, I., The Globus Striped GridFTP Framework and Server. *SC'2005*, 2005.
3. Allcock, W., Chervenak, A., Foster, I., Kesselman, C. and Livny, M., Data Grid Tools: Enabling Science on Big Distributed Data. *SciDAC Conference*, 2005.
4. Atkinson, M., Chervenak, A., Kunszt, P., Narang, I., Paton, N., Pearson, D., Shoshani, A. and Watson, P. Data Access, Integration, and Management. *The Grid: Blueprint for a New Computing Infrastructure*, Morgan Kaufmann, 2004.
5. Bernholdt, D., Bharathi, S., Brown, D., Chanchio, K., Chen, M., Chervenak, A., Cinquini, L., Drach, B., Foster, I., Fox, P., Garcia, J., Kesselman, C., Markel, R., Middleton, D., Nefedova, V., Pouchard, L., Shoshani, A., Sim, A., Strand, G. and Williams, D. The Earth System Grid: Supporting the Next Generation of Climate Modeling Research. *Proceedings of the IEEE, 93* (3). 485-495. 2005.

6. Chervenak, A., Deelman, E., Foster, I., Guy, L., Hoschek, W., Iamnitchi, A., Kesselman, C., Kunst, P., Ripenu, M., Schwartzkopf, B., Stockinger, H., Stockinger, K. and Tierney, B., Giggle: A Framework for Constructing Scalable Replica Location Services. *SC'02: High Performance Networking and Computing*, 2002.

7. Chervenak, A.L., Palavalli, N., Bharathi, S., Kesselman, C. and Schwartzkopf, R., Performance and Scalability of a Replica Location Service. *IEEE International Symposium on High Performance Distributed Computing*, 2004.

8. Dong, S., G, K. and Karonis, N. Cross-site computations on the TeraGrid. *Computing in Science & Engineering, 7* (5). 14-23. 2005.

9. Foster, I. Performance of Globus Toolkit Version 4. Globus Alliance, 2005. www.globus.org/alliance/publications.

10. Foster, I. Service-Oriented Science. *Science, 308.* 814-817. 2005.

11. Foster, I., Czajkowski, K., Ferguson, D., Frey, J., Graham, S., Maguire, T., Snelling, D. and Tuecke, S. Modeling and Managing State in Distributed Systems: The Role of OGSI and WSRF. *Proceedings of the IEEE, 93* (3). 604-612. 2005.

12. Foster, I. and Tuecke, S. Describing the Elephant: The Different Faces of IT as Service. *ACM Queue, 3* (6). 2005.

13. Harmer, T., Stell, A. and McBride, D. UK Engineering Task Force Globus Toolkit Version 4 Middleware Evaluation, UK Technical Report UKeS_2005-03, 2005.

14. Humphrey, M., Wasson, G., Jackson, K., Boverhof, J., Meder, S., Gawor, J., Lang, S., Pickles, S., McKeown, M. and Foster, I. A Comparison of WSRF and WS-Notification Implementations: Globus Toolkit V4, pyGridWare, WSRF:Lite, and WSRF.NET. *14th International Symposium on High Performance Distributed Computing*. 2005.

15. Karonis, N., Toonen, B. and Foster, I. MPICH-G2: A Grid-Enabled Implementation of the Message Passing Interface. *Journal of Parallel and Distributed Computing, 63* (5). 551-563. 2003.

16. Novotny, J., Tuecke, S. and Welch, V., An Online Credential Repository for the Grid: MyProxy. *10th IEEE International Symposium on High Performance Distributed Computing*, San Francisco, 2001, IEEE Computer Society Press.

17. Rodriguez, A., Sulakhe, D., Marland, E., Nefedova, V., Maltsev, N., Wilde, M. and Foster, I., A Grid-Enabled Service for High-Throughput Genome Analysis. *Workshop on Case Studies on Grid Applications*, Berlin, Germany, 2004.

18. Sotomayor, B. and Childers, L. *Globus Toolkit 4: Programming Java Services*. Morgan Kaufmann, 2005.

19. Welch, V. Globus Toolkit Version 4 Grid Security Infrastructure: A Standards Perspective, 2004. http://www.globus.org/toolkit/docs/4.0/security/GT4-GSI-Overview.pdf.

System Software for China National Grid

Li Zha[1], Wei Li[1], Haiyan Yu[1], Xianghui Xie[2], Nong Xiao[3], and Zhiwei Xu[1]

[1] Institute of Computing Technology, Chinese Academy of Sciences,
100080 Beijing, China
[2] JiangNan Institute of Computing Technology
[3] National University of Defense Technology

Abstract. The China National Grid project developed and deployed a suite of grid system software called CNGrid Software. This paper presents the features and implementation of the software suite from the viewpoints of grid system deployment, grid application developers, grid resource providers, grid system administrators, and the end users.

1 Introduction

The China National Grid project is a 4-year (2002-2005) R&D project sponsored by China Ministry of Science and Technology. It aims to constructing a wide-area national grid [1] environment to enable resource sharing and collaboration over the Internet, using standards-based components and novel technology developed by this project. Another main goal is to build up human resources in grid computing.

By August 2005, the CNGrid project has built such an environment, consisting of eight grid nodes (computing and data centers) spanning six cities in China. The total computing capability exceeds 20 Tflop/s, provided by domestic HPC systems such as Dawning 4000A (10 Tflop/s) and Lenovo 6800 (5 Tflop/s), as well as HPC systems from multinational vendors. Eleven domain-specific application grids are also running, from fields of scientific research, natural resource and environment, manufacturing, and the service sector.

A key ingredient of CNGrid is the CNGrid Software suite. It connects all the users (end users, grid application developers, grid resource providers, grid administrators) and resources (computing, storage, data, and applications software resources) into a uniform, coherent CNGrid environment.

The CNGrid Software suite employs a service-oriented architecture. It consists of three loosely coupled subsystems: the Vega GOS (grid operating system), the GriShield grid security software, and the GridDaEn data grid software. The current hosting environment is mainly Apache Tomcat/Axis, while providing connections to services running on Microsoft Windows platform.

In what follows, we present the main features of the CNGrid Software suite, from the users' viewpoints. We focus on showing how the CNGrid Software suite supports a loosely coupled architecture and dynamic changing nature of grids, while providing single system image and managed services, in a wide-area distributed environment wherein resource providers desiring autonomous control.

H. Jin, D. Reed, and W. Jiang (Eds.): NPC 2005, LNCS 3779, pp. 14 – 21, 2005.

2   CNGrid Software from Five Viewpoints

This section presents the salient features of the CNGrid Software suite from the viewpoints of grid system deployment, grid resource providers, grid system administrators, grid application developers, and the end users. The CNGrid software suite is meant to provide a tool set for users to build application grid systems, according to the users' business model. Therefore, there could be many alternatives. We will focus on typical scenarios.

2.1 Deployment

Before the CNGrid Software is deployed, CNGrid is the sum of two types of isolated resources: grid nodes and application grids. Grid nodes are HPC centers (e.g., Shanghai Supercomputing Center) or campus grids (e.g., Tsinghua University campus grid). An application grid is usually a distributed enterprise application system, such as the Simulation Grid for aviation/space industry. An application grid could have multiple intra-enterprise grid nodes. Currently, CNGrid has eight grid nodes and eleven application grids.

After the CNGrid Software is deployed, these isolated physical resources can be connected into a virtualized, uniform and coherent national grid environment. The deployment process usually consists of the following activities: install the CNGrid Software on grid nodes (typically one copy per grid node), and configure the initial grid system to create needed grid communities (called *agoras*). The CNGrid Software deployment in CNGrid environment is show in Fig.1. The following is a typical configuration seen by users:

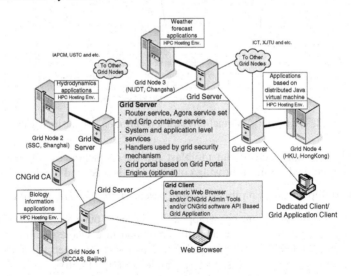

Fig. 1. National wide deployment of CNGrid software

- A single grid system called CNGrid, with its CA system.
- A CNGrid-wide virtual name space, implemented via a set of grid routers.
- One or more agoras. For instance, we could have an agora for each of the grid nodes and another "global" agora for CNGrid, giving nine agoras in total.

2.2 Resource Provider

The Effective-Virtual-Physical space model [2] (show in Fig.2.) implements resource virtualization. This EVP virtualization scheme is compatible with the OGSA 1.0 three-level naming scheme [3]. When a resource provider wants to add a new resource (or connect an existing resource) to CNGrid, he/she sees a grid-wide virtual address space and one or more agoras. A resource provider is responsible for two duties: (1) wrap the resource as a WS-I compliant Web service and connect it into the virtual name space; (2) register the service with one or more agoras, implying that the service can be shared by users in this agora according to the specified policies. The registration process has two aspects: deciding the virtualization mappings and selecting the access control policies. Let us use an example to illustrate virtualization.

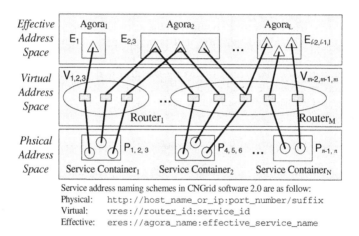

Service address naming schemes in CNGrid software 2.0 are as follow:
Physical: `http://host_name_or_ip:port_number/suffix`
Virtual: `vres://router_id:service_id`
Effective: `eres://agora_name:effective_service_name`

Fig. 2. The Effective-Virtual-Physical virtualization scheme in Vega GOS

The traditional approach to run mpiblast job on a machine is: login a frontend machine by telnet and submit following command to the backend batch system.

mpirun -np *nprocess* mpiblast -p *prog_name* -d *db_file* -i *in_file* -o *out_file*

The above command can be wrapped by general purposed batch service or dedicated one whose interfaces accept this command in a whole or all of the above parameters independently. Multiple such services can be connected and registered into virtual and effective name space, and build up one effective service named as mpiblast service with reduced interfaces. The Parameter Transformer (PT) in Vega GOS that resides on mappings between effective address and virtual address can eliminate the inconsistency at service interface level. In mpiblast case, the *nprocess, prog_name,* and *db_file* parameters in multiple services can be converted to uniformed ones by separate PT depending on practical situation. As listed below, the code accessing service can be highly reduced at effective layer.

```
...
// "mpiblastEAddr" is effective address of mpiblast
// service. The nprocess, prog_name, and db_file
// parameters are encapsulated behind it.
out_file = mpiblastClient(mpiblastEAddr, in_file);
...
```

2.3 Grid System Administrator

The grid system administrators manage users, resources, and policies via a Web based GUI tool or interfaces to agoras and grid routers. Each administrator can see one agora and its associated grid routers. The management functions include the following:

- Install, configure, and maintain GNGrid Software.
- Add, delete, and change attributes of users.
- Add, delete, and change attributes of resources (especially the EVP mappings of resources).
- Add, delete, and modify policies.

Currently, only two types of policies are supported. They are resource selection policies (e.g., random, FIFO) and access control policies.

2.4 Grid Application Developer

The Vega GOS allows grid application developers to see three levels of details: the effective, the virtual, and the physical levels. Many applications only need to see the effective level, which makes the following information available:

- An agora (with its specific policies and implied mappings to virtual services).
- All the effective services (resources) available in the agora, including system level services (e.g., meta file service and file service) and application level services (e.g., batch service).
- Interfaces to the GPE (Grid Portal Engine), if the developer wants the grid application to provide a presentation layer based on Web technology.
- Five Vega GOS interfaces to services and agora (see Fig. 4).

For example, a weather forecast and visualization grid application is supposed to be developed based on CNGrid Software. As the prerequisite, the weather forecast service and visualization service are developed and registered as effective service in an agora. The only thing that grid application developer needs to do is to integrate application logic flow with these two effective services, and, if the end user wants to submit weather forecast computation and views the graphical results by Web portal, Web pages (.jsp) constructing this grid application logic are needed. The main pseudo code is as below.

```
...
// Create a new grip under GPE's control.
GripClient gc = CreateGripUnderGPE;
// Upload weatherforecast required files to global user
// file space, and get back the global file addresses
// through the grip. The "hotfileEAddr" is the effective
// address of hotfile service.
weather_in_global = Upload(gc, hotfileEAddr,
                                          weather_in_local);
// Compose the weather forecast job description file.
weather_job_xml = weather_job_req + weather_in_global;
// Submit the job to effective weather forecast service
// by grip, and get back global result file addresses.
weather_out_global = JobSubmit(gc, weatherEAddr,
                                          weather_job_xml);
...
// Until weather forecast job finished, compose the
// visualization job description file.
viz_job_xml = viz_job_req + weather_out_global;
// Since the visualization input files are already
// existed in global space, directly submit the
// visualization job to effective visualization service,
// and get back the result.
viz_out_global = JobSubmit(gc, vizEAddr, viz_job_xml);
// Download result files in global space to portal side.
viz_out_local = Download(viz_out_global);
// Display the result at portal side.
Display(viz_out_local);
...
```

2.5 End User

An end user must go through an application/approval process (called user registration) to become a legitimate CNGrid user. Such a user has a certificate and proxy certificate (both GNGrid-wide unique), a home agora, and a user-name/password pair unique within the agora.

Users can log into CNGrid via a common grid portal or a customized client software (e.g., a Matlab client). When a user logs into CNGrid, he/she actually logs into an agora (the home agora by default). There he/she can see and utilize all the effective services (resources) available in the agora, subject to access control policies applied to this particular user. The most common usage scenario for an end user is to look for and utilize a pre-deployed application service. However, CNGrid provides several system level services (utilities) by default:

- A batch job service, which allows jobs to be submitted to the entire CNGrid, instead of a grid node or an application.
- A hotfile service, to allow location transparent access to files.
- GridDaEn data service, a more full-fledged data service than hotfile.

The hotfile services provide a location transparent file space for the users. Each user sees a tree of directories and files under a root "/", with the tree physically distributed across CNGrid.

3   Under the Hood

This section describes some implementation details of the CNGrid Software suite.

3.1   Architecture and Hosting Environment

Learned from computer systems [4], the CNGrid Software can be divided into four layers from bottom up [5]. They are CNGrid hosting environment, core layer, system layer and application layer (as show in Fig.1).

Currently, the CNGrid Software is hosted by J2SE/Tomcat environment, and can be easily migrated to other platforms, such as OMII, WSRF, even the .NET platform.

The core layer is something like OS kernel, provides common functionalities required by grid applications, such as layered service address management, grid user management and grid process (grip) manipulation. Also, the authentication and authorization are included in this layer.

The system layer provides a collection of basic libraries to help programmer developing grid application quickly. The services that shadowed will be gradually appended into this layer.

The application layer is not constructed by services, but by API provided by system layer and core layer. Grid portal developer or integrator can be benefited from Grid Portal Engine by avoiding using system or core layer API directly. GSML (Grid Service Markup Language) software suite is kind of client side service composition and collaboration toolkit which implements the GSML specification 1.0 and provides "on demand" programming environment.

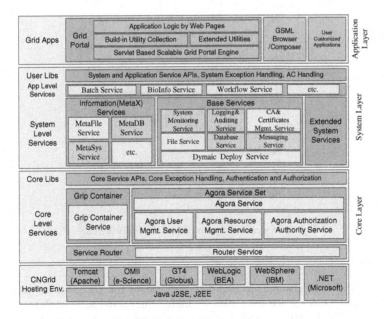

Fig. 3. Hierarchy of CNGrid Software

3.2 Grip, Agora and Router Service

The core layer composed by grip service, agora service set and router service with wrapped client side API; user authentication and service authorization mechanisms implemented by Axis handler chains; and the Vega GOS exception handling extends from the Axis fault which can help the developers accurately locating the service side exceptions and failures.

Aggregated by grip at runtime, agora service sets and router services implement the EVP space model. As show in Fig. 4, the grip client offers only five method calls. Behind these method calls, the grip container service accepts the requests and forwards the them to the agora service set or router service accordingly. When a grip created inside a grip container service, it will retain the information of login user and binding services in grip control block until a close operation is called. During the lifetime of a grip, user can access it at anytime and anywhere. When user is invoking the binding service through a grip, the grip will first resolve the virtual address to physical one, and then invoke the actual service by endpoint. At last, the grip will get back and cache the result of invocation for subsequent retrieval.

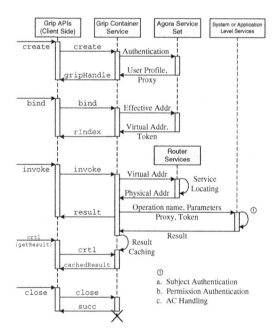

Fig. 4. Sequence diagram of CNGrid Software core

3.3 Security

Inside the CNGrid Software, GriShield is responsible for grid security issues. We have developed a CA service for certificate management, and have implemented WS-Security [6] conformed authentication, authorization, message level secure communication, access control by handler-chains of Axis.

4 Concluding Remarks

A main goal and feature of the CNGrid Software suite is loose coupling, achieved via virtualization and service orientation based on WS-I and OGSA standards. The three main modules, Vega GOS, Grishield security software, and GridDaEn data software are all loosely coupled, not critically depending on each other. The EVP model realizes resource (and service) virtualization, thus separate grid applications from physical resources. It is possible to run an application without changing its code even when the WSDL definition of a referenced physical service changes (location, operations, parameters, etc.).

Another feature of CNGrid is single system image. Once a user logs into CNGrid, he/she can use all available services in a location independent fashion. Furthermore, this capability is realized by the CNGrid system software, not as an application solution.

With the help of the Vega GOS core, agora and grip, the CNGrid API is also virtualized, compared to Web services interface. Application developers only need to understand the five interface calls provided via grip, with many details (including security and policy issues) automatically taken care of by the CNGrid software. Experiences show that it takes about 0.5-2 days to develop/deploy a simple grid application, including presentation, logic and data.

Acknowledgements

We acknowledge contributions by the CNGrid Software team and its users, especially Guangwen Yang, Hao Wang, Peixu Li, Mo Hai, Yanzhe Zhang and Honglei Dai. This work is supported in part by the China Ministry of Science and Technology 863 Program (Grant No. 2002AA104310), the National Natural Science Foundation of China (Grant No. 69925205), and the China National 973 Program (Grant No. 2003CB317000 and No. 2005CB321807), and Chinese Academy of Sciences Distinguished Scholars Fund (Grant No. 20014010).

References

[1] I. Foster, C. Kesselman (Eds.), The Grid 2: Blueprint for a New Computing Infrastructure, Morgan Kaufmann Publishers, San Francisco, 2004.
[2] W. Li, Z. Xu, A Model of Grid Address Space with Applications, Journal of Computer Research and Development, 2003, Vol. 40, No. 12, pp. 1756-1762.
[3] I. Foster et al (Eds.), The Open Grid Service Architecture 1.0, GGF document, Feb. 2005.
[4] Z. Xu, W. Li, et al., Vega: A Computer Systems Approach to Grid Computing, Journal of Grid Computing, 2004, Vol.2, Issue 2, pp. 109-120.
[5] L. Zha, W. Li, et al., Service oriented Vega grid system software design and evaluation, Chinese Journal of Computers, 2005, Vol. 28, No. 4, pp. 495-504.
[6] OASIS, Web Services Security: SOAP Message Security 1.0, http://docs.oasis-open.org/wss/2004/01/oasis-200401-wss-soap-message-security-1.0.pdf, 2004.3

CGSV*: An Adaptable Stream-Integrated Grid Monitoring System

Weimin Zheng[1], Lin Liu[1], Meizhi Hu[1], Yongwei Wu[1], Liangjie Li[1],
Feng He[1], and Jing Tie[2]

[1] Department of Computer Science and Technology,
Tsinghua University, 100084 Beijing, China
{zwm-dcs, wuyw}@tsinghua.edu.cn
{ll99, hmq02, liliangjie99,
hefeng04}@mails.tsinghua.edu.cn
[2] Cluster and Grid Computing Lab,
Huazhong University of Science and Technology,
430074 Wuhan, China
tiejing@gmail.com

Abstract. Grid monitoring is essential for the grid management and
efficiency improvement. ChinaGrid Super Vision (CGSV) is proposed for
ChinaGrid to collect status information of each entity (such as resources,
services, users, jobs, Network), and provide corresponding information data
query and mining services. In this paper, CGSV architecture and its
components are discussed. CGSV is featured by data stream integration and
adaptability to cope with dynamic measurement data and multiform query
requirements. Measurement data can be accessed quickly and easily through
WSRF-compliant services in CGSV. Transfer and control protocols are
brought forward to facilitate data stream querying and runtime producer
configuration in CGSV.

1 Introduction

1.1 ChinaGrid and CGSP

Grid computing has become the trend of distributed computing and Internet
applications. As a problem solving mechanism, the grid supports geographically
scattered communities to form Virtual Organizations [2], in order to achieve sharing
and coordination of heterogeneous resources and to provide a virtual uniform
application interface.

ChinaGrid (China Education and Research Grid) is the largest grid computing
project in China, which is launched by the Ministry of Education (MoE) of China in
2002[1]. ChinaGrid aims to provide the nationwide grid computing platform and
services for research and education purpose among 100 key universities in China.
ChinaGrid Support Platform (CGSP) is developed for this ambitious goal. CGSP

* This work is supported by ChinaGrid project of Ministry of Education of China, Natural
Science Foundation of China under Grant 60373004, 60373005, 90412006, 90412011, and
Nation Key Basic Research Project of China under Grant 2004CB318000.

H. Jin, D. Reed, and W. Jiang (Eds.): NPC 2005, LNCS 3779, pp. 22–31, 2005.

provides a set of tools for ChinaGrid application developers and specific grid platform constructors. CGSP organizes grid resources in several domains. Each domain has a complete set of grid components to be able to function relative independently. ChinaGrid SuperVision (CGSV) is designed and developed based on CGSP and provides monitoring functions for ChinaGrid.

1.2 Monitor Requirements and CGSV

Grids are large-scale distributed system, featured by dynamic and complex, which require monitoring system running on to track status information of system resources (e.g. hardware, network, services) and further to perform analysis and optimization. Grid monitoring differs from traditional cluster monitoring mainly in that the former require scalable support for both pull and push data delivery model that may be distributed across organizations, together with extensibility and self-description support of data format for interoperability [3].

In ChinaGrid, monitoring system is an essential part to keep such a complex distributed system efficient. Most CGSP components, including Job Manager, Storage Manager and Information Center, require a monitoring system to provide system status information for different purposes. CGSV is then designed for monitoring ChinaGrid. In addition to common inventory tracking tasks, ChinaGrid also require CGSV to have scalable support to different types of data request, an efficient approach of data processing and transmission must be developed. Moreover, CGSV is also required to be able to dynamically change its monitoring behavior, that is to say, to change monitor entity metadata.

To cope with the above requirements, CGSV is designed to be an adaptable, stream-integrated grid monitor system. A transfer and control protocol is designed in order to efficiently transfer various types of measurement data and perform modification over producer behavior in a unified way. Re-publishers are stream oriented, in that they are designed to support predicate-based processing over measurement data streams and SQL-like stream query interfaces.

1.3 Roadmap

In Section 2, CGSV's requirements, objective and position in ChinaGrid are overviewed. In Section 3, basic system architecture is given, followed by the detail design of system building blocks. Section 4 introduce the stream integration attempts in CGSV. Finally, Section 5 compares some related works correlated with our design and implementation, and in Section 6 a conclusion is summarized and future plan is listed.

2 Overview

2.1 Requirements and Objective

The final goal of CGSV is to implement a monitor and management module in ChinaGrid, which enable users or other grid modules in ChinaGrid to perform different level of system performance monitoring, analysis and optimization in a flexible way. Hardware resources, network condition, grid services and job status, the four main targets of ChinaGrid will be monitored in CGSV.

2.2 CGSV vs CGSP

CGSV will be implemented to be a control tower of ChinaGrid. The function of CGSV is distinguished from Information Center, but they also rely on each other. CGSV collects measurement data from hardware, Service Container, Job Manager, Storage Manager, and provides these data to Information Center. Domain monitoring services of CGSV acts like other system services in ChinaGrid, which rely on Information Center's domain topology information to locate monitoring services deployed in other domains. CGSV puts emphasis on dynamic monitor information while Information Center focuses relatively static information.

3 Architecture

CGSV is designed based on the Grid Monitoring Architecture [4] proposed by the Global Grid Forum. As Fig.1 shown above, CGSV is built up by several components, which can be divided into 3 layers, that is, collection layer, service layer and presentation layer. On the collection layer, sensors are deployed for measurement data collection. Sensor-I is responsible for collecting hardware resource information. Other sources of information including network condition and dynamic service information or data generated by other monitor tools are wrapped by an adaptor to unify the data monitor center, where Domain Registry Service and Monitor Services are deployed. A Message Gateway Service is provided to alleviate the communication cost of monitor services since over numbered notification and subscription will disastrously decease

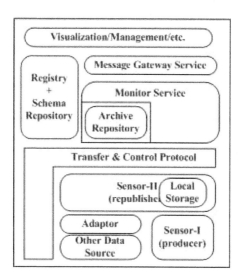

Fig. 1. Basic Architecture of CGSV Module Deployment

service performance. The top layer is the presentation layer, where data analysis, visualization work and management can be performed. Detailed description of sensors, protocol and stream-integration design will be discussed in the next section.

3.1 Collection Layer

For the purpose of both compactness and runtime controllability, we develop our own contributed sensors for measurement data collection.

Unlike many existing monitor tools, the most significant characteristic of our sensor is runtime configurable, which means that the monitor metadata, such as each metric's switch, collection frequency and granularity, is able to be changed over runtime on demand. For example, we demand turning off all the resource monitoring metrics except CPU load and also lower down the information collecting frequency to alleviate intrusiveness on some machines with heavy load. For many other monitor tools, configuration is written in files and is load only at startup; therefore the required action needs us to login on that computing node, shutdown the tool, change configuration file and start the tool again. This complicated work is not flexible for the dynamic environment of the grid, where similar scenarios are envisioned to occur frequently. In contrast, in CGSV, This action only needs us or grid system components to send a command according to our protocol. The sensors will then automatically change their configuration.

Configuration file is also used in our implementation, for initialization and logging configuration when changes occur. In other words, this file is the real-time hard-disk backup of sensor configuration, and is read only at startup. The configuration does not exist in any other materialized form even in memory.

There are 2 main types of sensors called sensor-I and sensor-II in CGSV. The difference between the 2 types is their function and deployment location in resource and network monitoring. For corresponding components in GMA, sensor-I is the actually producer and sensor-II can be treated as re-publisher.

Sensor-I is deployed on computing nodes of clusters and any PC resources. They are responsible for collecting resource information. Broadcast discovery and data transmission between Sensor-I are performed via UDP packets with the format specified in a message protocol.

Sensor-II is deployed on front-end node of clusters and any PC resources. They are responsible for pulling resource information from sensor-I like data sources (sensor-I also supports the pushing manner) through UDP messages and processing incoming data request through TCP massages. Dynamic information of web services are available through APIs of Service Container, so we can treat the APIs as sensors and wrap them with an adaptor, so that measurement data can go through a unified path. In addition, Sensor-II is also responsible for processing control messages and adjusting behaviors of Sensor-I. Sensor-II can also collect information from other sensor-like components. All the messages are under the protocol that will be discussed in 3.2.

Sensor-II can be connected hierarchically, but generally we do not advocate this method in CGSV for resources are autonomous and independent in ChinaGrid. So within each domain of ChinaGrid, Sensor-II are deployed flatly and connected to a single domain monitoring center.

3.2   Transfer and Control Protocol

A message protocol is designed for both measurement data transmission and sensor control. Inspired by the classical File Transfer Protocol (FTP) [14] and Supermon project [9], our protocol is a client-server protocol, based on symbolic expressions (or s-expressions). The underlying transfer protocol varies from UDP to TCP as described in the above paragraph.

S-expressions originated from LISP as a recursively defined, simple format for data representation. This format of data has the following features

- Extensibility: the protocol can be extended for new data types and new type of commands, which allows the system to be capable to evolve.
- Self-descriptive: each measurement data is associated with its metric name and timestamp, so the packet can be independently interpreted without any other knowledge, therefore increases the system's interoperability.
- Compactness: Though the packets are self-descriptive, the format is very compact comparing with XML. This feature saves network transmission bandwidth and memory cost for protocol interpretation, thus decrease the intrusiveness to host systems.
- Architecture independence: This is achieved by plain textual representation, which facilitates system portability.

Table 1. Five basic packets types implemented in CGSV protocol

Type	Packet example	Purpose	Comments
QUERY	(QUERY (get 1.2.3.4 *))	Issue a data query request for all measurement data of host 1.2.3.4	If this IP is a cluster, all back-end nodes' information are returned
DATA	(DATA (hostname 1.2.3.4)(timestamp 11 15715626)(OSType 1 10)(CPUNumber 2 10))	Data packet indica-ting 2 monitor items (OS type and CPU number) with host IP and collect time.	metric info tuple is composed by metric name, value and time difference with the complete timestamp.
SCHEMA	(SCHEMA (hostname 1.2.3.4)(OSType 1 1500)(CPULoad 0 15))	Schema packet indic-ating 2 metrics are supported on host 1.2.3.4 with their switches and monitor intervals	Metric schema tuple is composed by the name, switch flag and monitor interval in seconds
CTRL	(CTRL (close 1.2.3.4 4))	Issue a control request to switch MemFree metric off on host 1.2.3.4	"4" is predefined number for MemFree metric, full metric name is also accepted.
RESULT	(RESULT (1 (get 1.2.3.4 *)))	indicates execution result (1) of command "get 1.2.3.4 *"	"1" is predefined error code for success

For the convenience of protocol parsing, not only data and schema packets, but also command packets, including query, control and result, are encoded in s-expressions. So within each domain of ChinaGrid, all monitoring messages transferred are packets in the form of s-expression protocol. This unified data transmission and control method simplifies the implementation of monitoring components and naturally makes protocol interpretation and protocol execution logically separated.

This effort also makes CGSV components loose coupled and easy to collaborate with other monitor systems. Table 1 lists the basic packet types:

3.3 Service Layer

3.3.1 Registry

In each domain of ChinaGrid, we have a logical domain monitor center, where registry, archive module and monitor services are deployed.

Registry of CGSV performs 2 tasks. One is for producer/re-publisher registration, and to provide a lookup service for consumers to locate; the other task is to store producers' metric schema for system extension and modification. Since the adaptable implementation of sensors and protocol allows producers to accept control packets from any trusted source, the schema held by Registry needs to be synchronized periodically.

3.3.2 Archive

Archiving is an optional component. It periodically acquires measurement data from all data sources and stores them as historical information in DBMS. This mechanism works similar as registry schema synchronization. The different is that archive is much more costly and storage size increases quickly, so a distributed DBMS is used to share the loads when the domain grows larger.

3.3.3 Services and Message Gateway

Domain Monitor Services are WSRF-compliant services which are responsible for providing monitor information and management information interfaces. WSDM specification [6] has been studied and applied on monitor services for management issues. Each domain is treated as a WSDM manageability capability.

To alleviate the communication cost of monitor services, a message gateway service is used only for transmitting request and response between monitor services and grid users. As a result, data processing and data transmission are separated, and then service load is distributed.

3.4 Presentation Layer

Visualization work is implemented by http server plus servlet and java applet, to perform several forms (tables, histograms) of data presentation. Measurement data are retrieved from monitor services or monitoring service gateway. Users can view the grid by simply browsing the web pages. GIS (Geographical Information System) is introduced to locate resources from their geographical location on maps. An open source toolkit JFreeChart [16] is used for diagram plotting support. Basic Real-time visualization is implemented for dynamic resource information. To reveal relationship

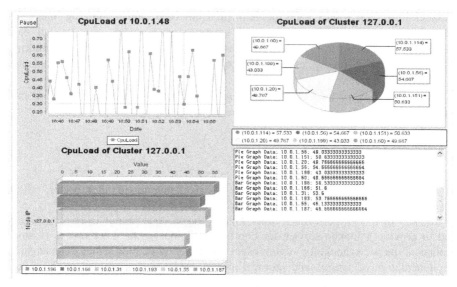

Fig. 2. Various visualization forms of CGSV implementation

between metrics, diagrams correlated with 2 or more metrics are designed for intuitive data analysis. Management actions can also be performed through the GUI client.

4   Stream-Orientated Scheme

Data Stream systems have been proven to be suitable for monitoring applications [12]. Research on data stream management system design and stream query model have attracted great effort of work and mature formal theory is proposed [11]. In CGSV, system monitor information is treated as a huge stream, which is composed of several levels of data streams. CGSV focuses on the stream-like features of monitor information and behaviors, such as trigger-oriented, real-time requirement. Two extreme viewpoints are avoided here. One is only to see the grid's instant status information, where instant data is not enough in many system usage scenarios such as failure analysis. The other is to view the grid as a virtual database, which often requires large storage and schema mapping and translation. This approach is feasible but often suffers from redundancy storage.

Stream integration in grid monitoring is a compromise of data storage, efficiency and functional capability. Stream processing should be put close to data source to distribute load and improve efficiency. For the sake of integration of any kinds of sensors, CGSV implements data stream on sensor-II, the actually re-publisher.

Fig. 3 shows the stream integration structure of re-publishers. Data streams come from Measure Data Puller, which pulls monitor information from producers. Data Stream Queue Manager holds two types of queues. Recent measurement information is kept in memory as buffer window queues, while outdated information is materialized in local storage. Since more recent information is usually more important and more frequently used, this division is reasonable. Both stream queues in memory and local storage form the input stream for processing. Queries coming from protocol interpreter give the system two input information. Data processing predicates are processed by Filter Inserter, and then are inserted to Predicate Manager. Predicate Manager maintains a predicate queue and also a processing plan by combination and optimization of predicates. Connection information is kept as channel queues. After processing of input streams, responses are sent to corresponding channel.

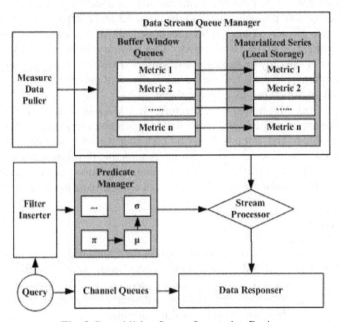

Fig. 3. Re-publisher Stream Integration Design

This structure has to coordinate with the proposed message passing protocol, in order to facilitate query parsing and data response transmission. The underlying Measure Data puller is a flexible component, which can be modified to combine any other monitor tools.

Stream query language is a set of SQL-like queries. The support to the language depends on the implementation of two components of Predicate Manager and Stream Processing. Single stream processing is supported currently.

5 Related Work

Grid monitoring is not a new issue. There are a large number of mature projects working on this area, but very few of them have a focus on stream integration for high efficiency and adaptability is seldom considered either. CGSV benefits from their efforts, and tries to naturally combine the outstanding features of some monitoring projects while avoiding their shortcomings. CGSV is made up as an adaptable and efficient grid monitoring framework based on ChinaGrid.

CGSV's design uses several monitoring tools and data stream projects as good references, integrates their features in one framework and also developed its own features. The feature of sensors' scalable broadcast discovery at cluster level is learned from Ganglia project [8]. Message protocol design is enlightened by Supermon [9]'s kernel mode protocol in the form of s-expression. Stream processing design is inspired by Aurora [12], a data stream project. Finally, MonALISA [10]'s intuitive and impressive visualization work, which has a rich set of visualization forms, has a great impact on CGSV presentation works. Besides, CGSV attempts to integrate data stream in re-publishers and has adaptable design of runtime configured sensors and extensible protocols for both data transfer and control.

The first two cluster monitor tools mentioned above has their problems in grid monitoring context. Ganglia has a registry-free arbitrary architecture with filter-free aggregation, so it can only be used as basic sensors. However, Ganglia sensors are not runtime configurable. Supermon uses a statically configured hierarchy of point-to-point connections which makes it less scalable.

Relational Grid Monitoring Architecture (R-GMA) is a grid monitor system considered stream integration problems. R-GMA perceives Grid monitoring as a data integration problem, and extends GMA by choosing the relational data model. They have performed some research on stream integration and developed basic techniques. [13] However, they ignore the activity of monitor information, and treat the data statically as a virtual database thus do not benefit from stream adequately.

6   Conclusion

CGSV is a complete set of grid monitor solution for ChinaGrid. In this paper, we first introduce the basic CGSV architecture, along with some detail design and implementation issues on system building blocks. CGSV focused on sensor controllability, adaptable message protocol and stream integration on re-publishers, and proposed a flexible mechanism for grid monitoring.

Our future plan of CGSV considers 4 research points.

- Data analysis, which assists decision making, and hence makes the behavior of our adaptable sensors automatic
- Scalable optimization of data stream model to cope with large number of queries and predicates.
- Security is also an important issue to be considered. The message protocol needs security data transfer to restrict access to sensors and re-publishers, and to protect sensitive measurement data.
- Measurement data precision representation and synchronization.

References

1. Hai, J.: ChinaGrid: Making grid computing a reality. Digital Libraries: International Collaboration and Cross-Fertilization, Proceedings, Vol. 3334. Springer-Verlag Berlin (2004) 13-24
2. Foster, I., Kesselman, C., et al.: The anatomy of the grid: Enabling scalable virtual organizations. International Journal of High Performance Computing Applications, 15(3). Sage Publications Inc (2001) 200-222

3. Zanikolas, S. and Sakellariou, R.: A taxonomy of grid monitoring systems. Future Generation Computer Systems, 21(1). Elsevier Science Bv (2005) 163-188
4. Tierney, B., Aydt, R., et al: A Grid Monitoring Architecture. GWDPerf-16–3, Global Grid Forum, August 2002. http://wwwdidc.lbl.gov/GGF-PERF/GMA-WG/papers/GWD-GP-16-3.pdf
5. Web Service Resource Framework (WSRF): http://www.globus.org/wsrf/
6. OASIS Web Services Distributed Management (WSDM): http://www.oasis-open.org/committees/tc_home.php?wg_abbrev=wsdm
7. GT Information Services: Monitoring & Discovery System (MDS): http://www.globus.org/toolkit/mds/
8. Massie, M. L., Chun, B. N., et al.: The ganglia distributed monitoring system: design, implementation, and experience. Parallel Computing, 30(7). Elsevier Science Bv (2004) 817-840
9. Sottile, M. J. and Minnich, R. G.: Supermon: A High-Speed Cluster Monitoring System. Proceedings of the IEEE International Conference on Cluster Computing. Washinton D.C. (2002) 39 IEEE Computer Society
10. Newman, H. B., Legrand, I. C., et al.: MonALISA: A Distributed Monitoring Service Architecture. Computing in High Energy and Nuclear Physics (CHEP03). La Jolla, California. (2003)
11. Babcock, B., Babu, S., et al.: Models and issues in data stream systems. Proceedings of the twenty-first ACM SIGMOD-SIGACT-SIGART symposium on Principles of database systems. Madison, Wisconsin. (2002) 1-16 ACM Press
12. Carney, D., Cetintemel, U., et al.: Monitoring Streams - A New Class of Data Management Applications. Proceedings of Very Large Databases (VLDB). HongKong. (2002)
13. Cooke, A., Gray, A. J. G., et al.: Stream integration techniques for Grid monitoring. Journal on Data Semantics Ii, Vol. 3360. Springer-Verlag Berlin (2005) 136-175
14. Postel, J., Reynolds, J.: File Transfer Protocol (FTP). Available from http://www.ietf.org/rfc/rfc959.txt
15. JFreeChart Project: http://www.jfree.org/jfreechart/index.html
16. ChinaGrid Project: http://www.chinagrid.edu.cn

Performance Modeling and Analysis
for Resource Scheduling in Data Grids*

Yajuan Li[1], Chuang Lin[1], Quanlin Li[2], and Zhiguang Shan[3]

[1] Department of Computer Science and Technology, Tsinghua University,
Beijing 100084, China
{yjli, clin}@csnet1.cs.tsinghua.edu.cn
[2] Department of Industrial Engineering, Tsinghua University, Beijing 100084, China
liquanlin@tsinghua.edu.cn
[3] Public Technical Service Department, State Information Center, Beijing 100045, China
shanzg@mx.cei.gov.cn

Abstract. Data Grids normally deal with large data-intensive problems on geo-graphically distributed resources; yet, most current research on performance evaluation of resource scheduling in Data Grids is based on simulation tech-niques, which can only consider a limited range of scenarios. In this paper, we propose a formal framework via Stochastic Petri Nets to deal with this problem. Within this framework, we model and analyze the performance of resource scheduling in Data Grids, allowing for a wide variety of job and data scheduling algorithms. As a result of our research, we can investigate more scenarios with multiple input parameters. Moreover, we can evaluate the combined effective-ness of job and data scheduling algorithms, rather than study them separately.

1 Introduction

A Data Grid [1] connects a collection of computational and data-resources distributed geographically among multiple sites, and enables users to share these resources. To use a Data Grid, users typically submit jobs. In order for a job to be executed, two types of resources are required: computing facilities, data access and storage. The Grid must make scheduling decisions for each job based on the current state of these resources. Different job and data scheduling algorithms may bring different perform-ance for the Data Grid.

Many research works have been done on the performance evaluation of Data Grids, but most of which use simulation techniques, which can only analyze a limited range of scenarios. For example, in [2], a special Data Grid simulator, called OptorSim, was designed to study the complex nature of a typical Grid environment and evaluate various data replication algorithms; in [3], a simulation work was developed to study

---

* This work is supported by the National Natural Science Foundation of China (No. 90412012, 60429202, 60372019 and 60373013), NSFC and RGC (No. 60218003), and the National Grand Fundamental Research 973 Program of China (No.2003CB314804).

H. Jin, D. Reed, and W. Jiang (Eds.): NPC 2005, LNCS 3779, pp. 32–39, 2005.

dynamic replication strategies; in [4], a discrete event simulator, called ChicagoSim, was constructed to evaluate the performance of different combinations of job and data scheduling algorithms. Furthermore, many related works are based on a single factor of job or data scheduling. In [2][3][5], performance is analyzed with the assumption that jobs have been allocated to certain computing elements. While in [6-9], performance is analyzed with the assumption that data have been accessed. The research to study the combined effectiveness of job and data scheduling strategies has been pointed out to be very complex [10].

We propose a formal performance evaluation framework that addresses the above mentioned issues. Within this framework, we can investigate more scenarios with multiple input parameters. Moreover, we can evaluate the combined effectiveness of job and data scheduling algorithms, rather than study them separately.

The rest of the paper is organized as follows. Section 2 describes the general and extensible scheduling architecture of Data Grids that we use for our modeling and analysis. Section 3 presents the performance model, while Section 4 analyzes the performance of the model. We conclude and point to future directions in Section 5.

2 Architecture

Our study is based on a general and extensible Data Grid scheduling architecture, which is inspired by the work presented in [4], and depicted in figure 1. The logic of the architecture can be encapsulated in three distinct modules:

- **Server.** Each server comprises a number of processors and storage. Due to the heterogeneousness of Grid environments, different server may have a different number of processors. The processors of a server can only access the local storage.

- **Client.** Each client submits jobs to schedulers. Then each job can be allocated to any of the servers and further dispatched to any of the processors of a server. Each job requires some specific data be available at the local storage before it can be executed.

- **Scheduler.** It is the core of the system and can be classified into three schedulers: external scheduler (ES), local scheduler (LS), and data scheduler (DS). (1) **External scheduler**. In the system, jobs can be classified depending on their different priority levels. Each job is submitted to some ES in terms of its priority. Once an ES receives a job, it immediately makes a decision on which server the job should be assigned to, according to some scheduling algorithm. It may use the global information, such as load of each server, and/or location of the data required by a job, as input to its decisions. (2) **Local scheduler**. When a job is delivered to some server, it is managed by the local scheduler of that server. The LS determines how to schedule the jobs allocated to it, according to its associated scheduling algorithm. It only uses the local information, such as load of each local processor, to guide its decisions. (3) **Data scheduler**. Each DS is responsible for determining if and from which server to replicate data according to some algorithm. When a job is allocated to some server, the DS in that server will query whether the data required to run the job is already present at the local storage. If not, the DS will use the global information, such as the

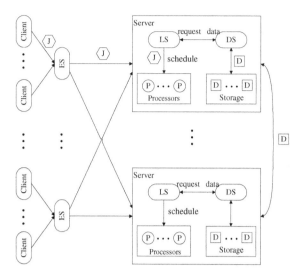

Fig. 1. A Data Grid Scheduling Architecture

availability of the required data in a remote server, and/or the distance between two servers, toreplicate the required data from some remote server to the local storage, before the job is executed.

3 SPN Model

To study the performance of resource scheduling in Data Grids, we adopt the modeling and analysis method, which allows for the performance evaluation in various scenarios. We choose the Stochastic Petri Net (SPN) [11] as the base for our study, since it is a powerful graphical and mathematical tool that is able to handle prioritized, concurrent, asynchronous, stochastic and nondeterministic events. In figure 2, we propose a SPN model of the Data Grid scheduling system.

Suppose there are n classes of jobs, the jobs in each class have the same priority level. The priority level values range from 1 (the highest priority) to n (the lowest one). Jobs with priority level i are denoted by r_i. In accordance, the clients in the system are classified into n categories. Each client in class i submits jobs r_i to ES_i according to a Poisson distribution with the same mean arrival rate.

The system consists of k servers, each of which contains a depository with an infinite capacity for storing data, and may have different compute power. To consider a general case, we assume that server x comprises m_x processors, for $1 \leq x \leq k$, and each processor provides the exponential distributed service durations with different mean rates for different priority-level jobs. In each processor, there are n waiting queues of jobs, each for one priority level and with an infinite capacity. Jobs in the same waiting queue are managed in FIFO (First-In-First-Out) order. If a job is in the turn to be scheduled, it can be executed only when the processor is free and its required data is available. Each processor can provide service for at most one job at any time, and the jobs from different waiting queues are selected for service according to their priorities, i.e., jobs with higher priorities have higher priorities to be executed.

There are n external schedulers, each for one priority level; k local schedulers, each distributed in one server; and k data schedulers, each for one server.

The meanings of the transitions and the places are described as follows, where variable i identifies priority level i ($1 \leq i \leq n$), x and y denote server x ($1 \leq x \leq k$) and storage y ($1 \leq y \leq k$) respectively, j indicates processor j of server x ($1 \leq j \leq m_x$), z indicates client z ($1 \leq z \leq l_i$).

- **Places.** f_i: the external job assigner, which holds jobs r_i; a_{ix}: the transmission link from ES_i to server x; f_{ix}: the local job assigner of server x, which holds jobs r_i; q_{ij}^x: the waiting queue, which holds jobs r_i in processor j of server x; w_{ij}^x: the running state of a job r_i at processor j of server x; v_j^x: the available state of processor j of server x; g_{ij}^x: the place holding execution results of jobs r_i in processor j of server x; sd_{ij}^{xy}: the place identifying for the processor j of server x whether the storage y possesses the data required by jobs r_i; dm_{ij}^x: the logical module of data manager x, which is responsible for jobs r_i on the local processor j; td_{ij}^{xy}: the transmission link for data required by jobs r_i, from storage y to processor j of server x; ls_{ij}^x: the place holding data required by jobs r_i, that is already allocated to processor j of server x.

- **Transitions.** c_{iz}: the exponential transition representing that client z submits jobs r_i, with mean firing rate λ_i; u_{ix}: the immediate transition denoting that ES_i dispatches jobs r_i to server x, according to some ES algorithm; e_{ix}: the exponential transition denoting the job transmission from ES_i to server x, with mean firing rate β_{ix}; d_{ij}^x: the immediate transition representing that LS_x allocates jobs r_i to the local processor j of server x, according to some LS algorithm; h_{ij}^x: the immediate transition which transfers jobs r_i in processor j of server x, from waiting state to execution state; s_{ij}^x: the exponential transition denoting that processor j of server x runs jobs r_i, with mean firing rate μ_{ij}^x; ud_{ij}^{xy}: the immediate transition representing that the data monitor of processor j of server x, which collects data information for jobs r_i from storage y once the state of storage y changes; rd_{ij}^{xy}: the immediate transition representing that DS_x schedules data required by jobs r_i, from storage y to processor j, according to some DS algorithm; od_{ij}^{xy}: the exponential transition denoting that the data transmission for jobs r_i, from storage y to processor j of server x, with mean firing rate δ_{ij}^{xy}.

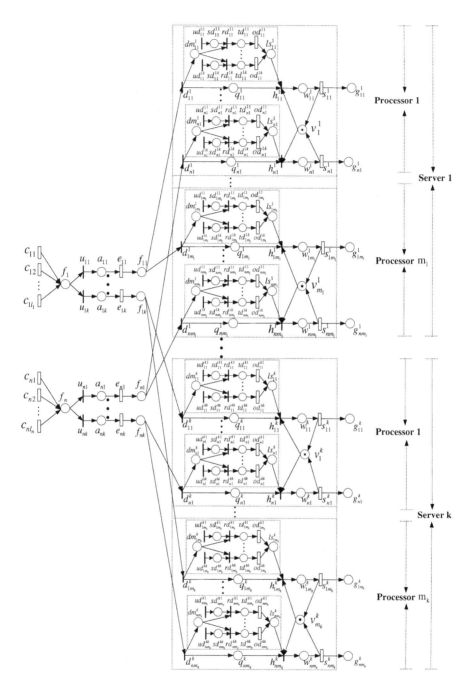

Fig. 2. A SPN Model of the Data Grid Scheduling System

4 Performance Evaluation

In SPN models, performance evaluation is based on steady-state probabilities. Since the model is very large and complicated, we adopt an approximate analysis technique to reduce the complexity of the model solution, presented as the following steps.

(1) **Refinement.** To simplify a complicated model into a relatively compact model, by deleting immediate transitions and transferring the enabling predicates associated with these immediate transitions to some exponential transitions.

(2) **Decomposition.** To decompose a model into several sub-models, by using independence and interdependence relations of the sub-models. A refined sub-model of the original model is generally described in figure 3, denoted as A_{ij}^{xy}, which represents the module that job r_i is submitted to processor j of server x, and its required data is replicated from storage y. The refined complete model is composed of $\sum_{i=1}^{k}(n \times k \times m_i)$ sub-models, which are independent with each other in structure. The interdependence relation of these sub-models is embodied by the enabling predicates associated with transitions.

(3) **Iteration.** For each sub-model, import parameters are from other sub-models; after computed, the solution result is again exported to other sub-models.

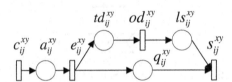

Fig. 3. A Refined Sub-Model of the Data Grid Scheduling System

It follows from the steady-state probabilities that system performance measures can be obtained.

(1) The average throughput for transition t in steady state is:

$$T(t) = \sum_{M \in H(t)} \Pr[M] \times \theta(t, M),$$

where $\Pr[M]$ is the steady-state probability of marking M, $\theta(t, M)$ is the firing rate of transition t in marking M, and $H(t)$ is the subset of reachable markings that enable t.

(2) The average number of tokens for place q in steady state is:

$$N(q) = \sum i \times \Pr[M(q) = i].$$

Following the above, we consider two important metrics of the Data Grid scheduling system: average system throughput and average job completion duration.

(1) **Average system throughput:**

$$T = \sum_{i=1}^{n} T_i,$$

where T_i is the throughput for job r_i and obtained by

$$T_i = \sum_{x=1}^{k}\sum_{j=1}^{m_x}\sum_{y=1}^{k} T\left(s_{ij}^{xy}\right).$$

(2) **Average job completion duration:**

$$JCD = \frac{\sum_{i=1}^{n} JCD_i \times T_i}{T},$$

where JCD_i is the job completion duration for job r_i and acquired by

$$JCD_i = SD_i + \sum_{x=1}^{k} PR_{ix} \times TD_{ix} + DT_i,$$

where SD_i: the submission duration of job r_i from client to ES_i, and

$$SD_i = \frac{1}{\sum_{x=1}^{k}\sum_{j=1}^{m_x}\sum_{y=1}^{k} T\left(c_{ij}^{xy}\right)},$$

PR_{ix}: the probability of job r_i being allocated to server x, and

$$PR_{ix} = \frac{\sum_{j=1}^{m_x}\sum_{y=1}^{k} T\left(s_{ij}^{xy}\right)}{\sum_{x=1}^{k}\sum_{j=1}^{m_x}\sum_{y=1}^{k} T\left(s_{ij}^{xy}\right)},$$

TD_{ix}: the transfer duration of job r_i from ES_i to LS_x, and

$$TD_{ix} = \frac{\sum_{j=1}^{m_x}\sum_{y=1}^{k} N\left(a_{ij}^{xy}\right)}{\sum_{j=1}^{m_x}\sum_{y=1}^{k} T\left(e_{ij}^{xy}\right)},$$

DT_i: the delay time of job r_i for all servers, and

$$DT_i = \frac{\sum_{x=1}^{k}\sum_{j=1}^{m_x}\sum_{y=1}^{k} N\left(td_{ij}^{xy}\right)}{\sum_{x=1}^{k}\sum_{j=1}^{m_x}\sum_{y=1}^{k} T\left(od_{ij}^{xy}\right)} + \frac{\sum_{x=1}^{k}\sum_{j=1}^{m_x}\sum_{y=1}^{k} N\left(q_{ij}^{xy}\right)}{\sum_{x=1}^{k}\sum_{j=1}^{m_x}\sum_{y=1}^{k} T\left(s_{ij}^{xy}\right)}.$$

5 Conclusions and Future Work

In this paper, we construct the SPN model based on a general and extensible schedul-ing architecture of Data Grids, and further evaluate the system performance. The performance metrics considered in this paper include the system throughput and the job completion duration experienced in system.

In future work, we want to develop an analysis tool to evaluate the performance of practical Grids. Particularly, this tool is planned to be able to plug in different algorithms for selecting the best server, the best processor, and the best replication. Another area for further research is to study the sensitivities with respect to all system parameters, which will be helpful to come up with more reasonable schemes for system designs.

References

1. Chervenak, A., Foster, I., Kesselman, C., Salisbury, C., Tuecke, S.: The Data Grid: Towards an Architecture for the Distributed Management and Analysis of Large Scientific Data Sets. J. Network and Computer Applications Vol. 23. No. 3. (2000) 187-200

2. William, H.B., David, G.C., Luigi, C., Paul, M.A., Kurt, S., Floriano, Z.: Simulation of Dynamic Grid Replication Strategies in OptorSim. In: Proceedings of the Third International Workshop on Grid Computing. Lecture Notes in Computer Science, Vol. 2536. Springer-Verlag, London, UK (2002) 46-57

3. Ranganathan, K., Foster, I.: Identifying Dynamic Replication Strategies for a High-Performance Data Grid. In: Proceedings of the Second International Workshop on Grid Computing. Lecture Notes in Computer Science, Vol. 2242. Springer-Verlag, London, UK (2001) 75-86

4. Ranganathan, K., Foster, I.: Simulation Studies of Computation and Data Scheduling Algorithms for Data Grids. Journal of Grid Computing, Vol. 1. No. 1. (2003) 53-62

5. Venugopal, S., Buyya, R., Lyle, J.W.: A Grid Service Broker for Scheduling Distributed Data-oriented Applications on Global Grids. In: Proceedings of the 2nd Workshop on Middleware for Grid Computing. ACM Press, USA (2004) 75-80

6. Hamscher, V., Schwiegelshohn, U., Streit, A., Yahyapour, R.: Evaluation of Job-Scheduling Strategies for Grid Computing. In: Proceedings of the First IEEE/ACM International Workshop on Grid Computing. Lecture Notes in Computer Science, Vol. 1971. Springer-Verlag, London, UK (2000) 191-202

7. James, H.A., Hawick, K.A., Coddington, P.D.: Scheduling Independent Tasks on Metacomputing Systems. Technical Report DHPC-066. University of Adelaide, Australia (1999)

8. Shirazi, B.A., Husson, A.R., Kavi, K.M. (eds.): Scheduling and Load Balancing in Parallel and Distributed Systems. IEEE Computer Society Press (1995)

9. Subramani, V., Kettimuthu, R., Srinivasan, S., Sadayappan, P.: Distributed Job Scheduling on Computational Grids Using Multiple Simultaneous Requests. In: Proceedings of the 11th IEEE International Symposium on High Performance Distributed Computing. IEEE Computer Society Press, Los Alamitos (2002) 359-367

10. Desprez, F., Vernois. A.: Simultaneous Scheduling of Replication and Computation for Data-Intensive Applications on the Grid. Technical Report RR2005-01 (2005)

11. Gianfranco, B.: Introduction to Stochastic Petri Nets. In: Lectures on Formal Methods and Performance Analysis: first EEF/Euro summer school on trends in computer science. Springer-Verlag, Berlin Heidelberg New York (2002)

Study on π-Calculus Based Equipment Grid Service Chain Model*

Yuexuan Wang, Cheng Wu, and Ke Xu

National CIMS Engineering Research Center, Department of Automation,
Tsinghua University, Beijing 100084, P.R. China
{wangyuexuan, wuc}@tsinghua.edu.cn

Abstract. The development of modern science requires the equipment grid to provide a scientific collaboration research platform, which can realize remote collaboration and sharing with the key instruments and equipment in wide areas. The reliability and high efficiency of a grid service chain model are key points in creation of a grid equipment system. The π-calculus as powerful process algebra has a specific advantage in modeling and testing the grid service chain model. This research investigates and improves a theoretical analysis and algorithm framework for the modeling, correctness checking and analysis of the π-calculus based equipment grid service chain model. It also studies on the analysis of its logistic structure and flexible modeling for the equipment grid. It would be beneficial to open up a new space in the theoretical and applied research on grid technology and formal methodology based on cross-disciplinary cooperation.

1 Introduction

With the development of scientific research and continuous emergency of cross-disciplinary research, it's highly necessary to share the related knowledge and various equipments. However, due to different communication protocols and data formats, information can not be easily integrated and understood with each other and has difficulty sharing with the equipment effectively [1].

The emergence and development of grid computing technology provides a revolutionary way to couple geographically distributed equipment resources and to solve large-scale resource sharing problems in wide area networks [2][3][4][5][6]. The equipment grid provides an abstraction of equipments, then presents and publishes their functionalities in the form of grid service to some granularity. Each service clearly shows its processing flow and value. Any service conforming to the specification can become an element in a workflow, and any change from one participant will not affect its cooperative counterpart. In this way, the unified operation and the cooperative sharing of equipment can be achieved [7][8][9][10].

* This paper is supported by China "211 project" "15" construct project: National Universities Equipment and Resource Sharing System and China Postdoctoral Science Foundation (No. 2003034155).

H. Jin, D. Reed, and W. Jiang (Eds.): NPC 2005, LNCS 3779, pp. 40–47, 2005.

Due to the complexity of wide areas distributed equipment, the equipment grid systems require high reliability. In order to accomplish a complicated task, equipment grid application often integrates a large number of grid services and equipment to conduct its inter-operation according to expected flow. On the other hand, with the increase of equipment resources and data, users will meet a large, dynamic and complex decision-making space. It is needed not only to select appropriate equipment service, but also to assure optimization of interoperation flow. Some of the key research problems on the equipment grid flow are as follows.

(1) As for the service chain model, how to check the correctness of its logical structure, such as no deadlock, being reachable to the end of the chain, compatibility between services, and whether the interaction of grid services meets the requirement of the pre-defined protocol, and etc.

(2) How to judge that a certain service chain model has the properties to meet the user's expectation. For example, whether the model can give the correct responses to user's requests, and whether the service in the model can be completed under the given time constraints or not.

(3) How to evaluate the working performance of a service chain, including the efficiency, cost and whether it has any space to perform further improvement or not.

(4) How to find a proper theoretical foundation for the modeling of the dynamic evolution characteristics of the equipment grid environment (service crash, new service and resource registration, alternative resource search tactics, selection of multiple optional services etc.) and depict the dynamical interaction and composition of the service and equipment resource.

Therefore, a complete theory system and related tools are urgently needed to answer the above questions. It is infeasible to analyze the above problems by simple manual methods. Firstly, the equipment grid system structure determines the complex alternative and coupling relations among the massive data, complicate equipment resources and services. Furthermore, the grid applications have their own complexity. Take E-science [11] [12] for an instance. The applications of the astronomical observation grid [13] of the disaster forecast grid [14] [15] are related to thousands of basic services. An equipment grid service chain model and its checking and reorganizing based on π-calculus are proposed in this paper.

This paper is organized as follows. In Section 2, some related work on grid service flow models is discussed. The equipment grid architecture and its 4-tuple are introduced in Section 3. A flexible equipment grid service chain model based on π-calculus is presented in Section 4. In Section 5, a proposal on a layered checking and analysis system for an equipment grid service chain model is explained. This study is a precondition for equipment grid service chain optimization. Finally, the conclusions of this research are presented in Section 6.

2   Related Work

Most existing work in grid service flow area is implementation specific, tailored to a particular grid application; almost every major grid project or system has its own flow language. Today, the idea based on services is the key concept of OGSA (Open Grid

Service Architecture). The OGSI (Open Grid Service Infrastructure) [16] has extended the WSDL (Web Service Definition Language) based on this idea and a defined grid service. The Global Grid Forum is working to develop a Web Services Flow Language (GSFL) that will provide a standard, platform-independent way to specify a grid services flow [17]. GSFL is an attempt to integrate efforts from the grid computing, Web services, and workflow areas. With the introduction of the WSRF (Web Service Resource Framework), the integration of grid computing and Web services has reached a new level.

The grid service flow management is a necessary phase in most grid systems including the Gridflow system by the NASA Ames research centre, the Pegasus system by USC information science association, and the grid workflow system by ChinaGrid (Education and Scientific Research Grid Project) support platform (CGSP) [18]. These systems can be grouped into two methods by the view of flow model validation and analysis. One is the semantic network [19][20] based research method. It is mainly applied in the Service Composition [21] and related service flow model analysis. The other benefits from the conventional workflow model validation method [22] that checks the related logical flow model. However, the above methods are only subset of the grid service flow model validation method. A completely grid service flow model validation system should include the application logical validation, service alternation protocol validation, service behavior and compatibility validation, and data and resource constraint validation, etc.

The π-calculus [23] proposed by Robin Milner is reputed for its powerful expressiveness. Through its mobility, π-calculus realizes the flexible description for the dynamical evolutionary system including grid systems and performs the equivalency analysis for alternative system behaviors. Through the mobility of π-calculus, the grid system dynamical properties such as new service register, service selection broker mechanism and disaster recover can be well described.

The direct support of π-calculus to the model checking technology provides good fundamentals for model analysis and validation. The composition operation defined in π-calculus supports the system structure decomposed and composed from the bottom to the top a natural and flexible description [24]. It is especially suitable to be used to depict the different composition and interaction in the grid service and also to model and optimize equipment grid service chain models.

3   Equipment Grid Service Architecture

The objective of equipment grid is to provide on-demand service according to user requirement. A user may query for a task which has to be carried out by several grid service cooperation together. The equipment grid has to find this set of services and propose a service chain in order to achieve the desired results. The equipment grid can be regarded as a 4-tuple: $DIG = \{U, R, P, M_\Pi\}$. Where:

U : A set of grid users, including the resource provider and the resource consumer and tagged U_{ProS} and, U_{ConS} respectively. $U = U_{ProS} \cup U_{ConS}$. For there might be some cases that a consumer is also a resource provider, we can see $U_{ProS} \cap U_{ConS} \neq \Phi$.

R : Resources in the system, including equipment resource set D and other assistant resource set A (such as network, etc.). The reason of dividing the resources in the system into two parts is that we will emphasize the main entity in the system: the sharing mechanism of equipment resource research. $D = \{T; Op(t \in T, u \in U_{ProS})\}$, T is type set of the equipment resources, u is subset of the resource provider, Op denotes the operation set offered by the t types of equipment resources provided by u. Following the trend of Service-Oriented Architecture (SOA) architecture, each sharing operation of each resource will publish a service in the equipment grid system. Therefore, the equipment resource set D equals the set of operation, that's to say $D = \{Op(u \in U_{ProS})\}$.

P : The sharing rule set of the resource set by the resource provider. It can be described as the following mathematical expression: $U_{ProS} * U_{ConS} * OP \rightarrow \{yes, no, N/A\}$, The value will certainly be N/A if a user who does not have the possession right $(U1, U2, op(t1, U1)) = N/A$, if $UI \neq U1$, as stated above, it shows that $U1$ does not have the possession right of the equipment resource belonging to UI.

M_Π : The set of the equipment service chain is based on work flow. It expresses the operation combination mode between the equipments, and it can be a combination of different functional operations of the same type of equipment or of different ones. So we can get $M_\Pi = \{op^+, op \in OP(t, u)\}$. M_Π is the key of the research project. It aims to record thoroughly the equipment service chain through the construct of equipment operations in the system using a flexible description to provide high layered service.

4 Flexible Equipment Grid Service Chain Model Based on π-Calculus

Based on the equipment grid 4-tuple model proposed in Section 3 and integrated with OGSI, GSFL and the semantic of π-calculus, a brief overview of our meta-model of the equipment grid service chain is illustrated in Fig. 1.

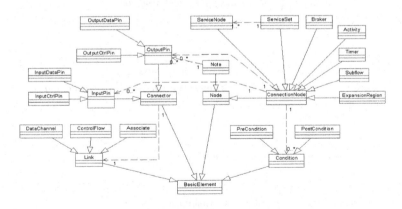

Fig. 1. Equipment gird service chain meta-model

In Fig. 1, *Activities* are the atomic building blocks of a service chain. *ServiceNodes* are bounded with the actual existing services that can be used to fulfill certain functionality of an activity, and it is the *Broker*'s job to select a *ServiceNode* from a set of alternative services to implement an activity.

Consequently, the formal semantics of the above meta-models are captured with π-calculus as a basis for the later process validation and verification. The polyadic version of π-calculus is used here [22] [24], whose syntax is concluded below.

$$P ::= \sum_{i=1}^{n} \pi_i.P_i \mid new \ \ x \ \ P \mid !P \mid P \mid Q \mid \phi P \mid A(y_1,...,y_n) \mid 0 \tag{1}$$
$$\pi_i ::= \overline{x} < y > \mid x(y) \mid \tau$$
$$\phi ::= [x = y] \phi \wedge \phi \mid \neg \phi$$

Limited by the length of the paper, part of the π-calculus formalization of elements in Fig. 2 is as follows.

Activity:

$$Act(inctrl,outctrl) = inctrl.new\ complete(Action(complete) \mid \overline{complete}.outctrl.Act) \tag{2}$$
$$Action(complete) = \tau.\overline{complete}.0$$

Decision, Fork, Merge, Join:

$$Decision \stackrel{def}{=} inctrl.\tau(\sum_{i=1} \overline{outctrl_i}) \tag{3}$$

$$Fork \stackrel{def}{=} inctrl.\tau(\prod_{i \in I}) \overline{outctrl_i} \tag{4}$$

$$Merge \stackrel{def}{=} (\sum_{i \in I} inctrl_i).\tau.\overline{outctrl} \tag{5}$$

$$Join \stackrel{def}{=} (\prod_{i \in I} inctrl_i.\overline{ack}).\underbrace{ack.....ack}_{i}.\tau.\overline{outctrl} \tag{6}$$

Timer:

$$Timer(inctrl, signal, timeout, outctl) = inctl.signal(message). \tag{7}$$
$$([message = timeout].\overline{outctrl}.Timer + [message \neq timeout].(inctrl \mid Timer))$$

DataStore:

$$Storage_0(put) \stackrel{def}{=} new\ x_1(put(x_1).Storage_1(in, x_1)) \tag{8}$$

$$Storage_n(put, get, reset, x_1,...,x_n) \stackrel{def}{=} new\ x_{n+1}(get(chan).\overline{chan} < x_1 >. \tag{9}$$
$$Storage_{n-1}(put, x_2,...,x_n) + put(x_{n+1}).Storage_{n+1}(in, x_1,...,x_{n+1})) + reset.Storage_0(put) \quad n \geq 1$$

Subflow:

The composition of all the connection nodes in the corresponding sub service chain model, with each name 'inctrl' and 'outctrl' in the sub-nodes of the sub-flow being restricted in the scope of the whole composed π-process.

5 Equipment Grid Service Chain Model's Layered Checking and Analysis System

Model checking techniques are applied to the verification of grid service chain model based on its formalized results with π-calculus as mentioned in the previous sections. The analysis and checking of an equipment grid chain can be divided into 3 levels: correctness checking, temporal constraint checking and equivalence analysis. Correctness checking indicates the logical properties including no deadlock, final state reachability, etc. Temporal constraint checking indicates temporal properties depicted by logical formulas using the formal techniques. Equivalence analysis judges whether there is the same behavior and same property between two models and it forms an important basis for service replacement, flow optimization and model integration.

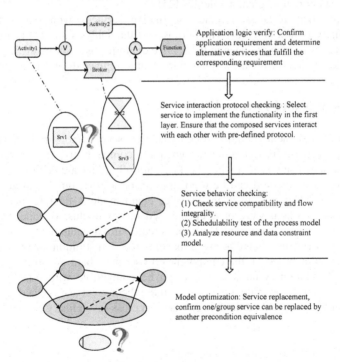

Fig. 2. Equipment grid service chain model's layered checking and analysis system

Applying model checking techniques in the field of grid systems raises new challenges as opposed to its traditional application domain of hardware design. Conventional model checking technology often counts on a holistic formal model which captures all the states or actions of the system as a whole. However, such a model for a grid system could be rather complicated. For example, it may involve the consideration of different system perspectives such as grid resources, security policies, and etc. Besides, the grid environment is dynamically evolving because of the life-cycle of grid services and the interactions among them.

Therefore, a layered verification architecture for grid environment based on above problem is needed as shown in Fig. 2. The layered verification idea includes not only the usage of model checking technique itself, but also the optimization techniques for the grid service chain model. The functions of each layer are described as follows.

Application logic verify layer: Confirm application requirement and determine alternative services that fulfill the corresponding requirement.

Service interaction protocol checking layer: Get service in accord with interaction protocol among optional services and compose service. In this layer, services are formalized with typed π-calculus and the correctness of the service interaction is thus ensured by the well-typeness of the composition of typed π-calculus processes.

Service behavior checking layer: Check service chain compatibility and integrity with model checking techniques based on the formal models of π-calculus. Schedulability test can also be carried out when real-time constraints are encountered with a timed version of original π-calculus [25].

Model optimization layer: Replace alternative services with the help of bi-simulation analysis in π-calculus. The purposes of the analysis are: (1) to find a safe substitution for an existing service in the service chain in case it is crushed; (2) to find a better service which fulfills the same requirement to replace the existing one.

6 Conclusions and Future Work

Grid system development should be emphasized on service mobility and interaction among grid services. Its correctness, logicality, compatibility, data property and related equipment state need to be checked carefully. The π-calculus as powerful formal specification method can be used to describe a grid complex system and its dynamic property. An equipment grid service chain model's flexible model and its layered checking system were developed based on π-calculus. By adopting the π-calculus based service chain model, we can create virtual equipments that integrate equipment resources distributed across a machine room, institution, or the globe. The study on π-calculus based on the equipment grid service chain model provides strict mathematic foundation. What's more, it can be compatible with other criteria. It would be beneficial to open up a new space in the theoretical and applied research on grid technology and formal methodology based on cross-disciplinary cooperation.

References

1. Jindong Wang, Hai Zhao, Guangjie Han, Jiyong Wang: Research of a SBDM model based on interoperable computing. Journal of China Institute of Communications. Vol. 25 No. 3 (2004) 84-93
2. Foster I, Kesselman C.: The Grid: Blueprint for a future Computing Infrastructure. USA: Morgan Kaufmann (1999)

3. Foster, I., Kesselman, C., et al.: The Anatomy of the grid: Enabling scalable virtual organizations. International Journal of Supercomputer Applications Vol. 15 No. 3 (2001) 200-222
4. Zhihui Du, Yu Chen, Peng Liu: Grid Computing. Publishing House of Tsinghua University (2002)
5. Ian Foster, Carl Kesselman. The Grid 2 : Blue print for a New Computing Infrastructure. USA:Morgan Kaufmann (2003)
6. Hai Jin, Pingpeng Yuan, Ke Shi: Grid Copmuting 2. Publishing House of Electronics Industry (2004)
7. Yuexuan Wang, Lianchen Liu, Xixiang Hu, Cheng Wu: The Study on Simulation Grid Technology for Equipment Resource Sharing System. In Proceedings of the 5th World Congress on Intelligent Control and Automation (2004) 3235-3239
8. Yuexuan Wang, Cheng Wu, Xixiang Hu, Lianchen Liu: The Study of Equipment Grid Based on Simulation Modeling. Computer Integrated Manufacturing Systems (2004) 10(9): 1031-1035
9. Yuexuan Wang, Lianchen Liu, Cheng Wu: Research on equipment resource scheduling in grids. The Third International Conference on Grid and Cooperative Computing (GCC 2004). Wuhan, China (2004) 927-930
10. Yuexuan Wang, Lianchen Liu, Cheng Wu: Research on Equipment Grid Platform for Resource Sharing. World Engineers Convention (WEC) Shanghai (2004) 148-151
11. Hey, A., and Trefethen, A. The UK e-Science Core Programme and the Grid. Future Generation Computer, Vol. 18 No. 8(2002) 1017-1031
12. Hey, A., Trefethen A.: The data deluge: An e-science perspective in Grid Computing: Making the Global Infrastructure a Reality. Wiley, New York (2003)
13. Yolanda, G., Ewa, D., et al.: Artificial Intelligence and Grids: Workflow Planning and Beyond. IEEE Intelligent Systems (2004) 19 (1): 26-33
14. Foster, I., Kesselman, C., et al.: The Philosophy of the Grid: An Open Grid Service Architecture for Distributed Systems. Global Grid Forum (2002)
15. Foster, I., Gannon, D., et al. : Open Grid Services Architecture Use Cases Version 1.0. Global Grid Forum public documents (GFD-I.029) (2004)
16. Tuecke, S., Czajkowski, K., et al.: Open Grid Services Infrastructure (OGSI) Version 1.0. Grid Forum public documents (GFD-I.015) (2003)
17. Sriram, K.; Patrick W.; et al. GSFL: A Workflow Framework for Grid Services. (2002) http://wwwunix.globus.org/cog/papers/gsfl-paper.pdf
18. ChinaGrid project: http://www.chinagrid.edu.cn.
19. Davies, N. J., Fensel, D. et al.: The future of Web Services. BT Technology Journal, Vol. 22, No.1 (2004) 118-130
20. Ding, Y.: A review of ontologies with the Semantic Web in view, Journal of Information Science, Vol. 27 No. 6 (2001) 377-384
21. Kouadri, M. S., Hirsbrunner, B.: Towards a Context-Based Service Composition Framework, Proceedings of the International Conference on Web Services (2003) 42-45
22. Van der Aalst: Verification of workflow nets. Lecture Notes in Computer Science (1997) 1248: 407
23. Milner, R.: Communicating and Mobile Systems: the π-calculus. Cambridge University Press (1999)
24. Milner, R.: Communication and Concurrency. Prentice Hall (1989)
25. Ke Xu., Lianchen Liu, Cheng Wu: Time Pi Calculus and Weak-timed Bisimulation Analysis. Compter Integrated Manufacturinig System. In press

A Performance-Based Parallel Loop Self-scheduling on Grid Computing Environments

Wen-Chung Shih[1], Chao-Tung Yang[2,*], and Shian-Shyong Tseng[1,3]

[1] Department of Computer and Information Science, National Chiao Tung University,
Hsinchu 300, Taiwan, R.O.C.
{gis90805, sstseng}@cis.nctu.edu.tw
[2] High-Performance Computing Laboratory,
Department of Computer Science and Information Engineering,
Tunghai University,
Taichung 407, Taiwan, R.O.C.
ctyang@thu.edu.tw
[3] Department of Information Science and Applications,
Asia University,
Taichung 413, Taiwan, R.O.C.
sstseng@asia.edu.tw

Abstract. Efficient loop scheduling on parallel and distributed systems depends mostly on load balancing, especially on heterogeneous PC-based cluster and grid computing environments. In this paper, a general approach, named Performance-Based Parallel Loop Self-Scheduling (PPLSS), was given to partition workload according to performance of grid nodes. This approach was applied to three types of application programs, which were executed on a testbed grid. Experimental results showed that our approach could execute efficiently for most scheduling parameters when estimation of node performance was accurate.

Keywords: Parallel loops, Loop scheduling, Self-scheduling, Grid computing, Globus, MPI.

1 Introduction

A promising approach to parallel computing is grid computing, which utilizes heterogeneous computers through the Internet to compute [2, 5, 6]. Traditional schemes for parallel loop scheduling include static scheduling and dynamic scheduling [8]. While the former might incur load imbalancing on heterogeneous environments, the latter has not been investigated thoroughly on grid environments.

Self-scheduling is a major class of dynamic loop scheduling schemes. Well-known self-scheduling schemes include Pure Self-Scheduling (PSS), Chunk Self-Scheduling (CSS), Guided Self-Scheduling (GSS) [9], Factoring Self-Scheduling (FSS) [7], and Trapezoid Self-Scheduling (TSS) [10]. These schemes partition work load according to a simple formula, not considering performance of processors.

---

* Corresponding author.

H. Jin, D. Reed, and W. Jiang (Eds.): NPC 2005, LNCS 3779, pp. 48 – 55, 2005.

In [11], a method (α self-scheduling) is proposed to improve well-known self-scheduling schemes. Although this scheme partition work load according to CPU clock speed of processors, CPU could not completely represent performance of processors. In [12], an approach is proposed to adjust α scheduling parameter, but performance is still estimated only by CPU speed. In [4], a class of self-scheduling schemes is extended to heterogeneous distributed systems.

In this paper, we address the performance estimation issue in parallel loop scheduling, and propose a general approach called Performance-Based Parallel Loop Self-Scheduling (PPLSS). This approach estimates the performance ratio of each node to partition loop iterations. For verification, this approach is applied to three types of application programs.

We organize the rest of this paper as follows. Section 2 describes the background about parallel loop self-scheduling schemes. Next, our approach is presented in section 3. In section 4, our system configuration is specified and experimental results on three application programs are also reported. Finally, the conclusion is given in the last section.

2 Background

In this section, related work on self-scheduling schemes is described. First, we review several well-known self-scheduling schemes. Next, two recently proposed schemes are introduced.

2.1 Well-Known Self-scheduling Schemes

Traditional self-scheduling schemes operate in common. At each step, the master assigns some amount of loop iterations to an idle slave. These schemes differ in the way how the master computes the amount to next idle slave. The well-known schemes include PSS, CSS, GSS, FSS and TSS. Table 1 shows the different chunk sizes for a problem with the number of iteration $N=1536$ and the number of processor $p=4$.

Table 1. Sample partition size

Scheme	Sample partition size
PSS	1, 1, 1, 1, 1, 1, 1, 1, 1, 1, ...
CSS(125)	125, 125, 125, 125, 125, 125, 125, 125, 125, ...
FSS	192, 192, 192, 192, 96, 96, 96, 96, 48, ...
GSS	384, 288, 216, 162, 122, 91, 69, 51, 39, ...
TSS	192, 180, 168, 156, 144, 132, 120, 108, 96, ...

2.2 Schemes for Cluster and Grid Environments

In [11], the authors revise known loop self-scheduling schemes for extremely heterogeneous PC-cluster environments. The algorithm is divided into two phases. In phase one, α% of workload is partitioned according to CPU clock of processors. Then, the rest of workload is scheduled according to some well-known selfscheduling in the second phase.

In [3, 12], a new scheme for heterogeneous grid computing environments is proposed. This scheme is still a two-phased approach. However, it can adjust the α scheduling parameter according to the relative heterogeneity of the environment.

3   Performance-Based Parallel Loop Self-scheduling (PPLSS)

In this section, the concept of performance estimation is presented first. After that, the algorithm of our approach is described.

3.1   Performance Estimation

We propose to estimate performance of each grid node, and assign work load to each node accordingly. In this paper, our performance function (PF) for node j is defined as

$$PF_j = w \times \frac{1/T_j}{\displaystyle\sum_{\forall node_i \in S} 1/T_i} \tag{1}$$

where

- S is the set of all grid nodes.
- T_i is the execution time (sec.) of node i for some application program, such as matrix multiplication.
- w is the weight of this term.

The performance ratio (PR) is defined to be the ratio of all performance functions. For instance, assume the PF of three nodes are 1/2, 1/3 and 1/4. Then, the PR is 1/2 : 1/3 : 1/4; i.e., the PR of the three nodes is 6 : 4 : 3. In other words, if there are 13 loop iterations, 6 iterations will be assigned to the first node, 4 iterations will be assigned to the second node, and 3 iterations will be assigned to the last one.

3.2   Algorithm

The algorithm of our approach is modified from [11], and master program and slave program are listed as follows.

Module MASTER
```
Gather performance ratio of all slave nodes
r = 0;
for (i = 1; i < number_of_slaves; i++) {
    partition α% of loop iterations according to the
performance ratio;
    send data to slave nodes;
    r++;
}
Partition (100-α)% of loop iterations into the task
queue using some known self-scheduling scheme
Probe for returned results
Do {
```

```
         Distinguish source and receive returned data
         If the task queue is not empty then
                Send another data to the idle slave
                r -- ;
              else
                send TAG = 0 to the idle slave
    } while (r > 0)
    END MASTER
```
Module SLAVE
```
  Probe if some data in
  While (TAG > 0) {
         Receive initial solution and size of subtask
  work and compute to fine solution
         Send the result to the master
         Probe if some data in
  }
  END SLAVE
```

4 Experimental Results

In this section, our grid configuration is presented. Then, experimental results for matrix multiplication, Mandelbrot and circuit satisfiability are shown respectively.

4.1 Grid Environments

The testbed grid includes three clusters which are located in three universities respectively. Cluster 1, located in Providence University, has five nodes. One of the nodes is designated as the master node. Cluster 2, located in Hsiuping Institute of Technology, has four nodes. Cluster 3, located in Tunghai University, also has four nodes. We use the following middleware to build the grid:

- Globus Toolkit 3.0.2
- Mpich library 1.2.6

For readability of experimental results, the naming of our implementation is listed in Table 2.

Table 2. Description of our implementation for all programs

AP	Name	Description
Matrix Multiplication,	G(F, T)SS	Dynamic scheduling G(F, T)SS
Mandelbrot, and	NG(F, T)SS	Fixed α scheduling + G(F, T)SS
Circuit Satisfiability	PG(F, T)SS	Our scheduling + G(F, T)SS

4.2 Application 1: Matrix Multiplication

The matrix multiplication is a fundamental operation in many applications. In this subsection, we investigate how scheduling parameters influence performance. In the experiment as shown in Fig. 1(a), we find NGSS get best performance when $\alpha = 50$.

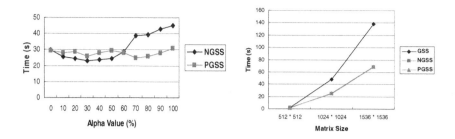

Fig. 1. (a)Execution time for different alpha values (b) Execution Time of Matrix Multiplication with GSS

Therefore, this value is adopted for the next experiment. Fig. 1(b) illustrates the result for $\alpha= 50$. Although both NGSS and our PGSS seem to perform well the same, PGSS is not restricted by the selection of α value. In other words, PGSS is more robust.

Fig. 2(a) illustrates the result for $\alpha= 30$. Although FSS, NFSS and our PFSS seem to perform well the same, PFSS is not restricted by the selection of α value. In other words, PFSS is more robust. Fig. 2(b) illustrates the result for $\alpha= 30$. Although TSS, NTSS and our PTSS seem to perform well the same, PTSS is not restricted by the selection of α value. In other words, PTSS is more robust.

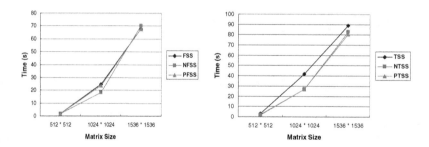

Fig. 2. (a) Execution Time of Matrix Multiplication with FSS (b) Execution Time of Matrix Multiplication with TSS

For application of Matrix Multiplication, experimental results show that our performance-based approach is efficient and robust.

4.3 Application 2: Mandelbrot

The Mandelbrot set is a problem involving the same computation on different data points which have different convergence rates [1]. In this subsection, we investigate how scheduling parameters influence performance. In the experiment as shown in Fig. 3(a), we find NGSS get best performance when $\alpha= 50$. Therefore, this value is adopted for the next experiment. Fig. 3(b) illustrates the result for $\alpha= 50$. Although both NGSS and our PGSS seem to perform well the same, PGSS is not restricted by the selection of α value. In other words, PGSS is more robust.

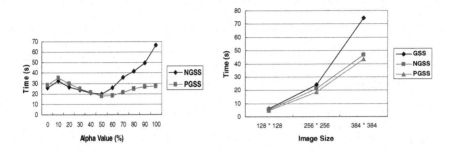

Fig. 3. (a)Execution time for different alpha values (b) Execution Time of Mandelbrot with GSS

Fig. 4(a) illustrates the result for $\alpha = 50$. Although FSS, NFSS and our PFSS seem to perform well the same, PFSS is not restricted by the selection of α value. In other words, PFSS is more robust. Fig. 4(b) illustrates the result for $\alpha = 50$. Although TSS, NTSS and our PTSS seem to perform well the same, PTSS is not restricted by the selection of α value. In other words, PTSS is more robust.

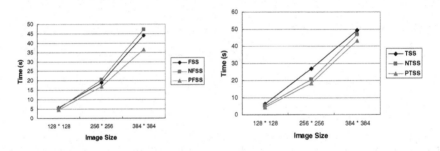

Fig. 4. (a) Execution Time of Mandelbrot with FSS (b) Execution Time of Mandelbrot with TSS

For application of the Mandelbrot set, experimental results show that our performance-based approach is efficient and robust.

4.4   Application 3: Circuit Satisfiability

The circuit satisfiability problem is one involving a combinational circuit composed of AND, OR, and NOT gates. In this subsection, we investigate how scheduling parameters influence performance. In the experiment as shown in Fig. 5(a), we find NGSS get best performance when $\alpha = 50$. Therefore, this value is adopted for the next experiment. Fig. 5(b) illustrates the result for $\alpha = 50$. Although both NGSS and our PGSS seem to perform well the same, PGSS is not restricted by the selection of α value. In other words, PGSS is more robust.

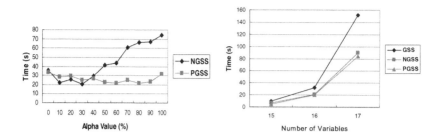

Fig. 5. (a)Execution time for different alpha values (b) Execution Time of Circuit Satisfiability with GSS

Fig. 6(a) illustrates the result for α= 50. Although FSS, NFSS and our PFSS seem to perform well the same, PFSS is not restricted by the selection of α values. In other words, PFSS is more robust. Fig. 6(b) illustrates the result for α= 50. Although TSS, NTSS and our PTSS seem to perform well the same, PTSS is not restricted by the selection of α value. In other words, PTSS is more robust.

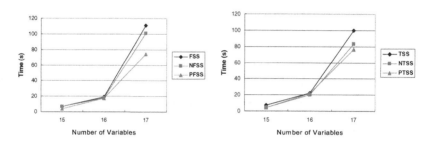

Fig. 6. (a) Execution Time of Circuit Satisfiability with FSS (b) Execution Time of Circuit Satisfiability with TSS

For application of the Circuit Satisfiability problem, experimental results show that our performance-based approach is efficient and robust.

5 Conclusions and Future Work

We have proposed a performance-based parallel loop self-scheduling (PPLSS) approach, which partitions work load according to performance ratio of grid nodes. It has been compared with previous algorithms by experiments on three types of application programs. In each case, our approach can obtain performance improvement on previous schemes. Besides, our approach is less sensitive to α values than previous schemes; in other words, it is more robust. In our future work, we will implement more types of application programs to verify our approach. Furthermore, we hope to find better ways of modeling the performance function, incorporating network information.

References

1. Introduction To The Mandelbrot Set, http://www.ddewey.net/mandelbrot/
2. What Is Grid Computing, http://www-1.ibm.com/grid/about_grid/what_is.shtml/
3. Kuan-Wei Cheng, Chao-Tung Yang, Chuan-Lin Lai, and Shun-Chyi Chang, "A Parallel Loop Self-Scheduling on Grid Computing Environments," *Proceedings of the 2004 IEEE International Symposium on Parallel Architectures, Algorithms and Networks*, pp. 409-414, KH, China, May 2004.
4. A. T. Chronopoulos, R. Andonie, M. Benche and D.Grosu, "A Class of Loop Self-Scheduling for Heterogeneous Clusters," *Proceedings of the 2001 IEEE International Conference on Cluster Computing*, pp. 282-291, 2001.
5. K. Czajkowski, S. Fitzgerald, I. Foster, and C. Kesselman, "Grid Information Services for Distributed Resource Sharing," *Proceedings of the 10th IEEE International Symposium on High-Performance Distributed Computing (HPDC-10)*, pp. 181-194, August 2001.
6. I. Foster, "The Grid: A New Infrastructure for 21st Century Science," *Physics Today*, 55(2):42-47, 2002.
7. S. F. Hummel, E. Schonberg, and L. E. Flynn, "Factoring: a method scheme for scheduling parallel loops," *Communications of the ACM*, vol. 35, 1992, pp. 90-101.
8. H. Li, S. Tandri, M. Stumm and K. C. Sevcik, "Locality and Loop Scheduling on NUMA Multiprocessors," *Proceedings of the 1993 International Conference on Parallel Processing*, vol. II, pp. 140-147, 1993.
9. C. D. Polychronopoulos and D. Kuck, "Guided Self-Scheduling: a Practical Scheduling Scheme for Parallel Supercomputers," *IEEE Trans. on Computers*, vol. 36, no. 12, pp. 1425-1439, 1987.
10. T. H. Tzen and L. M. Ni, "Trapezoid self-scheduling: a practical scheduling scheme for parallel compilers," *IEEE Transactions on Parallel and Distributed Systems*, vol. 4, 1993, pp. 87-98.
11. Chao-Tung Yang and Shun-Chyi Chang, "A Parallel Loop Self-Scheduling on Extremely Heterogeneous PC Clusters," *Journal of Information Science and Engineering*, vol. 20, no. 2, pp. 263-273, March 2004.
12. Chao-Tung Yang, Kuan-Wei Cheng, and Kuan-Ching Li, "An Efficient Parallel Loop Self-Scheduling on Grid Environments," *NPC'2004 IFIP International Conference on Network and Parallel Computing, Lecture Notes in Computer Science*, Springer-Verlag Heidelberg, Hai Jin, Guangrong Gao, Zhiwei Xu (Eds.), vol. 3222, pp. 92-100, Oct. 2004.

A Resource-Based Server Performance Control for Grid Computing Systems[*]

Naixue Xiong[1,3], Xavier Défago[1,2], Yanxiang He[3], and Yan Yang[4]

[1] School of Information Science,
Japan Advanced Institute of Science and Technology (JAIST), Japan
naixue@jaist.ac.jp
[2] PRESTO, Japan Science and Technology Agency (JST),
defago@jaist.ac.jp
[3] The State Key Lab of Software Engineering, Computer School,
Wuhan University, PR China
yxhe@whu.edu.cn
[4] Computer School, Wuhan university of science and technology, PR China
Y.Yang@mail.ccnu.edu.cn

Abstract. With the rapid advances in Internet and Grid technique, an increasing number of applications will involve computing systems. These applications in turn create an increasing demand for efficient resource management, request handling policies and admission control. In this paper, we propose an efficient admission control algorithm to protect the critical resource of server and improve the performance of the computing system. Stability of CPU utilization is aimed to protect the server from overload and under-load. It is then beneficial to keep a satisfactory response time of requests, high throughput and less potential loss of service. We analyze the stability in detail and present a method for tuning control gains in order to guarantee the system stability. Finally, we perform simulations to evaluate the performance of the proposed algorithm. Simulation results demonstrate that the proposed algorithm stabilizes the utilization of CPU in the computing system if the control gains are appropriately chosen on the basis of system stability. It then achieves satisfactory performance.

1 Introduction

With the rapid advances in Internet Application and Grid technique, the number of servers increased sharply in recent years, an increasing number of server applications will involve a large of computing systems. For every server, computing means consuming its resources, including CPU slot, memory, bandwidth and so on. When one or several kinds of resources are scare, the server will be regarded as overload. Because web server overload can lead to loss of service and even possible damage to some critical resources due to its over-utilization,

---

[*] This research is conducted as a program for the 21st Century COE Program by Ministry of Education, Culture, Sports, Science and Technology.

H. Jin, D. Reed, and W. Jiang (Eds.): NPC 2005, LNCS 3779, pp. 56–64, 2005.

web servers need to be protected from overload. Therefore, there is a need of efficient admission control to protect these resources and services in the above computing systems, especially during periods of peak server load. A number of admission control schemes have been studied in [1-6]. In these admission control methods, much attention has been paid to the context of performance metrics, such as the request response time, system throughput and efficient serving rate. The controller software process is embedded in Apache Server Linux OS in [7]. However, in [7], the stability of the network control system is not discussed, while this requirement to a control system in engineering is very important. Stability of control systems can protect the server from overload and under-load. It is then beneficial to keep a satisfactory response time of requests, high throughput and less potentially loss of service. The performance of an unstable system can severely and persistently diverge from the desired performance so as to cause system malfunctioning even worse to lead to the whole system break down [2]. Choosing the proper setting for tuning parameters is also very important for guaranteeing the stability of the whole system and achieving satisfactory performance.

In this paper, we propose an effective admission control scheme that utilizes the information about the resource consumption, which is indicated by CPU utilization. We call the approach resource-based admission control. Due to stability is a key requirement in admission control to achieve satisfactory performance, we focus on the stability analysis of the proposed network controller, and give a procedure for tuning the control gains in detail. The approach is shown by simulations to be able to avoid resource over-utilization and server overload and improve the computing system performance. Explicitly, we compare by simulations the system performance under various control schemes, namely the stable and unstable situations.

2   Design of Admission Controller

In controller design, an analysis of the computing system models leads to a controller that will achieve the service level objects. We report on an analysis of a closed-loop system using a proportional integral plus derivative (PID) control law. The object is to maintain the target CPU utilization. Using stability analyzing method in classical control theory, we are able to design a PID controller that leads the computing system to be stable and thus avoid the system oscillations in response to requests. Such oscillations are undesirable since they increase variability, thereby resulting in a failure to meet the service level objects.

2.1   Notations

Unless otherwise specified, the following notations are pertain to the considered computing system model:

$m(n)$: the number of maximum parallel threads in the nth interval;
$f(n)$:the feedback information on server's utilization in the nth interval;

u: the target CPU utilization ratio of genetic server;
$r(n)$: the number of requests in the nth interval;
k_P: the proportional control gain;
k_I : the integral control gain;
k_D : the Derivative control gain;
N: the duration of time slots.

2.2 Selection of Sampling Time

The choice of sampling time is a key factor that affects the performance of the admission controller [2]. In the controlled system, the sampling time not only determines the length of time between successive updates of the control inputs, but also the length of time system outputs are averaged over. In this sense, the sampling time is also an averaging interval. A short sampling time enables the controller to reacts to changes in the system quickly but increases measurement overhead. A long sampling time keeps the controller from overreacting to random fluctuations by averaging out the stochastic of the metrics, but will also yield a slow response. In order to balance these competing goals, the minimum sampling time in network control system must be larger than two special kinds of time [8]. One is the sampling time of SNMP (simple network management protocol) agent itself and the other is the Round Trip Time (RTT) between the controller and controlled device. The first one is easy to be found from the manuals of device, and the second one should be measured on Internet.

Some sampling rules about robustness can be supposed as below. If the sampling interval is less than the minimum RTT, the feedback will be regarded as the $(n+1)$th sampling results, because the $(n-1)$th feedback has been received and the $(n+1)$th sampling result is impossible to be retrieved so quickly. If the interval is equal to or more than the average RTT, the feedback will be regarded as the $(n+1)$th sampling results, because we suppose that the nth sampling result has been lost. On the basis of this simple and practical method, we design the PID controller.

2.3 Controller Design and Stability Analysis

The hardware and software in admission closed loop control system are distributed as shown in Fig. 1. The reference is the desired CPU utilization denoted by u. In this approach, the job of the administrator is shifted from directly setting the tuning parameters to supplying the desired utilization value. At the server, an admission control algorithm checks if the required CPU is available and determines if the arriving request can be admitted into the system. The server is able to service maximum number of requests in a round. The request will be admitted into the system if the number of requests currently being served plus one request is not more than the maximum number of requests. Because an inappropriately designed controller can overreact to performance errors and push a real-time system to unstable conditions, stability is a necessary condition for achieving the desired performance reference and is especially of importance.

Since the direct measurements of $m(n)$ and $f(n)$ is not be acquired, we can use the history values of $m(i)$ and $f(i)$ $(i = 1, 2, ..., N)$ to estimate $m(n)$ and $f(n)$. Therefore we can design a PID controller that can be better served to predict the number of maximum parallel threads in the nth interval than a simple proportional controller [7, 8].

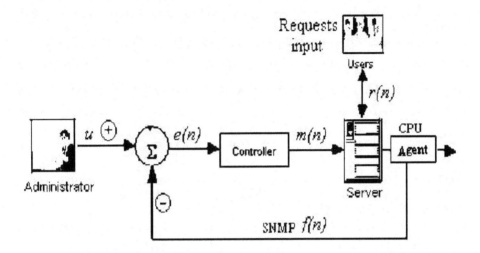

Fig. 1. Block diagram of feedback system for control of CPU utilization

In the following, we propose the PID controller, analyze its system stability and give the specific method for tuning control gains. The PID controller and the state equation of system are respectively described as follows:

$$m(n) = k_P(f(n) - u) + k_I \sum_{j=1}^{N} m(n - j) + k_D[f(n) - f(n - 1)]. \qquad (1)$$

$$f(n) = cf(n - 1) + am(n - 1) + b \sum_{j=2}^{N} m(n - j). \qquad (2)$$

Where a, b and c are constants that are estimated from statistical data. It is noted that the precise description given in (2) can be obtained by using some system identification method on the basis of statistical data. A statistical autoregressive-moving-average (ARMA) is established in [9] to fit the historical measurement. In this method, the procedure of estimating the parameters is as follows: First, measurement of the target system is obtained while configuring the input parameters in a controlled way. Second, the least-squares regression method is used to estimate a, b and c for different values of N. In general, the fit of the model improves as N is increased. For the concrete technique with regard to this modeling process, one is referred to [10].

For analysis purposes, it is much more convenient to convert the above two linear equations from the time domain into the z (frequency) domain, where z is a complex number. z-transfer function has several nice properties. For example, consider two linear systems with transforms $A(z)$ and $B(z)$. Then the transform of the system formed by connecting these two in series is $A(z)B(z)$. If outputs of the two systems are summed, then the combined system has the transform $A(z) + B(z)$. Also, if the input to $A(z)$ is multiplied by k, then the associated transform is $kA(z)$.

Applying these principles to equations (1) and (2), we obtain the z-transform:

$$M(z) = k_P(F(z) - uD(z)) + k_I \sum_{j=1}^{N} M(z)z^{-j} + k_D F(z)(1 - z^{-1}). \qquad (3)$$

$$F(z) = cF(z)z^{-1} + aM(z)z^{-1} + b\sum_{j=2}^{N} M(z)z^{-j}. \qquad (4)$$

Where
$M(z) = \sum_{n=0}^{\infty} m(n)z^{-n}$, $F(z) = \sum_{n=0}^{\infty} f(n)z^{-n}$, $D(z) = \frac{z}{1-z}$.
From (3), we can derive

$$M(z)(1 - k_I \sum_{j=1}^{N} z^{-j}) = k_P(F(z) - uD(z)) + k_D F(z)(1 - z^{-1}). \qquad (5)$$

By substituting (5) into (4), one yields

$$(1 - cz^{-1})(1 - k_I \sum_{j=1}^{N} z^{-j})F(z) = (az^{-1} + b\sum_{j=2}^{N} z^{-j})k_P(F(z) - uD(z))$$
$$+(az^{-1} + b\sum_{j=2}^{N} z^{-j})k_D F(z)(1 - z^{-1}). \qquad (6)$$

From (6), we can get

$$[(1 - cz^{-1})(1 - k_I \sum_{j=1}^{N} z^{-j}) - ak_P z^{-1} - bk_P \sum_{j=2}^{N} z^{-j} - ak_D z^{-1}(1 - z^{-1})$$
$$-bk_D(1 - z^{-1})\sum_{j=2}^{N} z^{-j}] \cdot F(z) = -uk_P D(z)(az^{-1} + b\sum_{j=2}^{N} z^{-j}). \qquad (7)$$

Both sides of (7) are multiplied by z , we can get

$$[(z - c)(1 - k_I \sum_{j=1}^{N} z^{-j}) - ak_P - bk_P \sum_{j=2}^{N} z^{1-j} - ak_D(1 - z^{-1})$$
$$-bk_D(z - 1)\sum_{j=2}^{N} z^{-j}] \cdot F(z) = -uk_P D(z)(a + b\sum_{j=2}^{N} z^{1-j}). \qquad (8)$$

Then the following description $\triangle(z)$ represents the characteristic polynomial of (7)

$$\triangle z = (z - c)(1 - k_I \sum_{j=1}^{N} z^{-j}) - ak_P - bk_P \sum_{j=2}^{N} z^{1-j}$$

$$-ak_D(1 - z^{-1}) - bk_D(z - 1)\sum_{j=2}^{N} z^{-j} \qquad (9)$$

$$= z - (k_I + bk_P + bk_D)\sum_{j=2}^{N} z^{1-j} + (ck_I + bk_D)\sum_{j=2}^{N} z^{-j}$$

$$-(k_I + c + ak_P + ak_D) + (ak_D + ck_I)z^{-1}.$$

The above characteristic polynomial is closely related to system stability. From control theory [10, 11], when all the zeros of this polynomial lie within the unit circle, the system governed by (1) and (2) is stable in terms of the server utilization. To yield a condition of stability, we let $k_I = bk_P/(c - 1)$, $a = b$ and $k_D = ck_P/(1 - c)$. The roots of the equation $\triangle z = 0$ are $z = c$. Therefore, we can get when $|c| < 1$, all roots are in the unit circle. In this case, the controlled computing system is stable in terms of the CPU utilization.

3   Performance Evaluation

In this section, we mainly consider the transient-state response and its stability. Transient-state response represents the responsiveness and efficiency of adaptive resource scheduling in reacting to changes in run-time conditions.

In the following experiments, we investigate if the proposed connection control scheme can be used to protect a web server from overload by a targeted

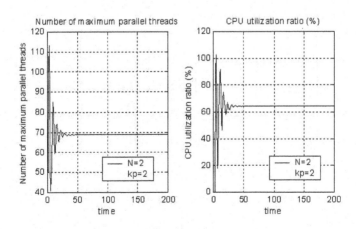

Fig. 2. Control effect of the scheme with parameters $N = 2$, $k_P = 2$ (stable fast responsive case)

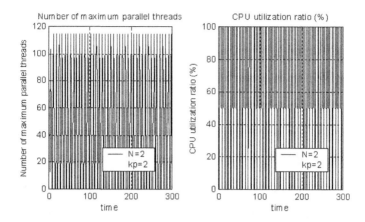

Fig. 3. Control effect of the scheme with parameters $N = 2$, $k_P = 2$ (unstable case)

control of high overhead requests. As mentioned in [8, 12], CPU utilization ratio between 60% and 70% is good for it to avoid damage after computing for a long time. Therefore, in our simulations the expected CPU utilization ratio u in simulation is set to be 65%. The values of a, b and c are similar to those suggested in [8, 12], i.e., $a = 0.5$, $b = 0.5$, $c = 0.6$. To simplify the control system, we measure the rule of input requests as "pulse signal" type. The period of such request is two minutes, in the first half period, there're one hundred requests per minute and in the second there are forty. The average input rate is seventy requests per minute.

We perform simulations for different values of a, b, c, k_I, k_P and k_D control gains. The simulation results are shown in Figures 2-5. Obviously, control gains

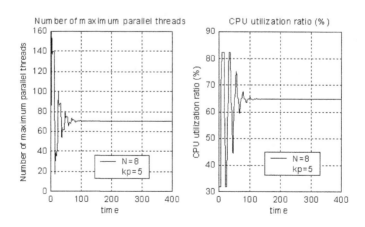

Fig. 4. Control effect of the scheme with parameters $N = 8$, $k_P = 5$ (Stable but sluggish case)

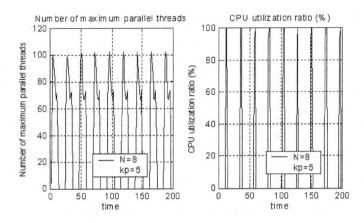

Fig. 5. Control effect of the scheme with parameters $N = 8$, $k_P = 5$ (unstable case)

determine the stability of system and the value of N influences the response of system. The smaller N is, the faster the system achieves steady state. When the control gains are chosen in the area of stability (see Figure 2 and Figure 4) based on the above stability condition, the CPU utilization rate is gradually becoming stable after adjusted for a short time. So is the number of maximum parallel threads. On the contrary, when control gains are not chosen in the area of stability (refer to Figure 3 and Figure 5), the system is unstable, and severe oscillations appear which will result in a failure to meet the service level objects.

The above performance profile establishes a set of metrics of adaptive real-time systems based on the specification of dynamic response in control theory. The metrics enables system designers to apply established control theory techniques to achieve stability, and meet transient and steady state specifications.

4   Conclusions

The widespread use of information technology has motivated the need of performance management of computing systems. In network control system, transfer function is not clear between input and output variables. Therefore, in this paper, we propose the use of a PID feedback control strategy to achieve the goal of optimized performance management. The proposed controller can protect the crucial resource of the server and enhance the performance of the server. Furthermore, systems administrator can translate desired performance into appropriate setting of available tuning parameters. Simulation results demonstrate the proposed algorithm can be applied into the server and can be very effective. Certainly, challenges still exist in the modeling and control of computing systems, for example computing systems generally exhibit stochastic behavior inspired by random requests from users and how to control the performance of them to scale such stochastic behavior would be a subject for future research.

References

1. P. Mundur, R. Simon, and A. Sood: Integrated Admission Control in Hierarchical Video-on-Demand Systems. In Proceedings of the IEEE International Conference on Multimedia Computing and Systems (ICMCS '99), pp. 220-225, Florence, Italy, June 7-11, 1999
2. N. Gandhi and DM Tilbury, Y. Diao, J. Hellerstein, and S. Parekh: MIMO Control of an Apache Web Server: Modeling and Controller Design. Proceedings of American Control Conference, May 2002
3. K. H Yum, E. J Kim, C. R Das, M. Yousif, and J. Duato: Integrated Admission and Congestion Control for QoS Support in Clusters. In Proceedings of IEEE International Conference on Cluster Computing, pp.325-332, September 2002, Chicago, Illinois, pp. 325
4. R. Mortier, I. Pratt, C. Clark, and S. Crosby: Implicit Admission Control. IEEE Journal on Selected Areas in Communications, Vol. 18, No.12, 2000
5. F. Kelly, P. Key, and S. Zachary: Distributed Admission Control. IEEE Journal on Selected Areas in Communications, Vol. 18, No. 12, Dec. 2000
6. R. J Gibbens, F. P Kelly, and P. B Key: A decision-theoretic approach to call admission control in ATM networks. IEEE Journal on Selected Areas of Communications, pp. 1101- 1114, August 1995
7. Thiemo Voigt, Gunningberg: Handling Multiple bottlenecks in web servers using adaptive inbound controls. Seventh International Workshop on Protocols for High-Speed Networks, Berlin, German, April 2002
8. Yijiao Yu, Qin Liu and Liansheng Tan: Application of server performance control with simple network management protocol. The Second International Workshop on Grid and Cooperative Computing, Shanghai, China, December 2003
9. Arnold Neumaier, Tapio Schneider: Estimation of parameters and eigenmodes of multivariate autoregressive models. ACM Transactions on Mathematical Software (TOMS), Volume 27, Issue 1, pp. 27 - 57, March 2001
10. J. L Hellerstein and S Parekh: An introduction to control theory with applications to computer science. ACM SIGMETRICS, 2001
11. W. Kamen, B. S. Heck: Fundamentals of Signals and Systems Using the Web and Matlab. Science Press and Pearson Education North Asia Limited, 2000
12. S. Parekh, N. Gandhi, J. Hellerstein, D. Tilbury, T. Jayram, and J. Bigus: Using control theory to achieve service level objectives in performance management. Journal of Real-time Systems, 23 (1/2), July 2002

IBP: An Index-Based XML Parser Model

Haihui Zhang[1], Xingshe Zhou [1], Yang Gang[1], and Xiaojun Wu [2]

[1] College of Computer Science, Northwestern Polytechnical University,
Xi'an, Shaanxi, China, 710072
zhh409@tom.com, zhouxs@nwpu.edu.cn, yang.gang@gmai.com
[2] College of Information Engineering, Chang'an University,
Xi'an, Shaanxi, China, 710064
depender@yahoo.com

Abstract. With XML widely used in distributed system, the existing parser models, DOM and SAX, are inefficient and resource intensive for applications with large XML documents. This paper presents an index-based parser model (IBP), which contains validation and non-validation modes, supports nearly all the XML characteristics. IBP has the characters of speediness, robustness and low resource requirement, which is more suitable for mass information parsing. We presents the application of IBP in a real-time distributed monitoring prototype system, the results have shown IBP effective.

1 Introduction

XML (Extensible Mark-up Language) is a meta-language to describe other markup languages. Since it appeared, XML has got greatly development and become standard of information exchange. Apart from traditional documents, it also comprises textual files describing graphical objects, transactions, protocol data units and all other kind of imaginable structured data. Despite XML's well known advantages, it has one key disadvantage: document size. Indeed, the XML standard explicitly states that markup terseness was *not* a design goal. Consequently, XML documents can be many times larger than equivalent non-standardized text or binary formats [2].

XML-conscious compression techniques have been well researched, XMLZIP, by XML Solutions [3], and Liefke and Suciu's XMILL[1], of which we are aware, also recently the Wireless Access Protocol standard group's Binary XML Content Format (WBXML) [4] and MHM[5] which based on Prediction by Partial Match (PPM). They are designed to reduce the size of XML documents with no loss of functionality or semantic information.

In a large-scale distributed system, it is always needed to exchange information with some applications that adopt original XML expression, so compression is not for all occasions. As Matthias[6] pointed out that in real-world experiences of using XML with databases, XML parsing was usually the main performance bottleneck. XML parser takes a most important role in XML applications. There are two models of XML parsers, DOM and SAX, which are proved to be ineffective for large XML database. Another feasible measure is to optimize the XML parser.

In our research, we develop Index-based Parser Model (IBP), which support almost whole XML specifications. With it, we can get element from the large XML file by

H. Jin, D. Reed, and W. Jiang (Eds.): NPC 2005, LNCS 3779, pp. 65–71, 2005.

its' multilevel index. It has the characteristic that parsing cost does not increase with the document size. Especially when parsing large XML file, it can get significant performance improvement compared to SAX and DOM.

2   Existing XML Parser Models

A XML parser is a basic but also very important tool. Publicly available parsers in use today, such as IBM's XML4J, Microsoft' MSXML, Oracle's XML Parser, Sun's Java[TM] Project X and some open source code parsers such as Expat, OpenXML, Xerces, SXP. Most XML parsing libraries use one of two interfaces, Simple API for XML (SAX) [7] and Document Object Model (DOM) [8]. XML parsing allows for optional validation of an XML document against a DTD or XML schema, so classified with validation and non-validation.

2.1   Document Object Model (DOM)

DOM is a standard tree-based API specification and under constant development by the Document Object Model working group at the W3C (World Wide Web Consortium). A tree-based parser parses and compiles an XML document into an internal, in-memory tree structure that represents the XML document's logical structure, which then is made available to the application. The current version is DOM Level 2 proposed recommendation [9], which is a platform-and-language-neutral interface that allows applications to dynamically access and update the content and structure of documents. DOM does allow applications to perform tree operations such as node additions, modifications, conversions and removals.

Since a DOM parser constructs an internal tree representation of the XML document content in main memory, it consumes memory proportional to the size of the document (2 to 5 times, hence unsuitable for large documents) [6]. Also, when a DOM parser constructs a tree, it will take account of all objects such as elements, text and attributes. But if applications only pay attention constantly to small proportion of total objects, the resource occupancy by which rarely or never used is striking. Lazy DOM parsers materialize only those parts of the document tree that are actually accessed, if most the document is accessed, lazy DOM is slower than regular DOM.

2.2   Simple API for XML (SAX)

SAX is a simple, low-level event-based API specification [7] and developed collaboratively by the members of the XML-DEV mailing list, hosted by OASIS. SAX 2.0 was released on the 5th of May 2000, and is free for both commercial and non-commercial use. SAX reports parsing events (such as the start and end of elements) directly to the application through callbacks. The application uses SAX parser to implement handlers to deal with different events. The memory consumption does not grow with the size of the document and it is possible to get the desired data without parsing the whole document. In general, applications requiring random access to the document nodes use a DOM parser while for serial access a SAX parser is better.

On the other hand, SAX has some disadvantages that restrict its application. SAX events are stateless, so, it may result in repeatedly parsing of the document to get multi-elements that scattered in the file. More serious is that events are only used to find the elements, applications must maintain lots of specially callback handles which are full of IF/ELSE structures. SAX is read only and difficult to carry out complex query.

3 Index-Based Parser Model (IBP)

Through our experiences of using XML with databases, we noted that XML documents contain one or more key tags just as index in relational database. So we introduce the index mechanism to the parsing process. There is an initial operation before the operation on XML document, during which key tag index tables and sub-tree index tables will be built. After that, IBP allow applications to perform operations based on these tables.

The following example shows the basic process of our IBP method. This is a simple XML document (named BookSet.xml) with DTD statements.

```
<?xml version="1.0" encoding="GB2312" ?>
<!ELEMENT BookSet (Book*)>
<!ELEMENT Book(ISBN, Name, Author+, Price*)>
<!ELEMENT ISBN(#PCDATA)>
<!ELEMENT Name(#PCDATA)>
<!ELEMENT Author(#PCDATA)>
<!ELEMENT Price(#PCDATA)>
<!ATTLIST Price currency (dollar | RMB | pound) 'Dollar'>
```

The IBP parser parses XML data and breaks the structural tree into many sub-trees with specified elements. In this document the best choice of element is 'Book', just logging all the positions of start tags (<Book>) and end tags (</Book>) to form sub-tree index table. If we know which sub-tree contains what we want, just search this one. How to know the sub-tree is just using the key tag index table. We can create index with any tag we needed, but the elements with exclusive text value are

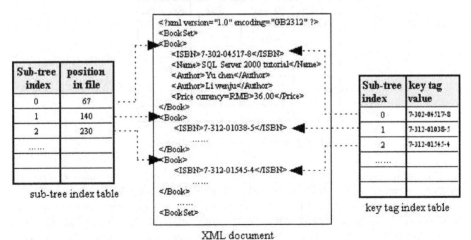

Fig. 1. Index tables after initial

recommendation. Therefore we take ISBN as the key tag and log the text between '<ISBN>' and '</ISBN>' as the value. After initial process, IBP builds the sub-tree index table and key tag index table (see Fig 1).

Now, if we want to find the author of a book with ISBN as '7-302-04517', we only load and search the fragment of document from position 67 to 140, just a string with length of 73.

3.1 Non-validation IBP

Non-validating parsers are only able to check if an XML document is well formed, whereas validating parsers can additionally check if the XML document conforms to its DTD (Document Type Definition).

IBP implements both modes. Non-validation mode of IBP (named IBP-nv), which works as above-mentioned, with which the XML document is read only. IBP-nv is suitable to lookup the XML database such as search tools and filters. IBP-nv is competent for the situation where SAX is used, but more efficient than SAX for its directly acquiring the special sub-tree by index tag, whereas SAX must parse the document at the beginning of the file.

After initial process, the optional operation can close the file handler, and reopen the file and read specified zone according to the sub-tree index table when needed. IBP-nv occupies very little memory, and it does not increase with the increase of file size.

3.2 Validation IBP

Validation mode of IBP (named IBP-v) does allow applications to perform updating operations such as node addition, modification, conversion and removal. In this mode, XML document is kept in memory, and the sub-tree index table is constructed in another way (see Fig 2).

Sub-tree index	Memory pointer	Size	Reallocated
0	0x0012fd40	73	False
1	0x0012fdb3	90	False
2	0x0012fd43	83	False
......			

Fig. 2. Sub-tree index table in IBP-v

After initial process, the XML document locates in a consecutive memory area. If an element needs to be modified, contents of the sub-tree must be copied to another reallocated memory first, and then change the sub-tree's memory pointer to the new address, and evaluate the 'Reallocated' with 'True' after update the element. The key of this mode is that a sub-tree is taken as an allocated memory unit, and memory pointer permanently points to the latest memory area. Before closing the file, all sub-tree will write back to the disk one by one according to the index.

Which one (IBP-nv or IBP-v) will be used in application depends on whether the XML need to be updated. If only parsing to search document, IBP-nv is recommended. The cost of validation, reparsing or revalidating a full document as part of a small update is sometimes unacceptable. After much experiment work, we find that parsing even small XML documents with validation can increase the CPU cost by 2 to 3 times or more.

4 XML Parser Performance

Parser performance always depends on document characteristics such as tag-to-data ratio, heavy vs. light use of attributes [6], amount of sub-trees vs. average size of sub-tree, etc, but we do not strive to quantify these dependencies here. In our project, we have developed a prototype system, which has the above-mentioned features. Our goal is to relate the cost of Microsoft's MSXML4.0, which is used in windows system widely, and support SAX and DOM parsers.

We still take BookSet.xml as our example, its DTD statements has been given above. First, we create 7 XML documents of 12KB, 115KB, 229KB, 458KB, 917KB, 1835KB, 4599KB, which contain different amount of elements. Then, we make quantitative analysis of the cost of parser initialization and parsing time, using MSXML4.0 and IBP respectively.

4.1 Analysis of Initialization Time

XML documents are initialized 5 times with DOM, SAX, and IBP parsers. The average times are listed in Fig 3.

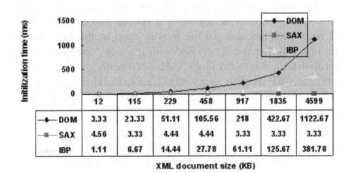

Initialization time (ms)	12	115	229	458	917	1835	4599
DOM	3.33	23.33	51.11	105.56	218	422.67	1122.67
SAX	4.56	3.33	4.44	4.44	3.33	3.33	3.33
IBP	1.11	6.67	14.44	27.78	61.11	125.67	381.78

XML document size (KB)

Fig. 3. Initialization times of DOM, SAX and IBP

In initial process, DOM needs to parse and compile a XML document into an internal, in-memory tree, the initial time is proportional to the size of the XML document. SAX only creates a handle to open the file, but does not read any data, so the cost is the least. IBP needs to parse and build index tables, so it takes more time.

4.2   Parsing Cost

The 7 XML documents are parsed 1,000 times, without grammar caching. Average
cost of 1000 times' random parsing can reflect moderately the parser's performance.

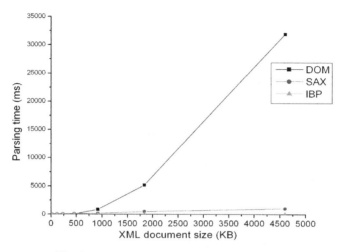

Fig. 4. Average parsing performance (1000 times)

DOM parser performs very well on small XML document, but cost for large
document exceeds the limit of our tolerance. SAX parser's performance is better than
DOM, but it is still not very efficient. After further research, we find DOM parser and
SAX parser have the approximately same costs when the XML document size is
720KB. During the IBP parser initialization process, it creates sub-tree index table
and key tag index table, so it's parsing process actually contain two operations:
lookup the tables and then matches element in special sub-tree. In IBP, index tables
are optimized with hash function, so the lookup time is almost invariable. And the
searching time in a sub-tree is only related with the tree' size. Therefore, IBP parser
has high performance even for very large XML documents.

In the worst case, IBP need to be re-initialized to build index table on a new tag.
We compare the initialization and parsing time of IBP with the parsing time of DOM
and SAX. IBP still has a better performance than DOM and SAX.

Document size (KB)	DOM (ms)	SAX(ms)	IBP(ms)
12	10	15.56	11.11
115	10	43.33	16.67
229	10	64.44	24.44
458	50	114.44	37.78
917	901	213.33	71.11
1835	5188	523.33	135.67
4599	31875	1034.33	391.78

Fig. 5. Average performance (1000 times): initialization and parsing time of IBP vs. parsing
time of DOM and SAX

5 Future Work

Future research directions concern both theoretical and practical aspects of the research carried out in this paper. We plan to keep on developing IBP API for full XML characteristic and research more flexible parsing model. Another interesting direction is tighter integration of database system with IBP.

6 Summary

We discuss common XML parser models, DOM and SAX, point out they are not suitable to large XML documents. Aiming at large-scale distributed systems, we present a new parser model called IBP, which has low resource requirement and good performance, regardless of the XML document size. For large XML files, IBP parses much more faster than DOM and SAX. Via API with C++, IBP can be widely used in various kinds of applications with low parsing time cost, and present a new idea for XML parsing.

References

1. H. Liefke and D. Suciu. Xmill. an efficient compressor for XML data. In Proceedings of the 2000 ACM SIGMOD International Conference on Management of Data, pages 153-164,2000.
2. James Cheney, Compressing XML with Multiplexed Hierarchical PPM Models, ICDE2001
3. XML Solutions. XMLZIP. http: //www.xmls.com/.
4. WAP Binary XML Content Format, W3C NOTE 24 June 1999, http://www.w3.org/TR/wbxml/
5. James Cheney, Compressing XML with Multiplexed Hierarchical Models, in Proceedings of the 2001 IEEE Data Compression Conference, pp. 163–172.
6. Matthias Nicola and Jasmi John. XML Parsing: A Threat to Database Performance, CIKM'03, November 3–8, 2003
7. Megginson, David, SAX 2.0: The Simple API for XML, http://www.megginson.com/SAX/
8. Extensible Markup Language (XML). 1.0 W3C Recommendation 10-Feb-98. http://www.w3.org/TR/1998/REC-xml-19980210.pdf.
9. World Wide Web Consortium. Extensible Markup Language (XML) 1.0 (Second Edition).http://www.w3.org/TR/2000/REC-xml-20001006.
10. Quanzhong Li and Bongki Moon, Indexing and Querying XML Data for Regular Path Expressions. Proceedings of the 27th International Conference on Very Large Databases (VLDB'2001), pages 361-370, Rome, Italy, September 2001.

A Stochastic Control Model for Hierarchical Grid Service*

Zhimin Tian, Li Liu, Yang Yang, and Zhengli Zhai

School of Information Engineering,
University of Science and Technology Beijing, Beijing, China
t_zhm@163.com

Abstract. In this paper, we introduce a model for deployment and hosting of a hierarchical gird service wherein the service provider must pay to a resource provider for the use of resources. Our model produces policies that balance the number of required resources with the desire to keep the cost of hosting the service to a minimum. In each layer of our framework, we quantify the cost increase of reserved resources caused by the fluctuation of the users' demand. A stochastic control algorithm is cast in order to resolve the problem. The results show that the model makes good decisions in the face of such uncertainties as random demand for the service.

1 Introduction

The success of OGSA (Open Grid Service Architecture) and web services has influenced grid applications [1]. Grid application designers are now beginning to make use of software services that provide a specific functionality to the application, such as solving a system of equations or performing a simulation remotely. Grid applications that make use of such services require consistent response time and high availability of those services. The service provider, who develops the service and its interface, may charge users through subscriptions to the service [2]. In turn, we assume that there is a cost to the service provider for maintaining the presence of a service in the grid. This cost is charged to the service provider by the owner and maintainer of the computational resources, the resource provider [3]. If there were no costs to maintain the presence of a grid service, then the service provider could simply deploy the service in as many places as possible and leave it running. Therefore, the service provider must balance the demand for service with the desire to keep the cost of providing it to a minimum. This work focuses on controlling the cost.

The amount of resources needed may vary over time and is a function of the demand for the service and the compute intensive nature of the service. We address the situation where the service demand and the execution time to process the service requests are unknown, but can be estimated. Even though the service provider will know the processing requirements for a typical invocation of the service, the execution time of any particular instantiation of the service can vary due to input data

* This work has been supported by National Natural Science Foundation of China. (No. 90412012).

H. Jin, D. Reed, and W. Jiang (Eds.): NPC 2005, LNCS 3779, pp. 72–79, 2005.

dependencies as well as resource contention with other services if, as is likely in a grid, the service is deployed in a time-sharing environment.

In this paper, we propose a layered model for service grid. The models are designed for a service grid focusing on business intelligence services that often involve a lot of data and many complex algorithms. The service Grid provides an economic platform for business intelligence services. In the model, the number of resources each tier provides is larger than that the users demand, because their demand is uncertain. i.e. the demand variability increases when it moves up a chain. This will make the cost increase. Our work is to control the cost by using the stochastic control theory.

The paper is organized as follows. Related works are reviewed in Section 2. In Section 3, a resource schedule framework of service grid is described. In Section 4, the stochastic control algorithms are discussed in details. Some simulation experiments are presented in Section 5. Finally, we draw some conclusions in Section 6.

2 Related Works

A number of works have proposed service-oriented architectures and have tested high-performance applications in those environments [4][5]. Weissman and Lee presented an architecture and middleware for dynamic replica selection and creation in response to service demand [6]. Their work answers the questions of when and where to deploy a grid service. In contrast, this work focuses on the question of how many resources are required to host a grid service in the presence of random demand and execution times. Buyya et. al.[7] and Wolski et. al. [8] examined the use of supply- and demand-based economic models for the purpose of pricing and allocating resources to the consumers of grid services. In this article we assume a supply- and demand-based economy in which both software services and computational resources are in demand. In particular, we assume a separation of interests between the service provider and the resource provider. The service provider obtains the necessary computational resources at a cost. The user then, is only concerned with the software services that are required for the application, rather than negotiating directly with a resource owner for computing time.

3 Grid Service Hierarchical Framework

Fig. 1 shows a layered architecture of a service Grid. Logically, the architecture is divided into four tiers: the User Tier, the Grid Tier, the Admin Domain Tier and the Node Tier. The Node Tier can be a computer, a service provider and a storage resource. It provides all kinds of resources for the upper tier. The Admin Domain Tier consists of machine groups, named as Admin Domains (AD), in which all nodes belong to one organization. For example in Fig. 1, AD1 belongs to the Computer Center and AD2 belongs to the Department of Computer Science. On the one hand, each AD can be regarded as a whole system, and all nodes in it have a common objective. On the other hand, an AD can fully centrally control the resources of its nodes but cannot operate the resources of nodes in the other ADs directly. In this view, all nodes are cooperative in the same AD. The ADs Tier not only provides service for the Grid Tier, but also reserves resource of the Node Tier. A Grid Service Tier can have many

ADs connected together and have good collaboration and trust relationship between the ADs. For example, Grid Service1 in Fig. 1 can be a Grid in Hong Kong and Grid Service2 is a Grid in Beijing, China. However, Grid services are independent from each other, the user can submit tasks to a Grid from its Portal. Likewise, the Grid Service Tier provides service for users.

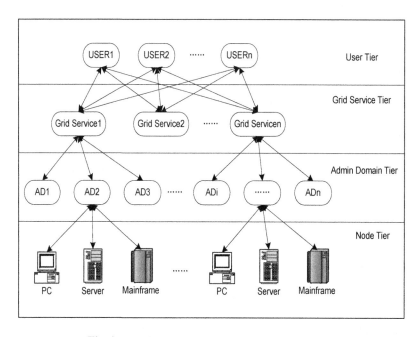

Fig. 1. The hierarchical framework for service grid

In this framework, the User Tier will subscribe services that the Grid Service Tier provides. Generally, what the Grid Service Tier provides is more than what the User Tier demands, or the application request can't be executed in time once some services halt. We define the offset as surplus resources. So is the Admin Domain Tier. Therefore, the surplus resources will become greater and greater from User Tier to Node Tier when the user's requests increase. The cost is also higher and higher. Our work is study how to control the cost by stochastic control theory.

4   Modeling for Hierarchical Grid Service

4.1 Modeling for Grid Service Chain

At first, we define the variables as follows:

$u_{1,k}^{s}$ ——denotes quantity of user demand; n-dimensional vector;

$x_{1,k}^{s}$ ——denotes surplus resources in grid service tier, n-dimensional vector;

$d_{1,k}$ ——denotes certainty of user demand, n-dimensional vector;

$u_{2,k}^{s}$ ——quantity of services that the Grid Service Tier subscribes in Admin

Domain Tier, m-dimensional vector;

$x^s_{2,k}$ ——the surplus resources of the Admin Domain Tier, m-dimensional vector;

L——m×n matrix;

$Lu^s_{1,k}$ ——quantity of user demand in the Admin Domain Tier.

So our system model is:

$$x^s_{1,k+1} = x^s_{1,k} + u^s_{1,k} - d_{1,k} \tag{1}$$

$$x^s_{2,k+1} = x^s_{2,k} + u^s_{2,k} - Lu^s_{1,k} \tag{2}$$

where L= $\begin{bmatrix} l_{11} & l_{12} & \cdots & l_{1n} \\ l_{21} & l_{22} & \cdots & l_{2n} \\ \cdots & \cdots & \cdots & \cdots \\ l_{m1} & m2 & \cdots & l_{mn} \end{bmatrix}$, $l_{ij} \geq 0, i = 1,2,\cdots,m; j = 1,2,\cdots,n.$ $\sum_i^m l_{ij} = 1$

L's row vector $(l_{i1}, l_{i2}, \cdots, l_{in})$ is a weight vector. It represents proportion of n users request in i node of the Admin Domain Tier.

Equation (1) denotes dynamic process in Grid Service Tier. Equation (2) denotes dynamic process in Admin Domain Tier. They are presented by matrix formal:

$$x^s_{k+1} = x^s_k + Bu^s_k + d_k \tag{3}$$

where $B = \begin{bmatrix} I & 0 \\ -L & I \end{bmatrix}$, $d_k = \begin{bmatrix} -d_{1,k} \\ 0 \end{bmatrix}$

When the user's requests change, w_k, the variety moves down from user tier to node tier, further, it will be greater. So, the state equation may be presented as:

$$x^f_{k+1} = x^s_k + Bu^f_k + d_k + w_k \tag{4}$$

where d_k is part of the certainty of the users' demand, n-vector, w_k is part of the uncertainty of users' demand, n-vector. Because of the change of the users' demand, the state variable, x^s_k, and the control variable, u^s_k produce variety. They turn into x^f_k, u^f_k respectively.

Now, we define the offset as follows:

$$x_k = x^f_k - x^s_k \tag{5}$$

$$u_k = u^f_k - u^s_k \tag{6}$$

Here, the system offset equation is:

$$x_{k+1} = x_k + Bu_k + w_k \tag{7}$$

where w_k is Gauss white noise, i.e. $w_k \sim N(0, \sigma_w^2)$, its covariance matrix is R_1.

In this hierarchical grid service system, the surplus resources offset of each tier is obtained by observation. So, it has noise effect:

$$y_k = x_k + v_k \qquad (8)$$

where y_k is an observation value, (n+m) dimensional vector; v_k is white noise, (n+m) dimensional vector, i.e. $v_k \sim N(0, \sigma_v^2)$, its covariance matrix is R_2.

4.2 Quantifying for Layered Grid System

The offset is used to quantificationally describe the situation which users' demand change affect each tier of hierarchical grid service system. Furthermore, the offset will be amplified from top to bottom. This is presented as follows:

$$y_1^2 = \frac{x_{1,k}^T Q_1 x_{1,k} + u_{1,k}^T u_{1,k}}{w_k^T w_k} \qquad (9)$$

$$y_2^2 = \frac{x_{2,k}^T Q_2 x_{2,k} + u_{2,k}^T u_{2,k}}{w_k^T w_k} \qquad (10)$$

where, Q is not negative definite matrix, and Q=diag(Q_1,Q_2), Q_1, Q_2 are also not negative definite matrix. y_1 denotes the effect of demand change in the Grid Service Tier; and y_2 denotes the effect of demand change in the Admin Domain Tier. The more y_1 and y_2 are, the greater the effect is. The less y_1 and y_2 are, the smaller the effect is.

5 Stochastic Control Strategies

The offset system equation (7), parameters y_1 and y_2 in equation (9), (10) have described the effect that the change of users' demand arouses the change of resources requirement. We should select a control u_k in order to make the effect minimum. In particular, the users' demand is random, and the external disturbance is also random. Therefore, our work is how to select u_k, such that:

$$\min_{u_k} J = E\{ \sum_{k=1}^{N-1} (x_k^T Q x_k + u_k^T u_k) + x_N^T Q x_N \} \qquad (11)$$

where Q is not negative define matrix. The objective function means how to select the control, u_k, so as to keep the surplus resources and the demand offset to a minimum .

The formulas (7), (8), (11) denote state equation, measurement equation and performance index function respectively. This is a Linear Quadratic Gaussian (LQG) model [9]. According to separate principle, the problem may be divided into feedback control and state estimate. The feedback state is Kalman Filter. In order to make equation (13) minimum, the optimal control is:

$$u_k = -F_k \hat{x}_{k|k-1} \tag{12}$$

where $\hat{x}_{k|k-1}$ denotes the estimate of state x_k. The feedback control gain is:

$$F_k = [I + B^T P_{k+1} B]^{-1} B^T P_{k+1} \tag{13}$$

$$\begin{cases} P_k = P_{k+1} + Q - P_{k+1} B_k [I + B^T P_{k+1} B]^{-1} B_k^T P_{k+1} \\ P_0 = Q \end{cases} \tag{14}$$

The state optimal estimate, $\hat{x}_{k|k-1}$, is:

$$\hat{x}_{k+1|k} = \hat{x}_{k|k-1} + B_k u_k + G_k [y_k - \hat{x}_{k|k-1}] \tag{15}$$

The gain of Kalman Filter is:

$$\begin{cases} G_k = S_{k|k-1} [R_2 + S_{k|k-1}] \\ S_{k+1|k} = S_{k|k-1} + R_1 - S_{k|k-1} [R_1 + S_{k|k-1}]^{-1} S_{k|k-1} \\ S_{1|0} = R_0 \end{cases} \tag{16}$$

where R_0 is the variance of random variable x_1.

Therefore, the surplus resources and the reserved resources of each tier of the hierarchical grid service system are:

$$\begin{cases} x_k^f = x_k + x_k^s \\ u_k^f = u_k + u_k^s \end{cases} \tag{17}$$

6 Simulation Analysis

In this section, we present results from a simulation study. The results show that by using the policy obtained from the stochastic control theory, we can not only maintain the system stability, but also reduce the variability caused by the input disturbance. As a result, the system can reduce the amount of uncertainty in the cost of hosting a grid service.

We assume the system has n=5 users, m=3 grid service nodes. In the noise condition, w_k submit to random normal distribution, i.e.

$w_k \sim N(0, \sigma_w^2)$, $\sigma_w^2 = 0.01$. The covariance matrix:
R_1=diag(0.0095,0.0088,0.0061,0.0071,0.0077,0.0102,0.0083,0.0124).
$v_k \sim N(0, \sigma_v^2)$, its covariance matrix :
R_2=diag(0.0083,0.0123,0.0072,0.0092,0.0063,0.0108,0.0080,0.0109).

The initial condition x_1^T =(0 1 1 0 0 0 1 0), its covariance matrix R_0=diag(0.05,0.05,0.05,0.05,0.05,0.1,0.1,0.1).
L=[0.2 0.4 0.2 0 0.1;0.6 0.5 0.8 1 0.8;0.2 0.1 0 0 0.1], k=7

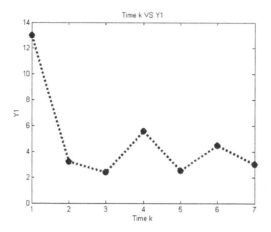

Fig. 2. The Curve of parameter y_1 with time k

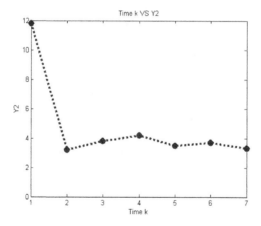

Fig. 3. The Curve of parameter y_2 with time k

Figure 2 and figure 3 show how the control strategy varies with the state. The parameter y_1 denotes the effect of the users demand disturbance in grid service tier, and y_2 does in AD tier. In both figures, x-axis presents time k, and y-axis presents y_1 or y_2. As shown in the plot, when time, k, increases, the effect factor of the system, y_1 or y_2, decreases. But the fluctuation in figure 2 is greater than that in figure 3. This shows that the effect subjected to in grid service tier is bigger than in the AD tier, i.e. the higher the tier is, the bigger the effect is. Therefore, we conclude that the stochastic control approach significantly reduces the disturbance of users demand of hosting of a dynamic grid service.

7 Conclusion

This work introduces a stochastic control model for deployment and hosting of a hierarchical grid service. The objective of the model is to produce policies to keep the costs to a minimum while maintaining the quality of service (QoS). The model is useful for making resource deployment decisions in the face of such uncertainties as random demand for the service. By employing a stochastic control approach, we obtain a solution of how to control the total cost in case of random users demand. When the users' demand produces a disturbance, the orders placed by the users will change. Meanwhile, this tier provides the downstream layer with users demand information. Furthermore, the disturbance will increase continuously from user tier to node tier. We quantify the effect by defining two parameters and produce a stochastic control algorithm. At last, a simulation experiment confirms that our mode can reduce the total cost and has a good performance.

Our work does not provide each tier of the hierarchical grid service framework with complete access to users demand information. When all layers of the framework share demand information, whether the effect still exists will be our future research topic.

References

1. I. Foster, C. Kesselman, and S. Tuecke. The anatomy of the grid: Enabling scalable virtual organizations. International Journal of Supercomputer Applications, 15(3), 2001.
2. I. Foster et al. Grid services for distributed system integration. Computer, 35(6), 2002.
3. D. England and J. B. Weissman, A Stochastic Control Model for the Deployment of Dynamic Grid Services, 5th. IEEE/ACM International Workshop on Grid Computing. 2004.
4. J. B. Weissman, S. H. Kim, and D. A. England. A Dynamic Grid Service Architecture. in submission, 2004.
5. J. B. Weissman and B. D. Lee. The service grid: Supporting scalable heterogenous services in wide-area networks. In IEEE Symposium on Applications and the Internet, 2001. San Diego, CA.
6. J. B. Weissman and B.-D. Lee. The virtual service grid: An architecture for delivering high-end network services. Concurrency: Practice and Experience, 14(4):287.319, Apr. 2002.
7. R. Buyya et al. Economic models for resource management and scheduling in grid computing. Concurrency and Computation: Practice and Experience, 14(13-15):1507.1542, 2002.
8. R. Wolski et al. Grid resource allocation and control using computational economies. In F. Berman, G. Fox, and A. Hey, editors, Grid Computing: Making the Global Infrastructure a Reality, chapter 32, pages 747~769. John Wiley and Sons, 2003.
9. Guo shanglai. A Stochastic Control, Tsinghua University, Beijing, 2000: 185~203.

Service-Based Grid Resource Monitoring with Common Information Model

Hongyan Mao, Linpeng Huang, and Minglu Li

Department of Computer Science and Engineering,
Shanghai Jiaotong University,Shanghai 200030, China
{mhy, lphuang, mlli}@sjtu.edu.cn

Abstract. The monitoring of grid environments helps administrators and users keep track of the availability and loading of resources, and the management of resources is dependent on the monitoring of information data. There is not an efficient and consistent monitoring mechanism to the manipulation of devices, resources and services in Grid computing. We propose a novel monitoring framework used to gather and retrieve monitoring information of Grid environments. The monitoring system RMCS integrates and extends the existing monitoring system using service-oriented mechanism and the common information model CIM. The RMCS defines a hierarchical structure of monitoring resources, and customizes the monitoring parameters and the display way. The adoption of CIM-based monitoring service enables compatible with other grid services such as grid portal, transaction or resource management and charging. The investigation shows that this monitoring approach provides the scalable monitoring capabilities, enables to exchange information in an unrestricted and flexible way, and improves grid performance and utilization.

1 Introduction

Grid technology enables sharing and accessing distributed resources that how to manage the performance and status of these resources is a challenging research [1]. The management of resources is dependent on the monitoring of information data that displays every node status, historical cpu and memory latency and network loading. GMA specification defines the Grid monitoring architecture in terms of the producer-consumer model [2]. The Ganglia system gives the graphics mode for monitoring the cpu, memory and loading performance of clusters and nodes [3]. M.A. Baker and G. Smith implement the monitoring prototype that provides the Grid sites map and the status of each site's MDS server [4]. The Vega project depicts the topology structure for the grid environments based on LDAP directory service [5]. There are limitations about the existed monitoring system and network. Administrators and users can only get and view the monitoring data in a fixed way, not customize the monitoring information according to domain-specific or user-specific favor. These approaches do not provide a general monitoring model that can be used in different scenarios and environments. We propose a novel monitoring strategy based on the common information model (CIM), which describes the overall management information of network and enterprise environment including devices, systems, applications. This monitoring

H. Jin, D. Reed, and W. Jiang (Eds.): NPC 2005, LNCS 3779, pp. 80 – 83, 2005.

system RMCS built on the services-oriented policy and CIM mechanism provides a standard and unified framework for monitoring logical and physical objects of grid environments. The RMCS organizes the monitoring object in a hierarchy structure that is scalable and extensible, building on which, we can set up the monitoring information according to diverse requirements.

Following the first section, section 2 briefly discusses the common information model. Section 3 elaborates the monitoring architecture, the representation of resources and the implementation mechanism. Finally, a short conclusion summarizes the work done and proposes the future research.

2   Common Information Model

The Common Information Model (CIM) is a model for describing information of network or enterprise environments [6]. An essential aspect of the CIM approach is the preservation and extension of traditional information resources. The CIM schema enables developers to describe monitoring data in a standard format so that it can be shared among a variety of applications. The CIM-XML encoding specification uses XML elements to represent CIM classes and instances. Aimed at particular grid environments, we design the schema of devices, system, network and applications by extending the core schema.

3   The Service-Oriented Resource Monitoring with CIM

3.1   The Resource Monitoring Architecture

In order to process raw information and efficiently analyze diverse network and applications, we propose a novel resource monitoring approach, which is based on CIM to describe and monitor information data. The architecture of the monitoring system RMCS is given in Fig.1.

There are many monitoring applications in grid and enterprise environments. The application generates requests to the CIM object management (CIMOM). The CIM-XML is responsible for the request and response of monitoring messages between Client and CIMOM. The CIMOM parses and handles these requests using the schema repository, and deals with communications between applications and providers. In the schema, the information of monitoring environments is organized consisting of a set of classes, properties, methods, and associations. The schema is intended as a basis for platform and domain-specific extensions. The schema information is stored in the repository. When the request coming, CIMOM searches the corresponding schema in repository. The provider interacts with monitoring objects such as operating system, network and application, and retrieves the information data. The separation of the abstract service description from a corresponding service implementation enables providers to realize services according to the local environment without restricting or implying a particular implementation.

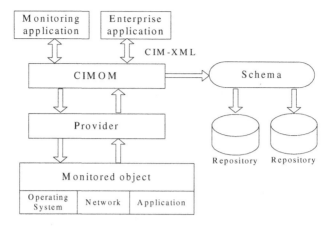

Fig. 1. The resource monitoring architecture

3.2 The CIM Based Monitoring Resource Representation of Grid Environments

In grid computing, we need to monitor and manipulate a large number of hardware and software components. Many resources possess the same properties and behaviors so that we adopt the hierarchical structure to depict grid elements. We use classes to describe resources, and associations to define the dependency and aggregation relationships between objects. Building on the common information model, the schema of every element is represented such as network card, disk, router and application. Every object is depicted using the Managed Object Format (MOF) description language [7, 8]. However CIM does not provide all the classes of various applications, so we have to extend CIM schema by adding new subclasses and associations with properties and methods to express the monitoring resources.

3.3 The Mapping Between Monitoring Object and CIM Schema

The operating system is investigated to show how to describe the monitoring object, and define the mapping from objects to CIM schema. The operating system is described a series of classes that Cpu, Memory and Process are subclass of Operating system. The Managed Object Format (MOF) files contain the definitions of class and instance, which are automatically imported into the CIMOM by management tool. The repository allows the extract from repository to MOF format containing usable monitoring data. CIMOM searches the registry information in the CIM schema repository.

3.4 The Implementation of RMCS

We have described the monitoring object and the schema, and then build the development in linux platform that uses Apache server as web server and Pegasus as CIM server. Pegasus is an open-source object manager for CIM objects. It includes the object manager, a set of defined interfaces, and SDKs for client, providers, and services extensions. The various monitoring services are automatically mapped to resource instrumentations. The provider returns the values of the monitoring component according to users' customized parameters and it contains a list of resources instances. The RMCS makes administrators and users define a wide variety of monitoring resources, specify the monitoring parameters and the display way.

4   Conclusions

We present a novel approach with CIM for the resource monitoring of grid environments. The resource monitoring system RMCS built on CIM and service is given that provides a general monitoring model for different scenarios and environments. It uses the hierarchical structure to define and represent the monitoring elements as classes and associations. The RMCS integrates the existing monitoring architecture, allows exchanging information in a flexible way. As well, the adoption of CIM-based monitoring service enables compatible with other grid services. In future, we will dedicate the perfection of the RMCS such as addressing the recovery of CIMOM failure, and apply to more grid and enterprise environments.

References

1. B. Bartosz, B. Marian Bubak, F. Włodzimierz et al. An infrastructure for Grid application monitoring. LNCS, Vol 2474 2002.
2. B.Tierney, R. Aydt, D. Gunter et al. A Grid Monitoring Service Architecture. Global Grid Forum White Paper, 2001.
3. M.L. Massie, B.N. Chun, D.E. Culler. The Ganglia Distributed Monitoring System: Design, Implementation, and Experience. Parallel Computing 30, pp 817–840, 2004.
4. M.A. Baker and G. Smith. A Prototype Grid-site Monitoring System. Version1. DSG Technical Report, January 2002.
5. http://www.vaga.com, VEGA GOS V1.1 manual.
6. Common Information Model (CIM) Specification. Distributed Management Task Force Version 2.2, 1999.
7. K. Alexander, K. Heather, S. Karl. Towards a CIM Schema for RunTime Application Management. 12th International Worshop on Distributed Systems: Operations and Management, France, 2001.
8. Specification for the Representation of CIM in XML Version 2.0. Distributed Management Task Force, July 1999.

Distributed Gridflow Model and Implementation

Cheng Bo, Qihe Liu, and Guowei Yang

College of computer science and engineering,
University of Electronic Science and Technology of China,
Chengdu 610059, P.R. China

Abstract. In this paper, we proposed distributed and adaptive grid
workflow net model. Which applies the Coloured Petri net as the formalism to describe grid process, and proposed the formal method for grid
services to composite the gridflows. And also proposed the multi-agent
based implementation for gridflow net model.

1 Introduction

The Open Grid Service Architecture (OGSA) tries to address the challenge to integrate services spread across distributed, heterogeneous, dynamic virtual organizations [1]. Which required to composite grid services into gridflows to gain grid
goals. Gridflow faces many uncertain factors such as unavailability, incomplete
information and local policy changes [2]. Therefore, we proposed the coloured
petri net based adaptive gridflow net model.

2 CPN Based Gridflow Net Model

CPN [3][4] which extends the formalism of classical Petri net [5] by allowing
a token to be of a specific distinguished colour. The sound mathematical foundation behind the CPN makes it a very useful tool for model distributed systems.

Definition 1. (Coloured Petri Net, CPN) A CPN is a tuple,

$$CPN = (\Sigma, P, T, A, N, C, G, E, I) \tag{1}$$

(1) Σ is a finite colour set specifying the type of tokens.
(2) (P, T, A) means basic Petri Net. P is the places set, T is the transitions set,
$A \subseteq T \times P \cup P \times T$ is the acres set.
(3) N is a node function defined from A into $P \times T \cup T \times P$.
(4) C is a colour function defined from P into C.
(5) G is a guard function from T to expression as such,
$$\forall t \in T : [Tpye(G(t)) = Boolean \wedge Type(Var(G(t))) \subseteq C]$$
(6) E is an arc function from A to expression as such,
$$\forall a \in A : [Tpye(E(a)) = C(p(a)) \wedge Type(Var(G(a))) \subseteq C]$$
(7) I is an initialization function from A into expression as,
$$\forall p \in P : [type(I(p)) = C(p)_{MS}]$$
where,$C(p)_{MS}$ denotes the multi-set over a set,$Type(v)$ denotes the type of
a variable , $var(exp)$ denote the type of variable in expression.

H. Jin, D. Reed, and W. Jiang (Eds.): NPC 2005, LNCS 3779, pp. 84–87, 2005.
© IFIP International Federation for Information Processing 2005

Definition 2. (Gridflow Net, GFN) A Distributed Gridflow Net is a tuple,

$$GFN = (CPN, i, o) \tag{2}$$

(1) IN and OUT are subsets of P, IN which has one element is a set of workflow start places, and OUT which may have one or many elements is a set of terminal places formal description. $IN, OUT \in P$: $\mid IN \mid= 1, \mid OUT \mid \geq 1$, and $\forall i \in IN, {}^{\bullet}i = \Phi; \forall o \in OUT, o^{\bullet} = \Phi$.

(2) $\forall x \in P \cup T \wedge x \in IN \wedge x \in OUT, x$ is on the path from $i \in IN$ to $o \in OUT$.

3   The Algebra of Gridflow Composition

Basic gridflow structure as sequence, parallelism, choice and iteration are foundations to composite the gridflow. The grammar is as such,

$$Grammar ::= GS \propto GS | GS \circ GS | GS \parallel GS | \lambda GS \tag{3}$$

where, GS represents a atomic grid service. $GS \propto GS$ represents sequence structrue which is defined as an ordered series of grid services. $GS \circ GS$ represents a choice structure which is selected to execute grid services at run-time when its associated conditions are true. $GS \parallel GS$ represents a parallel structure which means the grid services are performed concurrently. λGS represents a iteration structure which means to perform a grid service for certain number of times. The basic gridflow structure can be used to construct many complex grid workflows.

4   Formal Composition for Grid Services

Grid service can be mapped into a Petri net [6]. The basic control flows of grid services composition is represented as sequential,parallel, choice and repetition.

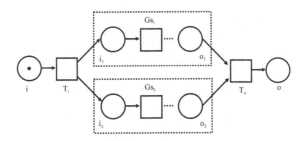

Fig. 1. The parallel composition for grid services

The parallel grid services composition $GS \parallel GS$ is as in Figure 1. Defined as,

$$GS_1 \parallel GS_2 = (ID, GSD, GSP, GRS, GFN) \tag{4}$$

where ID is the parallel grid workflow symbol. GSD is the grid services domain. GSP is the grid services prividers. $GRS = GR_1 \cup GR_2$ is the resources set which required by parallel grid workflow. $GFN = (CPN, i, o)$, where $\Sigma = S_1 \cup S_2$, $P = P_1 \cup P_2 \cup \{i, o\}, N = N_1 \cup N_2, T = T_1 \cup T_2 \cup \{T_i, T_o\}, A = A_1 \cup A_2 \cup \{(i, T_i), (T_i, i_1), (T_i, i_2), (o_1, T_o), (o_2, T_o), (T_o, O)\}$

5   Gridflow Net Model Implementation

Multi-agent based gridflow implementation built on Globus Toolkit and Aglet platforms. Globus Toolkit based on open-standard grid services which provide for resource monitoring, discovery, and management, security and so on. Aglets is a Java environment for mobile agents [7] development and implementation which is designed to exploit the strengths of platform independence, secure execution, dynamic class loading, multithreaded programming and object serialization[8]. The gridflow net implementation is as Figure 2.

Gca represents gridflow composition agent. Which is responsible to composite formal grid services into gridflow based on colour petri net, and also contains all necessary related information to be required by the grid workflow control agent. Mma represents monitoring mobile agent. Which is responsible for monitoring the grid nodes fault status periodically. The planning and checking algorithm [9] is embeded into Mma to detect the grid nodes fault status and share the status among grid domains. Wca represents gridflow control agent. Which is responsible for scheduling and rescheduling grid services to re-composite the gridflow dynamically. When demands from predefined gridflow occur, monitoring mobile agent can detect the deviations, then migrate to workflow control agent server to negotiate and decided which grid services should be invoked with the DAML-

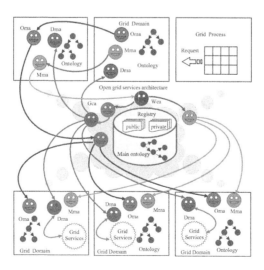

Fig. 2. Gridflow Net Model Implementation

S based ontology to adapt the dynamic changing grid. Then pass the related information to dispatch mobile agent. *Dma*, represents dispatch mobile agent. Which is responsible for interpreting the gridflow definition and controls the instantiation of gridflow processes. Which can migrate from one grid domain to the other domain to execute the corresponding grid services specified by *Gca*. *Oma*, represents ontology mobile agent. Different grid domain has different ontology. *Oma* can translate the similar concepts among grid domains. *Oma* can move to different grid domains to exchange and share the domains knowledge to make the similar concepts understandable in different grid domains.

6 Conclusions and Future Work

We mainly introduce the Coloured petri net based distributed Gridflow process model and describe the formal composition for Grid services. Also proposed agent-based adaptive Gridflow implementation. Gridflow security is a another key problem. In the future, we will focus on the access control for the gridflow.

References

1. Foster, I, et al: "The Physiology of the Grid: An Open Grid Services Architecture for Distributed Systems Integration". OGSA WG Global Grid Forum, June (2002)
2. Jia Yu and Rajkumar Buyya: "A Novel Architecture for realizing GridWorkflow using Tuple Spaces". In proceedings of the Fifth IEEE/ACM International Workshop on Grid Computing. (2000) 119-128
3. K. Jensen: "Coloured Petri Nets. Basic Concepts, Analysis Methods, and Practical Use". Monographs in Theoretical Computer Science. Springer Verlag. 1-3(1992-1997)
4. Dongsheng Liu: "Modeling workflow processes with colored Petri nets". computers in industry. 49(2002) 267-281
5. Zhijie Guan, Francisco Hernandez, and Purushotham Bangalore: "Grid-Flow: A Grid-Enabled Scientific Workflow System with a Petri Net-Based Interface". Accepted for publication in Concurrency and Computation: Practice and Experience, Special Issue on Grid Workflow. 2005
6. Rachid Hamadi, Boualem Benatallah: "A Petri Net-based model for Web service composition". In Proceedings of the 14th Australasian Database Conference. Australian Computer Society. February (2003) 191-200
7. Juan R. Velasco1 and Sergio F. Castillo: "Mobile agents for Web service composition". In Proceedings of 4th International Conference on E-Commerce and Web Technologies. Lecture Notes in Computer Science. september (2003) 135-144
8. Ian Gorton, Jereme Haack, and David McGee,et al: "Evaluating Agent Architectures: Cougaar, Aglets and AAA". Lecture Notes in Computer Science. Springer-Verlag. 2490(2004) 264-278
9. Alexander Lazovik: "Planning and Monitoring the Execution of Web Service Requests". Proceedings of international conference of Service-Oriented Computing. June (2003) 335-350

A Secure P2P Video Conference System for Enterprise Environments

Fuwen Liu and Hartmut Koenig

Brandenburg University of Technology Cottbus,
Department of Computer Science,
PF 10 33 44, 03013 Cottbus, Germany
{lfw, koenig}@informatik.tu-cottbus.de

Abstract. Many emerging group oriented and collaborative applications such as audio/video conferences use the peer-to-peer (P2P) paradigm. Confidentiality is an often demanded feature for such applications, e.g. in business meetings, to provide group privacy. How to build a secure P2P video conference system is still an open issue. In this paper several possible solutions are discussed. We present a security architecture used for P2P video conferences that ensures confidential talks in an enterprise environment whose branches might be geographically dispersed.

1 Introduction

Video conference technology has been well studied and standardized by ITU-T in the H.323 recommendation [1]. H.323 based systems adopt the client-server communication model in which two centralized servers are applied to supporting group meetings: the *gatekeeper* for the group management and the MCU (*multipoint control unit*) for the distribution of the media streams. Although these systems are widely available, they possess several technical drawbacks. They are subject to a single point of failure and might become a performance bottleneck. Moreover, they are still pretty expensive what limits their wide deployment.

A P2P conference system as alternative approach is characterized by a distributed approach. All group management and media distribution functions of the system are assigned to the peers. The communication runs directly between the peers without passing a server. Thus, the drawbacks of H.323 based systems are basically eliminated. Peer-to-peer conference systems are well suited to setting up spontaneous conferences, because they do not depend on a certain infrastructure. So far only a few P2P video conference approaches have been reported like BRAVIS [2], DAVIKO [3], and the P2P-SIP architecture [4].

Security is of primary concern for such conference systems which are mainly deployed in *closed environments*, e.g. an enterprise whose branches are geographically dispersed, where they are usually used to discuss or to negotiate business topics. To protect H.323 based systems ITU-T released the recommendation H.235 [5] which specifies a security framework. This framework is not applicable to P2P conferences. Approaches dedicated to securing P2P conference systems have not emerged, yet. In this paper, we propose such a security architecture and show how it can be incorpo-

H. Jin, D. Reed, and W. Jiang (Eds.): NPC 2005, LNCS 3779, pp. 88 – 96, 2005.

rated into a P2P conference system using our video conference system BRAVIS as example. The remainder of the paper is organized as follows. After introducing the P2P video conference system BRAVIS in Section 2 we briefly describe the security requirements for a P2P video conference in Section 3. Next in Section 4, we discuss possible solutions for this issue. In Section 5 we introduce appropriate security architecture and show how it has been integrated in the BRAVIS system. Final remarks conclude the paper.

2 BRAVIS

BRAVIS [2] is a P2P multiparty video conference system designed for supporting collaborative groups in closed environments over the Internet. The essential technical features of BRAVIS system are following.

Hybrid P2P Model
The P2P communication model distinguishes between pure and hybrid P2P models [6]. BRAVIS uses a hybrid P2P model. A SIP registrar is integrated in the system to allow peers registering their current IP address and retrieve the current IP addresses of the other peers for invitations. The hybrid model was chosen for two reasons. (1) No central authority is responsible for security related management functions like the identity management and the public key management in pure P2P systems what makes them prone to Sybil attacks [8], i.e. identity forgery. This allows an attacker to use different identities to attend conferences. To address this problem, a certificate authority (CA) was introduced in our system to centrally control the identities and the public keys. (2) Only one lookup operation is needed to locate a user when using the hybrid P2P model. In contrast, a pure P2P model like Chord [7] requires $O(logN)$ lookup operations for the same purpose.

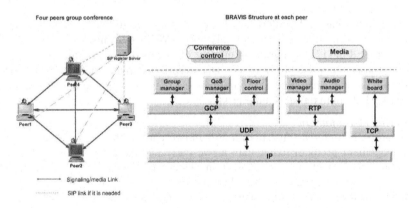

Fig. 1. Decentralized group management in the BRAVIS system

Figure 1 shows a four peer conference example and system structure at each peer. All peers of the group are assigned identical capabilities and properties. They use the same system structure, i.e. all system control modules (group management module, floor control module, QoS module), and the media modules (video manager, audio manager, and whiteboard) are available at each peer. Thus each peer has the ability to supervise the composition of the group, to control the access to shared resources, and to tune QoS parameter without calling any additional server. Furthermore, media data transmissions take place among the peers involved in the current conference directly.

The system control modules run on top of the decentralized group communication protocol GCP [9] [10] which ensures the consistency of the conference control data among the peers. Based on this all peers possess the same view on the actual group state and can uniquely decide all group related issues by themselves, e.g. QoS parameter settings or floor assignments. GCP achieves this by providing virtual synchrony [11] to the upper layer modules. It assures that no data are lost, that data are delivered in the order as they are sent, and that all peers are updated equally.

3   Security Requirements

Like other commonly used applications in the Internet, e.g. E-mail, a secure P2P conference has to support the well-known basic security features: *confidentiality*, *integrity*, *authentication*, and *access control*. Due to its decentralized structure and the real-time communication, a secure P2P conference system should meet some additional requirements beyond these basic demands:

End-to-End Security
Usually two kinds of security services can be offered in an enterprise network: end-to-end security, or site-to-site and site-to-end security, respectively. The so-called end-to-end security means that messages are securely delivered from the sender' host to the receiver's host and that they are not accessible to any intermediate node or server along the transmission path. Site-to-site and site-to-end security mean that messages are merely protected during WAN transmission, while they are transmitted in the plaintext form within the site scope.

It is obvious that P2P conferences have to apply end-to-end security for several reasons: (1) Security threats occur not only during WAN transmission but also at local site as indicated in [12]. A significant number of threats originate from insiders. (2) In order to protect enterprise business secrets, enterprises demand that business information should be only accessible to group members but not to people outside the group, even if they belong to the same enterprise.

Group Key Management
In a secure P2P conference usually more than two participants are involved. A group key management protocol rather than a two-party key exchange protocol has to be applied to securing group communication. Two-party key exchange protocols are inefficient for group communication, because each member has to negotiate an individual key with the other group members. Each message sent to the group has to be separately encrypted with the respective keys of the group members, i.e. n-1 encryptions are required. A group key needs only one encryption.

Flexible Security Policy Enforcement
The security policy determines the desired protection level of a conference and specifies the security algorithms to be applied. The security policy of a P2P conference should be determined by the participants themselves rather than by a dedicated net-

work administrator when running the conference, since a P2P conference is autonomous and consists of a transient group. The applied policy should be allowed to be attuned in the course of the conference to provide more flexibility for users.

Efficiency
Security always imposes additional processing burdens on the system. These burdens may pose a negative impact on the quality of service (QoS). For example, a secure conference incurs longer end-to-end communication delays due to message encryption/decryption. Therefore, the deployed algorithms and protocols should be efficient enough to meet the strict QoS requirements of real-time communication.

4   Overview of Possible Solutions

Nowadays virtual private networks (VPNs) are mostly applied for securing the communication across public networks. VPN functions can be introduced at different levels of the layered structure of the TCP/IP protocol stack. Correspondingly, there exist four kinds of VPNs: data link layer VPN, IPsec VPN, SSL VPN, and application layer VPN as shown in Figure 2.

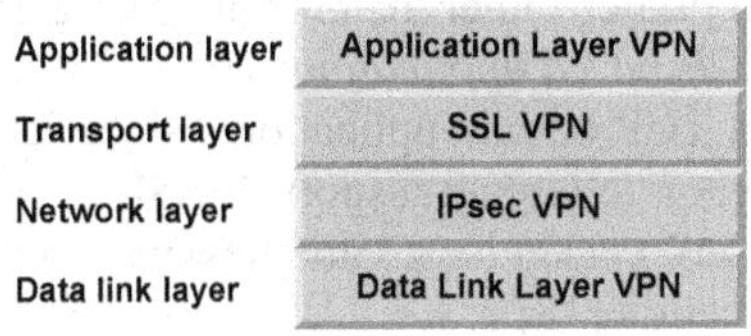

Application layer	Application Layer VPN
Transport layer	SSL VPN
Network layer	IPsec VPN
Data link layer	Data Link Layer VPN

Fig. 2. Kinds of VPNs

Data Link Layer VPNs
Data link layer VPNs could be constructed using one of three protocols: Point-to-Point Tunneling Protocol (PPTP) [13], Layer 2 Forwarding (L2F) [14], and Layer 2 Tunneling Protocol (L2TP) [15]. They were commonly applied to dial-up communications between a mobile user and the gateway of its enterprise network to provide site-to-end security rather than end-to-end security when they are used with IPsec together.

IPsec VPNs
IPsec VPNs are enterprise networks which are deployed on a shared infrastructure using IPsec technology. The most important advantage of IPsec is that it is transparent to applications. Any IP based applications without modifications can get total protection when it is deployed. However, several disadvantages inherently exist when it is used for a P2P conference.

> ➤ *Inflexible security policy enforcement*
>   Prior to the deployment of an IPsec VPN, the associated security policies must be manually configured in the related IP nodes. This specific task is usually only allowed for the network administrator but not for general users, because IPsec is implemented in the kernel [16].

➤ *Difficulty to offer end-to-end security*
IPsec VPNs operate at the network layer which is the lowest layer to provide end-to-end security in theory, but in practice IPsec VPNs rarely adopt a host-to-host architecture to provide end-to-end security for data transmission. This is because the configurations (e.g. security policy enforcement) on each host have to be manually carried out by the network administrator. This is an unbearable burden for the system administrator, especially for a large number of users [17].

➤ *Inefficient group communication*
Currently IPsec does not support a group key management but only a two-party key management.

SSL VPNs

SSL VPNs are based on the commonly used protocol SSL (*Secure Socket Layer*) for secure data transmissions at the transport level. It was standardized by IETF where it is called TLS [18]. SSL VPNs are extensively used in HTTP-based applications to provide end-to-end protection between client and server. Like IPsec VPNs, there are problems for their use in P2P conferences:

➤ *Inefficient group communication*
This is simply because the handshake protocol of SSL deals with the key management only for two parties rather than for the whole group members.

➤ *Merely supporting TCP-based applications*
SSL merely supports TCP based applications, since its design assumes that the underlying layer offers a reliable transport. If SSL is applied in connection with UDP based applications, packet losses are viewed as security breaks that force to release the communication [18].

Application Layer VPNs

Application layer VPNs use the security functions embedded in the respective applications. Due to its embedded implementation it can provide a more tailored protection compared to the underlying layer VPN technologies. Moreover, appropriate security algorithms and protocols such as a group key management protocol could be readily integrated into the system to meet the security requirements mentioned in Section 3. The major drawback of application layer VPNs is that some modifications have to be made in the applications to add these security functions. The designed security architecture is solely available for the designed application.

Table 1. Comparisons of VPNs

Security requirements	Date link layer VPN	IPsec VPN	SSL VPN	Application layer VPN
Basic security services	Yes	Yes	Yes	Yes
End-to-end security	No	Difficult	Yes	Yes
Group key management	No	No	No	Yes
Flexible security policy enforcement	No	No	Difficult	Yes
Supporting TCP and UDP-based applications simultaneously	Yes	Yes	TCP only	Yes
Transparent to applications	Yes	Yes	Yes	No

Summary
Table 1 shows that Data link layer VPNs and SSL VPNs are inappropriate for P2P conferences, because the first one does not provide end-to-end security and the latter one does not support UDP based applications. A straightforward solution would be the direct use of existing IPsec VPN infrastructure to support a P2P conference. Unfortunately, IPsec VPN is scarcely used in a host-to-host fashion to support the end-to-end security. Moreover, missing group key management and inflexible security policy enforcement make it difficult for IPsec VPNs to supporting P2P meetings in a dynamic and efficient manner. To fully meet the security requirements of P2P conferences the design of dedicated security architecture seems the most appropriate way, even it is more costly.

5 Secure BRAVIS System

In this section we introduce the security architecture designed for our P2P conference system BRAVIS. Our aim is to ensuring confidential P2P meetings on an end-to-end basis. For this purpose, a security layer has been inserted in the BRAVIS architecture presented in Section 2. It has been placed between the application and the communication layer. The resulting structure of the secure BRAVIS system is depicted in Fig. 3.

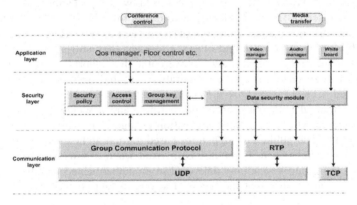

Fig. 3. Secure BRAVIS system

The security layer is composed of several modules. Each module fulfills a dedicated security function. They are shortly explained in the sequel.

Security Policy Module
This module decides which security level and what kind of security algorithm are enforced for the conference. Four security levels are distinguished. A *level zero* conference corresponds to a normal conference, where no special security function is applied. In a *level one* conference the joining of the group involves a mutual authentication, but the data exchange is not further protected. A *level two* conference besides the mutual authentication encrypts all signaling data and one or two media streams (video, audio, or whiteboard). *Level three* conferences are the most secure ones. All exchanged data are protected. The entrance into the conference is only allowed after

the successful mutual authentication. In addition, two different operation modes for managing the security policy were introduced: moderation and voting. In the moderation mode, one participant is designated as moderator who solely decides all security demands. When the moderator leaves the conference, he/she can hand over the moderation right to one of the remaining members. In the voting mode all group members share the same right to decide about the security policy. The security policy used in the conference is determined by voting.

Access Control Module

In BRAVIS the entrance into the meeting is by invitation. Each participant in the meeting can invite a new partner based on a social agreement with the other partners. No constraint is imposed on the callers for their calling activities, but an access control is applied to the invitee. Each participant on its own decides who can invite it. This is achieved by the use of an access control list (ACL) which is maintained by each participant. When a participant receives an invitation message, the required mutual authentication procedure is invoked. If this authentication is successful, the participant will check its ACL to examine whether the inviter has the right to call him/her. If true, it may accept this call.

Group Key Management Module

A decentralized group key exchange protocol used by group members to manage the group key themselves should be deployed to match the P2P communication model. Several protocols are available for this purpose such as TGDH [19], the protocol proposed by Rodeh et al. [20], and others. However, they still possess shortages in the respect of security and efficiency. To overcome these shortages we designed and implemented an efficient and secure decentralized group distribution protocol for our system, called VTKD (*virtual token based key distribution*) [21]. VTKD consists of two parts: a mutual authentication of the partners and a secure key renewal. The latter is triggered when the group composition changes, i.e. when members join or leave the group. The public key signatures based mutual authentication between the inviting group member and the invitee is invoked when a new member joins. This ensures that the group key is only delivered to an authenticated member, while the new member can be sure that the received key is in fact shared with the inviting parties.

Data Security Module

The data security module is used to ensure the data confidentiality and integrity during a conference. The participant can separately select different security algorithms for the protection of the four kinds of data (video, audio, whiteboard, signaling). Standard encryption algorithms are used to process audio, whiteboard, and signaling data in real-time due to their small data size. For the real-time video transmission, a specific encryption algorithm is needed to meet the stringent QoS requirements and to handle the large amounts of video data (the bit rate of a MPEG2 video stream typically ranges between 4 and 9 Mbps [22]). The end systems in a multiparty P2P video conference have to simultaneously compress/decompress and encryption/decryption the outgoing video stream and all incoming video streams in real-time. This imposes a high processing burden. Therefore, we developed a novel video encryption algorithm [23] which is fast enough to meet real-time demands with a sufficient security.

6   Final Remarks

P2P conference systems represent a new trend in the development of video conferencee systems. They provide a couple of interesting advantages compared to the traditional server based H.323 systems. Security is of primary concern for these systems to ensure the confidentiality of the talks, especially when applied in enterprise environments. In this paper we analyzed the feasibility of VPN technologies to secure P2P conferences. We showed that lower layer VPN technologies are not flexible enough for P2P conference applications. We argued that a security architecture especially designed for a P2P conference system (i.e. an application layer VPN) is a more appropriate solution to meet the stringent security and efficiency requirements. As example for such a security architecture, we presented the security solution applied in our P2P video conference system BRAVIS [2].

References

1.   ITU-T: Recommendation H.323 v5--Packet based multimedia communication systems. July 2003.
2.   The BRAVIS peer-to-peer video conference system. http://www.bravis.tu-cottbus.de.
3.   The DAVIKO system. http://www.daviko.com.
4.   D. A. Bryan and B. B. Lowekamp: Standards-Based P2P Communications Systems, Proceedings of the 2005 Virginia Space Grant Consortium Research Conference, April 2005
5.   ITU-T: Recommendation H.235v3-- Security and encryption for H-series (H.323 and other H.245-based) multimedia terminals. May 2003.
6.   D. S. Milojicic, V. Kalogerali, R. Lukose, K. Nagaraja, J. Pruyne, B. Richard, S. Rollins, Z. C. Xu: Peer-to-Peer Computing. HP white paper HPL-2002-57, March, 2002.
7.   I. Stocia, R. Morris, D. Karger, M. F. Kaashoek, and H. Balakrishnan: Chord: A scalable peer-to-peer lookup service for internet applications. In Proc. of ACM SIGCOMM 2001, pp 149-160, 2001.
8.   J. R. Douceur: The Sybil Attack. IPTPS'02, March 2002.
9.   E. C. Popovici, R. Mahlo, M. Zuehlke, and H. Koenig: Consistency Support for a Decentralized Management in Closed Multiparty Conferences Using SIP. In Proc. of IEEE ICON 2003, pp. 295 – 300.
10. M. Zuehlke and H. Koenig: A Signaling Protocol for Small Closed Dynamic Multi-peer Groups. In Z. Mammeri and P. Lorenz (eds.): HSNMC 2004, Springer LNCS 3079, pp. 973 – 984, 2004.
11. G. V. Chockler, I. Keidar, and R. Vitenberg: Group communication specifications: A comprehensive study. ACM Computing Suryes 4 (2001) 427-469.
12. ITU-T manual: Security in Telecommunications and Information Technology. December 2003.
13. K. Hamzeh, G. Pall, W. Verthein, J. Taarud, W. Little and G. Zorn: Point-to-Point Tunneling Protocol (PPTP). RFC 2637, July 1999.
14. A. Valencia and T. Kolar: Cisco Layer Two Forwarding (Protocol) "L2F", RFC 2341. May 1998.

15. W. Townsley, A. Valencia, A. Rubens, G. Pall, G. Zorn and B. Palter: Layer Two Tunneling Protocol "L2TP", RFC 2661. August 1999.
16. R. Perlman and C. Kaufman: Key Exchange in IPsec: Analysis of IKE. IEEE Internet Computing 2000
17. S. Frankel, K. Kent, R. Lewkowski, A. D. Orebaugh, R. W. Ritchey and S. R. Shama: Guide to IPsec VPNs. NIST Special Publication 800-77, January 2005.
18. T. Dierks and C. Allen: The TLS protocol Version 1.0. RFC 2246, January 1999.
19. Y. Kim, A. Perrig, and G. Tsudik: Simple and fault-tolerant key agreement for dynamic collaborative groups. ACM CCS 2000, pp. 235–244.
20. O. Rodeh, K. P. Birman, D. Dolev: Optimized Group Rekey for Group Communication Systems. In Proc. NDSS 2000, pp. 39-48.
21. F. Liu and H. Koenig: An efficient key distribution protocol for small closed peer groups. GI/ITG-workshop on peer-to-peer systems and applications. LNI Proceedings V.P-61, pp 163-167, 2005.
22. B. G. Haskell, A. Puri, and A. N. Netravali: Digital Video: An Introduction to MPEG-2. Kluwer Academic.
23. F. Liu and H. Koenig: A Novel Encryption Algorithm for High Resolution Video. In Proceeding of ACM NOSSDAV'05, Stephenson, WA, USA, June 2005.

Adaptive Query-Caching in Peer-to-Peer Systems*

Zuoning Yin, Hai Jin, Chao Zhang, Quan Yuan, and Chucheng Zhao

Cluster and Grid Computing Lab,
Huazhong University of Science and Technology, Wuhan, 430074, China
znyin@hust.edu.cn

Abstract. Peer-to-Peer (P2P) architectures are very prevalent in today's Internet. Lots of P2P file sharing systems using Gnutella protocol emerge out and draw attractions of millions of people. The "flooding" search mechanism of Gnutella makes it easy to be deployed, but also spawns numerous messages which leads to serious scalability problems. However, the locality discovered in both user's share files and queries, enables us to use query-caching to shorten the search length and reduce the messages traffic. This paper makes an extensive study of query-caching in P2P systems and proposes an adaptive query-caching mechanism to manage the cached query reply messages according to the heterogeneity of the uptime of different peers. Along with several other techniques we proposed, our approach achieves a 30% reduction of average search length and a 61% reduction of query message traffic comparing with the previous query-caching mechanisms in the simulation, which indicates that our approach makes Gnutella more scalable.

1 Introduction

There are mainly two kinds of P2P systems: unstructured [1] and structured [2][3], characterized by the search mechanism and the organization of peers. Due to the simplicity of the flooding search and loosely coupled structure, the unstructured P2P systems are more widely deployed than the structured ones. However the flooding search also spawns numerous messages, making the system not scalable. Lots of efforts have been made to tackle this problem, such as to limit the broadness of the searching, such as random k-walker [4] and routing index [5], to use expanding ring [4] and iterative deepening [6] to shorten the depth of the searching, to adjust the topology in order to reduce the message traffic [7]. Besides, replication [8] is used to enable peer to find desirable resources more quickly in time and shorter in distance. To achieve this, query-caching [9][10] caches query reply messages in a passive way.

In query-caching, peers cache the query reply messages they received. When a peer receives a query request, it searches its local share files as well as the cache. According to previous researches [11] on Gnutella workloads, the locality is a distinct characteristic in both users' queries and share files, which enables a considerable amount of queries hit in the cache. Hence the total message traffic and average search length can be reduced.

---

* This paper is supported by National Science Foundation of China under grant 60433040.

H. Jin, D. Reed, and W. Jiang (Eds.): NPC 2005, LNCS 3779, pp. 97–104, 2005.

However the current query-caching techniques [9][10] are rather simple and unfledged. The cache management policy is mainly controlled by a fix period of time. If a query reply message has stayed in the cache more than a threshold, the message is evicted from the cache. In Gnutella, the uptime of peers is heterogeneously distributed. Therefore, treating all cached query reply messages with the same deadline is too simple to match this heterogeneity, which leads to an ineffective exploitation of the contribution of query-caching. In this paper, we propose a new mechanism called Adaptive Eviction to take peers' heterogeneity of uptime into consideration and to evict a cached query reply message (a cached record) according to each peer's uptime. Besides, we propose some additional techniques, such as Exclude List and Cache Transfer. Exclude List is used to reduce the message duplication and Cache Transfer prolongs the use of valid cached records.

This paper is organized as follows. In section 2, we discuss all the issues related to the design of query-caching. In section 3, we perform the simulation to evaluate the performance. Finally, we conclude in section 4.

2   Design of Query-Caching

We made modifications on the client of Limewire [12] to turn it into a crawler of the Gnutella network. The crawling lasted for three weeks from April 5th to April 26th. After the crawling, we found some supportive evidences to query-caching:

1) *The uptime of a peer is growing longer.* Only 25% of total peers have a short uptime less than 30 minutes. Peers that have an uptime ranging from 1 hour to 8 hours account for 46% of total peers. The average uptime is 4.08 hours. This is very significant to the deployment of query-caching, because the longer the uptime of peers is, the better the overall performance of query-caching will be.

2) *During one full session, peers seldom delete their shared files.* More than 97% peers will not delete their shared files during one full session (from the join of a peer till its leave). Hence we can approximately regard that a peer will not delete its shared files during its current session. Therefore the life cycle of files can be ignored to simplify our design of the query-caching.

2.1   Design Considerations

Peers in Gnutella show a heterogeneous characteristic in uptime. Hence the design of query-caching should consider this heterogeneity. Previous techniques employ a fix time eviction policy. This strategy does reduce the average search length and the total message traffic, but due to its simple design, it has two primary drawbacks: 1) To those peers whose uptime is below the threshold, a cache hit gives false guidance, because the origin peer of the cached record may have already left the network. 2) To those peers whose uptime is beyond the fixed threshold. Eviction of such records limits their contribution in the future.

The previous approaches neglect the duplication of query reply messages generated by the cache. In Gnutella, a peer will not respond to the same query with duplicate reply. With cache support, the duplication may happen. Those duplicated messages increase the traffic on network, waste the processing capacity of peers and eventually dispel the benefit of query-caching.

A peer's cache will be inaccessible when the peer leaves the network. While the cached records may still be useful, how to make full use of these valuable records is also not addressed in previous approaches.

Our design tackles these problems, and Adaptive Eviction, Exclude List and Cache Transfer are proposed to deal with the above three issues respectively.

2.2 Adaptive Eviction

Adaptive Eviction is the core part of our design. The word "adaptive" means that the eviction is conducted according to each peer's uptime, rather than treating every peer uniformly. However, in the real environment, it is hard to attain the accurate uptime. So we try to predict the uptime of a peer's current session instead.

Every peer keeps track of the dynamic of its uptime. Then we get a sequence $Uptime_1$, $Uptime_2$, $Uptime_3$, ..., $Uptime_i$, representing its uptime in different days. We define transition Tr as a 2-tuple $(Uptime_i, Uptime_{i+1})$, where $Uptime_i$ and $Uptime_{i+1}$ are the uptime of two consecutive days (two consecutive sessions). If $Uptime_i > Uptime_{i+1}$, the transition is regarded as a decrease change. Otherwise the transition is regarded as an increase change. The value of a transition V_{Tr} is $\left| Uptime_i - Uptime_{i+1} \right|$. A peer calculates the value of *Decrease Change Ratio* ($Ratio_{DC}$) and *Average Decrease Change Range* ($AvgRange_{DC}$) as follows:

$$Ratio_{DC} = \frac{\text{the number of decrease changes}}{\text{the number of all transitions}}$$

$$AvgRange_{DC} = \frac{\sum V_{Tr} (Tr \in \text{decrease changes})}{\text{the number of decrease changes}}$$

A peer's uptime of current session $Uptime_{current}$ is predicted based on the peer's uptime of last complete session $Uptime_{last}$, $AvgRange_{DC}$, and $Ratio_{DC}$ as follow:

$$Uptime_{current} = Uptime_{last} \times (1 - Ratio_{DC} \times AvgRange_{DC}) \tag{1}$$

The $Uptime_{current}$ is always no more than $Uptime_{last}$ in Eq.1. But in many cases, the actual uptime of current session is longer than $Uptime_{last}$. Hence Eq.1 is a pessimistic prediction.

Based on our trace data, we study the transition of about 190,000 peers and find among all 13,467,602 transitions, over 65% are increase changes, 35% are decrease changes. The distribution of the $Ratio_{DC}$ is shown in Fig.1.

Fig.1 demonstrates that increase changes are more usual than decrease changes. Therefore, the $Uptime_{current}$ predicted in Eq.1 is a very conservative prediction and the probability that the $Uptime_{current}$ is longer than the accurate uptime can be low. Fig.2 shows the distribution of $AvgRange_{DC}$. There are over 30% peers with an $AvgRange_{DC}$ less than 0.3 and the average $AvgRange_{DC}$ is about 0.5.

Furthermore, we can predict the uptime more conservatively as follow:

$$Uptime_{current}' = Uptime_{last} \times (1 - AvgRange_{DC}) \tag{2}$$

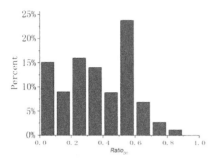

Fig. 1. The Distribution of $Ratio_{DC}$

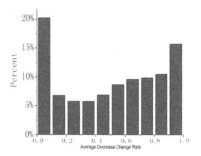

Fig. 2. The Distribution of $AvgRange_{DC}$

We use the real trace data to evaluate our prediction. We predict the uptime of the last 3 days based on the statistics of the uptime of the first 18 days. By using Eq.1, there are 22.7% predictions (totally 37,034,503 predictions) to be false predictions (the predicted uptime is longer than the actual uptime). While using Eq.2, there are only 10.3% predictions to be false predictions. This result proves that our conservative prediction is feasible, especially by using Eq.2. By using Eq.2, we also find that the average of predicted uptime is promising. The average of accurate uptime is 6.56 hours, while the average of predicted uptime is 3.92 hours.

Adaptive Eviction is enforced as follow:

1) When a peer receives a query to be responded, it calculates the time (T_{valid}) for the validation of a query reply according to the predicted $Uptime_{current}$ and the current on-line time $Uptime_{now}$ as $T_{valid} = Uptime_{current} - Uptime_{now}$. Then it adds T_{valid} to the query reply message.

2) When this query reply message is received, if T_{valid} is beyond a threshold h, the message will be cached. The use of threshold h is to avoid caching those messages with very small value of T_{valid}. Obviously, those query reply messages with a negative value of T_{valid} will not be cached, because their original peers are predicted to have left the network. The default threshold value here is set to half minute.

3) $Peer_j$ periodically examines the cached records. The T_{valid} of each record will be subtracted during every check operation. If T_{valid} is less then the threshold h, the corresponding record will be evicted.

2.3 Exclude List and Cache Transfer

Duplicating query reply messages caused by query-caching may increase the message traffic. So we add an exclude list to the query message. If a query is hit in a peer's cache, before the peer continues to flood the query to its neighbors, it adds the peers with corresponding records in the cache into the exclude list. Thus when the query is forwarded to next peer, the peers in the exclude list will be excluded from the searching scope. Although this approach could not solve the message duplication completely, it does provide an effective and light-weighted way to reduce a large fraction of duplication. Exclude List eliminates the message duplication in a depth-first way. To reduce duplication in a breadth-first way, random k-walker can be used together with Exclude List.

When a peer is about to leave the network, the information in its cache may still be valuable. So we can transfer the information of cache to some other peers that are still online in order to prolong their contribution. However we must take care of the choice of the destination of the transfer. We choose peers with a longer uptime. Because when the cache information is transferred to a peer that is ready to leave, we will face next transfer soon. Besides we should choose a peer with more connections. A peer with more connections usually has more queries through it. This enables the information to serve more queries. When most peers leave the network gracefully, that is, their leaves are under controlled and not caused by power failure, the Cache Transfer approach is a good supplement to query-caching.

2.4 Theoretical Analysis of Performance

We build a model to analyze the performance of query-caching. We use average search length to evaluate the performance. The average search length also influences the amount of message generated. We only consider a stable Gnutella network. We do not consider the initial stage of the establishment or the final stage of the demise of a Gnutella network. Due to the paper limitation, we only give the conclusions directly.

The average search length for fixed time eviction is:

$$L = 2 - \frac{T}{\Delta T} \tag{3}$$

The average search length for adaptive eviction is:

$$L = \frac{1}{(N+1)\Box T} \int_{t_0}^{t_0 + (N+1)\Box T} \left[P_t\{L=1\} + 2P_t\{L=2\} \right] dt$$

$$= \frac{1}{(N+1)\Box T} \int_0^{(N+1)\Box T} \left[P_t\{L=1\} + 2P_t\{L=2\} \right] dt \tag{4}$$

ΔT is the interval between the entering to a peer cache of two consecutive query reply messages containing the same keyword. N is a value determined by $N \Box T \le \max_{P_{K1}, P_{K2}, \cdots, P_{K_m}} T_{\text{valid}}(K_j) < (N+1)\Box T$, where P_{ki} stands for the peers whose shared files contain keyword K and T_{valid} is the time a record being cached. $P_t\{L=1\}$ stands for the probability that the search length is 1.

It can be observed that when the size of Gnutella network is big enough, $P_t\{L=1\}\uparrow\rightarrow1$, $P_t\{L=2\}\uparrow\rightarrow0$. While for Eq.3, $L_0\uparrow\rightarrow2$.

Therefore, Adaptive Eviction mechanism achieves considerable improvement over the performance of fixed time eviction. The larger the Gnutella network is, the more obvious the improvement is. However, the upper bound of the improvement is:

$$(2 - \frac{T}{\Delta T} - 1)/(2 - \frac{T}{\Delta T}) \uparrow \xrightarrow{M \to \infty} 50\%$$

3 Simulations

In order to further evaluate our algorithm, we have designed a simulation. We set up a network with 600 peers. 100 peers are ultra-peers and the rest are leaf nodes. The ultra-peers are organized in a random graph. This setting is very similar to the real setting of Gnutella network, the only deference is that all the parameters are reduced by a ratio. Therefore, though a small peer size, our simulation can also represent the condition of a network with a larger size.

Other parameters are set as follow: the number of files of a peer is conformed to the *Zipf(1.5, 25)*; the number of queries a peer issued is conformed to *Zipf(2.0, 20)*; the class level of keywords is conformed to *Zipf(1.8, 40)*; the uptime of peers is conformed to *Zipf(1.2, 86400)*.

The simulation is set to last for a virtual time of 24 hours. During the simulation, when a peer leaves, we add a new peer at the position where the previous peer was. This provides a simple way to keep the network with a stable peer size, meanwhile reflecting the dynamic of the Gnutella work. When a query has received 50 query reply messages from 50 different peers, we think the query is satisfied and then stop flooding of the query. Otherwise we continue flooding the query until the TTL of the query becomes zero.

We have done six different experiments based on six different situations. They are: 1) Basic (without query-caching); 2) Fixed Time Eviction with a 5 minutes threshold; 3) Fixed Time Eviction with a 10 minutes threshold; 4) Adaptive Eviction; 5) Adaptive Eviction plus Exclude List; 6) Adaptive Eviction plus Exclude List plus Cache Transfer.

As shown in Fig.3, the average search length of the basic algorithm (without query-caching) is 3.114 hops. When adopting the fixed time eviction with a 5 minutes threshold, the average search length drops to 1.749. However, when the threshold is set to 10 minutes, the average search length decreases to 1.614, which is only a 7.7% improvement. So for fixed time eviction, the performance bonus decrease with the increasing of the threshold. After the threshold reaches a certain value, continuous increasing it will not improve the performance much. This is because that when increasing the threshold, though the cache can store more query reply messages, it suffers more from the penalties which is to compensate the invalid records in the cache. With Adaptive Eviction, we can achieve an average search length of 1.128, which is a 30.1% reduction from the fixed time eviction with a 10 minutes threshold. This result demonstrates that Adaptive Eviction has considerable advantages over fixed time eviction. When adopting Cache Transfer, the average search length can be further reduced, while the reduction is not obvious, only 3.8%.

With the same parameters, we use Eq.3 and Eq.4 to calculate the theoretical value of average search length. We get ΔT=1904.4 seconds. Therefore when adopting the fixed time eviction with a 5 minutes threshold:

$$L_{5\,min} = 2 - \frac{T}{\Delta T} = 2 - \frac{300}{1904.4} = 1.84$$

When the threshold is 10 minutes,

$$L_{10\,min} = 2 - \frac{T}{\Delta T} = 2 - \frac{600}{1904.4} = 1.67$$

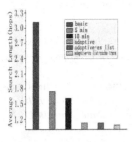 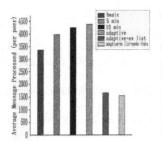 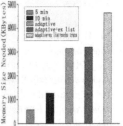

Fig. 3. Average Search Length **Fig. 4.** Average Messages Processed **Fig. 5.** Average Memory
Size

When adopting Adaptive Eviction, we get N as 4, and $L≈1.1172$. The improvement rate here is about 33.10%. The experimental data is very close to the theoretical value.

Fig.4 shows the messages processed per peer for different algorithms. The message here only includes query request and query reply messages. When adopting the basic algorithm, the average query messages processed per peer Avg_{QM} is 3352.2. When adopting the fixed time eviction, without using of Exclude List, Avg_{QM} increases to 3970.8 with a 5 minutes threshold. The Avg_{QM} continues increasing to 4245.5 with a 10 minutes threshold. However, when adopting the technique of Exclude List, the Avg_{QM} reduces to 1658.0. This is a 50.5% reduction from the basic algorithm and a 60.9% reduction from the fixed time eviction with a 10 minutes threshold, which indicate that Exclude List is very efficient in the reduction of message traffic.

Fig.5 shows the average memory a cache consumed. When adopting the fixed time eviction with a 5 minutes threshold, the average memory needed is about 575KB. With a 10 minutes threshold, the memory needed increases to 1265KB. When adopting Adaptive Eviction, the memory needed increases to 3146KB. Though Adaptive Eviction needs more memory for caching, a 3~4MB memory demand can be fulfilled easily for a state-of-art PC.

4 Conclusions and Future Works

Query-caching is an effective way to reduce the average search length and overall message traffics. However fixed time eviction mechanism has drawbacks and can not take full advantages of query-caching. By considering the heterogeneity of uptime, Adaptive Eviction is a more efficient approach to provide better performance. With the support of Exclude List and Cache Transfer, Adaptive Eviction is a good solution to query-caching.

In the future, we are looking forward to adopt our design in real environment in order to evaluate the practical effect to Gnutella. We are also trying to optimize our algorithm in order to make more accurate prediction of a peer's uptime, which will eventually give further improvement to the performance of system.

References

1. M. Ripeanu, "Peer-to-Peer Architecture Case Study: Gnutella", In *Proceedings of the International Conference on Peer-to-Peer Computing (P2P2001)*, Linkoping, Sweeden, Aug. 2001, pp.99-100

2. A. Rowstron and P. Druschel, "Pastry: Scalable, Distributed Object Location and Routing for Large-scale Peer-to-Peer Systems", In *Proceedings of the 18th IFIP/ACM International Conference on Distributed Systems Platforms (Middleware 2001)*, Nov. 2001, pp.329–350

3. I. Stoica, R. Morris, D. Karger, M. F. Kaashoek, and H. Balakrishnan, "Chord: A Scalable Peer-to-Peer Lookup Service for Internet Applications", In *Proceedings of ACM SIGCOMM 2001*, San Diego, CA, Aug. 2001

4. Q. Lv, P. Cao, E. Cohen, K. Li, and S. Shenker, "Search and Replication in Unstructured Peer-to-Peer Networks", In *Proceedings of the 2002 International Conference on Supercomputing*, June 2002, NY, USA, pp.84-95

5. A. Crespo and H. Garcia-Molina, "Routing Indices for Peer-to-Peer Systems", In *Proceedings of the 22nd International Conference on Distributed Computing Systems (ICDCS'02)*, July 2002, Vienna, Austria, pp.23-34

6. B. Yang and H. Garcia-Molina, "Efficient Search in Peer-to-Peer Networks", In *Proceedings of the 22nd International Conference on Distributed Computing Systems(ICDCS'02)*, July 2002, Vienna, Austria, pp.5-14

7. Y. Chawathe, S. Ratnasamy, L. Breslau, and S. Shenker, "Making Gnutella-like P2P Systems Scalable", In *Proceedings of ACM SIGCOMM 2003*, Aug. 2003, pp.407–418

8. E. Cohen and S. Shenker, "Replication Strategies in Unstructured Peer-to-Peer Networks", In *Proceedings of the ACM SIGCOMM 2002*, Aug. 2002, PA, USA, pp.177-190

9. K. Sripanidkulchai, "The Popularity of Gnutella Queries and Its Implications on Scalability", http://www-2.cs.cmu.edu/~kunwadee/research/p2p/gnutella.html

10. E. P. Markatos, "Tracing a Large-Scale Peer to Peer System: An Hour in the Life of Gnutella", In *Proceedings of 2nd IEEE International Symposium on Cluster Computing and the Grid (CCGrid 2002)*, May 2002, Berlin, pp.65-74

11. K. P. Gummadi, R. J. Dunn, S. Saroiu, S. Gribble, H. M. Levy, and J. Zahorjan, "Measurement, Modeling and Analysis of a Peer-to-Peer File-Sharing Workload", In *Proceedings of the 19th ACM symposium on Operating Systems Principles (SOSP03)*, pp.314-329

12. Limewire, http://www.limewire.org/

Design and Deployment of Locality-Aware Overlay Multicast Protocol for Live Streaming Services*

Xuping Tu, Hai Jin, Dafu Deng, Chao Zhang, and Quan Yuan

Cluster and Grid Computing Lab,
Huazhong University of Science and Technology, Wuhan, China, 430074
hjin@hust.edu.cn

Abstract. This paper presents the design and deployment of a locality-aware overlay multicast protocol called *Anysee*. The key idea of *Anysee* is to use the geometrical information of end hosts to construct the locality-aware overlay data delivery tree such that nearby users in the underlying network can be organized into nearby subtrees. The prototype of *Anysee* has been widely used in CERNET. Logging traces obtained from broadcasting 2004 Athens Olympic Games over 16 days have shown that the performance of *Anysee*, such as end-to-end delay and absolute data delivery delay, significantly outperforms that of randomly constructed overlay multicast.

1 Introduction

Network-level IP multicast [1] [7] was proposed over a decade ago. It seems (or, at least, was designed) to be the idea solution for efficiently disseminating real-time media content over Internet. However, the lack of high level features such as reliability, *quality of service* (QoS) control, and security, as well as the necessary of changes at the Internet infrastructure level make it very difficult to be widely deployed.

As a result, application level multicast protocols [2] [4] [5] [8] [9] [12] have gained tremendous momentum in recent years. In particular, for high-quality video streaming service, routing overhead is a key performance metric for the overlay video data disseminating tree since each stream tends to consume large amount of underlying bandwidth. If the overlay tree is constructed randomly, e.g. Coopnet [11], nearby hosts in the overlay tree may actually be far away in the underlying network. In this method, the QoS requirements for media data delivery is very difficult to be guaranteed.

End System Multicast (ESM) and its extension [4] [5] [6] give out *Narada* protocol and deployment for broadcasting video conference streams to a small (or moderate) group users. The main idea of ESM is that end-hosts exclusively exchange group membership information and routing information, build a mesh, and finally run a DVMRP-like(Distance Vector Multicast Routing Protocol) protocol to construct a overlay data delivery tree. ESM focuses on the out-going bandwidth limits of end hosts and the reduction of source to user latency. However, it does not address on large-scale issues.

Other schemes, such as Overcast [9], NICE [2], Zigzag [13], Scattercast [3], and TAG [10], present different optimization methods to extend the system to larger-scale

---

* This work is supported by National Science Foundation of China under grant No.60433040.

H. Jin, D. Reed, and W. Jiang (Eds.): NPC 2005, LNCS 3779, pp. 105–112, 2005.

cases under different conditions. However, as to our understand, all of them have not been widely deployed.

In this paper, we give out the design and deployment of a locality-aware multicast protocol called *Anysee*. *Anysee* is tailored to broadcast high-bandwidth video streams to a lager amount of users with low latency. The rest of this paper is organized as follows. Section 2 describes the locality-aware multicast protocol of *Anysee*, together with the prototype of *Anysee*, and gives out its performance analysis. Section 4 ends with conclusions.

2   Locality-Aware Overlay Multicast

The key idea of *Anysee* is to use the geometrical information of end hosts to construct the locality-aware overlay data delivery tree such that nearby users in the underlying network can be organized into nearby subtrees. It also supports *Network Address Translater* (NAT) traversals.

2.1   Tree Organization

To organize the overlay multicast tree into the locality-aware fashion, *Anysee* uses a L-parts *Global Unique Identify* (GUID) to identify the network position of an end host, where each part of the GUID value corresponds to the network and geometrical information. For example, we can statically divide the entire Internet to five-levels: the inter-country level, inter-ISP (*Internet Service Provider*) level, MAN (*Metropolitan-Area Network*) level, WAN (*Wide-Area Network*) level, and LAN (*Local-Area Network*) level, respectively. For each level, a corresponding part of GUID value of an end host is generated by the geometrical or network (i.e. ISP) information of that host.

Corresponding to the L-part GUIDs, the overlay multicast tree is also organized as a L-level hierarchy of subtrees. A subtree at level i is comprised of end hosts whose i^{th}

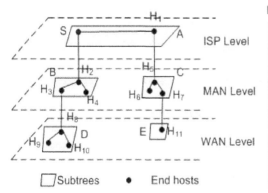

hosts	ISP Part GUID	MAN Part GUID	WAN Part GUID
S	0	0	0
H$_1$	1	0	0
H$_2$	0	0	0
H$_3$	0	1	0
H$_4$	0	2	0
H$_5$	1	0	0
H$_6$	1	1	0
H$_7$	1	2	0
H$_8$	0	1	0
H$_9$	0	1	1
H$_{10}$	0	1	2
H$_{11}$	1	2	2

Fig. 1. An example of 3-layer hierarchy of subtrees

part of GUID values are different from each other, and their $j^{th}(i < j \leq L - 1)$ part GUID values are the same as each other. Each host at layer $i(0 < i \leq L - 1)$ must reserve one out-degree for severing another host with the same i^{th} part GUID value.

Fig.1 illustrates an example of 3-level hierarchy of subtrees. In this case, hosts H_2, H_3, H_4, and S have the same inter-ISP level GUID value (i.e. H_2, H_3, H_4, and S are severed by the same ISP). Since they are located at different cities and have different MAN-level GUID values, they are organized into a subtree B at the MAN-level layer.

2.2 Tree Management

Initially, the entire tree contains a single subtree at the highest layer, consisting of a source host. The layer number of the source node is initialized as the serial number of the highest layer. To effectively construct and manage the overlay tree, an end host should maintain a small amount of state information–IP addresses and port number, layer number, connectivity constraints, and the GUID value of itself, its parent, grandparent, source host and children hosts.

New Host Joins: In our solution, we simply use the absolute difference value between GUIDs of any two hosts to predict their network distance. Given a new host X, it begins its join process by sending the *"Join"* message to the source node, where the *"Join"* message contains its GUID value and connectivity constraints information. Once an existing host Y at layer $i(0 < i \leq L - 1)$ receives the *"Join"* message sent by the new host, it uses the following rules to admit X and determine its level number. 1) If Y is the nearest host to X (comparing with its children), X will be admitted as a child of Y. In this case, the layer number of X is determined by the ith part GUID of X and Y. If the ith part GUID value of X is equal to that of Y, the layer number of X is assigned to $i - 1$. Otherwise, the layer number of X is equal to i. 2) If Y is not the nearest host but it has enough upload bandwidth to serve X, X will be admitted as a child at current level. 3) If Y has not enough remaining upload bandwidth to sever X and it has a child Z which is the nearest one to X, it sends *"Redirect"* message to the new host to redirect it to Z. 4) If X receives a *"Redirect"* message, it resents the *"Join"* message to the redirected host. The process repeats until X finds out its nearest parent. An except holds when the redirected one is a *freerider*. In this case, the new host is inserted between the existing host and the nearest *free-rider*. If the *"Join"* message is sent to a host located at layer 0, it simply uses the *First-Come-First-Sever* (FCFS) with randomly redirecting method to admit the new host.

Fig.2 shows an example of a join process. In this figure, the ISP-part, MAN-part, and WAN-part GUID values of the new host is 1, 2, and 3, respectively. It first contacts the source host S to initialize the join process. S finds out that the new host and its child H_1 are in the same ISP network. Thus, it redirects the new host to H_1. Based on the nearest parent selection principle, the new host will be redirected to H_5 and H_7, respectively, until it finds out the nearest parent H_{11}.

Host Departs: Host departure due to purposely leave or accidently failure can be detected by its children since the video data stream will be interrupted. Children of the departed host send *"Parent-Leave"* messages to their original grandparent to launch a

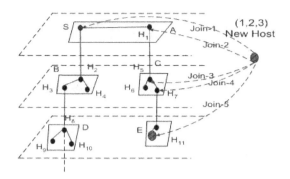

Fig. 2. An example of join process

recovery process. If unfortunately, the grandparent leaves at the same time, children should send "*Join*" message to the source node to rejoin the overlay tree.

Recovery from the departure of a host at layer 0 is trivial. The parent of the departure host randomly admits a grandchild to be its new child and redirects others to the admitted one. We propose the recovery process from the departure of a host at high layers. In this case, the parent of departed host sends a "*Probe*" message to that child. A non-leaf host forwards the message while the leaf node responses an "*Probe-Response*" message. Finally, the parent redirects other children of departed host to the promoted one.

Freeriders Supports: *Freeriders* can be detected by the *rendezvous point* (RP) when it requests the IP address and Port number of the source host. In particular, users behind NATs can be detected by comparing their public IP addresses and their private IP addresses (the private IP address is contained in their request message). This will be beneficial to admit more NAT-users since hosts behind the same NAT can be grouped into the same branch.

2.3   Prototype

The entire system is comprised of four components: a *rendezvous point* (RP), media sources, a monitor, and end systems. Source hosts are responsible for receiving the encoded video stream and promulgating them to end hosts. Each end system first accesses the RP machine to obtain the IP address and port number of source host and detect the connectivity constraints (i.e. whether the end host is behind NAT and firewall). Then, it joins the overlay network and periodically reports performance information to the monitor. The monitor is responsible for logging the performance information of joined hosts.

We implemented *Anysee*, and released the first version (v.1.0Beta) on August 12, 2004. This version runs on CERNET[1]. Each copy of end system software has combined

---

[1] CERNET stands for China Education and Research Network. It covers over 1000 colleges (or institutions) in China. More information can be found at http://www.cernet.edu.cn/

a pre-built IP-to-GUIDs database that contains all class **C** and class **B** IP addresses in CERNET.

The system has been used by HUSTOnline (http://www.hustonline.net) for broadcasting high-quality TV streams (near 512kbps bit-rate) to students. We have analyzed logging traces gathered from 13/8/04 to 29/8/2004. During this period, the 2004 Athens Olympic Games is broadcasted via four source hosts. Each of them corresponds to a unique TV channel.

2.4 Metrics

The metrics we are interest in the performance analysis are:

Control Overhead: This is measured by the time consumption of join processes, and time consumption of recovery processes.

Quality of Data Path: We evaluate the network proximity performance via the *End-to-End Delay* (EED) and the *Absolute Delay Penalty* (ADP) in the overlay multicast tree. EED is the *round-trip time* (RTT) between a parent and a child in the overlay multicast tree. It reflects QoS issues when a considerable end system buffer (20 seconds) has been used. ADP is defined as the cumulative latency to promulgate a data packet along the overlay path from the source host to an end host.

2.5 Analysis Methodology

Logging traces shows that almost 7200 users distributed among 40 colleges in 14 cities have enjoyed our contributions. The number of maximum concurrent users supported by the entire system is 3749, and the number of maximum concurrent users supported by a single overlay multicast tree is 1162. We use the tree with size of 1162 users for performance analysis. Fig.3 shows the changes of the number of maximum concurrent users over 16 days. We choose 10 different time intervals (length of each time interval is 40 minutes) to reconstruct the overlay multicast tree for detail analysis, while the

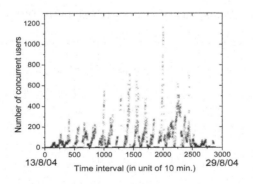

Fig. 3. The tree size vs. Time interval

tree sizes (i.e. numbers of concurrent users) at these time intervals are between 100 and 1162.

We choose the random construction method for comparison. In each time interval, we first compute the average end-to-end RTT and the average data promulgating delay between any two intra-region hosts and between any two inter-region hosts based on the measured latency information. Then, according to the real-life user accessing sequence, we reconstruct the overlay tree in the random fashion, where *free-riders* are processed by the method described in section 2. Finally, corresponding to the geometrical information of joined hosts, we assign the average end-to-end RTT value and the average data promulgating delay to neighbor hosts on randomly constructed trees to evaluate its data path quality.

2.6 Performance Results

Table 1 shows basic performance results of *Anysee* system. From this table, it can be seen that the join and recovery overhead of *Anysee* system is very low. Users can quickly find out their nearest parents for requesting video data. Theoretically, if the average number of hosts in a subtree of *Anysee* system is m and all joined hosts are uniformly distributed in different subtrees, we have $\sum_{i=1}^{L} m^i = N$, where N is total number of joined hosts. Thus, $m \leq \sqrt[L]{N}$. Since the average height of a subtree is in order of $O(\log m)$, the amortized height of the entire overlay tree is in order of $O(L \log \sqrt[L]{N})$. Consider that the *"Join"* message and *"Probe"* message will traverse the branch with maximum path length (i.e. tree height) in the join algorithm and the recovery algorithm, respectively. Thus, the time complexities of both join and recovery procedure are upperbounded by $O(L \log \sqrt[L]{N})$. As shown in Table 1, the mean time for join processes and recovery processes is less than 2 seconds. And the latter is larger than that for join processes. The main reason of this scenario is that lots of users tends to leave the

Table 1. Basic performance results, where m/n in the NAT column represents that m NAT-users come from n different NATs

Size	Date	Height	Mean join overhead (ms)	Mean recovery overhead (ms)	EED (ms)	ADP (ms)	NAT users	Firewall users
106	14/8/04	5	690	2,112	7.3	57.2	21/18	28
198	15/8/04	5	693	1,966	7.0	71.2	22/14	37
301	17/8/04	6	1,027	1,312	11.3	90.2	33/28	46
405	18/8/04	6	1,050	2,004	28.1	88.6	35/32	46
504	19/8/04	7	1,058	1,897	35.4	80.9	29/23	56
604	22/8/04	7	719	876	46.4	80.5	35/29	48
709	20/8/04	7	519	935	23.0	96.6	89/65	64
859	21/8/04	7	520	900	61.4	100.2	95/70	79
1038	24/8/04	7	1,018	2,338	62.7	114.3	108/76	103
1162	26/8/04	7	658	1,031	47.4	110.6	123/85	120

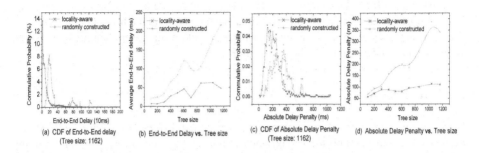

(a) CDF of End-to-End delay (Tree size: 1162)

(b) End-to-End Delay vs. Tree size

(c) CDF of Absolute Delay Penalty (Tree size: 1162)

(d) Absolute Delay Penalty vs. Tree size

Fig. 4. Comparison of data-path quality between locality-aware overlay multicast and randomly constructed overlay multicast

overlay in a short time interval when the interested media content has finished. In this case, children of leave hosts will rejoin the overlay tree.

Fig.4 (a) shows the comparison of cumulative distribution function of end-to-end delay between the locality-aware overlay and the randomly constructed overlay, with the overlay tree size 1162 users. In this figure, for locality-aware multicast, the end-to-end delays for almost 95% parent-to-child pairs are less than 100 ms. However, for randomly constructed overlay tree, almost 93% end-to-end delay values are within range $[100ms, 300ms]$. Fig.4 (b) shows clearly that the average end-to-end delay in locality-aware overlay tree is far less than that in randomly constructed tree.

As shown in Table 1, heights for locality-aware multicast trees with size between 106 and 1162 users are larger than or equal to 5. Obviously, the height of randomly constructed overlay tree is less than $\log_5 N$, where 5 is the out-degree of an end host and N is the amount of joined hosts. Thus, for randomly constructed overlay trees with size less than 1162, the corresponding height is also less than $log_5 1162 \leq 5$. Clearly, the larger height of locality-aware overlay multicast tree is resulted from which some out-degrees of inner-hosts are reserved for severing future nearest hosts and not used in the practice.

However, as shown in Fig.4 (c) and (d), the absolute delay penalty of locality-aware overlay tree is far less than that of randomly constructed overlay tree. In Fig.4 (c), for the tree with size 1162 users, the absolute delay penalties for most users in the locality-aware overlay tree are between 100ms and 400 ms, while the absolute delay penalties for most users in the randomly constructed overlay tree are between 200ms and 600ms. Fig.4 (d) shows a clear comparison of average absolute delay penalty between locality-aware overlay multicast tree and randomly constructed overlay multicast tree. From this figure, it can be seen that the average absolute delay penalty for randomly construction method is as three times as that for locality-aware construction method when the tree size is larger than 1000 users.

Network Address Translator (NAT) partially solves the address exhaustion problem of IPv4 and firewall gives out a solution for security issue. However, they create many challenges to peer-to-peer overlay applications since hosts behind NAT gateways or firewalls are often restricted to serve as receivers only, not suppliers. As our log indicates (shown in Table 1), near $20\% \sim 45\%$ *Anysee* users are behind NATs or firewalls. In our implementation, we use the inserting mechanism to make hosts behind NAT or firewalls as leaves of the overlay multicast tree. In additional, users behind same NAT gateway can be organized into the same subtree.

3   Conclusion

In this paper, we present a live streaming system called *Anysee*. *Anysee* uses a locality-aware overlay multicast protocol to broadcast high-quality video streams to large amount of users. It also supports NAT(or firewall)-traversals. We have studied the performance of *Anysee* based on logging traces of broadcasting 2004 Athens Olympic Games on CERNET.

References

1. T. Ballardie, P. Francis, and J. Crowcroft, "Core Based Trees (CBT): An Architecture for Scalable Multicast Routing", In *Proc. of ACM Sigcomm*, 1995.
2. S. Banerjee, B. Bhattacharjee, and C. Kommareddy, "Scalable application layer multicast", In *Proc. of ACM Sigcomm*, Aug. 2002.
3. Y. Chawathe, "Scattercast: An Architecture for Internet Broadcast Distribution as an Infrastruture Service", PH.D. Thesis, University of California, Berkeley, Dec. 2000.
4. Y.-H. Chu, S. G. Rao, and H. Zhang, "Enabling Conferencing Applications on the Internet Using an Overlay Multicast Architecture", In *Proc. of ACM Sigcomm*, Aug. 2001.
5. Y.-H. Chu, S. G. Rao, and H. Zhang, "A Case for End System Multicast", In *Proc. of ACM SIGMETRICS*, June 2000.
6. Y.-H. Chu, S. G. Rao, and H. Zhang, "Early deployment experience with an overlay based Internet Broadcasting System", In *Proc. of USENIX Annual Technical Conference*, June 2004.
7. S. Deering and D. Cheriton, "Multicast Routing in Datagram Internetworks and Extended LANs", In *ACM Transactions on Computer Systems*, May 1990.
8. P. Francis, "Yoid: Extending the Multicast Internet Architecture", *White paper*, http://www.aciri.org/yoid/, 1999.
9. J. Jannotti, D. Gifford, K. Johnson, M. Kaashoek, and J. O' Toole, "Overcast: Reliable Multicasting with an Overlay Network", In *Proc. of the 4th Symposium on Operating Systems Design and Implementation*, Oct. 2000.
10. M. Kwon and S. Fahmy, "Topology-aware Overlay Networks for Group Communication", In *Proc. of ACM NOSSDAV'02*, May 2002.
11. V. N. Padmanabhan, H. J. Wang, P. A. Chou, and K. Sripanidkulchai, "Distributing Streaming Media Content Using Cooperative Networking", In *Proc. of NOSSDAV'02*, USA, May 2002.
12. D. Pendarakis, S. Shi, D. Verma, and M. Waldvogel, "ALMI: An Application Level Multicast Infrastructure", In *Proc. of 3rd Usenix Symposium on Internet Technologies & Systems*, March 2001.
13. D. A. Tran, K. A. Hua, and T. T. Do, "A peer-to-peer architecture for media streaming," In *IEEE J. Select. Areas in Comm.*, Vol. 22, Jan. 2004.

Dynamic Thread Management in Kernel Pipeline Web Server[*]

Shan-Shan Li, Xiang-Ke Liao, Yu-Song Tan, and Jin-Yuan Liu

School of Computer, National University of Defense Technology,
ChangSha, China, 410073
{littlegege, xkliao}@263.net
{pine_tan, yuanchuangliu}@yahoo.com.cn

Abstract. With the development of high-speed backbone network, more and more traffic load is pushed to the Internet end system. The satisfactory execution of common business applications depends on the efficient performance of web server. In this paper, we propose a pipeline multi-thread kernel web server open KETA which divides the processing of a request into several independent phases. This architecture reduces parallelism granularity and achieves inner-request parallelism to enhance its processing capability. Furthermore, a thread allocation model is used to manage threads effectively in this special architecture. This model can adjust the thread allocation based on the server load and the work character of each phase so that the thread resource of web server can be utilized properly. Experimental result shows the capability of this web server and the zeffectiveness of the thread allocation model.

1 Introduction

Internet is undergoing substantial change from a communication and browsing infrastructure to a medium for conducting business and selling a myriad of emerging services. Because of the complexity of the web infrastructure, performance problems may arise in many aspects during a Web transaction. Although both network and server capacity have improved in recent years, the response time continues to be a challenge to the research on Web system. Some statistic shows that an e-commercial web site should guarantee its response in 7 seconds or it will lose more than 30% customers [1]. Recent measures suggest that web servers contribute for about 40% of the delay in a Web transaction and this percentage is likely to increase in the near future [2]. Some prediction estimated that network bandwidth would triple every year for the next 25 years. So far, this prediction seems to be approximately correct [3], while the Moore law estimates "just" a doubling of system capacity every 18 months. So we can see that the bottleneck is likely to be on the server side.

In order to solve above problem, some improvement should be made on web servers. There are mainly three ways to achieve this [4]:

---

[*] This work is supported by HI-TECH Research and Development Program of China (863 Program) under Grant No.2002AA1Z2101 and No. 2003AA1Z2060.

H. Jin, D. Reed, and W. Jiang (Eds.): NPC 2005, LNCS 3779, pp. 113–122, 2005.

- Improve the performance of a web server node at the software level, namely software scale-up.
- Upgrade web server's hardware such as CPU, memory and network interfaces to improve processing capability. This strategy, referred to as hardware scale-up, simply consists in expanding a system by incrementally adding more resources to an existing node.
- Deploy a distributed web system architecture consist of multiple server nodes where some system component such as a dispatcher can route incoming requests among different servers. The approach in which the system capabilities are expanded by adding more nodes, complete with processors, storage, and bandwidths, is typically referred to as scale-out.

Here we concentrate on the first method, software scale-up. Through comparison and analysis among some popular web servers' architecture and processing mechanism, we put forward a kernel pipeline web server open KETA (KErnel neTwork geAr). This web server divides the processing of a request into four phrases. Different phases of different requests can be executed concurrently like a pipeline on condition that there are no data or structure dependency. This architecture can reduce parallelism granularity effectively so that the resources of a web server can be utilized fully. Furthermore, the thread number of each phase is adjusted according to the server load dynamically in order to manage and schedule thread effectively.

The rest of this paper is organized as follows. In Section 2, we briefly describe some related work on the mainstream web server nowadays. The framework of open KETA and the thread management in open KETA are described in Section 3 and Section 4. In Section 5, some experimental results are presented.

2 Related Work

In view of the architecture, the mainstream web server can be classified into three categories: Single Process (SP), Symmetrical Multiple Threads (SMT) and Asymmetrical Multiple Threads (AMT).

In SP web server, a single process is responsible for the whole processing of all requests, including listening to the port, setting up connection, analyzing and processing requests, sending responses, etc. Some representative examples are μserver[5] , Zeus[6] and kHTTPd[7]. This kind of web server always uses non-blocking systems calls to perform asynchronous I/O operation. SP server is able to overlap all the operations associated with the serving of many HTTP requests in the context of a single process. As a result, the overheads of context switching and process synch- ronization in the MT and MP architectures are avoided. However, relied on operating system's well support for asynchronous disk operations, SP web server may only provide excellent performance for cached workloads, where most requested content can be kept in main memory.

On workloads that exceed that capacity of the server cache, servers with MT or MP architecture usually perform best. SMT web server employs multiple threads to process requests. Some representative examples are KNOT[8] and Apache[9]. SMT web server can overlap the disk activity, CPU processing and network connectivity concurrently so that it improves the server's parallelism capability. However, SMT web server ignores that the processing of a request also can be divided into several phases among which there are some potential parallelism.

AMT web server allocates different tasks to different thread. Flash [10] and Tux [11] are examples for this kind. They use one thread to process all connections and several helper threads to deal with the I/O operation. They decrease blocking time and improve the efficiency of the service. However, it increases IPC cost between threads and helper threads and can not utilize system resource fully like SMT architecture.

From the discussion above, we can see that most web servers have some parallelism capability and their parallelism granularity is request. Once a request is blocked on some operation, the thread will stop. It's well known that thread resource is limited and costly in web system so this paper tries to find a way to reduce parallelism granularity and achieve inner-request parallelism. Open KETA divides the processing of a request into four phrases. Thread in different phases performs different function and doesn't intervene with each other just like different pipeline phase. In this frame, even if a request is blocked in one phase, threads in other phases still can process other requests. So the whole system performance is improved. In the following section, framework of open KETA is presented in Detail.

3   Framework of Open KETA

Open KETA is a kernel web server, the original developing intention of which is to improve web server's performance by transferring the processing of static requests from user space to kernel space. When overloaded, performance of web server in user space is not so well due to much copy and syscall cost. Now many web servers are implemented in kernel space, such as kHTTPd and TUX. Considering system stability, kernel space web server only processes static requests instead of complex dynamic requests, and that dynamic requests are redirected to user space web server such as Apache. What's more, measurements [12, 13] have suggested that the request stream at most web servers is dominated by static requests. Serving static requests quickly is the focus of many companies. Figure1 shows the processing flow of open KETA. For Linux already has a kernel web server TUX to accelerate requests processing, FreeBSD doesn't have yet, open KETA is implemented in FreeBSD kernel.

As introduced above, Open KETA divides the processing of request into four phrases: Accept Connection (accept), Socket Recv (receive), Data Process and Send Response (send) each of which has its own thread pool. Threads of different phases run in a pipeline-like manner. Partition of pipeline phases is not at random but with some

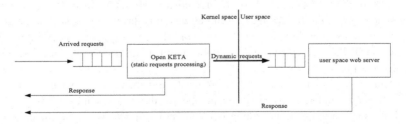

Fig. 1. Processing flow of open KETA

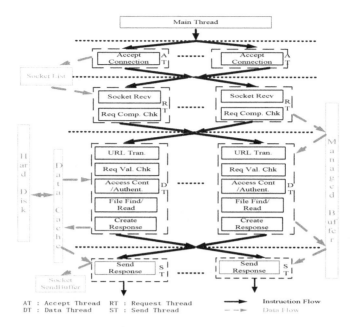

Fig. 2. Framework of open KETA

principle. Firstly, coupling degree of different phase should be relatively low so that threads in different phases could run concurrently. Secondly, depth of pipeline should be proper because too flat can't bring much parallelism and too deep will cause much scheduling cost.

Open KETA uses a managed buffer (MB) to transfer some control structures among all the phases. Furthermore, a software cache data cache (DC) is used to cache objects to reduce the times of disk access. DC and MB are initialized by a main thread as open KETA is loading. The framework of open KETA is presented in Figure 2.Main task of each phase is stated as followed:

- Accept phase is responsible for listening to the port. Applied with HTTP 1.1, once it finds a new arrived request which doesn't belong to an existing socket, it will create a new socket and set up connection, else if the socket is still keep alive, the request will stride over the accept phase and go to receive phase directly.
- Receive phase checks the completeness of http request and judges whether it's a static request. If not it will be redirected to web server in user space such as Apache. Here the socket the request belongs to is thrown to the socket list of user space web server directly in order to avoid the cost of recreating and destroying socket. If the arrived request is a static one, it is inserted to the task list of data process phase.
- Data process phase first validates requests and then judges whether the object requested is in DC or not by a hash map, if yes the response message is generated. It is worth saying that the response head is stored in DC as long as the object is in DC so that the response message can reuse the response head. Once the object is

not hashed in DC, get it from disk. If the conflict list of hash table is full or DC doesn't have enough space, some object will be washed out from DC.
- Just as its name implies, send phase sends the object requested back to clients. Open KETA utilizes Zero Copy which FreeBSD supports to reduce copy times and improve sending efficiency.

Owning to the Asymmetrical thread character, thread management is very important in open KETA. When should these threads be created, how to activate threads in each phase and how many threads should be allocated to each phase? The thread management will be presented in the following section.

4   Thread Management in Pipeline Architecture

4.1   Creation and Activation of Thread

In order to guarantee the real time service, all thread pools are initialized by a main thread when open KETA is loading. The number of thread is set empirically in a configuration file. As to the activation of threads, there are two ways in common: One is that a scheduler is specialized in this work in each thread group. After the execution, thread in previous group passes the result to the scheduler in this group. The scheduler will choose a thread based on some special rules. This method is extendable in implementation but the scheduler may be the bottleneck. Another way is that thread chooses the next-phase thread itself based on some rules. The advantage of this method is that cost of copy and control can be reduced but thread scheduling of each group is not transparent to other groups. Considering that open KETA is implemented in kernel, efficiency may be more important, so the latter is chosen and MB is used to transfer all control structures. When a thread has finished one task, it will check whether there are some unsettled tasks, if yes the thread continues to process another task else it will sleep and not wake up until thread in previous phases activate it.

4.2   Dynamic Tread Allocation

In section 3 the main task of each phase has been introduced respectively, from which we can see their burden is different owing to different length of execution code, different resource they mainly use, etc. With the changing of load, optimal thread number allocated to different phases is different. In this section, a feedback control model is proposed to control the thread allocation of each phase. First, we will analyze the runtime burden of each pipeline phase, from which thread allocation policy can be set with pertinence.

Burden Analysis. In web requests processing, CPU, memory and network bandwidth may be the consuming character of open KETA, threads in send phase may be first blocked in overloaded condition. Threads burden in data process are not as heavy as that in send phase since objects can be cached on DC. However, open KETA is running in kernel whose space can be used totally is 1G, so not all objects have chance to be cached in DC. In this case open KETA has to access disk at times to get the object requested and replace some other objects with it in DC. Threads in accept phase may be most light-burdened since their main task is only creating socket. Threads in receive phase examine socket list to see whether there are some new requests, if yes some prearrange checks will be done on these requests. Main resource receive phase uses is CPU. From these analysis, we can see that work process of open KETA is like a four level funnel, work burden is more and more heavy from accept phase to send phase. When system is overloaded, thread allocation should be adjusted based on this special character of open KETA.

Feedback Control Model of Thread Allocation. When open KETA is loading, all thread pools are initialized with some empirical value. Although these values can suit many load conditions, they cannot deal with all the cases. Ideally, threads allocated to each phase should be adjusted based on their task list and server utilization. Figure 3 presents a feedback control model to achieve this. From this figure, we can see that a load monitor in open KETA gathers the queue length of the task list of each phase and the server utilization periodically, based on which decision is made to adjust thread allocation.

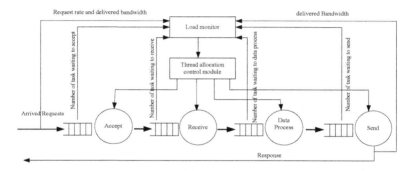

Fig. 3. Thread allocation feedback control model

1. Load Monitoring

The objective of load monitor is to inspect the task list of each phase and quantify server utilization with a single value that summarizes resource consumption. The queue length of each task list can be easily obtained. It's noticed that the service time of a request can be decomposed into a fixed overhead and an object size dependent overhead [14], that is:

$$T(x) = c_1 x + c_2 \qquad (1)$$

where x is the object size, c_1 and c_2 are platform constants

For summing the service time of n requests:

$$\sum_{k=1}^{n} T(x_k) = c_1 \sum_{k=1}^{n} x_k + k c_2$$

And dividing by the length of the period t we obtain the system utilization U:

$$U = \frac{\sum\limits_{k=1}^{n} T(x_k)}{t} = \frac{c_1 \sum\limits_{k=1}^{n} x_k + kc_2}{t} = c_1 \frac{\sum\limits_{k=1}^{n} x_k}{t} + c_2 \frac{k}{t} = c_1 W + c_2 R \qquad (2)$$

From the Eq. (2) we get the quantify guideline of server utilization. We can repeat the experiment with different concurrent connections or URL sizes. Each time a different Wmax and Rmax are recorded, every case is corresponding to a fully utilized server. i.e., U =100%.Thus, each experiment yields a different point (Rmax, Wmax), then using linear regression coefficient c1, c2 are found. These two constants are obtained off-line and written into a configuration file.

2. Thread Allocation Control Module

Just as its name implies, the main task of thread allocation control module is to adjust thread allocation based on the information load monitor provides and some special character of open KETA. In section 4.2.1 it has been analyzed that all the pipeline phases of open KETA make up a four level funnel like structure, bottleneck would easily appear in send phase when overloaded, data process phase followed and then does the receive and accept phase. The number of thread allocated to each phase should be in accordance with this character. In order to avoid resource wasting, the initial value should not be too large. Supposed that the maximal thread number of open KETA is M which can be configured based on server's hardware condition and that the initial number of phase k is P_k (k = 0...3, 0 is accept phase, 1 is receive phase, 2 is data process phase and 3 is send phase). When open KETA is loading, $\sum P_k$ is less than M. With the increase of concurrent connection, thread number of each phase is adjusted by the following formulas. Owning to the four level funnel structure the calculation sequence

of P_k^{i+1} is from P_3 to P_0:

$$\text{If } \sum_{n=0}^{k} P_n^i + \sum_{n=k+1}^{3} P_n^{i+1} + T_{i+1}(a_k + b_k \Delta W_{i+1}) \leq M$$

$$\text{then } P_k^{i+1} = P_k^i + T_{i+1}(a_k + b_k \Delta W_{i+1}) \qquad (3)$$

Else

$$P_k^{i+1} = M - \sum_{n=0}^{k-1} P_n^i \qquad (4)$$

$$P_k^{i+1} = M - \sum_{n=k+1}^{3} P_n^{i+1} \qquad (5)$$

$$P_k^{i+1} = M - \sum_{n=0}^{k-1} P_n^i - \sum_{n=k+1}^{3} P_n^{i+1} \qquad (6)$$

Here it means when some tasks are waiting, thread number of the corresponding phase will be increased but the total number should not exceed M. P_k^i is the current thread number of phase k and P_k^{i+1} is the new adjusted one. T_{i+1} is the queue length of the task list of phase k. ΔW_{i+1} represents W_{i+1}-W_i. If the P_k^{i+1} is not an interger, $\lceil P_k^{i+1} \rceil$ is taken. a_k, b_k can be well approached by some off-line experiment. But if $\sum_{k=0}^{3} P_k = M$, that thread number can not be increased, threads should be transferred from phase n (n<k) to phase k in order to release the burden of bottleneck phase. Thread number transferred is set empirically. It is worth saying that all threads can be implemented in a switch like manner to avoid destroying and creating thread frequently, here for limited length we do not discussed in detail. When Wi is low which means server is not so busy, thread number will be set back to the initial value by reducing the priority of some threads to a lower value of kernel thread just like destroying these threads so that other applications can utilize more system resource (because thread of other application can be schedule preferential). When the load of web server is increased again, Eq. (3) (4) (5) (6) are used to repeat the process.

5 Experimental Evaluation

The open KETA is implemented in FreeBSD 5.3 kernel. In order to contrast its performance with other web servers, we have done some experiments under different loads. In view of open KETA nature, all experiments are carried out only with static requests. The testing environment is made up of one server and three or five clients:

Table 1. Results of 300 concurrent connections (3 clients)

Tested object	Mean response time (ms)	Weighted bandwidth(bps)	Valid + Invalid	Conforming	Operations per second
Apache(freebsd)	410.0	303272.69	300+0	50	761
Apache(Redhat)	382.2	313600.49	300+0	56	765
Tux	320.4	373585.24	300+0	300	907
Zeus	342.5	357853.37	300+0	300	855
Open KETA	307.0	389930.76	300+0	300	954

Table 2. Results of 600 concurrent connections (3 clients)

Tested object	Mean response time (ms)	Weighted bandwidth(bps)	Valid + Invalid	Conforming	Operations per second
Apache(freebsd)	719.3	166083.41	600+0	0	771
Apache(Redhat)	758.2	157416.85	600+0	0	769
Tux	456.1	261535.11	600+0	600	1296
Zeus	536.1	228577.33	600+0	600	1100
Open KETA	352.4	356495.45	600+0	600	1702

Server: SMP with two xeon 2.0G hz cpus,2GB memory, 36G SCSI hard disk and 1000M network card;

Clients: 2.4G hz cpu, 512M memory, 40GB 5400 rpm hard disk and 10-100M adaptive network card;

A testing tool SPECWeb99 is used to test the performance of the web servers. Platform for these web servers are Apache, open KETA in FreeBSD 5.3, Apache, tux, Zeus in Redhat Enterprise Linux v3.0. Note that the results of Table1, 2, 3 for open KETA do not include the thread allocation control model.

Table 3. Results of 1000 concurrent connections (5 clients)

Tested object	Mean response time (ms)	Weighted bandwidth(bps)	Valid + Invalid	Conforming	Operations per second
Apache(freebsd)	1077.7	110974.79	983+17	0	773
Apache(Redhat)	1247.2	95514.28	989+11	0	750
Tux	791.1	150558.99	999+1	678	1244
Zeus	992.5	126145.36	996+4	565	987
Open KETA	437.7	290117.36	1000+0	35	2285

When the concurrent connections are 1000, client may be the bottleneck (due to 10-100M network card), so more clients are used.

We can see from the results, the performance of open KETA is much better than the web servers listed above. A simultaneous connection is considered conforming to the required bit rate if its aggregate bit rate is more than 320,000 bits/second, or 40,000 bytes/second. Other guidelines can be easily understood by their name. Table 4 presents the mean response time of open KETA with and without thread allocation model. Although thread adjustment brings additional system cost, we can see that the mean response time is reduced through the action of this model from the table.

Table 4. Mean response time of open KETA with and without thread control model

Concurrent connection / Policy	300	600	800	1000
Open KETA with thread allocation control model	307.0	352.4	391.2	437.7
Open KETA without thread allocation control model	307.0	350.1	386.8	430.2

6   Conclusion

In this paper, we proposed the pipeline framework of a kernel web server open KETA. This web server has a four level funnel like work flow architecture, based on which a Feedback control model is in action to control thread allocation. This model can adjust thread number of each pipeline phase with the change of server load. The experiment results showed in section 5 validate the effectiveness of the control model.

Finally, although the number of threads is allotted based on the queue length of task list and the change of server utilization, actually this method do not handle transient behavior very well. As a part of the future work, we will try to find the relation between thread allocation and mean response time in different server load, through which thread number can be adjusted to a proper value promptly.

References

1. SHAN Zhi-Guang, LIN CHuang, et. al.: Web Quality of Service :A survey. JOURNAL OF COMPUTERS, Feb, 2004
2. C. Huitema.: Network vs. server issues in end-to-end performance. Keynote speech at Performance and Architecture of Web Servers 2000, Santa Clara, CA. http://kkant.ccwebhost .com/PAWS2000/huitema _keynote.ppt.
3. J. Gray and P. Shenoy.: Rules of thumb in data engineering. In Proc. of IEEE 16th Int'l Conf. on Data Engineering, pages 3-10, San Diego, CA, Apr. 2000.
4. Valeria Cardellini, Emiliano Casalicchio.: The State of the Art in Locally Distributed Web-server Systems. IBM research report, Computer Science, RC22209 (W0110-048) October 16, 2001.
5. Philippe Joubert, Robert King, Richard Neves, Mark Russinovich, andJohn Tracey.: High-performance memory-baxde Web servers:Kernel and user-space performance. In Proceedings of the USENIX 2001 Annual Technical Conference, 2001.
6. Tim Brecht, David Pariag, Louay Gammo.: In:Proceedings of the USENIX 2004 Annual Technical Conference:General Track, June,2004.
7. Arjan wan de Ven.: kHTTPd Linux http accelerator. http://www.fenrus.demon.nl.
8. Rob von Behren, Jeremy Condit, et. al.: Why events are a bad idea for high- concurrency servers. In *9th Workshop on Hot Topics in Operating Systems (HotOS IX)*,2003.
9. The Apache Group.: Apache http server project. http://www.apache.org.
10. Vivek S.Pai, Peter Druschel, Willy Zwaenepoel.: Flash:An efficient and portable Web server. In Proceedings of the USENIX 1999 Annual Technical Conference, Monterey,CA,June 1999.
11. Red Hat, Inc. *TUX 2.2* Reference Manual, 2002.
12. B. Krishnamurthy and J. Rexford. Web Protocols and Practices:HTTP/1.1, Networking Protocols, Caching, and Traffic Measurement. Addison-Wesley, 2001
13. A. Feldmann. Web performance characteristics.: IETF plenary. http://www.research.att. com/anja/feldmann /papers.html.
14. Tarek F., Nina Bhatti.: Web server QOS management by adaptive content delivery.

QoS Aware Service Composition with Multiple Quality Constraints[*]

Bixin Liu, Quanyuan Wu, Yan Jia, and Bin Zhou

National University of Defense Technology, Changsha, China
{bxliu, qywu, yanjia, binzhou}@nudt.edu.cn

Abstract. Service composition has been recognized as a flexible way for resource sharing and application integration. Quality of service (QoS) is an important issue for composite services. In this paper, we address the issue of component services selection to ensures their composition satisfy given QoS constraints. We propose the concept of reduction tree as a general scheme to aggregate multi-dimensional quality. And then a heuristic algorithm MCSC_HEU is presented to find execution plans satisfying multiple QoS constrains, with the main idea of evaluating partial plans by a heuristic function during the course of reduction. The time complexity of MCSC_HEU is of polynomial level. Extensive evaluations show that MCSC_HEU succeeds in finding feasible plans with very high probability but demands much less time than exhausting search. So it is an efficient solution for QoS aware service selection with multiple constrains.

1 Introduction

Recently web services have been recognized as the next generation framework for building agile distributed applications over the Internet. Applications are provided as web services which can be discovered and composed into more coarse-grained services, called *composite service* [1]. Composite service is usually modeled as a business process build upon it component service. Instead of pre-established relationship between component services in the composition, service oriented computing advocates discovering and binding to services dynamically according to users' requirements on functional aspects as well as non-functional aspects, especially the quality of service (QoS).

Quality of service (QoS) of a web service typically includes a combination of several qualities or properties [2], such as service time, service cost, success rate and etc. Since QoS of a composite service is determined by the QoS of its underlying component services [3], the dynamic nature of composite services offers a good new chance to provide quality guarantee and service level agreement by selecting proper component services according to preferences and quality requirements set by the users. It has a good reason to believe that the quality aware service selection

---

[*] This work is supported by the National High-Tech Research and Development Plan of China under Grant No. 2004AA112020, No. 2003AA115210, 2003AA115410 and the National Natural Science Foundation of China under Grant No.90104020.

H. Jin, D. Reed, and W. Jiang (Eds.): NPC 2005, LNCS 3779, pp. 123–131, 2005.

mechanism will be an indispensable part for the QoS management framework for composite services. However, to decide which candidates should be chosen so as to satisfy the global constraints over the composite services is not an easy job, especially when multiple QoS dimensions are considered.

Issues of quality of a business process have been addressed in some earlier work on workflow, among which the METEOR system [5] has given a major contribution. A stochastic workflow reduction algorithm to compute multi-dimensional QoS of workflows has been proposed in METEOR and later extended to web service processes [6]. But service selection problems is absent from their research. Some recent work on web services composition has addressed the issue of QoS aware service selection. An extensible quality model has been proposed and a preference oriented service ranking approach has been presented in [4]. But they only concern selecting the best-qualified service for an activity. Such a local strategy can not handle the global constraints and preferences for the composite services. Limited work has addressed service selection issue in the global or end-to-end sense. A global planning approach based on multi choice decision making and integer programming has been studied in [7], with the objective to maximize the user preference. No domain specific efficient algorithms have been investigated. Similarly, [8] has proposed a utility based approach for service selection to ensure end-to-end response time constrain while maximizing the system benefit and minimizing the overall cost. It is solved by modeling the problem as a multiple choice knapsack problem. A simulated annealing approach for optimizing the performance cost ratio of composite services has been discussed in [9] with the background of grid computing. However the simulated annealing approach is usually not time-efficient.

In this paper, we investigate the issue of quality driven service selection for composite services to ensure multiple global QoS constraints. Compared with other work, the contribution of our research is as follows:

1. We have defined the generic quality-driven service selection problem as multi-constrained service composition (MCSC) problem, which is proved to be an NPC problem.
2. To aggregate the multi-dimensional QoS of composite services, we have explored a reduction based approach and proposed the *reduction tree* as a general QoS aggregation scheme for processes-based application. This concept can be easily extended to various quality metrics and process structures.
3. Based on the concept of reduction tree, we have proposed a heuristic which utilized a non-linear heuristic function to approximate the feasibility of execution plans. Time complexity of the heuristic algorithm MCSC_HEU is polynomial. Evaluations show that MCSC_HEU performs well both in its effectiveness and efficiency.

The rest of this paper is organized as follows. We present firstly the premises of our study and define the MCSC problem in section 2. Then in section 3, we introduce the concept of reduction tree and present the heuristic algorithm MCSC_HEU with its principle and complexity analysis. Extensive evaluations are presented in section 4. At the end, section 5 concludes the paper.

2 Premises and Problem Statement

Firstly, we assume that the composite service model is structured. That is to say the composite service model can be decomposed into substructures recursively according to predefined composition pattern, such as sequence, and-branch and or-branch, until all the substructures are atomic activities. Major composite service modeling languages provide building blocks for structured modeling, such as WSBPEL.

Secondly, general quality metrics are discussed. We consider n independent quality metrics $q^{(1)}, q^{(2)} \cdots q^{(n)}$. So the QoS of every candidate service s is represented as a quality vector $q(s) = < q^{(1)}(s), q^{(2)}(s) \cdots q^{(n)}(s) >$. We notice that some QoS metrics could be *negative* (the higher the value, the lower the quality), such as response time and cost, and others could be *positive*, such as success rate. The positive criteria can be converted to equivalent negative one or vice versa by using the reciprocal of its original value. So we assume all the QoS metrics are negative in the following discussion.

Thirdly, it is rational suppose that the quality of a structure in a composite service can be computed by aggregating the quality of its low-level substructures. The aggregation manner usually depends on both quality metrics and composition patterns, which has been discussed in [7,8]. We will not repeat to study specific aggregation rules, however, aggregation functions $f^{(x)}(pat, q_1^{(x)}, q_2^{(x)}, \cdots)$ for metric x are utilized to abstract the aggregation manners, where pat is flag of composition pattern, $q_1^{(x)}, q_2^{(x)}$ are the quality in dimension x for two low-level substructures, and $\cdots$ represents other potential parameters such as the execution probability of substructures. We demand that every $f^{(x)}$ is monotonous for all composition patterns:

$q_1^{(x)} \geq q_1'^{(x)}$ implies $f^{(x)}(*, q_1^{(x)}, q_2^{(x)}, \cdots) \geq f^{(x)}(*, q_1'^{(x)}, q_2^{(x)}, \cdots)$ and $q_2^{(x)} \geq q_2'^{(x)}$ implies $f^{(x)}(*, q_1^{(x)}, q_2^{(x)}, \cdots) \geq f^{(x)}(*, q_1^{(x)}, q_2'^{(x)}, \cdots)$.

Now we define the problem formally.

Definition 1. Consider a composite service with activity set $A = \{a_1, a_2, ..., a_N\}$ and their corresponding candidate sets $\{S_1, S_2, .., S_N\}$, its *partial execution plan p* is a partial function from A to $\bigcup_1^N S_i$ satisfying $p(a_i) \in S_i (i=1..N)$. If $Dom(p)=A$, we say p is an *execution plan*.

Because the QoS of composite service is related to specific execution plan, we denote the quality vector of a composite service with respect to (partial) execution plan p as $< q^{(1)}(p), q^{(2)}(p) \cdots q^{(n)}(p) >$.

Definition 2. Given a constrain vector $cons = < c^{(1)}, c^{(2)} \cdots c^{(n)} >$, where $c^{(i)} (i=1...n)$ is a real number, execution plan p is said to *satisfy cons* (or *cons* is satisfied by p) if for all $i=1..n$ $q^{(i)}(p) \leq c^{(i)}$.

Definition 3. Given a composite service with activity set $A = \{a_1, a_2, .., a_N\}$ and corresponding candidate sets $\{S_1, S_2, .., S_N\}$, the *multi-constrained service composition problem* (MCSC problem) is to find an execution plan p that satisfies the given constrain vector *cons*.

Theorem 1. The MCSC problem is NP-Complete.

Theorem 1 can be proved by converting a special case of MCSC problem which concerns sequentially connected activities to a typical scenario considered in the literature of QoS routing. Thus the problem becomes to find a path in a network of $M*N$ nodes that satisfies the given constraints, namely Multi-Constrain Path (MCP) problem [10], which has been proved to be NP-complete. So MCSC problem is NP-Complete too. Details are omitted for space limit.

3 Service Selection Algorithm for QoS Aware Service Composition

Before the service selection algorithms is presented, we introduce the concept reduction tree at first which acts as the QoS aggregation scheme for composite service and basic data structure in the algorithms.

3.1 Reduction Tree

Reduction tree is developed based on the reduction concept introduced in [5]. For composite services with well-structured model, once all the substructures' qualities in a structure are known, the quality of their composition can be calculated according to simple pre-defined rules. This procedure is called reduction. Reduction can be carried out repeatedly on two substructures in the reverse direction to decomposition and ends when the top structure, the whole process, is reached. Reduction tree captures the reduction procedure of a composite service.

Definition 4. The *reduction tree (R-Tree)* of a composite service is a binary tree in which the degree of each node is either 0 (leaf node) or 2 (non-leaf node). Leaf nodes represent activities of the process, and non-leaf nodes, annotated with workflow pattern flags denotes a substructure in the process. Every node in the R-Tree is weighted by a real number $prob_u$ which is the probability that the substructure denoted by u is visited if its parent is entered.

Reduction tree can be derived from the composite service model and the execution history of the service. Given the R-Tree of a composite service, we can compute its QoS w.r.t an execution plan by attaching a quality vector $q_u = (q^{(1)}_u, q^{(2)}_u \cdots q^{(n)}_u)$ to every node in the post order. Firstly, vectors of leaf nodes are set respectively to the quality vector of its assignment in the execution plan. Then vectors of those non-leaf nodes are determined by aggregating the vectors of their children according to pre-defined reduction rules. After the procedure is executed at the root, quality vector of the root is the quality of the process.

The left part of Fig.1 depicts an example R-Tree. Flags of " | ", " $\wedge$ "and " $\vee$ " in the non-leaf nodes represents sequence, AND-split/join and OR-split/join respectively.

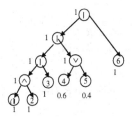

Fig. 1. Example of reduction tree

3.2 Heuristic Algorithm for Service Selection

Based on the concept of R-Tree, an exhausting search algorithm can be developed that every possible pair of partial plans are merged at every non-leaf nodes so that all the possible plans can be generated at the root. This simple algorithm is effective but not efficient enough because of its exponential complexity.

So we propose a heuristic algorithm MCSC_HEU that can solve the problem in polynomial time. The main idea of MCSC_HEU is to evaluate partial plans at non-leaf nodes by a heuristic function instead of comparing every pair of possible partial plans to decide which are the most promising combinations leading to the feasible solutions. The heuristic function to evaluate the favorableness of partial plan p on non-leaf node is defined as follows:

$$h(p) = \prod_{i=1}^{n} q^{(i)}(p)/c^{(i)}$$

Explanation of $h(p)$ is given in Fig. 2 which shows a simple case with only two dimensions. The square area ($\mathcal{F}$) represents the feasible region in the 2D space and the black dot represents a partial plan with normalized weight on each dimension. Every partial plan p determines a rectangle ($\mathcal{D}$) with the origin and two axes, filled with bias as shown in the Fig.2. In 2D space, the area of $\mathcal{D}$ indicates the cost of a partial plan with respect to $h(p)$. For n-dimensional cases, $\mathcal{D}$ is a n-dimensional hypercube and $h(p)$ represents the volume of the hypercube. So it is reasonable to suppose that the smaller $\mathcal{D}$ is, the better.

Because $g(p)$ is an approximation of the likelihood that a partial plan will be extended to a feasible plan, it is inevitable that the heuristic may fail in some cases. To improve performance MCSC_HEU search for the best k partial plans with respect

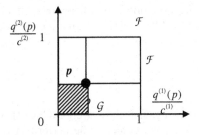

Fig. 2. Explanation of the cost function

MCSC_HEU (*Candidates[1..N],cons*)
FOR *all leaf node i in R-Tree*
  FOR *all* s_{ij} *in Candidates[i]*

  $P^i.insert(\{<i, s_{ij}>\}, q_{ij})$

FOR *all non-leaf node j in R-Tree*
  $P^j = null$
REDUCE (*RTree.root*);
IF *p in* P^{root} *and p<cons* RETURN *p*.

REDUCE (*u*)
IF *u is a leaf node* RETURN
REDUCE (*u.leftchild*);
REDUCE (*u.rightchild*);
FOR *all* p_m *in* P^l *of u.leftchild*

FOR *all* p_n *plan in* P^r *of u.rightchild*

  $p_u = p_m.plan \cup p_n.plan$
  FOR *every metric x* $q_u^{(x)} = f^{(x)}(flag, q^{(x)}(p_m), q^{(x)}(p_n), \cdots)$;

  $P^u.insert(p_u)$

sort entries in P^u *with increasing order w.r.t g(p)*
keep the first k *entries in* P^u *and delete others*

Fig. 3. Algorithm MCSC_HEU

to the heuristic function instead of the best one. When partial plans are merged at non-leaf nodes in the reduction procedure, k plans with minimum g are preserved and then contribute to their parents. Others are considered to be not good enough and discarded. The algorithm MCSC_HEU is presented in Fig. 3.

In MCSC_HEU k^2 partial plans are generated at each non-leaf node and the best k plans are selected by sorting technique. Because the time complexity for the best sorting algorithm is $o(n\log_2 n)$ where n is the number of items to be sorted, the time complexity of MCSC _HEU is $o(Nk^2 \log_2 k)$. Intuitively the efficiency of MCSC_HEU is related to k. The bigger k is, the less partial plans that may lead to feasible solutions will be dropped. But it is a contradiction that big k will increase the complexity. Fortunately, our evaluation experiments in section 4 show that a small k ($k=4$ for instance) is enough for MCSC_HEU to find the right solution with very high probability.

4 Evaluations

The goal of experiments is to evaluate how well MCSC_HEU algorithm performs regarding to various conditions. We compare the performance of MCSC_HEU with the exhausting search algorithm and define the *comparative ratio* as the performance metric which is the ratio that the feasible plan is found by the heuristic and exhausting search.

4.1 Experiments Setup

We study a special case of the 3-dimensional MCSC problem which considers three generic quality metrics: service time, service cost and success rate. Semantics of these quality metrics and their reduction rules can be referred to [5,7].

Experiments are conducted on composite service process templates generated at random. The QoS parameters for candidate services are generated stochastically too. Values of these quality parameters are uniformly distributed in [1,100], [101,200] and [0.1,1.0] respectively. Constraints $(c^{(t)}, c^{(c)}, c^{(r)})$ are randomly generated as follows:

$c^{(t)} = coef * \max(q^{(t)}(p_c), q^{(t)}(p_r))$, $c^{(c)} = coef * \max(q^{(c)}(p_t), q^{(c)}(p_r))$, $c^{(r)} = coef *$ $\max(q^{(r)}(p_t), q^{(r)}(p_c))$, where p_t , p_c and p_r are respectively the best plans w.r.t response time, cost and success rate, and $coef \in [0.5, 1, 5]$ is the adjustable relaxation coefficient that determines the feasible region. It can be understood that the smaller $coef$ is, the less possibly that the satisfying plan exists. The constraints selection scheme guarantees that at least one feasible plan exists when $coef$ is over 1.0.

4.2 Effectiveness and Scalability of MCSC_HU

The first experiment investigates effectiveness of the heuristic by changing the scale coefficient $coef$ and k. We construct process with 10 activities and 5 candidates for each activity. In the experiments $coef$ is set initially to be 0.5 and increased in step of 0.05. For every $coef$, the experiment results are collected by running two algorithms 1000 times with random reduction tree topologies, candidates' QoS parameters and corresponding constraints. The experiment are repeated several times with k= 1 to 128. Curves for comparative ratio are depicted in Fig. 4.

An approximate increasing trend with increasing $coef$ can be discovered in Fig.4. Due to the heuristic nature of MCSC_HEU, one can expect few anomalies in the general trend. Take the case that k is 4 for example. The comparative ratio is 0.925 when $coef$ is 1.0. So we can claim in the case that each non-leaf node maintains the best 4 plans, if only there is a plan satisfying given constraints, the probability that MCSC_HEU can find the solution is about 92%. It increases as the constraints are relaxed. We get nearly 100% comparative ratio when $coef$ is 1.5 which tells the fact that the heuristic performs almost as well as the exhausting search if the constraints are relaxed to a moderate level. Experiments with other k discover similar trends for comparative ratio in spite of some differences in detailed data.

Fig.4 also shows that the comparative ratio is closely relevant to the value of k. Generally speaking the bigger k is adopted, the better performance we get. For example, the comparative ratio is 87.8% when k =1 and $coef$ =1.0 while it goes up to 98.6% when k =128 and $coef$ =1.0. However we noticed that the performance improvement achieved by increasing k is distinct when k is below 8. It becomes unattractive if k increases to 16 or more although we can expect that the curve will

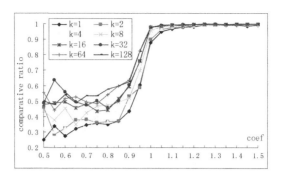

Fig. 4. Performance of MCSC_HEU

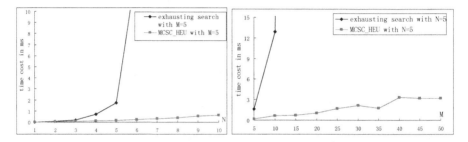

Fig. 5. Time cost comparison of exhausting search and MCSC_HEU

overlap that for the exhausting search algorithm if is k is set to be infinite. This inspires us that we should take a moderate table size in application to get satisfying performance and, at the same time, limit the complexity to a moderate level.

To test the time cost of MCSC_HEU regarding the scale of the problem, we set $coef =1.2$ and change the values of N and M. Fig. 5 shows the result. The curve for the exhausting search approach exhibits obvious exponential increase in its time cost while the curve for the heuristic algorithm indicates approximate linear increase with increasing N. Curves for different M also shows that MCSC_HEU demands much less time than the exhausting search does. When the problem scales, the advantage of MCSC_HEU in the execution time becomes more notable.

5   Conclusions

The emergence of web services has created unanticipated opportunities for establishing agile distributed applications by composing services dynamically to provide new functionality. We have addressed the issue of QoS aware service composition in this paper and raised the MCSC problem aiming at selecting proper component services to ensure their composition satisfy specified QoS constraints. Based on the concept of reduction tree, a heuristic service selection algorithm MCSC_HEU has been developed to solve the MCSC problem with polynomial time complexity. Experiments show that the heuristic performs well both in its effectiveness and efficiency. Furthermore, the approach presented is general and can be easily extended to deal with much wider scenarios.

References

1. B. Benatallah, M. Dumas, M.-C. Fauvet, F.A. Rabhi, Quan Z. Sheng. Overview of Some Patterns for Architecting and Managing Composite Web Services. ACM SIGecom Exchanges, Vol. 3, No. 3, (August 2002), Pages 9-16
2. Daniel A.Menascé, QoS Issues in Web Services, IEEE INTERNET COMPUTIN, NOVEMBER • DECEMBER 2002, Published by the IEEE Computer Society
3. Daniel A.Menascé ,Composing Web Services: A QoS View, IEEE INTERNET COMPUTIN, NOVEMBER • DECEMBE,R 2004, Published by the IEEE Computer Society.
4. Yutu Liu,Anne H.H. Ngu,Liangzhao Zeng，QoS Computation and Policing in Dynamic Web Service Selection, WWW2004, New York, New York, USA.
5. Cardoso, J., A. Sheth and J. Miller. Workflow Quality of Service. International Conference on Enterprise Integration and Modeling Technology and International Enterprise Modeling Conference (ICEIMT/IEMC'02), Valencia, Spain, Kluwer Publishers.
6. Jorge Cardoso, Amit Sheth, John Miller, Jonathan Arnold, and Krys Kochut，Quality of Service for Workflows and Web Service Processes，Journal of Web Semantics, 2004
7. Liangzhao Zeng, Boualem Benatallah,Anne H.H. Ngu, et. al, QoS-Aware Middleware for Web Services Composition, IEEE TRANSACTIONS ON SOFTWARE ENGINEERING, VOL. 30, NO. 5, MAY 2004
8. Tao Yu, Kwei-Jay Lin, Service Selection Algorithms for Web Services with End-to-end QoS Constaints, in Proc. of the IEEE International Conference on E-Commerce Technology, 2004
9. H. Jin, H.H. Cheng, Z.P. Lu,X.M. Ning.Qos Optimizing Model and Solving for Composite Service in CGSP Job Mananger. Chinese Journal of Computers, Apr.2005, Vol 28. No.4. P578-588
10. Yuan, X., Liu, X. Heuristic algorithms for multi-constrained quality of service routing, In Proceedings of the IEEE INFOCOM 2001. Piscataway, NJ: IEEE Communication Society, 2001. 844~853.

Performance Modelling and Optimization of Memory Access on Cellular Computer Architecture Cyclops64

Yanwei Niu, Ziang Hu, Kenneth Barner, and Guang R. Gao

Department of ECE, University of Delaware, Newark, DE, 19711, USA
{niu, hu, barner, ggao}@ee.udel.edu

Abstract. This paper focuses on the Cyclops64 computer architecture and presents an analytical model and performance simulation results for the preloading and loop unrolling approaches to optimize the performance of SVD (Singular Value Decomposition) benchmark. A performance model for dissecting the total execution cycles is presented. The data preloading using "memcpy" or hand optimized "inline" assembly code, and the loop unrolling approach are implemented and compared with each other in terms of the total number of memory access cycles. The key idea is to preload data from offchip to onchip memory and store the data back after the computation. These approaches can reduce the total memory access cycles and can thus improve the benchmark performance significantly.

1 Introduction

The design concept of computer architecture over the last two decades has been mainly on the exploitation of the instruction level parallelism, such as pipelining,VLIW or superscalar architecture. For the next generation of computer architecture, hardware threading multiprocessor is becoming more and more popular. One approach of hardware multithreading is called CMP (Chip MultiProcessor) approach, which proposes a single chip design that uses a collection of independent processors with less resource sharing. An example of CMP architecture design is Cyclops64 [1,2,3,4,5], a new architecture for high performance parallel computers being developed at the IBM T. J. Watson Research Center and University of Delaware. More details of Cyclops64 architecture are described in Section 2.

This paper focuses on the Cyclops64 computer architecture and presented performance model and simulation results for the preloading and loop unrolling approach to optimize the performance of SVD benchmark. The key idea is to preload data from offchip to onchip memory and store the data back after the computation. The contributions include: (1) a performance model for dissecting the total execution cycles; (2) detailed analysis of the tradeoff of the data preloading approaches using "memcpy" or hand optimized "inline" assembly code, and the loop unrolling approach.

The remainder of this paper is organized as follows. The target platform Cyclops64 will be introduced in Section 2. The SVD benchmark and the GaoThomas algorithm are presented in Section 3. Different memory access approaches are introduced in Section 4 and detailed analysis of these approaches in Section 5. Simulation results and validation of the analysis are shown in Section 6. The conclusions are summarized in Section 7.

H. Jin, D. Reed, and W. Jiang (Eds.): NPC 2005, LNCS 3779, pp. 132–143, 2005.
© IFIP International Federation for Information Processing 2005

2   Cyclops64 Hardware and Software

Cyclops64(C64) is a petaflop supercomputer project under development at IBM research Laboratory. The Cyclops64 project is a renovative idea to explore the thread-level parallelism. Figure.1 shows the hardware architecture of a Cyclops64 chip, the main component of a Cyclops64 node. Each Cyclops64 chip has 80 processors, each consisting of two thread units, a floating-point unit and two SRAM memory banks of 32KB each. A 32KB instruction cache, not shown in the figure, is shared among five processors. In a Cyclops64 chip architecture there is no data cache. Instead a half of each SRAM bank can be configured as scratch-pad memory. Such a memory provides a fast temporary storage to exploit locality under software control. The latency of onchip scratch-pad memory is 2 cycles. Cyclops64 system also has offchip memory modules. The default offchip latency is 36 cycles. It could become larger when there is heavy load of memory accesses from many thread units. This parameter can be preset in the Cyclops64 simulator. In this paper, we preset the offchip latency to be 36 or 80.

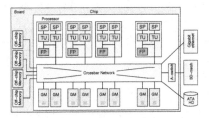

Fig. 1. Cyclops64 Chip

On the software side, one important part of the Cyclops64 system software is the Cyclops64 thread virtual machine. CThread is implemented directly on top of the hardware architecture as a micro-kernel/run-time system that fully takes advantage of the Cyclops64 hardware features. Cyclops64 thread virtual machine includes a thread model, a memory model and a synchronization model. The details of those models are explained in [6]. Suffice it to say that, the Cyclops64 chip hardware supports a shared address space model: all on chip SRAM and off-chip DRAM banks are addressable from all thread units/processors on the same chip.

3   SVD for Complex Matrices

In our implementation, we will focus on the one sided Jacobi SVD method since it is most suitable for parallel computing. The idea is to generate an orthogonal matrix V such that the transformed matrix $AV = W$ has orthogonal columns. Normalizing the Euclidean length of each nonnull column of W to unity, we will get the relation:

$$W = U\Sigma, \qquad (1)$$

where the U is a matrix whose nonnull columns form an orthonormal set of vectors and Σ is a nonnegative diagonal matrix. Since $V^H V = I$, where I is the identity matrix, we have the SVD of A given by $A = U\Sigma V^H$.

Hestenes [7] uses plane rotations to construct V. He generates a sequence of matrices $\{A_k\}$ using the rotation

$$A_{k+1} = A_k Q_k \qquad (2)$$

where the initial $A_1 = A$ and Q_k is a plane rotation matrix. The post-multiplication by Q_k affects only two columns, denoted by u and v, for real matrices, we have:

$$(u', v') = (u, v) \begin{pmatrix} c & s \\ -s & c \end{pmatrix}. \qquad (3)$$

For complex matrices, we have

$$(u', v') = (u, v) \begin{pmatrix} e^{j\beta} & 0 \\ 0 & 1 \end{pmatrix} \begin{pmatrix} c & s \\ -s & c \end{pmatrix} \begin{pmatrix} e^{-j\beta} & 0 \\ 0 & 1 \end{pmatrix}. \qquad (4)$$

where the angel β is from w: $w = |w|e^{j\beta}$, the formulas to get c and s are:

$$\alpha = \frac{y - x}{2|w|}, \qquad \tau = \frac{sign(\alpha)}{|\alpha| + \sqrt{1 + \alpha^2}}$$

$$c = \frac{1}{\sqrt{1 + \tau^2}}, \qquad s = \tau c. \qquad (5)$$

We set $c = 1$ and $s = 0$ if $|w| = 0$. The peudocode of the one-sided Jacobi routine for complex matrices is show in Listing.1.1, which we refer to as "basic rotation routine".

```
1    Rotation_of_two_column(colu, colv)
2    {
3        /* colu and colv are two  columns of complex numbers */
4        w=inner_product(colu, colv);
5        if(|w| <= delta)  {converged <- true; return;};
6        x=inner_product(colu, colu);
7        y=inner_product(colv, colv);
8
9        computer rotation parameter c,s from w, x, y according to Equation 5;
10       update colu, colv according to rotation Equation 4;
11   }
```

Listing 1.1. Rotation of two column of complex numbers

3.1 GaoThomas Algorithm

The plane rotations have to be applied to all column pairs exactly once in any sequence (a sweep) of $n(n-1)/2$ rotations. Several sweeps are required so that the matrix converges. A simple sweep can be a cyclic-by-rows ordering. For instance, let us consider a matrix with 4 columns, with the cyclic-by-rows order, the sequence of a sweep is:

$$(1, 2), (1, 3), (1, 4), (2, 3), (2, 4), (3, 4). \qquad (6)$$

```
1    Rotation_of_two_column(colu, colv)
2    {
3
4        Allocate local_colu, local_colv
5        on the scratch-pad;
6
7        memcpy (local_colu <-colu);
8        memcpy (local_colv <-colv);
9
10       conduct three inner products and
11       column rotation on local_colu, local_colv
12       as in Listing.1.1
13
14       memcpy (colu <-local_colu);
15       memcpy (colv <-local_colv);
16   }
```

Listing 1.2. Basic rotation routine with preloading using "memcpy"

It is easy to see some pairs are independent and may be executed in parallel if we change the order in the sequence. Another possible sequence for a sweep can group independent pairs and executes them in parallel:

$$\{(1, 2), (3, 4)\}, \{(1, 4), (2, 3)\}, \{(1, 3), (2, 4)\}, \tag{7}$$

where the pairs in curly brackets are independent.We call each of these groups a step.

In this research, we implemented the GaoThomas algorithm. This algorithm computes the pairs of n elements on $n/2$ processors when n is a power of 2. A sweep is composed of $n - 1$ steps, each step consisting of $n/2$ pairs of rotations. Therefore, one sweep consists of $n(n - 1)/2$ rotations. In our shared memory implementation, the number of slave threads p can be set to be equal to the number of available processors. All the column pairs in one step can be treated as a work pool, the works in this work pool are shared among the p slave threads, where $1 \leq p \leq \frac{n}{2}$.

GaoThomas algorithm can compute $n(n-1)/2$ rotations of a matrix with n columns on $n/2$ processors. When the size of the matrix increases, group based GaoThomas algorithm can be adopted. For instance, when the matrix size is now $2n$ and we only have $n/2$ processors, we can group two columns together and treat them as one single unit. Generally speaking, for a matrix with n columns, if we group g columns together as a group, then we have n/g groups and can use the basic GaoThomas algorithm for n/g elements, except now each element is a group. For a matrix with n columns and group size g, one sweep contains $n/g - 1$ steps, each step contains $n/2g$ instances of a rotation of two groups, which can run in parallel on maximum $n/2g$ processors. The rotation of two groups includes the rotation of all possible pairs of matrix columns in these two groups.

4   Optimization of Memory Access

4.1   Naive Approach

The default memory allocation using "malloc()" in the Cyclops64 simulator is from the offchip memory, while the local variables are allocated from the stack located on the onchip scratch-pad memory. Assuming that the matrix data originally reside on the offchip memory, we implemented an SVD program where all the memory accesses are from the offchip memory. This implementation is referred to as the naive version in the following discussions. Also, the loop within the inner product computation of the rotation routine is implemented without any loop unrolling in the naive approach.

4.2 Preloading

In order to reduce the cycles spent on memory accesses, we can preload the data from the offchip memory to the onchip scratch-pad memory. Thus the data accesses in the computation part of the rotation routine are directly from the onchip memory. The updated data are then stored back to the offchip memory.

There are two ways to preload data. The simplest way is to use the "memcpy" function from the C library. The pseudo-code for the "memcpy" preloading in the two-column rotation routine is shown in Listing 1.2. We refer to the code segment from the line 10 to line 12 as the "computation core", which consists of the computation of three inner products and a column rotation. Preloading for the group based rotation routine is similar, except that two "groups" of columns are preloaded. The "memcpy" function based preloading has the problem of paying extra overhead of function calling. Additionally, the assembly code of the "memcpy" function is not fully optimized, which is shown with analysis in the next section.

To overcome these two problems, we implement preloading by using an optimized inline assembly code instead of a function call. We refer to this approach as the "inline" approach. For this approach, each "memcpy" function call is replaced with a segment of inline assembly code. The assembly code segment for the "memcpy" and "inline" preloading approaches (either group based rotation routine or basic rotation routine) are shown in Listing 1.4 and Listing 1.5. From the listings, we can see that memcpy and inline approaches have different instruction scheduling. The effect of different ways of instruction scheduling on the total memory access cycles is analyzed in Section 5.

4.3 Loop Unrolling of Inner Product Computation

There are three inner product function calls in the rotation routine. We implemented two versions of loop unrolling for the loop in the inner product computation: unrolling the loop body 4 times or 8 times. The idea is that loop unrolling makes it possible to schedule instructions from multiple iterations, thus facilitating the exploitation of instruction level parallelism.

5   Performance Model

5.1 Dissection of Execution Cycles

We begin with a simple execution trace example in Listing 1.3 to illustrate how to dissect total execution cycles into several parts. In the listing, the first column is the current cycle number. We notice that at cycle 98472, there is a note "DLL = 1", which means that there is a one-cycle latency related to memory access. The reason is that at cycle 98472, the instruction needs the operand R9, which is not ready at cycle 98472 because the LDD instruction at cycle 98470 has two cycles of latency. Similarly, at cycle 98475, the FMULD instruction needs the input operand R8 generated by the FDIVD instruction at cycle 98469. R8 is not ready at cycle 98475 and needs an extra latency of 25 cycles since the FDIVD instruction has 30 cycles of latency from the float point unit. Counting the total number of cycles from cycle 98469 till cycle 98501, there are 33 cycles which include 7 instructions, 1 cycle of "DLL" and 25 cycles of "DLF". The integer unit may also cause certain latency called "DLI", which is similar to the "DLF" in the trace example. Therefore, we have the following equation:

$$
\begin{aligned}
Total \quad cycles = \quad & INST \\
& + \quad DLL + \quad DLF + \quad DLI,
\end{aligned}
\tag{8}
$$

where the "INST" part stands for the total number of instructions, "DLL" represents the cycles spent on memory access, "DLF" represents the latency cycles related to floating point instructions, and "DLI" represents the latency cycles related to integer instructions.

98469	FDIVD	R8,R60,R8	
98470	LDD	R9,R3,96	
98471	ORI	R21,R0,0	
98472	FDIVD	R20,R9,R62	DLL = 1
98474	LDD	R60,R3,104	
98475	FMULD	R6,R61,R8	DLF = 25
98501	STD	R8,R3,160	

Listing 1.3. Example of dissection of execution cycles

5.2 Analysis of Naive Approach

All memory accesses in the naive approach are from the offchip memory and the computation core part has a large number of "DLL" latency cycles. We denote the size of the matrix as $n \times n$. Each element of this matrix is a double complex number. We focus on one sweep that consists of $\binom{n}{2}$ basic rotations for either the non-group based approach or the group based approach. A basic rotation, as shown in Listing 1.1 consists of two different parts, the inner product part and the column rotation part. We analyze the total "DLL" latency cycles for both of them in this subsection.

First, there are three inner product function calls in the basic rotation routine. Each one of them consists of n iterations, each iteration producing a multiplication of two complex numbers and adding it to the sum. From the trace of the innermost iteration (the offchip latency is set to be 80 cycles), we see that the innermost iteration has a "DLL = 76". In general, if we preset the offchip latency to be L cycles, then the total number of "DLL" cycles in each iteration is $L - 4$. Therefore, in one sweep, the total number of "DLL" cycles within the inner product part is:

$$
DLL_{innerproduct} = \binom{n}{2} \times 3 \times n \times (L - 4),
\tag{9}
$$

Second, for the column rotation part in the basic rotation routine, we conduct a similar analysis. The total number of "DLL" cycles of this part is:

$$DLL_{column\_rotation} = \binom{n}{2} \times n \times (L - 4).$$ (10)

Therefore the total number of "DLL" cycles in the naive implementation of GaoThomas algorithm (either group based or non-group based, just one sweep) including both inner product and column rotation is:

$$\begin{aligned} DLL_{naive} &= DLL_{innerproduct} + DLL_{column\_rotation} \\ &= \binom{n}{2} \times n \times (4L - 16). \end{aligned}$$ (11)

5.3   Analysis of "Memcpy" Approach

Using either the "memcpy" or "inline" preloading approach, the computation core accesses data from the onchip memory. The "DLL" part in the computation core is roughly zero due to the overlap of the short onchip memory access latency (2 cycles) with the float point unit latency. Therefore, from the program without preloading to the program with preloading, the decrease of the total number of "DLL" cycles in the computation core is DLL_{naive}, which is the cycles we save by using preloading, and thus the gain we expect to get.

Moving data from the offchip memory to the onchip memory results in an extra cost, which consists of two parts: the first part is the total "DLL" cycles in the code segment that is responsible for moving data, and the second part is the extra instructions incurred. The equation for the first part is derived as follows.

First, we derive the total number of "memcpy" function calls (which are responsible for loading data "in"). For the basic non-group-based GaoThomas algorithm, there are totally $\binom{n}{2}$ basic rotations (shown in Listing 1.1) in one sweep. A basic rotation needs to load in two columns, each of length n. Loading a double complex number needs two "LDD" instructions. Therefore, the total number of "LDD"s for preloading data is:

$$\begin{aligned} LDD_{memcpy\_no\_group} &= \binom{n}{2} \times 2 \times n \times 2 \\ &= \binom{n}{2} \times 4n, \end{aligned}$$ (12)

where the first "2" stands for loading "two" columns, n is that the length of the column, and the second "2" means that loading a double complex number needs two LDDs.

For the group based algorithm, if the group size is g, there are totally $\binom{n/g}{2}$ group based rotations. At the beginning of each group based rotation, we need to load in two groups of columns (i.e, $2 \times g$ columns) and each column needs $n \times 2$ LDDs. Therefore, the total number of LDDs for preloading data during one sweep is:

$$\begin{aligned} LDD_{memcpy} &= \binom{n/g}{2} \times 2g \times n \times 2 \\ &= \binom{n/g}{2} \times g \times 4n. \end{aligned}$$ (13)

If we treat the non-group-based GaoThomas algorithm as a group-based algorithm with group size one, then we can use (13) for either the group based algorithm or non-group-based algorithm.

Second, we compute the latency incurred by the LDDs. The execution trace segment of the assembly code for the "memcpy" function is shown in Listing 1.4, with the offchip latency set to be 80. From the Listing 1.4, we observe that each LDD instruction causes a long latency of 80 cycles, which is reflected where the "STD" instructions exist. If we preset the offchip latency to be L, then each "LDD" causes a latency of L cycles. So the total number of "DLL" cycles for preloading data using "memcpy" is:

$$
\begin{aligned}
DLL_{memcpy} &= LDD_{memcpy} \times L \\
&= \binom{n/g}{2} \times g \times 4n \times L.
\end{aligned}
\tag{14}
$$

In addition to the change in the total "DLL"s, we also observe the increase in the total instruction count as:

$$
Total \quad INST \quad increase = \binom{n/g}{2} \times g \times 4n \times 2 \times 2,
\tag{15}
$$

where the first part $\binom{n/g}{2} \times g \times 4n$ is the total number of "LDD"s for preloading data. We need a same amount of "STD", thus a multiplication by 2. Also we need to use "LDD" and "STD" to store data back, thus another multiplication by 2.

5.4 Analysis of "Inline" Approach

The total amount of data preloaded for the "inline" preloading approach is the same as the "memcpy" approach. Therefore the total number of "LDD"s of the inline approach is the same as the "memcpy" approach:

$$
LDD_{inline} = \binom{n/g}{2} \times 2g \times n \times 2
\tag{16}
$$

In the "inline" approach, 8 LDDs in a row are followed by 8 STDs in a row, as shown in Listing 1.5. From the trace we can see that we will have one "DLL=73" every 8 LDDs if we preset the offchip latency to be 80. If the offchip latency is L cycles, there is a "DLL=$L - 7$" every 8 "LDD" instructions. Therefore, the total number of "DLL" cycles for preloading data using the "inline" approach is:

$$
\begin{aligned}
DLL_{inline} &= LDD_{inline}/8 \times (L - 7) \\
&= \tfrac{1}{8} \times \binom{n/g}{2} \times g \times 4n \times (L - 7).
\end{aligned}
\tag{17}
$$

From (17), we can see very clearly that preloading data using the "inline" approach is better than using the "memcpy" approach because DLL_{inline} is approximately $1/8$ of DLL_{memcpy}.

5.5 Analysis of the Loop Unrolling

The loop unrolling method only affects the inner product routine. For unrolling 4 times, eaczzzh inner product routine now contains $n/4$ iterations, each iteration consisting of computation of the sum of 4 multiplications of complex number. Based on the trace

```
105375    LDD      R6,R9,0
105376    STD      R6,R7,0        DLL = 80
105457    ADDI     R9,R9,8
105458    ADDI     R7,R7,8
105459    LDD      R6,R9,0
105460    STD      R6,R7,0        DLL = 80
105541    ADDI     R9,R9,8
105542    ADDI     R7,R7,8
105543    LDD      R6,R9,0
105544    STD      R6,R7,0        DLL = 80
105625    ADDI     R9,R9,8
105626    ADDI     R7,R7,8
105627    LDD      R6,R9,0
105628    STD      R6,R7,0        DLL = 80
```

Listing 1.4. Trace of the memcpy approach

```
112688    LDD      R16,R9,0
112689    LDD      R17,R9,8
112690    LDD      R18,R9,16
112691    LDD      R19,R9,24
112692    LDD      R20,R9,32
112693    LDD      R21,R9,40
112694    LDD      R22,R9,48
112695    LDD      R28,R9,56
112696    STD      R16,R6,0       DLL = 73
112770    STD      R17,R6,8
112771    STD      R18,R6,16
112772    STD      R19,R6,24
112773    STD      R20,R6,32
112774    STD      R21,R6,40
112775    STD      R22,R6,48
112776    STD      R28,R6,56
```

Listing 1.5. Trace of the "inline" approach

of the innermost iteration, the "DLL" incurred inside the inner product part can be summarized in (18):

$$DLL_{innerproduct\_unroll4} = \binom{n}{2} \times 3 \times \frac{n}{4} \times (L - 8). \qquad (18)$$

Similar analysis of unrolling 8 times can give us:

$$DLL_{innerproduct\_unroll8} = \binom{n}{2} \times 3 \times \frac{n}{8} \times (L - 13). \qquad (19)$$

6   Simulation Result

6.1   Cyclops64 Simulation Environment

The software tool chain of Cyclops64 platform currently provides a compiler, linker and simulator for users. A number of optimization levels are supported by the compiler. A multi-chip multi-threading functional accurate simulator (FAST) is also provided. We

Table 1. Model validation

		Latency=36		Latency=80	
		STD related DLL Latency	Computation core DLL Latency	STD related DLL Latency	Computation core DLL Latency
naive	Measured	52416	16646112	52416	39354336
memcpy	Measured	19664064	2016	42372288	2016
	Change from Naive	19611648	16644096	42319872	39354336
	Predicted change	18579456	16515072	41287680	39223296
	Diff percentage	5.41%	0.78%	2.47%	0.33%
inline	Measured	1943424	2016	4781952	2016
	Change from Naive	1891008	16644096	4729536	39354336
	Predicted change	1870848	16515072	4709376	39223296
	Diff percentage	1.08%	0.78%	0.43%	0.33%
unroll 4	Measured	46368	6711264	46368	16646112
	Change from Naive	6048	9934848	6048	22708224
	Predicted change	-	9676800	-	22450176
	Diff percentage	-	2.63%	-	1.14%
unroll 8	Measured	46368	5114592	46368	12920544
	change from Naive	6048	11531580	6048	26433792
	Predicted change	-	11273472	-	26175744
	Diff percentage	-	2.26%	-	0.98%

developed a Trace Analyzer that can take the output trace from the simulator and generate the dissection of execution cycles and analysis of the code simulated. The analyzer can generate statistics about the total "DLL" related to a certain instruction. For instance, in the example shown in Listing 1.5, the "DLL" latencies caused by the "LDD" instruction are reflected in the STD instruction. we call such latencies "related/associated" to the STD instruction.

6.2   Model Validation

Table 1 shows the change of total "DLL"'s for different approaches with the group size set to be one. In the table, for the preloading based approaches (memcpy or inline), the change of the "STD associated DLL latency" is the cost we pay for preloading, as shown in the third and fifth column of this table. The predicted value of this part is computed using (14) for the memcpy approach, and (17) for the "inline" approach. The change of the total "DLL"'s in the computation core (inner product and column rotation) is the gain we achieved. Without preloading the equation for this part is (11), with preloading, the number of total "DLL" cycles in this part is approximately zero. Therefore, for two preloading approaches, the equation for the cycles saved in the computation core is (11).

The difference percentage between the measured value from the simulation trace and the predicted value from the equations is computed using the following equation:

$$Diff.Percentage = \frac{|Measurement - Prediction|}{(Measurement + Prediction)/2}. \tag{20}$$

From the table, we can see the predicted value is very close to the measured value and the difference percentage is quite small. The prediction for the "memcpy" approach has a relatively bigger difference percentage since the extra overhead of function calling is not accounted for in our simplified model.

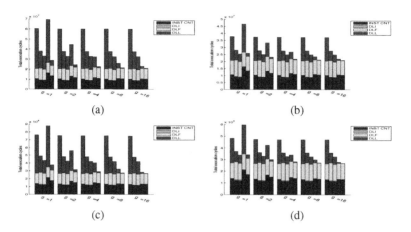

Fig. 2. comparison of different approaches (a)Problem size 64 by 64, L=80 (b) Problem size 64 by 64, L=36, (c) Problem size 32 by 32, L=80 (d) Problem size 32 by 32, L=36

6.3   Comparison of Different Approaches

Figure. 2 shows the comparison of total execution cycles and the dissection to four parts as in (8). Each figure is composed of five clusters of stacked bars. Within each cluster, the leftmost stacked bar is the microlevel breakdown of the naive approach, the second from the left shows the four times unrolling approach, the third one is the eight times unrolling approach, the fourth one is the "memcpy" approach, the fifth one is the "inline" approach. The first cluster shows the five approaches when group size equals one, the second cluster has group size 2, so on so forth. Within each stacked bar, the brown bar (the top bar) shows the total "DLL" cycles, the deep blue bar (the bottom bar) shows the total number of instructions, the light blue bar shows the total "DLI" latency, the yellow bar (in the middle) shows the total "DLF" float point unit latency.

There are several observations from the figures. (1) All the proposed approaches have performance improvement over the naive approach except the "memcpy" method (for group size 1). (2) The figure also shows how the "DLL" cycles change with the increase of the group size. For preloading based approaches ("memcpy" and "inline"), as the group size doubles, the "DLL" will reduce to one half. The loop unrolling based approach does not change with the change of the group size because the loop unrolling based approach only change the inner product routine of the basic rotation routine of two columns and the total number of basic rotations within one sweep is not changed when the group size changes. (3) This figure also shows the total instructions change for different approaches. It can be seen that for preloading based approaches, the total number of instructions increases from the naive approach due to the extra instructions for preloading. On the other hand, the loop unrolling approach can reduce the total instruction count from the naive approach since the loop unrolling reduces the total numbers that the loop control statement are executed. (4) The "DLF" part in the figure roughly does not change no matter what approach we are using. This is true because the "DLF" is related to the floating point instructions in the computation core, which is kept unchanged. (5) It can be seen the "inline" preloading approach performs the best out of all five approaches.

7   Conclusions

This paper focus on the Cyclops64 computer architecture and presented an analytical model and performance simulation results for the preloading and loop unrolling approach to optimize the performance of SVD benchmark. The major contributions include: (1), We developed a performance model and trace analyzer to dissect the total execution cycles. This model allows us to study the application performance tradeoff for different algorithm or architectural design ideas. (2), We presented a clear understanding of SVD benchmark. (3), We used cycle accurate simulator to validate the model and compare the effect of four approaches on the "DLL" part and the total execution cycle. We find the hand optimized "inline" method can improve the performance significantly and performs best among several approaches. We would like to thank Juan B. del Cuvillo, Fei Chen, Weirong Zhu, and other members in the CAPSL (Computer Architecture and Parallel Systems Laboratory) group for their help.

References

1. C. Cascaval, J. G. C. nos, L. Ceze, M. Denneau, M. Gupta, D. Lieber, J. E. Moreira, K. Strauss, and H. S. W. Jr., "Evaluation of a multithreaded architecture for cellular computing," in *HPCA*, 2002, pp. 311–322.
2. G. Almái, C. Cascaval, J. G. Castaños, M. Denneau, D. Lieber, José E. Moreira, and J. Henry S. Warren, "Dissecting cyclops: a detailed analysis of a multithreaded architecture," *SPECIAL ISSUE: MEDEA workshop*, vol. 31, pp. 26 – 38, 2003.
3. G. S. Almasi, C. Caşcaval, J. E. Moreira, M. Denneau, W. Donath, M. Eleftheriou, M. Giampapa, H. Ho, D. Lieber, D. Newns, M. Snir, and J. Henry S. Warren, "Demonstrating the scalability of a molecular dynamics application on a petaflop computer," in *ICS '01: Proceedings of the 15th international conference on Supercomputing*.   New York, NY, USA: ACM Press, 2001, pp. 393–406.
4. J. del Cuvillo, W. Zhu, Z. Hu, and G. R. Gao, "Fast: A functionally accurate simulation toolset for the cyclops-64 cellular architecture," in *Workshop on Modeling, Benchmarking and Simulation (MoBS), held in conjunction with the 32nd Annual Interantional Symposium on Computer Architecture (ISCA'05)*, Madison, Wisconsin, June 4 2005.
5. ——, "Tiny threads: a thread virtual machine for the cyclops64 cellular architecture," in *Fifth Workshop on Massively Parallel Processing (WMPP), held in conjunction with the 19th International Parallel and Distributed Processing System*, Denver, Colorado, April 3 - 8 2005.
6. J. B. del Cuvillo, Z. Hu, W. Zhu, F. Chen, and G. R. Gao, "Toward a software infrastructure for the cyclops64 cellular architecture," 2004, CAPSL Memo 55, Department of ECE, Universisty of Delaware.
7. M. R. Hestenes, "Inversion of matrices by biorthogonalization and related results," *J. Soc. Induct. Appl. Math.*, vol. 6, pp. 51–90, 1958.

TCP-ABC: From Multiple TCP Connections to Atomic Broadcasting*

Zhiyuan Shao, Hai Jin, Wenbin Jiang, and Bin Cheng

Cluster and Grid Computing Lab,
Huazhong University of Science and Technology, Wuhan, 430074, China
zyshao@mail.hust.edu.cn

Abstract. In this paper, we propose a novel scheme, named as TCP-ABC, which replicates the server side TCP connections among multiple server nodes of a cluster. By guaranteeing atomic request delivery, and consensus on responses, this scheme provides the legacy server applications running on the server nodes with multiple active backups in a transparent fashion. By failing the connections over healthy units, the scheme enhances the service and data availability of the cluster. By conducting experiments on the prototype system of a cluster up to four nodes, we find TCP-ABC results in small performance lost while greatly enhances the service and data availability.

1 Introduction

With the popularity of using clusters built with COTS components, more and more efforts need to be done to enhance the availability of the cluster systems. For the considerations of cost and portability, clusters always adopt mature legacy server applications, such as Apache, Q-Mail, to provide the services. Most of these applications follow the client/server model, and use TCP to implement their communication module. However, few of these applications provide active or standby backups to tolerate the faults so as to enhance the availability of a cluster. Although achieving fault-tolerance of the application by totally replacing its communication module sounds feasible, it involves huge effort. The most ideal way to improve fault-tolerance of the application and availability of the cluster is to employ solutions transparent to these legacy applications.

Generally, the availability of a cluster system has two aspects: the service availability and the data availability. Nowadays, front-end solutions, such as LVS [13], are used to achieve the service availability of a cluster, and a series of TCP fault-tolerance schemes [2][7][9], are proposed to do it at finer granularity, i.e., TCP connections. However, few legacy application transparent solutions are forwarded to enhance the data availability for the share-nothing clusters.

Active and semi-active replications methods [12] provide strong data consistency among the copies, which are the most ideal choices to implement the data availability of the clusters. However, both classes of these schemes require support from the

---

* This paper is supported by National 863 Hi-Tech R&D Project under grant No.2002AA1Z2102.

H. Jin, D. Reed, and W. Jiang (Eds.): NPC 2005, LNCS 3779, pp. 144–152, 2005.

communication layer, i.e., atomic multicasting (broadcasting) [1][4]. In order to be transparent to the legacy applications, converting the TCP connections at the server side to atomic multicasting is the prerequisite of deploying these replication methods.

In this paper, we propose a novel scheme, namely TCP-ABC, which replicates the server side TCP connections among multiple server nodes of a cluster. By guaranteeing atomic request delivery, and consensus on responses, this scheme provides the legacy server applications running on the server nodes with multiple active backups in a transparent fashion. By failing the connections over healthy units, the scheme enhances the service and data availability of the cluster.

We organize this paper as the followings. In section 2, the scenario of research is presented. In section 3, we discuss the mechanisms employed by TCP-ABC during the failure-free phase, and consider the possible failures in section 4. To evaluate this scheme, we conduct experiments on real implementations, and present the results in section 5. In section 6, we present a briefly survey of the related works and conclude the paper in section 7.

2   Scenarios of Research

We take the share-nothing cluster shown in Fig. 1 as the scenario of our research. Among the server nodes, there is a unique primary server and multiple backup servers. The primary server possesses the *Portal IP* of the cluster. All the server nodes in the cluster have their own IP addresses (*IP1, IP2 .... IPn*), which belong to a same private subnet. The switch (or router), which connects the server nodes of the cluster with the outside world, supports IP multicasting (which is widely supported by varieties of network standards today) as well as point-to-point communication.

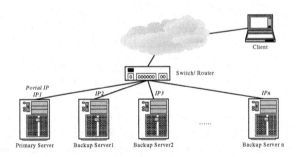

Fig. 1. Scenarios of Research

Data on the server nodes can only be modified by the server side applications by processing the requests of the clients. After processing each request, the server side application sends a response back to the client to indicate the result of the operation (Interactive Communication), and the requests and responses are sent via the estab-lished TCP connections. In this paper, we only consider the TCP connections initiated by the clients to the cluster. Regarding the server side applications, we consider only those processing the incoming requests in a non-stop fashion, i.e., the request messages are delivered in the order they are received.

For convenience of discussion, we assume the execution of the application is deterministic (Deterministic), and the server node delivers the received messages if it does not fail (Self-delivery). We assume the network is always available and will not be partitioned. Messages sent from one server node to another will eventually arrive at its destination (Live Network). Moreover, we assume the failures are crashes (Failure Stop) of the server nodes, and after failure, they will never come back. As our scheme can adopt any independent failure detector, we assume the failure detector used in our scheme is eventually perfect [5], i.e., it can diagnose the faults correctly.

3   Failure-Free Phase

Although the servers can obtain the incoming request messages at ease by simply programming the switch [7], guaranteeing the atomicity of request delivery turns difficult. In TCP-ABC, incoming requests are sequenced at the primary server and then propagated, while the responses from the server nodes converge at the primary server to form a unique response. The communication paradigm of TCP-ABC is shown in Fig. 2, where Pi (i =1~8) and Bj (j =1~9) are the processing steps at the primary and backup respectively.

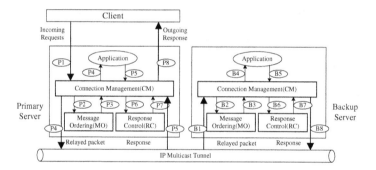

Fig. 2. Communication Paradigm of TCP-ABC

From Fig. 2 we can see that each server node of the cluster consists of *Connection Management* (CM), *Message Ordering* (MO) and *Response Control* (RC) module.

When the primary server receives an incoming TCP request packet from one of the clients, its CM module intercepts the packet and conducts legality check on the packet according to the connections. After that, the packet is given a global ordering number by MO module of the primary server, and then relayed to the backup servers. Section 3.1 will explain the ordering and delivery mechanisms in detail.

When responses are generated, they will be intercepted by the local CM modules and further handled by RC modules to figure out to the ordering number of the incoming request packet the response is for (the response number). Then, the response together with the response number will be sent to the primary server, which will decide the final version. Section 3.2 will explain this procedure in detail.

3.1 Message Ordering and Delivery Strategy

In TCP-ABC, each incoming TCP request packet from the clients is ordered by MO module of the primary server. To explain the ordering method, we illustrate the message exchange pattern of a typical TCP connection [10] in Fig. 3.

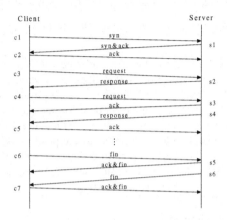

Fig. 3. The Message Exchange Pattern of a Typical TCP Connection

During the connection, MO module of the primary server gives the request packets ($c1$, $c2$ ... in Fig. 3) from the client the ordering numbers provided they are not the retransmitted packets or pure ACKs. In TCP-ABC, the ordering number grows monotonically and re-folds at a boundary, and fragments of the same request packet are given the same ordering number.

Regarding the pure ACK request packets, such as $c5$ in Fig. 3, we give them a special ordering number that does not fall in the range of ordinary ordering numbers. When received by the server nodes, they are simply delivered if no request packets are pending before them. MO module of primary server will have the FIN packets as $c6$ in Fig. 3 ordered before dissemination. If a server node receives the final request packet, i.e., $c7$ in Fig. 3, and makes sure that all other nodes have also received the packet, the resources used by the corresponding connection will be reclaimed.

After being properly ordered, each incoming TCP request packet (except for the pure ACK and $c7$) forms a *decision message* as $<n, m, p>$, where n denotes the ordering number allocated by the primary, p denotes the request packet while m denotes the connection number the packet belongs to. The backup servers in TCP-ABC receive the decision messages by a monotonically increasing order. If decision message is received in disrupted order, the backup server will stop message delivering and send NAK messages to the primary server for retransmissions, which requires the primary to log incoming requests. As communication is interactive, the size of buffer used for logging on the primary should be the number of connections, and this buffer is replicated among all the backup servers to tolerate faults.

In TCP-ABC, all the server nodes of the cluster only deliver the decisions by a monotonically increasing order. Before delivering, the server nodes should make sure the decision is *stable*, i.e., all the others have received the decision. TCP-ABC requires all the backups to send a positive ACK message with the ordering number to other nodes after having received a decision. Each node delivers the decision only after having gathered all corresponding positive ACKs from the backups. As receiving ACK message with higher ordering number from a backup, each backup employs a simple time-out mechanism to retransmit the positive ACK message with the latest ordering number to guarantee the reliable dissemination of its positive ACK messages.

Theorem 1. *TCP-ABC guarantees the atomicity of message delivery for request packets at the server nodes.*

Proof. A multicast protocol is atomic if it satisfied three properties: *Self-delivery*, *All-or-nothing* and *Message ordering*. Self-delivery is assumed in section 2. Since a fixed sequencer (i.e., the primary) is used to order all incoming requests, which means TCP-ABC satisfied FIFO ordering. In case a decision message is lost at some nodes, the rest of the server nodes can delivery this decision only after the decision is received by all the server nodes, as they cannot receive all the positive ACKs. If one of server nodes crashes on the fly, the employed failure detector will eventually confirm the failure, exclude the server node from the cluster, and awake the rest of the server nodes. By this way, the all-or-nothing property is satisfied.

3.2 Response Control (Consensus)

In active replication schemes (e.g. [3]), with the deterministic assumption, server nodes always send their responses directly back to the clients, and the client picks up the fastest one. This method, however, does not fit TCP-ABC, as if it was employed, the processing and communication speed will be decided by the fastest node, and the slower nodes will lose pace. In TCP-ABC, a consensus on the responses at each turn of the iterations of communication is required to synchronize the server nodes.

Response numbers are used to differentiate the iterations. TCP-ABC computes the response number by comparing the ACK number of the response packet and the sequence number of the request packets in history. Response packets of the server nodes together with their individual response numbers will converge at the primary, which decide the final version of response for each response number by comparing the response packets with the same response number. TCP-ABC drops the pure ACK responses of the backups, and sends only those of the primary back to the clients.

With this consensus stage, TCP-ABC actually implements a semi-active replication mechanism to guarantee the data consistency of the replicas [12].

4 Failures

There are two typical types of failures in our scheme: failure of backup server and that of the primary. Crash failure of one of the backups makes the cluster stop working temporarily, since the rest healthy server nodes cannot receive the positive ACKs for the decisions and the responses from the failed backup. System continues to work until the failure detector diagnoses the failure, and after that, server nodes in the cluster will not wait messages from it anymore.

TCP-ABC handles the failure of primary by electing a new primary server among the healthy backups. The one with highest ordering number will be chosen as the new primary so as to keep the existing ordering number of the decisions. If more than one backup satisfy this criteria, the one with the smallest private IP address wins the election. Portal IP address of the cluster will be bound to the NIC of the new primary (IP-takeover). The retransmission mechanism of TCP assures that the unacknowledged requests of the clients will arrive at the new primary.

5   Performance Evaluation

To evaluate performance of TCP-ABC, we implement a prototype with a cluster up to four server nodes. In section 5.1, we will discuss the penalty on communication. In section 5.2, we will discuss the performance of MySQL cluster, which employs TCP-ABC to achieve high availability. The server nodes of the cluster are PC servers running Redhat Linux with kernel version 2.4.7-10, the hardware configuration is Intel Pentium III 1GHz CPU, 512MB Memory and 100Mbps Intel EEPro NIC. The client machines are PCs running Windows 2000 Professional (service pack 4) with hardware of Intel Celeron 1.7GHz CPU, 512MB Memory and RTL8139A NIC. We use 3COM 100Mbps switch to connect the clients and the server nodes.

5.1   Communication Penalty

In Fig. 4, we compare the performance of TCP connections under different cluster configurations. TCP-ABC is used when there is more than one server node. The *round trip time* (RTT) between the client and the cluster is used to demonstrate the latency of communication, and Netpipe-2.4 [11] is used as the benchmark.

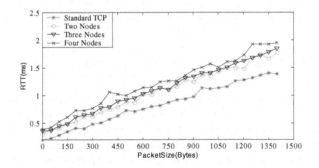

Fig. 4. Communication Penalty of TCP-ABC

From Fig. 4, we can see that when there are two server nodes in the cluster, the latency increases about 20~30% compared with that of the standard TCP. The latency increase is due to message ordering operations on the primary and the time paid at waiting for the positive ACKs and responses from the backup.

When the number of server nodes increases to four, the latency turns higher than that of two. But from Fig. 4, we can observe that compared with that of two nodes, the latency of four nodes only increases about near 10%. The increment is resulted for more time spent on waiting for the positive ACKs and responses from the backup servers.

5.2 Performance of MySQL Cluster

As an open source database management system, MySQL server [8] has been gaining more and more users around the world. In common installations, it is used as backend server providing data to the other server nodes. However, the crash of MySQL server will result in unavailability of the whole cluster. Build-in program of MySQL package can provide the users with a standby backup, and the failover mechanism is not automatic and seamless. We use TCP-ABC to provide multiple active replicas for MySQL server. In our experiment, MySQL server 3.23.41 runs on the server nodes, and the client machine connects to the cluster with MySQL ODBC 3.51.10.

A thread is invoked at the client to create and drop 1000 tables, each of which has ten integer fields. A *test table* with ten integer fields is created for further experiments. We invoke another thread to insert and delete 10000 rows into and out from the test table. The performance of update is obtained by updating a random row within the test table for 1000 times. For all these tests, average response time is obtained to indicate the performance, shown in Fig. 5.

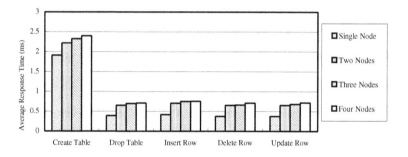

Fig. 5. Performance of MySQL Cluster on Update Operations

Fig. 5 shows that creating of table is the most time consuming. This is because MySQL server needs I/O operations when creating new files to hold newly created tables. The other update operations cost less time since the file is always open before operation. Larger sacrifice on the performance of the update operations consuming less time than those consuming more can be observed. Since penalty put on communication can be better masked by the time consumed on the operations. This means, to the complex operations (e.g., updates on multi-table), the sacrifice is less than that of the simple ones in the experiments.

6   Related Works

Atomic Multicast schemes [1][4] and View Synchronous Communication [6] are two important communication abstractions that have been extensively considered in the context of asynchronous fault-tolerant distributed systems. However, besides the disadvantages for practical applications, such as heavy-weighted, prolonged delivery time and complexity, both of these two abstractions take stateless communication protocols (i.e. UDP) as their basis. This inevitably jeopardizes the transparency if they are applied to the legacy applications using TCP.

TCP Fault-tolerance Schemes [2][7][9] were proposed within the past a few years. Most of them were implemented by providing primary server that actually handled the connection with an active fully replicated backup. However, these schemes suffered some common drawbacks, such as long failover time [2], unreasonable assumption on the processing speed of replicas [7], heavy load on the primary [9]. Moreover, these schemes considered only the service availability.

7 Conclusions

In this paper, we propose a scheme to replicate the server side TCP connections among multiple server nodes of a cluster so as to make failover at TCP connection granularity possible. By guaranteeing atomic request delivery, and consensus on responses, a semi-active replication mechanism is formed to guarantee the data consistency of the server nodes. By conducting experiments on the prototype system of a cluster up to four nodes, especially the MySQL cluster, we find our scheme results in small performance lost while greatly enhances the service and data availability.

References

1. D. A. Agarwal, L. E. Moser, P. M. Melliar-Smith, and R. K. Budhia, "The Totem multiple-ring ordering and topology maintenance protocol", *ACM Transactions on Computer Systems*, May 1998, 16(2):93-132
2. L. Alvisi, T. C. Bressoud, A. El-Khashab, K. Marzullo, and D. Zagorodnov, "Wrapping Server-Side TCP to Mask Connection Failures", In *Proceedings of IEEE INFOCOM*, Anchorage, Alaska, USA, 2001, pp.329-337
3. Y. Amir, D. Dolev, P. M. Melliar-Smith, and L. E. Moser, "Robust and Efficient Replication using Group Communication", *Technique Report CS94-20*, Institute of Computer Science, Hebrew University, 1994
4. K. Birman, A. Schiper, and P. Stephenson, "Lightweight Causal and Atomic Group Multicast", *ACM Transactions on Computer Systems*, 1991. 9(3):272-314
5. T. D. Chandra and S. Toueg, "Unreliable failure detectors for reliable distributed systems", *Journal of the ACM*, March 1996, 43(2):225-267
6. G. V. Chockler, I. Keidar, and R. Vitenberg, "Group Communication Specifications: A Comprehensive Study", *ACM Computing Surveys*, December 2001, 33(4):1-43
7. M. Marwah, S. Mishra, and C. Fetzer, "TCP Server Fault Tolerance Using Connection Migration to a Backup Server", In *Proceedings of the 2003 IEEE International Conference on Dependable Systems and Networks (DSN)*, San Francisco, CA, USA, 2003, pp.373-382
8. MySQL server, http://www.mysql.com
9. Z. Shao, H. Jin and B. Chen, J. Xu, and J. Yue, "HARTS: High Availability Cluster Architecture with Redundant TCP Stacks", In *Proceedings of the International Performance Computing and Communication Conference (IPCCC)*, Phoenix, Arizona, USA, 2003, pp.255-262

10. W. R. Stevens, *TCP/IP illustrated. Volume 1: The protocols*, Addison-Wesley, 1994
11. Q. O. Snell, A. Mikler, and J. L. Gustafson, "Netpipe: A Network Protocol Independent Performace Evaluator", In *Proceedings of IASTED International Conference on Intelligent Information Management and Systems*, June 1996, pp.196-204
12. M. Wiesmann, F. Pedone, A. Schiper, and B. Kemme, "Understanding replication in databases and distributed systems", In *Proceedings of the 20th IEEE International Conference on Distributed Computing Systems (ICDCS)*, Taipei, Taiwan, 2000, pp.264-274
13. W. Zhang, "Linux Virtual Server for Scalable Network Services", In *Proceedings of Ottawa Linux Symposium*, Ottawa, Canada, 2000, pp.212-221

A Parallel File System Based on Spatial Information Object

Keying Huang[1,2], Guoqing Li[2], Dingsheng Liu[2] , and Wenyi Zhang[2]

[1] Graduate School of the Chinese Academy of Sciences (GSCAS)
kyhuang@ne.rsgs.ac.cn
2 Key Laboratory, China Remote-Sensing Satellite Ground Station,
Chinese Academy of Sciences
{gqli, dsliu, wyzhang}@ne.rsgs.ac.cn

Abstract. In this paper we introduced a parallel file system based on the spatial information object storage, the PIPFS system. PIPFS is a special-purpose parallel file system which designed in view of the remote sensing image processing. It uses the server/client pattern and bases on the metadata mechanism. It simultaneously accesses disks on several nodes for application I/O operations, which improves the efficiency of the operation on large scale data. A high performance is shown on high-data-complexity application, such as remote sensing image processing.

1 Introduction

1.1 Spatial Information Data Characteristics

Remote sensing technology is developing on the filed of spatial resolution, spectrum resolution, time resolution and weather condition, model, rate of observation, with which the data scale is expanding rapidly. A single scene of TM image with 7 bands can reach 280MB. The large mosaic image can be several gigabytes[1]. Different from general file data, the image data structure of remote sensing is quite complicated. The data type which is used to save pixel of remote sensing image data may be 8bit integrated, 16bit integrated, 32bit integrated or complex number and the organizational form may be BIP, BIL or BSQ. Moreover, a group of remote sensing image data often contains the same spatial attribute information.

The traditional file system is unable to combine and save the remote sensing images with their attribute information. They can be only saved separately as different files. In the remote sensing image processing process, we should keep the maximum spatial information which the image contained in order to keep the high-usability of the spatial data. Because each pixel in the image represents some spatial information, the image processing is aim at the raw form image. This limits the use of image compression technology, especially the loss-compression technology. Therefore, the remote sensing image data characteristics and data processing force us to face the problems of computing and saving the magnanimous special structure data.

H. Jin, D. Reed, and W. Jiang (Eds.): NPC 2005, LNCS 3779, pp. 153–162, 2005.
© IFIP International Federation for Information Processing 2005

1.2 The Storage Pattern Used in High Performance Computing

Facing the computing and saving problems of magnanimous spatial information data, high performance computing has took one good way which applied in spatial information processing and service. In high performance computing, data storage pattern affects the overall performance directly. General high performance computing storage pattern mainly includes two kinds of network storage system: (1) parallel and distributed file system, (2) data and computation separated system. The architecture of parallel and distributed file system is mainly based on computing servers. In other words, the storage and the computing are both in the same group servers. The representatives of this storage pattern are[2] message sharing mechanism such as NFS[3], Coda[4], XFS[5] and storage sharing mechanism such as VMS[6] and SFS[7]. There are two kinds of mainstream network storage construction. They are distinguished by the command collection[8]. One kind is the high-bandwidth, low-detention but high-price and bad-extension SAN（Storage Area Network) structure. The other is good-extension, low-price, easy-manage but high-protocol-spending, low-bandwidth and heavy-delay NAS（Network Attached Storage) Structure.

In view of the insufficiency of above storage pattern, the research aim at a new Linux cluster file system, object storage file system, has been launched.

1.3 From the File System Angle to Accelerate the Remote Sensing Image Parallel Processing

When the remote sensing image parallel processing algorithm executes on traditional file system, the data operation model is distribution - computing - collection. With this model, data distribution and collection process is the bottleneck of entire procedure. For example, in the image rotate algorithm which using small buffer, data I/O cost takes almost 60% of the whole time used by application[9]. Using the traditional file system and existing parallel computing model can not solve this problem. Therefore, the key job is to study a file system which adapts the characteristics of remote sensing image parallel process. This new parallel file system saves the remote sensing image data in cluster according to some distribution rules and manages the relevant spatial information and physical data distribution information in unison. In the process, through the algorithm control, the majority of data which each computing node needs can be read from local hard disk, thus reduces the network transmit time which cased by using traditional file system. The new file system can effectively accelerate the data accessing speed and the application execution.

2 PIPFS: A Parallel File System Based on the Spatial Information Object Storage

PIPFS（Parallel Remote Sensing Image Processing File System) is a parallel file system on Linux cluster, which based on spatial information object storage. In the following, we will introduce PIPFS system from tow aspects: the system structure and its support to the remote sensing image parallel process.

2.1   System Structure

As figure 1, PIPFS adopts client-server pattern based on metadata. File metadata information is managed by metadata server. Physical data is stored with distributed mode. Physical files distributed on different nodes are looked as a whole logic file. This can shield the network transfers to developers and reduce the complexity of programming and file management. PIPFS system contains three parts: metadata server, storage servers and the clients.

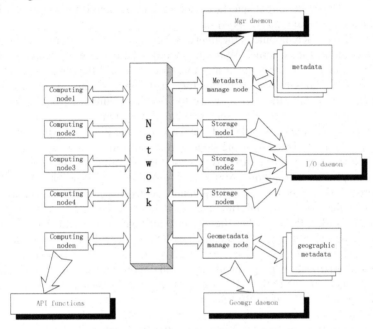

Fig. 1. Structure of PIPFS System

2.1.1   Metadata Server
The management daemon Mgrd (Metadata Manager daemon) is running on the metadata server. It is responsible for storing and managing the ordinary metadata and the spatial information metadata, doing any kind of operations on metadata, such as create, read or modify. Ordinary metadata includes the physical distributing information of image data which is distributed stored. Spatial information metadata includes the spatial attribute information that the remote sensing image has. In PIPFS, we adopt metadata centralized management--there is a unique metadata server in cluster. On one hand, it can apply a foundation for cluster to distributed store and read remote sensing data. On the other hand, it can apply convenience for users to unified manage the image data.

2.1.2   Storage Servers
In PIPFS, the physical data is distributed in storage servers which named I/O servers. The physical data management daemons Iod (I/O daemon) are running on these

servers. They are responsible for real read and write operations on local files and communication with clients. In fact, these servers create new files on local file system and access files with common operations, such as read(), write() and mmap(). It means that any local file system can store PIPFS files, such as ext2, ext3 and so on. Furthermore, we can realize fault tolerance by hard RAID or soft RAID which can create extern large file system.

2.1.3 Clients

The clients include the kernel interface module and the application program library (the application program interfaces APIs).

The kernel interface module is the interface between PIPFS system and file system manage module in Linux kernel. With this module, there are two advantages. One is that PIPFS system can be mounted as same directory in different clients. Then the users can use the files in the same directory at different clients. After installed the kernel interface module, the user may use the familiar command, such as ls, cd, rm, etc. to manage files. Most of present parallel file systems can not be visited via different operation system. Another advantage is that the directory which attached to PIPFS system can be visited by using samba protocol from windows system.

The application program library has provided the function interfaces which can be called by application programs. Application programs access all kinds of data in PIPFS through the APIs. The operations mainly consist of three kinds: operating on ordinary metadata, on spatial information metadata and accessing distributed physical data. Visiting files through the file system manage module increases the time expenses of kernel. But in PIPFS, the application program library provides a shortcut for programs to visit storage servers directly. It saves more resources for the computation. Application program library is analogous to the file system interface function library of UNIX\Linux system. This has facilitated users to develop application programs based on PIPFS system.

2.2 Support to Remote Sensing Image Parallel Processing

2.2.1 To Parallel Processing

In PIPFS, the storage server is also the computing server. In this way, the application programs can get distribution information of physical data through the metadata and control the parallel processing. As a result, the majority of data that each computing server needs can gain from local hard disk, little part of data gains from other storage servers via PIPFS. Thus, it reduces the time spend in data distributing and collecting, which caused by using traditional file system and the distribution – computing – collection pattern. Parallel programs furthest use the data exchange and manage protocol of PIPFS to improve the efficiency. The parallel disk I/O operations in different nodes accelerate accessing data in file system. Therefore, PIPFS can improve the application performance.

2.2.2 To Spatial Information Object

The spatial information object is PIPFS system fundamental unit. An object is a combination of some spatial attribute information and remote sensing image data files. But in traditional system, the file and the block are basic storage units. Users should track the relevant spatial information while access the images. But in PIPFS system, the spatial information objects manage their attribute information via file system. And all spatial information objects have a unique object marking. Through the object marking, the users can access and operate the spatial information objects easily. Besides the I/O function interfaces which are analogous to UNIX\Linux system, PIPFS also provides some new functions which fit the remote sensing image processing:

1. Read-write data by block. Traditional file system read/write function only can read/write continual data that starts from an assigned address. A remote sensing image actually is a two-dimensional or multi-dimensional array. It frequently uses BIL or BSQ as its data organization form. Read and write data by block is the basic data accessing mode. In this mode, the efficiency of read function in traditional file system is very low. It leads to frequent I/O operations and memory redundancy. Using the read/write functions by block that provided by PIPFS system, users can access the assigned region data easily.

2. Distribution strategy control. In common parallel file system, the users almost can not control the distribution strategy of a file. They only can make some adjustments in the file distribution number or the partition size but unable to control the storage location of block data. In PIPFS system, there is a default distributed strategy, but users are able to control the distribution through APIs, too.

3. Sampling reading. For better supporting remote sensing image processing application, PIPFS system also add some commonly used functions, such as image sampling, to the file system. Users can gain the sampling date but need not to read the distributed date to local node. This facilitates developers and enhances the system's efficiency. It also avoids the frequency I/O operations and lightens the load of master node.

4. Support to save large size spatial information object. Because the using of advanced remote sensing technologies, for example high spectrum, high resolution and so on, now the single spatial information object size may amount to several hundred Megabyte. The size of spatial information object that has been processed is possible to reach several Gigabyte even dozens of Gigabyte. On the traditional file system, it is difficult to save or operate a file bigger than one Gigabyte. But in PIPFS system, the physical data are distributed, so it theoretically can save and operate arbitrary size spatial information object as will.

3   Experiments

The experimental environment is:

Meta data server is equipped with dual Xeon 2.4G processors, 2GByte ECC ram, 146GByte 1000RPM SCSI hard disk, and a 1000MBps Ethernet card.

Storage servers and computing servers constitute 8 nodes. Each node is equipped with dual Xeon 2.4G processors, 1GByte ECC ram, 160GByte 7200RPM Ultra IDE (ATA133) hard disk, and a 1000MBps Ethernet card.

The operating system is Redhat Linux 7.3.

3.1   Throughput

There is only one application program operated the data in this test. Parallel operation will be displayed in the expansibility test (see Sect. 3.3).
We compared the throughput of PIPFS with NFS in the testing environment.

Table 1. Throughout data ranged of PIPFS and NFS

Unit:MB/s

Filing system		Data scale				Read-write speed Mean value
		100MB	500MB	1GB	5GB	
NFS	Reading	21.76	23.50	21.12	20.05	21.61
	Reads in	43.52	36.83	37.05	34.81	38.05
PIPFS	Reading	21.38	22.84	22.31	21.20	21.93
	Reads in	53.91	52.45	51.62	52.03	52.50

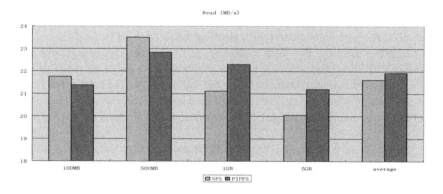

Fig. 2. Read speed of PIPFS and NFS

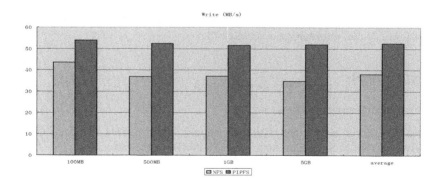

Fig. 3. Write speed of PIPFS and NFS

From the result we can see that NFS and PIPFS can perform the full performance on the Giga Ethernet. The result from different size of data indicated that when handles big data the throughput of PIPFS is much better. That is because NFS only can operate one file and PIPFS on a group of files. In the experiment we adopt NFS version3, which is an asynchronous write mode. PIPFS is built on local ext3 file system and applies asynchronous write mode in real write procedure. Therefore the write speed of NFS and PIPFS is both higher than read.

3.2   Combine PIPFS with Remote Sensing Image Processing Algorithm

The experiment explained the advantages of PIPFS combined with algorithms. The testing algorithms we chose are: (1) image rotate algorithm whose local hit rate is small in image processing algorithms, (2) unsupervised classify algorithm which the data needed by computing is stored in local storage.

3.2.1   Image Rotate Algorithm

In the experiment we used a single wave band TM image whose size is 5728*6920 pixels and rotated it 45 degree in the counterclockwise. The output image is an 8942*8941 pixels image. We use cubic convolution algorithm and gained two rotate program's run time in different parallel scales.

Table 2. Execute time of two rotate functions

Unit: Second

Function name	Parallel scale and running time			
	5 nodes	6 nodes	7 nodes	8 nodes
Rotate (MPI) *	79.5	71.0	64.9	61.7
Rotate (PIPFS)	25.2	23.6	19.8	18.1

* rotate (MPI) A function in PIPS system

In the experiment rotate algorithm is a reduced local retrieve algorithm. That algorithm's characteristic is that each computing node just deals with the local retrieve area. That brings the treatment simpler and avoids transferring the whole image to each computing node. But in PIPS system's rotate algorithm, the data is distributed by the master process through MPI. That consumes network bandwidth and computing node's memory. There is certain of resource waste. When dealing with pictures oversize there is some limits. Recur to PIPFS system, we can access the spatial information object via its global control ability. The master process's task is limited to little message transfer. The data operations are achieved by several storage servers in parallel. This can radically avoid block and improve the algorithm's efficiency. From table 2 we can see that the rotate algorithm combined with PIPFS is faster 2/3 running time than that with MPI to distribute data. We can conclude that the algorithms combined with PIPFS can obviously improve the performance.

3.2.2 Unsupervised Classify Algorithm

In the experiment, we used a single wave band TM image whose size is 5728*6920 pixels. We separated the image into 8 classes, iterative time is 10 and the threshold is 0.01. We compared algorithm using MPI with that combined with PIPFS in the main procedure's running time. Because the massage transfer time is microsecond, we ignored it.

Table 3. Execute time of tow class functions

Unit: Second

Function name		Class (MPI)	Class (PIPFS)
Master process	Read/ write	0.98	
	Transmission	4.17	
	Processing	10.32	13.38
	Receive	5.72	
slave process	Receive /Reads	3.89	3.60
	Processing	11.35	10.06
	Transmission /Writes	6.04	1.28
total		42.47	28.32

The parallel unsupervised classify algorithm's procedure is: The slave process deals with the clustering center of the image area which is distributed in each iterative. When accomplished the slaves send the result to the master. Then the master deals with the clustering center received from each slave and returns the new center to them. The slave deals with data according to the new cluster center. From table 3 we can see the algorithm with PIPFS can save the master's read/write and send/receive time compared with that using MPI. The slave's read/write time also smaller. Therefore in the whole procedure we can save above 40% time using PIPFS and the result will be much evident when dealing with bigger data.

3.3 File System Regarding Parallel Scale Extended Test

The experiment environment is:

Meta data server is equipped with two Xeon 2.4G processor, 2GByte ECC ram, 160GByte 7200RPM Ultra IDE (ATA 133) hard drive, and a 1000MB Ethernet card. The operating system is Redhat Linux 7.3.

Storage servers and compute servers constitute 8 nodes. Each node is equipped with two Xeon 2.4G processor, 1GByte ECC ram, 160GByte 7200RPM Ultra IDE (ATA133) hard drive, and a 1000MB Ethernet card. The operating system is Redhat Linux 7.3.

In remote sensing image processing, read operation is more than write. However in parallel algorithm, parallel reading the same file in the meantime is a basic operation. Therefore read performance, especially parallel read, is important to the

Table 4. Expansibility of NFS and PIPFS

Unit:MB/s

Filing system	Parallel scale			
	1 node	2 nodes	4 nodes	8 nodes
NFS	21.56	7.61	6.19	4.07
PIPFS	20.67	21.13	22.03	21.84

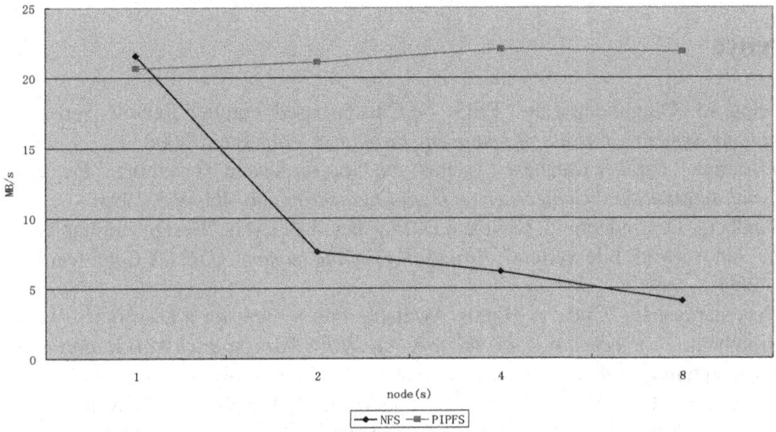

Fig. 4. Read speed of NFS and PIPFS while parallel scale increase

performance of a file system. This test assumes that the number of storage servers and computing servers is linearity grows. In this condition, compare the read speed of the bottleneck nodes in NFS and PIPFS.

From table 4 and figure 4, the test result showed that the support of NFS to the parallel scale extended was far inferior to PIPFS. PIPFS has used the multi-thread response mechanism, and the data distributed to different server. So concurrently reading can fully use the network band width. Therefore, when the parallel scale is growing, PIPFS had a higher reading speed than NFS. This test also showed that under the certainly parallel scale, PIPFS system has a good extension and it can provide an effective performance platform for the remote sensing image parallel processing.

4 Conclusion

From above tests, we can find that the efficiency of remote sensing image processing algorithm in PIPFS system is higher than the algorithm in traditional file system, because the algorithm used file system to control and operate the spatial information object. Storage based on spatial information object shield physical distribution detail and the network transmission to the developers. It greatly reduces the complexity of programming and file management. The developer need not to consider the distribution and parallel operations on data. The application program can execute the parallel process just by calling PIPFS system interface functions and synchronizing the messages. So the entire development mode in PIPFS is even more similar to the development mentality of serial programming.

What's more, combined with Linux kernel, management of spatial information object in PIPFS is more convenient and direct-viewing. Users can operate the data but need not to enter each storage server. They can complete the operation through the metadata server. At the same time, this also increased data security on the storage server.

Reference

1. Guoqing Li, DingSheng Liu, "PIPS: A Cluster-based Parallel Remote Sensing Image Processing System", *Journal of Image and Graphics*, Vol.5 Supp. 2000
2. P. Valduriez, "Parallel Database Systems: the case for shared–something," *Proceedings of the Ninth International Conference on Data Engineering*, pp. 460-465, 1993.
3. R. Sandberg, D. Goldberg, S. Kleiman, D. Walsh and B. Lyon, "Design and Implementation of the Sun Network File System", *Proceedings of the Summer USENIX Conference*Pp. 119 - 130, 1985.
4. M. Satyanarayanan, "Coda: A Highly Available File System for a Distributed Workstation Environment, " *Proceedings of the Second IEEEWorkshop onWorkstation Operating Systems*September 1989.
5. T. Anderson, M. Dahlin, J. Neefe, D. Patterson, D. Roselli, and R.Wang, "Serverless Network File System," *ACM Operating Systems Review*Vol. 29, no. 5, December 1995.
6. *Digital Technical Journal*, VAXcluster Systems, September 1987. Special Issue - Number 5.
7. K. Matthews, "Implementing a Shared File System on a HIPPI Disk Array," *Fourteenth IEEE Symposium on Mass Storage Systems*, pp. 77-88, 1995.
8. Wu Qingbo, "Linux Object storage file system research",*Http://www-900.Ibm.Com/developerWorks/cn/linux/l-ofs/index.Shtml*, 2004.10
9. Zhu Yaofei, " research and experiment in remote sensing data parallel processing file system ", *Master's degree paper,* Chinese remote sensing satellite earth station, 2002.7

Topology-Aware Multi-cluster Architecture
Based on Efficient Index Techniques

Yun He, Qi Zhao, Jianzhong Zhang, and Gongyi Wu

Department of Computer Science and Technology, Nankai University,
Tianjin 300072, China
{hey1630, qizhao6688}@mail.nankai.edu.cn
{zjz, wgy}@nankai.edu.cn

Abstract. In this paper, we focus on how to construct an efficient unstructured P2P system. The main contributions of our proposal are two-fold. First, aiming at alleviating the topology mismatch problem between the P2P logical overlay network and the physical underlying network, we proposed a Topology-aware Multi-cluster Overlay (TMO) architecture where peers self-organize into clusters based on network locality. Second, in order to further improve the search efficiency of the TMO architecture, we present two novel index techniques, namely, cluster-index technique and topic-index technique. The two different techniques are highly effective in different application domains in which the TMO architecture is deployed. The simulation results indicate that our proposed schemes are efficient in both resource usage and data retrieval.

1 Introduction

In recent years, there has been much interest in peer-to-peer (P2P) systems because they provide a good substrate for building large scale data sharing and content distribution applications. P2P systems can be broadly classified into two categories: unstructured and structured P2P systems.

Unstructured P2P systems, like Gnutella [1] and KaZaA [2], organize peers in a random graph and use flooding on the graph to query documents stored at overlay peers. The floods support arbitrary queries, but are not scalable because they cause exponentially increased network traffic. In contrast, structured P2P systems are developed to perform key queries by constructing Distributed Hash Tables (DHTs), such as Chord [3], CAN [4], and Pastry [5], etc. Although such schemes provide good performance for exact match queries, they almost don't work for range, approximate, or text queries. Thus, many agree that unstructured P2P systems are more suitable for mass-market file sharing applications.

In traditional unstructured P2P systems, the mechanism of a peer randomly joining and leaving causes topology mismatch between the P2P logical overlay network and the physical underlying network [6]. This topology mismatch problem causes a large amount of unnecessary traffic, which brings great stress on the Internet infrastructure.

The objective of this paper is to construct an efficient unstructured P2P system. We propose an application architecture called Topology-aware Multi-cluster Overlay (TMO), which has two levels. Peers in the lower level self-organize into clusters based

H. Jin, D. Reed, and W. Jiang (Eds.): NPC 2005, LNCS 3779, pp. 163–171, 2005.
© IFIP International Federation for Information Processing 2005

on network locality, aiming at alleviating the topology mismatch problem. The clusters are organized into the upper level overlay defined by a directed graph (e.g. DTH graph) such that the efficient routing between clusters can be easily achieved.

In order to further improve the search efficiency of the TMO architecture, we present two novel index techniques, namely, *cluster-index technique* and *topic-index technique*. In the cluster-index technique, each cluster has content indices from all peers of some other clusters. When a query is submitted, full search scope can be achieved even though some of the clusters are directly probed. In the topic-index technique, all the documents stored in the network are classified into topics. Each document's index is sent to the cluster responsible for the topic that the document belongs to. A query probes only a few clusters that have the largest number of results under a particular topic. The two different techniques are highly effective in different application domains in which the TMO architecture is deployed.

The rest of the paper is organized as follows. Section 2 introduces related work. Section 3 describes the TMO architecture in details. Section 4 and Section 5 describes the cluster-index technique and the topic-index technique, respectively. In Section 6, the simulation results are presented, followed by conclusions in Section 7.

2   Related Work

There are several P2P systems that use indexing approaches. For example, Napster [7] is a centralized system that uses specialized peers to maintain the indices of the documents available in the overlay network. To find a document, the user queries an index peer to identify peers having documents with the content of interest. KaZaA [2] is a popular super-peer network where a super-peer acts as a centralized server to a subset of clients. In order to process queries for its clients, a super-peer keeps an index over its clients' documents.

Although original Gnutella does not build indices, some indexing approaches have been proposed to make Gnutella scalable. For example, in Local Indices policy proposed in [9], each peer indexes the files stored at all peers within a certain radius r and can answer queries on behalf of all of them. The work in [10] proposes 3 types of Routing Indices (RIs), namely compound RIs, hop-count RIs and exponential RIs to facilitate search in Gnutella. In particular, peers forward queries to their neighbors based on their own RIs. Ways to improve searching has been extensively studied using Search/Index Links (SIL) [8]. SIL points out that a parallel search cluster based P2P network is superior to a super-peer network for several important scenarios. However, the mechanism of how to break the P2P networks into multiple clusters has not been mentioned yet.

3   Topology-Aware Multi-cluster Overlay

We begin by presenting a general framework for TMO. We assume that each participating peer has an IP address. The peers are organized into clusters. Each cluster has a unique cluster id. We let N denote the number of clusters, and C_i denote both cluster i and the id of cluster i. The clusters are organized by a graph (X, U), where $X = \{C_0, C_1, ..., C_{N-1}\}$ is the set of all clusters and U is a given set of virtual edges between the nodes (that is, clusters) in X. The edges in U may be unidirectional or not. We believe that DHT graphs [3, 4, 5] can be efficiently used as the graph (X, U). In this paper, we use the Chord DHT graph as an example.

TMO consists of two kinds of links. *Short-distance links* connect peers within a cluster. *Long-distance links* connect pairs of peers from different clusters. Two peers are *short-distance neighbors* if they are connected by a short-distance link. We require that if p_i is a peer in C_i, and (C_i, C_j) is a unidirectional edge in U, then p_i knows the IP address of a peer $p_j \in C_j$. With this knowledge, p_i establishes a long-distance link to p_j, and p_j becomes a *long-distance neighbor* of p_i. It is important to note that p_i keeps only one long-distance neighbor in each of C_i's neighboring clusters. In addition, if C_j is the successor node of C_i in Chord DHT graph [3], we will say that p_j is p_i's *first long-distance neighbor*. Of course, each peer has only one first long-distance neighbor, which plays the key role in the cluster-index technique that will be described in Section 4.

Figure 1 shows an example of TMO architecture. Four clusters C_0, C_1, C_2 and C_3 are organized by a Chord graph. Each peer in cluster C_0 selects a long-distance neighbor from both C_1 and C_2, because the neighboring clusters of C_0 are C_1 and C_2.

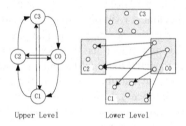

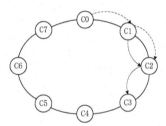

Fig. 1. A TMO architecture (N=4)   **Fig. 2.** A TMO-CI system (N=8, d=2)

3.1 TMO Construction

One key idea of TMO is that it partitions peers into clusters by network locality. We use the landmark clustering method proposed in [6] to generate topology information for clustering physically close peers. Landmark clustering method requires a set of well-known landmark nodes spread across the Internet. A peer measures the network-level Round-Trip-times (RTTs) to each of these landmark nodes and sorts the landmark nodes in terms of increasing RTTs. Peers with the same or similar landmark ordering are considered close to each other, and are expected to join the same cluster. The interested reader is referred to [6] for these details.

When a new peer wants to join a TMO system, it first measures RTTs to all landmark nodes to get a landmark ordering, which assigns it to a specific cluster. Then the new peer sends a JOIN message destined for the target cluster. The message is sent into TMO via any existing peer. Peers receiving the message use Chord routing mechanism to forward the message via long-distance links, until it reaches a random peer in the target cluster. A new peer can only join one cluster at the same time.

After the new peer has joined the target cluster, it gets short-distance neighbors in the Gnutella fashion, and gets long-distance neighbors as follows. If x is the new peer in cluster C_i, it will send request messages to its short-distance neighbors for the IP addresses of their long-distance neighbors. If x gets the IP address of another peer y belonging to cluster C_j, which is a neighboring cluster of C_i, then x will try to connect y. If the attempt succeeds, y will become x's long-distance neighbor for cluster C_j, or else y will send the IP address of its short-distance neighbors to x, then x will try to connect these peers for long-distance neighbors. It is enough for x to keep only one long-distance neighbor in each of C_i's neighboring clusters. But in practice, x may cache more than one candidate peer in each cluster to improve system tolerance.

There are two reasons for why we use the Chord graph to organize clusters. First, using the Chord graph can maintain network connectivity and route queries in a few hops without requiring too many long-distance links per peer. Second, the Chord graph is able to embed the two index techniques that we will describe later.

4   Cluster-Index Technique

In this section we present an efficient index technique: cluster-index technique (TMO-CI). Let us suppose that peer x constructs content index over its own documents soon after it joins a cluster. The content index, which is used to assist in answering queries, may be inverted lists of words, sets of metadata or simply a list of filenames. The peer x will send its content index to its first long-distance neighbor. The peer that receives x's content index will cache the index and select its first long-distance neighbor to relay the index. The whole process is repeated until d different peers have received x's content index, where d is a system-wide variable known as the *depth parameter*. If these d peers receive queries, they can process the queries on behalf of x. It is important to note that a peer does not send any content indices to other long-distance neighbors except its first long-distance neighbor.

4.1   Select the Directly Probed Clusters

Using the cluster-index technique, a cluster can be *directly probed* or *indirectly probed*. Figure 2 shows a TMO-CI system where the depth parameter d is set to 2. So each peer in cluster C_i sends its content index to its first long-distance neighbor in cluster C_{i+1} and in turn to a peer in cluster C_{i+2}. Hence, we can deduce that the cluster C_{i+2} has content indices of all peers in cluster C_i and C_{i+1}. If a query is propagated in cluster C_{i+2}, we will say that cluster C_{i+2} is directly probed, and will say that cluster C_i and C_{i+1} are indirectly probed. For a query, it is unnecessary to require a cluster to be directly probed if it has been indirectly probed already.

A probe to a directly probed cluster proceeds in two steps. First, the Chord routing mechanism in system's upper level makes sure that the query message is routed to the target cluster. Next, an intra-cluster flood mechanism is used to further propagate the query within the cluster. Although, we implement only the intra-cluster flood mechanism, the TMO system can also use other search mechanisms, such as Random Walks [11] or Gossip [12], to propagate queries within a cluster.

We propose that the selection of directly probed clusters should follow two criterions. First, with the same number of probed clusters, minimize the number of directly probed clusters, aiming to reduce query traffic. Second, make sure that the query messages sent from the source peer to these directly probed clusters traverse as few long-distance links as possible, aiming to shorten the query response time.

For example, illustrating in figure 2, if a peer in cluster C_0 submits a query and requires all of the eight clusters to be probed, then the cluster C_0, C_2 and C_5 are selected as the directly probed clusters according to our criterions.

5 Topic-Index Technique

In this section, we present another index technique for the TMO architecture: topic-index (TMO-TI). In the TMO-TI system, all the documents stored in the network are classified into topics. For example, for a music sharing application, TMO-TI may create topics like "Rock", "Heavy metal", "Classical" and so forth. Each document belongs to one or more topics. For each topic, there are one or more clusters responsible for it. A cluster collects the indices of documents belong to specific topics that it is responsible for. An index of a document may be an inverted list of words or simply the name of the document. We let M denote the number of topics, T_i ($0{\leq}i{\leq}M$-1) denote topic i, and S_i ($0{\leq}i{\leq}M$-1) denote the set of clusters responsible for T_i. It is obvious that $S_i \subseteq \{C_0, C_1,\ldots, C_{N-1}\}$.

A peer will classify its own documents after it joins a cluster. If some documents do not belong to the topics that the peer's cluster is responsible for, the peer will send these documents' indices to the responsible clusters. To explain, we assume p is a peer in cluster C_i, for each document D_i stored on p, if $D_i \in T_i$ and $C_i \notin S_i$, then the index of D_i will be send to a cluster $C_j \in S_i$.

A query is also classified into one or more topics, and the clusters responsible for the topics will be directly probed. The classification of documents and queries can be done manually or automatically. However, classifiers may make mistakes by returning the wrong topics for a query or document. In the simulations we will study how much the system is affected in the presence of classifier mistakes.

6 Simulations

The two types of topologies, physical topology and logical topology are needed in the simulation. A transit-stub topology [15] of approximately 35,000 nodes is generated as the physical topology in which the delays of intra-transit domain links, stub-transit links and intra-stub domain links are set to 20, 5 and 2ms respectively. We generate a flat logical topology with average connectivity degree of 6 for measuring Gnutella search. This logical topology has 16,000 peers, each of which is uniquely mapped to one physical node. In order to measure our TMO search, we randomly select 8 physical nodes as the landmark nodes, and partition all the logical peers into 8-32 clusters based on locality.

We distribute 3,000 different documents of varying popularity in the simulation. A zipfian distribution is used to model both the replication distribution and the query distribution to achieve results similar to the results in [13]: The most popular 10% of documents amount for 50% of the total number of stored documents and account for over 50% of total queries. The documents are classified into 50 different topics, each of which only one cluster is responsible for.

The quality of a search mechanism is judged by the following metrics:

➤   Traffic cost: We define traffic cost as $\sum_{i=1}^{N_m} y_i s_i$, where N_m is the number of messages, s_i is the size of message i, and y_i is the delay of the link which message i traverses. Implicit here is the assumption that links with higher delay and messages with larger size tend to be associated with higher traffic cost.

➤   Hits: We define hits as the size of total result set for a query.

➤   Response Time: We define response time as the time that has elapsed from when the query is submitted by the peer, to when the peer receives the first result.

6.1 Results of Gnutella Search

We conduct our simulations to evaluate the performance of TMO search against Gnutella search. In the first simulation, we examine the performance of Gnutella search with different TTLs. The simulation results in Table 1 indicate that increasing the TTL of Gnutella search increases the traffic cost quickly, but results in more hits and better response time as we model the network delay in the simulation.

Table 1. Results for Gnutella search

Scheme	Cost	Hits	Time	Scheme	Cost	Hits	Time
TTL=7	3275376	52.76	354	TTL=5	799886	24.75	404.8
TTL=6	1955845	43.49	393.2	TTL=4	183658	7.34	406

6.2 Effectiveness of TMO-CI

In this subsection, we examine the effectiveness of TMO-CI search with different TTLs (that is, TTLs of intra-cluster floods used within each cluster). Here we representatively present the results based on 16 clusters only, since changing the number of clusters produces similar results. We set the depth parameter d to from 0 (means the degenerate TMO case without cluster-index technique) to 7. When a query is submitted, we require all the clusters to be probed, aiming to get full search scope.

Figure 3, figure 4 and figure 5 show the average query traffic cost, query hits and response time, respectively. Based on these simulation results, we make the following inferences on TMO-CI search.

➤   Similar to Gnutella search, increasing the TTL of TMO-CI search also increases traffic cost, but results in more hits and better response time.

➤   Compared with Gnutella search, by appropriately selecting TTLs the TMO-CI search really reduces the average traffic cost while achieving the same or similar query hits. Furthermore, increasing the value of d usually results in larger reduction of query traffic cost. For example, when TTL= 5, the strategies that setting d to from 0 to 7 achieve similar query hits of Gnutella search with TTL=7, but reduce average traffic cost by from 38% to 90%. In fact, the traffic cost each query generates largely depends on the number of directly probed clusters, which is equal to $\lceil N/(d+1) \rceil$, where N is the number of clusters.

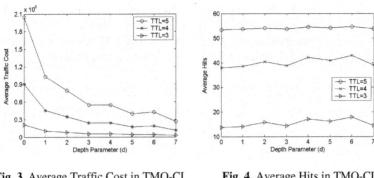

Fig. 3. Average Traffic Cost in TMO-CI   **Fig. 4.** Average Hits in TMO-CI

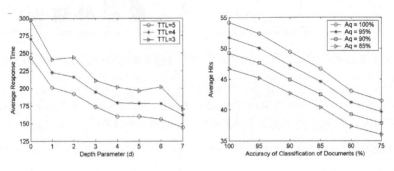

Fig. 5. Average Response Time in TMO-CI   **Fig. 6.** Average Hits in TMO-TI

➤ The TMO-CI search can shorten the response time, since it takes the physical network topology into consideration when the overlay is constructed. Besides, increasing the value of d usually results in better response time, since a peer can answer queries for many other peers when d is set to a large value. For example, compared with Gnutella search, the strategies that setting d to from 0 to 7 in TMO-CI search can shorten the response time by from 31% to 59%.

➤ It may be difficult to choose the appropriate TTL for TMO-CI search. Empirically, we would choose a smaller TTL when the number of clusters is large, and a larger TTL when in the contrast case. However, we also believe that it is difficult to choose the appropriate TTL for the Gnutella search.

6.3 Effectiveness of TMO-TI

In this subsection, we examine the effectiveness of TMO-TI search. We let A_d denote the accuracy of classification of documents, and A_q denote the accuracy of classification of queries.

We representatively present the results based on TTL=5 only. Figure 6 illustrates the average query hits of TMO-TI. Different curves correspond to the performance on different A_q with different value of A_d. If classifiers don't make mistake, the TMO-TI search achieves similar query hits compared with Gnutella search. However, with the decrements of A_q and A_d, the query hits also decreases. For example, TMO-TI search achieves 67% query hits of Gnutella search when A_q=85% and A_d=75%.

Figure 7 shows the average response time for TMO-TI search. We can see that decreasing the values of A_q and A_d results in a little longer response time.

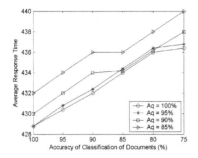 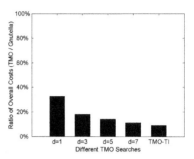

Fig. 7. Average Response Time in TMO-TI   **Fig. 8.** Ratio of Overall Traffic Costs

In the simulation, we find that TMO-TI search only generates around 5% of the average query traffic cost of Gnutella search. Changing the values of A_q and A_d has little influence on the average traffic cost that the queries generate.

6.4   The Impact of Index Update

One of the key factors that affect the performance of TMO system is the frequency of index update operations, which heavily depends on the dynamic nature of overlay network. In a real environment, the source peer should do index update operations periodically, which incurs extra traffic cost. Especially, in the TMO-CI system, increasing the depth parameter d could increase the extra traffic cost proportionally.

In the simulation, we assume that each peer executes 10 index update operations per minute. We also assume that each peer issues 0.3 queries per minute, which is calculated from the observation data shown in [14], i.e., 12,805 unique IP addresses issued 1,146,782 queries in 5 hours. Figure 8 shows the ratio of the overall traffic costs in different TMO systems to the overall traffic cost in Gnutella system. Compared with Gnutella system, our TMO-CI system can reduce overall traffic cost by at least 67%, and TMO-TI system can reduce overall traffic cost by 90%. Thus, the search improvements afforded by TMO and the two index techniques are seldom outweighed by the extra traffic cost of index update operations.

Based on the observations above, we believe that the strength of the cluster-index technique lies in that it can help the TMO system to reduce both query traffic cost and response time without decreasing the query hits. Thus, it is highly effective in the applications where 100% recall is required, for example, a patent information sharing application. The advantage of the topic-index technique is that it can help the TMO system to reduce a quite large amount of traffic cost, though it may result in reduction of query hits. Thus, it is highly effective in the applications where users are satisfied with tens of (but not all) results, such as the music sharing application.

7   Conclusion

In this paper, we proposed TMO, a topology-aware multi-cluster overlay architecture which using a hierarchical structure with two levels. Furthermore, we present two novel index techniques, namely cluster-index technique and topic-index technique that can be incorporated into the TMO system to enhance search efficiency. From our simulation results we conclude that TMO with index techniques offers significant improvements versus Gnutella-like overlay networks. We believe that the TMO system and the two index techniques can help improve the search performance of current and future P2P systems.

References

1. Gnutella. http://gnutella.wego.com/
2. KaZaA. http://www.kazaa.com/
3. I. Stoica, R. Morris, D. Karger, F. Kaashoek, and H. Balakrishnan, "Chord: A scalable peer-to-peer lookup service for Internet applications," In *Proceedings of ACM SIGCOMM*, 2001.
4. S. Ratnasamy, P. Francis, M. Handley, R. Karp, and S. Shenker, "A scalable content -addressable addressable network," In *Proceedings of ACM SIGCOMM*, 2001.
5. A. Rowstron and P. Druschel, "Pastry: Scalable, distributed object location and routing for large-scale peer-to-peer systems," In *Proceedings of International Conference on Distributed Systems Platforms*, 2001.
6. S. Ratnasamy, N. Handley, R. Karp, and S. Shenker, "Topologically-Aware Overlay Construction and Server Selection," In *Proceedings of IEEE INFOCOM*, 2002.
7. Napster. http://www.napster.com/
8. B. F. Cooper and H. Garcia-Molina, "Studying search networks with SIL," In *Proceedings of IPTPS*, 2003.
9. B. Yang and H. Garcia-Molina, "Improving Search in Peer-to-Peer Networks," In *Proceedings of IEEE ICDCS*, 2002.
10. A. Crespo and H. Garcia-Molina, "Routing indices for peer-to-peer systems," In *Proceedings of 22nd International Conference on Distributed Computing Systems*, 2002.
11. C. Lv, P. Cao, E. Cohen, K. Li, and S. Shenker, "Search and replication in unstructured peer-to-peer networks," In *Proceedings of ACM ICS*, 2002.
12. Kermarrec, A.-N., Massoulie, L., and Ganesh, A. J, "Probabilistic reliable dissemination in large-scale systems," *IEEE Transactions on Parallel and Distributed Systems*, 2003.
13. J. Chu, K. Labonte, and B. Levine, "Availability and Locality Measurements of Peer-to-Peer File Systems," In *Proceedings of SPIE*, 2002.
14. K. Sripanidkulchai, "The popularity of Gnutella queries and its implications on scalability," In *Proceedings of O'Reilly's Peer-to-Peer and Web Services Conference*, 2001.
15. E. W. Zegura, K. L. Calvert, and S. Bhattacharjee, "How to Model An Internetwork," In *Proceedings of IEEE INFOCOM*, 1996.

A Parallel Routing Algorithm on Circulant Networks Employing the Hamiltonian Circuit Latin Square

Dongkil Tak[1], Yongeun Bae[1], Chunkyun Youn[2], and Ilyong Chung[1,*]

[1] Department of Computer Science, Chosun University, Kwangju, Korea
iyc@chosun.ac.kr
[2] Information Technology Division, Honam University, Kwangju, Korea
chqyoun@itc.honam.ac.kr

Abstract. Double-loop and 2-circulant networks are widely used in the design and implementation of local area networks and parallel processing architectures. In this paper, we investigate the routing of a message on circulant networks, that is a key to the performance of this network. We would like to transmit 2k packets from a source node to a destination node simultaneously along paths on $G(n; \pm s_1, \pm s_2, ..., \pm s_k)$, where the ith packet will traverse along the ith path ($1 \leq i \leq 2k$). In oder for all packets to arrive at the destination node quickly and securely, the ith path must be node-disjoint from all other paths. For construction of these paths, employing the Hamiltonian Circuit Latin Square(HCLS) we present $O(n^2)$ parallel routing algorithm on circulant networks.

1 Introduction

The intense interest in interconnection network used graph-theoretic properties for its investigations and produced various interconnection schemes. Many of these schemes have been derived to optimize important parameters such as degree, diameter, fault-tolerance, hardware cost, and the needs of particular applications. Double-loop[1] and 2-circulant networks(2-CN)[2] are widely used in the design and implementation of local area networks and parallel processing architectures. These networks are defined as follows. Let n, s_1, s_2 be positive integers such that $0 < s_1 < s_2 < n/2$. A double-loop network is a directed graph $G(n; s_1, s_2)$, where n nodes labeled with integers modulo n, and 2 links per vertex such that each node i is adjacent to the 2 other nodes $i+s_1$, $i+s_2$. In the undirected case, which is known as a 2-circulant network and is denoted by $G(n; \pm s_1, \pm s_2)$. It is well known that $G(n; s_1, s_2)$ and $G(n; \pm s_1, \pm s_2)$ are connected iff $\gcd(n, s_1, s_2) = 1$.

The routing of message is thus a key to the performance of such networks. There are routing algorithms using well-known methods, such as the Shortest Path Algorithm(the Forward Algorithm)[3], the Backward Algorithm[4], the

---

* Corresponding author.

H. Jin, D. Reed, and W. Jiang (Eds.): NPC 2005, LNCS 3779, pp. 172–175, 2005.

Spanning Tree Algorithm[8]. These algorithms provide for only sequential transmission, from the source node to the desired node in a short time. We now look for algorithms that are capable of handling, multiple data items simultaneously transmitted from the staring(source) node to the destination node. There are a few algorithms on the n-dimensional hypercube network[5]-[6] that allow us to locate n disjoint paths such as the Disjoint Path Algorithm[7] and the Hamiltonian path Algorithm [8]. In this paper, we propose the algebraic approach to the routing of message on the $G(n; \pm s_1, \pm s_2, ..., \pm s_k)$. As described above, $2k$ packets are simultaneously transmitted from the starting(source) node to the destination node. In order for all packets to arrive at the destination node quickly and securely, the ith path must be node-disjoint from all other paths.

2 Design of the Hamiltonian Circuit Latin Square to the Parallel Routing Algorithm on Circulant Networks

Let A and B be any two nodes on $G(n; \pm s_1, \pm s_2, ..., \pm s_k)$. The paper's objective is to find algorithms that will facilitate the transmission of data from node A to B in that network. In order for the data to traverse from node A to node B, it must cross, successively, intermediate nodes along a path.

Definition 1. The routing function R for $\pm s_i$ is as follows:

$$R(A) = A \pm s_i \text{ (mod n)}, \text{ where A is node address}$$

Definition 2. The relative address r of nodes A and B on $G(n; \pm s_1, \pm s_2, ..., \pm s_k)$ is computed as the value of difference between A and B.

$$r = B\text{-}A$$

Let two addresses of node A and node B be 1 and 3. What is the relative address of two nodes? The value of the relative address is 2.

Definition 3. Let T(A,S) be the logical transmission path of data starting from node A to the destination node B, where S is a multiset and a sequence of operations, via which data can reach at the destination node. T(A,S) is determined by the order of the elements in the set S. between A and B.

The ith packet is transmitted along the ith path, the first intermediate node of which is obtained from applying the ith operation at a starting node and the last intermediate node transmits the packet to a destination node by applying the ith operation. In some cases, the two operations can be the same.

Definition 4. Let O^s be a set of operations occurring at a starting node when four packets are transmitted simultaneously and Let O^d be a set of operations occurring at a destination node when four packets arrive. These sets are defined as follows:

$O^s = \{s_1, \text{-}s_1, s_2, \text{-}s_2, ..., s_k, \text{-}s_k\}$
$O^d = \{p_1, p_2, p_3, p_4, ..., p_{2k-1}, p_{2k}\}$
$O^s = O^d$

We now apply the HCLS(Hamiltonian Circuit Latin Square) to find a set of m shortest and node-disjoint paths.

Definition 5. The HCLS M^1 is constructed as follows: Given distinct m points $a_0, a_2, ... , a_{m-2}, a_{m-1}$, a Hamiltonian circuit $a_i \rightarrow a_j \rightarrow ... \rightarrow a_k \rightarrow a_i$ is randomly selected. On the circuit each row of M can be obtained from the Hamiltonian path, starting at any position $a_k(0 \leq k \leq m\text{-}1)$, under the condition that no two rows begin at the same position. If a Hamiltonian path is $a_i \rightarrow a_j \rightarrow ... \rightarrow a_k$, then the row obtained from it is $[a_i, a_j, ..., a_k]$

Definition 6. Given the HCLS $M^1 = [a_{i,j}]$, the MHCM M^2 is constructed as follows: $M^2 = [A_{i,j}]$, $A_{i,j} = \{a_{i,0}, a_{i,1}, ... , a_{i,j-1}, a_{i,j}\}$, $0 \leq$ i,j $\leq$ m-1.

We now propose a parallel routing algorithm that generates a set of m minimum-distance and node-disjoint paths for the network.

*CN_Routing_*Algorithm

A ← an address of a starting node A
B ← an address of a destination node B
O^s ← a set of operations occurring at a starting node A
O^d ← a set of operations requisite for reaching to a destination node B

begin

(1) Compute the relative address R of nodes A and B; R = B-A
(2) Using the relative address R, a sequence S of operations to arrive at node B in a short time are produced
(3) In order to design a set of shortest and node-disjoint paths, find a set S_1 of distinct elements in S. A set of $|S_1|$ shortest and node-disjoint paths are generated. Each path of length is $|S|$,

(3-1) Using the set S_1, (n×n) HCLS is constructed, where n = $|S_1|$.
(3-2) Operations in the ith row of the HCLS are performed for traversal of the ith packet and the remaining operations in S should be executed at the point except the first and the last points.
(3-3) $O^s \leftarrow O^s$ - S_1 and $O^d \leftarrow O^d$ - S_1.

(4) Construct two node-disjoint paths, each path has length $|S|+2$.

(4-1) If $O^s = \phi$, the process is finished.
(4-2) If a set of $\{s_i, \text{-}s_i\}$ is found in O^s , then these operations are performed at the first and the last steps of two paths newly designed, and operations in S at the middle steps of them, otherwise go to (5).
(4-3) $O^s \leftarrow O^s$ - $\{s_i, \text{-}s_i\}$, $O^d \leftarrow O^d$ - $\{s_i, \text{-}s_i\}$ and go to (4-1).

(5) Generate the remaining paths.

(5-1) If $O^s = \phi$, the process is finished.
(5-2) Produce a sequence S_2 of minimum number of operations by reducing the size of $S \cup \{-s_i,-s_i\}$, $s_i \in O^s$, $S_2 = \{s_i, \min(S \cup \{-s_i,-s_i\}),$ $s_i\}$.
(5-3) Operation g_i is performed at the first and the last steps at traversal and operations of S_2 are executed at the middle steps.
(5-4) $O^s \leftarrow O^s - \{s_i\}$, $O^d \leftarrow O^d - \{s_i\}$ and go to (5-1).

end.

3   Conclusion

In this paper, we present the algorithm that generates a set of 2k shortest and node-disjoint paths on G(n; $\pm s_1, \pm s_2, ..., \pm s_k$), employing the Hamiltonian Circuit Latin Square(HCLS). Even n and k are fixed values, the algorithm can be easily extended on arbitrary circulant networks. Important steps for determining time complexity requisite for the algorithm are two things. One is to design the HCLS, which needs O(n). The other is to execute Step (5) of $CN\_Routing\_$Algorithm, which requires $O(n^2)$. Therefore, we can create $O(n^2)$ parallel routing algorithm for constructing 2k shortest and node-disjoint paths.

References

1. Bermond, J., Comellas, F., Hsu, D., "Distributed Loop Computer Networks: A Survey," J. Parallel and Distributed Computing, Academic Press, no. 24, pp.2-10, 1995.
2. Park, J., "Cycle Embedding of Faulty Recursive Circulants," J. of Korea Info. Sci. Soc., vol.31, no. 2, pp. 86-94, 2004.
3. Basse, S., Computer Algorithms : Introduction to Design and Analysis, Addition-Wesley, Reading, MA, 1978.
4. Stallings, W., Data and Computer Communications. Macmillan Publishing Company, New York, 1985.
5. Bae, M. and Bose, B., "Edge Disjoint Hamiltonian Cycles in k-ary n-cubes and Hypercubes," IEEE Trans. Comput., vol. 52, no. 10, pp. 1259-1270, 2003.
6. Thottethodi, M., Lebeck, A., and Mukherjee, S., "Exploiting Global Knowledge to Achieve Self-Tuned Congetion Control for k-ary n-cube Networks," IEEE Trans. Parallel and Distributed Systems, vol 15, no. 3, pp. 257-272, 2004.
7. Johnson, S.L. and Ho, C-T., "Optimum Broadcasting and Personalized Communication in Hypercube," IEEE Trans. Comput., vol. 38, no. 9, pp. 1249-1268, Seep. 1989.
8. Rabin, M.O., "Efficient Dispersal of Information for Security, Load Balancing, and Fault Tolerance," J. ACM, vol. 36, no. 2, pp. 335-348, Apr. 1989.

An Efficient Load Balancing Algorithm for Cluster System

Chunkyun Youn[1,*] and Ilyoung Chung[2]

[1] Department of Internet Software, Honam University, Kwangju, Korea
chqyoun@honam.ac.kr
[2] Department of Computer Science, Chosun University, Kwangju, Korea
iyc@mail.chosun.ac.kr

Abstract. Load balancing is one of the best efficient methods for performance improvement of cluster system. Recently, WLC algorithm is used for the load balancing of cluster system. But, the algorithm also has load imbalance between servers, because it uses inaccurate static load status of servers. In this paper, I suggest a more efficient dynamic load balancing algorithm base on various load status information of servers by real time. It shows that load imbalance phenomenon is improved greatly and response time is also improved compare with WLC algorithm.

1 Introductions

Fast growing Internet user and huge amount of multimedia data are rapidly increasing network traffic. Servers and network are bottle-neck in this situation. Now a days, performance elevation and high availability of server are important to solve the problem [1]. Various cluster systems are used as suitable solution of it [2, 3]. Among them, load sharing cluster system consists of several low-cost servers which are connected to high speed network, and applies load balancing technique between servers. It offers high computing power and high availability.

The load balancing algorithm is core function of the cluster system. Many techniques were studied. Well known algorithms are round-robin (RR) scheduling [4], weighted round-robin (WRR) scheduling [5], least-connection (LC) scheduling [6] and WLC (Weighted Least Connection) scheduling [7]. The WLC is widely used now among them.

Above load balancing algorithms select a server according to fixed weights which are calculated by server's physical processing capacity and the number of established connections mainly. Such methods can't know server's load state exactly, because those are not considered various load elements of real servers. And measuring time is not suitable, because Director gets the connection number of real servers periodically. So, it is not correct load of real servers. That is, inaccurate load status and unsuitable measuring time are the cause of load imbalance.

---

* Corresponding author.

H. Jin, D. Reed, and W. Jiang (Eds.): NPC 2005, LNCS 3779, pp. 176 – 179, 2005.

2   Proposal of an Efficient Load Balancing Algorithm

2.1   Various Load Elements Investigation and Application Plan

In this paper, various load elements of UNIX web server are considered to measure exact load situation. CPU, memory and network are selected as influential suitable elements among them. The detail statuses of main load elements are followings;

CPU load. Usually, we have to collect whole CPU usage, average CPU load and CPU usage of each process etc to measure CPU load. When a client requests connection, correct present CPU load of real servers is very important to decide which server will handle the request. Numbers of waiting process is suitable for that purpose. It can be different according to cluster system configuration, number of users and concurrent connection ratio etc. Usually, connection requests are processed without waiting because servers are very powerful. Therefore, if there is waiting processes that mean the CPU is busy. So, we can select which server has lower load [8, 9].

Load of memory. We can use virtual memory amount of processes, free memory amount and paging activity that are performed in the latest 20 seconds from memory. We can confirm relatively exact present memory load by the free memory amount among them [8, 9].

Load of network. Packet I/O amount of each network interface, packet error rate and collision rate are available for load status of network. We can estimate that a network interface is over load if collision rate approaches to 5 ~ 10%, and use packet I/O amount if necessary [8, 9].

2.2   Dynamic Load Measuring and Balancing Algorithm

I propose a dynamic load measuring algorithm (Fig. 1) that can collect load status of server base on the selected elements by real time. It will be loaded on each real server and called using broadcasting RPC by Director. A called real server collects own load status according to Fig. 1 algorithm and transmits it to the director. The value "Y" and "Init_Average" should be adjusted properly according to configuration of cluster system and users' environment after system configuration.

Fig. 3 shows the proposed load balancing algorithm that handles user's request with real time load status of servers.

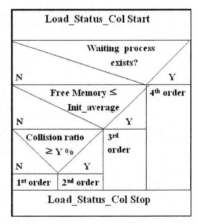

Fig. 1. Load measuring algorithm

Fig. 2 and 3 show the proposed prototype modules configuration and load balancing algorithm.

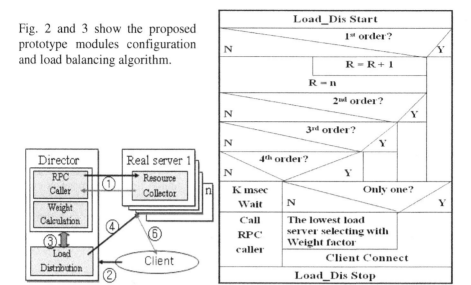

Fig. 2. Prototype module configuration   **Fig. 3.** Load balancing algorithm

3   Test and Results Analysis

I use the WLC which is the most efficient among existing algorithms for performance comparative test of the proposed algorithm. Comparison items are free memory change of each real server and response time of cluster system for the two algorithms.

3.1   Test Result Analysis for Free Memory

When number of concurrent connecters is below 200, free memory difference of each server is not so big in the WLC and the proposed algorithm. But, when the number is

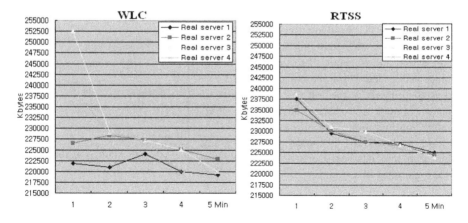

Fig. 4. Free memory changes of WLC and the proposed algorithm (at 400 numbers)

400, server's free memory of the WLC is not even, while it is similar in the proposed algorithm (RTSS) as shown Fig. 4. This means that more efficient load balancing was done by the proposed algorithm.

3.2 Test Result Analysis for Response Time

Fig. 5 shows the test result for average response time of two algorithms by the number of concurrent connecters. Response time of the proposed algorithm (RTSS) is improved 9.3msec than existing algorithm (WLC) in case of 100, while it is improved 203msec in case of 400.

When the number of concurrent connecter is few, the response time is not so big different. But, when it is increased, the difference is big. This means performance of cluster system is optimized well in the proposed algorithm.

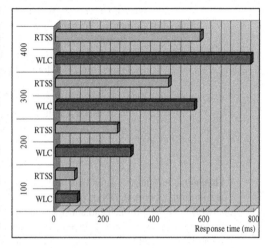

Fig. 5. Results of response time comparison

4   Conclusions

I proposed an efficient load balancing algorithm to improve the performance of cluster system. The WLC algorithm tries to balance load according to the fixed physical resources of real servers' and connection numbers. On the other hand, the proposed algorithm measures waiting process, free memory and collision rate by real time to get more accurate load state of real servers, and used them to balance load efficiently.

References

1. Delivering High Availability Solutions with Red Hat Enterprise Linux AS 2.1, RedHat (2003)
2. Jian liu, Lorghu Xu, Baogen Gu, Jing Zhang, A scalable, high performance Internet cluster server, High performance computing in the Asia-Pacific region, 2000 Proceedings. The firth International Conference/ Exhibition, Vol.2, (2000) 941-944
3. OYoung Kwon, Cluster system introduction Korea institute of science and technology information news letter (2000)

A Greedy Algorithm for Capacity-Constrained Surrogate Placement in CDNs

Yifeng Chen[1], Yanxiang He[2], Jiannong Cao[3], and Jie Wu[4]

[1] State Key Laboratory of Water Resources and Hydropower Engineering Science,
Wuhan University, Wuhan 430072, Hubei, China
[2] School of Computer, Wuhan University, Wuhan 430072, Hubei, China
{Csyfchen, Yxhe}@whu.edu.cn
[3] Department of Computing, Hong Kong Polytechnic University,
Hung Hom, Kowloon, Hong Kong, China
Csjcao@comp.polyu.edu.hk
[4] Department of Computer Science & Engineering, Florida Atlantic University,
Boca Raton, FL 33431, USA
Jie@cse.fau.edu

Abstract. One major factor that heavily affects the performance of a content
distribution network (CDN) is placement of the surrogates. Previous works take a
network-centric approach and consider only the network traffic. In this paper, we
propose solutions to optimal surrogate placement, taking into consideration both
network latency and capacity constraints on the surrogates. For CDNs with a tree
topology, an efficient and effective greedy algorithm is proposed which minimizes network traffic while at the same time maximizing system throughput.
Simulation results show that the greedy algorithm is far better than the existing
optimal placement scheme that makes decisions based solely on network traffic.
This suggests that capacity constraints on surrogates or server bottlenecks should
be considered when determining surrogate placement, especially when the capacities of CDN servers are limited.

1 Introduction

A content distribution network (CDN) is a network optimized to deliver specific content such as static Web pages, streaming media, or real-time video or audio. The design
of a CDN aims at quickly providing users with the most current content in a highly
available fashion [1]. This is achieved by pushing hosted content from the origin
server(s) to a set of surrogates located at the edge of the Internet closer to clients. For
any client request, an appropriate surrogate is selected to deliver the requested content
to the client on behalf of the origin server(s) [2]. Besides speeding up content delivery,
CDNs can also reduce server workload and alleviate network congestion.

The performance of a CDN can be significantly affected by the decisions on 1) how
many surrogates are needed, and 2) where they should be placed. Previous studies
typically formulate this decision problem as the minimum k-median problem [3,4], the

H. Jin, D. Reed, and W. Jiang (Eds.): NPC 2005, LNCS 3779, pp. 180–188, 2005.
© IFIP International Federation for Information Processing 2005

facility location problem [3], the minimum k-center problem [5], or for simple network topologies (e.g., line, ring, or tree), the dynamic programming problem [3,6-9].

All of these previous works [3-9], however, take a network-centric view of the issue of surrogate placement, assuming that a client's requests can always be directed to the surrogates closest to the client. Consequently, they consider only the network latency factor and the resultant placement scheme may very likely lead to an undesirable load concentration on some surrogates. In this paper, we argue that, in order to minimize the network traffic and maximize the system throughput, load balancing among surrogates should also be considered in surrogate placement. We call this problem the *capacity constrained surrogate placement problem* (CCSP).

In this paper, we focus on a simplified version of the CCSP problem in the context of *transparent data replication* [8-10], in which the access paths to a Web site are arranged as a tree with the origin server at the root. The aim of transparent data replication is to reduce the management overhead incurred by client redirection and to simplify the design of surrogate cooperation and load balancing. Fig. 1 illustrates a surrogate hierarchy for transparent data replication. A collection of surrogates, together with the origin server, is placed on {1, 6, 10, 15, 20}. The request issued from node 11 is forwarded toward the origin server along the unique path from 11 to 1. Normally, the surrogate placed on node 10 will intercept the request and immediately satisfy the request on behalf of the origin server. However, if the surrogate is overloaded, the request will be forwarded up the tree, until another available surrogate, say node 6, is able to serve the request. For any update activity, the update message will first be propagated from root, (i.e., the origin server node 1) to its immediate descendant surrogate node 6, and node 20. Then the update message will continue to be propagated down the surrogate hierarchy from node 6 to nodes 10 and 15.

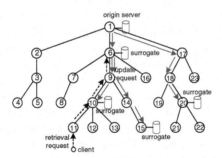

Fig. 1. Request-routing and consistency maintenance under transparent data replication

We employ queuing theory [11] to model server throughput and achieve load balancing among surrogates by redirecting part of the client requests initially assigned to the heavily loaded surrogates to other lightly loaded ones according to transparent data replication. We propose an efficient greedy algorithm to solve the CCSP problem. The performance of the proposed algorithm is evaluated in terms of communication cost and system throughput. We compare our algorithm with an existing optimal placement scheme that solely minimizes the communication cost and a random placement scheme that uniformly chooses sites to place surrogates. The simulation results show that our proposed CCSP approach significantly outperforms these two benchmarks.

2 Problem Formulation

In this section, we first develop a queuing model of the throughput of CDN servers, and then formulate the CCSP problem for tree networks.

We model each CDN server as an M/G/1/K*PS queuing system [11]. The arrival process of HTTP requests is assumed to be Poissonian with rate $(\lambda+\mu)$ (λ is the read rate, μ the write rate), whereas the service time has a general distribution with mean $\bar{x}$. The service discipline is processor sharing. The total number of requests that can be processed at one time is limited to K ($\bar{x}$ and K represent the processing power of each CDN server). Denoting the blocking probability by $P^{b'}$, we have

$$P^{b'} = \frac{(1-\rho)\rho^{K}}{(1-\rho^{K+1})} \tag{1}$$

where $\rho=(\lambda+\mu)\bar{x}$. Thus, the rate of blocked requests is given by $(\lambda+\mu)P^{b'}$. A CDN increases the throughput of the whole system by enabling the surrogates to cooperate for redirecting the overloaded amount of requests (i.e., $(\lambda+\mu)P^{b'}$) that have routed to one surrogate to other lightly loaded ones. Note that update requests should always be served locally and only retrieval requests can be redirected. Thus, if we define $P^{b} = (1+\mu/\lambda)P^{b'}$, the request blocking rate can be represented as λP^{b}. This transformation is reasonable, since the CDN servers are typically dominated by retrieval requests.

The network is modeled as a tree $T_r(V,E)$, where V is a set of nodes, $E \subseteq V \times V$ is a set of edges and $r \in V$ is the root where the origin server is located. Each node represents an autonomous system (AS) and each edge corresponds to a physical link connecting two AS's. For any node $v \in T_r$, we denote by T_v the subtree of T_r rooted at v.

Assume that the origin server holds N objects. The size of each object i is denoted by $s_i(1 \le i \le N)$. For each object i, every node v is associated with a nonnegative retrieval rate $\lambda_{v,i}$. The origin server is responsible for propagating update information down the surrogate hierarchy and is additionally associated with a nonnegative update rate μ_i for object i. Any link (u,v) in E is associated with a distance metric $d(u,v)$, which could be interpreted as bandwidth, hop counts, link cost, etc. Assuming that $\pi_{x,y}$ is a path between node x and y, the distance associated with path $\pi_{x,y}$ could be represented as $d(x,y)=\sum_{(u,v)\in\pi_{x,y}}d(u,v)$. We use $f(s_i,d(u,v))$ to denote the data transmission cost for object i traverses link (u,v) or path $\pi_{u,v}$, which measures the resource utilization on that link or path for transferring object i from node u to v.

Suppose M surrogates are to be placed on a set of domains $P(P \subseteq V, r \in P$ and $|P|=M)$. For any node $v \in T_r$, we say a node is the *parent surrogate* of v, denoted by $C(v,P)$, if it is the first node in $P \setminus \{v\}$ that is seen while going up from v to the root r, i.e., the lowest ancestor of v which is contained in $P \setminus \{v\}$. Also, the *immediate descendant surrogates* of any v, denoted by $D(v)$, is defined as follows. If $v \notin P$, $D(v)=\{u: u \in P \wedge u \in T_v \wedge C(u,P)=C(v,P)\}$; if $v \in P$, $D(v) = \{u: u \in P \wedge C(u,P)=v\}$.

Now, suppose a set of surrogates P are placed on the network, the reduction of data transfer cost, denoted by $Cost(T_r,P)$, is ready to be obtained by:

$$Cost(T_r,P) = \sum_{i=1}^{N} \sum_{v \in P \backslash \{r\}} ((1-P_v^b) \lambda_{v,i}^t f(s_i, d(v,r)) - u_i f(s_i, d(v, C(v,P)))) \quad (2)$$

where the first term corresponds to the total decrease of retrieval cost and the second term represents the total increase of update cost due to the placement of surrogates. $\lambda_{v,i}$ denotes the access rate to object i issued from node v. $\lambda_{v,i}^t$ denotes the total retrieval requests for object i that traverse node v:

$$\lambda_{v,i}^t = \lambda_{v,i} + \sum_{u \in B_v} P_u^b \lambda_{u,i}^t \quad (3)$$

where B_v is the children of v, and P_v^b is the blocking probability of v. Here we extend the concept of blocking probability: If v is a surrogate node (i.e., $v \in P$), P_v^b would be derived via a queuing model; otherwise, P_v^b is set to one, meaning that, for the nodes where no surrogates are located, all the incoming requests will be forwarded to their parent nodes. We define $\lambda_v^t = \sum_{i=1}^{N} \lambda_{v,i}$ and $\mu = \sum_{i=1}^{N} \mu_i$ to compute P_v^b.

Under the given request-routing mechanism, the drop of requests occurs only if the origin server is overloaded. The total requests blocked in the CDN therefore is

$$Block\ (T_r, P) = P_r^b \lambda_r^t \quad (4)$$

where λ_r^t denotes the total retrieval request rate directed to r after placing a set of surrogates P. Now, we are ready to define the CCSP problem in tree topologies: *Given $T_r(V,E)$, traffic pattern, and surrogate capacity constraints, find a set of M surrogates $P(P \subseteq V, r \in P, |P|=M)$ such that the objective function (5) is satisfied.*

$$Obj(T_r,P) = \underset{P \subseteq V, |P|=M, r \in P}{Max} (Cost(T_r,P) - \gamma Block(T_r,P)) \quad (5)$$

γ in (5) is a penalty coefficient to make a tradeoff between traffic reduction and load balancing among surrogates.

3 A Greedy Algorithm

From the computation of P_v^b, it's easy to verify that the CCSP problem for tree topologies can not be solved via a dynamic programming approach similar to that used in [8]. In this section, we develop an efficient greedy algorithm.

The greedy algorithm is illustrated in *Algorithm 1*. Initially, we set $P=\{r\}$ and the network cost reduction to zero. The objective is determined by the dropped requests. Then the algorithm iterates and chooses one surrogate in each step until M surrogates are chosen. In each iteration, for $\forall v \in V \backslash P$, we compute the objective increment assuming v is added to P. The node that yields the maximum objective increment is chosen and added to P. The objective increment of candidate node v, besides the contribution of v itself, includes (a) modifying the retrieval cost reduction of v's ancestor surrogates (the ratio of the request directed to and the blocking probabilities of these surrogates will change when a surrogate is placed on v); and (b) modifying the update cost of immediate descendant surrogates whose parent surrogate is $C(v,P)$ (their parent surrogate has changed from $C(v,P)$ to v).

The objective increment can be computed in the following fashion. Suppose a set of surrogates $P (P \subset V, |P| < M, r \in P)$ has been placed over the network, and a candidate node $v (v \in V \backslash P)$ is intended to join P. Define by $A(v)$ the ordered ancestor nodes of v, $v \notin A(v)$, i.e., the elements in $A(v)$ are the nodes ordered as seen while going up from v to the root r. Obviously, the first element in $A(v)$ is the parent of v, and for any successive node u and w in $A(v)$, w is the parent of u. After the candidate v joins in P, the increment of data transfer cost reduction $\Delta Cost(T_r, P \cup \{v\})$ and that of objective $\Delta Obj(T_r, P \cup \{v\})$ can be obtained by the following steps.

Step 1: compute the contribution of v itself
$$\Delta Cost(T_r, P \cup \{v\}) = \sum_{i=1}^{N}((1-P_v^b)\lambda_{v,i}^t f(s_i, d(v,r)) - \mu_i f(s_i, d(v, C(v,P))))$$

Step 2: modify the retrieval cost reduction of ancestor surrogates of v

Let $\Delta \lambda = -(1-P_v^b)\lambda_v^t$, $\Delta \lambda_i = -(1-P_v^b)\lambda_{v,i}^t$

Then obtain a node u from $A(v)$ in order until all the elements are traversed. Note that the variable with a superscript of *new* corresponds to the case where v has joined in P.

If $u \notin P$, set $\lambda_u^{t,new} = \lambda_u^t + \Delta \lambda$, $\lambda_{u,i}^{t,new} = \lambda_{u,i}^t + \Delta \lambda_i$

Otherwise if $u \in P$, set $\lambda_u^{t,new} = \lambda_u^t + \Delta \lambda$, $\lambda_{u,i}^{t,new} = \lambda_{u,i}^t + \Delta \lambda_i$, compute $P_u^{b,new}$ by $\lambda_u^{t,new}$

$\Delta \lambda = \Delta \lambda - (1-P_u^{b,new})\lambda_u^{t,new} + (1-P_u^b)\lambda_u^t$
$\Delta \lambda_i = \Delta \lambda_i - (1-P_u^{b,new})\lambda_{u,i}^{t,new} + (1-P_u^b)\lambda_{u,i}^t$

$\Delta Cost(T_r, P \cup \{v\}) = \Delta Cost(T_r, P \cup \{v\}) + \sum_{i=1}^{N}(((1-P_u^{b,new})\lambda_{u,i}^{t,new} - (1-P_u^b)\lambda_{u,i}^t)f(s_i, d(u,r)))$

Step 3: modify the update cost of the immediate descendant surrogates of v
$$\Delta Cost(T_r, P \cup \{v\}) = \Delta Cost(T_r, P \cup \{v\}) + |D(v)|\sum_{i=1}^{N}\mu_i f(s_i, d(v, C(v,P)))$$

Step 4: compute $Block(T_r, P \cup \{v\})$ and $\Delta Obj(T_r, P \cup \{v\})$
$Block(T_r, P \cup \{v\}) = P_r^{b,new}\lambda_r^{t,new}$
$\Delta Obj(T_r, P \cup \{v\}) = \Delta Cost(T_r, P \cup \{v\}) - \chi(Block(T_r, P \cup \{v\}) - Block(T_r, P))$

Algorithm 1. The greedy algorithm for surrogate placement

set $P = \{r\}$, set $\lambda_{v,i}^t = \sum_{u \in T_v}\lambda_{u,i}$, $\lambda_v^t = \sum_{i=1}^{N}\lambda_{v,i}^t$, for $\forall v \in T_r$, $\forall i$ $(1 \leq i \leq N)$,
set $Cost(T_r, P) = 0$, compute $Block(T_r, P)$, $Obj(T_r, P)$;
while($|P| \leq M$){
    for $\forall v \in V \backslash P$, compute $\Delta Cost(T_r, P \cup \{v\})$, $Block(T_r, P \cup \{v\})$ and $\Delta Obj(T_r, P \cup \{v\})$;
    find $v \in V \backslash P$ such that $\Delta Obj(T_r, P \cup \{v\})$ is maximized;
    $P \leftarrow P \cup \{v\}$, $Cost(T_r, P) \leftarrow Cost(T_r, P) + \Delta Cost(T_r, P)$,
    $Obj(T_r, P) \leftarrow Obj(T_r, P) + \Delta Obj(T_r, P)$;
    for $\forall u \in A(v)$, update λ_u^t, $\lambda_{u,i}^t$ in order;
    for $\forall u \in D(v)$, $C(u,P) \leftarrow v$; }

4   Performance Evaluation

We have evaluated the performance of the proposed algorithm through simulations, in comparison with two baseline algorithms: a random algorithm and a throughput-oblivious dynamic programming (DP) algorithm.

We use synthetic tree topologies and traffic pattern to evaluate the algorithms, as in [8]. Tree topologies are created randomly in a breadth-first manner with two parameters: the total number of nodes (treeSize) and the maximum degree of a tree node (treeDegree). Each tree edge is associated with a distance randomly distributed in (0,1). Every node v is associated with a retrieval rate λ_v and values, $\bar{x}$ and K, uniformly distributed in (minSvTime, maxSvTime) and in (minJobLimit, maxJobLimit), respectively. The root r is further associated with an update rate of μ uniformly distributed in (minWtRate, maxWtRate).

The origin server holds a collection of N Web objects. The access popularity of the objects follows a Zipf-like distribution [12,13] with a parameter of θ_r for retrieval and θ_w for update. Each object i is assigned an object size of s_i, whose distribution has been found to be heavy-tailed [13]. The cumulative distribution function is given by

$$F(s)=1-(s_0/s)^{\beta} \quad \beta, s_0>0, s\geq s_0 \qquad (6)$$

where β is known as the tail index, and s_0 represents the smallest possible value of the random object size in the heavy-tailed distribution. For simplicity, we set $f(s_i,d(u,v))= s_i*d(u,v)$. Default parameter settings are summarized in Table 1.

We vary the number of nodes from 60 to 1000 and examine the impacts on surrogate placement decision of the penalty coefficient, traffic volume, and server capacity. Fig. 2 shows a typical simulation result on a 600-node tree with $M=0.3*treeSize$.

We have made the following observations: (1) The greedy algorithm significantly outperforms the benchmarks in both network cost reduction and dropped request rate; (2) The greedy algorithm is not very sensitive to the penalty coefficient. A larger γ, however, will lead to a decrease in blocked requests at slight cost of network traffic; (3) When the traffic is relatively small, adding one more surrogate can absorb a significant amount of traffic and remarkably improve the performance of the system. As traffic increases, more surrogates are needed to achieve the same normalized performance; (4) When candidate surrogates are configured powerful (i.e., set $\bar{x}$ close to zero), the

Table 1. Default simulation parameter settings

Parameter	Setting	Parameter	Setting	Parameter	Setting
minRdRate	1	minSvTime	0.0001	θ_r	0.8
maxRdRate	80	maxSvTime	0.01	θ_w	0.4
minWtRate	1	minJobLimit	50	β	1.2
maxWtRate	80	maxJobLimit	300	s_0	4
treeDegree	6	N	1000	γ	10

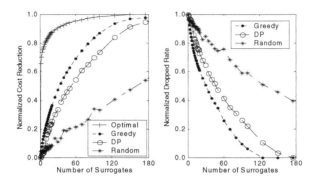

Fig. 2. Traffic reduction (normalized by "optimal" measure of placing a maximum of M surrogates) and blocked request rate (normalized by "optimal" measure of placing only a single surrogate at the root of the tree)

greedy algorithm can offer a performance close to optimal. Otherwise, the network cost reduction has to be traded off against the system throughput; (5) Heterogeneity in CDN servers and skewness in traffic pattern do not hurt the performance of the proposed greedy algorithm.

5   Conclusion

In this paper, we have investigated the capacity constrained surrogate placement problem (CCSP), aiming at minimizing the network traffic while maximizing the throughput of a CDN. An efficient greedy algorithm is developed to solve the problem in the context of transparent data replication.

The performance of the proposed algorithm is compared with a random solution and a dynamic programming based optimal solution, that makes decisions considering only data transmission cost. The simulation results demonstrate that the proposed greedy algorithm has a performance close to optimality and can find the placement scheme that remarkably increases the throughput of the system. Therefore, capacity constraints on surrogates or server bottlenecks should be integrated into the surrogate placement decision. This is especially the case when the power of CDN servers is limited for some reason. If the traffic volume increases roughly in proportion in the domains, an incremental or amortized surrogate placement scheme will be appropriate, just as the proposed greedy algorithm does.

Acknowledgement

This work is supported in part by the University Grant Council of Hong Kong under the CERG grant PolyU 5075/02E, the Hong Kong Polytechnic University under the grant G-YY41 and the National Natural Science Foundation of China under the grant 90104005.

References

1. Lazar, I., Terrill, W.: Exploring Content Delivery Networking. IEEE IT Pro. (2001) 47-49
2. Day, M., Cain, B., Tomlinson, G., Rzewski, P.: A Model for Content Internetworking. RFC 3466. Network Working Group (2003)
3. Qiu, L., Padmanabhan, V.N., Voelker, G.M.: On the Placement of Web Server Replicas. Proc. IEEE INFOCOM'01, Vol. 3 (2001) 1587-1596
4. Li, Y., Liu, M.T.: Optimization of Performance Gain in Content Distribution Networks with Server Replicas. Proc. 2003 Symp. Applications and the Internet (2003)
5. Cronin, E., Jamin, S., Jin, C., Kurc, A.R., Raz, D., Shavitt, Y.: Constrained Mirror Placement on the Internet. IEEE J. Select. Areas Commun., Vol. 20. **7** (2002) 1369-1381
6. Li, B., Golin, M.J., Italiano, G.F., Deng, X., Sohraby, K.: On the Optimal Placement of Web Proxies in the Internet. Proc. IEEE INFOCOM'99 (1999) 1282-1290
7. Jia, X., Li, D., Hu, X., Du, D.: Placement of Read-Write Web Proxies on the Internet. Proc. IEEE ICDCS'01 (2001) 687-690
8. Xu, J., Li, B., Lee, D.L.: Placement Problems for Transparent Data Replication Proxy Services. IEEE J. Select. Areas Commun., Vol. 20. **7** (2002) 1383-1398
9. Krishnan, P., Raz, D., Shavitt, Y.: The Cache Location Problem. IEEE/ACM Trans. Networking, Vol.8. **5** (2002) 568-582
10. Heddaya, A., Mirdad, A.: WebWave: Globally Load Balanced Fully Distributed Caching of Hot Published Documents. Proc. IEEE ICDCS'97 (1997) 160-168
11. Cao, I., Andersson, M., Nyberg, C., Kihl, M.: Web Server Performance Modeling Using an M/G/1/K*PS Queue. Proc. 10th Int'l Conf. Telecommunications, Vol. 2. (2003) 1501-1506
12. Breslau, L., Cao, P., Fan, L., Phillips, G., Shenker, S.: Web Caching and Zipf-like Distributions: Evidence and Implications. Proc. IEEE INFOCOM'99, New York (1999) 126-134
13. Mahanti, A., Williamson, C., Eager, D.: Traffic Analysis of a Web Proxy Caching Hierarchy. IEEE Network (2000) 16-23

Appendix: Correctness Proof for Algorithm 1

Theorem 1. Algorithm 1 is correct, and can be computed in $O(ML)$ time. L is the *path length* of T_r, which is defined as the sum over T_r of the number of ancestors of each node.

Proof. The time complexity of the algorithm is straightforward. The proof for the correctness can be reduced to proving that for $\forall u \in A(v)$, the computation of $\lambda_u^{t,new}$ (and similarly $\lambda_{u,i}^{t,new}$ for $\forall i(1 \leq i \leq N)$) is correct. We first prove the following Lemma.

Lemma 1. For any surrogate placement scheme P in tree topologies, there holds

$$\lambda_v^t = \lambda_v^{t,0} - \Sigma_{u \in D(v)} \lambda_u^{t,0} + \Sigma_{u \in D(v)} P_u^b \lambda_u^t, \text{ for } \forall v \in T_r \quad (7)$$

where $\lambda_v^{t,0}$ is the corresponding result after execution of the first step in *Algorithm 1*.

Proof. The proof is done by induction.
(1) Basis: when $P=\{r\}$, we have $D(v)=\varnothing$, $\lambda_v^t = \lambda_v^{t,0}$ for $\forall v \in T_r$. Thus (7) trivially holds.
(2) Induction: Suppose (7) holds when a set of surrogates $P(P \subset V, |P| < M, r \in P)$ is placed over the network. Now we prove that (7) still holds after any node $v(v \in V\backslash P)$ is added to P.

First, according to the request-routing mechanism, placing a surrogate on v can only affect the retrieval requests of its ancestor nodes $A(v)$. Therefore, based on the induction hypothesis, (7) holds for $\forall u \in T_r \backslash A(v)$, and $\lambda_u^{t,new} = \lambda_u^t$. For $A(v)$, we first consider the first element u in $A(v)$, i.e., the parent of v. Obviously, $D(v) \subseteq D(u)$. Now due to the join of v, $D^{new}(u) = (D(u) - D(v)) \cup \{v\}$. According to the algorithm, $\lambda_u^{t,new} = \lambda_u^t + \Delta\lambda = \lambda_u^t - (1 - P_v^b)\lambda_v^t$. By $\lambda_u^t = \lambda_u^{t,0} - \Sigma_{w \in D(u)} \lambda_w^{t,0} + \Sigma_{w \in D(u)} P_w^b \lambda_w^t$ (induction hypothesis)

$$\lambda_u^{t,new} = \lambda_u^{t,0} - \Sigma_{w \in D(u)-D(v)}\lambda_w^{t,0} + \Sigma_{w \in D(u)-D(v)}P_w^b\lambda_w^t + (\lambda_v^{t,0} - \Sigma_{w \in D(v)}\lambda_w^{t,0} + \Sigma_{w \in D(v)}P_w^b\lambda_w^t - \lambda_v^{t,0}) - (1-P_v^b)\lambda_v^t$$
$$= \lambda_u^{t,0} - \Sigma_{w \in D^{new}(u)}\lambda_w^{t,0} + \Sigma_{w \in D^{new}(u)} P_w^b\lambda_w^t$$
$$= \lambda_u^{t,0} - \Sigma_{w \in D^{new}(u)}\lambda_w^{t,0} + \Sigma_{w \in D^{new}(u)} P_w^{b,new}\lambda_w^{t,new}$$

(7) holds. Then for the successive element x of u in $A(v)$, if $u \notin P$, it is completely the same as u. Otherwise, if $u \in P$, there is evidently $u \in D(x)$, but $D(u) \not\subset D(x)$. Therefore, $D^{new}(x) = D(x)$. According to the algorithm, $\lambda_x^{t,new} = \lambda_x^t + \Delta\lambda = \lambda_x^t - (1-P_v^b)\lambda_v^t - (1-P_u^{b,new})\lambda_u^{t,new} + (1-P_u^b)\lambda_u^t$. By $\lambda_x^t = \lambda_x^{t,0} - \Sigma_{w \in D(x)}\lambda_w^{t,0} + \Sigma_{w \in D(x)} P_w^b \lambda_w^t$ (induction hypothesis) $\lambda_x^{t,new} = \lambda_x^{t,0} - \Sigma_{w \in D(x)}\lambda_w^{t,0} + \Sigma_{w \in D(x)-u}P_w^b\lambda_w^t + P_u^b\lambda_u^t - (1-P_v^b)\lambda_v^t - (1-P_u^b)\lambda_u^{t,new} + (1-P_u^b)\lambda_u^t$

$$= \lambda_x^{t,0} - \Sigma_{w \in D^{new}(x)}\lambda_w^{t,0} + \Sigma_{w \in D^{new}(x)}P_w^{b,new}\lambda_w^{t,new} + \lambda_u^t - (1-P_v^b)\lambda_v^t - \lambda_u^{t,new}$$
$$= \lambda_x^{t,0} - \Sigma_{w \in D^{new}(x)}\lambda_w^{t,0} + \Sigma_{w \in D^{new}(x)}P_w^{b,new}\lambda_w^{t,new}$$

(7) holds. Based on this approach, we can prove one by one that (7) holds for all the elements in $A(v)$. Thus *Lemma 1* is true. Noticing that (7) is equivalent to $\lambda_v^t = \sum_{i=1}^N \lambda_{v,i}^t$, where $\lambda_{v,i}^t$ is computed by (3), it can be trivially inferred that *Theorem 1* is true.

An Improved Scheme of Wavelength Assignment for Parallel FFT Communication Pattern on a Class of Regular Optical Networks[*]

Yawen Chen and Hong Shen

Japan Advanced Institute of Science and Technology,
Asahidai 1-8, Nomi-Shi, Ishikawa, Japan, 923-1292
{yawen, shen}@jaist.ac.jp

Abstract. Routing and wavelength assignment (RWA) is a central issue to increase efficiency and reduce cost in Wavelength Division Multiplexing (WDM) optical networks. In this paper, we propose an improved scheme of wavelength assignment of parallel FFT communication pattern on a class of regular optical networks. With our new scheme, the numbers of wavelengths required to realize parallel FFT communication pattern with 2^n nodes on WDM linear arrays, rings, 2-D meshes and 2-D tori are $\left\lfloor 2^{n-2}+1 \right\rfloor$, $\left\lfloor 2^{n-3}+1 \right\rfloor$, $\left\lfloor 2^{\max(k,n-k)-2}+1 \right\rfloor$ and $\left\lfloor 2^{\max(k,n-k)-3}+1 \right\rfloor$ respectively, which are about one-third less for linear arrays and meshes, and a half less for rings and tori, than the known results. Our results have a clear significance for applications because FFT represents a common communication pattern shared by a large class of scientific and engineering problems and WDM optical networks as a promising technology in networking has an increasing popularity.

Keywords: Parallel FFT, wavelength assignment, optical networks, Wavelength Division Multiplexing (WDM), network embedding.

1 Introduction

Fast Fourier Transform (FFT) plays an important role in numerous scientific and technical applications [1]. While the application fields of FFT are growing rapidly, the amount of data to be transformed is also increasing tremendously. Hence, there has been a great interest in implementing FFT on parallel computers and some parallel computers have been specially designed to perform FFT computations [2]. With the increasing computation power of parallel computers, interprocessor communication has become an important factor that limits the performance of supercomputing systems. Optical communication, in particular, Wavelength Division Multiplexing (WDM) technique, has become a promising technology for many emerging networking and parallel/distributed computing applications because of its huge bandwidth. Parallel FFT is often implemented on dense interconnection networks such as hypercube and

---

[*] This work is supported by the 21st Century Center of Excellence Program in JAIST on "Verifiable and Evolvable e-Society".

H. Jin, D. Reed, and W. Jiang (Eds.): NPC 2005, LNCS 3779, pp. 189–196, 2005.

shuffle-exchange networks [2], instead of simple connected networks such as linear arrays and rings. Since WDM divides the bandwidth of an optical fiber into multiple wavelength channels so that multiple devices can transmit on distinct wavelengths through the same fiber concurrently [3], these dense networks can be simplified to simple regular topologies by realizing connections in parallel FFT communication patterns in optical lightpaths. A connection or a lightpath in a WDM network is an ordered pair of nodes (x, y) corresponding to that a packet is sent from source x to destination y. In this paper, we assume that no wavelength converter facility is available in the network. Thus, a connection must use the same wavelength throughout its path. Routing and wavelength assignment (RWA) is a key problem for increasing the efficiency of wavelength-routed all-optical networks. RWA can be described as follows [4]: Given a set of all–optical connections, the problem is to (a) find routes from the source nodes to their respective destinations, and (b) assign channels to these routes so that the same channel is assigned to all the links of a particular route. (c) The goal of RWA is to minimize the number of assigned channels. Numerous research studies have been conducted on the RWA problem [3-8]. A popular approach to tackle this problem is to apply integer programming technique, which, however, does not always lead to efficient solution. In [5], the problem of wavelength assignment for realizing parallel FFT communication pattern on a class of regular optical WDM networks was addressed and two methods, sequential mapping and shift-reversal mapping, were proposed. By sequential mapping, the numbers of wavelengths required to realize parallel FFT communication pattern of 2^n nodes on WDM linear arrays, rings, 2-D meshes and 2-D tori are 2^{n-1}, 2^{n-1}, $2^{\max(k,n-k)-1}$ and $2^{\max(k,n-k)-1}$ respectively. By shift-reversal mapping, the numbers of wavelengths required are $\max(3\times 2^{n-3},2)$, 2^{n-2}, $\max(3\times 2^{\max(k,n-k)-3},2)$ and $2^{\max(k,n-k)-2}$ respectively. In this paper, we design a new scheme to realize parallel FFT communication pattern on a class of regular optical WDM networks and results show that our new scheme significantly improves the known results in [5].

2   Wavelength Assignment of Parallel FFT Communication Pattern

2.1 Problem Definition

The so-called butterfly representation [2] of FFT algorithm is a diagram made up of blocks representing identical computational units (*butterflies*) connected by arrows that show the flow of data between the blocks. Assuming that N is the length of the sequence to be transformed (N is an integer power of two), then the diagram with $N(log_2N+1)$ nodes arranged in N rows and log_2N+1 columns is made of log_2N stages of $N/2$ butterflies each. The butterfly representation clearly shows the great potential of FFT for parallel processing. Generally, the FFT is implemented stage by stage, i.e. any stage of calculation cannot proceed until all the results of its previous stage have been completed. In this paper, we consider one dimensional data sequence of size $N=2^n$. If the butterfly representation is viewed as a process graph, i.e. each row of the butterfly is implemented by a process and each arrow by a communication channel, the butterfly can map onto a WDM hypercube perfectly those links connecting the nodes having an address that differs by only one bit at each stage. However, if a WDM hypercube is used, only the ith dimensional links are used with one wavelength during the ith stage whereas other $(n-1) \times 2^{n-1}$ links are vacant during this stage, which may lead to wasting of wavelength channels.

As we know, a connection in the hypercube communication pattern is called a *dimensional i connection* [4] if it connects two nodes that differ in the ith bit position, where $1 \leq i \leq n$. In a network of size 2^n, the set DIM_i is defined as the set of all dimension i connections and H_n is defined as the hypercube communication pattern which contains all connections in the hypercube. That is, $H_n = \bigcup_{i=1}^{n} DIM_i$ and

$DIM_i = \{(j, j + (-1)^{\lfloor j/2^{n-i} \rfloor} \times 2^{n-i}) \mid 0 \leq j \leq 2^n - 1\}$. With 2^n input data distributed on 2^n processors, the set of all communications during n stages of parallel FFT is equivalent to H_n, and the set of communications during the ith stage is equivalent to DIM_i. Clearly, parallel FFT has a regular communication pattern which we denote by $FFT_n (n \geq 2)$. We model a network as a directed graph $G (V, E)$. Nodes in V are switches and edges in E are links. Since the n stages of parallel FFT communications should be implemented stage by stage, the number of wavelengths required to realize FFT_n on optical WDM networks is the maximum number among the wavelengths required by the n stages. Let $W_e(G', G)$ denote the number of wavelengths to realize communication pattern G' on network G by embedding scheme e. Thus, $W_e(FFT_n, G) = \max_{1 \leq i \leq n}(W_e(DIM_i, G))$.

2.2 Linear Arrays

At first, we introduce the definition of cross mapping on linear arrays. Assume that N_L and N_R are two node arrangements with 2^{n-1} nodes numbered from left to right in ascending order starting from 0. If we put node i of N_R between node $2^{n-2}+i$ and node $2^{n-2}+i+1$ of N_L for $i=0, 1, 2, ..., 2^{n-2}-2$, and nodes $2^{n-2}-1$ till $2^{n-1}-1$ of N_R consecutively after node $2^{n-1}-1$ of N_L. By symmetry, this is equivalent to placing node $2^{n-2}+i+1$ of N_L between node i and node $i+1$ of N_R, and nodes 0 till $2^{n-2}-2$ of N_L consecutively before node 0 of N_R. We call the above operation *cross operation* and denote the obtained node arrangement $Cross(N_L, N_R)$. Assume that X_n is the increasing order of indices in binary representations of 2^n nodes. For example, X_2=00, 01, 10, 11. We define the *cross order* of a linear arrays with 2^n nodes, $C_n (n \geq 1)$, as follows:

$C_n = \begin{cases} X_n, n \leq 2 \\ Cross(0X_{n-1}, 1X_{n-1}), n \geq 3 \end{cases}$. For example, $C_4 = Cross(0X_3, 1X_3) = Cross$

((0000, 0001, 0010, 0011, 0100, 0101, 0110, 0111), (1000, 1001, 1010, 1011, 1100, 1101, 1110, 1111)) =0000, 0001, 0010, 0011, 0100, 1000, 0101, 1001, 0110, 1010, 0111, 1011, 1100, 1101, 1110, 1111.

Assume that the nodes of WDM linear arrays are numbered from left to right in ascending order starting from 0, and that the links are numbered from left to right starting from 1. If the ith node of C_n for FFT_n is mapped onto the ith processor of the WDM network G, we establish the 1-1 mapping from the nodes of FFT_n to the nodes of G. We define such an embedding *cross mapping* on WDM linear arrays. Figure 1 shows cross mapping of FFT_3 on 8-node linear array.

Fig. 1. Cross mapping on 8-node linear array

Theorem 1. By cross mapping, the number of wavelengths required to realize FFT_n on an 2^n-node WDM linear array is $\lfloor 2^{n-2} + 1 \rfloor$.

Proof. When $n=1$ and 2, it is easy to know the results are true. In the following, we consider the numbers of wavelengths required during the n stages when $n \geq 3$.

When $n \geq 3$, the ith node of N_L ($0X_{n-1}$) communicates with the ith node of N_R ($1X_{n-1}$) during the first stage. Assuming that the number of nodes in N_L on the left side of the ith link on the linear array is l_i^l by cross mapping, and the number of nodes in N_R on the left side of the ith link is r_i^l, then the number of wavelengths required on the ith link during the first stage is $l_i^l - r_i^l$. It can be calculated that the number of wavelengths required during the first stage on the ith link, denoted by w_{il}, is

$$w_{il} = \begin{cases} i, 1 \leq i \leq 2^{n-2} \\ 2^{n-2}, 2^{n-2} + 1 \leq i \leq 3 \times 2^{n-2} - 1 \text{ and } i \text{ is even} \\ 2^{n-2} + 1, 2^{n-2} + 1 \leq i \leq 3 \times 2^{n-2} - 1 \text{ and } i \text{ is odd} \\ 2^n - i, 3 \times 2^{n-2} \leq i \leq 2^n - 1 \end{cases}$$

. Therefore, the number of wavelengths required during the first stage is $2^{n-2} + 1$. During the second stage, there is no communications between the nodes of N_L and N_R. If the cross operation is not implemented, communications within nodes of N_L and nodes of N_R are equivalent to the communications of FFT_{n-1} mapped on 2^{n-1}-node linear arrays by sequential mapping [5]. So, the number of wavelengths required on the ith link of the two 2^{n-1}-node linear arrays is i for $1 \leq i \leq 2^{n-2} - 1$ and $2^{n-1} - i$ for $2^{n-2} \leq i \leq 2^{n-1} - 1$. If the cross operation is implemented between these two 2^{n-1}-node linear arrays, the relative positions between the nodes within N_L and N_R are not changed and the number of wavelengths required on each link is the sum of wavelengths required on the corresponding links which are overlapped between the two 2^{n-1}-node linear arrays. Assuming that the number of nodes in N_L on the right side of the ith $(2^{n-2}+1 \le i \le 3 \times 2^{n-2}-1)$ link on linear arrays is l_i^r by cross mapping and the number of nodes in N_R on the left side of the ith link is r_i^l, the number of wavelengths required on the ith link during the second stage is $l_i^r + r_i^l$. It can be calculated that the number of wavelengths required during the second stage on the ith link, denoted by w_{i2}, is

$$w_{i2} = \begin{cases} i, 1 \le i \le 2^{n-2} \\ 2^{n-2}, 2^{n-2}+1 \le i \le 3 \times 2^{n-2}-1 \text{ and } i \text{ is even} \\ 2^{n-2}-1, 2^{n-2}+1 \le i \le 3 \times 2^{n-2}-1 \text{ and } i \text{ is odd} \\ 2^n - i, 3 \times 2^{n-2} \le i \le 2^n -1 \end{cases}$$. Therefore, the number of

wavelengths required during the second stage is 2^{n-2}.

During the jth stage for $3 \le j \le n$, the number of wavelengths required is 2^{n-j} on each of N_L and N_R before the cross operation [5]. After the cross operation, the numbers of wavelengths required during stage from 3 to n are less than $2 \times 2^{n-j} \le 2 \times 2^{n-3} = 2^{n-2}$ because the number of wavelengths required on the 2^n-node linear array is not more than the double of the wavelengths required on each of N_L and N_R in the worst case. Therefore, the maximum number of wavelengths required during all stages by cross mapping is $\lfloor 2^{n-2}+1 \rfloor$.

Clearly, realizing FFT_n on an 2^n-node WDM linear array by cross mapping requires $2^{n-3}-1$ fewer wavelengths than that by shift-reversal mapping mentioned in [5] when $n \ge 4$.

2.3 Rings

If we exchange node i of N_L with node 2^{n-1}-i of N_R and exchange node 2^{n-1}-i of N_L with node i of N_R for each $i=1, 3, 5,..., 2^{n-3}$-1, we call such an operation *exchange operation* and denote the obtained node arrangement $Exchange(N_L, N_R)$. Assume that C^{-1} is the reversal arrangement of C. For example, if $C = a,b,c,d$, then $C^{-1} = d,c,b,a$. Thus, we define the *cross order* on rings, denoted by $CR_n (n \ge 1)$ as follows:

$$CR_n = \begin{cases} 0C_{n-1}, 1C_{n-1}^{-1}, n \le 3 \\ Exchange(0C_{n-1}, 1C_{n-1}^{-1}), n \ge 4 \end{cases}$$. For example, $CR_4 = Exchange(0C_3, 1C_3^{-1}) =$

Exchange (0(000, 001, 010, 100, 011, 101, 110, 111), 1(000,001,010,100,011, 101,110,111)$^{-1}$) =0000, 1000, 0010, 0100, 0011, 0101, 0110, 1110, 1111, 0111, 1101, 1011, 1100, 1010, 1001, 0001. Assume that the nodes of WDM rings are numbered clockwise starting from 0, and the links starting from 1. If we map the ith node on CR_n of FFT_n onto the ith processor of WDM rings, we establish the 1-1 mapping from the nodes of FFT_n to the nodes of rings. We define such an embedding *cross mapping* on rings.

Theorem 2. By cross mapping, the number of wavelengths required to realize FFT_n on an 2^n-node WDM ring is $\lfloor 2^{n-3}+1 \rfloor$.

Proof. It is easy to know the numbers of wavelengths required on the rings for $n=1$, 2 and 3 are 1, 1, and 2 respectively. In the following, we consider the numbers of wavelengths required during the n stages when $n \geq 4$.

During the first stage, the ith node of N_L communicates with node 2^{n-1}-1-i of N_R. Exchange operation results that the ith node on the ring communicates with node $i+1$ for $i \in \{2k | 0 \leq k \leq 2^{n-4}-1, 3\times 2^{n-4} \leq k \leq 5\times 2^{n-4}-1, 7\times 2^{n-4} \leq k \leq 2^{n-1}-1\}$. As those communications take place between the neighborhood nodes, the number of wavelengths required is 1. At the same time, the ith node on the ring communicates with node 2^{n-1}-i for $2^{n-3} \leq i \leq 3\times 2^{n-3}-1$, which requires 2^{n-3} wavelengths. Therefore, the number of wavelengths required during the first stage is $2^{n-3}+1$.

During the stages from 2 to n, there is no communications passing through the links of 2^{n-1} and 2^n if the exchange operation is not implemented. If we ignore these two links, the ring can be regarded as two 2^{n-1}-node linear arrays. By the definition of cross mapping on rings, realizing the stages from 2 to n can be regarded as realizing FFT_{n-1} on each 2^{n-1}-node linear array by cross mapping before the exchange operation, which requires $2^{n-3}+1$ wavelengths by Theorem 1. In the following, we prove that the number of wavelengths is still $2^{n-3}+1$ after exchange operation.

Due to the symmetry of the ring, the numbers of wavelengths required on the links clockwise from $7\times 2^{n-3}$ to 2^n and 1 to 2^{n-3} are equal with those on the links clockwise from $3\times 2^{n-3}$ to $5\times 2^{n-3}$. So, we only take the links from $7\times 2^{n-3}$ to 2^n and 1 to 2^{n-3} for example. Before the exchange operation, the maximum number of wavelengths required on the ith ($1 \leq i \leq 2^{n-3}$, $7\times 2^{n-3} \leq i \leq 2^n$) link of the ring, denoted by w_i, satisfies $w_i \leq \begin{cases} i, 1 \leq i \leq 2^{n-3} \\ 2^n - i, 7\times 2^{n-3} \leq i \leq 2^n \end{cases}$. After the exchange operation,

the exchange between node i and node $2^n - i$ results that the numbers of wavelengths required on the links clockwise from $2^n - i$ to 2^n and from 1 to i increase by 1 for each $i=1, 3, 5,..., 2^{n-3}$-1 in the worst case. So, the number of additional wavelengths passing through the ith link caused by the exchange operation, denoted by Δw_i,

satisfies $\Delta w_i \leq \begin{cases} 2^{n-3} - i, 1 \leq i \leq 2^{n-3} \text{ and } i \text{ is even} \\ 2^{n-3} - i - 1, 1 \leq i \leq 2^{n-3} \text{ and } i \text{ is odd} \\ i - 7\times 2^{n-3}, 7\times 2^{n-3} \leq i \leq 2^n \text{ and } i \text{ is even} \\ i - 7\times 2^{n-3} - 1, 7\times 2^{n-3} \leq i \leq 2^n \text{ and } i \text{ is odd} \end{cases}$. Therefore, the

maximum number of wavelengths required on the ith links is not more than

$$w_i + \Delta w_i \le \begin{cases} 2^{n-3}, 1 \le i \le 2^{n-3} \text{ and } i \text{ is even} \\ 2^{n-3} - 1, 1 \le i \le 2^{n-3} \text{ and } i \text{ is odd} \\ 2^{n-3}, 7 \times 2^{n-3} \le i \le 2^n \text{ and } i \text{ is even} \\ 2^{n-3} - 1, 7 \times 2^{n-3} \le i \le 2^n \text{ and } i \text{ is odd} \end{cases}$$
. It can be concluded that the

maximum number of wavelengths required on the links clockwise from $7 \times 2^{n-3}$ to 2^n and 1 to 2^{n-3} is not more than $2^{n-3} + 1$. Therefore, the number of wavelengths required on WDM rings with 2^n nodes is $\lfloor 2^{n-3} + 1 \rfloor$. From the above discussion, we know that the wavelengths required to realize FFT_n in WDM ring with 2^n nodes by cross mapping is $2^{n-3} - 1$ less wavelengths than that by shift-reversal mapping when $n \ge 4$.

We denote sizes of meshes and tori as $N = 2^k \times 2^{n-k}$. For simplicity, the details of the definition for the cross mapping on meshes and tori are ignored here.

Theorem 3. By cross mapping, the numbers of wavelengths required to realize FFT_n on a $2^k \times 2^{n-k}$ mesh and torus are $\lfloor 2^{\max(k,n-k)-2} + 1 \rfloor$ and $\lfloor 2^{\max(k,n-k)-3} + 1 \rfloor$ respectively.

3   Comparisons

It can be seen that cross mapping outperforms shift-reversal mapping and sequential mapping on the number of wavelengths, as shown in Fig. 2 for linear arrays. The analysis can be obtained similarly for other topologies.

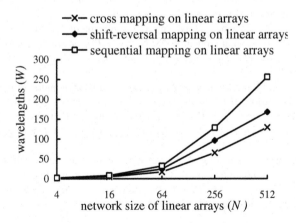

Fig. 2. Comparisons of wavelengths required on liner arrays

4 Conclusions

In this paper, we proposed an improved scheme of wavelength assignment for parallel FFT communication pattern on a class of regular optical networks. By the improved mapping method, the numbers of wavelengths required to realize parallel FFT communication pattern with 2^n nodes on WDM linear arrays, rings, 2-D meshes and 2-D tori are $\left\lfloor 2^{n-2}+1 \right\rfloor$, $\left\lfloor 2^{n-3}+1 \right\rfloor$, $\left\lfloor 2^{\max(k,n-k)-2}+1 \right\rfloor$ and $\left\lfloor 2^{\max(k,n-k)-3}+1 \right\rfloor$ respectively, which improved the results in [5]. Our results have a clear significance for applications because FFT represents a common communication pattern shared by a large class of scientific and engineering problems and WDM optical networks as a promising technology in networking has an increasing popularity. Future work may include other type of optical networks and other RWA problems. Another interesting issue is to find the lower bound for this problem and the improved schemes which can achieve the lower bound.

References

1. Rami A, AL-Na'mneh, W. David Pan, and B. Earl Wells. Two parallel implementations for one dimension FFT on symmetric multiprocessors. *ACM Southeast Regional Conference*, pp. 273-278. ACM Press. New York, NY, USA, 2004.
2. F. T. Leighton. *Introduction to Parallel Algorithms and Architectures: Arrays, Trees, Hypercubes*. Morgan Kaufmann Publishers, Inc., 1992.
3. Hui Zang, Jason P. Jue, and Biswanath Mukherjee. A review of routing and wavelength assignment approaches for wavelength-routed optical WDM networks. *SPIE Optical Networks Magazine*, 1(1):47-60, 2000.
4. Yuan X and Melhem R. Optimal Routing and Channel Assignments for Hypercube Communication on Optical Mesh-like Processor Arrays. *Proceedings of the 5th International Conference on Massively Parallel Processing Using Optical Interconnection*, pp.110-118. IEEE Computer Society Press. Las Vegas, NV, 1998.
5. Fangai Liu and Yawen Chen. Wavelength Assignment of Parallel FFT Communication Pattern in a Class of Regular Optical WDM Network. *Proceedings of the IEEE International Symposium on Parallel Architectures, Algorithms, and Networks*, 495-500. IEEE Computer Society. Hong Kong, 2004.
6. Zhou Chunling and Yang Yuanyuan. Wide-Sense nonblocking multicast in a class of regular optical WDM networks. *IEEE Transactions on Communications*, 50(1):126-134, 2002.
7. H. Shen, Y. Pan, J. Sum and S. Horiguchi, Multicasting in multihop optical WDM networks with limited wavelength conversion. *IEICE Transactions on Information and Systems*, E86-D(1):3-14, 2003.
8. Yawen Chen and Fangai Liu. A Wavelength Assignment Algorithm of Parallel LU Decomposition Communication Pattern On WDM Ring Interconnection Network. *International Symposium on Distributed Computing and Applications to Business, Engineering and Science*, pp. 366-370. Wuhan, China, 2004.

A Parallel $O(n2^{7n/8})$ Time-Memory-Processor Tradeoff for Knapsack-Like Problems

Ken-Li Li[1,2], Ren-Fa Li[1], Yang Lei[1], and Yan-Tao Zhou[1]

[1] School of Computer and Communication,
Hunan University,
Changsha, 410082, China
{jt_lrf, jt-yl, jt_zyt}@hnu.cn
[2] Department of Computer Science,
University of Illinois at Urbana-Champaign,
Champaign, 61801,USA
kenlili@uiuc.edu

Abstract. A general-purpose parallel three-list four-table algorithm that can solve a number of knapsack-like NP-complete problems is developed in this paper. Running on an EREW PRAM model, The proposed parallel algorithm can solve this kind of problems of size n in $O(n2^{9n/20})$ time, with $O(2^{13n/40})$ shared memory units and $O(2^{n/10})$ processors, and thus its time-space-processor tradeoff is $O(n2^{7n/8})$. The performance analysis and comparisons show that the proposed algorithms are both time and space efficient, and thus is an improved result over the past researches. Since it can break greater variables knapsack-based cryptosystems and watermark, the new algorithm has some cryptanalytic significance.

1 Introduction

Every NP-complete problem can be solved in $O(2^n)$ time by exhaustive search, but this complexity becomes prohibitive when n exceeds 70 or 80. Assuming that NP $\neq$ P, we cannot hope to find algorithms whose worst-case complexity is polynomial, but it is both theoretically interesting and practically important to determine whether substantially faster algorithms exist. In this paper we describe a parallel algorithm which can solve the knapsack problem. But owing to the work done by Schoreppel and Shamir [1], our proposed algorithm actually can solve a fair number of NP-complete problems including knapsack, partition, exact satisfiability, set covering, hitting set, disjoint domination in graphs, etc, which can be related by the *composition operator* [1]. Although the proposed algorithm is a versatile algorithm, to make this algorithm more easily be understood, we only take the knapsack problem as the representative to narrate this algorithm.

Given n positive integers $W = (w_1, w_2, ..., w_n)$ and a positive integer M, the knapsack problem is the decision problem of a binary n-tuple $X = (x_1, x_2, ..., x_n)$ that solves the equation: $\sum_{i=1}^{n} w_i x_i = M$. This problem was proved to be NP-complete. Solving the

H. Jin, D. Reed, and W. Jiang (Eds.): NPC 2005, LNCS 3779, pp. 197 – 204, 2005.
© IFIP International Federation for Information Processing 2005

knapsack problem can be seen as a way to study some large problems in number theory and, because of its exponential complexity, some public-key cryptosystem are based on it [2-3]. Branch and Bound algorithms were proposed, but the worst case complexity is still $O(2^n)$ [4]. A major improvement in this area was made by Horowitz and Sahni [4], who drastically reduced the time needed to solve the knapsack problem by conceiving a clear algorithm in $O(n2^{n/2})$ time and $O(2^{n/2})$ space. It is known as the *two-list* algorithm. Based on this algorithm, Schrowppel and Shamir [1] reduced the memory requirements with the *two-list four-table* algorithm which needs $O(2^{n/4})$ memory space to solve the problem in still $O(n2^{n/2})$ time. Using unbalanced four tables, an adaptive algorithm is presented in [5], which can solve the knapsack-like problems according to the available computation source. Although the above algorithm is by far the most efficient algorithm to solve the knapsack problem in sequential, it can not solve any instances where the size n is great.

With the advent of the parallelism, much effort has been done in order to reduce the computation time of problems in all research areas [6-14], most of which are based on CREW (concurrent read exclusive write) PRAM (parallel random access machine) model. Karnin [6] proposed a parallel algorithm that parallelizes the generation routine of the *two-list four-table* algorithm. In his algorithm the knapsack problem could be solved with $O(2^{n/6})$ processors and $O(2^{n/6})$ memory cells in $O(2^{n/2})$ time. The algorithm proposed by Amirazizi and Helman [7] runs in $O(n2^{\alpha n})$ time, $0 \le \alpha \le 1/2$, by allowing $O(2^{(1-\alpha)n/2})$ processors to concurrently access a list of this same size. They also present a more feasible *Time-Space-Processor* (*TSP*) model for evaluation of performance of different algorithms for the solution of knapsack-like NP-complete problems [7]. Ferreira [8] proposed a parallel algorithm that solves the knapsack problem of size n in time $T = O(n(2^{n/2})^\varepsilon)$, $0 \le \varepsilon \le 1$, when $P = O((2^{n/2})^{1-\varepsilon})$ processors $S = O(2^{n/2})$ memory units are available. Chang et al. [9] presented another parallel algorithm where the requirement of the sharing memory is $O(2^{n/2})$ by using $O(2^{n/8})$ processors to solve the knapsack problem still in $O(2^{n/2})$ time. Thereafter, based on Chang et al.'s parallel algorithm, Lou and Chang [10] successfully parallelize the second stage of the *two-list* algorithm. Regretfully, it is independently found in [11] and [12] that the analysis of the complexity of the Chang et al.'s algorithm was wrong. In addition to pointing out the wrong in literature [9], we also proposed a CREW-PRAM cost-optimal parallel algorithm [11], and thereafter, a cost-optimal algorithm without memory conflicts was further presented in [13]. It must be pointed out that the space complexity is very important when solving the knapsack-like problems [6,15]. However, because the memories required in both of these two cost-optimal parallel algorithms are still $O(2^{n/2})$, it make the available memory cells a bottleneck when using these algorithms to break practical knapsack based cryptosystem.

Therefore, to further reduce the required memory units for the solution of this kind of NP-complete problems, based on Ferreira's CREW based parallel *three-list* algorithm [14], we proposed a new parallel *three-list four-table* algorithm. The main properties of the proposed algorithm are as follows:

(i) With this algorithm, we can solve knapsack-like problems in $O(n2^{9n/20})$ time, $O(2^{13n/40})$ shared memory units when $O(2^{n/10})$ processors are available. It results in an $O(n2^{7n/8})$ *TSP* trade off, which is considerably better than those of all similar algorithms published so far.

(ii) It can be performed on an EREW (exclusive read exclusive write) PRAM machine model, and thus is a totally without memory conflicts algorithm. Furthermore, the algorithm is completely practical in the sense that it is easy to program and it can handle problems which are almost 1.5 times as big as those handled by previous algorithms.

The rest of this paper is organized as follows. Section 2 explains the parallel *three-list* algorithm, on which the proposed algorithm is based. The proposed parallel algorithm is described in Section 3. Then, in Section 4, the performance comparisons follow. Finally, some concluding remarks are given in Section 5.

2   The Parallel Three-List Algorithm

In 1995, Ferreira presented a parallel *three-list* algorithm, which is based on a CREW PRAM model [14]. The number of processor, time complexity, and space requirements in it are $O(2^{\beta n})$, $O(n2^{(1-\varepsilon/2-\beta)n})$, $O(n2^{\varepsilon n/2})$, $0 < \varepsilon < 1, 0 \le \beta \le 1-\varepsilon/2$, respectively. It is viewed as an important breakthrough in the research of knapsack-like problems for it can solve the knapsack-like problems in a way of both time and space effective [14]. Because our parallel algorithm is based on this algorithm, we introduce it. To make it easy be understood, let the number of processors be $O(2^{n/10})$.

Algorithm 1. The *Three-list* algorithm
  Generation stage

  1. Divide W into three parts: $W_1 = (w_1, w_2, \ldots, w_{9n/20}), W_2 = (w_{9n/20+1}, w_{9n/20+2}, \ldots,$ $w_{18n/20}), W_3 = (w_{18n/20+1}, w_{18n/20+2}, \ldots, w_n)$.
  2. Form all possible subset sums of W_1, W_2, then sorted them in an nondecreasing order and store them as $A = [A_1, A_2, \ldots, A_{2^{\frac{9n}{20}}}]$ and $B = [B_1, B_2, \ldots, B_{2^{\frac{9n}{20}}}]$, respectively.
  3. Form all possible subset sums of W_3, and store them as $C = [C_1, C_2, \ldots, C_{2^{\frac{n}{10}}}]$.

  Search stage

  1. For all C_i in C where $1 \le i \le 2^{n/10}$
  2. C_i execute the binary search over $A + B$:
  3. If a solution is found: then stop, output the solution
  4. If a solution cannot be found: then stop: output that there is no solution.

The time and space complexity of this algorithm are $O(n \times 2^{11n/20})$ and $O(2^{9n/20})$ [14].

Based on its serial algorithm, Ferreira's parallel algorithm is very direct. It runs on a CREW model. The subset sums in list A and B which hold $2^{9n/20}$ subset sums respectively are stored in the shared memory. And each processor $P_i (1 \le i \le P)$, which holds the subset sum C_i, execute a "virtual" binary search on the list $A + B$ to make sure whether $A[j] + B[l] = M - C_i$ is satisfied, $1 \leq j, l \leq 2^{9n/20}$. The parallel *three-list* algorithm consists of the following three main steps [14].

Algorithm 2. Parallel *three-list* algorithm

for all P_i where $1 \leq i \leq 2^{n/10}$ **do**
  1. Generation of the two lists A, B and C
  2. Sorting of the two lists
  3. Binary search over $A + B$
end

The time and space needed in this algorithm are $O(n \times 2^{9n/20})$ and $O(2^{9n/20})$ [14].

3 The Proposed Parallel Algorithm

Although Ferreira's above algorithm is considered as a main breakthrough for the researches on the knapsack problem, it still have an obvious shortcoming, i.e. the *TSP* tradeoff is $O(n \times 2^n)$, which is greater than that of the recent parallel algorithms in [11,14] by a factor n. To overcome this shortcoming, we redesign the two main stages of the parallel *three-list* algorithm. In list generation stage, we introduce four tables to produce two ordered list A and B dynamically. Doing so we can reduce the space complexity from $O(2^{9n/20})$ to $O(2^{13n/40})$. While in list search stage, we replace the matrix search way in [14] with the *two-list* like search algorithm, which is more simply and can reduce the time needed by a factor $O(n)$ in search stage.

In our proposed algorithm, each of the two lists stored in shared memory have a size of $O(2^{9n/20})$, whose elements will be dynamically generated one by one, by using only $O(2^{13n/40})$ shared memory units. Now consider the two stages of the algorithm.

3.1 The Generation Stage

Using the selection technique [14], Ferreira's parallel search algorithm is subtle. For it reduced the time needed otherwise for direct enumerating on the virtual list $A + B$ from $O(2^{9n/10})$ to $O(n \times 2^{9n/20})$. However, it is a little complicated for it concerns the search of "virtual" matrix [14]. Now we use the simply *two-list* like search to fulfill the list search stage.

Suppose the two ordered list A and B exist before the following algorithm 3 executes. We can use the following *two-list* like search algorithm to make sure that for any $C[k]$, $1 \leq k \leq 2^{n/10}$ whether exist $A[i]$ and $B[j], 1 \leq i, j \leq 2^{9n/20}$, such that the formula $A[i] + B[j] + C[k] = M$ can be satisfied.

Algorithm 3. Parallel two-list like search algorithm
  The subset sums in list A and B are sorted in increasing and decreasing order

for all processors P_k where $1 \leq k \leq 2^{n/10}$ **do**
  1. $i = 1, j = 1$.
  2. **If** $A[i] + B[j] = M - C[k]$, **then stop**: a solution is found, and **write** the result into the shared memory.
  3. **If** $A[i] + B[j] < M - C[k]$, **then** $i = i + 1$; **else** $j = j + 1$.

   4. **If** $i > 2^{9n/20}$ **or** $j > 2^{9n/20}$ **then stop**: there is no solution.
   5. **Goto** Step 2.
   End

Lemma 1. Let all elements in list A and B are given, the time needed to perform the algorithm 3 is at most $2 \times 2^{9n/20}$.

Proof. The condition that the loop ends shows that once the variables i or j is greater than $2^{9n/20}$, the algorithm terminates. While for each computation step, the value of one of the above two variables must increase by 1. So it is obvious that the maximum of the needed time to perform the algorithm 3 is $2 \times 2^{9n/20}$.

   Compared with the Ferreira's search algorithm [14], the search time needed here is reduced by a factor $O(n)$. But the space requirements do not increase.

3.2   The Search Stage

We discuss how to produce all elements of lists A and B stored in the shared memory. Note that in list search algorithm 3, each processor accesses the elements of the sorted lists A and B sequentially, and thus there is no need to store all the possible subset sums of A and B simultaneously in the shared memory—what we need is the ability to generate them quickly (on-line, upon request) in sorted order. So if we generate the two ordered lists dynamically, the needed space will reduced greatly. To implement this key idea, we explore the thoughts in [1] where four tables are used to dynamically produce the two sorted lists. Use *four tables* T_1, T_2, and T_3 , T_4 to produce the two sorted lists A and B, where T_1 includes all possible subset sums of knapsack entries $(w_1, w_2, ..., w_{9n/40})$, ..., T_4 includes all sums of $(w_{27n/40 + 1}, w_{27n/40 + 2}, ..., w_{36n/40})$. let $e = 2^{9n/40}$, and mark $T_i = (t_{i1}, t_{i2}, ..., t_{ie})$, $i = 1,2,3,4$. We first sort all sums in T_1 in an increasing order. Then use a priority queue Q_1 which has a length of $O(2^{9n/40})$. At start, Q_1 stores all pairs of first (T_1) and all elements t_{2i}. It can be updated by two operations *deletion* and *insertion*, which enables arbitrary insertions and deletions to be done in logarithmic time of the length of the queue, and makes the pair with the smallest $t_{1i} + t_{2j}$ sum accessible in constant time. Through the efficient heap implementations of priority queues [1], the following algorithm is designed to dynamically produce all sums of $T_1 + T_2$ in an increasing order. For the processes to generate list A and B are similar, we focus on the procedures on the process to generate list A.

Algorithm 4. Algorithm for generating all sums of $T_1 + T_2$ dynamically
   Tables $T_1 = (t_{11}, t_{12}, ..., t_{1e})$, $T_2 = (t_{21}, t_{22}, ..., t_{2e})$ are given

   (1)   **sort** T_1 into increasing order;
   (2)   **insert** into Q_1 all the pairs (first (T_1), t_{2i}) for all $t_{2i} \in T_2$;
   (3)   **Repeat** until Q_1 becomes empty.
      (t_1, t_2) ← pair with smallest $t_1 + t_2$ sum in Q_1;
      S_1 ← $(t_1 + t_2)$
      if S_1 is needed and used for the objectivity of computation;
      delete (t_1, t_2) from Q_1;
      if the successor t_1^{1} of t_1 in T_1 is defined,
      insert (t_1^{1}, t_2) into Q_1;

Lemma 2. One element in $T_1 + T_2$ can be produced in $O(9n/40)$ time; while all $2^{9n/20}$ elements can be dynamically generated in $O(n2^{9n/20})$ time with $O(2^{9n/40})$ shared memory units.

Proof. According to the theory of heap [1], one time of deletion and insertion on the heap can be performed with logarithmic time of the size of the heap. Since the heap constructed in algorithm 4 has a size of $2^{9n/40}$ and the combinations of $T_1 + T_2$ have $2^{9n/20}$ elements. It validates the results of lemma 2.

To make the search algorithm perform successfully, we must prepare two queues (heaps) for each processor. As a result, in parallel case, the shared memory must have more memory units than that needed in sequential case.

Combine the above discussions into a whole; we get the final parallel *three-list four-table* algorithm and an overall conclusion on the solution of knapsack-like NP-complete problems.

Algorithm 5. An EREW based parallel three-list four-table algorithm

for all processors P_k where $1 \leq k \leq 2^{n/10}$ **do**
   1. generate list C and four tables T_1, T_2 and T_3, T_4 and sort T_1 and T_3 in parallel.
   2. construct one *min* heaps for queue Q_1, and one *max* heaps for queue Q_2.
   3. perform algorithm 4.
   4. perform two-list like search algorithm (algorithm 3).
end

Theorem 1. n-variable knapsack-like problems can be solved on EREW model in $O(n2^{9n/20})$ time when $O(2^{n/10})$ processors and $O(2^{13n/40})$ memory units are available.

Proof. Producing list C and tables T_2 and T_4 can be finished in n and $2n \times 2^{5n/40}$ time, while tables T_1 and T_3 can be sorted in $4 \times 2^{5n/40}$ time [13]. Each processor will take $2 \times 2^{9n/40}$ time to construct two heaps. Following the lemmas 1 and 2, the total needed time is: $n + 2n \times 2^{5n/40} + 4 \times 2^{5n/40} + 2 \times 2^{9n/20} \times (\frac{9n}{40}) = O(\frac{9n}{40} \times 2^{9n/20})$.

The linear factor has little impact on the time complexity and thus is usually omitted [6-9,14]. So the time complexity of the proposed parallel algorithm is $O(2^{9n/20})$. As for the space complexity, since there are $2^{n/10}$ processors, and each of them need $2 \times 2^{9n/40}$ for the construction of heaps, the total space requirements is $O(2^{13n/40})$. To avoid memory conflicts, at first, we copy the knapsack vector W and scalar M for each processor, which doesn't affect the overall complexity of the proposed algorithm. Thereafter, each processor access and update its own heaps, so it is obvious that all processors have no memory conflicts, and it can be performed on EREW PRAM machine model.

4   Performance Comparisons

For the importance of the space complexity [6,15], we adopt the time-space-processor tradeoff (*TSP* tradeoff) [10], as the criterion of evaluation of relevant algorithms.

The *TSP* tradeoff of Karnin's parallel algorithm is $O(2^{5n/6})$ [6]. The number of processor, time complexity, and the *TSP* tradeoff of Ferreira's parallel *three-list* search algorithm in [14] are $O(2^{\beta n})$, $O(n2^{(1-\varepsilon/2-\beta)n})$, $0 \le \beta \le 1-\varepsilon/2$, and $O(n2^n)$, respectively. The parallel algorithm [7] runs in $O(n2^{\alpha n})$ time, $0 \le \alpha \le 1/2$, by allowing $O(2^{(1-\alpha)n/2})$ processors to concurrently access a list of this same size, hence the *TSP* tradeoff of this algorithm is also $O(n2^n)$. Ferreira's parallel *one-list* algorithm [8] bears $O(n2^n)$ *TSP* tradeoff. The performance of Chang et al.'s parallel algorithm [9] is $T = O(2^{n/2})$, $P = O(2^{n/8})$, and $S = O(2^{n/2})$, thus results in a *TSP* tradeoff of $O(2^{9n/8})$. The parallel algorithm Lou and Chang presented had a same performance as Chang et al.'s algorithm. In addition, both of the algorithms in [11] and [13] have a *TSP* tradeoff of $O(2^n)$. From our parallel *three-list four-table* algorithm, one can get a *TSP* tradeoff of $O(9n/40 \times 2^{n/10} \times 2^{13n/40} \times 2^{9n/20}) = O(n2^{7n/8})$.

Among all algorithms that have been published, the *TSP* tradeoff of Karnin's algorithm [6] is the lowest, which is $O(n2^{5n/6})$. However, it has an obvious defect that it can't reduce the execution time even in parallel. In spite of our proposed algorithm is not cost optimal, it go further on the overall time and memory performance than Ferreira's parallel *three-list* algorithm did. Moreover, our algorithm is totally without memory conflicts when different processors access the shared memory.

For the purpose of clarity, the comparisons of the main parallel algorithms published by far for solving the knapsack-like problems are depicted in Table 1. It is obvious that our parallel algorithm outtakes undoubtedly other parallel algorithms in the overall performance.

Table 1. Comparisons of the parallel algorithms for solving the knapsack-like problems

Algorithm	Model	Processor	Time	Memory	*TSP* tradeoff
1 [6]	*CREW*	$O(2^{n/6})$	$O(2^{n/2})$	$O(2^{n/6})$	$O(2^{5n/6})$
2 [7]	*CREW*	$O(2^{(1-\alpha)n/2})$	$O(2^{\alpha n})$	$O(2^{(1-\alpha)n/2})$	$O(2^n)$
3 [14]	*CREW*	$O(2^{\beta n})$	$O(2^{(1-\varepsilon/2-\beta)n})$	$O(2^{\varepsilon n/2})$	$O(2^n)$
4 [8]	*CREW*	$O(2^{(1-\varepsilon)n/2})$	$O(2^{\varepsilon n/2})$	$O(2^{n/2})$	$O(2^n)$
5 [9]	*CREW*	$O(2^{n/8})$	$O(2^{n/2})$	$O(2^{n/2})$	$O(2^{9n/8})$
6 [10]	*CREW*	$O(2^{n/8})$	$O(2^{n/2})$	$O(2^{n/2})$	$O(2^{9n/8})$
7 [11]	*CREW*	$O((2^{n/4})^{1-\varepsilon})$	$O(2^{n/4}(2^{n/4})^{\varepsilon})$	$O(2^{n/2})$	$O(2^n)$
8 [13]	*EREW*	$O((2^{n/4})^{1-\varepsilon})$	$O(2^{n/4}(2^{n/4})^{\varepsilon})$	$O(2^{n/2})$	$O(2^n)$
Ours	*EREW*	$O(2^{n/10})$	$O(2^{9n/20})$	$O(2^{n/4})$	$O(2^{7n/8})$

Notation: $0 \le \varepsilon \le 1$, $0 \le \alpha \le 1/2$, $0 \le \beta \le 1-\varepsilon$. The linear factor n in algorithms numbered by 1-6 and ours has been ignored for its little impact on the overall performance [6-9,14].

5 Conclusions

A new parallel *three-list four-table* algorithm for solving the knapsack-like problems is presented. Through dynamically producing the elements of the two lists which is to be searched in our *two-list* like search algorithm, we dramatically reduce the space requirements from $O(2^{9n/20})$ in *three-list* algorithm in [14] to $O(2^{13n/40})$. Moreover, the memory conflicts in [14] are also avoided by leave different memory address segment for different processors, permitting the algorithm being able to perform on an EREW machine model. Performance comparisons shows our proposed algorithm greatly outweighs the parallel algorithms presented by far, and thus it is an improved result over the past researches. To our knowledge it is the first time that the knapsack-like problems can be solved without memory conflicts with less than $O(2^{n/2})$ running time when the hardware is also much smaller than $O(2^{n/2})$. Since it can solve problems that are almost 1.5 times as big as those handled by previous algorithms, it has some importance in research of cryptosystem.

References

1. Schroeppel, R., Shamir, A. A $T = O(2^{n/2})$, $S = O(2^{n/4})$ algorithm for certain NP-complete problems. SIAM J. Comput, 1981,10(3):456-464.
2. Chor, B., Rivest, R.L. A knapsack–type public key cryptosystem based on arithmetic in finite fields. IEEE Trans. Inform. Theory, 1988,34(5):901-909.
3. Zhang, B., Wu, H.J., Feng, D.G, Bao, F. Cyptanalysis of a knapsack based two-lock cryptosystem. ACNS 2004, Lecture Notes in Computer Science, Vol. 3089. Springer-Verlag, Berlin Heidelberg New York (2004) 303-309.
4. Horowitz, E., Sahni, S. Computing partitions with applications to the knapsack problem. J. ACM, 1974,21(2): 277-292.
5. Li, K.L, Li,Q.H., Dai, G.M. An adaptive algorithm for the knapsack problem. Journal of Computer Development and Research, 2004,12(7): 1024-1029.
6. Karnin, E.D. A parallel algorithm for the knapsack problem. IEEE Trans, Comput, 1984, 33(5): 404-408.
7. Amirazizi, H.R., Hellman, M.E. Time-Memory-Processor trade-offs, IEEE Transactions on Information Theory, 1988,34(3):505-512.
8. Ferreira, A.G. A parallel time/hardware tradeoff $T \cdot H = O(2^{n/2})$ for the knapsack problem. IEEE Trans. Comput, 1991,40(2):221-225.
9. Chang, H.K.-C., Chen, J.J.-R., Shyu, S.-J. A parallel algorithm for the knapsack problem using a generation and searching technique. Parallel Computing, 1994,20(2):233-243.
10. Lou, D.C., Chang, C.C. A parallel two-list algorithm for the knapsack problem. Parallel Computing, 1997,22(14): 1985-1996.
11. Li, K.L, Li Q.H., Jiang, S.Y. An optimal parallel algorithm for the knapsack problem. Journal of Software, 2003,14(5): 891-896. (in Chinese)
12. Aanches, C.A., Soma, N.Y., Yanasse, H.H. Comments on parallel algorithms for the knapsack problem. Parallel Computing, 2002,28(10): 1501-1505.
13. Li, K.L., Li, Q.H., Li, R.F. Optimal parallel algorithm for the knapsack problem without memory conflicts. Journal of Computer Science and Technology. 2004,19(6): 760-768
14. Ferreira, A.G, Work and memory efficient parallel algorithms for the knapsack problem. International Journal of High Speed Computing, 1995,7(4): 595-606.
15. Woeginger G.J. Space and time complexity of exact algorithms: some open problems. In: R. Downey etc. Proceeding of IWPEC 2004, Lecture Notes in Computer Science, Vol. 3162. Springer-Verlag, Berlin Heidelberg New York (2004) 281–290.

Improving Parallelism of Nested Loops
with Non-uniform Dependences

Sam Jin Jeong and Kun Hee Han

Division of Information and Communication Engineering,
Cheonan University Anseo-dong 115, Cheonan City, Korea 330-704
{sjjeong, hankh}@cheonan.ac.kr

Abstract. This paper defines the properties of FDT (Flow Dependence Tail set) and FDH (Flow Dependence Head set), and presents two partitioning methods for finding two parallel regions in two-dimensional solution space. One is the region partitioning method by intersection of FDT and FDH. Another is the region partitioning method by two given equations. Both methods show how to determine whether the intersection of FDT and FDH is empty or not. In the case that FDT does not overlap FDH, we will divide the iteration space into two parallel regions by a line. The iterations within each area can be fully executed in parallel. So, we can find two parallel regions for doubly nested loops with non-uniform dependences for maximizing parallelism.

1 Introduction

The evolutionary transition from sequential to parallel computing offers the promise of quantum leap in computing power [1]. In the past few years, many techniques for exploiting parallelism within nested loops have been developed, and they have been automated and collected to form parallelizing compilers.

Example l.

$$
\begin{aligned}
&\text{do } i = 1, 10\\
&\quad \text{do } j = 1, 10\\
&\quad\quad A(2i+3, j+1) = \ldots\\
&\quad\quad\quad\quad \ldots = A(i+2j+1, i+j+1)\\
&\quad \text{enddo}\\
&\text{enddo}
\end{aligned}
$$

Several works has been done for loops with non-uniform dependences, but show us poor performance. Some techniques, based on Convex Hull theory [5] that has been proven to have enough information to handle non-uniform dependences, are the minimum dependence distance tiling method [4], the unique set oriented partitioning method [3], and the three region partitioning method [2], [7].

Fig. 1(a) shows the dependence patterns of Example 1 in the iteration space.

This paper will focus on parallelization of flow and anti dependence loops with non-uniform dependences. Especially, it shows us two partitioning methods to find two parallel regions in doubly nested loops with non-uniform dependences.

H. Jin, D. Reed, and W. Jiang (Eds.): NPC 2005, LNCS 3779, pp. 205–212, 2005.

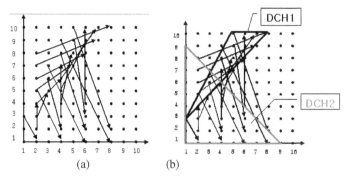

Fig. 1. (a) Iteration Spaces (b) CDCH of Example 1

The rest of this paper is organized as follows. Chapter two describes our loop model, and introduces the concept of Complete Dependence Convex Hull (CDCH). In chapter three, we define the properties of FDT (Flow Dependence Tail set) and FDH (Flow Dependence Head set), and show how to find FDT and FDH. We also present two partitioning methods to find two parallel regions in the given space. Chapter four shows comparison with related works. Finally, we conclude in chapter five with the direction to enhance this work.

2   Program Model and Dependence Analysis

The loop model considered in this paper is doubly nested loops with linearly coupled subscripts and both lower and upper bounds for loop variables should be known at compile time. The loop model has the form in Fig. 2, where $f_1(I, J)$, $f_2(I, J)$, $f_3(I, J)$, and $f_4(I, J)$ are linear functions of loop variables.

$$
\begin{aligned}
&\text{do } I = l_1, u_1 \\
&\quad \text{do } J = l_2, u_2 \\
&\qquad A(f_1(I, J), f_2(I, J)) = \ldots \\
&\qquad \ldots = A(f_3(I, J), f_4(I, J)) \\
&\quad \text{enddo} \\
&\text{enddo}
\end{aligned}
$$

Fig. 2. A doubly nested loop model

The loop in Fig. 2 carries cross iteration dependences if and only if there exist four integers (i_1, j_1, i_2, j_2) satisfying the system of linear diophantine equations given by (1) and the system of inequalities given by (2). The general solution to these equations can be computed by the extended GCD or the power test algorithm [6] and forms a **DCH** (Dependence Convex Hull).

$$f_1(i_1, j_1) = f_3(i_2, j_2) \text{ and } f_2(i_1, j_1) = f_4(i_2, j_2) \tag{1}$$

$$l_1 \le i_1, i_2 \le u_1 \text{ and } l_2 \le j_1, j_2 \le u_2 \tag{2}$$

From (1), (i_1, j_1, i_2, j_2) can be represented as

$$(i_1, j_1, i_2, j_2) = (g_1(i_2, j_2), g_2(i_2, j_2), g_3(i_1, j_1), g_4(i_1, j_1))$$
where g_i are linear functions.

From (2), two sets of inequalities can be written as

$$l_1 \le i_1 \le u_1 \text{ and } l_2 \le j_1 \le u_2 \text{ and} \tag{3}$$

$$l_1 \le g_3(i_1, j_1) \le u_1 \text{ and } l_2 \le g_4(i_1, j_1) \le u_2$$

$$l_1 \le i_2 \le u_1 \text{ and } l_2 \le j_2 \le u_2 \text{ and} \tag{4}$$

$$l_1 \le g_1(i_2, j_2) \le u_1 \text{ and } l_2 \le g_2(i_2, j_2) \le u_2$$

And, (3) and (4) form DCHs denoted by DCH1 and DCH2, respectively [3]. Clearly, if we have a solution (i_1, j_1) in DCH1, we must have a solution (i_2, j_2) in DCH2, because they are derived from the same set of equations (1). The union of DCH1 and DCH2 is called Complete DCH (**CDCH**), and all dependences lie within the CDCH. Fig. 1(b) shows the CDCH of Example 1.

If iteration (i_2, j_2) is dependent on iteration (i_1, j_1), then we have a dependence vector $d(i_1, j_1) = (d_i(i_1, j_1), d_j(i_1, j_1)) = (i_2-i_1, j_2-j_1)$

So, for DCH1, we have

$$d_i(i_1, j_1) = g_3(i_1, j_1) - i_1 = (\alpha_{11} - 1)i_1 + \beta_{11}j_1 + \gamma_{11} \text{ and} \tag{5}$$

$$d_j(i_1, j_1) = g_4(i_1, j_1) - j_1 = \alpha_{12}i_1 + (\beta_{12} - 1)j_1 + \gamma_{12}$$

For DCH2, we have

$$d_i(i_2, j_2) = i_2 - g_1(i_2, j_2) = (1 - \alpha_{21})i_2 - \beta_{21}j_2 - \gamma_{21} \text{ and} \tag{6}$$

$$d_j(i_2, j_2) = j_2 - g_2(i_2, j_2) = -\alpha_{22}i_2 + (1 - \beta_{22})j_2 - \gamma_{22}$$

We can write these dependence distance functions in a general form as

$$d(i_1, j_1) = (d_i(i_1, j_1), d_j(i_1, j_1)), d(i_2, j_2) = (d_i(i_2, j_2), d_j(i_2, j_2)) \tag{7}$$

$$d_i(i_1, j_1) = p_1 * i_1 + q_1 * j_1 + r_1, d_j(i_1, j_1) = p_2 * i_1 + q_2 * j_1 + r_2$$

$$d_i(i_2, j_2) = p_3 * i_2 + q_3 * j_2 + r_3, d_j(i_2, j_2) = p_4 * i_2 + q_4 * j_2 + r_4$$

where p_i, q_i, and r_i are real values and i_1, j_1, i_2, and j_2 are integer variables of the iteration space. The properties of DCH1 and DCH2 can be found in [3].

The set of inequalities and dependence distances of the loop in Example 1 are computed as follows.

$$\text{DCH1} : 1 \le i_1 \le 10, 1 \le j_1 \le 10$$
$$1 \le -2i_1 + 2j_1 - 2 \le 10, 1 \le 2i_1 - j_1 + 2 \le 10$$
$$d_i(i_1, j_1) = -3i_1 + 2j_1 - 2, d_j(i_1, j_1) = 2i_1 - 2j_1 + 2$$
$$\text{DCH2} : 1 \le i_2/2 + j_2 - 1 \le 10, 1 \le i_2 + j_2 \le 10$$
$$1 \le i_2 \le 10, 1 \le j_2 \le 10$$
$$d_i(i_2, j_2) = i_2/2 - j_2 + 1, d_j(i_2, j_2) = -i_2$$

3 Region Partitioning Methods for Two Parallel Regions

In this section, we propose two partitioning methods to find two parallel regions in the given space. One is the region partitioning method by intersection of FDT and FDH. Another is the region partitioning method by two given equations. Both methods show how to determine whether the intersection of FDT and FDH is empty or not.

3.1 Region Partitioning Method by Intersection of FDT and FDH

We define the flow dependence tail set (FDT) and the flow dependence head set (FDH) as follows.

Definition 1. *Let L be a doubly nested loop with the form in Fig. 2. If line* $d_i(i_1, j_1) = 0$ *intersects DCH1, the flow dependence tail set of the DCH1, namely* **FDT(L)**, *is the region H, where H is equal to*

$$DCH1 \cap \{(i_1, j_1) \mid d_i(i_1, j_1) \geq 0 \text{ or } d_i(i_1, j_1) \leq 0 \} \qquad (8)$$

Definition 2. *Let L be a doubly nested loop with the form in Fig. 2. If line* $d_i(i_2, j_2) = 0$ *intersects DCH2, the flow dependence head set of the DCH2, namely* **FDH(L)**, *is the region H, where H is equal to*

$$DCH2 \cap \{(i_2, j_2) \mid d_i(i_2, j_2) \geq 0 \text{ or } d_i(i_2, j_2) \leq 0 \} \qquad (9)$$

Property 1. *Suppose line* $d_i(i, j) = p*i+q*j+r$ *passes through CDCH. If* $q > 0$, *FDT(FDH) is on the side of* $d_i(i_1, j_1) \geq 0$ $(d_i(i_2, j_2) \geq 0)$, *otherwise, FDT(FDH) is on the side of* $d_i(i_1, j_1) \leq 0$ $(d_i(i_2, j_2) \leq 0)$.

We can form two regions, FDT and FDH, by the algorithm of finding FDT or FDH in two-dimensional solution space in Fig. 3, which is similar to the algorithm presented in [5].

Fig. 4 shows the head and tail sets of flow dependence, anti dependence, and FDH and FDT of the loop in Example 1.

By Property 1, we can know the area of the flow dependence head set (FDH) of DCH1 and the flow dependence tail set (FDT) of DCH2 in Example 1 as shown in Fig. 4. In this example, because the intersection of FDT and FDH is empty, FDT does not overlap FDH and the iteration space is divided into two parallel regions by the line $d_i(i_2, j_2) = 0$. From equation (7), we can get $d_i(i_2, j_2) = i_2/2 - j_2 + 1$, and the equation is $j = i/2+1$. So, the iteration space is divided into two parallel regions, AREA1 and AREA2, by the line $j = i/2+1$. The execution order is AREA1 $\rightarrow$ AREA2.

Transformed loops are given as follows.

```
/* AREA1 – parallel region */              /* AREA2 – parallel region */
doall i    l₁ u₁                           doall i    l₁ u₁
   doall j    max(l₂,⌈i/2+1⌉), u₂             doall j    l₂ min(u₂,⌈i/2+1⌉)
      A(2i+3, j+1) = . . .                       A(2i+3, j+1) = . . .
          . . . = A(i+2j+1, i+j+1)                   . . . = A(i+2j+1, i+j+1)
   enddoall                                   enddoall
enddoall                                   enddoall
```

```
Algorithm FDT (or FDH)
Input: A list of 9 half spaces (Def. 1 or 2)
Output: An FDT (or FDH);
            struct node {
               float (x, y);
               int zoom;
               struct node *next;
                 struct node *prev; };
            max = 9999999;
BEGIN
Build the initial FDT (or FDH) ring which is composed of four
nodes:
    (x₁, y₁) = ( max,  max);
    (x₂, y₂) = ( max, -max);
    (x₃, y₃) = (-max, -max);
    (x₄, y₄) = (-max,  max);
  while (the input list is not empty)
    Pop a half space from the list, named HS;
    Scan the ring;
      { Determine the zoom value for each node; }
      if ((x, y) ∈ HS ) then
         zoom = 0;
      else
         zoom = 1;
    if (the zoom is different from previous node)then
        { Compute the intersection point
           and give it zoom = 0;
           Insert it into the ring between the
           current node and the previous node };
      endif
    Scan the ring again;
      { Remove the nodes with zoom = 1 };
    if (the ring is empty) STOP;
  end while
END FDT
```

Fig. 3. Algorithm of finding FDT (or FDH) in two-dimensional solution space

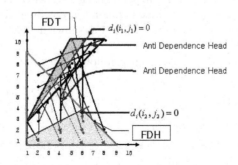

Fig. 4. FDT and FDH in Example 1

3.2 Region Partitioning Method by Two Given Equations

In our proposed algorithm in Fig. 5, Algorithm Region_Partition, we can determine whether the intersection of FDT and FDH is empty by position of two given lines $d_i(i_1, j_1) = 0$ and $d_i(i_2, j_2) = 0$, and two real values q_1 and q_3 given in (7). If the intersection of FDT and FDH is not empty, we divide the iteration space into two parallel regions and one serial region by two appropriate lines as given in the three region partitioning method [2], [7]. If the intersection of FDT and FDH is empty, we divide the iteration space into two parallel regions by the line $d_i(i_1, j_1) = 0$ or $d_i(i_2, j_2) = 0$.

```
Algorithm Region_Partition
INPUT: two lines (d_i(i_1, j_1) = 0, d_i(i_2, j_2) = 0) and two real values
(q_1, q_3)
OUTPUT: two parallel regions
BEGIN
If (line d_i(i_1, j_1) = 0 is on the left side of line d_i(i_2, j_2) =0)
      If (q_1 > 0 and q_3 < 0){
            /* AREA1 does not overlap AREA2 */
            AREA1: {(i_1, j_1) | d_i(i_1, j_1) ≥ 0}
            AREA2: {(i_1, j_1) | d_i(i_1, j_1) < 0} }
Else if (d_i(i_1, j_1) = 0 is on the right side of d_i(i_2, j_2) = 0)
      If (q_1 < 0 and q_3 > 0) {
            /* AREA1 does not overlap AREA2 */
            AREA1: {(i_1, j_1) | d_i(i_1, j_1) ≤ 0}
            AREA2: {(i_1, j_1) | d_i(i_1, j_1) > 0} }
Else Call Three Region Partitioning Method
END Region_Partition
```

Fig. 5. Algorithm of determining the intersection of FDT and FDH

From property 1, we know that the real value $q_1(q_3)$ determines whether the position of FDT(FDH) is on side of the line $d_i(i_1, j_1) \geq 0$ $(d_i(i_2, j_2) \geq 0)$ or not. The line is the bounds of two parallel loops.

In this algorithm, the line $d_i(i_1, j_1) = 0$ is expressed by $j = Ai+B$, where $A = (1 - \alpha_{11})/\beta_{11}$, $B = -\gamma_{11}/\beta_{11}$, which are derived from (5). We know that the line can be the upper or lower bound in the transformed loops based on the corresponding region of the loop technique. The line $d_i(i_1, j_1) = 0$ is the upper boundary in AREA2 and lower boundary in AREA1 in Example 1. In this case, the iteration space is divided into two parallel regions, AREA1 and AREA2, by line $j = 3/2*i+1$ as shown in Fig 4. The execution order is AREA1 → AREA2.

Transformed loops are loops are given as follows.

```
/* AREA1 – parallel region */
doall i     l_1  u_1
    doall j     max(l_2, ⌈3/2*i+1⌉), u_2
        A(2i+3, j+1) = ...
            ... = A(i+2j+1, i+j+1)
    enddoall
enddoall
```

```
/* AREA2 – parallel region */
doall i     l_1  u_1
    doall j     l_2  min(u_2, ⌈3/2*i+1⌉)
        A(2i+3, j+1) = ...
            ... = A(i+2j+1, i+j+1)
    enddoall
enddoall
```

4   Performance Analysis

Theoretical speedup for performance analysis can be computed as follows. Ignoring the synchronization, scheduling and variable renaming overheads, and assuming an unlimited number of processors, each partition can be executed in one time step. Hence, the total time of execution is equal to the number of parallel regions, N_p, plus the number of sequential iterations, N_s. Generally, speedup is represented by the ratio of total sequential execution time to the execution time on parallel computer system as follows:

$$Speedup = (N_i * N_j)/(N_p + N_s)$$

where N_i, N_j are the size of loop i, j, respectively

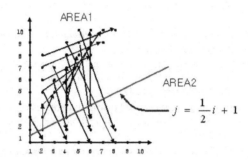

Fig. 6. Regions of the loop partitioned by the unique sets oriented partitioning in Example 1

By using an example given in Example 1, the unique set oriented partitioning method [3] divides the iteration space into one parallel region, AREA2, and one serial region, AREA1, as shown in Fig. 6. So, the speedup is $(10*10)/(1+69) = 1.4$.

Applying the minimum dependence distance tiling method to this loop illustrates case 2 of this technique [4], which is the case that line $d_i(i, j) = 0$ and $d_j(i, j) = 0$ pass through the IDCH. The minimum values of $d_i(i, j)$, d_{imin}, and $d_j(i, j)$, d_{jmin}, occur at the extreme point $(1, 1)$ and both $d_{imin} = 1$ and $d_{jmin} = 1$. There is only serial region, and no speedup for this method.

Our proposed two methods divide the iteration space into two parallel areas by line $j = 1/2*i+1$ and line $j = 3/2*i+1$, respectively. The speedup for these methods is $(10*10)/2 = 50$.

5   Conclusions

In this paper, we have studied the parallelization of flow and anti dependence loops with non-uniform dependences to improve parallelism.

By variable renaming, there remains only flow dependence sets in the nested loop. We then divide the iteration space into the flow dependence head and tail sets.

We defined the properties of FDT (Flow Dependence Tail set) and FDH (Flow Dependence Head set), and show how to find FDT and FDH in two-dimensional solution space. We also present two partitioning methods to find two parallel regions in the given space. One is the method by intersection of FDT and FDH. Another is the method by two given equations. Both methods show how to determine whether the intersection of FDT and FDH is empty or not. If FDT does not overlap FDH, a line $d_i(i,j) = 0$ between two sets divides the iteration space into two areas. The iterations within each area can be fully executed in parallel. So, we can find two parallel regions for doubly nested loops with non-uniform dependences.

In comparison with some previous partitioning methods, our proposed methods give much better speedup and extract more parallelism than other methods in the case which FDT does not overlap the FDH. Our future research work is to develop a method for improving parallelization of higher dimensional nested loops.

References

1. V. Kumar, A. Grama, A. Gupta, and G. Karypis, *Introduction to Parallel Computing*, The Benjamin/Cummings Publishing Company, Inc., 1994.
2. C. K. Cho and M. H. Lee, "A loop parallelization method for nested loops with non-uniform dependences", in *Proceedings of the International Conference on Parallel and Distributed Systems,* pp. 314-321, December 10-13, 1997.
3. J. Ju and V. Chaudhary, "Unique sets oriented partitioning of nested loops with non-uniform dependences," in *Proceedings of International Conference on Parallel Processing*, vol. III, pp. 45-52, 1996.
4. S. Punyamurtula and V. Chaudhary, "Minimum dependence distance tiling of nested loops with non-uniform dependences," in *Proceedings of Symposium on Parallel and Distributed Processing*, pp. 74-81, 1994.
5. T. Tzen and L. Ni, "Dependence uniformization: A loop parallelization technique," *IEEE Transactions on Parallel and Distributed Systems*, vol. 4, no. 5, pp. 547-558. May 1993.
6. M. Wolfe and C. W. Tseng, "The power test for data dependence," *IEEE Transactions on Parallel and Distributed Systems*, vol. 3, no. 5, pp. 591-601, September 1992.
7. A. Zaafrani and M. R. Ito, "Parallel region execution of loops with irregular dependences," in *Proceedings of the International Conference on Parallel Processing*, vol. II, pp. 11-19, 1994.

A Static Data Dependence Analysis Approach
for Software Pipelining

Lin Qiao, Weitong Huang, and Zhizhong Tang

Department of Computer Science and Technology,
Tsinghua University, Beijing, 100084, PR China
{qiaolin, hwt}@cic.tsinghua.edu.cn, tzz-dcs@tsinghua.edu.cn

Abstract. This paper introduces a new static data dependence constraint, called dependence difference inequality, which can deal with coupled subscripts for multi-dimensional array references. Unlike direction vectors, dependence difference inequalities are related to not only the iteration space for a loop program but also the operation distance between two operations. They are more strict than other methods, and can act as additional constraints to each variable in a linear system on their own or with others. As a result, the solution space for a linear system can be compressed heavily. So long as dependence difference inequalities do not satisfy simultaneously, the loop can be software-pipelined with any initiation interval even if there exists a data dependence between two operations. Meanwhile, by replacing direction vectors with dependence difference inequalities some conservative estimations made by other traditional data dependence analysis approaches can be eliminated.

1 Introduction

Data dependence analysis plays an important role in automatic detection of implicit parallelism in programs written in conventional sequential languages. Dependence analysis techniques estimate, at compile-time, the run-time interactions between different operations or between different instances of the same operation [1].

It is at the core of data dependence analysis strategies to estimate data dependence between two operations in which multi-dimensional array references are involved. General speaking, the question of whether multi-dimensional array references with coupled linear subscripts can be parallelized depends upon the resolution of multi-dimensional array aliases. The resolution of multi-dimensional array aliases is to ascertain whether or not the two references to the same multi-dimensional array within a general [nested] loop can refer to the same element of that multi-dimensional array [2].

The paper focuses on a new data dependence analysis technique for an interlaced inner and outer loop software pipelining algorithm. Our approach, called dependence difference inequalities, can deal with coupled subscripts for multi-dimensional array references statically. This paper is organized as follows. Section 2 introduces related work and background, while Section 3 discusses dependence difference inequalities. Section 4 draws a conclusion.

H. Jin, D. Reed, and W. Jiang (Eds.): NPC 2005, LNCS 3779, pp. 213–220, 2005.

2 Related Work and Background

This section introduces a novel software pipelining algorithm and gives a brief description of data dependence analysis techniques.

2.1 Interlaced Inner and Outer Loop Software Pipelining Algorithm

Software pipelining algorithms currently pursued in the world exploit the instruction-level parallelism of loop program by overlapping the operations of different loop bodies. Using software pipelining, a loop is transformed into a semantics-equivalent program consisting of a new loop, a prologue and an epilogue.

Several effective software pipelining algorithms have been presented to optimize innermost loops, such as Modulo Scheduling [3] and GURPR* [4]. In most cases, however, actual programs always contain nested loops. Optimization performance of existed algorithms is fairly insufficient when they are used to optimize nested loop programs, so it is the key to develop new algorithms that can efficiently optimize these nested loop programs.

Interlaced inner and outer Loop Software Pipelining (ILSP) is an efficient algorithm that can optimize operations in nested loops with various loop structures. In order to make the ILSP algorithm work efficiently and correctly, corresponding control mechanism, which combines software pipelining techniques with several hardware features, is introduced in [5]. In [6], Rong and his co-operators introduces a single-dimension software pipelining algorithm, which can be outlined as a brief version of the ILSP algorithm. Their algorithm chooses the most profitable loop level in the loop nest and software-pipelines it, which has been implemented as a tool set on an IA-64 Itanium workstation.

The ILSP algorithm is different from any traditional software pipelining algorithms of nested loops. ILSP does not execute the nested loops in the traditional sequence of completing the inner loop first and then executing the outer loop. It breaks the boundary of the different loop bodies of the nested loop, and can overlap the inner loop bodies of different outer loop bodies. Thus, ILSP makes it possible to optimize nested loops with various loop structures.

Consider the nested loop example as shown in Fig. 1. It can be performed well using the ILSP, as shown in Table 1.

By the example, we can describe the basic principle of the ILSP as follows. The ILSP is a software pipelining algorithm that is suitable for the nested loops with various loop structures. When each loop body of the nested loops is pipelined, the ILSP pipelines the nested loop as if the inner loops of this loop were executed only once. Whenever a new execution pattern made up of operations of an inner loop appears, in other words, the inner loop becomes active, the execution of the outer loop will be temporarily stopped. At this moment the software pipelining of the inner loop will be continuously executed until it is ready to enter its epilogue stage and to return to its outer loop or until another inner loop becomes active. When the inner loop begins to execute, the outer loop gives all its function units to the inner loop, and when the inner loop is completed, it will give all function units back to the outer loop, and the execution of the outer loop will be continued.

In one word, the foundation of the ILSP algorithm is to perform the nested loops as a whole. In order to form an effective pipeline along different loop bodies of the nested loop, it is very necessary to feed it with enough operations. A data dependence analysis approach has to meet the demand.

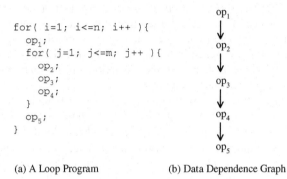

```
for( i=1; i<=n; i++ ){
    op₁;
    for( j=1; j<=m; j++ ){
        op₂;
        op₃;
        op₄;
    }
    op₅;
}
```

(a) A Loop Program   (b) Data Dependence Graph

Fig. 1. A nested loop example

Table 1. Execution result of the example

Clock	Operations					Comments
0	$op_1(1,-)$					Prologue of the outer loop begins
1	$op_1(2,-)$	$op_2(1,1)$				Prologue of the inner loop begins
2	$op_1(3,-)$	$op_2(2,1)$	$op_3(1,1)$			
3	$op_1(4,-)$	$op_2(3,1)$	$op_3(2,1)$	$op_4(1,1)$		The inner becomes active; switches to it
4		$op_2(1,2)$	$op_3(3,1)$	$op_4(2,1)$		The inner executes; the outer pauses
5		$op_2(2,2)$	$op_3(1,2)$	$op_4(3,1)$		
...	...	...	...	...		
$3m$		$op_2(3,m)$	$op_3(2,m)$	$op_4(1,m)$		The inner completes; system returns
$3m+1$	$op_1(5,-)$	$op_2(4,1)$	$op_3(3,m)$	$op_4(2,m)$	$op_5(1,-)$	The first epilogue of the inner begins
$3m+2$	$op_1(6,-)$	$op_2(5,1)$	$op_3(4,1)$	$op_4(3,m)$	$op_5(2,-)$	Epilogue of the outer begins
$3m+3$	$op_1(7,-)$	$op_2(6,1)$	$op_3(5,1)$	$op_4(4,1)$	$op_5(3,-)$	The second epilogue of the inner begins
$3m+4$		$op_2(4,2)$	$op_3(6,1)$	$op_4(5,1)$		The inner executes again; the outer pauses
...	...	...	...	...	...	
nm		$op_2(n,m)$	$op_3(n-1,m)$	$op_4(n-2,m)$		
$nm+1$			$op_3(n,m)$	$op_4(n-1,m)$	$op_5(n-2,-)$	Epilogue of the whole nested loop
$nm+2$				$op_4(n,m)$	$op_5(n-1,-)$	
$nm+3$					$op_5(n,-)$	

2.2 Data Dependence Analysis

Suppose op_1 and op_2 be two operations within a n-nested loop which refer to a m-dimensional array simultaneously. Each iteration of the loop is identified by an *iteration vector* whose elements are the values of the iteration variables for that iteration. We have

Definition 1. Let $op_1(i)$ and $op_2(j)$ respectively denote the instance of the operation op_1 during the iteration $i = (i_1, i_2, ..., i_n)$ and that of the operation op_2 during the iteration $j = (j_1, j_2, \ldots, j_n)$. There exists an *partial order* between the two operation instances, $op_1(i) < op_2(j)$, if (*a*) for given an r where $1 \le r \le \min\{m, n\}$, $i_r = j_r$ and $i_k \le j_k$ ($1 \le k < r$) hold, or (*b*) for $m \le n$, $i_r = j_r$ ($1 \le r \le m$) holds.

Practically an partial order $op_1(i) < op_2(j)$ means that $op_1(i)$ precedes $op_2(j)$. If the instance of the operation $op_2(j)$ uses the element of the array defined first by the instance of the operation $op_1(i)$, then $op_2(j)$ is true-dependent or write-read-dependent on $op_1(i)$. If the instance of the operation $op_2(j)$ defines the element of the array used first by the instance of the operation $op_1(i)$, then $op_2(j)$ is anti-dependent or read-write-dependent on $op_1(i)$. If the instance of the operation $op_2(j)$ redefines the element of the array defined first by the instance of the operation $op_1(i)$, then $op_2(j)$ is output-dependent or write-write-dependent on $op_1(i)$.

In general, suppose the n-nested loop have linear lower bounds and upper bounds, f_k denote the lower bound function for the k-th level nested loop, and g_k the upper bound function. It is obvious that $f_k \le i_k, j_k \le g_k$, $1 \le k \le n$, hold simultaneously. By replacing i_k with x_{2k-1} and j_k with x_{2k}, the problem mathematically can be reduced to that of checking whether or not a system of m linear equations with $2n$ unknown variables has a simultaneous integer solution, which satisfies the constraints for each variable in the system. The m linear equations in the system can be written as

$$\begin{cases} a_{1,0} + a_{1,1}x_1 + a_{1,2}x_2 + \ldots + a_{1,2n}x_{2n} = 0 \\ a_{2,0} + a_{2,1}x_1 + a_{2,2}x_2 + \ldots + a_{2,2n}x_{2n} = 0 \\ \ldots \\ a_{m,0} + a_{m,1}x_1 + a_{m,2}x_2 + \ldots + a_{m,2n}x_{2n} = 0 \end{cases} \tag{1}$$

where each $a_{i,j}$ is a constant integer for $1 \le i \le m$ and $1 \le j \le 2n$. $i = (x_1, x_3, \ldots, x_{2n-1})$ and $j = (x_2, x_4, \ldots, x_{2n})$ denote two iteration vectors, $op_1(i)$ and $op_2(j)$, respectively. Constraints to each variable in Eq. (1) can be represented as

$$\begin{cases} P_{1,0} \le x_1, x_2 \le Q_{1,0} \\ P_{k,0} + \sum_{s=1}^{k-1} P_{k,s}x_{2s-1} = f_k(x_1, x_3, \ldots, x_{2k-3}) \le x_{2k-1} \le g_k(x_1, x_3, \ldots, x_{2k-3}) = Q_{k,0} + \sum_{s=1}^{k-1} Q_{k,s}x_{2s-1}, \ 2 \le k \le n \\ P_{k,0} + \sum_{s=1}^{k-1} P_{k,s}x_{2s} = f_k(x_2, x_4, \ldots, x_{2k-2}) \le x_{2k} \le g_k(x_2, x_4, \ldots, x_{2k-2}) = Q_{k,0} + \sum_{s=1}^{k-1} Q_{k,s}x_{2s}, \ 2 \le k \le n \end{cases} \tag{2}$$

where $P_{r,0}, Q_{r,0}, P_{r,s}, Q_{r,s}$ are constant integers for $1 \le r \le n$. If each of $P_{r,s}$ and $Q_{r,s}$ is zero, the Eq. (2) will be reduced to

$$P_{k,0} \le x_{2k-1}, x_{2k} \le Q_{k,0}, \ 1 \le k \le n. \tag{3}$$

That is, the bounds for each variables are constants.

Definition 2. A vector of the form $e = (e_1, e_2, \ldots, e_n)$ is termed a direction vector from $op_1(i)$ to $op_2(j)$ if for $1 \le k \le d$, $i_k e_k j_k$, i.e., the relation e_k is defined by

$$e_k = \begin{cases} < & \text{if } i_k < j_k \\ = & \text{if } i_k = j_k \\ > & \text{if } i_k > j_k \\ * & \text{any one of } \{<, =, >\} \end{cases} \tag{4}$$

There are several well-known data dependence analysis algorithms exploited for practical parallelizing compilers. The Banerjee Inequalities can handle one linear equation under the bounds of Eq. (3) and Eq. (4), and the Banerjee Algorithm can deal with one linear equation under the bounds of Eq. (2) and Eq. (4) [7]. When applied to practical cases, the Banerjee Test (the Banerjee Inequalities and the Banerjee Algorithm) may lose accuracy. The I Test and the Direction Vector I Test are a combination of the Banerjee inequalities and the GCD Test [8] [9]. They determine integer solutions for a linear equation with constant bounds and given direction vectors. The Lambda Test extends the Banerjee Inequalities to allow m linear equations in Eq. (1) under the constraints of Eq. (3) and Eq. (4) to be tested simultaneously [10]. And the Generalized Lambda Test allows m linear equations in Eq. (1) under the constraints of Eq. (2) and Eq. (4) to be tested simultaneously [2]. More precise results can be obtained by judging the consistency of a linear system of equations and inequalities inexpensively.

All of above data dependence analysis methods, however, are exploited for general parallelizing compilers, and they ignore the fact that the software pipelining technique *per se* has an impact on instruction-level parallelism. The next section will prove that for instruction-level parallelizing compilers more interesting results can be achieved under additional constraints of dependence difference inequalities.

3   Dependence Difference Inequalities

This section introduces a kind of additional constraints, called *dependence difference inequalities*, for software pipelining techniques. Under these additional constraints the solution space for a linear system can be compressed heavily.

3.1   Relationship Between Software Pipelining and Data Dependence

In general, the ILSP algorithm overlaps adjacent iterations of a nested loop program. The *initiation interval* of these adjacent iterations, denoted by II, is only restricted by resource limit, denoted by II_{res}, and sequential semantics of the loop program, denoted by II_{sem}, i.e., $\text{II} = \max\{\text{II}_{\text{res}}, \text{II}_{\text{sem}}\}$. For the sake of clarity the paper only concentrates on II_{sem} since II_{res} can always be released by using more function units.

Definition 3. Let op_1 and op_2 be two operations of a loop program. The number of operations between op_1 and op_2 plus 1 is referred to as *operation distance*, denoted by $\text{dis}(op_1, op_2)$.

Definition 4. If $op_2(j)$ is dependent on $op_1(i)$, $i = (x_1, x_3, \ldots, x_{2n-1})$ and $j = (x_2, x_4, \ldots, x_{2n})$, then $i - j = (x_1 - x_2, x_3 - x_4, \ldots, x_{2n-1} - x_{2n})$ is referred to as *dependence difference vector*, denoted by $\text{dif}(op_1, op_2)$, and $i_k - j_k = x_{2k-1} - x_{2k}$ is referred to as the dependence difference in the k-th level nested loop, denoted by $\text{dif}_k(op_1, op_2)$. If $\text{dif}_k(op_1, op_2) = 0$ then $op_2(j)$ is intra-loop-dependent on $op_1(i)$ otherwise inter-loop-dependent.

For the ILSP algorithm intra-loop-dependences have no impact on II_{sem} but those inter-loop-dependences may make a strong impact on II_{sem}.

Lemma 1 [11]. Let op_1 and op_2 be two operations, both belonging to the same k-th level nested loop. If $0 < \mathrm{dif}_k(op_1, op_2) \leq \mathrm{dis}(op_1, op_2)$ does not hold, then the loop program can be software-pipelined with $\mathrm{II}_{sem} = 1$.

Lemma 1 shows that the loop program can not be software-pipelined with $\mathrm{II}_{sem} = 1$ where $0 < \mathrm{dif}_k(op_1, op_2) \leq \mathrm{dis}(op_1, op_2)$ holds. However, it does not imply that the loop program can not be software-pipelined with a greater one.

Definition 5. An inequality of the form $1 \leq \mathrm{dif}_k(op_1, op_2) \leq \mathrm{dis}(op_1, op_2)$ is termed a *dependence difference inequality* for $1 \leq k \leq n$.

Theorem 1 [11]. Let op_1 and op_2 be two operations, both belonging to the same n-nested loop program whose loop labels are denoted by $L_1, L_2, \ldots, L_n$ in turn. The loop can be software-pipelined with any value of initiation interval if the following dependence difference inequalities

$$1 \leq \mathrm{dif}_k(op_1, op_2) \leq \mathrm{dis}(op_1, op_2), \ 1 \leq k \leq n, \tag{5}$$

do not satisfy simultaneously.

Theorem 1 implies that dependence difference inequalities can act as, on their own or with other constraints, additional constraints to each variable in a linear system. If there does not exist any integer solution for the linear system under these constraints, the loop can be software-pipelined with $\mathrm{II}_{sem} = 1$ even if a data dependence between two operations exists.

3.2 Dependence Difference Inequalities vs. Direction Vectors

In general, a direction vector $e = (e_1, e_2, \ldots, e_n)$ bounds the solution space for a linear system with $i_k < j_k$ or $i_k > j_k$ for $1 \leq k \leq n$. $i_k = j_k$ means two operations are intra-loop-dependent on each other, and thus the dependence can be ignored when the loop is software-pipelined by the ILSP algorithm.

Suppose $i_k > j_k$. When using a direction vector as a constraint we have $f_k(x_2, x_4, \ldots, x_{2n}) \leq j_k < i_k \leq g_k(x_1, x_3, \ldots, x_{2n-1})$, i.e.,

$$1 \leq i_k - j_k \leq g_k(x_1, x_3, \ldots, x_{2n-1}) - f_k(x_2, x_4, \ldots, x_{2n}). \tag{6}$$

On the other hand, by using dependence difference inequalities as constraints we have

$$1 \leq i_k - j_k \leq \mathrm{dis}(op_1, op_2). \tag{7}$$

It is shown that dependence difference inequalities are more strict than direction vectors since in most cases $g_k(x_1, x_3, \ldots, x_{2n-1}) - f_k(x_2, x_4, \ldots, x_{2n})$, as an iteration counter, is far greater than $\mathrm{dis}(op_1, op_2)$. In one word, these dependence difference inequality constraints make our data dependence analysis algorithm more powerful.

Table 2 gives a practical loop example where op_2 is anti-dependent on op_1 and $\mathrm{dis}(op_1, op_2) = 3$. The corresponding data dependence equation of the loop program is $2i_1 + 1 = j_1$, i.e., $2i_1 - j_1 = -1$. Because $\gcd(2, 1) = 1$, the GCD Test draws a conclusion that op_1 is dependent on op_2 and the loop can not be parallelized. On the other hand, it can be derived that $-90 \leq 2i_1 - j_1 \leq 195$ from $5 \leq i_1, j_1 \leq 100$, namely, $-90 \leq -1 \leq 195$, which makes the Banerjee Test also draws a conclusion that the loop can not be parallelized. Furthermore, when a direction vector $i_1 < j_1$ is applied we first have $-95 \le i_1 - j_1 \le -1$, and second $-106 \le i_1 - j_1 \le -6$ from $i_1 - j_1 = -i_1 - 1$. The Banerjee Test still draws the same conclusion since the interaction of the solution spaces for the two inequalities is not empty.

Table 2. Dependence difference inequalities are more strict tha`n direction vectors

`for(L1=5;L1<=100;++L1)`
`{`
`    op₁: X = A[2L1+1];`
`    Y = X + 5;`
`    Z = Y * 3;`
`    op₂: A[L1] = Z;`
`}`
	Clock	Iteration			

		$i = 5$	$i = 6$	$i = 7$	$i = 8$
	1	`X=A[11];`			
	2	`Y=X+5;`	`X=A[13];`		
	3	`Z=Y*3;`	`Y=X+5;`	`X=A[15];`	
	4	`A[5]=Z;`	`Z=Y*3;`	`Y=X+5;`	`X=A[17];`
	5		`A[6]=Z;`	`Z=Y*3;`	`Y=X+5;`
	6			`A[7]=Z;`	`Z=Y*3;`
	7				`A[8]=Z;`
(a) A loop program	(b) Correct software pipelining with $\mathrm{II}_{sem} = 1$				

When replacing the direction vector with a dependence difference inequality, we can clearly find the interaction of the solution spaces for the two inequalities, $1 \le i_1 - j_1 \le \mathrm{dis}(op_1, op_2) = 3$ and $-106 \le i_1 - j_1 \le -6$, is empty. Thus our data dependence analysis algorithm determines that the loop can be paralleled, as shown in Table 2.

4 Conclusion

This paper has presented a new static data dependence analysis approach, called dependence difference inequality, for our software pipelining algorithm ILSP for nested loops. Our data dependence analysis approach can deal with coupled subscripts for multi-dimensional array references statically.

Conceptually, unlike a direction vector, a dependence difference inequality is not only related to the iteration space for a loop program but also related to the operation distance between two operations. Dependence difference inequalities can act as additional constraints to each variable in a linear system on their own or with other constraints, such as direction vectors. They are more strict than a direction vector and make our data dependence analysis algorithm more powerful. As a result, the solution space for the linear system can be compressed heavily.

Under constraints of dependence difference inequalities, so long as these inequalities do not satisfy simultaneously, the loop can be software-pipelined with any value of initiation interval even though there exists a data dependence between two operations. The paper has also shown that some conservative estimations made by other traditional data dependence analysis approaches can be eliminated by replacing a direction vector with a dependence difference inequality.

Further experimental results are reported in [12]. On the other hand, a dynamic data dependence analysis approach is presented in [13], which can work with this method together to coping with data dependencies for software pipelining.

Acknowledgement

This work was partially supported by National Nature Science Foundation, grant number 60173010, of *P. R. China.*

References

1. Petersen, P. M., Padua, D. A.: Static and Dynamic Evaluation of Data Dependence Analysis Techniques. IEEE Transactions on Parallel and Distributed Systems 7 (1996) 1121–1132
2. Chang, W. L., Chu, C. P., Wu, J.: The Generalized Lambda Test: A Multi-Dimensional Version of Banerjee's Algorithm. International Journal of Parallel and Distributed Systems and Networks 2 (1999) 69–78
3. Rau, B.R.: Iterative Modulo Scheduling. Technical Report HPL-94-115. Hewlett-Packard Laboratory, Palo Alto, CA (1994)
4. Su, B., Ding, S., Wang, J., Xia, J.: GURPR — A Method for Global Software Pipelining. ACM SIGMICRO Newsletter 19 (1988) 32–36
5. Qiao, L., Tang, Z. Z., Wang, S. Y.: Control Strategies of Software Pipelining: Dealing with the Prologue and the Epilogue of Nested Loops. In: Zhou, X., Xu, M., Lou, S., Yang, X. (eds.): Proceedings of the 3rd Workshop on Advanced Parallel Processing Technologies, 19-21 Oct. 1999, Changsha, China. Publishing House of Electronics Industry, Beijing (1999) 177–181
6. Rong, H. B., Tang, Z. Z., Govindarajan, R., Douillet, A., Gao, G. R.: Single-Dimension Software Pipelining for Multi-Dimensional Loops. In: Proceedings of the 2nd IEEE/ACM International Symposium on Code Generation and Optimization, 21-24 Mar. 2004, San Jose, CA. IEEE Computer Society, Los Alamitos, CA (2004) 163–174
7. Banerjee, U.: Dependence Analysis. Kluwer Academic Publishers, Norwell MA (1997)
8. Kong, X, Klappholz, D., Psarris, K.: The I Test. IEEE Transactions on Parallel and Distributed System 2 (1991) 342–359
9. Kong, X, Klappholz, D., Psarris, K.: The Direction Vector I Test. IEEE Transactions on Parallel and Distributed System 4 (1993) 1280–1290
10. Li, Z., Yew, Y. C., Zhu, C. Q.: An Efficient Data Dependence Analysis for Parallelizing Compilers. IEEE Transactions on Parallel and Distributed System 1 (1990) 26–34
11. Qiao, L.: On Data Dependencies in Software Pipelining. Doctorial Dissertation, Department of Computer Science, Tsinghua University, Beijing (2001)
12. Qiao, L., Huang, W. T., Tang, Z. Z.: Coping with Data Dependencies of Multi-Dimensional Array References. In: Jin, H., Reed, D., Jiang, W. (eds.): Proceedings of IFIP International Conference on Network and Parallel Computing, Beijing, Lecture Notes in Computer Science. Springer-Verlag, Berlin Heidelberg New York (2005) accepted by NPC'05
13. Qiao, L., Huang, W. T., Tang, Z. Z.: A Dynamic Data Dependence Analysis Approach for Software Pipelining. In: Jin, H., Reed, D., Jiang, W. (eds.): Proceedings of IFIP International Conference on Network and Parallel Computing, Beijing, Lecture Notes in Computer Science. Springer-Verlag, Berlin Heidelberg New York (2005) accepted by NPC'05

A Dynamic Data Dependence Analysis Approach for Software Pipelining

Lin Qiao, Weitong Huang, and Zhizhong Tang

Department of Computer Science and Technology, Tsinghua University,
Beijing, 100084, PR China
{qiaolin, hwt}@cic.tsinghua.edu.cn, tzz-dcs@tsinghua.edu.cn

Abstract. This paper presents a run-time pointer aliasing disambiguation method for software pipelining techniques. By combining hardware with software, the method is better than run-time checking method or run-time compensation method, which is capable of dealing with irreversible code, and has limited compensation code space without serious rerollability problem. The new method solves pointer aliasing problem efficiently and makes it possible to obtain potential instruction-level parallel speedup. In this paper instruction-level parallel speedups of the new method are analyzed in detail. Three theoretical speedups, i.e., *general speedup, probabilistic speedup* and *mean speedup with probability*, are given, which will be helpful for studying and evaluating instruction-level parallelism of the new method.

1 Introduction

To exploit instruction-level parallelism (ILP), compilers for a very-long instruction word (VLIW) machine often employ static code scheduling and software pipelining [1] [2] [3] [4]. It is, however, restricted by ambiguous dependencies between memory fetches. Even though great progress has been made in the analysis of static aliases among arrays, analysis of pointer aliasing is a formidable task for most compilers. In order to solve this key problem to achieving the potential speedup in instruction-level parallel processing, two types of run-time disambiguation (RTD) methods, i.e., run-time checking and run-time compensation, have been presented in [5].

When applying both of the run-time disambiguation methods to software pipelining, however, the run-time compensation approach allows speculative memory fetch but is suitable only for reversed code, while the run-time checking approach can be used for any code but has serious rerollability problem. Moreover, both of the run-time disambiguation methods have code space problem. In particular, when applying run-time disambiguation to global software pipelining the space of compensation code could be tremendous.

Followed Su and his co-operators [6], the paper presents a new hardware/software combined method. The basic ideas are as follows. First, during run time, let the function units execute NOP operations instead of using compensation code to implement the postponement of the incorrect memory load operation and its successive operations. Second, to guarantee the consistency of the execution sequence of all postponed operations, the order of function units that execute NOPs and the number of NOPs must be determined during compiler time.

H. Jin, D. Reed, and W. Jiang (Eds.): NPC 2005, LNCS 3779, pp. 221–228, 2005.

This paper is organized as follows. Section 2 discusses the hardware support for the RTPAD method before how to use the RTPAD method is discussed by a sample example in detail in Section 3. Section 4 presents three theoretical parallel speedups and analyzes the example. Section 5 gives some experimental results while Section 6 draws conclusions.

2 Hardware Architecture

Fig.1 illustrates a hypothetical VLIW architecture that has ten function units: two ALU, two multipliers (MUL), two memory ports (MEM), and four branch-and-loop-control units (BRLC). In addition, the hardware support of the RTPAD method includes an instruction buffer (IB) storing postponed operations, a multiplexer set (MUX) selecting operations from regular instruction memory or from instruction buffer, an RTPAD control instruction buffer, and a read register called RTPAD WORD. This VLIW processor is capable of starting four integer operations, two memory operations, and four branch operations every cycle.

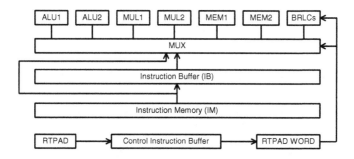

Fig. 1. Hardware support for the RTPAD method

3 Using the RTPAD Method

The RTPAD method has been used for software pipelining of non-loop programs in [7] [8] [9]. This paper extends the work by using it for software pipelining of loop programs.

Table 1 and Table 2 illustrates how to use the RTPAD method for software pipelining algorithms. Fig. 2 shows the original code and Fig. 3 shows the modified code into which RTPAD operations are inserted.

Because the software pipelining algorithm overlaps several iterations, some RTPAD operations are inserted before the ambiguous load operation as shown in Fig. 3. Table 1 shows the normal execution sequence of the result of software pipelining when no address conflict is detected, where $op_i^{(j)}$ denotes operation op_i belongs to the j-th iteration of the loop.

Table 1. The result of software pipelining without address conflicts

CLK	ALU1	ALU2	MUL1	MUL2	MEM1	MEM2	BRLC0	BRLC1	BRLC2
1			$op_1^{(1)}$						
2			$op_1^{(2)}$		$op_5^{(1)}$				$RTPAD(op_5^{(2)}, op_8^{(1)})$
3	$op_6^{(1)}$		$op_1^{(3)}$		$op_5^{(2)}$			$RTPAD(op_5^{(3)}, op_8^{(1)})$	$RTPAD(op_5^{(3)}, op_8^{(2)})$
4	$op_6^{(2)}$	$op_7^{(1)}$	$op_1^{(4)}$		$op_5^{(3)}$		$RTPAD(op_5^{(4)}, op_8^{(1)})$	$RTPAD(op_5^{(4)}, op_8^{(2)})$	$RTPAD(op_5^{(4)}, op_8^{(3)})$
5	$op_6^{(3)}$	$op_7^{(2)}$	$op_1^{(5)}$		$op_5^{(4)}$	$op_8^{(1)}$	$RTPAD(op_5^{(5)}, op_8^{(2)})$	$RTPAD(op_5^{(5)}, op_8^{(3)})$	$RTPAD(op_5^{(5)}, op_8^{(4)})$
6	$op_6^{(4)}$	$op_7^{(3)}$	$op_1^{(6)}$	$op_9^{(1)}$	$op_5^{(5)}$	$op_8^{(2)}$	$RTPAD(op_5^{(6)}, op_8^{(3)})$	$RTPAD(op_5^{(6)}, op_8^{(4)})$	$RTPAD(op_5^{(6)}, op_8^{(5)})$
7	$op_6^{(5)}$	$op_7^{(4)}$	$op_1^{(7)}$	$op_9^{(2)}$	$op_5^{(6)}$	$op_8^{(3)}$	$RTPAD(op_5^{(7)}, op_8^{(4)})$	$RTPAD(op_5^{(7)}, op_8^{(5)})$	$RTPAD(op_5^{(7)}, op_8^{(6)})$
8	$op_6^{(6)}$	$op_7^{(5)}$	$op_1^{(8)}$	$op_9^{(3)}$	$op_5^{(7)}$	$op_8^{(4)}$	$RTPAD(op_5^{(8)}, op_8^{(5)})$	$RTPAD(op_5^{(8)}, op_8^{(6)})$	$RTPAD(op_5^{(8)}, op_8^{(7)})$
9	$op_6^{(7)}$	$op_7^{(6)}$	$op_1^{(9)}$	$op_9^{(4)}$	$op_5^{(8)}$	$op_8^{(5)}$	$RTPAD(op_5^{(9)}, op_8^{(6)})$	$RTPAD(op_5^{(9)}, op_8^{(7)})$	$RTPAD(op_5^{(9)}, op_8^{(8)})$

Table 2. An address conflict between $op_5^{(6)}$ and $op_8^{(4)}$ is detected

CLK	ALU1	ALU2	MUL1	MUL2	MEM1	MEM2	BRLC0	BRLC1	BRLC2
6	$op_6^{(4)}$	$op_7^{(3)}$	$op_1^{(6)}$	$op_9^{(1)}$	$op_5^{(5)}$	$op_8^{(2)}$	$RTPAD(op_5^{(6)}, op_8^{(3)})$	$RTPAD(op_5^{(6)}, op_8^{(4)})$	$RTPAD(op_5^{(6)}, op_8^{(5)})$
7	$op_6^{(5)}$	$op_7^{(4)}$	NOP	$op_9^{(2)}$	NOP	$op_8^{(3)}$	$RTPAD(op_5^{(7)}, op_8^{(4)})$	$RTPAD(op_5^{(7)}, op_8^{(5)})$	$RTPAD(op_5^{(7)}, op_8^{(6)})$
8	NOP	$op_7^{(5)}$	NOP	$op_9^{(3)}$	NOP	$Op_8^{(4)}$	$RTPAD(op_5^{(8)}, op_8^{(5)})$	$RTPAD(op_5^{(8)}, op_8^{(6)})$	$RTPAD(op_5^{(8)}, op_8^{(7)})$
9	NOP	NOP	$op_1^{(7)}$	NOP	$op_5^{(6)}$	NOP	NOP	NOP	NOP
10	$op_6^{(6)}$	NOP	$op_1^{(8)}$	NOP	$op_5^{(7)}$	NOP	NOP	NOP	NOP
11	$op_6^{(7)}$	$op_7^{(6)}$	$op_1^{(9)}$	$op_9^{(4)}$	$op_5^{(8)}$	$op_8^{(5)}$	$RTPAD(op_5^{(9)}, op_8^{(6)})$	$RTPAD(op_5^{(9)}, op_8^{(7)})$	$RTPAD(op_5^{(9)}, op_8^{(8)})$

```
for( i=0; i<n; i++ )
{
    R2 = 2 * R1
    R1 = M(P)
    R4 = R2 - R1
    R4 = R4 + R3
    M(Q) = R6
    R7 = R4 * R5
}
```

Fig. 2. Th eoriginal code

```
for( i=0; i<n; i++ )
{
    op1: R2 = 2 * R1
    op2: RTPAD
    op3: RTPAD
    op4: RTPAD
    op5: R1 = M(P)
    op6: R4 = R2 - R1
    op7: R4 = R4 + R3
    op8: M(Q) = R6
    op9: R7 = R4 * R5
}
```

Fig. 3. After RTPAD inserted

The prologue stage of the loop is from cycle 1 to cycle 5, and the pipelining stage of the loop begins from cycle 6. In Table 1, each VLIW instruction executes 6 operations belonging to adjoining iterations, namely, it takes a VLIW CPU one cycle to complete an iteration of the loop. Assume that l be the loop length and n be the loop counter. If $n \gg l$, the corresponding parallel speedup is l approximately.

Three RTPAD operations are inserted to determine whether memory address conflict between the ambiguous load operation of the iteration and store operations of previous three iterations, respectively. As Table 2 shows, all operations at cycle 11 are the same as original run-time VLIW code at cycle 9, which means that all operations within cycle 7 and cycle 8 in Table 1 are performed within cycle 7 to cycle 10 in Table 2. All data dependencies of these operations are guaranteed by the order of inserted NOP operations. The RTPAD method totally needs two extra cycles to complete compensation NOP operations, which is equal to the compensation code measure, when the address conflict is detected.

It takes a sequential CPU $6n$ cycles to execute the original code as shown in Fig. 2. When the RTPAD method is used, it takes a VLIW CPU n cycles to execute the corresponding VLIW code in parallel if no address conflict is detected. Thus, the speedup of the VLIW code is 6 approximately.

4 Theoretical Speedups

Because of the indeterminacy of parallel execution of programs, it is very difficult to precisely analyze the complexity and code space of the final VLIW code. The results we obtained are related to probabilities of events that address conflicts occur.

For the sake of clarity, assume that (*a*) all operations complete within one cycle, (*b*) all PEs share only one memory bank, and (*c*) each of PEs have a memory read unit, a memory load unit and four BRLC units. Proofs of theorems can be found in [8].

Definition 1. Let op_1 and op_2 be two operations of a program. The number of operations between op_1 and op_2 plus 1 is referred to as *operation distance*, denoted by $dis(op_1, op_2)$.

Definition 2. Let op_1 and op_2 be two operations of a VLIW program, and operation op_1 executes before operation op_2 in the original sequential code. If op_1 and op_2 have been arranged and the number of VLIW instructions between these two operations is N, *arrangement distance* of these two operations, denoted by $d(op_1, op_2)$, is

$$d(op_1, op_2) = \begin{cases} N+1, & \text{if } op_1 \text{ executes before } op_2, \\ -N-1, & \text{if } op_1 \text{ executes after } op_2, \\ 0, & \text{otherwise.} \end{cases} \tag{1}$$

Definition 3. Let op_1 and op_2, respectively, be two ambiguous store and load operations. Let the arrangement distance $d(op_1, op_2) < 0$. When an address conflict is detected during run-time, some NOP operations are inserted to implement the postponement of the incorrect memory load operation and its successive operations. The number of inserted NOP operations is called *compensation code measure*, denoted by Ω.

Definition 4. The duration when compensation NOP operations are executed before op_2 is referred to as *pre-compensation period*, denoted by D_1. Similarly, the duration when compensation NOP operations are executed after op_1 is referred to as *post-compensation period*, denoted by D_2.

Given a loop program, an operation has different arrangement place in different iterations. The following definition presents specific arrangement information of operations in different iterations.

Definition 5. For any op_1 and op_2 belonging to a loop whose loop counter is n, suppose that $op_1^{(k)}$ and $op_2^{(j)}$ denote the k-th iteration of op_1 and the j-th iteration of op_2, respectively, where $1 \le j \le n$ and $1 \le k \le n$. If $j \ne k$, $d(op_1^{(k)}, op_2^{(j)})$ is referred to as *inter-body arrangement distance*. Otherwise, $d(op_1^{(k)}, op_2^{(j)})$ is referred to as *inner-body arrangement distance*.

Any modulo scheduling algorithm of a loop has to determine the initial interval, II, of the loop before scheduling it. That is, the modulo scheduling algorithm has to determine the inter-body arrangement distance of the first operation in two adjoining iterations, $d(op_1^{(k)}, op_1^{(k+1)})$. It is easily found that the inner-body arrangement distance of op_1 and op_2 in different iterations are the same, abbreviated as $d_{inn}(op_1, op_2)$. If op_1 executes before op_2 in the original code, $op_1^{(j)}$ executes before $op_2^{(j)}$ in the VLIW code when software pipelining algorithm is applied, i.e., $d_{inn}(op_1, op_2) > 0$.

Theorem 1. Let II = 1. Suppose that l be the length of the sequential code of the loop and n be the loop counter. $op_1^{(k)}$ and $op_2^{(j)}$ are two arranged ambiguous load and store operations, respectively, and their inner-body arrangement distance is $d_{inn}(op_1, op_2) = d$. After some address conflicts have occurred, that is, the address conflict whose body difference is i has occurred j_i times, where $1 \le i \le d$ for any i, the parallel speedup of the VLIW program, called *general speedup*, is

$$S = \frac{ln}{n + 2l - 4 + \sum_{i=1}^{d} j_i (d - i + 1)}. \tag{2}$$

After address conflicts have occurred m times, the average value of general speedups is of the form

$$\overline{S(m)} = \frac{2ln}{2n + md + m + 4l - 8}. \tag{3}$$

Theorem 2. Suppose that probabilities of events that address conflicts between any two different iterations occur are independent of each other and probabilities of events that address conflicts with different body differences in an iteration occur are mutual. Let p_i be the probability of the event that an address conflict whose body difference is i, occur in an iteration, where $1 \le i \le d$ for any i. Other assumptions of the theorem are the same as those of Theorem 1. If address conflicts occur m times with probability, the compensation code measure, $\Omega_P(m)$, is related to m's probability, that is,

$$\Omega_P(m) = \sum_{\substack{j_1 + j_2 + \ldots + j_d = m \\ 0 \le j_1, j_2, \ldots, j_d \le m}} \left(\binom{n}{j_1, j_2, \ldots, j_d, n - m} \left(1 - \sum_{i=1}^{d} p_i \right)^{n-m} \prod_{i=1}^{d} p_i^{j_i} \sum_{i=1}^{d} j_i (d - i + 1) \right). \tag{4}$$

The corresponding parallel speedup with probability, called *probabilistic speedup*, is of the form

$$S_P(m) = \frac{l \times n}{\Omega_P(m) + n + 2l - 4}. \tag{5}$$

Parallel speedups of the VLIW program are different from each other when distinct address conflicts occur. Being the means of estimating speedup before program execution, the probabilistic speedup $S_P(m)$ denotes the expected value of the parallel speedup. The probabilistic speedup is an important parameter to show the efficiency of the RTPAD method.

Theorem 3. Assumptions of the theorem are the same as Theorem 2. The average value of parallel speedups when some address conflicts occur with probability, called *mean speedup with probability*, is

$$\overline{S} = \frac{ln}{\overline{\Omega} + n + 2l - 4} , \qquad (6)$$

where $\overline{\Omega}$ is the average value of compensation code measures with probability and

$$\overline{\Omega} = \frac{n\sum_{i=1}^{d} p_i(d - i + 1)}{1 - \left(1 - \sum_{i=1}^{d} p_i\right)^n} .$$ Convergence of mean speedup with probability is

$$\lim_{n \to \infty} \overline{S} = \frac{l}{1 + \sum_{i=1}^{d} p_i(d - i + 1)} . \qquad (7)$$

The mean speedup with probability $\overline{S}$ denotes the average value of the parallel speedups, which is an important parameter to show the average performance of the RTPAD method. When the probability of events that address conflicts occur is 0, convergence of mean speedup with probability is l.

5 Experiment Results

This section briefly introduces and analyzes experimental results of the RTPAD algorithm for the sample code. For load operations which can possibly result in run-time address conflicts, the method inserts some RTPAD instructions before them. For the sake of the clarity, we only discuss the loop program shown in Fig. 3. More detailed experimental results and practical applications can be seen in [8].

The RTPAD method inserts three RTPAD operations before op_5. That is, there exist three probabilistic parameters, p_1, p_2 and p_3, when software pipelining is applied. Suppose that $p_1 = p_2 = p_3$, and $p_1 + p_2 + p_3 = p$. We executes the compiled code of the loop program 10,000 times repeatedly where the loop counter $n = 10,000$.

Fig. 4 illustrates the speedups of the compiled code shown in Fig. 3, while the p-axis denotes the probability of occurring address conflicts between two iterations, and the S-axis means the speedup. In Fig. 4 max, min, and mean denote the maximum speedup, minimum speedup, and mean speedup obtained through 10,000 times executions respectively, while $\lim S$ denotes convergence of mean speedup with probability obtained by Theorem 3. The experiment shows that the RTPAD method works very well.

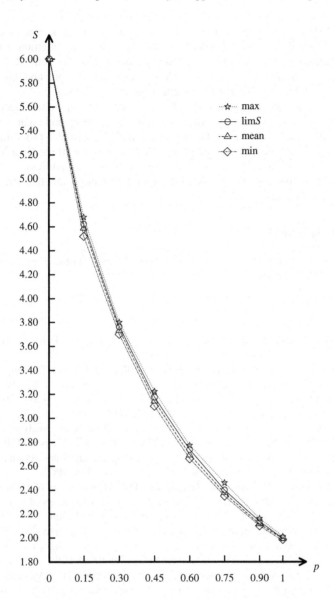

Fig. 4. Speedups of the compiled code shown in Fig. 3

6 Conclusion

This paper has proposed a method of run-time pointer aliasing disambiguation, RTPAD. Applying the RTPAD approach to a typical loop example, this paper has indicated that it has solved pointer aliasing problem with the same speed as software pipelining only applying compensation approach.

The RTPAD approach presented in this paper has its own advantages. First, it is good for irreversible code because the run-time checking method has no redo problem. Second, the code space for compensation code is limited because any RTPAD operation only needs one RTPAD control instruction. and last, it has no rerollability problem that other run-time checking methods have.

In addition, this paper has theoretically described three parallel speedups of the RTPAD approach, *i.e.*, general speedup, probabilistic speedup and mean speedup with probability. Because of the indeterminacy of parallel execution of programs, it is very difficult to precisely analyze the complexity and code space of the final VLIW code. The obtained results are related to probabilities of events that address conflicts occur. These theoretical speedups will be helpful for studying and evaluating the instruction-level parallel techniques.

Acknowledgement

This work was supported by National Nature Science Foundation, grant number 60173010, of *P. R. China*.

References

1. Rau, B. R., Fisher, A.: Instruction-Level Parallel Processing: History, Overview, and Perspective. Journal of Supercomputing 7 (1993) 9–50
2. Rong, H. B., Tang, Z. Z., Govindarajan, R., Douillet, A., Gao, G. R.: Single-Dimension Software Pipelining for Multi-Dimensional Loops. In: Proceedings of the 2nd IEEE/ACM International Symposium on Code Generation and Optimization, 21-24 Mar. 2004, San Jose, CA. IEEE Computer Society, Los Alamitos, CA (2004) 163–174
3. Qiao, L., Huang, W. T., Tang, Z. Z.: A Static Data Dependence Analysis Approach for Software Pipelining. In: Jin, H., Reed, D., Jiang, W. (eds.): Proceedings of IFIP International Conference on Network and Parallel Computing, Beijing, Lecture Notes in Computer Science. Springer-Verlag, Berlin Heidelberg New York (2005) accepted by NPC'05
4. Qiao, L., Huang, W. T., Tang, Z. Z.: Coping with Data Dependencies of Multi-Dimensional Array References. In: Jin, H., Reed, D., Jiang, W. (eds.): Proceedings of IFIP International Conference on Network and Parallel Computing, Beijing, Lecture Notes in Computer Science. Springer-Verlag, Berlin Heidelberg New York (2005) accepted by NPC'05
5. Nicolau, A.: Run-Time Disambiguation: Coping with Statically Unpredictable Dependencies. IEEE Transactions on Computers 38 (1989) 663–678
6. Su, B., Hu, E. W., Najarian, J.: Technical Description of SPLIT – A Hardware/Software Combined Approach for Run-Time Pointer Aliasing Disambiguation. Tech. Rep. 108, Department of Computer Science, William Paterson University, NJ (1996)
7. Qiao, L., Tang, Z. Z., Wang, S. Y.: Control Strategies of Software Pipelining: Dealing with the Prologue and the Epilogue of Nested Loops. In: Zhou, X., Xu, M., Lou, S., Yang, X. (eds.): Proceedings of the 3rd Workshop on Advanced Parallel Processing Technologies, 19-21 Oct. 1999, Changsha, China. Publishing House of Electronics Industry, Beijing (1999) 177–181
8. Qiao, L.: On Data Dependencies in Software Pipelining. Doctorial Dissertation, Department of Computer Science, Tsinghua University, Beijing (2001)
9. Qiao, L., Zou, H. X., Wen, Q., Tang, Z. Z.: Exploiting Instruction-Level Parallelism for the FM^{M}let Transformation. In: Ip, H. S., Shi, Y. C., Zhang, X. J., (eds.): Proceedings of the 10th Joint International Computer Conference, 4-6 Nov. 2004, Kunming, China. International Academic Publishers, Word Publishing Corporation, Beijing (2004) 587–592

A Parallel and Distributed Method for Computing High Dimensional MOLAP*

Kongfa Hu[1,2], Ling Chen[1], Qi Gu[1], Bin Li[1], and Yisheng Dong[2]

[1] Department of Computer Science and Engineering, Yangzhou University
[2] Department of Computer Science and Engineering, Southeast University
kfhu@seu.edu.cn

Abstract. Data cube has been playing an essential role in fast OLAP(on-line analytical processing) in many multidimensional data warehouse. We often execute range queries on aggregate cube computed by pre-aggregate technique in MOLAP. For the cube with d dimensions, it can generate 2^d cuboids. But in a high-dimensional data warehouse (such as the applications of bioinformatics and statistical analysis, etc.), we build all these cuboids and their indices and full materialized the data cube impossibly. In this paper, we propose a multi-dimensional hierarchical fragmentation of the fact table based on dimension hierarchical encoding. This method partition the high dimensional data cube into shell mini-cubes. Using dimension hierarchical encoding and pre-aggregated results, OLAP queries are computed online by dynamically constructing cuboids from the fragment data cubes. Such an approach permits a significant reduction of processing and I/O overhead for many queries by restricting the number of fragments to be processed for both the fact table and bitmap encoding data. This method also supports parallel I/O and parallel processing as well as load balancing for disks and processors. We have compared the methods of our parallel method with the other existed ones such as partial cube by experiment. The analytical and experimental results show that the method of our parallel method proposed in this paper is more efficient than the other existed ones.

1 Introduction

Data warehouses integrate massive amounts of data from multiple sources and are primarily used for decision support purposes. They have to process complex analytical queries for different access forms such as OLAP, data mining, OLAM(on-line analytical mining) etc. Since the advent of data warehousing and online analytical processing (OLAP) [1], data cube has been playing an essential role in the implementation of fast OLAP operations [2]. Materialization of a data cube is a way to pre-compute and store multi-dimensional aggregates so that multi-dimensional analysis can be performed on the fly. For this task, there have been many efficient cube

---

* The research in the paper is supported by the National Natural Science Foundation of China under Grant No. 60473012; the Natural Science Foundation of Jiangsu Province under Grant No. BK2005047, BK2004052 and BK2005046; the National Tenth-Five High Technology Key Project of China under Grant No. 2003BA614A; the Tenth-Five High Technology Key Project of JiangSu Province of China under Grant No. BG2004034.

H. Jin, D. Reed, and W. Jiang (Eds.): NPC 2005, LNCS 3779, pp. 229–237, 2005.

computation algorithms proposed, such as ROLAP-based multi-dimensional aggregate computation [3], BUC [4], H-cubing [5], and Star-cubing [6]. Since computing the whole data cube not only requires a substantial amount of time but also generates a huge number of cube cells, there have also been many studies on partial materialization of data cubes [7], computation of condensed[8], dwarf[9], or quotient cubes [10], and computation of approximate cubes [11].

Besides large data warehouse applications, there are other kinds of applications like bioinformatics, statistical analysis, and text processing that need the OLAP data analysis. However, data in such applications usually are high in dimensionality, e.g., over 100 dimensions, and moderate size, e.g., around 10^6 tuples. This kind of datasets behaves rather differently from the datasets in a traditional data warehouse which may have about 10 dimensions but more than 10^9 tuples. Since a data cube grows exponentially with the number of dimensions, it is too costly in both computation time and storage space to materialize a full high-dimensional data cube. For example, a data cube of 100 dimensions, each with 10 distinct values, may contain as many as 11^{100} aggregate cells. If we consider the dimension hierarchies, the aggregate cell will increase by 2^h times. Although the adoption of iceberg cube[5,6], condensed cube[8], or approximate cube[11] delays the explosion, it does not solve the fundamental problem. No feasible data cube can be constructed with such data sets. In this paper we will address the problem of developing an efficient algorithm to perform OLAP on such data sets.

The paper focuses on the design and evaluation of suitable data allocation methods for the fact table and bitmap indices to allow an efficient parallel processing of OLAP queries. We propose a multi-dimensional hierarchical fragmentation of the fact table based on multiple dimension attributes and their dimension hierarchical encoding. Such an approach permits a significant reduction of processing and I/O overhead for many queries by restricting the number of fragments to be processed for both the fact table and bitmap data. Such savings are achieved not only for the fragmentation attributes themselves but also for attributes at different levels of a dimension hierarchy. The proposed data allocation and processing model also supports parallel I/O and parallel processing as well as load balancing for disks and processors.

2 Parallel Shell mini-Cubes

OLAP Queries tend to be complex and ad hoc, often requiring computationally expensive operations such as joins and aggregation. Those queries must be performed on tables having potentially millions of records. The OLAP query that accesses a large number of fact table tuples that are stored in no particular order might result to much more many I/Os, causing a prohibitive long response time. Due to the huge size of the fact table, such full scans are very costly and must be avoided whenever possible even when parallel scans can be utilized. This is also because for most queries, only a small fraction of the fact data is relevant. To illustrate the method ,a tiny database, Table 1, is used as a running example.

Table 1. A sample database with two measure values

TID	DimProduct			dimRegion			dimTime			Measure	
	Category	Class	Product	Country	Province	City	Year	Month	Day	Count	SaleNum
1	Office	OA	Computer	China	Jiangsu	Nanjing	1998	1	1	1	20
2	Office	OA	Computer	China	Jiangsu	Nanjing	1998	1	2	1	60
3	Office	OA	Computer	China	Jiangsu	Yangzhou	1998	1	2	1	40
4	Office	OA	Computer	China	Jiangsu	Yangzhou	1998	1	3	1	20
...	...	...	...	...	...	...	...	...	...	...	...
367	Office	OA	Computer	China	Jiangsu	Nanjing	1999	1	2	1	60
...	...	...	...	...	...	...	...	...	...	...	...

From the RPT Cube, we would compute eight cuboids:{(P,R,T),(P,R,All), (P,All,T),(All,R,T),(P,All,All), (All,R,All), (All,All,T), (All,All,All)}.To the cube of d dimensions, it would create 2^d cuboids (The P dimension in these cuboids would be {P, All},such as the R and T dimension .The aggregate cuboids is $\prod_{i=1}^{d} 2 = 2^d$).

For the cube with d dimensions $(D_1,D_2,...,D_d)$ and $|D_i|$ distinct values for each dimension D_i, it can generate 2^d cuboids and $\prod_{i=1}^{d}(|D_i|+1)$ cells. If we consider the dimension hierarchies of each dimension, the cube would generate cuboids $\prod_{i=1}^{d}(h_i+1)$ and $\prod_{i}^{d}\prod_{j=1}^{h_i}(|L_j^i|+1)$ cells. (where h_i is the dimension hierarchy levels of the dimension D_i, $|L_j^i|$ is he max number of the distinct member of the hierarchy L_j^i).

For example, the RPT cube in figure 1 has three dimensions: *DimProduct, DimRegion* and *DimTime*. The *DimProduct* dimension has three hierarchies as (*Category,Class,Product*),the *DimRegion* dimension has three hierarchies as (*Country,Province,City*),and the *DimTime* dimension has three hierarchies as (*Year,Month,Day*). Thus this cube would generate $\prod_{i=1}^{d}(h_i+1)=(3+1)*(3+1)*(3+1)=64$ cuboids such as {(*Product,City,Day*),(*Product,City,Month*),(*Product,City,Year*), (*Product,City,All*),...,(*All,All,All*)}.But in a high-dimensional database with many cuboids, it might not be practical to build all these cuboids and their indices. Furthermore, reading via an index implies random access for each row in the cuboid, which could turn out to be more expensive than a sequential scan of the raw data.

A partial solution, which has been implemented in some commercial data warehouse systems is to compute a thin cube shell. For example, one might compute all cuboids with 3 dimensions or less in a 30-dimensional data cube. There are two disadvantages to this approach. First, it still needs to compute $C_{30}^3 + C_{30}^2 + C_{30}^1 = 4525$ cuboids. Second, it does not support OLAP in a large portion of the high-dimensional cube space. If we consider the dimension hierarchies, the cuboids is vary much. So we can use the shell mini-Cubes.

For example, for a database of 30 dimensions, D_1, D_2, ..., D_{30}, we first partition the 30 dimensions into 10 fragments(mini-Cubes) of size 3: (D_1,D_2,D_3), (D_4,D_5,D_6), ... , (D_{28},D_{29},D_{30}). For each fragment, we compute its full data cube while recording the inverted indices. For example, in fragment mini-Cube (D_1,D_2,D_3), we would compute eight cuboids: $\{(D_1,D_2,D_3),(D_1,D_2,All),(D_1,All,D_3),(All,D_2,D_3),(D_1,All,All), (All,D_2,All),(All,All,D_3),(All,All,All)\}$. An inverted encoding index is retained for each cell in the cuboids.

The benefit of this method can be seen by a simple calculation. For a base cuboid of 30 dimensions, there are only 8*10 = 80 cuboids to be computed according to the above shell fragment partition. Comparing this to 4525 cuboids for the cube shell of size 3, the saving is enormous.

As we will see, our multi-dimensional fragmentation permits eliminating some bitmaps, thus improving storage and access overhead. We propose this novel hierarchical encoding on each dimension table. The encoding is implemented through the assignment of a special surrogate key on each dimension table tuple, called dimension hierarchical encoding.We can create the *dimRegion*, *DimTime* and *dimProduct* dimension hierarchy encoding shown in Table 2, Table 3 and Table 4.

Table 2. *DimTime* dimension hierarchy encoding

TimeID	Year	Month	Day	B^{TimeID}
	yyy	mmmm	ddddd	yyymmmmddddd
1	98	Jan	1	001000100001
2	98	Jan	2	001000100010
3	98	Jan	3	001000100011
...	...	...	...	...

Table 3. The *dimRegion* dimension hierarchy encoding

RegionID	Country	Province	City	$B^{RegionID}$
	uuuuuuu	vvvvv	cccc	uuuuuuuvvvvvcccc
1	China	Jiangsu	Nanjing	0000001000010001
2	China	Jiangsu	Yangzhou	0000001000010010
...	...	...	...	...

Table 4. The *dimProduct* dimension hierarchy encoding

ProductID	Category	Class	Product	$B^{ProductID}$
	gggg	aaaaa	ppppppp	ggggaaaaappppppp
1	Office	OA	Computer	0001000010000001
2	Office	OA	Printer	0001000010000010
...	...	...	...	...

By using dimension hierarchical encoding, we can register a list of tuples IDs (tids) associated with the dimension members for each dimension. For example, the TID list associated with the *dimProduct* , *dimRegion* and *dimTime* dimension are shown in Table 5, Table 6 and Table 7 in turn. To compute a data cube for this database with the measure avg() (obtained by sum()/count()), we need to have a tid-list for each cell: $\{tid_1, \ldots, tid_n\}$. Because each tid is uniquely associated with a particular set of measure values, all future computations just need to fetch the measure values associated with the tuples in the list. In other words, by keeping an array of the ID-measures in memory for online processing, one can handle any complex measure computation. Table 8 shows what exactly should be kept, which is substantially smaller than the database itself.

Table 5. *dimProduct* dimension TID

$B^{ProductID}$	TID List
0001000010000001	1-2-3-4-367
...	...

Table 6. *dimRegion* dimension TID

$B^{RegionID}$	TID List
0000001000010001	1-2-367
0000001000010010	3-4
...	...

Table 7. *dimTime* dimension TID

B^{TimeID}	TID List
001000100001	1
001000100010	2-3
001000100011	4
...	...

Table 8. TID- measure array of Table 2

tid	Count	SaleNum
1	1	20
2	1	60
3	1	40
4	1	20
...	...	...

In our study , the method can rapidly retrieve the matching dimension member hierarchical encoding and evaluate the set of query ranges for each dimension and improve the efficiency of OLAP queries by using dimension hierarchical path prefix and encoding prefix.

By using encoding prefix, we can register the dimension hierarchy encoding and its TID list for every dimension hierarchy for each dimension. For example, the dimension hierarchy encoding and its TID list associated with the dimension hierarchies *Month* and *Province* are shown in Table 9 , and so on.

For each fragment, we compute the complete data cube by intersecting the TID-lists in the dimension and its hierarchies in a bottom-up depths-first order in the cuboid lattice (as seen in [6]). For example, to compute the cell {0001000010000001, 0000001000010001, 0010001}, we intersect the TID lists of $B^{ProductID}$ =0001000010000001, $B^{RegionID}$ =0000001000010001, and $Bprefix(B^{TimeID}, Month)$= 0010001 to get a new list of {1,2}.

Table 9. *Month* hierarchy encoding *Prefix* AND its TID

B^{TimeID}	Bprefix(B^{TimeID},Month)	TID List
001000100001		
001000100010	0010001	1-2-3-4
001000100011		
...	...	...
010000100001	0100001	367
...	...	...

3 Parallel and Distributed MOLAP Aggregation Algorithm

The data cube can be distributed across a set of parallel computers by parallel constructing the segment Cubes. Therefore, for the end-user and other potential applications, we consider this data cube as one large virtual cube, which is distributed across a set of parallel computers, which manage the creation, updates and querying of the associated cube portions. To develop appropriate scheduling mechanisms for these management tasks, we consider that the virtual cube is split into several smaller parts, called mini-Cube segments. But a mini-Cube segment could furthermore also be split into smaller segments and so on, till we achieve the level of chunks. They can then be assigned to parallel computers, having sequential or parallel computing power, which are responsible for their management. The algorithm for shell cube segment parallel computation can be summarized as follows.

Algorithm 1 (Parallel Shell mini-Cube Computation)
Input: A base cuboid BC of n dimensions:$(D_1; ... ;D_n)$.
   { partition the set of dimensions :$(D_1; ... ;D_n)$ into a set of k mini-Cube fragments
     $\{P_1;..., P_k\}$;
   scan base cuboid BC once and do the following with parallel processing
    { insert each <tid, measure> into ID-measure array;
      for each attribute value a_i of each dimension D_i;
        build an dimension hierarchy encoding index entry: <B; TID list>;}
     parallel processing all fragment partition P_i as follows
        {build a local fragment mini-cubes MC_i by intersecting their corresponding tid-lists and computing their measures;
        build MC_i's aggregate cuboids by the cuboid lattice;}

We can parallel construct the high dimensional cube with the Cube segments parallel construction. The system architecture of these shell mini-Cube segment parallel construction is shown in Figure 2.

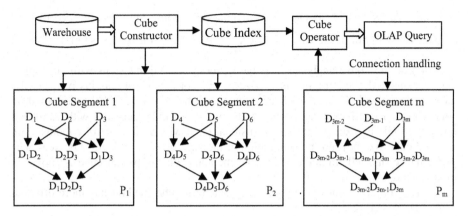

Fig. 2. The system architecture of these shell Cube segment parallel construction

4   Performance Analysis

The bitmap encoding index table uses the same amount of storage space as the original database. Since we have |T| tuple IDs in total, the entire inverted index will still only need $d\times|T|$ bitmap encoding indices. The amount of memory needed to store the

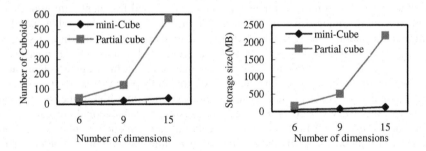

Fig. 3. Cuboids of mini-Cube   **Fig. 4.** Storage size of mini-Cube

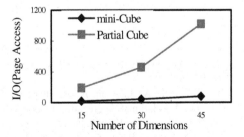

Fig. 5. Average I/Os

shell mini-cubes of size f is $O(|T|*(2^f*d/f))$,but the amount of storage needed to store partial cube with f dimensions is $O(|T|*(\sum_{i=1}^{f} C_d^i))$,and the full cube's is $O(|T|*(2^d))$.

Based on the above analysis, for a base cuboid of 30 dimensions with 10^6 tuples, our precomputed shell fragments of size 3 will consist of 80 cuboids plus one ID measure array, with the total estimated size of roughly $320 + 12 = 332$ MB in total. In comparison, a shell cube of size 3 will consist of 4525 cuboids, with estimated roughly 18 GB in size. A full 30-dimensional cube will have $2^{30}= 10^9$ cuboids, with the total cube size beyond the summation of the capacities of all storage devices. The performance of shell fragment mini-cube method with the partial cube is shown in Figure 3- Figure 5.

Figure 3-Figure 5 show the shell fragment mini-cube method has more efficient than other existed ones.

5 Conclusion

Data cube has been playing an essential role in fast OLAP in many multidimensional data warehouse. We often execute range queries on aggregate cube computed by pre-aggregate technique in MOLAP. For the cube with d dimensions, it can generate 2^d cuboids. But in a high-dimensional data warehouse(such as the applications of bioinformatics and statistical analysis, etc.), while full materialization of the data cube is impossible, we have proposed a reasonable method to partition the high dimensional cube into a set of disjoint low dimensional cubes (i.e., shell fragment mini-cubes). We propose a multi-dimensional hierarchical fragmentation of the fact table based on multiple dimension attributes and their dimension hierarchical encoding. Using inverted hierarchical encoding indices and pre-aggregated results, OLAP queries are computed online by dynamically constructing cuboids from the fragment data cubes. With this method, for high-dimensional OLAP, the total space that needs to store such shell-fragment mini-cubes is negligible in comparison with a high-dimensional cube. Moreover, the query I/O costs for large data sets are reasonable and are comparable with reading answers from a materialized data cube, when such a cube is available. We have compared the methods of parallel shell mini-cubes with the other existed ones such as partial cube by experiment. The analytical and experimental results show that the methods of our parallel shell mini-cubes proposed in this paper are more efficient than the other existed ones.

References

1. Chaudhuri, U., Dayal, U.: Data Warehousing and OLAP for Decision Support. ACM SIGMOD Record 26 (1997) 507-508
2. Gray, J., Chaudhuri, S., Bosworth, A., Layman, A., Reichart, D., Venkatrao, M., Pellow F., Pirahesh, H.: Data Cube: A Relational Aggregation Operator Generalizing Group-by, Cross-tab and Subtotals. Data Mining and Knowledge Discovery 1(1997)29-54
3. Agarwal, S., Agrawal, R., Deshpande, P. M., Gupta, A., Naughton, J. F., Ramakrishnan, R., Sarawagi, S.: On the Computation of Multidimensional Aggregates. VLDB(1996) 506-521

4. Beyer, K., Ramakrishnan, R.: Bottom-up Computation of Sparse and Iceberg Cubes. ACM SIDMOD (1999) 359-370
5. Han, J., Pei, J., Dong, G., Wang, K.: Efficient Computation of Iceberg Cubes with Complex Measures. ACM SIGMOD (2001)1-12
6. Xin, D., Han, J., Li, X., Wah, B. W.: Star-cubing:Computing Iceberg Cubes by Top-down and Bottom-up Integration. VLDB(2003) 476-487
7. Harinarayan, V., Rajaraman, A., Ullman, J. D.: Implementing Data Cubes Efficiently. ACM SIGMOD (1996) 205-216
8. Wang, W., Lu, H., Feng, J., Yu, J. X.: Condensed Cube: An Effective Approach to Reducing Data Cube Size. ICDE(2002) 155-165
9. Sismanis, Y. , deligiannakis, A., Kotidis, Y., Roussopoulos, N.: Hierarchical Dwarfs for the Rollup Cube.VLDB(2004) 540-551
10. Lakshmanan, L. V. S., Pei, J., Zhao, Y.: Q-trees: An Efficient Summary Structure for Semantic OLAP. ACM SIGMOD(2003) 64-75
11. Shanmugasundaram, J., Fayyad, U. M., Bradley, P. S.: Compressed Data Cubes for OLAP Aggregate Query Approximation on Continuous Dimensions. ACM SIGKDD(1999) 223-232

An Improved ACO Algorithm
for Multicast Routing

Ziqiang Wang and Dexian Zhang

School of Information Science and Engineering, Henan University of Technology,
Zheng Zhou 450052,China
wzqagent@xinhuanet.com

Abstract. The multicast routing problem with quality of service (QoS) constraints is a key requirement of computer networks supporting multimedia applications. In order to resolve Qos multicast routing effectively and efficiently, an improved ant colony optimization (ACO) algorithm is proposed to resolve this problem.The core idea of improved ACO algorithm is mainly realized through pheromone local and global updating rule.Experimental results show that this algorithm can find optimal solution quickly and has a good scalability.

1 Introduction

As a result of the emergence of many kinds of high-speed communication systems, such as ATM, and increasing demands of distributed multimedia applications, such as video on demand, multimedia conference, efficient and effective support of quality of service (QoS) has become more and more essential, these multimedia applications all require multicast support. Multicast employs a tree structure of the network to efficiently deliver the same data stream to a group of receivers. In multicast routing, one or more constraints must be applied to the entire tree. Multicast service is becoming a key requirement of computer networks supporting multimedia applications. In the past, the multicast routing problem has been formulated as the minimum cost multicast tree problem[1], i.e., the Steiner tree problem, which is well-known to be NP-complete[2].Over the past decades, many works have done to solve multicast routing problems using conventional algorithm, such as exhaustive search routing and greedy routing. But due to the high degree of complexity, it is not practical to use these algorithms in real-time multicast routing. Recently, some nature-based algorithms[3] have been proposed. but these algorithms too complex and lower the efficiency of the algorithm.

Ant Colony Optimization (ACO) algorithm is a novel population-based metaheuristic search algorithm[4] for solving difficult discrete optimization problems, inspired by the foraging behavior of real ant colonies. It has been applied to TSP, QAP, scheduling and graph coloring, etc. In this paper, we develop an efficient heuristic ant colony algorithm for multicast routing. This paper is organized as

H. Jin, D. Reed, and W. Jiang (Eds.): NPC 2005, LNCS 3779, pp. 238–244, 2005.

follows: The multicast routing model is described in section 2.The ACO algorithm are analyzed in section 3.The multicast routing algorithm based on ACO algorithm are presented in section 4. Experimental results are given in section 5. Conclusions and future works are presented in section 6.

2   Multicast Routing Model

Communication network can be modeled as an undirected graph $G =< V, E >$, where V is a finite set of vertices (network nodes) and E is the set of edges (network links) representing connection of these vertices.Each link in G has three weights $(B(x,y), D(x,y), C(x,y))$ associated with it, in which positive real values $B(x,y), D(x,y), C(x,y)$, denote the available bandwidth, the delay and the cost of the link respectively. Given a path $P(x,y)$ connected any two nodes x, y in G, it can be presumed that:

1)The delay of a path is the sum of the delays of the links $(a, b) \in P(x,y)$:

$$Delay(P(x,y)) = \sum D(a,b) \tag{1}$$

2)The available bandwidth of $(a, b) \in P(x,y)$ is considered as the bottle neck bandwidth of $P(x,y)$:

$$Width(P(x,y)) = min(B(a,b)) \tag{2}$$

In Qos transmission of real time multimedia service, the optimal cost routing problem with delay and bandwidth constrained can be described as follows.Given $G =< V, E >$, a source node s, and a multicast member set $M \subseteq V - \{s\}$,the problem is to find the multicast tree $T = (V_T, V_E)$ from source s to all destinations $v \in M$ and T must satisfy the following conditions:

$$Cost(T) = min(\sum_{(x,y) \in (E_T)} C(x,y)) \tag{3}$$

$$\sum_{(x,y) \in (E_T)} D(x,y) \le D_{max}, \forall v \in M \tag{4}$$

$$Width(P_T(s,v)) \ge W_{min}, \forall v \in M \tag{5}$$

where $P_T(s, v)$ is the set of links in the path from source nodes s to destination v in the multicast tree.Relation (3) means that the cost of multicast routing tree should be minimum. Relation (4) means that the delay requirement of Qos, in which D_{max} is the permitted maximum delay value of real time services. And relation (5) guarantees the bandwidth of communication traffic, in which W_{min} is the required minimum bandwidth of all applications.

3   The Ant Colony Optimization(ACO) Algorithm

3.1   The Ant System

The Ant Colony Optimization(ACO) technique[5] has emerged recently as a new meta-heuristic search methods for hard combinatorial optimization problems. ACO algorithms have been inspired by the behavior of real ant colonies, in particular, by their foraging behavior. Real ants communicate with each other using an chemical substance called pheromone, which they leave on the paths they traverse. In the absence of pheromone trails ants more or less performance a random walk. However, as soon as they sense a pheromone trail on a path in their vicinity, they are likely to follow that path, thus reinforcing this rail. More specifically, if ants at some point sense more than one pheromone trail, they will choose one of these trails with a probability related to the strengths of the existing trails. This idea has first been applied to the TSP, where an ant located in a city choose the next city according to the strength of the artificial trails.

3.2   The ACO Algorithm Description

Informally, the ACO algorithm works as follows: m ants are randomly positioned on n cities. Each ant builds a tour path (i.e.,a feasible solution to the TSP) by repeatedly applying a state transition rule. While constructing its tour, an ant also modifies the amount of pheromone on the visited edges by applying the local updating rule. Once all ants have finished their tours, the amount of pheromone on edges is modified again by applying the global updating rule. In the following, we firstly describe the ACO algorithm procedure, then we discuss the core steps of ACO algorithm: the state transition rule, the global updating rule, and the local updating rule.

Algorithm 1. The ACO Algorithm.
   Initialize;
   Loop;
   Each ant is positioned on a starting node;
   Loop;
   Each ant applies a state transition rule to incrementally build a solution;
   And a local pheromone updating rule ;
   Until all ants have built a complete solution;
   A global pheromone updating rule is applied ;
   Until End condition.

3.3   State Transition Rule

While building a tour, ant k situated in city r moves to city s using the follow state transition rule:

$$s = \begin{cases} arg\,max_{u \in J_k(r)}\{[\tau(r,u)] \cdot [\eta(r,u)]^\beta\} : q \leq q_0 \\ S : \qquad\qquad\qquad\qquad\qquad\qquad otherwise \end{cases} \qquad (6)$$

where $J_k(r)$ is the set of cities not visited by ant k, $\tau(r, u)$ is the amount of pheromone trail on edge, $\eta(r, u)]$ is a heuristic function which is the inverse of distance between city r and u, β is a parameter which determines the relative importance of pheromone versus distance, q is a random number uniformly distributed in [0,1], q_0 is a parameter $(0 \le q_0 \le 1)$,and S is a random variable selected according to the probability distribution given by Equation (7) which gives the probability with which an ant k in city r choose the city s to move to:

$$p_k(r, s) = \begin{cases} \frac{[\tau(r,u)] \cdot [\eta(r,u)]^\beta}{\sum\limits_{u \in J_k(r)} \tau(r,u)] \cdot [\eta(r,u)]^\beta} : S \in J_k(r) \\ 0 : \qquad\qquad otherwise \end{cases} \tag{7}$$

3.4   Local Updating Rule

While building a solution of the TSP, ants visit edges and change their amount of pheromone trail by applying the local updating rule of Equation (8):

$$\tau(r, s) \leftarrow (1 - \rho) \cdot \tau(r, s) + \rho \cdot \tau_0 \tag{8}$$

where $\rho(0 < \rho < 1)$ is the pheromone decay parameter, τ_0 is an initial pheromone level.

3.5   Global Updating Rule

Global updating rule is performed after all ants have completed their tours. The pheromone level is updated by applying global updating rule of Equation(9).

$$\tau(r, s) \leftarrow (1 - \alpha) \cdot \tau(r, s) + \alpha \cdot \Delta_k \tau(r, s) \tag{9}$$

where $\alpha(0 < \alpha < 1)$ is the pheromone decay parameter,

$$\Delta_k \tau(r, s) = \begin{cases} (L_{gb})^{-1} : (r, s) \in global\_best\_tour \\ 0 : \qquad otherwise \end{cases} \tag{10}$$

and L_{gb} is the length of global best tour from the beginning of the trail. Equation (9) indicates that only those edges that belong to the global best tour will receive reinforcement.

4   The ACO Algorithm For Multicast Routing

The proposed ACO algorithm steps for multicast routing are as follows:

Step 1: Initialize network nodes;
Set $NC:=0$; $\tau_0:=c$;
Put m ants to the source node;

Step 2: Check bandwidth of all edges, deletes those edges that do not satisfy the bandwidth require;

Step 3: Setup tabu table;
Set $r:=1$;
For $k:=1$ to m
Put the value of source node into tabu table $tab_k(r)$;

Step 4: Repeat this step until the tabu table $tab_k(r)$ is full;
Set $r:=r+1$;
For $k:=1$ to m
Random choose q and compare with q_0;
If $q \leq q_0$
Then choose the next node s according to

$$s := arg \max_{u \in J_k(r)} \{[\tau(r,u)] \cdot [\eta(r,u)]^{\beta}\} \tag{11}$$

Else choose the node s according to the probability distribution given by Equation (7).
Compute the delay to reach node s, and compare the result with delay D_{max};
If the result exceeds the constraints D_{max}
Then the kth ant choose a new node;
Else
{
The kth ant moves to node s, and put s into $tab_k(r)$;
Pheromone local updating according to

$$\tau(r,s) := (1-\rho) \cdot \tau(r,s) + \rho \cdot \tau_0 \tag{12}$$

}

Step 5: Compute $\Delta_k \tau(r,s)$ and pheromone global updating;
For $k:=1$ to m set

$$\Delta_k \tau(r,s) := \begin{cases} (L_{gb})^{-1} : (r,s) \in global\_best\_tour \\ 0 : \qquad otherwise \end{cases} \tag{13}$$

$$\tau(r,s) := (1-\alpha) \cdot \tau(r,s) + \alpha \cdot \Delta_k \tau(r,s) \tag{14}$$

$NC:=NC+1$;

Step6: Check stop condition;
If $(NC < NC_{max})$
Then empty all tabu table, and goto Step3;
Else Print the minimum cost multicast tree.

5   Experimental Results

We have performed simulation to investigate the performances of multicast routing algorithms based on ACO algorithm. A random generator developed by

Table 1. CPU Time of ACO Algorithm

Nodes	Edges	Time(s)
20	32	0.27
40	89	0.45
80	172	1.42
120	239	2.68
160	336	5.37
180	371	8.19
200	427	9.73

Salama[2] is used to create links interconnecting the nodes. The random graphs are generated using the above graph generator with an average degree 4,which have the appearance roughly resembling that of geographical maps of major nodes in the Internet .The source and the destination are randomly generated. D_t for destination t is uniformly distributed in range [30ms,160ms].The bandwidth and delay of each link are uniformly distributed in range [10,50]and [0,50ms] respectively. The cost of each link is uniformly distributed in range [0,200]. In Table 1, we have compared the CPU times of ACO algorithm for different combinations of node and edge.

Table 2. Predictive Accuracy Comparison

Algorithm	Optimal Solutions	Sub-optimal Solutions	Invalid Solutions
HNN	75.6%	21.5%	2.9%
GA	78.4%	19.4%	2.2%
IA	78.9%	19.6%	1.5%
ACO	79.9%	18.2%	1.9%

Table1 results clearly show that the running time of ACO algorithm grows very slowly with the size of the network. Therefore, our algorithm is very effective.

Furthermore, for the same multicast routing, we made 300 simulations by ACO algorithm against Hopfield Neural Networks(HNN)[6],GA[7] and immune algorithm(IA)[8]. The computation results are shown in Table 2.We can find that ACO algorithm performances better than HNN,GA and IA. So our proposed algorithm has good performance.

6   Conclusions

Multicast routing arises in many multimedia communication applications, and this problem has been proved to be NP-Complete. In this paper, we studied the bandwidth-delay-constrained least-cost multicast routing problem, and present an ACO algorithm to solve the problem. The simulation results show that this

algorithm is an efficient algorithm. For further research, we will improve the ef-
fectives of ACO algorithm and study the multicast routing problem with general
constraint.

References

1. Wang,Z.,Crowcroft,J.:Quality of service for supporting multimedia applica-
   tions.IEEE Journal on Selected Areas in Communications.14(1996)1228–1234
2. Salama,H.F.,Reeves,D.S.,Viniotis, Y.:Evaluation of multicast routing algorithms for
   real-time communication on high-speed networks. IEEE Journal on Selected Areas
   in Communications. 15(1997)332–345
3. Wang,Z.,Shi,B.:Solution to Qos multicast routing problem based on heuristic genetic
   algorithm. Journal of Computer.24(2001)55–61
4. Dorigo,M.,Maniezzo,V. and Colomi A.:The ant system: optimization by a colony of
   cooperation agents. IEEE Transaction on System, Man, and Cybernetics-Part B.
   26(1996)1–13
5. Dorigo,M.,Gambardella, L.M.: Ant colony system:a cooperative learning approach to the traveling salesman problem.IEEE Transaction on Evolutionary
   Computation.1(1997)53–66
6. Chotipat,P.,Goutam,C.,Norio S.:Neural network approach to multicast routing algorithms for real-time communication on high-speed networks.IEEE Journal on Selected Areas in Communications.15(1997)332–345
7. Feng,X.,Li,J.Z.,Wang J.V.,et al.:Qos routing based on genetic algorithm. Computer
   communication.22(1999)1392–1399
8. Liu,F.,Feng,X.J.:Immune algorithm for multicast routing.Chinese Journal of
   Computer.26(2003)676–681

Performance Modelling of Pipelined Circuit Switching in Torus with Hot Spot Traffic*

F. Safaei[1], A. Khonsari[1], M. Fathy[2], and M. Ould-Khaoua[3]

[1] Institute for Studies in Theoretical Physics and Mathematics (I.P.M.)
[2] Dept. of Computer Engineering, Iran Univ. of Science and Technology, Tehran, Iran
[3] Dept. of Computing Science, University of Glasgow, UK
{safaei, ak}@ipm.ir, mahfathy@iust.ac.ir, mohamed@dcs.gla.ac.uk

Abstract. This paper proposes a new analytical model of PCS in torus in the presence of hot spot traffic pattern. Results from simulation experiments show close agreement with those predicted by the analytical model.

1 Introduction

Gaughan and Yalamanchili [1] have proposed PCS that combines aspects of *Circuit Switching* (CS) and *Wormhole Switching*. When a message header encounters blocking and cannot progress towards its destination, it releases the last reserved channel by backtracking to the previous node, and then continues its search from that node to find an alternative path. Recent studies [2, 3] have revealed that the performance advantages of adaptive routing are more noticeable when traffic is non-uniform due to the presence of hot spots [4]. This paper proposes a new analytical model of PCS for computing the average message latency in the presence of hot spot traffic in torus.

2 The Analytical Model

PCS and the router structure are discussed in detail in [1, 3]. The model is based on the following assumptions.

i) The traffic model is based on Pfister and Norton approach [4]. In their method, each generated message has a finite probability θ of being directed to the hot spot node and probability $(1-\theta)$ of being directed to other network nodes. We usually refer to these types of messages as *hot spot* and *regular*, respectively.

ii) Nodes generate traffic independently of each other, which follows a Poisson process with a mean arrival rate of λ_g messages per node per cycle including regular and hot spot fractions, $\theta \lambda_g$ and $(1-\theta \lambda_g)$, respectively. Message length is M flits, each of which requires one cycle to cross from one node to the next.

iii) L virtual channels $(L{\geq}1)$ are used per physical channel.

---

* This research was in part supported by a grant from I.P.M. (No. CS1384-3-01).

H. Jin, D. Reed, and W. Jiang (Eds.): NPC 2005, LNCS 3779, pp. 245–248, 2005.

The average message latency is composed of the average network latency, $\overline{T}$, and the average waiting time seen by a message at the source node, $\overline{W}$. However, to capture the effects of virtual channels multiplexing, the average message latency has to be scaled by a factor, $\overline{L}$, representing the average degree of virtual channels multiplexing that takes place at a given physical channel. Therefore, we can write [2]

$$Latency = (\overline{T} + \overline{W})\overline{L} \quad where \quad \overline{T} = (1-\theta)\overline{T_r} + \theta\,\overline{T_\theta} \tag{1}$$

In the above equation, $\overline{T_r}$ and $\overline{T_\theta}$ denote the average network latency for regular and hot spot messages, respectively. The average number of hops that a regular message makes across one dimension and across the network, $\overline{k}$ and $\overline{d_r}$ respectively, are [3]

$$\overline{k} = (k-1)/2 \quad , \quad \overline{d_r} = 2\overline{k} \tag{2}$$

Since each regular message travels, on average, $\overline{d_r}$ hops to cross the network, the rate of regular messages received by each channel, λ_r, can be written as

$$\lambda_r = (1-\theta)\lambda_g \overline{d_r}/2 = (1-\theta)\lambda_g \overline{c_r}/4 \tag{3}$$

Where, $\overline{c_r}$ is the average time needed to setup a path for a regular r-hop header. The number of source nodes for which one of $2N_{j-1}$ channels can act as intermediate channel to reach the hot spot node is given by [2]

$$N - \sum_{r=0}^{j-1} N_r = \sum_{r=j}^{2(k-1)} N_r \quad ; \quad N_r = 0 \quad if\ r > 2k-2, N_r = \begin{cases} r+1 & r < k \\ 2k-r-1 & k \le r \le 2k-2 \end{cases} \tag{4}$$

The overall traffic rate, on the channel located j hops from the hot spot node, is

$$\lambda_j = \lambda_r + \lambda_{\theta_j} \quad where \quad \lambda_{\theta_j} = (\theta\lambda_g \sum_{r=j}^{2(k-1)} N_r)/(2N_{j-1}) \tag{5}$$

In the above equation, each node generates, on average, $\theta\,\lambda_g$ hot spot messages in a cycle, and λ_{θ_j} is the rate of hot spot traffic on a channel located j hops away from hot spot node. In PCS, the network latency of an r-hop regular message can be written as

$$\overline{T_r} = M + r + \overline{c_r} \tag{6}$$

The latency seen by a hot spot message that is j hops a way from the hot spot node is

$$\overline{T_{\theta_j}} = M + j + \overline{c_\theta} \tag{7}$$

Where, $\overline{c_\theta}$ is the average time needed to setup a path for a hot spot message header. When a regular (or hot spot) message reaches a channel that is j hops away from the hot spot node, the mean service time at the channel, considering both regular and hot spot message with their appropriate weights, can be written as

$$\overline{T_j} = (\lambda_c/\lambda_j)\overline{T_r} + (\lambda_{\theta_j}/\lambda_j)\overline{T_{\theta_j}} \tag{8}$$

Finally, by averaging all possible values of $\bar{c}_r$ and $\bar{c}_\theta$ yields the overall average time to set up a path, $\bar{c}$, is given by

$$\bar{c} = (1 - \theta)\bar{c}_r + \theta\, \bar{c}_\theta \qquad (9)$$

The average network latency seen by a hot spot message can be written as

$$\bar{T}_\theta = \sum_{j=1}^{2(k-1)} p_{\theta_j} \bar{T}_{\theta_j} \quad where \; p_{\theta_j} = N_j / (N - 1) \qquad (10)$$

We model the header behaviour as a Random Walk problem [3]. $\bar{c}_j$ which is the average time interval to reach the destination, satisfies the following equation

$$\bar{c}_j = 0 \;\; if \; j = r \;\; otherwise \quad \bar{c}_j = \begin{cases} (1 - pb_0)(c_1 + 1) + pb_0 \bar{c}_0 & j = 0 \\ (1 - pb_j)\bar{c}_{j+1} + pb_j \bar{c}_{j-1} + 1 & 1 \le j \le r-1 \end{cases} \qquad (11)$$

The average time to setup a path for an r-hop regular message and the time is needed to setup a reserved path for hot spot message that is j hops away $(1 \le j \le 2(k-1))$ from the hot spot node are given by

$$\bar{c}_r = \bar{c}_0 + r \quad , \bar{c}_{\theta\, j} = \bar{c}_0 + j \qquad (12)$$

The probability of blocking, can therefore written as

$$pb_j = pass_j^0 \cdot (P_L)^2 + pass_j^1 \cdot P_L \quad ; pass_j^0 = (1 - \bar{k})^2 , pass_j^1 = 2(1 - \bar{k}) / \bar{k} \qquad (13)$$

Where $pass_j^0$ and $pass_j^1$ are the probability that a message has to visit one dimension and the probability that it still has to visit both dimensions, respectively. To determine the average time, $\bar{W}$, that a message sees in the source node before entering into the network, the injection channel is treated as an M/G/1 queue with a mean time waiting of [2]

$$\bar{W} = \rho\bar{T}(1 + C_{\bar{T}}^2) / (2(1 - \rho)) \;\; , \;\; \rho = \lambda_g \bar{T} \;\; , \;\; C_{\bar{T}}^2 = \sigma_{\bar{T}}^2 / \bar{T}^2 \qquad (14)$$

Where $\sigma_{\bar{T}}^2$ is the variance of the service distribution. The average arrival rate on each virtual channel is λ_g / L and service time, $\bar{T}$, with an approximated variance $(\bar{T} - M - 3\bar{d} + 1)^2$ yields the mean waiting time as

$$\bar{W} = \bar{T}^2 (\lambda_g / L)[1 + (\bar{T} - M - 3\bar{d} + 1)^2 / \bar{T}^2] / (2[1 - \bar{T}(\lambda_g / L)]) \qquad (15)$$

The probability, P_{l_j}, that l virtual channels are busy at the physical channel that is j hops away from the hot spot node, can be determined as follows

$$P_{l_j} = (1 - \lambda_j \overline{T_j})(\lambda_j \overline{T_j})^l \quad if \quad 0 \le l < L \quad otherwise \quad P_{l_j} = (\lambda_j \overline{T_j})^l \qquad l = L \qquad (16)$$

And the average multiplexing rate through the network is

$$\overline{L} = \sum_{j=1}^{2(k-1)} p_{\theta_j} \overline{L}_j \quad where \quad \overline{L}_j = \sum_{l=1}^{L} l^2 P_{l_j} \Big/ \sum_{l=1}^{L} l P_{l_j} \qquad (17)$$

Fig. 1 shows the latency results predicted by the model against those provided by the simulator for Network size $N = 8\times8$ torus, Message length is $M=32$ and 64 flits, number of virtual channels $L= 6$, and fractions of hot spot traffic is $\theta=0.05$ and 0.2.

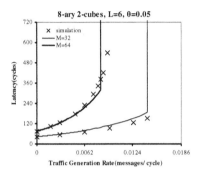 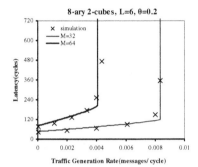

Fig. 1. Average message latency calculated by model vs. simulation

3 Conclusions

In this paper we proposed a new analytical model to compute the average message latency of PCS in two-dimensional torus in the presence of hot spot traffic. Simulation experiments have revealed that the results predicted by the model are in good agreement with those obtained through simulations under different working conditions.

References

1. P.Gaughan, S. Yalamanchili, "A family of fault-tolerant routing protocols for direct multiprocessor networks", *IEEE TPDS,* 6(5): 482-497, 1995.
2. H. Sarbazi-Azad, L. Mackenzie, M. Ould-Khaoua, "Hot Spot Analysis in Wormhole-routed Tori", *IPCCC 2000. Conference proceeding of the IEEE International*, 337-343, 2000.
3. F. Safaei, A.. Khonsari, M. Fathy, M. Ould-Khaoua, "An analytical model of Pipelined Circuit Switching in hypercubes in the presence of hot spot traffic", *ICPP 2005 conference proceedindg of the IEEE international*, 485-492, June 2005.
4. G.J. Pfister, V.A. Norton, "Hot spot contention and combining in multistage interconnection networks", *IEEE Trans. Computers,* 34(10): 943-948, 1985.

An Incremental Compilation Approach for OpenMP Applications

Maurizio Giordano and Mario Mango Furnari

Istituto di Cibernetica "E. Caianiello" - C.N.R.,
Via Campi Flegrei 34, 80078 Pozzuoli, Naples - Italy
{m.giordano, m.mangofurnari}@cib.na.cnr.it

Abstract. This work presents a new approach to software development framework design for parallel programming: the *Graphical Parallelizing Environment*[1] (*GPE*). It adopts an incremental compilation process for OpenMP programming based on automatic detection of parallelism and user interaction for its calibration. GPE is extensible via plug-in modules providing new capabilities. It is an experimental OpenMP programming framework targeting shared-memory multiprocessors and clusters of PCs.

1 Introduction

In past years, several techniques were developed in the area of program automatic parallelization, like *data and control dependence analysis* [1], *symbolic and interprocedural analysis* [3,4]. Several research projects [5,6] dealt with the development of parallelizing compilers implementing most of these techniques.

Multithreaded applications, that were specifically targeted to shared-memory, may now use Software DSM to run in distributed settings. There are proposals [8,9] to adopt a single programming paradigm, like OpenMP, independently from where the application will run, that is a multiprocessor, SMP or a cluster.

In this context, a pure automatic compiler-based approach to program parallelization has proved to be insufficient, since compilers cannot use information available only to users. This is even worst if the same parallel program will run on different multiprocessor architectures, or even on clusters of PCs.

In recent years, an alternative approach was proposed [5,6] that combines automatic and manual parallelization: the programmer interacts with the compiler to supply his knowledge of the application. This additional information helps the compiler in carrying on the hard task of parallelism analysis and discovery.

We developed a new environment for program parallelization, named *Graphical Parallelizing Environment* (*GPE*). It adopts an incremental approach for the parallelization of programs based on both parallelism automatic detection (done by a parallelizing compiler) and the user intervention to drive code restructuring as well as parallelism annotation before generation of program executables.

The rest of the paper is so organized: section 2 describes the GPE architecture; section 3 gives and overview of the GPE modules for the visualization and modification of program parallelism; section 4 reports some conclusive remarks.

---

[1] GPE software is a result of the POP European project: IST-2001-3307.

H. Jin, D. Reed, and W. Jiang (Eds.): NPC 2005, LNCS 3779, pp. 249–252, 2005.

2   GPE Program Development Cycle

According to the GPE approach, OpenMP program parallelization is the result of a cyclic process in which, at each round, the following activities (see figure 1) are carried out:

1. *OpenMP program editing* - first, the programmer writes the FORTRAN source code with OpenMP annotations.
2. *Compilation* - the compiler performs data & control dependence analysis and detects program parallelism accounting also for OpenMP parsed directives.
3. *Parallelism visualization* - program parallelism and its sources are shown to users in a *Hierarchical Task Graph* [2] representation.
4. *Parallelism modification* - users restructure parallelism annotating the code with OpenMP directives and transforming loops to extract/tune parallelism.
5. *Parallel code generation* - OpenMP annotated program tasks are translated to FORTRAN code plus calls to a multithreaded library [7].

Steps 3 to 4 can be iterated to further tune application parallelism. Each modification to the source is saved in a program new version and version history is kept by the GPE *versioning module*. The multithreaded code produced in step 5 is compiled on the target architecture to generate the executable. Performance measurements and execution traces can be used in next rounds of the tuning.

Parallelism detection and task formation is done by the *POP compiler* [9]. It is a source-to-source parallelizer that uses an aggressive approach for dependence testing. Parallelism detection is synthesized in a compiler internal representation: the *Hierarchical Task Graph (HTG)* [2]. User-compiler interaction relies on HTG handling: parallelism visualization/calibrating is based on graph-manipulation. We think that the HTG could be considered the intermediate program representation closer to the user conceptual view of the application parallel execution.

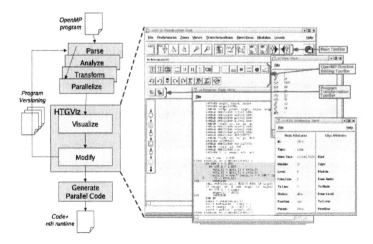

Fig. 1. The GPE architecture

3   GPE Modules

The GPE first design aimed to provide visualization and navigation of the program HTG, that synthesizes results of compiler analysis and parallelism discovery. We experienced that OpenMP program parallelization is often an incremental process involving both compiler techniques and programmer's restructuring decisions. The process is time-consuming as it implies hand-coding of many versions of the same program corresponding to different parallelization strategies.

Therefore, we redesigned the GPE to be an environment supporting the iterative process of OpenMP programming and extensible with new functionalities, added as plug-ins to the core system. With this new design the GPE has become a framework in which new capabilities and tools can be quickly developed and experimented. In what follows we describe the main GPE modules.

Visualization module - The GPE visualization module, named *Hierarchical Task Graph Visualization Tool* (*HTGViz*), displays compiler analysis (parallelism detection) results and provides facilities to navigate and correlate different information about the application parallelism discovered by the compiler. HTGViz offers three views of the application, that are hereafter described.

The *HTG Visualization View* is the main interface where HTGs of program subroutines are drawn. It allows to navigate through the HTG structure across hierarchy levels by means of a task expanding/collapsing facility. This feature simplifies HTG navigation when the program size and complexity increases.

The *Program Code View* illustrates the code in textual format. The interface shows the correspondence between program statements and HTG nodes during all user actions, like HTG navigation and directive insertion.

The *Vars View* shows, for each task node, the list of variables used (read/ written) and their occurrences in the program. This helps the programmer in detecting variables to privatize or share in OpenMP parallel sections and loops.

Modification modules - The *Program transformation module* supports the set of loop transformations more frequently used by POP users during the experience in OpenMP programming, i.e *loop interchange, blocking* and *coalescing* [10].

Transformation capabilities are based on graph-manipulation with the possibility to choose different equivalent patterns. The module implements checks on transformation applicability and inputs mainly based on data and control dependence analysis. If the compiler detects constraint violations the transformation is forbidden; otherwise the system allows the programmer to apply it.

The *OpenMP editing module* is a GPE extension providing an easy-to-use editor, based on graph manipulation, to assist users in inserting/modifying OpenMP annotations. The module allows to restructure and overwrite parallelism specification in terms of directives during compilation, before parallel code generation.

The editing tool partially automatizes the task of OpenMP directive insertion/modification. It assists the user in generating well-formed directives offering commands for fast pre-formatted editing operations. Upon directive insertion, a form-like interface is prompted for the input of clauses and their arguments: it displays the variables used (read/written) in the code enveloped by the directive. This information is useful to set variables as private or shared in the parallel threads. The tool performs directive applicability checks and syntax control.

The *Program versioning module* supports the tracking and re-using of intermediate versions during program development. Each code modification or OpenMP editing is saved in a program new version. The module maintains a history of program versions that can be navigated back and forth.

After the generation of the multithreaded binary and its execution, programmers may use runtime performance analysis information to restart application tuning from an intermediate version. To this aim the versioning module has a facility to store/reload program versions and history in/from a "project file".

4   Conclusions

The main novelty of GPE is its design as an extensible environment to support the incremental development cycle of OpenMP programs. At each round of the cycle, the user interacts with the compiler to tune the detected parallelism according to his knowledge of the application. GPE is extensible since new modules and tools can be implemented and plugged-in the GPE core to offer new functionalities, like modules supporting new analysis and transformation techniques.

Experiences of GPE usage in parallelizing OpenMP applications from NAS and SPEC95 benchmarks proved that performance measurements and trace data analysis are crucial to identify sources of performance drawbacks and to further improve program parallelization in next compilation steps. The *Program versioning* module was developed and integrated in GPE to facilitate this task.

References

1. Banerjee, U.: Dependence analysis for supercomputing. Kluwer Academic Publishers, (1988)
2. Girkar, M., Polychronopoulos, C.D.: The hierarchical task graph as a universal intermediate representation. Int. J. Parallel Programming **22** (1994) 519–551
3. Hall, M.W., *et al.*: Interprocedural Compilation on Fortran D. Journal of Parallel Distrib. Comput. **38**(2) (1996) 114–129
4. Haghighat, M.R., Polychronopoulos, C.D.: Symbolic analysis for parallelizing compilers. ACM Trans. on Programming Languages **18** (1996) 477–518.
5. Hall, M.W., *et al.*: Experience Using the ParaScope Editor. Proc. of Symp. Principles and Practice on Parallel Programming (1993)
6. Liao, S., *et al.*: Suif explorer: An interactive and interprocedural parallelizer. Proc. of Symp. on Principles and Practice of Parallel Programming (1999)
7. Martorell, X., *et al.*: A Library Implementation of the Nano-Threads Programming Model. Proc. of the 2nd Intern. Euro-Par Conf. (1996) 644–649
8. Omni OpenMP compiler project. `http:/phase.hpcc.jp/Omni/`
9. POP Esprit Project IST 2001-3307: Performance Portability of OpenMP. `http://www.cepba.upc.es/pop`
10. Wolfe, M.: High performance compilers for parallel computing. Addison–Wesley Publishing Company (1995)

Enhanced Congestion Control Algorithm for High-Speed TCP

Young-Soo Choi, Sung-Hyup Lee, and You-Ze Cho

School of Electrical Engineering and Computer Science,
Kyungpook National University, Korea
{yschoi, tenetshlee, yzcho} @ee.knu.ac.kr

Abstract. Current TCP congestion control can be inefficient and unstable in high-speed wide area networks due to its slow response with
a large congestion window. Several congestion control proposals have
already been suggested to solve these problems. In this paper, we propose a new variant of TCP for a high-speed network, which combines
delay-based congestion control with loss-based congestion control. Our
simulation results show that the proposed scheme performs better than
the existing high-speed TCP protocols in terms of fairness, stability, and
scalability, while providing TCP friendliness at the same time.

1 Introduction

The demand for high-speed applications such as bulk-data transfer, storage area
network, and grid networking has increased. It, however, has been reported that
as the bandwidth-delay product continues to grow, TCP underutilizes the bandwidth and it will eventually become a performance bottleneck itself [1]. Recently,
various schemes have been designed. Such schemes include HSTCP [1], STCP [2],
and BIC [3] and two properties have been considered: TCP friendliness and scalability. This is to ensure that a protocol does not take away too much bandwidth
from TCP, while utilizing a bandwidth of high speed networks efficiently.

In this paper, we propose a new variant of HSTCP, called eHSTCP (enhanced
HSTCP), which is a hybrid scheme of loss-based congestion control and delay-
based congestion control. First, we develop mechanism which avoids the effect
of backward path congestion. Second, eHSTCP refines the Additive Increase
Multiplicative Decrease (AIMD) mechanism of HSTCP to enhance scalability,
TCP friendliness, stability, and fairness.

The remainder of this paper is organized as follows: Section II introduces
the eHSTCP protocol. Section III presents the simulation results, and finally
conclusions are given in Section IV.

2 eHSTCP Protocol

If network congestion occurs in the backward path, delay-based congestion control protocols may overestimate RTT and unnecessarily decrease the congestion

H. Jin, D. Reed, and W. Jiang (Eds.): NPC 2005, LNCS 3779, pp. 253–256, 2005.
© IFIP International Federation for Information Processing 2005

window. By using the TCP timestamp option, our mechanism obtains samples of queueing delay on the forward and backward paths separately. Note that the sender and receiver clocks do not have to be synchronized since we are only interested in the relative time difference. We define the effective RTT (eRTT) as

$$eRTT = RTT - d_{b,q} \tag{1}$$

$$d_{b,q} = d_b - min(d_b) \tag{2}$$

where RTT is a newly measured round-trip time, $d_{b,q}$ is the backward queueing delay, d_b is a measured backward delay and $min(d_b)$ is the minimum of all measured backward delays. Consequently, the $eRTT$ indicates a round trip time when there is no backward path congestion.

Because previous research has shown that the HSTCP provides acceptable performances, we adopt the HSTCP as our baseline congestion control algorithm throughout this paper. In order to improve scalability, fairness, and stability, the proposed scheme uses the RTT which has up-to-date information about congestion levels and the HSTCP's AIMD mechanism is modified as follows.

Since random noise in RTT measurements cannot be avoided in practice, we use the RTT as a binary feedback signal in additive increase mechanism. To prevent throughput degradation from the reverse cross-traffic, we define N' as follows:

$$N' = (Expected - \frac{cwnd}{eRTT}) \times RTT_{min} = cwnd \times d_{f,q}/eRTT \tag{3}$$

where $Expected$ is the current congestion window size divided by RTT_{min} (the minimum of all measured RTTs) and $d_{f,q}$ is the forward queue delay. Consequently, according to the Little's Law, N' indicates the measured backlog when there is no backward queueing delay.

If the measured backlog (N') is lower than threshold (N^*), we assume that the network is underutilized and the HSTCP's congestion control algorithm is used. When the network is fully utilized, eHSTCP behaves like TCP Reno. eHSTCP stays at the fully utilized region longer, because eHSTCP does not increase its window size as quickly as HSTCP does when the critical region is reached. This mechanism not only reduces packet loss, but also improves stability by avoiding unnecessary decrease of the congestion window. Additionally, this mechanism leaves a buffer space for other traffic and thus makes eHSTCP TCP friendly. From the equation (3), since each source behaves like TCP Reno at the same throughput for a given queueing delay, the proposed mechanism can significantly correct the RTT fairness problem as compared with other protocols.

Setting (1-β) as RTT_{min} divided by RTT_{max} ensures that the buffer is empty while preventing buffer underflow (for more detail, see [5]). To prevent link underutilization and exclude the effect of backward pach congestion, eHSTCP uses:

$$1 - \beta_{eHSTCP} = \frac{RTT_{min}}{eRTT} \tag{4}$$

Note that we use $eRTT$ instead of RTT_{max}. By inspecting the raw data from our simulation results, we found that the measured RTTs are frequently smaller than the maximum RTT when a packet loss occurs. The main reason behind this phenomenon is TCP burstiness [4].

To provide TCP friendliness which is comparable to that of HSTCP, we employ the following compensation algorithm. After a packet loss, if β_{eHSTCP} is smaller than β_{HSTCP}, eHSTCP reduces its congestion window using β_{eHSTCP} and it enters a safety check phase. At the same time, w_{desg} is calculated using β_{HSTCP}. During this safety check phase, eHSTCP does not increase its congestion window but monitor the backlog. If N' exceeds N^* in the safety check phase, eHSTCP assumes that β_{eHSTCP} is too aggressive and reduces its congestion window to w_{desg}. Therefore, it takes one RTT time for eHSTCP to decrease its window size to the size of HSTCP. Otherwise, after the safety check phase, eHSTCP enters the additive increase phase.

3   Simulation Results and Discussion

We use ns simulator and the topology used for the simulation is dumbbell network. For background traffic, web traffic, 25 small TCP flows with a limited congestion window size under 64, and 4 long lived TCP flows are created in both directions. We use $N^*=10$ and the safety check phase $=5 \times RTT_{max}$.

In order to evaluate bandwidth scalability, we measure utilization and the average packet loss rate of the bottleneck link. So as to evaluate stability for high-speed TCP, we use the sample standard deviation normalized by the average throughput of high-speed flows. Table 1 shows that link utilization of eHSTCP is relatively comparable to that of STCP. Also, eHSTCP shows a good performance among all protocols under the packet loss rate evaluation criterion. Additionally, we found that eHSTCP showed the best stability.

In this experiment, two high speed flows with a different RTT are used. The RTT of flow 1 is 40ms, while we vary the RTT of flow 2 between 120ms and 240ms. Table 2 depicts that eHSTCP outperforms other high-speed protocols in terms of RTT fairness.

Fig. 1 shows the percentage of the bandwidth shared by each flow type with different bottleneck bandwidth. For 20Mbps, all high-speed TCP protocols show similar TCP friendliness. As the bandwidth increases, the share of the bandwidth taken by the background traffic is substantially reduced due to the TCP scalability problem. Note that, under 2.5Gbps, eHSTCP flows achieve slightly higher throughput than HSTCP flows. The increase in eHSTCP bandwidth shares is

Table 1. Comparison of utilization, fairness, packet loss ratio, and stability under 2.5Gbps bottleneck link

	HSTCP	STCP	BIC	eHSTCP
Link utilization	0.92	0.99	0.95	0.99
Packet loss ratio(%)	0.0197	0.1281	0.0206	0.0065
Normalized standard deviation	0.148	0.149	0.107	0.047

Table 2. The throughput ratio of two high-speed flows over various RTT ratios under 1Gbps bottleneck link

	HSTCP	STCP	BIC	eHSTCP
RTT ratio = 3	42.46	111.45	12.03	3.88
RTT ratio = 6	197.80	341.65	84.65	4.77

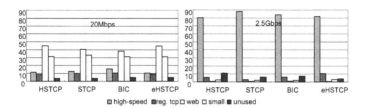

Fig. 1. A comparison of TCP friendliness for various bandwidth networks

due to the better utilization of the available bandwidth. In most cases, eHSTCP shows good TCP friendliness but we did not present simulation results with various bandwidth here due to lack of space.

4   Conclusion

In this paper, we propose a new variant of TCP for a high-speed network which combines delay-based congestion control with loss-based congestion control. We define the effective RTT and adopt it to refine the HSTCP's AIMD mechanism. We have shown that the proposed scheme outperforms other high-speed protocols about fairness, scalability, and stability, while offering TCP friendliness.

Acknowledgement

This work was supported in part by the ITRC of the Ministry of Information and Communication (MIC), Korea.

References

1. S. Floyd, "HighSpeed TCP for Large Congestion Windows," *RFC3649*, 2003.
2. T. Kelly, "Scalable TCP: Improving Performance in Highspeed Wide Area Networks", *ACM SIGCOMM Computer Communication Review*, vol.33, pp. 83-91, 2003.
3. L. Xu, K. Harfoush, and I. Rhee, "Binary Increase Congestion Control for Fast, Long Distance Networks," In *Proceedings of IEEE Infocom*, 2004.
4. Y. Choi, K. Lee, and Y. Cho, "Performance Evaluation of High-Speed TCP Protocols with Pacing," *Lecture Notes in Computer Science*, 2004.
5. R. Shorten and D. Leith, "H-TCP: TCP for high-speed and long-distance networks," In *Proceedings of the PFLDnet*, 2004.

Advanced Software On-Demand Based on Functional Streaming

Jeong Min Shim, Won Young Kim, and Wan Choi

Electronics and Telecommunications Research Institute (ETRI), Daejeon, South Korea
{jmshim, wykim, wchoi}@etri.re.kr

Abstract. Streaming is a technology that enables either real-time or on-demand distribution of multimedia contents over network. Recently streaming technology has been applied onto applications, and many deployment tools for enterprise applications have been developed. Software streaming is a technology to provide software whichever users need on-demand in real-time by using streaming technology without downloading and installing a full package in advance before its use. Software streaming technology has many issues that are application load time, network fault-tolerant and etc. In this paper, we discuss issues for software streaming technology. Then, we propose a new SOD system based on functional streaming called *Advanced Software On-Demand (ASOD)* system. Also, we present schemes to solve issues that are application load time and network fault-tolerant.

1 Introduction

Streaming is the process of playing application while it is still downloading [1] [2]. Streaming has been mostly found on streaming media that lets users listen to or view the digitized contents such as sound, animation and video, as it is being downloaded.

Recently streaming technology has been applied onto applications, and many companies have developed deployment tools for enterprise applications such as AppStream's AppStream.NOW platform [3], Softricity's SoftGrid platform [4], Stream Theory's AppExpress platform [5] and SoftOnNet's Z!Stream [6]. Software streaming is a technology to provide software whichever users need on-demand in real-time by using streaming technology without downloading and installing a full package in advance before its use.

Software streaming technology still has many issues that are application load time, network fault-tolerant and etc. To solve these problems, we will define software by differentiating environment for launching, basic function and additional functions. Basic function is first and certainly necessary contents to launch an application. Additional functions are contents for each component (a set of the menus).

In this paper, we discuss issues for software streaming technology, and present advanced Software On-Demand (ASOD) system based on functional streaming using basic function and additional functions. Also, we present schemes to solve issues that are application load time and network fault-tolerant.

H. Jin, D. Reed, and W. Jiang (Eds.): NPC 2005, LNCS 3779, pp. 257–260, 2005.

2 Issues in Existing Software On-Demand (SOD) Service

In existing SOD system, the client requests page contents to the streaming server (only, when the page contents are not found in the local cache) when an application tries to process a function of the application streamed to execute. To get contents, client will send one or more request messages to the streaming server. Operation of an application is suspended until the client receives all required contents.

We performed experiments to measure necessary contents to launch an application. Table 1 show results of *Application Launching Size* (ALS) for Linux Application. As shown in Table 1, in all application, a lot of contents are required when the application is launched. This fact implies that a client must send a lot of page requests. Also, users must wait for a long time after they request service.

Network is one of the important issues in SOD service. If a client loses connection with a streaming server, it is not able to request a page to the streaming server. If users try to use the function which is not stored in a local cache, the application will be destroyed or the client system may be crashed. Consequently, if network connection fails, the service has to be stopped although users can use a function which is stored pages in a local cache.

Table 1. Application Launching Size (ALS) versus total size of an application

Application	Application Launching Size	Total size
CBtracker	3.1 MB, of total size 100%	3.1 MB
Bubble Shooter	6.03 MB, of total size 99%	6.1 MB
Abiword	4.6 MB, of total size 15.7%	29.4 MB
OpenOffice	98.3 MB, of total size 41.5%	236.3 MB

3 Advanced Software On-Demand Based on Functional Streaming

3.1 Architecture of the ASOD System Based on Functional Streaming

To provide SOD service based on functional streaming, preliminary work that analyzes an application is needed. First, we define new transmission unit between a client and a streaming server, named Functional Unit (FUint). The FUnit consists of contents for one or more menus. There are two kinds of FUnit: (1) basic FUnit and (2) extra FUnit. Basic FUnit is first and certainly necessary contents to launch an application. Extra FUnit is contents for each component (a set of the menus). We analyze software execution and extract necessary information for functional streaming. We should be able to extract this information by extracting statistical data from simulations.

Figure 1 is architecture of client and streaming server based on functional streaming. A client system in SOD system consists of the following components: (1) Streaming Application (SA), (2) Event Hooker (EH), (3) Application Streaming File System (ASFS) and (4) Streaming Data Manager (SDM). SA is an application running through SOD service. EH intercepts functionality, is selected by user, of an application when network fault occurs. ASFS communicates with the streaming server to get FUnits. SDM stores FUnits and information for FUnits streamed from the streaming server, and maintains information for all FUnits of an application. SDM also maintains relationship between the FUnits and functionalities.

A streaming server consists of (1) Streaming Data Package (SDP) and (2) Data Package Information (DPI). SDP is FUnits, are extracted through *Software Analyzer*, for applications. DPI maintains information for application packages and FUnits. DPI is used to find out FUnit which is corresponding to function required from the client.

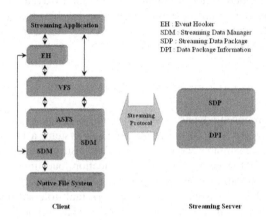

Fig. 1. Architecture of client and streaming server in the ASOD system

3.2 Techniques in the ASOD System Based on Functional Streaming

As experimental result in section 2.1, most applications need contents, called basic FUnit, above 40% of the total software size to launch an application. An application cannot launch until basic FUnit completely are arrived. In existing SOD system, a client sends page request message of several tens and hundreds to streaming server to get basic FUnit. Therefore, whenever the client requests the page, the streaming server searches it and then transmits it to the client.

In the proposed system, application load time can be reduced by using basic FUnit. When a client requests a software streaming service to the streaming server, a streaming server sends immediately basic FUnit and FUnit information for the application to launch the application to the client without another request of the client. Accordingly, application load time must be reduced significantly.

The proposed SOD system supports network fault-tolerant. If a client loses its connection to the streaming server, the client will be notified of the situation and client may continuously use the application with the functionality that it might have. If a menu clicked by a user is not in a local cache, process for the menu is ignored by EH. Consequently, users can continuously use the application, although network fault occurs.

In the proposed SOD system, we use a prefetching technique to reduce an application suspension time. The prefetching is a technique that sends the FUnit to be expected from the streaming server to the client without user's demand in advance. There are three different ways to apply prefetching: (1) prediction by producers, (2) prediction by static statistics, and (3) prediction by dynamic statistics. Prediction by producers is that the order of FUnits for the application is decided by producers without any statistics. A streaming server sends FUnit to a client in sequence when a service is begun by request of a user. Prediction by static statistics is that content providers or packers decide a transmission-priority by using statistics collected from each user. When an application through the SOD service is launched, the streaming server first sends basic FUnit, and extra FUnits are transmitted by decided priority after. After a priority is decided, it doesn't change. Prediction by dynamic statistics is similar to prediction by static statistics. But, prediction by dynamic statistics updates a priority of extra FUnits by using statistics continuously collected from each user that uses an application provided through SOD service.

4 Conclusion

In this paper, we proposed advanced SOD system based on functional streaming for more efficient SOD service. In the proposed SOD system, a transmission unit between a client and streaming server is FUnit. We also presented schemes to solve issues in existing SOD system. To reduce application load time, a streaming server sends basic FUnit without to wait for request message of a client when a service begins. The proposed SOD system supports network fault-tolerant that users can continuously use functions which is stored in the local cache although network fault occurs. Therefore, we introduce prefetching technique based on statistical information to reduce the application suspension time significantly.

References

1. Bitpipe, "Streaming Media Services," http://www.bitpipe.com.
2. California Software Labs (CSWL), "Basic Streaming Technology and RTSP Protocol," http://www.cswl.com.
3. AppStream Inc., "AppStream Technology," http://www.appstream.com.
4. Softricity Inc., "The SoftGrid Application Virtualization Platform," http://www.softricity.com/home/index.asp.
5. Stream Theory, "The Enterprise Software Distribution Platform," http://www.streamtheory.com.
6. SoftonNet Inc., "Z!Stream Technology," http://www.softonnet.com.

Can Out-of-Order Instruction Execution in Multiprocessors Be Made Sequentially Consistent?

Lisa Higham[1] and Jalal Kawash[2]

[1] Department of Computer Science,
The University of Calgary, Canada
higham@cpsc.ucalgary.ca
[2] Department of Computer Science,
American University of Sharjah, UAE
jkawash@aus.edu

Abstract. We investigate all possible combinations of re-ordering of read and write instructions and their effects on the correctness of programs that are designed for sequential consistency. With certain combinations of re-orderings, any program that accesses shared memory through only reads and writes and that is correct assuming sequential consistency, can be transformed to a new program that does not use any explicit synchronization, and that remains correct in spite of the instruction re-ordering. With other combinations of re-ordering, such transformations do not exist, without resorting to explicit synchronization.

1 Introduction

Designers of concurrent algorithms typically assume sequential consistency, a consistency model that is formalized by Lamport [11]. Sequential consistency requires that memory operations of all processors appear to be "executed in some sequential order, and the operations of each processor appear in this sequence in the order specified by its program" (program order). Sequential consistency is intuitive, but disallows many possible hardware and software optimizations.

Adve and Gharachorloo [1] identify several optimization techniques that cause instructions to be re-ordered so that they appear to execute out of program order. This is called *instruction re-ordering*. Write buffers with read bypasses, overlapping writes, non-blocking reads, and optimizing compilers can lead to all forms of instruction re-ordering. They also cite many commercial multiprocessors that utilize instruction re-ordering, such as the AlphaServer 8200/8400, Cray T3D/T3E, and SparcCenter 1000/2000 (See Figure 1). Other examples include the Java Virtual Machine (JVM), IBM PowerPC, Intel Itanium, and .Net. Instruction re-ordering aims at improving the system's performance but it relaxes sequential consistency, making the job of programming multiprocessors even harder.

H. Jin, D. Reed, and W. Jiang (Eds.): NPC 2005, LNCS 3779, pp. 261–265, 2005.
© IFIP International Federation for Information Processing 2005

Architecture	write-read re-ordering	write-write re-ordering	read-write re-ordering	read-read re-ordering
IBM 370 [1]	√			
SPARC TSO [14,7]	√			√ [10]
SPARC PSO [14,7]	√	√	√ [10]	√ [10]
SPARC RMO [14,5]	√	√	√	√
IBM PowerPC [2]	√	√	√	√
DEC Alpha [3,5]	√	√	√	√
JVM [12,6]	√	√	√	√
Intel Itanium[9]	√	√	√	√
.Net [13]	√	√	√	√

Fig. 1. Examples of some commercial systems that utilize instruction re-ordering

Multiprocessor machines that incorporate instruction re-ordering are also equipped with more powerful instructions than reads and writes, such as read-modify-write and memory barrier instructions. These synchronization primitives can be used to enforce orderings on instructions that otherwise might be re-ordered causing incorrect computation. Using these powerful instructions, however, is expensive; excessive use can result in inefficient implementations, possibly defeating the purpose of instruction re-ordering altogether.

Other related studies (see the full version of the paper for a bibliography [8]) provide programming strategies for high performance multiprocessors most of which rely on the wise usage of synchronization.

2   Summary of Results

We assume that multiprocessors are *coherent* [4], requiring execution order to maintain program order of instructions applied to the same memory location. If a read of one memory location precedes in program order a write to a different memory location and this read appears after this write in execution order, this is called *read-write re-ordering*. Reordering types *write-read, write-write, and read-read* are defined similarly. Call a shared memory multiprocessor program whose shared memory consists of only atomic locations (that is, variables that support only read and write instructions) a *(read/write) multi-program*. The fundamental question guiding this work is:

> Under what conditions is there a general transformation that transforms any read/write multi-program that is correct under sequential consistency to another read/write multi-program that is still correct in spite of possible instruction re-ordering?

Such a transformation is called a *read/write transformation* and constitutes inserting only additional read and write operations to a given read/write multi-program, which solves some problem $\mathcal{P}$ under sequential consistency, but without altering its original semantics. Hence, the transformed multi-program is also a read/write multi-program. The purpose of these additions is to restore program order and maintain sequential consistency in spite of instruction re-ordering. Since the semantics of the original program are maintained, the transformed program still solves problem $\mathcal{P}$.

single type	two combinations	three combinations
read-read $\sqrt{}$	read-read, write-write $\sqrt{}$	read-read, write-write, write-read $\times$
write-write $\sqrt{}$	read-read, read-write $\times$	read-read, write-write, read-write $\times$
read-write $\sqrt{}$	read-read, write-read $\times$	read-read, read-write, read-write $\times$
write-read $\sqrt{}$	read-write, write-read $\sqrt{}$	write-write, read-write, write-read $\sqrt{}$
	write-write, write-read $\sqrt{}$	
	write-write, read-write $\sqrt{}$	

Fig. 2. Summary of results

The results of this investigation are summarized in Figure 2. The possibilities (represented by $\sqrt{}$) in Figure 2 indicate the existence of a general read/write transformation for any sequentially consistent program to a program that is still correct in spite of the indicated instruction re-ordering combination.

The impossibilities of Figure 2 (represented by $\times$) indicate that there is no *general* read/write transformation for the indicated combinations of instruction re-ordering. That is, any read/write transformation fails to transform at least one multi-program that is known to be correct for sequential consistency. Such general transformations for the indicated combinations of instruction re-orderings must augment the specified program with explicit synchronization operations.

More precisely, let $\mathcal{A}$ be an arbitrary read/write multi-program that solves a problem $\mathcal{P}$, under sequential consistency. The results of our research are:

1. For any combination of re-ordering types that excludes read-read re-ordering, there exists a read/write transformation, which transforms $\mathcal{A}$ to a read/write program $\mathcal{A}'$ that solves $\mathcal{P}$ in spite of the re-ordering. The transformation is general; it is correct for any read/write multi-program under any combination of read-write, write-read, and write-write re-orderings.
2. The exclusion of the read-read re-ordering is sufficient but not necessary. For any combination of read-read and write-write re-ordering only, such a read/write transformation still exists.
3. If both read-read and read-write (or both read-read and write-read) re-ordering combinations are possible, there is no general read/write transformation. Any correct general transformation must use stronger operations than reads and writes, such as read-modify-write and memory barrier instructions, for at least some programs.

3   Conclusion

The transformations we used are simple and general; they can be applied to any read/write multi-program that is correct for sequential consistency. They are also optimal for general transformations — these that apply to *any* multi-program that is correct for sequential consistency. However, optimality for general transformations does not necessarily imply optimality for individual multi-program instances. When given a *fixed* instance, it may be possible to apply further optimizations that exploit information from the given multi-program and the problem it solves. Such information (from both programs and problems) is unavailable to general transformers.

Our results imply that the IBM PowerPC, DEC Alpha, JVM, and SPARC TSO, PSO, and RMO (Figure 1) require the use of explicit synchronization in order to solve certain problems. Hence, one of our future research directions is to augment the target program with memory barrier instructions and to minimize the number of such instructions.

References

1. S. Adve and K. Gharachorloo. Shared memory consistency models: A tutorial. *IEEE Computer*, pages 66–76, December 1996.
2. F. Corella, J. Stone, and C. Barton. A formal specification of the PowerPC shared memory architecture. Technical Report RC18638, IBM, 1994.
3. C. C. Corportaion. *The Alpha Architecture Handbook*. Compaq Computer Corporation, 1998. Order number: EC-QD2KC-TE.
4. M. Frigo. The weakest reasonable memory model. Master's thesis, Department of Electrical Engineering and Computer Science, MIT, 1998.
5. L. Higham, L. Jackson, and J. Kawash. Specifying memory consistency of write buffer multiprocessors. Technical Report 2004-758-23, Department of Computer Science, The University of Calgary, August 2004. Submitted for publication.
6. L. Higham and J. Kawash. Java: Memory consistency and process coordination (extended abstract). In *Proc. 12th Int'l Symp. on Distributed Computing, Lecture Notes in Computer Science volume 1499*, pages 201–215, September 1998.
7. L. Higham and J. Kawash. Memory consistency and process coordination for SPARC multiprocessors. In *Proc. of the 7th Int'l Conf. on High Performance Computing, Lecture Notes in Computer Science volume 1970*, pages 355–366, December 2000.
8. L. Higham and J. Kawash. Impact of instruction re-ordering on the correctness of shared-memory programs. Technical Report 2005/794/25, Department of Computer Science, The University of Calgary, July 2005.
9. Intel Corporation. Intel Itanium architecture software developers manual, volumes 1-3. 2002.
10. J. Kawash. *Limitations and Capabilities of Weak Memory Consistency Systems*. Ph.D. dissertation, Department of Computer Science, The University of Calgary, January 2000.
11. L. Lamport. How to make a multiprocessor computer that correctly executes multiprocess programs. *IEEE Trans. on Computers*, C-28(9):690–691, September 1979.

12. T. Lindholm and F. Yellin. *The Java Virtual Machine Specification*. Addison-Wesley, 1997.
13. A. D. Robison. Memory consistency and .Net. *Dr. Dobb's Journal*, pages 46–50, April 2003.
14. D. Weaver and T. Germond, editors. *The SPARC Architecture Manual version 9*. Prentice-Hall, 1994.

Efficiently Passive Monitoring Flow Bandwidth*

Zhiping Cai, Jianping Yin, Fang Liu, Xianghui Liu, and Shaohe Lv

School of Computer, National University of Defense Technology,
Changsha, 410073, China
caizhiping_nudt@163.com, jpyin@nudt.edu.cn,
fangl_nudt@163.com, liuxh@tom.com, chi.shaohe@gmail.com

Abstract. Using the flow-conservation law, we could reduce the number
of activated monitor agents used to monitor link bandwidth usage. In
this paper, we address the problem of efficiently passive monitoring flow
bandwidth based on flow-conservation, which could be reduced to weak
vertex cover problem. And the weak vertex cover problem is NP-hard.
We give an approximation algorithm with approximation ratio 2 to solve
the problem. The effectiveness of our monitoring algorithm is validated
by simulations evaluation over a wide range of network topologies.

1 Introduction

Bandwidth utilizations are critical for numerous important network management
tasks. Some novel tools and infrastructures for measuring network bandwidth
have been developed and proposed by researchers and industries.

The number of placed monitors of a monitoring system should be kept as
small as possible in order to reduce the deployment cost and the actual monitoring operating cost [1]. Several measurements over backbone routers show each
IP router satisfies a flow-conservation law that, the sum of the traffic flowing
into router is approximately the same as those of the traffic flowing out [2]. The
problem of efficiently monitoring the network flowing based on flow-conservation
could be reduced to the weak vertex cover problem.

The paper is structured as follows. The weak vertex cover problem is brought
forward, and some approximation results for the weak vertex cover problem are
listed in the section 2. In next section, we give an approximation algorithm to
solve the weak vertex cover problem with approximation ratio 2. The effectiveness of our monitoring algorithm is validated by simulations evaluation over a
wide range of network topologies in section 4. And we depict our further research
in the last section.

2 Weak Vertex Cover Problem

The problem of efficiently passive monitoring the network flowing based on flow-
conservation could be reduced to the weak vertex cover problem, which is NP-
hard [2],[3].

---

* This work is supported by the National Natural Science Foundation of China under
Grant No. 60373023.

Definition 1. *(Weak Vertex Cover) Given an undirected graph $G = (V, E)$, where $\forall v \in V$, $d(v) \geq 2$ holds, we say $S \subseteq V$ is a weak vertex cover Set of G, if and only if every edge in G can be marked by performing the following three steps:*

(1) Mark all edges that are incident on vertices in S;

(2) Mark the edge if it is the only unmarked edge among all of the edges that are incident on the same vertex;

(3) Repeat step (2) until no new edge can be marked.

For solving the problem of finding the minimum weak vertex cover set, Xianghui Liu et al. [3] brought forward a greedy approximation algorithm which gives an approximation ratio $2(1 + \ln d)$, where $d = \max_{v \in V} \{d(v)\}$. And Xianghui Liu et al. [4] proved that the weak vertex cover problem is NP-complete. Yong Zhang et al. [5] gave an approximation algorithm with approximation ratio $1 + \ln d$. Zhiping Cai et al. [6] gave an approximation preserving reduction from the vertex cover problem to the weak vertex cover problem. Due to this reduction, it implied that it is difficult to get an approximation algorithm with approximation ratio small than 2.

3   An Approximation Algorithm

We give a 2-approximation algorithm for the weak vertex cover by using the primal-dual method for approximation algorithms, which has been used to derive approximation algorithms for network design problems [7-9].

At the beginning, we give some inequalities that will be needed in proving the performance guarantees of the algorithms and in giving the integer programming formulation. In fact, we could get different primal-dual algorithms by using different integer programming formulation [9].

Given a subset S of vertices, let $E[S]$ denote the subset of edges that have both endpoints in S. Let $G[S]$ denote the subgraph $(S, E[S])$ induced by G, and let $d_s(v)$ denote the degree of v in $G[S]$. We let $b(S) = |E[S]| - |S| + 1$ and $b(V) = |E| - |V| + 1$. Observe that if F is a weak vertex cover for G, then $F \cap S$ is clearly a weak vertex cover for $G[S]$. Hence we have following theorem. The details of this proof are omitted due to space limitations.

Theorem 1. *Let F be any weak vertex set. Then for any $S \subseteq V$, $E[S] \neq 0$,*

$$\sum_{v \in F \cap S} (d_s(v) - 1) \geq |E[S]| - |S| + 1 = b(S)$$

By Theorem 1, the integer programming formulation of the weak vertex cover problem is the following:

$$\text{Min} \sum_{v \in V} w_v x_v$$

Subject to:

(IP) $$\sum_{v \in S} (d_s(v) - 1)x_v \geq b(S) \qquad S \subseteq V, E[S] \neq 0$$
$$x_v \in \{0,1\} \qquad v \in V.$$

We construct a feasible solution to the dual of the linear programming relaxation of (IP). The linear programming relaxation is

$$\text{Min} \sum_{v \in V} w_v x_v$$

Subject to:

(LP) $$\sum_{v \in S} (d_s(v) - 1)x_v \geq b(S) \qquad S \subseteq V, E[S] \neq 0$$
$$x_v \geq 0 \qquad v \in V.$$

And its dual is

$$\text{Max} \sum_{S} b(S)y_s$$

Subject to:

(D) $$\sum_{v \in S} (d_s(v) - 1)y_s \leq w_v \qquad v \in V$$
$$y_s \geq 0 \qquad S \subseteq V, E[S] \neq 0.$$

Then an approximation algorithm is given as follows:
Algorithm WeakCover $(G = (V, E))$:

1. $y = 0; F = 0; l = 0$;
2. $V' = V; E' = E$;
3. While F is not a WVC for G
   (a) $l = l + 1$;
   (b) Recursively remove degree one vertices and incident edges from V' and E';
   (c) $S = Endblock(V', E')$;
   (d) Increase y_S until $\exists v_l \in S, s.t. \sum_{T:v_l \in T} (d_T(v_l) - 1)y_T = w_{v_l}$
   (e) $F = F \cup \{v_l\}$
   (f) Remove v_l from V' and attached edges from E'.
4. For $(j = l; j > 0; j - -)$
   (a) if $F - \{v_j\}$ is a WVC then $F = F - \{v_j\}$
5. $F' = F$

And the *Endblock* procedure is defined as follows:

Procedure Endblock (V', E'):

1. Return the vertices of an endblock of (V', E');

Note that the worst-case time complexity of the algorithm can be shown to be $O(|V||E|)$.And the algorithm computes a 2 approximation for the Weak Vertex Cover problem.The details of this proof are omitted due to space limitations.

4 Simulations

The effectiveness of our monitoring algorithm is validated by simulations evaluation over a wide range of network topologies generated using the Waxman Model [10]. Simulation result has been omitted due to paper size limitations and the simulation shows the our proposed algorithmic solutions are not only theoretically sound but also they could give significant benefits over naive solutions in practice for a wide variety of realistic network topologies.

5 Conclusions

In this paper, we have addressed the problem of efficiently passive monitoring flow bandwidth. This problem could be abstracted to the weak vertex cover problem, which is NP-hard. We have proposed a 2-approximation algorithm to solve Weak Vertex Cover problem. Finally, we have verified the effectiveness of our approximation algorithms through simulations evaluation.

Further research would be conducted to exploit knowledge of traffic flows in the network to further reduce the required overhead for monitoring flow bandwidth.

References

1. Kyoungwon Suh, Yang Guo, Jim Kurose, and Don Towsley. Locating Network Monitors: Complexity, Heuristics, and Coverage. In Proc. IEEE INFOCOM 2005.
2. Breitbart Y., Chan CY., Garofalakis M., Rastogi R., Siberschatz A.: Efficiently Monitoring Bandwidth and Latency in IP Networks. In Proc. IEEE INFOCOM 2001.
3. Xianghui Liu, Jianping Yin, Lele Tang: Analysis of Efficient Monitoring Method for the Network Flow. *Journal of Software*, 2003,14(2): 300-304(in Chinese with English abstract).
4. Xianghui Liu, Jianping Yin, Xicheng Lu: A Monitoring Model for Link Bandwidth Usage of Network Based on Weak Vertex Cover. *Journal of Software*, 2004,15(4): 545-549(in Chinese with English abstract).
5. Yong Zhang and Hong Zhu: Approximation Algorithm for Weighted Weak Vertex Cover. *Journal of Computer Science and Technology*, 2004,19(6): 782-786.
6. Zhiping Cai, Jianping Yin, Fang Liu, Xianghui Liu, Shaohe Lv: Efficiently Monitoring Link Bandwidth in IP Networks. In Proc. IEEE GLOBECOM 2005.
7. Dorit S. Hochbaum: Approximation Algorithm for *NP*-Hard Problems. PWS Publishing Company,1997.
8. A. Becker and D. Geiger: Approximation Algorithms for the Loop Cutest Problem. In Proc. 10th Conference on Uncertainty in Artificial Intelligence.
9. F. A. Chudak, M. X. Goemans, D. S. Hochbaumn, and D. P. Williamson: A Primal-Dual Interpretation of Two 2-Approximation Algorithms for the Feedback Vertex Set Problem in Undirected Graphs. *Operations Research Letters*, 1998, 22 :111-118.
10. B.M.Waxman: Routing of Multipoint Connections. IEEE Journal on Selected Areas in Communications, 1988, 6(9):1617-1622.

A Heuristic for Scheduling Parallel Programs with Synchronous Communication Model in the Network Computing Environments

Mingyu Zhao and Tianwen Zhang

School of Computer Science and Technology Harbin, Institute of Technology,
Harbin 150001,China
zhmy@21cn.com

Abstract. Most heuristics for scheduling address asynchronous communication DAG, but they are not suitable for the synchronous ones. The proposed PRGSC algorithm avoids the deadlock that is caused by the synchronous communication, but also it can alleviate impact of synchronous communicating delay. Simulation shows that the PRGSC algorithm has better performance than the CASC algorithm which deals with the same type of problems.

1 Introduction

Scheduling problem is fundamental and highly important in the parallel system research domain [1]. Most of scheduling heuristics target to the asynchronous scheduling problems. But applications in the network computing environment may depend on the synchronous communication to ensure the reliability. Nevertheless, synchronization introduces delay for the sender. Furthermore, synchronization may result in deadlock situations between communicating tasks.

With regards to synchronous scheduling, there have been few researches and algorithms proposed [3, 4]. Although these algorithms studied deadlock detection, they can merely manage the direct deadlock between processors, but not the circular deadlock among multiprocessors.

This paper proposed a heuristic: Parameters Relation Graph based Synchronous Clustering (PRGSC) for the synchronous scheduling problems. It can fully detect and avoid the deadlock situation, while has better scheduling quality.

2 Definitions

Parallel applications can be depicted as weighted Directed Acyclic Graph, $G = (V, E, \tau, \beta)$, where $V = \{n_1, n_2, \ldots, n_v\}$ represents the set of tasks to be executed, and the weighted, directed edges $(n_i, n_j) \in E$ represents communication between tasks. The weight of task n is $w(n)$, representing the execution time. Edge (n_i, n_j) represents a message sent from n_i to n_j , and the weight of the edge refers to the message transportation time, denoted $\beta(n_i, n_j)$. We use $tlevel(n_i) + blevel(n_i)$

H. Jin, D. Reed, and W. Jiang (Eds.): NPC 2005, LNCS 3779, pp. 270–273, 2005.

to evaluate node n_i's relevant importance, where tlevel and blevel are defined in [1]. The execution of task can be divided into three phases: receiving, computing and sending. Therefore, four attributes are required to measure the start time and finish time of these three phases:

Definition 1. $r(v)$ *is the time that v starts receiving messages.*

Definition 2. $R(v)$ *is the time that v finishes receiving messages, and it is also the start time of computing phase.*

Definition 3. $s(v)$ *is the time that v starts sending messages, and it is also the finish time of computing phase.*

Definition 4. $S(v)$ *is end of the sending phase of a task when it receives acknowledgments from all the recipient tasks.*

These values can be evaluated by the equations defined in [3].

3 The Proposed Heuristic

3.1 Selection of Nodes and Processors

In the synchronous scheduling, unlike the asynchronous one, scheduling a node changes not only the time properties of unscheduled nodes, but also those of scheduled nodes. Thus, except for decreasing the start time of unscheduled part, every scheduling step has to evaluate the impact on scheduled part in synchronous model.

Therefore, PRGSC tries four methods of scheduling a node in every scheduling step:

1. Among the edges between scheduled nodes and ready nodes, choose the one (n_p, n_f) with highest priority. An edge's priority is defined as the sum of two nodes' priorities.
2. Choose n_p with highest priority among the scheduled nodes which have ready child nodes, firstly; then, select the critical child node n_f in the ready child nodes set of n_p.
3. Choose n_f with highest priority among the ready nodes, then select the critical parent nodes n_p in the set of parent nodes of n_f.
4. Assign the ready node with highest priority onto a new processor without changing the makespan.

PRGSC compares each zeroing result and uses the one that produces the lowest makespan and no deadlock in each step. PRGSC zeros the edge (n_p, n_f) by adding n_f into cluster $clust(n_p)$, i.e., setting n_f rightly behind the last node n_l. If n_l isn't a parent of n_f in the original DAG, produce a pseudo-edge (n_l, n_f) with weight of zero.

3.2   Deadlock Detection

Definition 5. *Deadlock is a status. Under this status, there is a subset D of tasks. For every element that belongs to D, its complete time is decided by the others. That is, $D = \{v_i : 1 \le i \le m, m \ge 2\} \in V$, for every task $v_i \in D$, $S(v_i) = f_i(S(v_1), S(v_2), S(v_{i-1}), S(v_{i+1}), \ldots, S(v_m))$, where f_i is a function.*

Every step changes the scheduling by zeroing a certain edge or adding a pseudo-edge. Represent the scheduled graph of step k with $G_k(V, E_k)$. Say that assign node n_f to processor P at step k, and n_l is the last node on P at step $k-1$, then $E_k = E_{k-1} - (n_i, n_f) + (n_l, n_f)$, where $n_i \in P$, $(n_i, n_f) \in E_k$, and $\beta(n_l, n_f) = 0$. Provide the definition accordingly:

Definition 6. *In the kth step, Parameters relation graph is $G'_k(V', E'_k)$, where the elements of set V' are values of r,R, s and S of nodes n in V, denoted as $n.r$, $n.R$, $n.s$ and $n.S$ respectively. If the value of element a has some effect on that of element b, then $(a, b) \in E'_k$. All possible members of E'_k are listed below:*

1. *$\{(n.r, n.R), (n.R, n.s), (n.s, n.S)\} \subseteq E'_k, n \in V$.*
2. *If $(n, c) \in E_k$ and $\beta(n, c) \ne 0$, then $\{(n.s, c.R), (c.r, n.S)\} \subseteq E'_k$.*
3. *If $(n, c) \in E_k$ and $\beta(n, c) = 0$, then $(n.S, c.r) \in E'_k$.*

According to definition 1-4 and the assumption that tasks on the same processor have no communication cost, E'_k of step k can be incrementally derive from E'_{k-1}: $E'_k = E'_{k-1} - \{(n_i.s, n_f.R), (n_f.r, n_i.S)\} + \{(n_l.S, n_f.r)\}$.

Due to the construction scheme, we can derive two theorems following:

Theorem 1. *G'_k includes a circuit, iff the current schedule is deadlock.*

Theorem 2. *The schedule is deadlock, iff there is a circuit in G'_k through $n_f.r$.*

For the sake of space, the proofs are ignored.

As it need to traverse the PRG G'_k breadth-first to compute all the parameters and determine if exist a circuit in current schdule, the complexities of parameters computing and deadlock detection are both $O(v+e)$. For every node scheduling, deadlock determination and time parameters update are the major operations. Thus, the complexity of PRGSC is $O(v(v+e))$.

4   Simulation Experiment

250 random generated graphs are used for validating the performance of PRGSC. These graphs are separated into 5 groups according to their CCR [5], values of which are 0.1, 0.5, 1.0, 2.0 and 10.0 respectively. Each group has 50 graphs, which are separated into 10 subgroups according to the number of nodes, valuing from 50 to 500, 50 incremental. Every subgroup contains 5 graphs.

Among all the previous researches, CASC is most similar to ours, but it can only determine and avoid the direct deadlock between 2 processors. We replace the deadlock detection function in CASC with the one mentioned above. Table 1

Table 1. The average improving comparisons for random generated DAGs

Size	CCR=0.1	CCR=0.2	CCR=1.0	CCR=2.0	CCR=10.0
50	10.13%	10.08%	13.78%	12.56%	9.28%
100	4.58%	6.69%	13.11%	11.70%	17.33%
150	6.31%	5.76%	10.33%	9.02%	9.28%
200	4.65%	7.72%	5.75%	10.36%	12.23%
250	2.08%	5.21%	6.05%	5.38%	9.51%
300	-0.07%	3.55%	5.55%	7.18%	7.36%
350	2.11%	3.15%	6.50%	5.15%	6.39%
400	3.03%	1.73%	3.80%	6.67%	5.49%
450	3.30%	3.78%	4.75%	4.45%	5.35%
500	3.47%	3.82%	3.32%	5.95%	6.82%

is the comparison of the scheduling quality of PRGSC and modified CASC. The measures in the table are the average makespan improvement of the 5 graphs in every subgroup. We can conclude from these experiment results that PRGSC has better performance than CASC consistently, except for the situation of CCR=0.1 and graph size of 300.

5   Conclusions

Parallel computing in the synchronous communication environment has different impacts on scheduling method. This paper presents a scheduling algorithm used for parallel application in synchronous communication, proves the validity of the deadlock determination method analytically and its efficiency experimentally. PRGSC has lower complexity, breaks the limitation of direct deadlock determination and has better scheduling result than CASC.

References

1. Y.K. Kwok and I. Ahmad, Static Scheduling Algorithms for Allocating Directed Task Graphs to Multiprocessors, ACM Computing Surveys, Dec.1999, vol.31, no.4, pp. 406–471.
2. A. Gerasoulis and T. Yang, A Comparison of Clustering Heuristics for Scheduling DAGs on Multiprocessors, J. Parallel and Distributed Computing, Dec. 1992, vol. 16, no. 4, pp. 276–291.
3. D. Kadamuddi and J. Tsai, Clustering Algorithm for Parallelizing Software System in Multiprocessors, IEEE Transactions on Software Engineering, Apr.2000, vol. 26, pp. 340–361.
4. B.R. Arafeh, A Task Duplication Scheme for Resolving Deadlocks in Clustered DAGs, Parallel Computing, 2003, vol. 29, pp. 795–820.
5. Y.K. Kwok and I. Ahmad, Benchmarking and Comparison of the Task Graph Scheduling Algorithms, J. Parallel and Distributed Computing, Dec. 1999, vol.59, no. 3, pp. 381–422.

A Formal Model for Network Processor Workload[*]

Xiao Ming Zhang, Zhi Gang Sun, and Min Xuan Zhang

School of Computer, National University of Defense Technology,
410073, Changsha, China
xiaomingzone@gmail.com

Abstract. Due to the heterogeneity of network processor architectures and constantly evolving network applications, it is currently a challenge to characterize the network processor workloads. In this paper, we formally model the task-level workloads of network processors as reactive dataflow process network (RDPN). RDPN is a suitable model of computation for formally describing the behaviors of packet-level parallel processing and event interaction with control point of network processors. We extend the expressive capability of RDPN by using three transformations (i.e., clustering, decomposing and duplicating) to analyze the model and support the further design space exploration of network processors.

1 Introduction

A router in core/edge networks is functionally split into control plane (also known as control point) and data plane. Network processors (NPs) are usually located on data-plane of routers and implements functional processing tasks, i.e. packet forwarding, security control and QoS (Quality of Service). Control plane and data plane of routers are interacted with each other in event-driven mode. A special case of interactive transaction would be that control plane constantly updates the forwarding tables of the data plane. These packet processing tasks and interactive transactions are called workloads of NPs. Due to the heterogeneity of network processor architectures and constantly evolving network applications, it is currently a challenge to characterize the network application workload.

Applications based on dataflow processing can be formally modeled by some MoC (Model of Computation) [1, 2, 3, 4, 5, 6]. In this paper, we introduce a novel dataflow process network (DPN) [7] model called Reactive DPN (RDPN) to model application workloads in NP domains. In RDPN model, reactive interfaces are added to basic DPN process and used for describing interactive events between control and data planes, while packet dataflow processing in data plane is still modeled as basic DPN. The remarkable work on this model is that we introduce three transformations (i.e., clustering, decomposing and duplicating) to analyze the model and support the further development of network processor design space.

---

[*] The work has been co-supported by National Sciences Foundations of China (NSFC) under grant No.2003CB314802, Hi-Tech Research and Development Program of China (863) under grant No.2003AA115130.

H. Jin, D. Reed, and W. Jiang (Eds.): NPC 2005, LNCS 3779, pp. 274–277, 2005.

The remainder of this paper is structured as follows. Section 2 presents the basic structure of our RDPN model. Section 3 then describes three transformations of RDPN. Section 4 explores some implementations of RDPN. Finally, we draw some conclusions in Section 5.

2 RDPN Model

The NP application workload represents a serial of packet processing functions. It can be naturally represented by DPN model, which makes parallelism and communication within an application explicit. A single functional task in the workloads is defined as a process and communicates with other processes through unbounded FIFO channels. All elements stored on the channels will be abstracted as tokens, including packets, events and control information.

However, DPN model has vulnerability to describing interactive behaviors between data plane and control plane because of its dataflow-aware feature. A DPN process referring to a task of data plane interacts with control plane through control channels, and with other process of data plane through data channels. We call this special DPN model as *reactive* DPN (RDPN). A single process model is illustrated in Fig. 1(a), where CI,CO respectively denote the input and output control channels between data and control planes, and DI,DO respectively denote input and output dataflow channels in data plane. The process consists of read channel actions, write channel actions and a set of internal function actions { $f_0, f_1, f_2 \cdots$ } mapping input channels to output ones.

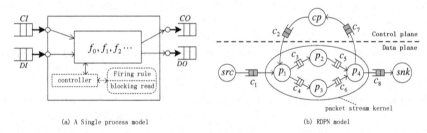

(a) A Single process model   (b) RDPN model

Fig. 1. The structure of our RDPN model, where (a) is the structure of a single process and (b) is the whole RDPN model of the packet processing structure in NP domains

Within our single process model, there is an implicit controller with the function firing rules and blocking read restriction drawn with dashed boxes. The controller itself checks firing rules of every function in a sequential order with blocking reads. When a function is activated, it reads input channels with blocking read and write output channels with non-blocking write. When all input arguments are present the function will be evaluated instantaneously. After evaluating the function, the controller checks the firing rules again until a valid firing is found.

From the single process model, the NP workloads can be described by the RDPN model, which is defined as multiple processes connected with each other according to the process network topology. Our RDPN is an open system, which interacts with external environments through channels. Fig. 1(b) shows an example of RDPN for NP workloads, where *src* and *snk* processes respectively denote input and output packet streams of data plane, while *cp* process denotes the control plane. The packet stream kernel represents the packet processing workload, consisting of process $p_1 \sim p_4$ and channel $c_3 \sim c_6$. Channel c_1, c_2, c_7 and c_8 are environmental interactive channels.

When there is no interaction between data and control planes, the behaviors of our RDPN model act as DPN. There are two types of interactive events between data and control plane: *down events* are used for control plane downloading control information (i.e. NP configuration or routing update) to data plane; *up events* are used for data plane uploading local information (i.e. local states or packets) to control plane. Down events will disrupt the pipelining of packet flow and deadlines of packet processing, while up events not do so. We handle these two types of interactive events in two different ways: (1) the up events are only treated in the same way as normal dataflow throughout the RDPN. (2) we use *event reactive point* (ERP) to control the moment when down events would be applied within the data plane. In more details, before processing an input event the packet input to the network conceptually needs to be frozen and all data must be processed internally. Only when all data has been processed, the event can be applied and the dataflow can be continued.

3   Transformation of RDPN

RDPN model is constructional and hierarchical. We address three transformations of RDPN: clustering, decomposing and duplicating. Clustering and decomposing are used to support hierarchical modeling. Duplicating is used to develop task-level parallelism on the network processor architectures.

When multiple processes communicate with each other frequently or exchange a large amount of dataflow between them, clustering these processes into a single process can avoid the overhead of communication through channels.

A complex process in RDPN can be discomposed into several relatively simple processes in order to analyze the feature and structures of RDPN and develop the task-level parallelism of the network processor workload. We assume that a single process of RDPN is a program described with some kind of programming language (such as C /C ++). Thus decomposing of a process is the same action as translating a program into RDPN, which provides a bridge between the actual workload programs and our formal RDPN model.

A complex task would be distributed to multiple components for parallel implementation. Duplicating a single process of RDPN is used to support this situation. To transform a process into multiple duplicates, we introduce a *switch* process which plays the role of schedulers to map input channels to the duplicates, and a *select* process which selects one duplicate to output its processing results. A RDPN model with duplicating structure can be easy to be mapped into NP architectures based on multi-processors.

4   Implementation of RDPN

We implement RDPN software framework in C++ programming environment by using concepts of object-oriented approach. All Processes of RDPN are implemented by classes. The behaviors of the classes depend on the operational semantics of RDPN. Actions in RDPN are implemented by member functions of the classes. Similarly, all channels are implemented as classes in which these channels are implemented by dynamic lists with FIFO operation.

In our RDPN software framework, every process is treated as an instantiation of its corresponding class, which is assigned a separate thread of execution. To implement event interactions between data and control planes, three threads are introduced to monitor *src*, *snk* and *cp* process in NP domains (referring to Fig. 1(b)). In the RDPN framework, the run-time environment coordinates the execution of all these threads.

5   Conclusion

In this paper, we have proposed a formal model for NP workloads, called RDPN. Our RDPN is used to describe packet processing behavior in data plane as well as the interactive transactions between data and control planes. Transformations of RDPN can extend the expressive capability of RDPN and support design space exploration of NP architectures. Furthermore, modeling NP workloads as RDPN is a start-point of our design space exploration of NP architectures. The next work will be to use the model for application optimization, allocation of processing tasks, developing novel NP architectures and mapping applications to NP architecture.

References

1. G. Kahn. The Semantics of a Simple Language for Parallel Programming. In J.L. Rosenfeld, editor, Information Processing 74, Proceedings, pages 471–475, Stockholm, Sweden, August 1974. North-Holland, Amsterdam, The Netherlands, 1974
2. E. Lee. Overview of the Ptolemy project. Technical Memorandum UCB/ERL No. M01/11, University of California, EECS Dept., Berkeley, CA, March 2001
3. A. Girault, B. Lee, and E. Lee. Hierarchical finite state machines with multiple concurrency models. IEEE Transactions on Computer-aided Design of Integrated Circuits and Systems, 18(6):742-760, June 1999
4. K. Strehl, et al. FunState - an internal design representation for codesign. IEEE Transactions on Very Large Scale Integration (VLSI) Systems, 9(4):524–544, Aug. 2001
5. B. Kienhuis, E. F. Deprettere. Modeling Stream-Based Applications using the SBF model of computation. IEEE Workshop on Signal Processing Systems (SIPS 2001), Antwerp, Belgium, September 26-28, 2001
6. M.C.W. Geilen, T. Basten. Reactive Process Networks. In Fourth ACM International Conference on Embedded Software, Proceedings, pages 137–146. Pisa, Italy, 27-29 September, 2004. ACM Press, New York, NY, USA, 2004
7. E. A. Lee and T. M. Parks. Dataflow Process Networks. Proceedings of the IEEE, May 1995. (http://ptolemy.eecs.berkeley.edu/papers/processNets)

Coping with Data Dependencies
of Multi-dimensional Array References

Lin Qiao, Weitong Huang, and Zhizhong Tang

Department of Computer Science and Technology,
Tsinghua University, Beijing, 100084, PR China
{qiaolin, hwt}@cic.tsinghua.edu.cn,
tzz-dcs@tsinghua.edu.cn

Abstract. This paper presents a new static data dependence analysis approach, Dependence Difference Inequality Test, which can deal with coupled subscripts for multi-dimensional array references for software pipelining techniques for nested loops. The Dependence Difference Inequality Test (DDIT) replaces direction vectors with dependence difference inequalities as constraints to variables in a linear system. The method presented in this paper extends the applicable range of the Generalized Lambda Test and seems to be a practical scheme to analyze data dependence. Experimental results show that the number of data independences checked by the DDIT algorithm is slightly smaller than that manually. It is also shown that our method is better than other traditional data dependence analysis methods without increasing time cost: it increases the success rate of the Generalized Lambda Test by approximately 14.19%.

1 Introduction

Data dependence analysis plays an important role in automatic detection of implicit parallelism in programs written in conventional sequential languages. Dependence analysis techniques estimate, at compile-time, the run-time interactions between different operations or between different instances of the same operation [1]. It is at the core of data dependence analysis strategies to estimate data dependence between two operations in which multi-dimensional array references are involved [2].

Mathematically the problem can be reduced to that of checking whether or not a system of m linear equations with $2n$ unknown variables has a simultaneous integer solution, which satisfies the constraints for each variable in the system. It has been proved that a loop can be software-pipelined with any value of initiation interval if the dependence difference inequalities do not satisfy simultaneously [3]. That is to say, dependence difference inequalities can act as additional constraints to each variable in the system of m linear equations on their own or with other constraints, such as direction vectors.

The paper is the ongoing work of [3]. We focuses on applying dependence difference inequalities for analyzing data dependence. The algorithm the paper presents, called Dependence Difference Inequality Test (DDIT), can handle coupled

H. Jin, D. Reed, and W. Jiang (Eds.): NPC 2005, LNCS 3779, pp. 278–284, 2005.

subscripts for multi-dimensional array references statically. Experimental results shows that our method is better than the Generalized Lambda Test.

This paper is organized as follows. Section 2 first introduces the Lambda Test and the Generalized Lambda Test, and then Section 3 discusses the Dependence Difference Inequality Test. Section 4 gives experimental results. The Last section draws a conclusion.

2 The Lambda Test and the Generalized Lambda Test

This section introduces the Lambda Test and the Generalized Lambda Test that are the cornerstone of the DDIT algorithm.

Geometrically, a linear equation in the system defines a hyperplane π in $\mathbf{R}^{2n}$ spaces. The intersection S of m hyperplanes corresponds to the common solutions to all linear equations in the system [2] [4]. It is obvious that there exists no data dependence if S is empty. The bounds introduced by the Lambda Test or by the Generalized Lambda Test, with any given direction vectors, define a bounded convex set V in $\mathbf{R}^{2n}$. If any of hyperplanes in the system does not intersect V, it is clear that S can not intersect V. However, even if every hyperplane intersects V, it is still possible that S and V are disjoint. And if S and V are disjoint, there exists a hyperplane which contains S and is disjoint from V. Furthermore, the hyperplane is a linear combination of hyperplanes in the system. On the other hand, if S intersect V, there is no such a linear combination [2].

In summary, the Lambda Test or the Generalized Lambda Test first applies the Banerjee Inequalities to test each hyperplane in the system, and then checks these hyperplanes simultaneously if every hyperplane intersects V. These two methods are efficient and precise to analyze the system beneath V. In fact, they are equivalent to a multi-dimensional version of the Banerjee Inequality because they can determine simultaneous constrained real-valued solutions. The tests form linear combinations of coupled references that eliminate one or more instances of index variables when direction vectors are not considered. On the other hand, once direction vectors are considered, they can generate new linear combinations that use a pair of relative index variables. Simultaneous constrained real-valued solutions exist if and only if the Banerjee Inequalities find solutions in all linear combinations generated [2].

3 Dependence Difference Inequality Test

This section takes account of m linear equations, $m \geq 2$, and gives a detailed description of the Dependence Difference Inequality Test.

Without losing generality, all m linear equations are assumed to be connected; otherwise they be partitioned into smaller systems. Furthermore, it is hypothesized that there are no redundant equations. An arbitrary linear combination of m linear equations can be written as $\sum_{i=1}^{m} \lambda_i F_i = 0$ where $F_i = a_{i,0} + \boldsymbol{a}_i \boldsymbol{x}$, $\boldsymbol{a}_i = (a_{i,1}, a_{i,2}, \dots, a_{i,2n})$ for $1 \leq i \leq m$, and $\boldsymbol{x} = (x_1, x_2, \dots, x_{2n})^{\mathrm{T}}$. The domain of $\boldsymbol{\lambda} = (\lambda_1, \lambda_2, \dots, \lambda_m)$ is the whole $\mathbf{R}^m$ space. Let $F_\lambda = -\lambda \boldsymbol{b} + (\lambda \boldsymbol{a}_1{}', \lambda \boldsymbol{a}_2{}', \dots, \lambda \boldsymbol{a}_{2n}{}') \boldsymbol{x}$ where $\boldsymbol{b} = (-a_{1,0}, -a_{2,0}, \dots, -a_{m,0})^{\mathrm{T}}$

and $a_k' = (a_{1,k}, a_{2,k}, ..., a_{m,k})^T$ for $1 \leq k \leq 2n$. It needs to be determined whether or not $F_\lambda = 0$ intersects V in $\mathbf{R}^{2n}$ space for arbitrary λ.

Definition 1. The coefficient of each variable in F_λ is a linear function of λ in $\mathbf{R}^m$ which is $\psi_k = \lambda a_k'$ for $1 \leq k \leq 2n$. The equation $\psi_k = 0$ is termed a ψ-equation, which corresponds to a hyperplane in $\mathbf{R}^m$, called a ψ-plane. Let $\phi_k = \psi_{2k-1} + \psi_{2k}$ for $1 \leq k \leq n$. The equation $\phi_k = 0$ is called a ϕ-equation, which still corresponds to a hyperplane in $\mathbf{R}^m$, called a ϕ-plane.

In general, each ψ-plane or ϕ-plane divides $\mathbf{R}^m$ into two closed half-spaces, i.e., $\psi_k^+ = \{\lambda | \psi_k \geq 0\}$, $\psi_k^- = \{\lambda | \psi_k \leq 0\}$, $\phi_k^+ = \{\lambda | \phi_k \geq 0\}$, and $\phi_k^- = \{\lambda | \phi_k \leq 0\}$. These ψ-planes and ϕ-planes divide the whole space into some regions, denoted by $(\cap_{1 \leq k \leq 2n} \psi_k^*)$ $\cap (\cap_{1 \leq k \leq n} \phi_k^*)$ for $\psi_k^* \in \{\psi_k^+, \psi_k^-\}$ and $\phi_k^* \in \{\phi_k^+, \phi_k^-\}$. It is obvious that each region is a cone in $\mathbf{R}^m$ space. Furthermore, every region has several hyperlines as the frames of their boundaries. Note that such a hyperline can be determined by $m - 1$ hyperplanes in $\mathbf{R}^m$ space uniquely, there are at most $\binom{3n}{m-1}$ hyperlines. As a special case, there are at most $3n$ lines in $\mathbf{R}^2$ space if $m = 2$.

Definition 2. A hyperline determined by arbitrary $m - 1$ ψ-planes and/or ϕ-planes in $\mathbf{R}^m$ space is termed a λ-line which corresponds to a λ-equation, that is,

$$\begin{cases} \xi_1 = 0 \\ \xi_2 = 0 \\ \cdots \\ \xi_{m-1} = 0 \end{cases}, \tag{1}$$

where $\xi_i \in \{\psi_1, \psi_2, ..., \psi_{2n}\} \cup \{\phi_1, \phi_2, ..., \phi_n\}$ and $\xi_i \neq \xi_j$ for $1 \leq i, j \leq m - 1$, $i \neq j$.

Mathematically Eq. (1) can be represented as

$$\xi = U\lambda^T = 0, \tag{2}$$

where $\xi = (\xi_1, \xi_2, ..., \xi_{m-1})^T$, $U = \begin{pmatrix} u_{1,1} & \cdots & u_{1,m} \\ \vdots & \ddots & \vdots \\ u_{m-1,1} & \cdots & u_{m-1,m} \end{pmatrix}$, and $\lambda = (\lambda_1, \lambda_2, ..., \lambda_m)$. On the other hand, it can also be of the form

$$\frac{\lambda_1}{v_1} = \frac{\lambda_2}{v_2} = ... = \frac{\lambda_m}{v_m} \tag{3}$$

since it passes through the origin of the coordinates, where $v = (v_1, v_2, ..., v_m)$ denotes the direction vector of the λ-line. Let $u_i = (u_{i,1}, u_{i,2}, ..., u_{i,m})$ be the normal vector of the hyperplane determined by the equation $\xi_i = 0$ for $1 \leq i \leq m - 1$. We have v is orthogonal with every u_i for $1 \leq i \leq m - 1$ because the λ-line belongs to every hyperplane, i.e.,

$$v = u_1 \times u_2 \times \ldots \times u_{m-1}. \tag{4}$$

Thus, we have

$$v\lambda^{\mathrm{T}} = \begin{vmatrix} \lambda \\ u_1 \\ \ldots \\ u_{m-1} \end{vmatrix} = \begin{vmatrix} \lambda_1 & \lambda_2 & \ldots & \lambda_m \\ u_{1,1} & u_{1,2} & \ldots & u_{1,m} \\ \ldots & \ldots & \ldots & \ldots \\ u_{m-1,1} & u_{m-1,2} & \ldots & u_{m-1,m} \end{vmatrix} = \sum_{j=1}^{m} v_j \lambda_j, \tag{5}$$

where

$$v_j = (-1)^{j+1} \begin{vmatrix} u_{1,1} & \ldots & u_{1,j-1} & u_{1,j+1} & \ldots & u_{1,m} \\ \ldots & \ldots \ldots & \ldots & \ldots \ldots \\ u_{m-1,1} & \ldots & u_{m-1,j-1} & u_{m-1,j+1} & \ldots & u_{m-1,m} \end{vmatrix}. \tag{6}$$

Definition 3. Given an equation of the form $v\lambda^{\mathrm{T}} = 0$ where $\lambda = (\lambda_1, \lambda_2, \ldots, \lambda_m)$, $v = (v_1, v_2, \ldots, v_m)$, and $v_1, v_2, \ldots, v_m$ are not zero simultaneously, a canonical solution of the equation is defined as

$$\begin{cases} \lambda_i = 1, \lambda_j = 0, & \text{if } \exists v_i = 0 \text{ and } \forall v_j \neq 0 \text{ for } 1 \leq i, j \leq m \\ \lambda = (v_2, -v_1, 0, \ldots, 0) & \text{if } \forall v_i \neq 0 \text{ for } 1 \leq i \leq m \end{cases}. \tag{7}$$

Definition 4. The set Λ is denoted to be the set of all canonical solutions to ψ-equations and ϕ-equations. The hyperplane in $\mathbf{R}^{2n}$ corresponding to $F_\lambda = 0$, where λ is a canonical solution in the Λ set, is called a λ-plane.

Theorem 1 [5]. Suppose that a bounded convex set V is defined by the limit of Eq. (2) and Eq. (5) presented in [3]. Given a line in $\mathbf{R}^m$ corresponding to an equation $v\lambda^{\mathrm{T}} = 0$, if $F_\lambda = 0$ intersects V in $\mathbf{R}^m$ for any fixed point $\lambda \neq \mathbf{0}$ in the line, such as its canonical solution, then for every λ in the line $F_\lambda = 0$ also intersects V.

Theorem 1 shows that there are at most $2n$ ψ-planes and n ϕ-planes, and there are no more than $\binom{3n}{m-1}$ λ-lines determined by these hyperplanes. Each of λ-line generates a canonical solution according to Definition 3, and each canonical solution forms a λ-plane in light of Definition 4. That is, there are at most $\binom{3n}{m-1}$ λ-planes to be tested, which is the same as the number of λ-planes checked by the Lambda Test and the Generalized Lambda Test.

4 Experimental Results

We test the DDIT through the NASA benchmark code. For the sake of clarity, we just draw out 100 loops at random, in which the number of operations varies from 17 to 354. As shown in Table 1, among these loops only 3 loops are above 4-level-nested, including two 5-level-nested loops and one 6-level-nested loops. In addition, when a data dependence analysis approach is applied, total 45154 pairs of array references with coupled subscripts have to be tested, 62.57% of which is 3-dimensional.

Table 1. Statistics of extracted loops

		Levels of nested loops				
	Total	1	2	3	4	Others
Number of loops	100	18	25	29	25	3
		Dimension of arrays				
	Total	1	2	3	4	5
Pairs of array references tested	45154	3178	5484	28252	6888	1352

In order to reduce the number of variables of linear systems and to validate our static data dependence analysis approach, we employ an innerprocedural constant propagation technique, manually, before invoking the DDIT algorithm. Except that, no other symbolic value propagation techniques or interprocedural dependence analysis techniques [6] are applied even if they are able to improve on the DDIT algorithm.

Table 2 reveals the success rate of the DDIT algorithm for multi-dimensional array references, by which we mean how often the DDIT detects a case where there is no data dependence. In the table *dependences proved* means they have been checked manually or by the DDIT algorithm; *dependences assumed* means they have been assumed to be dependent because of lacking of further detailed information, which can be found when nonlinear coupled subscripts are involved in pairs of array references or coupled subscripts can not be determined at compile-time at all; and *independences proved* means these data independences have been confirmed.

Table 2. The success rate of the DDIT for multi-dimensional array references

		Dependences proved		Dependences assumed		Independences proved	
		Number	Percent	Number	Percent	Number	Percent
2-dimensional	Manually	722	13.16	154	2.81	4608	84.03
	Checked by DDIT	786	14.33	235	4.29	4463	81.38
3-dimensional	Manually	5612	19.86	945	3.35	21695	76.79
	Checked by DDIT	6481	22.94	1060	3.75	20711	73.31
4-dimensional	Manually	984	14.29	336	4.88	5568	80.83
	Checked by DDIT	1011	14.68	360	5.23	5517	80.09
5-dimensional	Manually	90	6.66	135	9.98	1127	83.36
	Checked by DDIT	90	6.66	141	10.63	1121	82.91

Manual analysis results show that for the 2-dimensional array references 84.03% of them can be parallelized by the ILSP algorithm, for the 3-dimensional 76.79%, for the 4-dimensional 80.83%, and for the 5-dimensional 83.36%. When the DDIT is applied it is founded that 81.38% of pairs of 2-dimensional array references, 73.31% of pairs of the 3-dimensional, 80.09% of pairs of the 4-dimensional, and 82.91% of pairs of the 5-dimensional are independent. That is, the DDIT algorithm detects no data dependences for 31812 pairs of multi-dimensional array references, 75.79% of overall 41976 pairs. It is shown that the number of data independences checked by the DDIT algorithm is slightly smaller than that manually.

We use the Generalized Lambda Test to test the same dataset, as shown in Table 3. When the Generalized Lambda Test is applied it is founded that 78.52% of pairs of 2-dimensional array references, 57.60% of pairs of the 3-dimensional, 61.21% of pairs of the 4-dimensional, and 78.55% of pairs of the 5-dimensional are independent. That is, the Generalized Lambda Test detects no data dependences for 25857 pairs of multi-dimensional array references, 61.60% of overall 41976 pairs. It can be concluded that the number of data independences checked by the DDIT algorithm is significantly greater than that checked by the Generalized Lambda Test: the increasing success rate was about 14.19%. It is satisfying.

Table 3. The success rate of the GLT for multi-dimensional array references

	Dependences proved		Dependences assumed		Independences proved	
	Number	Percent	Number	Percent	Number	Percent
2-dimensional array references	913	16.65	265	4.83	4306	78.52
3-dimensional array references	9543	33.78	2436	8.62	16273	57.60
4-dimensional array references	1824	26.48	848	12.31	4216	61.21
5-dimensional array references	109	8.06	181	13.39	1062	78.55

5 Conclusion

This paper has presented a new data dependence analysis approach, Dependence Difference Inequality Test, for our software pipelining algorithm ILSP. The DDIT extends the applicable range of the Generalized Lambda Test and is able to deal with linear coupled subscripts for multi-dimensional array references by employing dependence difference inequalities as constraints to variables in a linear system on their own or with others.

As the same as the Generalized Lambda Test, The DDIT only ascertains whether or not real-valued solutions exist because it is based on equality consistency checking. However, it is implemented for the ILSP algorithm in particular. Experimental results shows that compared to the Generated Lambda Test the DDIT increases the success rate without increasing time cost. Therefore, the DDIT seems to be a practical scheme to analyze data dependence for the ILSP algorithm.

On the other hand, a dynamic data dependence analysis approach is presented in [7], which can work with this method together to coping with data dependencies for software pipelining.

Acknowledgement

This work was partially supported by National Nature Science Foundation, grant number 60173010, of *P. R. China*.

References

1. Petersen, P. M., Padua, D. A.: Static and Dynamic Evaluation of Data Dependence Analysis Techniques. IEEE Transactions on Parallel and Distributed Systems 7 (1996) 1121–1132
2. Chang, W. L., Chu, C. P., Wu, J.: The Generalized Lambda Test: A Multi-Dimensional Version of Banerjee's Algorithm. International Journal of Parallel and Distributed Systems and Networks 2 (1999) 69–78
3. Qiao, L., Huang, W. T., Tang, Z. Z.: A Static Data Dependence Analysis Approach for Software Pipelining. In: Jin, H., Reed, D., Jiang, W. (eds.): Proceedings of IFIP International Conference on Network and Parallel Computing, Beijing, Lecture Notes in Computer Science. Springer-Verlag, Berlin Heidelberg New York (2005) accepted by NPC'05
4. Li, Z., Yew, Y. C., Zhu, C. Q.: An Efficient Data Dependence Analysis for Parallelizing Compilers. IEEE Transactions on Parallel and Distributed System 1 (1990) 26–34
5. Qiao, L.: On Data Dependencies in Software Pipelining. Doctorial Dissertation, Department of Computer Science, Tsinghua University, Beijing (2001)
6. Johnson, S. P., Cross, M., Everett, M. G.: Exploitation of Symbolic Information in Interprocedural Dependence Analysis. Parallel Computing 22 (1996) 197–226
7. Qiao, L., Huang, W. T., Tang, Z. Z.: A Dynamic Data Dependence Analysis Approach for Software Pipelining. In: Jin, H., Reed, D., Jiang, W. (eds.): Proceedings of IFIP International Conference on Network and Parallel Computing, Beijing, Lecture Notes in Computer Science. Springer-Verlag, Berlin Heidelberg New York (2005) accepted by NPC'05

QoS-Based Dynamic Channel Allocation
for GSM/GPRS Networks

Jun Zheng[1] and Emma Regentova[2]

[1] Department of Computer Science,
Queens College - The City University of New York, USA
zheng@cs.qc.edu
[2] Deaprtment of Electrical and Computer Engineering,
University of Nevada, Las Vegas, USA
regent@egr.unlv.edu

Abstract. Efficient channel allocation is important for meeting the quality of service (QoS) requirements of both GSM voice calls and GPRS packets in integrated GSM/GPRS networks. In this paper, we propose a new dynamic channel allocation scheme with guard channel, channel de-allocation/re-allocation for voice call and packet queue for GSM/GPRS networks. An analytic model with general GPRS channel requirement is developed to evaluate the performance of the proposed scheme. Numerical results demonstrate that the scheme can adapt to different QoS requirements of the system by adjusting the number of guard channels and the size of packet queue. Compared to some conventional schemes, the proposed scheme achieves better performance of QoS provisioning.

1 Introduction

General Packet Radio Service (GPRS) utilizes the existing GSM network infrastructure to provide end-to-end packet-switched service [1]. To ensure the required quality of service (QoS) of the voice and data in the integrated GSM/GPRS networks, the channel allocation scheme has to optimally use the scarce radio resource. Dynamic resource allocation is believed to be a judicious solution for the problem.

Dynamic channel allocation in GSM/GPRS networks has received a considerable attention in recent studies. For example, Lin et al. [2] investigated four resource allocation algorithms, i.e., fix resource allocation (FRA), fix resource allocation with queue capability (FRAQ), dynamic resource allocation (DRA) and dynamic resource allocation with queue capability (DRAQ). In the dynamic schemes, partial resources can be allocated to the GPRS packet request. This kind of dynamic allocation can substantially reduce the GPRS dropping probability. It is also indicated that the voice queuing mechanism could significantly lower the GSM voice call incompletion probability. In [3], Lin et al. studied the buffering mechanisms for the dynamic resource allocation by employing both the voice queue and the packet queue. The results have demonstrated that packet

H. Jin, D. Reed, and W. Jiang (Eds.): NPC 2005, LNCS 3779, pp. 285–294, 2005.
© IFIP International Federation for Information Processing 2005

queuing greatly reduces the GPRS packet dropping probability while the performance of the voice call slightly degrades. Chen et al. [4] proposed a channel de-allocation scheme (DAS) which decreases the GSM voice call incompletion probability by de-allocating a channel from on-going GPRS packet to new arrived GSM voice call if there is no free channel in the system. In [5], the authors employed both DAS and packet queue. It was shown that although the packet buffering mechanism can lessen the packet dropping probability, it increases the voice call incompletion probability even with the DAS in use. Recently, Zhang and Soong [6] introduced a channel re-allocation scheme (RAS) that re-allocates released idling channels to the GPRS data using partial resources. Results confirm that RAS sharply decreases the GSM voice call incompletion probability at the expense of the slight increment of the GPRS packet dropping probability.

In all the above studies, the new and handoff GSM voice calls are not differentiated. However, in the real systems, handoff calls always have a higher priority than new voice calls. This is because termination of a former is more noticeable, hence more annoying for users than blocking of a new call. In this paper, we enforce the priority of handoff voice calls, and propose a dynamic channel allocation scheme with guard channel, channel de-allocation/re-allocation for voice call and packet queue. In the proposed scheme, the guard channel is for lowering the dropping probability of handoff calls. Channel de-allocation/re-allocation for voice call lessens both the new and handoff voice call blocking probabilities and the packet queuing is used for reducing the packet dropping probability. By dynamically adjusting the guard channel capacity and the packet queue size, the scheme can adapt to the QoS requirements of the system on the new/hadnoff voice call blocking probability and GPRS packet dropping probability.

To study the system performance under the proposed dynamic channel allocation scheme, we derive an analytic model. In contrast with the models in [2][3][4][5] that have adopted a specific maximum numbers of channels for GPRS packet for the sake of analytical simplicity, we derive a model with generalized GPRS channel requirement based on the one presented in [6]. That offers more versatility to the performance analysis.

The rest of this paper is organized as follows. In the next section, we introduce the QoS-based dynamic channel allocation scheme with guard channel, channel de-allocation/re-allocation for voice call and packet queue. The analytical model for evaluating the performance of the proposed scheme is developed in Section 3. Numerical results are presented and discussed in Section 4, and followed are the conclusions drawn in Section 5.

2   QoS-Based Dynamic Resource Allocation Scheme

We consider the GSM/GPRS network is homogeneous such that we only need to analyze one cell case. Assume the base station (BS) of each cell has C channels shared by GSM voice calls and GPRS data packets. The maximum number of channels for data packet transmission is M. A type-m GPRS call is the GPRS packet transmitted using $m(m = 1, ..., M)$ channels. Assume the number of free channels in the system is C_F which equals to $C - n_{vn} - n_{vh} - \sum_{m=1}^{M} m n_{g_m}$, where n_{vn} is the number of new voice calls in service, n_{vh} is the number of handoff voice calls, n_{g_m} is the number of type-m ongoing GPRS packet transmissions. The proposed scheme reserves g channels as guard channels only for serving handoff GSM voice calls. The remaining $(C - g)$ channels are shared by both new/handoff GSM voice calls and GPRS calls. The size of the packet queue is B, and the number of GPRS calls buffered in the packet queue is denoted as n_{PQ}.

The state of the system changes according to the arrival and the completion of new/handoff GSM voice call and GPRS call. For the new GSM voice call arrival, the call will be served if $C_F > g$. The handoff voice call will be served if $C_F > 0$. Upon arrival of GPRS packet, M channels are allocated if $C_F \geq M + g$. If $g < C_F < M + g$, $(C_F - g)$ channels are allocated to the GPRS call. If $C_F \leq g$ and the number of buffered GPRS calls is less than B, the GPRS call will be buffered in the packet queue. Otherwise, the GPRS packet is dropped. For a new arrived voice call, if $C_F \leq g$, channel de-allocation allows one channel from an ongoing type-m $(m > 1)$ GPRS call (or degradable GPRS call) to service the arrived voice call. If no degradable GPRS call exists, the arrived new voice call will be blocked. For handoff voice call, if $C_F = 0$, channel de-allocation will be applied to service the call if there exists a degradable GPRS call in the system. Otherwise, the handoff voice call will be forced to terminate. Note that the channel is de-allocated from the GPRS call with the highest number of channels, e.g. a type-m GPRS call can be degraded if there is no type-q $(q = m + 1, ..., M - 1, M)$ GPRS call in the BS. Upon the channel release due to the GSM voice call termination or handoff or completion of the GPRS packet transmission, if there are degraded GPRS calls in the system and no GPRS call buffered in the packet queue, the released channels will be re-allocated to upgrade the transmission of these calls. The re-allocation is performed using "worst degraded first upgrading" policy [6]. That is, a type-m GPRS call can be upgraded if all type-q $(q = 1, 2, ..., m - 1)$ GPRS calls have been upgraded to type-M. If there are GPRS calls buffered in the packet queue, the released channels are used to service the buffered GPRS call instead of re-allocating for degraded on-going GPRS calls.

To demonstrate the performance of the proposed scheme, we compare it with three other dynamic resource allocation schemes described below.

(1) Scheme 1 (referred as DRA1) is the same as the DRA proposed in [2];
(2) Scheme 2 (referred as DRA2) is the same as the scheme with channel de-allocation/re-allocation for voice call in [6];
(3) Scheme 3 (referred as DRA3) is similar to the proposed scheme except the channel de-allocation/re-allocation for voice call is not applied.

3   Analytic Model

For the purpose of performance analysis of the proposed dynamic channel allocation scheme, we develop an analytic model. We assume that the new GSM voice call, the handoff GSM voice call and the GPRS packet all follow the Poisson process with arrival rate λ_{vn}, λ_{vh} and λ_g, respectively. The voice call holding time and the cell residence time are assumed to be exponentially distributed with means $1/\mu_{ch}$, $1/\mu_{cr}$, respectively. Then the channel holding time for voice call is exponentially distributed with rate $\mu_v = \mu_{ch} + \mu_{cr}$. If one channel is allocated to a GPRS packet, the packet transmission is assumed to follow the exponential distribution with mean $1/\mu_g$. Thus the mean packet transmission time is also exponentially distributed with mean $1/m\mu_g$ when m channels are allocated. The handoff of the GPRS packet transmission is not considered, because the transmission time of individual packet is negligible, and transmission is completed before the handoff procedure starts [3].

The dynamic resource allocation scheme is modeled as a $(M + 3)$-dimension Markov process. A state in this process is denoted as $s = (n_{vn}, n_{vh}, n_{g_1}, n_{g_2}, ..., n_{g_{M-1}}, n_{g_M}, n_{PQ})$. The state space $\boldsymbol{S}$ of the Markov process is given by

$$
\begin{aligned}
\boldsymbol{S} = \Big(& s = (n_{vn}, n_{vh}, n_{g_1}, n_{g_2}, ..., n_{g_{M-1}}, n_{g_M}, n_{PQ}) \mid \\
& 0 \le n_{vn} + n_{vh} + \sum_{k=1}^{M} k n_{g_k} \le C - g, 0 \le n_{vn} \le C - g, \\
& 0 \le n_{vh} \le C - g, 0 \le n_{g_k} \le \lfloor \tfrac{C-g}{k} \rfloor (k = 1, 2, ..., M), n_{PQ} = 0 \Big) \\
\bigcup \Big(& s = (n_{vn}, n_{vh}, n_{g_1}, n_{g_2}, ..., n_{g_{M-1}}, n_{g_M}, n_{PQ}) \mid \\
& 0 \le n_{vn} + \sum_{k=1}^{M} k n_{g_k} \le C - g, C - g < n_{vn} + n_{vh} + \sum_{k=1}^{M} k n_{g_k} \le C, \\
& 0 \le n_{vn} \le C - g, 0 \le n_{vh} \le C, 0 \le n_{g_k} \le \lfloor \tfrac{C}{k} \rfloor (k = 1, 2, ..., M), n_{PQ} \ge 0 \Big)
\end{aligned}
\tag{1}
$$

Denote the steady state probability for state s as π_s. For all states $s \in \boldsymbol{S}$, $\sum_{s \in \boldsymbol{S}} \pi_s = 1$. To find the steady state probability matrix $\boldsymbol{\Pi}$, we need to obtain the generator matrix $\boldsymbol{Q} = [q_{s \to s'}]_{s \in \boldsymbol{S}, s' \in \boldsymbol{S}}$, where $q_{s \to s'}$ ($s \in \boldsymbol{S}, s' \in \boldsymbol{S}$) is the transition rate from state $s = (n_{vn}, n_{vh}, n_{g_1}, n_{g_2}, ..., n_{g_{M-1}}, n_{g_M}, n_{PQ})$ to state $s' = (n'_{vn}, n'_{vh}, n'_{g_1}, n'_{g_2}, ..., n'_{g_{M-1}}, n'_{g_M}, n'_{PQ})$.

Given below are some definitions for deriving the generator matrix $\boldsymbol{Q}$.

- I_A: The indicator function which equals to 1 (0) when the event A is true (false).
- n_{g_α}: The first non-zero value in the sequence $(n_{g_M}, n_{g_{M-1}}, ..., n_{g_2})$, where $\alpha = \max(m \mid n_{g_m} > 0, m = M, M - 1, ..., 2)$. For $(n_{g_M}, n_{g_{M-1}}, ..., n_{g_2}) \equiv 0$, α is set to -1. Thus if $\alpha \ge 2$, there exists a degradable GPRS call.
- n_{g_β}: The first non-zero value in the sequence $(n_{g_1}, n_{g_1}, ..., n_{g_{M-1}})$, where $\beta = \min(k \mid n_{g_k} > 0, k = 1, 2, ..., M - 1)$. For $(n_{g_1}, n_{g_2}, ..., n_{g_{M-1}}) \equiv 0$, β is set to -1. Thus if $\beta \ge 0$, there exists a degraded GPRS call.
- $\boldsymbol{M}$: The state space of the GPRS call type, $\boldsymbol{M} = (1, 2, ..., M - 1, M)$.

To obtain the transition rate $q_{s \to s'}$, we consider two cases according to the arrival and completion events of new/handoff GSM voice call and GPRS call.

Case 1: New/handoff GSM voice call and GPRS call arrival

The transitions from state s to all possible next state s' for new/handoff GSM voice call and GPRS call arrival are shown in Table 1, where the first column shows the changes between s and s' followed with the condition for the transitions, transition rates and the event related to the transition.

Case 2: New/handoff GSM voice call and GPRS call completion

Table 2 shows the state transitions under new/handoff GSM voice call and GPRS call completion. Here we discuss in detail the case of type-m GPRS call completion and $n_{PQ} = 0$ that channel re-allocation can be used by allocating the released m channels to upgrade degraded GPRS calls in the system. In this case, upon the type-m GPRS call completion, the new state becomes s_1 = $(n_{vn}^*, n_{vh}^*, n_{g_1}^*, ..., n_{g_m}^*, ..., n_{g_M}^*, n_{PQ}^*)$, where $n_{vn}^* = n_{nv}$, $n_{vh}^* = n_{vh}$, $n_{g_m}^* = n_{g_m} - 1$, $n_{g_k}^* = n_{g_k} (k \in \mathbf{M} - \{m\})$, $n_{PQ}^* = n_{PQ}$. An index θ $(1 \le \theta \le M - 1)$ is introduced such that

$$\sum_{k=1}^{\theta-1} n_{g_k}^* (M - k) \le m \le \sum_{k=1}^{\theta} n_{g_k}^* (M - k). \tag{2}$$

Inequality (2) implies that when a type-m GPRS call leaves the BS, all the type-1 to type-$(\theta - 1)$ GPRS calls and some of the type-θ GPRS calls can be upgraded to type-M GPRS calls. Denote

$$\delta = \lfloor \frac{m - \sum_{k=1}^{\theta-1} n_{g_k}^* (M - k)}{M - \theta} \rfloor$$

as the number of type-θ calls that can be upgraded to type-M calls. $\delta_r = \delta - \delta(M - \theta)$ is the number of channels that can upgrade a type-θ call to type-$(\theta + \delta_r)$. If $\sum_{k=1}^{M-1} n_{g_k}^* (M - k) \le m$ which means that all the type-1 to type-$(M - 1)$ calls can be upgraded to type-M calls, we set θ to M. If $\beta = 0$ which means that there is no data call in the BS or all the data calls are type-M, we set θ to -1.

The transition rate $q_{s \to s}$ can be obtained as

$$q_{s \to s} = - \sum_{s' \ne s, s \in S, s' \in S} q_{s \to s'} \tag{3}$$

Table 1. Transitions from s to s' for new/handoff GSM voice call and GPRS call arrival. A: New GSM voice call, B: Handoff GSM voice call, C: Type-m GPRS call.

Next state s'	Condition	Rate	Event
$n_{vn}' = n_{vn} + 1$	$C_F > g$	λ_{vn}	A
$n_{vn}' = n_{vn} + 1, n_{g_\alpha-1}' = n_{g_\alpha-1} + 1,$ $n_{g_\alpha}' = n_{g_\alpha} - 1$	$C_F \le g$ and $\alpha \ge 2$	λ_{vn}	A
$n_{vh}' = n_{vh} + 1$	$C_F > 0$	λ_{vh}	B
$n_{vh}' = n_{vh} + 1, n_{g_\alpha-1}' = n_{g_\alpha-1} + 1,$ $n_{g_\alpha}' = n_{g_\alpha} - 1$	$C_F = 0$ and $\alpha \ge 2$	λ_{vh}	B
$n_{g_M}' = n_{g_M} + 1$	$C_F \ge M + g$	λ_g	C
$n_{g_{C_F-g}}' = n_{g_{C_F-g}} + 1$	$g < C_F < M + g$	λ_g	C
$n_{PQ}' = n_{PQ} + 1$	$C_F \le g, B > 0$ and $n_{PQ} < B$	λ_g	C

Table 2. Transitions from s to s' for new/handoff GSM voice call and GPRS call completion. D: New GSM voice call, E: Handoff GSM voice call, F: Type-m GPRS call.

Next state s'	Condition	Rate	Event
$n'_{vn} = n_{vn} - 1, n'_{g_1} = n_{g_1} + 1,$ $n'_{PQ} = n_{PQ} - 1$	$n_{PQ} > 0$	$n_{vn}\mu_v$	D
$n'_{vn} = n_{vn} - 1, n'_{g_\beta} = n_{g_\beta} - 1,$ $n'_{g_{\beta+1}} = n_{g_{\beta+1}} + 1$	$n_{PQ} = 0$ and $\beta > 0$	$n_{vn}\mu_v$	D
$n'_{vn} = n_{vn} - 1$	$n_{PQ} = 0$ and $\beta = -1$	$n_{vn}\mu_v$	D
$n'_{vh} = n_{vh} - 1, n'_{g_1} = n_{g_1} + 1,$ $n'_{PQ} = n_{PQ} - 1$	$C_F \geq g$ and $n_{PQ} > 0$	$n_{vh}\mu_v$	E
$n'_{vh} = n_{vh} - 1, n'_{g_\beta} = n_{g_\beta} - 1,$ $n'_{g_{\beta+1}} = n_{g_{\beta+1}} + 1$	$C_F \geq g, n_{PQ} = 0$ and $\beta > 0$	$n_{vh}\mu_v$	E
$n'_{vh} = n_{vh} - 1$	$C_F \geq g, n_{PQ} = 0$ and $\beta = -1$	$n_{vh}\mu_v$	E
$n'_{vh} = n_{vh} - 1$	$C_F < g$	$n_{vh}\mu_v$	E
$n'_{PQ} = n_{PQ} - 1$	$n_{PQ} > 0$	$n_{g_m} m\mu_g$	F
$n'_{g_m} = n_{g_m} - 1$	$n_{PQ} = 0$ and $\theta = -1$	$n_{g_m} m\mu_g$	F
$n'_{g_k} = 0(k = 1, 2, ..., \theta - 1),$ $n'_{g_\theta} = n_{g_\theta} - \delta - 1,$ $n'_{g_{\theta+\delta_r}} = n_{g_{\theta+\delta_r}} + 1,$ $n'_{g_M} = n_{g_M} + \sum_{k=1}^{\theta-1} n_{g_k} + \delta$	$n_{PQ} = 0$ and $1 \leq \theta \leq M - 1$	$n_{g_m} m\mu_g$	F
$n'_{g_k} = 0(k \in \mathbf{M} - \{M\}),$ $n'_{g_M} = \sum_{k=1}^{M} n_{g_k} - 1$	$n_{PQ} = 0$ and $\theta = M$	$n_{g_m} m\mu_g$	F

From Table 1 and 2 and Eq. (3), we can derive the generator matrix $\mathbf{Q}$ for the $(M+3)$-dimension Markov chain. To obtain the steady-state probability matrix $\mathbf{\Pi}$, we need to solve the linear equation $\mathbf{\Pi e} = 1$ and $\mathbf{\Pi Q} = 0$, where $\mathbf{e}$ is a unary column vector. This is done using a numerical method introduced in [7].

Knowing the steady-state probability π_s of the Markov chain, we can calculate the handoff GSM voice call arrival rate as

$$\lambda_{vh} = \sum_{s \in S} (n_{vn} + n_{vh})\pi_s \mu_{cr} \qquad (4)$$

Since the steady-state probability π_s and the handoff call arrival rate λ_{vh} are mutually related, an iterative algorithm is applied to compute π_s and λ_{vh} as in [8].

To measure the performance of the proposed scheme, we use the following performance metrics - new GSM voice call blocking probability P_{vn}, handoff GSM voice call forced termination probability P_{vh}, GPRS packet dropping probability P_g and channel utilization u.

The new GSM voice call will be blocked if the number of free channels $C_F \leq g$ and the GPRS calls in the BS are all type-1. Then, the new GSM voice call blocking probability P_{vn} is represented as

$$P_{vn} = \sum_{n_{PQ}=0}^{B} \sum_{\substack{n_{vn}+n_{vh}+n_{g_1} \geq C-g, \\ n_{g_k}=0(k\in M-\{1\}), s\in S}} \pi_s \tag{5}$$

The handoff GSM voice call will be forced to terminate if the number of free channels $C_F = 0$, and the GSM calls in the BS are all of type-1. The handoff GSM voice call dropping probability P_{vh} is obtained as

$$P_{vh} = \sum_{n_{PQ}=0}^{B} \sum_{\substack{n_{vn}+n_{vh}+n_{g_1}=C, \\ n_{g_k}=0(k\in M-\{1\}), s\in S}} \pi_s \tag{6}$$

The GPRS packet will be dropped if the number of free channels $C_F \leq g$ and the packet queue is full. The GPRS packet dropping probability P_g is then represented as

$$P_g = \sum_{\substack{n_{vn}+n_{vh}+n_{g_1} \geq C-g, \\ n_{PQ}=B, s\in S}} \pi_s \tag{7}$$

The channel utilization u can be expressed as

$$u = \frac{\sum_{s\in S}\left(n_{vn} + n_{vh} + \sum_{k=1}^{M} k n_{g_k}\right)\pi_s}{C} \tag{8}$$

It should be noted that the above-mentioned performance metrics are influenced by the number of guard channels g and the packet queue size B. To measure the QoS of the system, we use a system award Q which is expressed as

$$Q = \alpha(1 - P_{vn}) + \beta(1 - P_{vh}) + \gamma(1 - P_g) \tag{9}$$

where α, β and γ are weighting factors which indicate the contribution of P_{vn}, P_{vh} and P_g to the system's QoS, respectively. Notice that $\alpha + \beta + \gamma = 1$. The weighting factors are determined by the system's overall revenue and service objectives. A larger Q indicates higher performance of the scheme.

4   Numerical Results

Based on the derived analytic model, we can evaluate the performance of the proposed dynamic resource allocation scheme. We normalize the parameters λ_{vn}, λ_g, μ_{cr} and μ_g by μ_{ch} as done in [2][3]. The number of channels C in the BS is assumed to be 7.

Figures 1(a) through 1(d) compare the performance of the proposed scheme with that of other three schemes under different GPRS traffic load ρ_g. The parameters are set as $M = 2$, $B = 4$, $g = 1$, $\mu_{ch} = 1/180$, $\mu_{cr} = 0.2\mu_{ch}$, $\mu_g = 100\mu_{ch}$ and $\rho_v = 2$. Fig. 1(a) shows that DRA1 and DRA2 without packet queue capability have a higher P_g compared to that of DRA3 and the proposed scheme

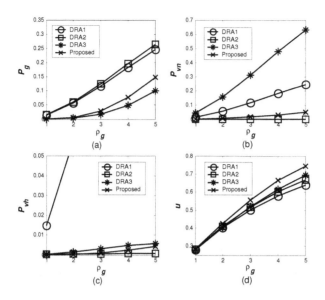

Fig. 1. Performance comparison for different schemes. (a) P_g, (b) P_{vn}, (c) P_{vh}, (d) u.

with packet queue. DRA3 has lower P_g than that of the proposed scheme because DRA3 does not use channel de-allocation/re-allocation for voice calls. From Fig. 1(b), we can see that P_{vn} is ranging from low to high for DRA2, the proposed scheme, DRA1 and DRA3. By using channel de-allocation/re-allocation for voice call, DRA2 and the proposed scheme achieves lower P_{vn}. Since the proposed scheme employs the packet queue and guard channels that results in higher P_{vn}, DRA2 outperforms the proposed scheme in terms of P_{vn}. DRA3 has the highest P_{vn} because it uses the packet queue and guard channels without channel de-allocation/re-allocation for voice call. Fig. 1(c) shows that P_{vh} ranging from low to high are DRA2, the proposed scheme, DRA3 and DRA1. From Fig. 1(d), one can observe that the proposed scheme achieves the best channel utilization. Followed are DRA3, DRA2 and DRA1.

Figure 2(a) to 2(d) show the system award Q as a function of B and g for different system QoS requirements. They correspond to four cases with varying weight factors for the system award Q: (a) $\alpha = 0.8$, $\beta = 0.1$ and $\gamma = 0.1$, (b) $\alpha = 0.1$, $\beta = 0.8$ and $\gamma = 0.1$, (c) $\alpha = 0.1$, $\beta = 0.1$ and $\gamma = 0.8$ and (d) $\alpha = 0.4$, $\beta = 0.3$ and $\gamma = 0.3$. Other parameters are set as $M = 2$, $\mu_{ch} = 1/180$, $\lambda_{vn} = 2\mu_{ch}$, $\lambda_g = 200\mu_{ch}$, $\mu_{cr} = 0.4\mu_{ch}$, $\mu_g = 100\mu_{ch}$, $0 \le g \le 5$, $0 \le B \le 6$. For Fig. 2(a), we can find $g = 0$ and $B = 1$ produce the best value of Q. This is due to the fact that P_{vn} is the most important factor in the system award Q ($\alpha = 0.8$) and larger g and B will result in higher P_{vn}. In Fig. 2(b), the best Q is achieved for $g = 1$ and $B = 3$. In this case, the system emphasizes P_{vh} ($\beta = 0.8$) and one channel is reserved only for handoff voice calls. Fig. 2(c) shows the best Q produced when $g = 0$, $B = 6$. In this case, the system prefers GPRS packet to GSM voice call ($\gamma = 0.8$) and a larger packet queue size is used to reduce

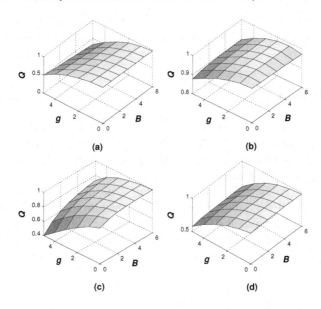

Fig. 2. System award Q vs. B and g for (a) $\alpha = 0.8$, $\beta = 0.1$ and $\gamma = 0.1$, (b) $\alpha = 0.1$, $\beta = 0.8$ and $\gamma = 0.1$, (c) $\alpha = 0.1$, $\beta = 0.1$ and $\gamma = 0.8$ and (d) $\alpha = 0.4$, $\beta = 0.3$ and $\gamma = 0.3$

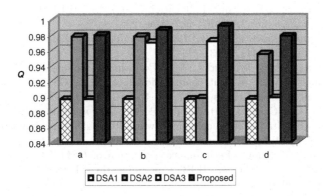

Fig. 3. System award comparison for different schemes. (a) $\alpha = 0.8$, $\beta = 0.1$ and $\gamma = 0.1$, (b) $\alpha = 0.1$, $\beta = 0.8$ and $\gamma = 0.1$, (c) $\alpha = 0.1$, $\beta = 0.1$ and $\gamma = 0.8$ and (d) $\alpha = 0.4$, $\beta = 0.3$ and $\gamma = 0.3$.

P_g. Finally, for the case shown in Fig. 2(d), the system has no preferences for new/handoff GSM voice call or GPRS packet, we can find that the best Q is achieved by $g = 0$, $B = 4$.

We then compare the system award Q of the four dynamic resource allocation schemes as shown in Fig. 3 for the same four cases and parameters as for Fig 2. Q values of DSA3 are obtained using the optimal combination of g and B. The results demonstrate that the proposed scheme always outperforms other three reference schemes because it is furnished by the capability of adjusting the number of guard channels g and packet queue size B to meet the system's QoS requirements.

5 Conclusion

In the integrated GSM/GPRS networks, the GSM voice and the GPRS packet services use the same resources that makes the channel allocation a critical issue for the QOS provisioning for both. In this paper, we have discussed a new dynamic channel allocation scheme with guard channel, channel de-allocation/re-allocation for voice call and packet queuing. The developed analytical model with generalized GPRS data channel requirement has allowed for evaluating the performance of the proposed scheme. The numerical results indicate that by adjusting the number of guard channels and the size of the packet queue, one can attain dynamical adaptation to different QoS requirements of the system.

References

1. Y.-B. Lin, H. C.-H. Rao and I. Chlamtac, "General Packet Radio Service (GPRS): architecture, interfaces and deployment," Wirel. Commun. Mob. Comput., vol. 1, pp. 77-92, 2001.
2. P. Lin and Y. -B. Lin, "Channel allocation for GPRS," IEEE Trans. on Vehicular Technology, vol. 50, no. 2, pp. 375-387, Mar. 2001.
3. P. Lin, "Channel allocation for GPRS with buffering mechanisms," Wireless Networks, vol. 9, pp. 431-441, 2003.
4. W. Y. Chen, J.-L. C. Wu and L. Lu, "Performance comparison of dynamic resource allocation with/without channel de-allocation in GSM/GPRS networks," IEEE Communications Letters, vol. 7, no. 1, pp. 10-12, Jan. 2003.
5. W. Y. Chen, J.-L. C. Wu and H. H. Liu, "Performance analysis of dynamic resource allocation with finite buffers in cellular networks," IEICE Trans. Fundementals, vol. E87-A, no. 7, pp. 1692-1699, July 2004.
6. Y. Zhang and B. Soong, "Performance evaluation of GSM/GPRS networks with channel re-allocation scheme," IEEE Communications Letters, vol. 8, no. 5, pp. 280-282, May 2004.
7. W. J. Stewart, Introduction to the Numerical Solution of Markov Chains, Princeton University Press, 1994.
8. Y. -B. Lin, "Performance modeling for mobile telephone networks," IEEE Network Magazine, vol. 11, no. 6, pp. 63-68, 1997.

Distributed Active Measuring Link Bandwidth in IP Networks*

Zhiping Cai, Jianping Yin, Fang Liu, Xianghui Liu, and Shaohe Lv

School of Computer, National University of Defense Technology, China
caizhiping_nudt@163.com, jpyin@nudt.edu.cn, fangl_nudt@163.com,
liuxh@tom.com, chi.shaohe@gmail.com

Abstract. Link bandwidth is obviously critical for numerous network management tasks. Taking into account the issues of measuring costs and network-wide view for large IP network, a distributed measuring system would be an ideal monitoring architecture for active measuring link bandwidth. In this paper, we address the problem of efficiently measure assignment, which optimizing goal is to reduce the cost of measuring all links bandwidth. We show that this problem is NP-hard and propose an approximation algorithm with approximation ratio 2. The effectiveness of our measuring algorithm is validated by simulations evaluation over a wide range of network topologies.

1 Introduction

Link bandwidth is obviously critical for numerous network management tasks, including identifying and relieving congestion points, proactive and reactive resource management and traffic engineering, as well as providing and verifying QoS guarantees for end-user applications. Some novel tools and infrastructures for measuring network bandwidth have been developed and proposed by researchers and industries, like as SNMP and RMON measurement probes [1], Cisco's NetFlow tools [2], the IDMaps [3], [4], packet-pair algorithms for measuring link bandwidth [5], [6] and the Pathchar [7] tool for estimating Internet link characteristics.

These measurement tools periodically query and collect detailed traffic data on packet flows for monitoring and measuring network flows and bandwidth usage. Unfortunately, probes processing queries can adversely impact routers performance and active probe message transfers can result in significant volumes of additional network traffic [8].

As an example, Pathchar [7] is unique in its ability to measure the bandwidth of every link on a path accurately while requiring special software on only one host. This mean it could easily be widely deployed. Although excellent as a testing tool, the problem with Pathchar is that it is slow and can consume significant amounts of network bandwidth [6]. The distance between measuring

---

* This work is supported by the National Natural Science Foundation of China under Grant No. 60373023.

H. Jin, D. Reed, and W. Jiang (Eds.): NPC 2005, LNCS 3779, pp. 295–302, 2005.

station and destination link is greater, the probe messages would consume more bandwidth. So using a distributed active measuring architecture can reduce the overall measuring cost and the impact on network bandwidth.

Another key consideration in using the distributed measuring architecture is these measurement tools can only measure links included in the routing trees of the measuring stations [9]. To measure all link of the network, it must install some distributed measuring stations. Thus, taking into account the issues of measuring costs and network-wide view for large service provider network, a distributed measuring system would be an ideal monitoring architecture for active measuring link bandwidth.

The costs of measuring the same link bandwidth are different in sending probe messages from different measuring stations. Hence, once we have selected a set of measuring stations, we need to determine the measurement strategies to minimize the measuring cost for measuring all link of a network. Our work focuses on optimizing the measure assignment for measuring all links bandwidths.

The main contributions of our work are as follows: We first show that the problem of minimizing the measuring costs in a given network with some given measuring stations is NP-hard. Then using greedy heuristics and dynamic programming, we propose an approximation algorithm with an approximation ratio 2. The effectiveness of our measuring algorithm is validated by simulations evaluation over a wide range of network topologies.

The paper is structured as follows. We bring forward the measure assignment problem and provide the integer programming formulation in the section 2. In next section, we give an approximation algorithm to solve the measure assignment problem. The result of simulations evaluation is shown in section 4. And we depict our further research in the last section.

1.1 Related Work

Y. Bejerano et al. [8] and J. Walz et al. [10] study link monitoring and delays in IP networks based on a single Network Operations Center(NOC) . In order to monitor links not in its routing tree, the NOC uses the IP source routing option to explicitly route probe packets along the links [8]. Unfortunately, due to security problems, many routers frequently disable the IP source routing option. Consequently, approaches that rely on explicitly routed probe packets for delay and fault monitoring may not be feasible in today's ISP and Enterprise environments [11]. On the other hand, the distributed monitoring infrastructures would be better than a single point-of-control due to reducing the measurement cost.

There is recently significant interest in developing network monitoring infrastructures that allow ISPs to monitor their network links [12]. A key consideration in the design of monitoring infrastructures is to develop low-cost solution. In particular, the idea of placing and operating monitors at all nodes in a network is not cost-efficient. Instead, there has been significant recent in replying on tomographic techniques that use only a few probing nodes (beacons) for monitoring the health of all network links [12], [13], [14], [15],[16].

Once the beacons are located, the smallest set of probes must still be determined. Our work focuses on determining and optimizing the probes assignment for measuring the link bandwidths. The majority of work on network tomography on either topology discovery [4], [17] or link delay monitoring [11]. Some recent research showed that active measurements can also be used to pinpoint failure in IP networks [11], [18]. For measuring link bandwidths, the measuring model and cost are different from that of topology discovery or link delay monitoring. We develop different strategies and algorithms based on different bandwidth measuring technology.

2   Bandwidth Measure Assignment Problem

2.1   Problem Formulation

A number of tools estimate network link bandwidth using Variable Packet Size (VPS) probing technology, like as Pathchar [7], Clink [19] and Pchar [20]. The key element of the technique is to measure the RTT from the measuring station to each hop of the path as a function of the probing packet size [9]. VPS uses the Time-To-Live field of the IP header to force probing packets to expire at a particular hop. The router at that hop discards the probing packets, returning ICMP "Time-exceeded" error messages back to the measuring station. The measuring station uses the received ICMP packets to measure the RTT to that hop.

We model the Service Provider or Enterprise IP network by an undirected graph $G(V, E)$, where the graph nodes V, denote the network routers and the edges, E, represent the communications links connecting them. For measuring the bandwidth of a link $e \in E$, a measuring station s must be selected firstly for sending probe message, where $s \in V$ such that e belongs to s's routing tree (i.e., $e \in T_s$). Consequently,the measuring station s must send two probe messages to the end-points of e, which travel almost identical routes except for the link e.

Once having selected a set S of monitoring stations, a measuring system designated for measuring the bandwidths of all network links has to find a measure assignment $M \subseteq \{m(s, u) | s \in S, u \in V\}$, where each message $m(s, u)$ represents a probe message that is sent from the measuring station s to node u.The measure assignment M are required to satisfy a covering assignment constraint which ensures that for every edge $e = (u, v) \in E$, there is a measuring station $s \in S$ such that $e \in T_s$ and M contains the messages $m(s, u)$ and $m(s, v)$. The covering assignment constraint essentially ensures that every link is measured by some stations. Note that although we only consider the problem of measuring all network links in this paper, our results also apply to the problem of measuring only a subset of links of interest.

We associate a positive cost $c_{s,t}$ with sending a probe message along the path $P_{s,t}$ between any pair of nodes $s, t \in V$. For every intermediate node $x \in P_{s,t}$ both $c_{s,x}$ and $c_{x,t}$ are at most $c_{s,t}$ and $c_{s,x} + c_{x,t} \geq c_{s,t}$. Typical example of this cost model are the fixed cost model, where all messages have the same cost, and the hop count model, where the message cost is the number of hops in its route. Moreover, we denote by $h_{s,t}$ the number of hops in path $P_{s,t}$.

Definition 1 (Measure Assignment). *Given an undirected graph $G = (V, E)$, where V denotes the set of nodes, E represents the edges between two nodes. Let T_v be a route tree for every node $v \in V$. And $S \subseteq V$ denotes a set of measuring stations. We say $M \subseteq \{m(s,u)|s \in S, u \in V\}$ is a Measure Assignment, if there is a measuring station $s \in S$ for every edge $e = \{u,v\} \in E$ such that $e \in T_s$ and $m(s,u) \in M, m(s,v) \in M$. The cost of a Measure Assignment M is $COST_M = \sum_{m(s,u) \in M} c_{s,u}$.*

To reduce the network burden, the measuring cost is preferable to as few as possible. We are interested in the following optimization problem.

Definition 2 (Measure Assignment Problem-MA). *Given an undirected graph $G = (V, E)$ and a routing tree T_v, for every node $v \in V$. Let $S \subseteq V$ denotes a set of measuring stations. The Measure Assignment problem is to determine the measure assignment with the minimum cost.*

2.2 Integer Programming Formulation for the MA Problem

Given an undirected graph $G = (V, E)$, where V denotes the set of nodes, E represents the edges between two nodes. Let T_v be a route tree for every node $v \in V$. And $S \subseteq V$ denotes a set of measuring stations. Let M denotes a Measure Assignment. The binary variable $x_{s,u}$ indicates whether there is a probe message from s to u in M. And the binary variable $y_{s,u,v}$ indicates whether the routing tree of s includes edge (u,v). We give the integer programming formulation of the measure assignment problem as follows.

$$\text{Min} \sum_{m(s,u) \in M} c_{s,u}$$

Subject to:

$$\sum_{s \in S} x_{s,u} x_{s,v} y_{s,u,v} \geq 1, \quad \text{for each } \{u,v\} \in E \tag{1}$$

$$x_{s,u} \in \{0,1\}, \quad \text{for each } u \in V, s \in S \tag{2}$$

$$y_{s,u,v} \in \{0,1\}, \quad \text{for each } \{u,v\} \in E, s \in S \tag{3}$$

The first constraint makes sure that each edge can be measured from at least one measuring station which routing tree constains this edge.

2.3 Hardness of the MA Problem

The MA problem could be proved to be NP-hard by presenting a polynomial reduction from the well-known Vertex Cover problem [21] to the MA problem. The details of this proof are omitted due to space limitations.

Theorem 1. *Given a set of measuring stations S, the MA problem is NP-hard.*

3   Approximation Algorithm for Measure Assignment Problem

We give a 2-approximation algorithm for the measure assignment problem using dynamic programming strategy.

3.1   An Approximation Algorithm

For measuring the bandwidth of any edge $e \in E$, at least one station $s \in S$ must send two probe message, one to each end point of e. So the measuring cost is the sum of two probe message cost, i.e. $c_{s,u} + c_{s,v}$. Note that $c_{s,u}$ is zero while $s = u$. While the probe assignment M has contained one probe message $m_{s,u}$ or $m_{s,v}$, the measuring cost would be $c_{s,v}$ or $c_{s,v}$ respectively. We pick a station to minimize the measuring cost for every edge by using dynamic programming strategy. And the approximation algorithm is given as follows.

Algorithm $(G = (V, E), S \subseteq V, \{c_{s,u} | s \in S, u \in V\})$:

1. $M = \Phi$;
2. $E' = E$;
3. for each edge $(u, v) \in E$;
    (a) $Cost(u, v) = min_{(u,v) \in T_s}(c_{s,u} + c_{s,v})$;
4. while $(|E'| \neq 0)$
    (a) Pick $min_{(u^*,v^*) \in E'} Cost(u^*, v^*)$
    (b) $E' = E' - (u^*, v^*)$
    (c) $M = M \cup \{m(s^*, u^*), m(s^*, v^*)\}$
    (d) for each edge $(u', v') \in E' \cap T_{s^*}$, s.t. $u' \in \{u^*, v^*\}$ or $u' \in \{u^*, v^*\}$. Suppose that $u' \in \{u^*, v^*\}$.

        i. $Cost(u', v') = min_{(u,v) \in T_s}\{(c_{s,u'} + c_{s,v'}), c_{s^*,v'}\}$;

It is not hard to see that this algorithm is effectively equivalent to the following: start with $M = \Phi$ and $E' = E$. Compute the measuring cost for each edge. The measuring cost of each edge is the sum of two probe message cost, i.e. $c_{s^*,u} + c_{s^*,v}$, while s^* is the station which minimize the measuring cost. Pick one edge (u^*, v^*) from E' that achieves the minimum the measuring cost. Let it be measured by station s^*. Add these two probe messages $m(s^*, u^*)$, $m(s^*, v*)$ to the Measure Assignment M. And remove the edge u^*, v^* from E'. Adjust the measuring cost of these edges which incident with the picked edge. Repeat until M cover all links.

Note that there exists a implementation of this algorithm takes $O(|E|^2)$ time. Then we prove the algorithm is a 2-approximation algorithm.

Theorem 2. *The approximation ratio of the approximation algorithm is 2.*

Proof. In any measuring assignment, at least one probe message can be associated with each edge e. Let it be the message that is sent to the farthest endpoint of e from the measuring station. Let M'' be the optimal probe assignment and let

s''_e be the station that measures edge e in M''. So, in M'', the cost of measuring edge $e = (u, v)$ is at least $max\{c_{s''_e,u}, c_{s''_e,v}\}$. Let s^* be the selected station for measuring edge e in the assignment M returned by the approximation measure assignment algorithm. So we have the following inequality:

$$Cost(u, v) \le c_{s*_e,u} + c_{s*_e,v} \le c_{s''_e,u} + c_{s''_e,v} \le 2max\{c_{s''_e,u}, c_{s''_e,v}\}. \quad (4)$$

Thus, we have $COST_M \le 2COST_{M''}$.   □

4   Simulations

In this section, we present simulation results of comparing the performance of the various algorithms that solve the measure assignment problem. The main objective of the simulations is to demonstrate that our proposed algorithmic solutions are not only theoretically sound but also they could give significant benefits over naive solutions in practice for a wide variety of realistic network topologies. The simulations are based on network topologies generated using the Waxman Model [22], which is a popular topology model for networking research. Different network topologies are generated by varying three parameters: (1)n, the number of nodes in the network graph; (2)α, a parameter that controls the density of short edges in the networks; and (3)β, a parameter that controls the average node degree.

We compare the performance of three algorithms: the naive random assignment algorithm, the simple probe assignment algorithm [16] and our approximation algorithm. The comparison is in terms of the total measuring cost. We denote the cost of measuring all link for these algorithms by $COST_r$, $COST_s$ and $COST_a$ respectively.

Table 1 presents one set of simulation results. We have obtained similar results for other parameter settings. The third and fourth columns in the table represent the maximum and average degree of the nodes in the generated network graph respectively. Our results indicate that using our approximation algorithm can reduce measuring cost. And the result of our algorithm is better than is better than the other two algorithms.

We have obtained the other simulation result by adjusting the number of measuring stations. We compute the measuring cost on having selected 50,75,100,125, 150 measuring stations respectively. From figure 1, we can know that the measuring cost would be reduced by adding the number of measuring stations. And our algorithm is better than the naive assignment.

Table 1. Comparisons of Measuring Algorithms on Different Topologies

n	α	β	Maximum Degree	Average Degree	$COST_r$	$COST_s$	$COST_a$
400	0.1	0.06	8	2.45	723	616	503
400	0.5	0.02	11	3.43	901	844	711
400	0.5	0.06	26	4.94	1988	1773	1475

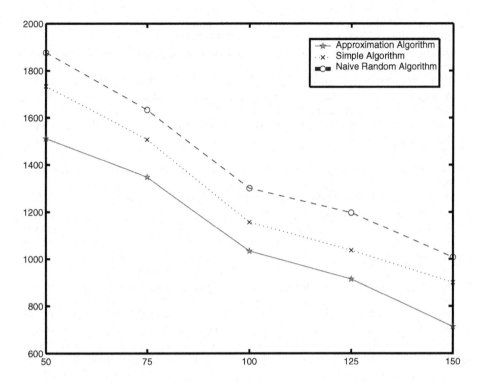

Fig. 1. Measuring Cost on Different Algorithms

5   Conclusion

In this paper, we have addressed the problem of efficiently measure assignment
in IP networks. This problem is shown NP-hard. We have proposed an approximation algorithm with approximation ratio 2 to solve the measure assignment
problem. Finally, we have verified the effectiveness of our approximation algorithms through simulations evaluation. This work is helpful to efficiently measure
link bandwidth in IP networks.

Further research would be conducted to develop novel algorithms based on
different measuring technology.

References

1. W. Stallings: SNMP, SNMPv2, SNMPv3, and RMON 1 and 2. Addison-Wesley
   Longman, Inc., 1999.
2. Cisco Systems: NetFlow Services and Applications, White Paper, 1999
3. P. Francis, S. Jamin, V. Paxson, L. Zhang, D.F.Gryniewicz, and Y. Jin: An Architecture for a Global Internet Host Distance Estimation Service. In Proc. IEEE
   INFOCOM 1999.

4. S. Jamin, C. Jin, Y. Jin, Y. Raz, Y. Shavitt, and L. Zhang: On the Placement of Internet Instrumentation. In Proc. IEEE INFOCOM 2000.
5. J.C.Bolot: End-to-End Packet Delay and Loss Behavior in the Internet. In. Proc. ACM SIGCOMM 1993.
6. K. Lai and M. Baker: Measuring Bandwidth. In Proc. IEEE INFOCOM 1999.
7. V.Jacobsen: Dynamic   Distance   Maps   of   the   Internet   Paths, ftp://ftp.ee.lbl.gov/pathchar, April 1997.
8. Breitbart Y., Chan CY., Garofalakis M., Rastogi R., Siberschatz A.: Efficiently Monitoring Bandwidth and Latency in IP Networks. In Proc. IEEE INFOCOM 2001.
9. R.S. Prasad, M. Murray, C. Dovrolis, K. Claffy: Bandwidth Estimation: Metrics, Measurement Techniques, and Tools. IEEE Network, 2003, 17(6):27-35.
10. J. Walz, B. Levine: A Hierachical Multicast Monitoring Scheme. In Proc. Networked Group Communication 2000.
11. Y. Bejerano, R.Rastogi: Robust Monitoring of Link Delays and Faults in Networks. In Proc. IEEE INFOCOM'03, 2003.
12. R. Kumar, J. Kaur: Efficient Beacon Placement for Network Tomography. In Proc. ACM Internet Measurement Conference 2004, October 2004.
13. K. Claffy, T.E. Monk, D. McRobb: Internet Tomography, Nature, January, 1999.
14. J. D. Horton, A. Lopez-Ortiz: On the Number of Distributed Measurement Points for Network Tomography. In Proc. ACM SIGCOMM IMC'03. 2003,pp.204-209.
15. Kyoungwon Suh, Yang Guo, Jim Kurose, and Don Towsley. Locating Network Monitors: Complexity, Heuristics, and Coverage. In Proc. IEEE INFOCOM 2005.
16. M. Adler, T. Bu, R.K. Sitaraman, D. Towsley: Tree Layout for Internal Network Characterizations in Multicast Network. In Proc. Networked Group Comm,2001.
17. N. Spring, R. Mahajan, D. Wetherall: Measuring ISP Topologies with Rocketfuel. In Proc. ACM SIGCOMM'02. 2002.
18. H. X. Nguyen, P. Thiran: Active Measurment for Multiple Link Failure Diagnosis in IP Networks. In Proc. PAM'04. April, 2004.
19. A. B. Doweny: Using Pathchar to Estimate Internet Link Characteristics. In Proc. ACM SIGCOMM'99. Sept,1999.
20. CAIDA: http://www.caida.org/tools/. Oct, 2002.
21. Dorit S. Hochbaum: Approximation Algorithm for *NP*-Hard Problems. PWS Publishing Company,1997.
22. B.M.Waxman: Routing of Multipoint Connections. IEEE Journal on Selected Areas in Communications, 1988, 6(9):1617-1622.
23. Zhiping Cai, Jianping Yin, Fang Liu and Xianghui Liu: Distributed Monitoring Model With Bounded Delay For Evolving Networks. *Journal of Software*, 2005,11.
24. Zhiping Cai, Wentao Zhao, Jianping Yin and Xianghui Liu: Using Passive Measuring to Calibrate Active Measuring Latency. In Proc. ICOIN2005, *Lecture Notes in Computer Science 3391*, C.Kim(eds.), Springer-Verlag, 2005.
25. Zhiping Cai, Jianping Yin, Fang Liu, Xianghui Liu, Shaohe Lv: Efficiently Monitoring Link Bandwidth in IP Networks. In Proc. IEEE GLOBECOM 2005.

Preferential Bandwidth Allocation
for Short Flows with Active Queue Management

Heying Zhang, Liu Lu, Liquan Xiao, and Wenhua Dou

School of Computer, National University of Defense Technology, 410073,
Changsha, Hunan, China
hey_zhang@hotmail.com, douwh@vip.sina.com

Abstract. Several fair queueing mechanisms based on stateless core (SCORE)/dynamic packet state (DPS) architecture have been proposed to address the scalability problem of stateful architectures. However, most of these mechanisms indiscriminatingly label every packet in edge routers while only a small fraction of the packets that come from fast flows will be dropped by core routers. Moreover, these mechanisms usually apply simple techniques to detect congestion, which makes them unable to control the queue length. In this paper, a new fair bandwidth allocation mechanism is proposed. In the new mechanism, edge routers only label the packets of long flows so that the bandwidth is preferentially allocated to short flows and the remaining is fairly allocated among the competing long flows. Furthermore, routers can keep the queue length at a reference value using active queue management (AQM) algorithm. The simulation results show that this mechanism performs well in many aspects.

1 Introduction

In current Internet, routers simply forward each incoming packet to its destination, regardless of which flow it belongs to. Therefore, some greedy, unresponsive flows will unfairly obtain more bandwidth than the conservative, responsive ones when congestion occurs. Such a situation will probably cause the danger of congestion collapse and the starvation of conformant flows.

The stateless core architecture, or SCORE for short, is proposed to achieve approximate fairness and reasonable scalability simultaneously. The key technique used to implement the SCORE network is the dynamic packet state (DPS), which inserts the flow state information into the header of packets. In the SCORE/DPS network architecture, routers are divided into edge routers and core routers. Edge routers maintain per-flow state and insert it into the header of the incoming packet [1-4]. Core routers use the simple first-in first-out (FIFO) queueing and drop the incoming packet based on the state information carried in its header when congestion occurs.

Unfortunately, the existing mechanisms based on SCORE/DPS architecture have the following limitations. First, they label every packet passing through edge routers, which is not really necessary since only packets of high-bandwidth flows will be

H. Jin, D. Reed, and W. Jiang (Eds.): NPC 2005, LNCS 3779, pp. 303 – 309, 2005.

dropped probabilistically when the network becomes congested. Moreover, it is showed by recent measurement that most of the traffic is actually carried by a small number of flows, while the large remaining amount of flows is very small both in size and lifetime [5,6]. So it is reasonable to just maintain the state of these minority flows that tend to occupy more bandwidth than others and label their packets. Second, these mechanisms treat short flows and long flows equally. In fact, the throughput and delay of the short-lived TCP (Transmission Control Protocol) flows will deteriorate severely when competing with the long-lived flows due to lack of sufficient packets to activate duplicate acknowledgments and the dependence on timeout to detect packet loss. Although several approaches have been proposed to deal with short flows preferentially, they cannot allocate bandwidth fairly among the competing long flows [7,8]. Third, to the best of our knowledge, none of these proposed SCORE/DPS mechanisms applies specific approach to control the queue length, which corresponds to the queueing delay experienced by the backlogged packets.

In order to address these issues, we propose a new fair bandwidth sharing mechanism in this paper. The features of the new mechanism include simplifying the operation of routers, protecting short flows and achieving fairness among long flows. We use a well-designed AQM (Active Queue Management) algorithm, called proportional integral based series compensation and position feedback compensation (PIP), to detect congestion and control queue length [9]. So the proposed mechanism is called FPIP (fair PIP).

The rest of the paper is organized as follows. In section 2, we describe FPIP in detail, including the core router and edge router. In section 3, we evaluate the performance of FPIP through extensive simulations. Finally, we conclude in section 4.

2   FPIP Framework

In this section, we present FPIP, a packet labeling and queue management mechanism that significantly simplifies the operation of routers without affecting the performance by taking into account the ubiquitous heavy-tailed distribution of the Internet traffic. We apply the network model comprised of edge routers and core routers. For each active flow, the edge routers maintain a traffic counter that tracks how many bits have been observed so far and determine whether the flow is short or long. When a packet comes from a short flow, the traffic counter of the flow increases. Otherwise, the flow rate is estimated and inserted into the header of the packet. The routers estimate the aggregate arrival rate of short flows and the number of active long flows, and then calculate the fair share based on them. In addition, a notable feature of FPIP is the use of AQM algorithm in detecting congestion and controlling the queue length, from which the delay-sensitive applications such as Web or Telnet can benefit.

2.1   Estimating the Flow Arrival Rate

To protect short flows, we should distinguish them from long flows at first and then decrease their loss rates. In our mechanism, the edge router maintains a traffic counter for each active flow, which is used to record the number of the bits sent by this flow. Once the traffic counter exceeds a certain "bit threshold", noted as *bitThresh*, the flow will be considered long. Otherwise, it is considered short. For the long flows, the edge routers estimate their arrival rates and label their packets. Instead, for the short flows, only their traffic counters increase.

We use the exponential averaging formula to estimate the long flow arrival rate. Let Δt_i^k be the time interval between the kth and the $(k\text{-}1)^{th}$ packet of flow i. The estimated rate of flow i is calculated as

$$r_i^{new} = (1 - e^{-\Delta t_i^k/K_r})\, l_i^k \big/ \Delta t_i^k + e^{-\Delta t_i^k/K_r} r_i^{old} \ . \tag{1}$$

where l_i^k is the length of the kth arrival packet of flow i and K_r is a constant.

2.2 Estimating the Aggregate Arrival Rate of Short Flows

To calculate the bandwidth that can be allocated to long flows, we should estimate the aggregate arrival rate of short flows at first. For each arrival packet, the router checks its label to see which kind of flow it comes from. If the packet label equals to zero, the packet is thought of as coming from short flow. Let l be the length of the arrival packet and Δt be the inter-arrival time of the consecutive packets that come from short flows. The router calculates the aggregate arrival rate of short flow, denoted by *sRate*, as follows

$$sRate = (1 - e^{-\Delta t^k/K_s})\, l^k \big/ \Delta t^k + e^{-\Delta t^k/K_s} sRate \ . \tag{2}$$

where K_s is a constant.

If the label of the arrival packet is greater than zero, the packet is thought of as coming from long flow. *sRate* is also updated according to (2), where l equals to zero. By doing so, *sRate* will reflect the real aggregate arrival rate of short flows even if there have been no packets from short flows for a long period of time.

Now, the bandwidth that can be obtained by long flows is readily available:

$$C_l = \max\{0, C - sRate\} \ . \tag{3}$$

2.3 Estimating the Number of Active Long Flows

In FPIP, the routers calculate the fair share rate based on two variables: the bandwidth allocated to long flows and the number of the active long flows (*Nactivel*). The former has been determined easily, while the latter is a lot harder to estimate. Several approaches have been proposed previously to address this issue [10-12]. Since these approaches are motivated by some specific goals, none of them can be copied here.

In this paper, we introduce a new method to estimate the number of the active long flows. According to our method, the router is required to maintain a state table for tracking the arrival time (denoted by *prevtime*) of the packet that has lately arrived from each long flow. For each arrival packet, if its label is greater than zero, the *prevtime* of the corresponding flow in the state table is checked. If it equals to zero, the number of active long flows increases and the *prevtime* is set to the current time. Otherwise, only the *prevtime* is replaced by the current time. In order to estimate the number of the flows sharing the bandwidth during a longer period of time rather than that of the flows currently having packets in the buffer, the flow table is not updated when there is packet leaving the queue. Instead, it is updated periodically with a constant frequency, which can be viewed as a background task, for it is shifted from the high-speed data-forwarding path. When the update timer expires, entries of the table are checked one by one. If the interval between the current time and the *prevtime* of a flow is greater than a certain threshold (*Tn*), which means there is no packet from that flow in the last *Tn* time units, the flow is considered terminated. Thus, *Nactivel* is reduced and the *prevtime* of the flow is reset to zero.

2.4 Estimating and Adjusting the Fair Share Rate

The problem of the fair bandwidth sharing occurs along with the presence of the network congestion, and the estimation of the fair share rate depends further on it. Therefore, it is of great importance to correctly detect congestion. In this paper, we apply AQM algorithm in congestion detection for the following reasons: (1) The packet drop probability calculated by AQM is a good representation of the congestion degree; (2) AQM algorithm is able to detect congestion and control queue length simultaneously. In our mechanism, we use a robust AQM algorithm called PIP [9].

The packet drop probability $p(k)$ determined by PIP is regarded as a measure of congestion. When $p(k)$ is greater than a random variable, it is likely that the link is congested and the fair share rate (R_{fair}) should be calculated. Let the capacity of the output link be C. Suppose *sRate* is less than C. R_{fair} is calculated as

$$R_{fair} = \frac{C - sRate}{Nactivel} \qquad Nactivel > 0 .$$ (4)

When $p(k)$ is less than a random variable, the link is considered uncongested. To avoid under-utilization of the link, when the estimated rate of the accepted traffic (*cRate*) is less than the output link capacity C, the fair share rate is adjusted as follows

$$R_{fair}^{new} = \min\{C, \frac{C}{cRate} R_{fair}^{old}\} .$$ (5)

The accepted rate is also estimated by exponential averaging:

$$cRate = (1 - e^{-\Delta t^k / K_c}) l^k / \Delta t + e^{-\Delta t^k / K_c} cRate .$$ (6)

The implications of the parameters in (6) are similar to those in (1). Now, the incoming packet of the long flow will be dropped with the following probability

$$prob = \max\{0, \frac{r_i - R_{fair}}{r_i}\} .$$ (7)

3 Simulations

In this section, we use NS simulator to evaluate the performance of FPIP and compare with CSFQ and RED [13]. In the simulations, we use the network topology with multiple congested links shown in Fig.1. The number of congested links varies from one to five. The capacities of all the access links are 30 Mbps, and those of the congested links are 10 Mbps. The propagation delay of each link is 5 ms. Each router is connected with five UDP flows which terminate at the next router and send at 4 Mbps. Thus, all the links between neighboring routers are congested.

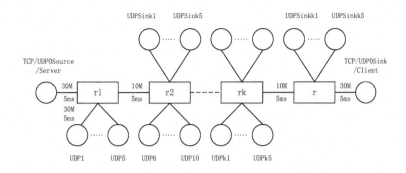

Fig. 1. Network topology used in the simulations

In the first experiment, a TCP flow traverses all the congested links. Fig.2 shows the bandwidths achieved by the TCP flow as a function of the number of congested links. We compare the bandwidth achieved by each flow through the normalized bandwidth, which is defined as the ratio of the allocated bandwidth to the ideal bandwidth. In RED, the TCP flow is submerged by the high-speed unresponsive flows. The TCP flow achieves more bandwidth under FPIP than that under CSFQ. Fig.3 shows the queue dynamics in router r under CSFQ and FPIP when the number of the congested links is 5. For CSFQ, the queue length of each router is about 300 Kbytes in steady state, while for FPIP, the queue length is 25 Kbytes.

In the second experiment, the TCP flow is replaced by a UDP flow (denoted by UDP0 in Fig. 1) sending at its fair share rate 1.67 Mbps. Fig. 4 shows the normalized bandwidth achieved by UDP0. Similarly, RED has the worst performance. FPIP performs slightly better than CSFQ.

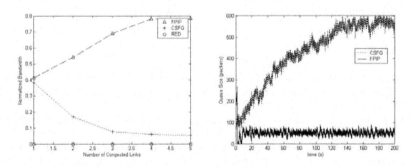

Fig. 2. Bandwidth achieved by TCP flow   **Fig. 3.** The queue dynamics of CSFQ and FPIP

In the last experiment, a Web flow traverses all the congested links. Fig. 5 shows the response time of the Web flow traversing different numbers of congested links. We cannot show the result under RED, for the client of the Web flow cannot even receive a single response from the server. For the other two mechanisms, when the

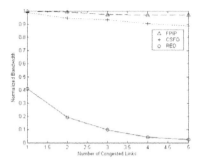
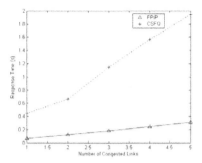

Fig. 4. Bandwidth achieved by UDP flow   **Fig. 5.** The response time of web flow

number of the congested links increases, the response time of the Web flow also increases. Moreover, the increase under CSFQ is faster than that under FPIP.

4   Conclusions

In this paper, we present a new fair bandwidth allocation mechanism called FPIP. By labeling only the packets of long flows at edges, the mechanism greatly reduces the amount of flow state required and the processing done on it. In the core of the network, routers only drop packets from long flows with probability, while short flows will not be dropped as long as the capacity of the output link will satisfy their bandwidth demand. Furthermore, to provide low delay service, the core routers apply AQM mechanism to detect congestion and control queue length, which is beneficial to the adaptive flows and delay-sensitive applications. The results of simulations show that FPIP can obtain approximate fairness among long flows, keep queue length at a desired value and reduce the response time of Web flows.

References

1. Stoica, I., Shenker, S., Zhang, H.: Core-stateless Fair Queueing: Achieving Approximately Fair Bandwidth Allocations in High Speed Networks. In Proceedings of ACM SIGCOMM 1998, Vancouver (1998) 118-130
2. Cao, Z., Wang, Z., Zegura, E.: Rainbow Fair Queueing: Fair Bandwidth Sharing Without Per-flow State. In Proceedings of IEEE INFOCOM 2000, Tel-Aviv, Israel (2000) 922-931
3. Clerget, A., Dabbous, W.: Tag-based Fair Bandwidth Sharing for Responsive and Unresponsive Flows. In Proceedings of IEEE INFOCOM 2001, An-chorage, AK (2001)
4. Ngin, H.T., Tham, C.K.: A Control-Theoretical Approach for Achieving Fair Bandwidth Allocations in Core-Stateless Networks. Computer Networks, Vol.40, (2002) 727-741
5. Mahajan, R., Floyd, S.: Controlling High Bandwidth Flows at the Congested Router. AT&T Center for Internet Research at ICSI (ACIRI), TR-01-001 (2001)
6. Brownlee, N., Claffy, K.C.: Understanding Internet Traffic Streams: Dragonflies and Tortoises Brownlee. IEEE Communications Magazine, Vol.40, (2002) 110-117
7. Zhang, Y., Qiu, L., Keshav, S.: Speeding up Short Data Transfers: Theory, Architecture Support, and Simulation Results. In Proceedings of NOSSDAV 2000, Chapel Hill, NC, USA (2000)

8. Guo, L., Matta, I.: The War Between Mice and Elephants. Technical Report BU-CS-2001-005, Boston University (2001)

9. Zhang, H.Y., Liu, B.H., Dou, W.H.: Design of a Robust Active Queue Management Algorithm Based on Feedback Compensation. In Proceedings of ACM SIGCOMM 2003, Karlsruhe, Germany (2003) 277-286

10. Lin, D., Morris, R.: Dynamics of Random Early Detection. In Proceedings of ACM SIGCOMM 1997, Cannes, France (1997) 127-137

11. Li, J.S., Leu, M.S.: Network Fair Bandwidth Share Using Hash Rate Estimation. Networks, Vol. 40, (2002) 125-141

12. Ott, T.J., Lakshman, T.V., Wong, L.: SRED: Stabilized RED. In Proceedings of IEEE INFOCOM 1999, New York, USA (1999) 1346-1355

13. Floyd, S., Jacobson, V.: Random Early Detection Gateways for Congestion Avoidance. IEEE/ACM Transactions on Networking, Vol.4, (1993) 397-413

A New Self-tuning Active Queue Management Algorithm Based on Adaptive Control

Heying Zhang[1], Baohong Liu[2], Liquan Xiao[1], and Wenhua Dou[1]

[1] School of Computer, National University of Defense Technology, 410073,
Changsha, Hunan, China
hey_zhang@hotmail.com, douwh@vip.sina.com
[2] Institute of Automation, National University of Defense Technology, 410073,
Changsha, Hunan, China
liu_baohong@hotmail.com

Abstract. Most Active Queue Management (AQM) algorithms based on control theory have difficulty in obtaining desirable performance once the network conditions or the traffic patterns change out of the presumed ones they are designed for. To address these problems, a new self-tuning AQM algorithm called STR is proposed in this paper. STR has the ability of keeping minimum variance between the instantaneous queue length of the router and the reference value by estimating the parameters of the model of controlled object online and adjusting the packet drop probability accordingly. The performance of STR is evaluated through extensive simulations. The results show that STR is robust against the great changes of the network parameters and the traffic load.

1 Introduction

Congestion control is very important to the stability and scalability of Internet. To improve the performance of traditional end-to-end congestion control, IETF (Internet Engineering Task Force) strongly suggests using active queue management (AQM) in routers [1]. RED (Random Early Detection) is one of the well-known AQM algorithms [2]. Many simulations and tests show that the performance of RED is very sensitive to its parameter settings [3]. This is considered partly due to lack of systematic analysis during the design of RED. In view of this, many AQM algorithms based on control theory have been proposed in recent years [4-11]. These algorithms are usually characterized by simple implementation and easy configuration. However, they have some disadvantages. For example, these algorithms are usually designed based on the linearized model of the controlled object, which is made up of TCP (Transmission Control Protocol) and the queue dynamics. While the accurate model of the controlled object is nonlinear and time-varying in real networks. The inaccuracy of the model will lead to dissatisfied performance for AQM algorithms especially in terms of robustness and stability. Moreover, the parameters of most AQM algorithms are determined according to some specific network conditions. When the real network condition is far from that presumed, the performance of the algorithm will become unpredictable. In view of the fact that AQM algorithms with

H. Jin, D. Reed, and W. Jiang (Eds.): NPC 2005, LNCS 3779, pp. 310–316, 2005.
© IFIP International Federation for Information Processing 2005

fixed parameters are not very suitable for the highly variable network conditions, some adaptive AQM algorithms have been proposed recently [12]. Unfortunately, they cannot solve the problems thoroughly.

The rest of this paper is organized as follows. In section 2, we describe the design of STR in detail. In section 3, the performance of STR is evaluated through simulations. Finally, we give the conclusions in section 4.

2   The Self-tuning Active Queue Management

Through detailed analyses, we find that it seems impossible to establish accurate model of TCP and the queue dynamics with fixed parameters. To efficiently control congestions even if the network conditions change widely, the AQM algorithm should identify the parameters of the controlled object timely and adjust the control laws, i.e. the packet drop probability, accordingly. So we use the self-tuning regulator to design AQM algorithm, which combines the recursive least square parameter identification and the minimum variance control as illustrated in Fig.1. In TCP/AQM system, the reference input r of the system is the reference queue length. The controlled object is made up of TCP window adjustment scheme and the queue dynamics. And the input u and output y of the controlled object is the packet drop probability and the queue length respectively. The estimator identifies the parameters of the model of controlled object. The regulator adjusts the packet drop probability according to the identified parameters. The estimator and regulator compose the self-tuning AQM algorithm.

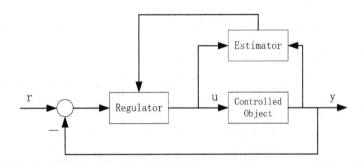

Fig. 1. Structure of self-tuning regulator

Now we will give the design of STR in detail. First of all, two key parameters of the system should be determined. One is the order n of the controlled object. The other is the delay d from the input of the controlled object to its output. If the parameters n and d of a system are unknown, it is feasible to select large values for them [13]. In [6], the differential equation model of TCP and queue dynamics is linearized about the operating point and a second-order system model is gained. So n can be selected as 2. Considering the stochastic disturbance frequently occurred in the network, we choose $n=3$ to guarantee the convergence of the parameter identification. In TCP/AQM system, the packet drop rate will delay one RTT (Round Trip Time) before affecting the queue length. To decrease the number of parameters which require identifying, we choose the sample cycle T=RTT. Then the delay between the packet drop and the change of the queue length is one sample cycle, namely d=1.

After determining n and d, the controlled object can be repr esented by:

$$q(k) + a_1 q(k-1) + a_2 q(k-2) + a_3 q(k-3) = b_0 p(k-1) + \tag{1}$$
$$b_1 p(k-2) + b_2 p(k-3) + b_3 p(k-4)$$

where $q(k)$ is the queue length and $p(k)$ is the packet drop probability.

Equation (1) can be rewritten as:

$$q(k+1) = b_0 p(k) + \varphi^T(k)\theta . \tag{2}$$

where

$$\theta = [-a_1, -a_2, -a_3, b_1, b_2, b_3]^T \tag{3}$$

$$\varphi(k) = [q(k), q(k-1), q(k-2), p(k-1), p(k-2), p(k-3)]^T$$

Calculating the variance between $q(k+1)$ and the reference value q_0, we yield:

$$E[q(k+1) - q_0]^2 = E[b_0 p(k) + \varphi^T(k)\theta - q_0]^2 . \tag{4}$$

We have the following condition when the minimum variance is gained:

$$b_0 p(k) + \varphi^T(k)\theta - q_0 = 0 \tag{5}$$

Then, we get the packet drop probability of STR:

$$p(k) = \frac{1}{\hat{b}_0}[q_0 - \varphi^T(k)\hat{\theta}] . \tag{6}$$

where $\hat{b}_0$ is the estimated value of b_0 and $\hat{\theta}$ is the estimated value of θ. To simplify the parameter identification and guarantee its convergence, we will determine the value of b_0 by experiments and use the basic least squares method to estimate θ. Since θ is variable rather than constant in real networks, we will use the recursive parameter identification algorithm with forgetting property which is suitable for the slowly variable parameter estimation. The estimation method is represented by:

$$\begin{cases} \hat{\theta}(k) = \hat{\theta}(k-1) + K(k)[q(k) - \hat{b}_0 p(k-1) - \varphi^T(k-1)\hat{\theta}(k-1)] \\ K(k) = H(k-1)\varphi(k-1)[\lambda(k) + \varphi^T(k-1)H(k-1)\varphi(k-1)]^{-1} \\ H(k) = \frac{1}{\lambda(k)}[I - K(k)\varphi^T(k-1)]H(k-1) \end{cases} \tag{7}$$

where λ is the "forgetting factor" ranging between 0.95 and 1. Generally, let $\hat{\theta}(0) = 0$, $H(0) = \alpha I$, where α is positive and large enough and I is a unit matrix. In TCP/AQM system, we will change the value of λ as follows [13]:

$$\lambda(k+1) = \begin{cases} \lambda(k)(1 - \lambda_0) + \lambda_0 & |\varepsilon(k)| \le E \\ \lambda_0 & |\varepsilon(k)| > E \end{cases} \tag{8}$$

where, λ_0 is the lower bound of λ and set to 0.95. E is a constant. $\varepsilon(k)$ is the prediction error and defined as follows:

$$\varepsilon(k) = q(k) - \hat{b}_0 p(k-1) - \varphi^T(k-1)\hat{\theta}(k-1)$$
(9)

3 Simulations

We implement STR algorithm in NS simulator and compare its performance with PI and ARED. The network topology is shown in Fig.2. The propagation delays of connections range between 40 ms and 240 ms. The link between routers r1 and r2 is the only congested link with the capacity being 100 Mbps and the delay being 10 ms. The buffer size of the routers is 800 packets, with the average packet size being 500 bytes. The flows from s_i to d_i are forward, while those from d_i to s_i are backward. The reference queue length of STR and PI is 100 packets. For STR, $E=20$, $\hat{b}_0 = -10^4$. The parameters of PI are selected according to [7]. The minimum and maximum queue thresholds of ARED are 50 packets and 150 packets respectively.

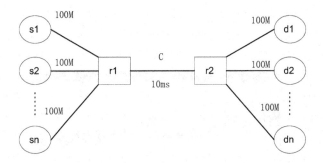

Fig. 2. Network topology used in the simulations

In the first experiment, we evaluate the responsiveness and robustness of STR when the traffic load changes. At the beginning of the simulation, there are 500 forward TCP flows. At t=100s, 450 TCP flows stop. And at t=200s, the stopped 450 TCP flows started again. The queue dynamics of STR, PI and ARED are depicted in Fig.3. It's easy to find that STR can keep small queue length and oscillations in either heavy or light load condition. For PI, the buffer is almost full when the traffic load is heavy. It however becomes empty frequently when the traffic load is light. For ARED, the queue oscillations are very large in heavy load condition.

The second experiment evaluates the performance of STR when the unresponsive flows and short TCP flows exist. At the beginning of the simulation, there are 100 FTP flows. At t=100s, 50 ON/OFF flows based on UDP protocol and 300 web flows based on HTTP protocol started simultaneously. The queue dynamics of STR, PI and ARED are shown in Fig.4. We can find that the queue length of PI increases abruptly and changes in a wide range when the ON/OFF flows and web flows exist. The queue

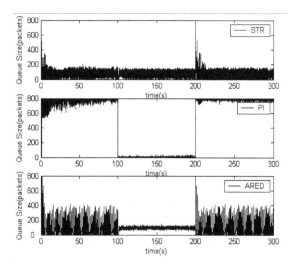

Fig. 3. Queue dynamics when the traffic load changes

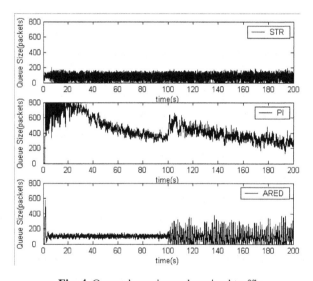

Fig. 4. Queue dynamics under mixed traffic

oscillations of ARED become large. On the contrary, both the queue length and oscillations of STR remain small all the time.

In the last experiment, all the routers in Fig.2 use AQM algorithm with the same configuration. At the beginning of the simulation, there are 100 forward TCP flows. At $t=100$s, 100 backward TCP flows joined. The queue dynamics of STR, PI and ARED are shown in Fig.5. When the backward traffic is active, the queue length of PI becomes unstable and the queue oscillations of ARED also become large. In contrast, both the queue length and the oscillations of STR have no evident changes.

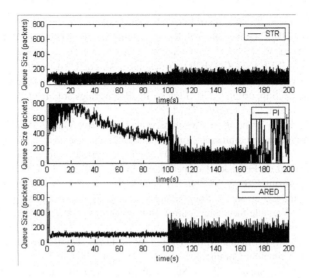

Fig. 5. Queue dynamics under bi-directional traffic

We also evaluate the performance of STR when the capacity of the bottleneck link is small, i.e. 15 Mbps. The results are similar to those described above. For space limitation, we don't show them here.

4 Conclusions

This paper proposes a new self-tuning active queue management algorithm called STR. Through estimating the parameters of the model of controlled object online and adjusting the packet drop probability accordingly, STR can minimize the variance between the transient queue length and the reference queue length, and eliminate the limitation of configuring AQM algorithms according to some specific network conditions. The results of the extensive simulations indicate that STR can keep the queue length at low level and achieve high link utilization simultaneously even when the network conditions change widely.

References

1. Braden, B., et al.: Recommendations on Queue Management and Congestion Avoidance in the Internet. RFC2309, (1998)
2. Floyd, S., Jacobson, V.: Random Early Detection Gateways for Congestion Avoidance. IEEE/ACM Transactions on Networking, Vol.1, (1993) 397-413
3. Firoiu, V., Borden, M.: A Study of Active Queue Management for Congestion Control. In Proceedings of IEEE INFOCOM 2000, Tel-Aviv, Israel (2000) 1435-1444
4. Misra, V., Gong, W.B., Towsley, D.: Fluid-based Analysis of a Network of AQM Routers Supporting TCP Flows with an Application to RED. In Proceedings of ACM SIGCOMM 2000, Stockholm, Sweden (2000) 151-160

5. David, L., Steven, L.: Random Early Marking for Internet Congestion Control. In Proceedings of IEEE Globecom1999, Rio de Janeiro, Brazil (1999) 1747-1752

6. Hollot, C., Misra, V., Towsley, D., Gong, W.B.: A Control Theoretic Analysis of RED. In Proceedings of IEEE INFOCOM 2001, Anchorage, Alaska, USA (2001) 1510-1519

7. Hollot, C., Misra, V., Towsley, D., Gong, W.B.: On Designing Improved Controllers for AQM Routers Supporting TCP Flows. In Proceedings of IEEE INFOCOM2001, Anchorage, Alaska, USA (2001) 1726-1734

8. Ren, F.Y., Lin, C.: Speed up the Responsiveness of Active Queue Management System. IEICE Transactions on communication, Vol.2, (2003) 630-636

9. Zhang, H.Y., Liu, B.H., Dou, W.H.: Design of a Robust Active Queue Management Algorithm Based on Feedback Compensation. In Proceedings of ACM SIGCOMM2003, Karlsruhe, Germany (2003) 277-286

10. Ren, F.Y., Lin, C., et al.: A Robust Active Queue Management Algorithm Based on Sliding Mode Variable Structure Control. In Proceedings of INFOCOM2002, New York, USA (2002) 64-79

11. Ren, F.Y., Ren, Y., Shan, X.M.: Design of a Fuzzy Controller for Active Queue Management. Computer Communications, Vol.25, (2002) 874-883

12. Wu, W., Ren, Y., Shan, X.M.: A Self-configuring Proportional-Integral Controller for AQM Routers Supporting TCP-like Flows. In Proceedings of 7th Asia Pacific Conference on Communications. Tokyo, Japan (2001) 368-371

13. Wu, G.Y.: System Identification and Adaptive Control. Harbin Institute of Technology Press, Harbin, China (1987) (in Chinese)

Research on Multi-agent System Automated Negotiation Theory and Model

Weijin Jiang[1], Yusheng Xu[2], Ding Hao[1], and Shangyou Zhen[2]

[1] Department of computer, Zhuzhou Institute of Technology, Zhuzhou 412008, P.R. China
jwjnudt@163.com
[2] College of Mechanical Engineering and Applied Electronics,
Beijing University of Technology, Beijing 100022, P.R. China
yshxu520@163.com

Abstract. The communication between agents has some special requirements. One of them is asynchronous communication. Used communication sequence process (CSP) to descript a model of agents communication with shared buffer channel. The essence of this model is very suitable for the multi-agents communication, so it is a base for our next step job. Based on the communication model, explored the distributed tasks dealing method among joint intention agents and with description of relation between tasks we give a figure of agents' organization. Agents communicate with each other in this kind of organization. The semantics of agent communication is another emphasis in this paper. With the detailed description of agents' communication process, given a general agent automated negotiation protocol based on speech act theory in MAS, then we use CSP to verify this protocol has properties of safety and liveness, so prove it is logic right. At last a frame of this protocol's realization was given.

1 Introduction

The theory of Multi-Agent Automated Negotiation involves extensive applying fields and many kinds of methods. The theory mainly lies in Argument Based Automated Negotiation, Game Theoretic Models and Heuristic Approaches. In application, it can be divided into two categories, Agent's Negotiation within MAS and Self-interested between different MAS. Those theories supporting the interior collaboration of MAS are like Self-interested, Joint Intentions and Shared Plans, no matter which are have differences, they have been working under the premise of identical intention and target of Agent within MAS. This text will discuss the Joint Intentions in Multi-Agent Automated Negotiation of MAS[1-4].

If Multi-Agent in MAS interacts successfully, there must be three conditions demanded to be satisfied as below:

1) Communication Structure, that is, how to dispatch and take over information between Agent ;
2) Communication Language, that is, Agent is required to understand the signification of the information;
3) Interaction Rules, that is, how to organize the conversation between Agent.

H. Jin, D. Reed, and W. Jiang (Eds.): NPC 2005, LNCS 3779, pp. 317–320, 2005.
© IFIP International Federation for Information Processing 2005

Regarding to the research of Agent Communication Structure, we have proposed TTMAS communication model in the previous parts. In the second section, it will be stressed to analyze Agent's asynchronous communication mechanism[5,6]. As to the research of Agent Communication Language, presently there have been many abroad, like KQML, FIPA, ACL, Agent Talk, etc., so the language is not the emphasis in our text. Then, research of Interaction Rules is the second emphasis in the text. In the third part, the text will set forth the agreement of Agent Automated Negotiation and its validation. In the forth part, it illustrates and analyzes the complete frame of Agent Automated Negotiation. The fifth is the conclusion of the text.

2 Agent Communication Mechanism Analyses

Definition 1. Agent is a status course which can accomplish the task automatically with the ability and agreement of communication, for example, P_A represents the course of Agent A.

Definition 2. The course of Agent make the Agent's ability which can be marked as $Ability_{P_A}$ and $TASK_{P_A}$ means to be able to fulfill the task.

The moving status of the static Agent in MAS can be classified as Active, Wait and Run. Agent in the Wait status will be activated after receiving the requests from other Agent and then run. Agent in Run status will negotiate with other Agent or provide services according to the Try-best principle. $State_{outer}$ stands for the Run status of Agent:

$$State_{outer} :: =Wait \mid Active \mid Run$$

Agent's collaborating course observed from the outer MAS is the process that Agent runs in the $I_{outer}=State_{outer}*$

Definition 3. Contain the protocol system extremely locking the state, including STOP process in its CSP expression formula.

Definition 4. Contain alive protocol system that lock, its CSP expression formula will certainly include part exported to have pass ring of returning.

Theorem 1. In an Agent's collaborating process with Safety and Liveness, the circulation of $Wait \rightarrow Active \rightarrow Run \rightarrow Wait$ in I_{outer} will appear at least once to Agent's launch and acceptance.

Attestation： Obviously, in the circulation of $Wait \rightarrow Active \rightarrow Run \rightarrow Wait$, if any one part of Agent can not fulfill the circulation, it means something happened unexpectedly cause the deadlock or livelock to the system during the collaborating process, so the theorem attested.

Definition 5. Buffer channel C is such an Agent which set independent state switch and message buffer to all its relevant Agents and transmit messages for these Agents.

3 MAS Interior Agent Cooperation Model

When Multi-Agent in MAS begins cooperation, for the reason that there is a conform joint intension between Agent, the process of Multi-Agent in MAS works according to the principal of "From each according to his ability, abide by the law and behave oneself", that is, each Agent is trying its best to cooperated with other Agent[7,8].

3.1 Automatic Negotiation in Agent Protocol

Agent automatic negotiation is the main method for multi-Agent to negotiate, which focus on three aspects lieing in negotiation protocol, negotiation object and negotiation policy. Negotiation protocol and negotiation object act as the textual points, but the negotiation policy is clampinged how to look for in Agent each from of negotiation space best in order to reach consistence, concretion content visible literature cited.

Present hypotheses 1 to ensure negotiation agent could each other have partner faith in against due to MAS interior Agent according to Try-Best principle proceed synergic, furthermore MAS possess concurrent combine intent.

Hypotheses 1. Negotiation Agent knows each other in negotiation policy.

Be on the negotiation with the result that decision agent toward inter network communication negotiatory condition of Agent automatic negotiatory course mission due to specific assignment require different communication quality guarantee AND specific network insurance. Text take mission negotiation AND inter network communication negotiation as agent automatism negotiation in process two phase.

Definition 6. MAS interior agent automatic negotiation course could include two phases. The first phase is based on multi-Agent automatic negotiation whose negotiation object includes task starting time, task ending time and the relation of the tasks; The second phase is the negotiation of Agent's communicating conditions whose negotiation object include corresponding security policy and network service quality (Q_oS) .

According to the top analysis talks about with the correlative language behavior academic theories, we say the Agent automatic negotiation correspondence in the procedure to state row word certain for: request, promise, refuse, advise, counter advise. In view of agreement presence overtime event and agent unsolicited message transmission, so increase overtime (timeout) status and inform (inform) state row word that. Communication protocol engine of the communication process state as follows of the agent :

$State_{inner}$ $::=$ $Started|$ $Requested$ | $Accepted$ | $Refused$ | $Promised$ | $Informed$ | $Advised$ | $CAd\text{-}vised$ | $Timeout$ | $Stopped$

Agent automatic negotiation protocol can be divided into information transmission layer, buffer channel layer and Agent negotiation protocol layer from bottom to top, of which buffer channel layer C is one of the needed layers between Agents to realize asynchronous communication. If it will realize point-to-point synchronous communication between Agents, it can do communication directly through channel C. As to the description of Agent automatic negotiation, it mostly focus on Agent negotiation protocol layer, while for the other layers, it only describes their services and running environment in brief. In essence, the function of Agent negotiation protocol layer is the description of process.

The service provided by each protocol layer:

a. Information transmission layer: being in position to transmit information data between Agents in sequential way and correctly;
b. Buffering channel C0 and C1 layer: providing Agent automatic negotiation layer with the services described in 2.2.;
c. Agent automatic negotiation protocol layer : supplying Agent with credibility, efficient negotiation control and policy.

4 Conclusions

This text provides a common and communication-based Agent cooperation mode by studying mutual behavior of Agent cooperation. The text also uses some effective format ways to depict automatic negotiation protocol of Agent process and verify the validity of the protocol's logic. Finally, the text makes an implementation frame for this agreement. While using blackboard mode to realize buffer channel in this implementation frame, it provides a deployed agreement stack extra and at last it presents performance analysis and expandable analysis. In addition, as to negotiation between Agent in MAS, because the advantage difference of Agent group negotiating with Agent which has a conform joint intension has great differences on negotiation principle and strategy, the self-interested Agent's negotiation agreement between MAS is our next work under research.

References

1. Jennings N R ,Faratin P, Lomuscio A R et al.: Automated negotiation: prospects. Methods and challenges[C]. Pacific Rim International Conference on Artificial Intelligence, (2000)
2. Grosz B, Sidner C.: Plans for discourse[A]. In: P. Cohen, Morgan J, Pollack M. eds. Intentions in communication [M]. Bradford Books, MIT Press, (1990)
3. Wang Bin . Zhang Yao-xue, Chen Song-qiao: A communication method of MAS based on blackboard architecture[J]. Mini-Micro Systems, 23(11), (2002) 1355-1358
4. In G. Agha and F.: Decindio, editors, Concur-rent Object-Oriented Programming and Petri Nets, Lecture notes in Computer Science[M]. Springer-Verlag, Berlin, (1998)
5. Jiao Wen-pin, Shi Zhong-Zhi.: Modeling dynamic architectures for multi-agent system[J]. Chinese Journal of Computers, 23(7),(2000) 732-737
6. Mao Xin-jun: Anon-terminating active computing model in multi-agent systems[J]. Journal of Computer Research & Development, 36(7) , (1999) 769-775
7. Jiang Weijin: Modeling and Application of Complex Diagnosis Distributed Intelligence Based on MAS. Journal of Nanjing University(Natural Science), 40(4) ,(2004) 483-496
8. Jiang Weijin: Research on Diagnosis Model Distributed Intelligence and Key Technique Based on MAS. Journal of Control Theory & Applications, 20(6), (2004) 231-236

Adaptive Congestion Control in ATM Networks

Farzad Habibipour, Mehdi Galily, Masoum Fardis, and Ali Yazdian

Iran Telecommunication Research Center, Ministry of ICT,
Tehran, IRAN
habibipor@itrc.ac.ir

Abstract. In this paper an adaptive minimum variance controller is proposed to minimize the rate of stochastic inputs from uncontrollable high priority sources. This method avoids the computations needed for pole placement design of the minimum variance controller, and utilizes an online recursive least squares algorithm in direct tuning of the controller parameters.

1 Introduction

Congestion control of ATM (Asynchronous Transfer Mode) network with its wide use in high bandwidth communication systems is the source of attention and subject of active research [1]. There are different types of communication services which are categorized in high priority sources including Constant Bit Rate (CBR) and Variable Bit Rate (VBR), and best effort sources often considered as Available Bit Rate (ABR) sources. On the basis of QoS (Quality of Service) requirements, congestion control is possible by regulating the queue length at bottleneck nodes via active controlling of Available Bit Rate (ABR) [2]. Another important factor is the unavoidable delay of closed loop systems in high speed links such as satellite ATM networks or IP ATM. The Round Trip Time (RTT) delay is the time from the moment control information is sent to the source until an appropriate action takes place, and is the source of instability in simple control systems [3]. In this paper, a direct minimum variance self tuning regulator is proposed to be used with an online recursive least squares algorithm to estimate the appropriate control parameters and to adaptively regulate the queue length to the nominal value. The simulation results show the efficiency of the method in comparison to a proportional-integral rate matching controller.

2 Queue Length Dynamics

Each bottleneck node of an ATM network has an output buffer to prevent cell loss, but the queue length of cells in the limited size buffer should be controlled to avoid overflow. Denoting the queue length at time n by $q(n)$, the queue length dynamics is written by a simple linear equation

$$q(n+1) = q(n) + r(n) - \mu(n) \qquad (1)$$

H. Jin, D. Reed, and W. Jiang (Eds.): NPC 2005, LNCS 3779, pp. 321–326, 2005.

where $r(n)$ is the total number of cells receiving in the time interval $[n, n+1)$, and $\mu(n)$ is the number of cells that depart from this node at the same time. The rate of input cells to the buffer, $r(n)$, consists of inputs from M controllable ABR sources and a rate of cells from uncontrollable high priority sources (CBRs and VBRs) denoted by $r^u(n)$. Clearly:

$$r(n) = \sum_{m=1}^{M} r_m^c(n) + r^u(n) \tag{2}$$

A high performance tracking control method, actually results in optimal use of buffer and network capacity. $q(n)$ is referred to as the controlled variable and $r_m^c(n)$s are the M control signals. The available bandwidth for ABR, $\mu(n) - r^u(n)$, is a stochastic value since the rate of VBR traffic is time varying. Therefore the uncontrolled traffic, $r^u(n)$, can be simply modeled by a filtered random disturbance sequence to the system.

There are noticeable round trip time delays in a congestion controlled feedback loop:

$$r_m^c(n) = u_m(n - d_m) \tag{3}$$

where $u_m(n)$ is the available bit rate to the mth source calculated at time n, but is considered by the source d_m time units later. We suppose minimum and maximum limits for these time delays:

$$0 \le d_{min} \le d_1 \le d_2 \le \cdots \le d_M \le d_{max} \tag{4}$$

By defining a nominal queue length value (Q), and the error variable $q(n) - Q$, a simple proportional integral control law can be used

$$u_m(n) = a_m \left[u_m(n-1) + k_1 q(n) + k_2 q(n-1) - (k_1 + k_2)Q \right] \tag{5}$$

where a_m is the rate allocation coefficient for source m, and k_1 and k_2 are control parameters which are constant for all of the sources. Typically

$$\sum_{m=1}^{M} a_m = 1 \tag{6}$$

The control signals of the different sources are computed by dividing a unified control signal proportional to the rate allocation coefficients:

$$r_m^c(n + d_m) = u_m(n) = a_m u(n) \tag{7}$$

To design the pole placement controller, the queue length dynamics are reformulated in frequency domain (Z-domain). A colored noise process is first assumed for the rate of uncontrolled sources:

$$r^u(n) = C(z)e(n) \tag{8}$$

Where $e(n)$ denotes a Gaussian random sequence. By definition of $y(n) = q(n) - Q$, the tracking problem is simplified to the regulation problem, and the dynamical model is described by

$$A(z)y(n) = B(z)u(n) + C(z)e(n) \tag{9}$$

in which

$$A(z) = z^{d_{max}+1} + z^{d_{max}} \quad ; \quad \deg(A(z)) = d_{max} + 1 \tag{10}$$

and

$$B(z) = a_d z^d + a_{d-1} z^{d-1} + \ldots + a_0 \quad ; \quad \deg(B(z)) = d = d_{max} - d_{min} \tag{11}$$

3 Minimum Variance Controller

The minimum variance control law is designed to minimize the cost function defined as the expectation of the controlled signal in equation 9:

$$J = E\{y^2(n)\} \tag{12}$$

Equation (9) is then reconfigured as

$$y(n + d_0) = \frac{B(z)}{A(z)} u(n + d_0) + \frac{C(z)}{A(z)} e(n + d_0) \tag{13}$$

where $d_0 = d_{min}$ is the minimum time delay for a control action to appear in output, and hence is the prediction horizon of the minimum variance controller. Equation (13) can be further modified to yield

$$y(n + d_0) = \frac{B(z)}{A(z)} u(n + d_0) + F(z)e(n+1) + \frac{zG(z)}{A(z)} e(n) \tag{14}$$

$F(z)$ and $G(z)$ are computed as the quotient and remainder polynomials of dividing $z^{d_0-1}C(z)$ to $A(z)$ from the following Diophantine equation:

$$z^{d_0-1}C(z) = A(z)F(z) + G(z) \tag{15}$$

By a few mathematical manipulations through the noise innovation model, the following equation is obtained [4]:

$$y(n+d_0) = F(z)e(n+1) + \frac{zB(z)F(z)}{C(z)}u(n) + \frac{zG(z)}{C(z)}y(n) \qquad (16)$$

The second part of which is considered as the prediction model

$$\hat{y}(n+d_0|n) = \frac{zB(z)F(z)}{C(z)}u(n) + \frac{zG(z)}{C(z)}y(n) \qquad (17)$$

And to minimize the prediction error, $y(n+d_0) - \hat{y}(n+d_0|n)$, the minimum variance control law is obtained

$$u(n) = -\frac{G(z)}{B(z)F(z)}y(n) \qquad (18)$$

4 Self Tuning Regulator

The pole placement design of the minimum variance controller via equations (15) and (18) is just applicable if the polynomials of the model in equation (9), i.e. $A(z)$, $B(z)$, and $C(z)$, are definite; but this is not the case in real situation. So there is a need to utilize an estimation method either for these parameters or directly for the control parameters in equation (18). Using an identification method to estimate the parameters of the model in equation (9) is followed by the hard computation of the Diophantine equation and is not efficient. Another approach is the direct tuning of the controller parameters. To start, equation (16) is parameterized in backward difference form as follow

$$y(n+d_0) = \frac{1}{C^*(z^{-1})}\left(R^*(z^{-1})u(n) + S^*(z^{-1})y(n)\right) + R_1^*(z^{-1})e(n+d_0) \qquad (19)$$

in which $R_1^*(z^{-1}) = F^*(z^{-1})$. Recursive Least Squares (RLS) algorithm is proposed to estimate the polynomials $R^*(z^{-1})$ and $S^*(z^{-1})$ as the coefficients of the regressors of input ($u(n)$) and output ($y(n)$). The $\frac{1}{C^*(z^{-1})}$ coefficient can be considered as a filter on regressors, and is commonly replaced by a stable filter of the rational form $\frac{Q^*(z^{-1})}{P^*(z^{-1})}$:

$$u_f(n) = \frac{Q^*(z^{-1})}{P^*(z^{-1})}u(n) \quad and \quad y_f(n) = \frac{Q^*(z^{-1})}{P^*(z^{-1})}y(n) \qquad (20)$$

Therefore the RLS algorithm is formulated to estimate the coefficients of $R^*\left(z^{-1}\right)$ and $S^*\left(z^{-1}\right)$ in the following model

$$y\left(n+d_0\right)= R^*\left(z^{-1}\right)u(n)+S^*\left(z^{-1}\right)y(n)+\varepsilon\left(n+d_0\right) \qquad (21)$$

where

$$R^*\left(z^{-1}\right)= r_0 + r_1 z^{-1} +\ldots+ r_k z^{-k}$$
$$S^*\left(z^{-1}\right)= s_0 + s_1 z^{-1} +\ldots+ s_l z^{-l} \qquad (22)$$

The recursive least squares estimation is performed via

$$\varepsilon(n)= y(n)-R^*\left(z^{-1}\right)u_f\left(n-d_0\right)-S^*\left(z^{-1}\right)y_f\left(n-d_0\right)= y(n)-\phi^T\left(n-d_0\right)\hat{\theta}(n-1)$$
$$\phi^T(n)=\left[u(n) \quad \ldots \quad u(n-k) \quad y(n) \quad \ldots \quad y(n-l)\right] \qquad (23)$$
$$\theta^T =\left[r_0 \quad \ldots \quad r_k \quad s_0 \quad \ldots \quad s_l\right]$$

5 Simulation Results

Three ABR sources with different round trip time delays are assumed, one of which has an allocation rate coefficient of 0.5 and the others have equal coefficients of 0.25. The output service rate of the node is 10000 cells per time unit and the traffic of high priority sources is modeled as a filtered random process with a Gaussian input sequence (m_x=5000, σ_x=2500). Nominal time delays of ABR sources are $d_1 = 3$, $d_2 = 4$, $d_3 = 5$; $M = 3$, and the desired queue length is 3000. The nominal queue length is 3000 and the maximum buffer size is 5000. Simulation results of the proposed controller are compared to the simple control structure of equation (4). Fig. 1 presents a comparison of the queue length values for the proportional integral control method, and the adaptive minimum variance controller. Both methods have

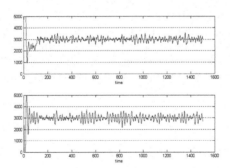

Fig. 1. Tracking control of queue length, Upper: Control feedback loop, Lower: The self tuning minimum variance regulator

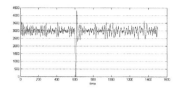 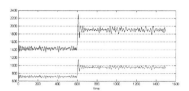

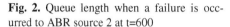

Fig. 2. Queue length when a failure is occurred to ABR source 2 at t=600

Fig. 3. Bit rate available to ABR sources

regulated the queue length to 3000, but their mean values and standard deviations are different. Obviously, the minimum variance controller has resulted in lower variance of the queue length about the nominal value. Figs. 2 and 3 depict the robustness of the system when one of the ABR sources is failed.

6 Conclusions

The self tuning minimum variance regulator proposed in this article, is designed to minimize the effect of stochastic disturbance inputs of the high priority sources to the system. While the queue length dynamics at bottleneck nodes is undetermined and the round trip time delays are uncertain and time varying for controlled ABR sources, an online recursive least squares algorithm can directly tune the control parameters to achieve the desired performance. The proposed controller is automatic and just needs good estimations of the minimum and maximum limits of the time delays. This adaptive system is also robust to the changes in network conditions, and the failure of ABR sources, to prevent buffer overflow and efficient use of network resources.

Reference

1. Imer O.C., Compance S., Basar T., Srikant R.: Available bit rate congestion control in ATM networks, IEEE Control Systems Magazine, Vol. 135, (2001) 38-56
2. Altman E., Basar T., Srikant R.: Congestion control as a stochastic control problem with action delays, Automatica, Vol. 35, (1999) 1937-1950
3. Liansheng Tan, Yang S.H.: Rate-based congestion controllers for high speed computer networks, IFAC 15th Triennial World Congress, (2002) Barcelona, Spain
4. Astrom K.J., Wittenmark B.: Adaptive Control, Addison-Wesley, 2nd Edition, (1995)

Secure Password Pocket for Distributed Web Services[*]

Jae Hyung Koo[1] and Dong Hoon Lee[2]

[1] Center for Information Security Technologies (CIST),
Korea University, Seoul, Korea
ideao@cist.korea.ac.kr
[2] Graduate School for Information Security (GSIS),
Korea University, Seoul, Korea
donghlee@korea.ac.kr

Abstract. Password authentication (PA) is a general and well-known technique to authenticate a user who is trying to establish a connection in distributed web services. The main idea of PA is to remove complex information from users so that they can log on servers only with a human-memorable password at anywhere. So far, many papers have been proposed to set up security requirements and improve the efficiency of PA. Most papers consider practical attacks such as password guessing, impersonation and server compromise which occur frequently in the real world. However, they missed an important and critical risk. A revealed password of a user from a server may affect other servers because most people tend to use a same password on different servers. This enables anyone who obtains a password to easily log onto other servers. In this paper, we first introduce a new notion, called "password pocket" which randomizes user's password even if he/she types a same password on different servers. When our password pocket is used, an exposed password does not affect other servers any more. The cost of a password pocket is extremely low since it needs to store only one random number securely.

1 Introduction

In a client-server environment, there exist several mechanisms to authenticate a client trying to log on a server such as cryptographic secure module, biometric data, information which only legitimate user knows and so on. Cryptographic module adopts mathematically secure algorithms such as message authentication code [7,15] and digital signature in public key infrastructure (PKI) [10,11]. In spite of providing very strong user authentication, cryptographic module is not widely installed in many servers because of its high cost and difficulty in key management. Biometric authentication [6,12] is also hard to take in since installation cost is too high. Furthermore, users generally do not like to give their

---

[*] This work was supported (in part) by the Ministry of Information&Communications, Korea, under the Information Technology Research Center (ITRC) Support Program.

H. Jin, D. Reed, and W. Jiang (Eds.): NPC 2005, LNCS 3779, pp. 327–334, 2005.

biometric information because of privacy. Password based authentication is a typical technique using information which a person knows and does not require high cost for additional devices such as biometric information scanner. The only requirement for users is to memorize passwords which they registered in server. Thus, password authentication is the most attractive one.

Although password based authentication (shortly PA in this paper) is a nice solution, PA still has a drawback. If a user wants to log on multiple servers, he/she should memorize a number of passwords. Obviously, it is hard for user to memorize several passwords. One approach to remedy the drawback is single-sign-on (SSO in short) [14]. As the name denotes, a user can get services from different servers without logging on separately. When a user logs on SSO gateway, he/she automatically logs on other servers which he/she has permission. SSO is a very convenient tool from the user's point of view but it has important problem. An exposed password may harm entire SSO system since anyone with the password can use all applications from servers in which the password is registered. We note that even if a user does not use SSO, the problem happens very often. In other word, many users set a same password on different servers. A simple but bad solution is to let users memorize multiple passwords. As we mentioned, memorizing several passwords is not so easy for user. So, it is desirable to design a method to achieve two goals simultaneously: i)*set user free from memorizing multiple passwords* and ii) *guarding user's passwords in other servers from a revealed password.*

Smartcard [5] is one of hardware solutions to protect secret information from out side attack. Also, it provides portability so that the owner can use the secret information for authentication at anywhere. It is possible for a user to store a number of passwords in a smartcard. However, to use a smartcard, every computer has to be equipped with a smartcard reader. Another adoptable device may be a universal serial bus (USB) [16]. Recently, most computers have USB and lots of users use the device. Therefore, saving passwords into a USB seems to be the best way for password based authentication for distributed services without additional equipments. But, the device should guarantee the confidentiality of the passwords and linkability to match each password with its corresponding server. Confidentiality of passwords is necessary because USB can be stolen. A very simple method to achieve confidentiality is to encrypt all passwords with a symmetric key which is securely managed in USB. The key also could be encrypted with a password [9] for user authentication. Obviously, it requires memory spaces. Furthermore, although a user does not need to memorize multiple passwords, he/she has to generate different passwords. Making several passwords is not easy for human-being.

Our goal is to build a mechanism to randomize a user's password even though he/she enters a same password on different web sites. We adopt an *one-to-one one-way random mapping function* $h(\cdot)$ in which same input results in same output but it is hard to guess pre-image from function value, e.g. m from $h(m)$. The word 'random mapping' means, even only one bit changes, it is computationally infeasible to guess the function value. We use a USB device but it just stores a random number in a secure area. So our idea is also memory efficient. More detailed description is shown in Sect. 3.

1.1 Related Works

A password is widely used in a client-server setting for user authentication. Basic idea is to allow permission to a person who exactly knows password registered in a server by comparing it with the entered password. To enhance security, i.e. to protect communication between a client and a server, a secure channel is usually constructed through an encryption scheme. The key used in the encryption scheme is derived from a password. By checking the validity of the encryption and additional message, the server decides to open connection. The key is continuously used after authentication until current connection is closed. This mechanism is very popular especially in internet banking to prevent user's information from being disclosed. There have been lots of papers to build password based authentication with secure channel. Most of the papers focus on finding security breaches in password based schemes such as guessing password and remedying them [1,2,3,4]. Unfortunately, all of them do not consider the situation of password exposure. Although their schemes are secure, whenever a user stores a same password on different servers and the password is revealed, anyone with the password can easily log onto the servers as though he/she is the owner of the password.

Single sign on (SSO) [14] is a cost-effective password management which concentrates on enhancing user's convenience. It is very attractive in enterprise environment with various servers or distributed web services. In a distributed web services without SSO, a user has to log on as many servers as the number of services he/she wants to get. For example, if a user tries to transfer money to an account registered in an auction server, buy a goods from a merchant and receive a receipt through email, then he/she must log on three servers, on-line banking server, auction server and email server. SSO removes the tiresome login phases based on the assumption that all of the servers are registered in the SSO gateway. I.e. whenever a user logs on the gateway, he/she can automatically logs on other servers registered in the gateway. However, as we mentioned, instead of setting a user free from memorizing multiple passwords it has critical security breach when a password is stolen. In our scheme, we adopt the basic idea of SSO but use a portable USB in place of SSO gateway.

Our contributions are two folds.

- We pointed out potential risk of a disclosed password in distributed web services which is more critical in SSO. As we noted, even though a password based authentication scheme is secure, we can easily logs on servers with a obtained password if the owner set a same password on different servers
- We propose a new and practical concept, called 'password pocket' in which even a user types a same password, the actual passwords used to authenticate user to servers are different. The actual password depends on the server's

internet address (i.e. URL : uniform resource locator). The password pocket does not store all passwords. It keeps only a random number in its secure area. Hence, the required size of memory is very small.

2   Preliminaries

We briefly introduce several building blocks which are adopted in our scheme.

One-to-One One-Way Random Mapping Function. The notion of *one-wayness* is that if we know input value it is very easy to compute the result but it is infeasible to compute the value of an inverse function. *One-to-one random mapping* guarantees two properties: i) same input always derives same output, ii) even if only one bit of input changes the output is not predictable. There exist several practical functions with the above properties such as SHA-1 [13].

Password Authenticated Key Agreement. Password authenticated key agreement is widely adopted to construct a secure channel only with a password. Basically, the secure channel consists of encryption algorithms and the key used in the algorithms is derived from the password and some related information. Following is a simple method to build a secure channel between a user U and a server S. pw denotes user's password and g^a, g^b are the result of cryptographic operation with random inputs a, b.

- **U → S** : $E_{h(pw)}(g^a)$ where $E(\cdot)$ is a symmetric algorithm and $h(\cdot)$ is a hash function.
- **U ← S** : $E_{h(pw)}(g^b)$, $MAC_K(g^a)$ where $K = h(g^{ab})$.
- **U → S** : $MAC_K(g^b)$.

MAC is a cryptographically secure message authentication code [7,15] in which only a person knows actual key (K) and input message can generate a correct value.

3   Password Pocket for Distributed Servers

In this section, we introduce a password pocket. As we mentioned in Sect. 1, we use a USB as a portable device. The structure of a password pocket is simple. There are one small secure memory (128 bits is sufficient) for a random number and relatively large general memory for one-to-one one-way random mapping function and temporal values. General memory does not need to be secure but it should guarantee read-only property for the area in which the function is stored. In fact, we only consider randomizing passwords. So we do not deal with the way to send a password to a server securely. There are many schemes providing methods to transmit data to a server in a secure manner and we can adopt one of them to enhance the security.

In the initial phase, a user $\mathcal{U}$ registers a randomized password on a server $\mathcal{S}$ as followings:

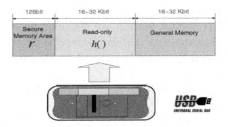

Fig. 1. Structure of Password Pocket

1. $\mathcal{U}$ chooses a password pw from password dictionary $\mathcal{D}$. In the real world, pw could be a meaningless word generated by $\mathcal{U}$.
2. $\mathcal{U}$ enters pw into a password pocket with his/her ID and $\mathcal{S}$'s address (it can be URL or IP address) Svr_Addr.
3. The password pocket fetches a random number r stored in the secure area and computes $h(ID\|pw\|r\|Svr\_Addr)$.
4. $\mathcal{U}$ registers $h(ID\|pw\|r\|Svr\_Addr)$ on $\mathcal{S}$.

We assume that there is no attack while r is used to generate a randomized password. $h(\cdot)$ is the function we explained in Sect. 2. We note that even if same pw is used for multiple servers, each server gets a different password because of the different addresses (Svr_Addr).

Whenever $\mathcal{U}$ wants to log onto a server, he/she just needs to type ID and pw into the password pocket. Then, the password pocket sets ID, pw, r, Svr_Addr as input values and returns $h(ID\|pw\|r\|Svr\_Addr)$. An essential assumption is that a secure module guards r and pw from attacks such as memory dump and data capture.

Remark 1. [Random number escrow and update]: Even though the probability is low, a password pocket could be broken or stolen. We provide two mechanisms: i) random number escrow for 'broken' and ii) random number update for 'stolen'. For the former one, we can use a key escrow technique [8] in which a user escrows his/her secret key to prepare the case of losing the key. So, after reconstructing the random number, the user installs it into a new device and uses a password pocket as before. For the latter one, a user may want to change the random number. In fact, updating the random number is very complex because all passwords registered in servers should be also updated. We note that the user may not need to update the random number since the probability of guessing correct password is very low. More detailed explanation for the security against the stolen password pocket is showed in Sect. 4.

4   Security Analysis of Password Pocket

Basically, we assume that there exists a cheap USB device with secure area and insecure area. The secure area may be very small but it is tamper-proof. A random number r is stored in the secure area and it is infeasible to find or get r. For the security of password pocket, we consider *password exposure from a server* and *password guessing with a stolen password pocket*. Because of the lack of pages, we omit the security proof but it will be shown in final paper.

5   Efficiency of Password Pocket

Password pocket is cost and memory efficient idea. It requires only a quite small secure memory for guarding a random number r and a little larger general memory for storing $h(\cdot)$ and computing values. So it can be installed in a small size USB device and a user can carry the device by inserting it into a key-holder. In this paper, we set the length of r as 128 bit and it is sufficient because the probability of guessing correct r is $\frac{1}{2^{128}}$. Only tens of kilo-bits of general memory is required to manage and execute a function $h(\cdot)$. Usually, a mapping does not require much time ($1.25 \times \frac{1}{10^6}$ second to execute a hash function SHA-1[13] on 3.21GHz Pentium 4 processor with 1 Gbyte RAM). In fact, we also consider a method to adopt our password pocket, called *virtual password pocket* (VPP). We will provide the description of VPP in the final paper. Table 3 shows the property comparison among the mechanisms. PP denotes a password pocket. In general, a smartcard authenticates a user with the owner's password pre-set in it. Therefore, if the stolen password from a server is same as or similar to the owner's password, all passwords could be revealed. As we mentioned, secure memory is tamper-proof and an encryption key (smartcard) or a random number

Table 1. Property comparisons

	Password-only	*Smartcard*	*PP*
secure for stolen password	X	△	O
secure memory	X	O (encryption key)	O(random number)
additional memory	X	O (encrypted passwords)	O ($h(\cdot)$)
additional device	X	O(reader)	O(USB port)
password guessing attack	feasible	infeasible	infeasible
memorable	easy	irrelevant	easy
cost	very low	high	low

Table 2. Simulation results. The values of random numbers and P_Passwords are hexadecimal.

ID	Password	Random number (128 bit)	Server's Address	P_Password
Robert	Password	00112233445566778899aabbccddeeff	*www.security.com*	f001e795ac95f23a
Robert	Password	00112233445566778899aabbccddeeff	*www.npc05.org*	073e160a41738cd2
bobert	Password	00112233445566778899aabbccddeeff	www.security.com	9ba86eb376b36756
Robert	*Passpord*	00112233445566778899aabbccddeeff	www.security.com	128d6116fb2faa8c
Robert	Password	*ff*112233445566778899*aabbccddeeff*	www.security.com	1060904b14a42155

(PP) should be managed in this area. In a smartcard, because all encrypted passwords should be stored, a sufficient size of additional memory is required. Our password pocket needs a USB as a portable device but almost all of the computers adopt USB port. Hence, using USB does not require additional cost. All mechanisms in Table 1. excluding 'password-only' guarantee security against password guessing attack.

We simulated our password pocket with a hash function, SHA-1 [13]. Table 1. shows the results.

5.1 Other Application of Password Pocket

Password pocket is applicable even in home network environment. If a password pocket is embedded in a mobile equipment such as a cellular phone, a user can control the devices at home from remote outside with randomized passwords. In this case, two of the input values should be changed. $Time_{Current}$ denoting current time and Cmd representing user's command are inserted instead of ID and Svr_Addr. And we set a control server at home which has the same random number and the password pocket which the user takes. Simply Cmd consists of device name (DN) and type of command (TC). The role of the server is to interpret user's command, activate a device connected to home network and report the result to the user. The messages from a user to the server are $h(Time_{Current}||pw||r||Cmd)$, $Time_{Current}, Cmd$. If the value of $h(\cdot)$ is correct, then the server extracts DN and TC to operate command. Clearly, since only who knows the password pw and the random number r can compute the function value, no one without permission can access to the devices at user's home.

6 Conclusion

We pointed out a potential but critical security breach in password based authentication which frequently occurs in distributed web services where a user only uses a same password on different servers. To remedy the security breach, we proposed a practical method, called 'password pocket' which randomizes a password so that a user can register different passwords on multiple servers only with a memorable password. Furthermore, the only requirement for the password pocket is very small secure memory to keep a random number in a secure manner. Hence, password pocket is a practical idea for distributed web services.

Acknowledgements

We really thank the reviewers for their helpful advices. Our scheme is general and can be used in all password based key agreement schemes without modification. So it is hard to compare our scheme with password based key agreement schemes. The entire security of our scheme is similar to that of smartcard. However, usually the computation power and storage ability of USB are much higher than those of smartcard.

We also want to give thanks to Bum Han Kim and Sang Pil Yun for their advice and assistance for the system-design.

References

1. M. Bellare, D. Pointcheval and P. Rogaway. Authenticated Key Exchange Secure against Dictionary Attacks. Eurocrypt '2000, 2000.
2. V. Bokyo, P. Mackenzie, and S. Patel. Provably Secure Password-Authenticated Key Exchange using Diffie-Hellman. Eurocrypt 2000
3. E. Bresson, O. Chevassut and D. Pointcheval. Security Proofs for an Efficient Password-based Key Exchange. ACM CCS 03, 2003.
4. E. Bresson, O. Chevassu and D. Pointcheval. New Security Results on Encrypted Key Exchange. PKC 2004, vol. 2947 of LNCS, 2004.
5. The ISO 7816 Smart Card Standard. Available at ``http://www.cardwerk.com/sma-rtcards/smartcard_standard_ISO7816.aspx".
6. A. Jain and S. Prabhakar. Biometrics Authentication. INSIGHT: A Publication of the Institute for the Advancement of Emerging Technologies in Education, Vol. 2, pp. Vision 29-52, EdPress, Jan 2003.
7. B. Kaliski Jr. and M. Robshaw. Message Authentication with MD5, CryptoBytes (1) 1, Spring 1995.
8. Key Escrow. Available at "http://www.epic.org/crypto/key_escrow/".
9. RFC 2898PKCS #5: Password-Based Cryptography. Available at "http://ww-w.f-aqs.org/ rfcs/rfc2898.html".
10. P1363 Standard Specifications for Public-Key Cryptography. Available at "http://grouper.ieee.org/groups/1363/".
11. Public-Key Infrastructure (X.509) (pkix). Available at ``http://www.ietf.org/html.charters/pkix-charter.html".
12. S. Qidwai, K. Venkataramani and B. Kumar. Face Authentication from Cell Phone Camera Images with Illumination and Temporal Variations. Proc. First International Conference Biometric Authentication (ICBA), Springer Verlag, LNCS 3072, 2004.
13. Secure Hash Standard (SHA1). Available at ``http://www.itl.nist.gov/fipspubs/fi-p180-1.htm"
14. Single Sign on. Available at "http://www.opengroup.org/security/sso/".
15. D. Stinson. Cryptography - Theory and Practice, CRC Press, Boca Raton, 1995.
16. Universal Serial Bus. Available at "http://www.usb.org/".

The Modified DTW Method for On-Line Automatic Signature Verification

Dong Uk Cho, Young Lae J. Bae, and Il Seok Ko

Dept. of Information & Communications Engineering,
Chungbuk Provincial University of Science & Technology, Chungbuk, Korea
{ducho, yljb, isko}@ctech.ac.kr

Abstract. Dynamic Programming Matching (DPM) is a mathematical optimization technique for sequentially structured problems, which has, over the years, played a major role in providing primary algorithms in pattern recognition fields. Most practical applications of this method in signature verification have been based on the practical implementational version proposed by Sakoe and Chiba [1], and is usually applied as a case of *slope constraint p* = 0. We found, in this case, a modified version of DPM by applying a forward seeking implementation is more efficient, offering significantly reduced processing complexity as well as slightly improved verification performance.

1 Introduction

Dynamic Programming Matching (DPM) is a mathematical optimization technique for sequentially structured problems, which has, over the years, played a major role in providing primary algorithms for automatic signature verification [1], [2], [3], [4]. In the pattern recognition field, it has been particularly used to eliminate the timing differences between two differently originating pattern signals. Hence it is called as the *Dynamic Time Warping* (DTW) method owing to its non-linear time-normalization function. Most practical applications of this method in signature verification [2], [5], [6] have been based on the practical implementational version proposed by Sakoe and Chiba [1], which is an analytical optimization method unlike others' rather heuristic approaches[1]. For practical use in signature verification, it is usually applied as a case of *slope constraint p* = 0 as, apart from the fact that this provides the simplest and the fastest implementation owing to the least constraint (see Fig. 1), the slope constraint on the warping function has been noted to be merely time-consuming. The problem in the DPM application to signature verification was that many writers have an unstable pattern of signature writing, which confuses the DTW mechanism. A different approach from the opposite perspective to investigate the DTW function is performed by applying a forward seeking implementation of DTW under the assumption that the applied patterns satisfy the preconditions for the DTW function, i.e., the patterns have only a monotonic and continuous shift on the time axis. Thus a modified version of

---

[1] Other elastic matching methods include *the peak matching technique*, a finite state machine approach and *regional correlation*.

H. Jin, D. Reed, and W. Jiang (Eds.): NPC 2005, LNCS 3779, pp. 335–342, 2005.

DPM in this context is developed. To verify the proposed method, experiments are applied under the same conditions and using the same data base to standardize and simplify the test for both conventional and proposed DTW methods. The results have proved the proposed method to be efficient, offering significantly reduced processing complexity as well as slightly improved verification.

2 DPM for Signature Verification

2.1 DPM Basics [1, 2]

Consider two different signals as sequences of feature vectors:

$$A = a_1.a_2, ..., a_i, ..., a_I \qquad (1)$$
$$B = b_1, b_2, ..., b_j, ..., b_I .$$

These two patterns, A and B, can be depicted in an i-j plane as shown in Fig. 2, where two patterns are represented along the i-axis and j-axis, respectively, and their matching stages are by a sequence of points $S(k)$, where $S(k) = (i(k), j(k))$.

To normalize these two signals with a N-stage decision process, a sequence of decision functions can be expressed as:

$$D_{(k, x_k)} = \sum_{k=1}^{N} C_k(q_k, x_k). \qquad (2)$$

where Ck is a contribution function at kth stage for the decision vector qk and the state vector $xk(ai,bj)$.

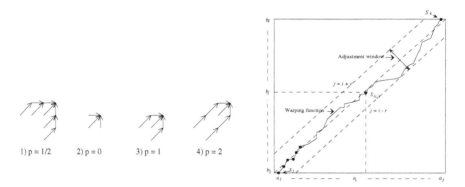

1) p = 1/2   2) p = 0   3) p = 1   4) p = 2

Fig. 1. DTW slope constraint   **Fig. 2.** DTW mechanism for time alignment

DP matching seeks to find the optimum function $D(k,xk)$ at the kth stage:

$$D_{(k, x_k)} = \frac{Optimum}{q_k} \left[D_{(k-1, x_{k-1})} + C_k(q_k, x_k) \right]. \qquad (3)$$

In the context of the DTW algorithm, this problem of determining the optimal sequence corresponds to finding a minimum sequence of warping function $F(i(k),j(k))$, which is normally composed of two components:

$$F_k = d_{(i_k, j_k)} * w_{(i_k, j_k)} . \tag{4}$$

where $d(i_k, j_k)$ is the k_{th} occupancy cost and $w(i_k, j_k)$ is the corresponding weight.
Then the optimal objective function at the k_{th} stage, Df_k, is given as:

$$D_{f_k} = \frac{Min}{F_k} \left[D_{f_{k-1}} + F_k \right] . \tag{5}$$

The optimal value of this function will be the result of the sequence of recursive functions:

$$D_{f_k} = \frac{Min}{F} \sum_{l=1}^{k} \left[\frac{\sum_{l=1}^{k} d_{i_l j_l} * w_{i_l j_l}}{\sum_{l=1}^{k} w_l} \right] . \tag{6}$$

This is expanded as follows.

1. Initial condition:

$$D_{f_1} = d(f_1) * w(f_1). \tag{7}$$

2. DP-equation:

$$D_{f_k} = \frac{Min}{F_k} [D_{f_{k-1}} + d(f_k) * w(f_k)]. \tag{8}$$

3. Time-normalized distance:

$$D_{i_k j_k} = \tfrac{1}{N} D_{f_k} . \tag{9}$$

where $N = \sum_{l=1}^{k} w(f_l)$

2.2 DPM Implementation

Sakoe and Chiba [1] provided a practical solution for Equation (6), which originally was proposed for speech recognition. Since then, this method has been extended for use in signature verification and has been widely accepted for practical applications.

Restrictions on the warping function
To provide a safeguard against unusual deviations during the warping process and to keep a desirable warping gradient, two conditions are imposed on the warping function:

1. Adjustment window (see Fig. 2)

$$| i(k) - j(k) | \leq r. \tag{10}$$

where r is an adequate value for the window size.

This is to prevent unusual deviations from the warping function, which is based on the assumption that the normal time-axis fluctuation does not cause an excessive timing difference.

2. Slope constraint

An appropriate slope constraint is imposed to keep the warping gradient from an undesirable time warping (see Fig. 1).

Let the pattern at kth stage, (i_k, j_k), be a simplified term, (i, j), then Equation (9) becomes:

1) $p = 1/2$

$$D_{ij} = Min \begin{bmatrix} D_{(i-1,j-3)} & + & 2d_{(i,j-2)} & + & d_{(i,j-1)} & + & d_{(i,j)} \\ D_{(i-1,j-2)} & + & 2d_{(i,j-1)} & + & d_{(i,j)} \\ D_{(i-1,j-1)} & + & 2d_{(i,j)} \\ D_{(i-2,j-1)} & + & 2d_{(i-1,j)} & + & d_{(i,j)} \\ D_{(i-3,j-1)} & + & 2d_{(i-2,j)} & + & d_{(i-1,j)} & + & d_{(i,j)} \end{bmatrix}. \tag{11}$$

2) $p = 0$

$$D_{ij} = Min \begin{bmatrix} D_{(i,j-1)} & + & d_{(i,j)} \\ D_{(i-1,j-1)} & + & 2d_{(i,j)} \\ D_{(i-1,j)} & + & d_{(i,j)} \end{bmatrix}. \tag{12}$$

3) $p = 1$

$$D_{ij} = Min \begin{bmatrix} D_{(i-1,j-2)} & + & 2d_{(i,j-1)} & + & d_{(i,j)} \\ D_{(i-1,j-1)} & + & 2d_{(i,j)} \\ D_{(i-2,j-1)} & + & 2d_{(i-1,j)} & + & d_{(i,j)} \end{bmatrix}. \tag{13}$$

4) $p = 2$

$$D_{ij} = Min \begin{bmatrix} D_{(i-2,j-3)} & + & 2d_{(i-1,j-2)} & + & 2d_{(i,j-1)} & + & d_{(i,j)} \\ D_{(i-1,j-1)} & + & 2d_{(i,j)} \\ D_{(i-3,j-2)} & + & 2d_{(i-2,j-1)} & + & 2d_{(i-1,j)} & + & d_{(i,j)} \end{bmatrix}. \tag{14}$$

For practical use in signature verification, it is usually applied as a case of *slope constraint $p = 0$* as in Equation (12) as, apart from the fact that this provides the simplest and the fastest implementation owing to the least constraint (see Fig. 1), the slope constraint on the warping function has been noted to be merely time-consuming.

Sakoe and Chiba [1] gave an example of practical implementation of DTW. The flow of the DTW solution for Equation (6) is diagrammed from the initialization according to Equation (7) to the time-normalization as in Equation (9). Unlike Equation (6), which uses variable "k", for indexing from the first stage, 1, to the final stage, "K", this implementation uses two indices, "i, j", to iterate "J" times the DP-equation (8) (see Fig. 2) for the sequential solution. The adjustment window size is applied as variable "r".

2.3 Experimentation

An experiment was performed to investigate how the nature of signatures affects the performance of DTW. It was relevant to the issue about the vulnerability of the DTW mechanism to relatively variable signature patterns. For this experiment, the data base consists of two contrasting types of signature sample groups:

1. Group I has the members who have relatively "stable" signature patterns.

2. Group II members have relatively "unstable" patterns in signature writing.

Group I has a membership of 15 writers and Group II 24. A total of 50 signatures was collected from each member in five sessions. Each individual donated ten signatures in each session. Random forgeries, i.e., signatures generated by others, were used for the forgery samples, on the same grounds. To eliminate effects arising from the variation of magnitude and orientation, a precise normalization process in the spatial domain was performed. The performance in terms of the equal error rate was measured as a function of the adjustment window size applying the $f(x,y)$ function. Fig. 3 is the DPM performance result from Group I and Fig. 4 is from Group II.

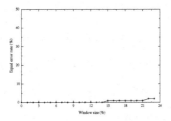   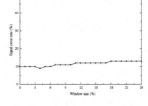

Fig. 3. Group I DPM result   **Fig. 4.** Group II DPM result

From these results, it has been observed that the nature of signature samples has a considerable effect on the DTW performance:

1. For Group I, in which each member has a stable signature pattern, DTW has ideally functioned at zero error rates with smaller window sizes. Increasing the window size over 14% has caused the degradation of the error rate performance.

2. For Group II, in which most members have variable signature patterns, the DPM performance has been considerably degraded. The window size of 4% has recorded the best result at the equal error rate of 9%, which is slightly better than the results of 10% with neighbouring window sizes.

3   Development of Modified DPM

The problem in the DPM application to signature verification in the preceding sections, which applied the implementational version proposed by Sakoe and Sato [1], was that many writers have an unstable pattern of signature writing, which confuses the DTW mechanism. In this section, a different approach from the opposite perspective to investigate the DTW function is performed by applying a heuristic (forward seeking) implementation of DTW under the assumption that the applied patterns satisfy the preconditions for the DTW function, i.e., the patterns have only a monotonic and continuous shift on the time axis. Under such ideal conditions, there is little necessity of DTW functioning for all cases at the preceding stage (see Equation (8)) as the function is continuously increasing.

Algorithm

If the optimal objective function at the k-1_{th} stage, Df_{k-1}, has been correctly selected, and the function satisfies the necessary conditions of continuity and monotonicity for DTW [1] and it does not have an abnormal (excessive) fluctuation[2] on the time axis, then Equation (8) can be alternatively expanded as:

$$D_{f_k} = D_{f_{k-1}} + \underset{F_k}{Min}\left[d\left(f_k\right)^* w\left(f_k\right)\right] \tag{15}$$

A *slope constraint* then can be imposed as in Fig. 5 to maintain a normal time warping gradient, which corresponds to the slope constraint for Sakoe's version as in Fig. 1.

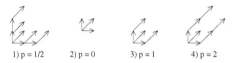

1) p = 1/2   2) p = 0   3) p = 1   4) p = 2

Fig. 5. MDTW *slope constraint*

For the practical application, it is implemented as follows:

1) $p = 1/2$

$$D_{i_k j_k} = d_{i_{k-1} j_{k-1}} + Min \begin{bmatrix} d(i_{k-1}+3, j_{k-1}+1) + d(i_{k-1}+2, j_{k-1}+1) + d(i_{k-1}+1, j_{k-1}+1) \\ d(i_{k-1}+2, j_{k-1}+1) + 2d(i_{k-1}+1, j_{k-1}+1) \\ 3d(i_{k-1}+1, j_{k-1}+1) \\ d(i_{k-1}+1, j_{k-1}+2) + 2d(i_{k-1}+1, j_{k-1}+1) \\ d(i_{k-1}+1, j_{k-1}+3) + d(i_{k-1}+1, j_{k-1}+2) + d(i_{k-1}+1, j_{k-1}+1) \end{bmatrix} \tag{16}$$

2) $p = 0$

$$D_{i_k j_k} = D_{i_{k-1} j_{k-1}} + Min \begin{bmatrix} d(i_{k-1} & , & j_{k-1}+1) \\ d(i_{k-1}+1 & , & j_{k-1}+1) \\ d(i_{k-1}+1 & , & j_{k-1}) \end{bmatrix} \tag{17}$$

3) $p = 1$

$$D_{i_k j_k} = D_{i_{k-1} j_{k-1}} + Min \begin{bmatrix} d(i_{k-1}+1 & , & j_{k-1}+2) \\ d(i_{k-1}+1 & , & j_{k-1}+1) \\ d(i_{k-1}+2 & , & j_{k-1}+1) \end{bmatrix} \tag{18}$$

4) $p = 2$

$$D_{i_k j_k} = D_{i_{k-1} j_{k-1}} + Min \begin{bmatrix} d(i_{k-1}+2 & , & j_{k-1}+3) \\ d(i_{k-1}+1 & , & j_{k-1}+1) \\ d(i_{k-1}+3 & , & j_{k-1}+2) \end{bmatrix} \tag{19}$$

---

[2] This was assumed for DTW mechanism in Sakoe and Chiba [1] and became the ground for implementing the adjustment window condition.

Equation (15) in the modified DPM (MDPM) version, firstly, has a strong point compared to Equation (8) in the conventional DPM (CDPM) as it requires only one DTW process at each decision stage while the conventional one requires this process as many times as the window size. Hence, this alternative method can reduce the computational complexity.

4 Experimentation

To compare the performances of both DPM methods, the same error rate performance tests were applied to the modified DPM (MDPM) for the two groups. Fig. 6 is the result for Group I and Fig. 7 is for Group II.

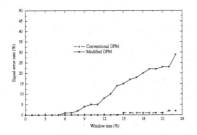
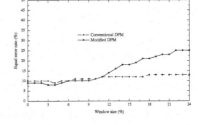

Fig. 6. Group I MDPM result

Fig. 7. Group II MDPM result

For both of the two groups, the modified DPM (MDPM) method has shown an equal or better performance compared to the conventional DPM (CDPM) method with smaller window sizes while it has a considerably degraded performance with larger window sizes. For Group I, MDPM as well as CDPM has recorded a zero error rate: for stable signature patterns, MDPM performs well as CDPM does. But its performance becomes degraded as the window size increases. For Group II, the best performance has been recorded by MDPM with the window size of 4 percent: for unstable patterns, MDPM has a slightly better performance than CDPM with smaller window sizes. Through all experiments, MDPM has shown equal or better performance than CDPM.

5 Conclusion

During the experiments for CDPM, it was observed that applying precise normalization such as preprocessing results in both an improvement in error rate performance and a smaller optimal window size. Accordingly, it was thought that the time domain fluctuation can also originate from the attitude variation during signature collection as the normalization process mainly reduces this geometrical variation. The results from the MDPM, which has been proposed for stable patterns satisfying the preconditions for DPM, applied under the same conditions as for CDPM, have also confirmed these implications as all the results have corresponded to the previous results for CDPM.

Some results have even emphasized the assumed trends, e.g., if normalization is more precisely carried out, the optimal window size is reduced.

The results from the experiments have shown that:

1. The temporal variations are ideally applied to DTW. Patterns which are affected only by these variations produce a good DTW result. (See the experimental results for Group I.)

2. The geometrical variations due to attitude change can be removed by using precise normalization, which correspondingly improves the error rate performance.

3. The random variations cannot be corrected. Patterns which are severely affected by these variations produce the worst DTW results. (See the experimental results for Group II.) Their influence can be minimized by reducing the adjustment window size.

References

1. H. Sakoe and S. Chiba: Dynamic Programming Algorithm Optimization for Spoken Word recognition, IEEE Trans. on ASCP, Vol.26, No.1 (1978)
2. M.C. Fairhust, S. Ng: Management of access through biometric control: A case study based on automatic signature verification, Universal Access in the Information Society, vol. 1, no. 1 (2001) 31-39
3. C. Lee:, Applications of Dynamic Programming to Speech and Language Processing, AT & T Technical Journal, May/June (1989) 115-130
4. H. F. Silverman and D. P. Morgan: The Application of Dynamic Programming to Connected Speech Recognition, IEEE ASSP Magazine, Jul (1990) 6-24.43
5. Parizeau and R. Plamondon: A Comparative Analysis of Regional Correlation, Dynamic Time Warping and Skeletal Tree Matching for Signature Verification, IEEE Trans. on PAMI, Vol.12, No.7 (1990)
6. Y. Sato and K. Kogure: On-Line Signature Verification based on Shape, Motion and Handwriting Pressure, Proc. 6th Int. Conf. on Pattern Recognition, Vol.2, München (1982) 823-826

A Secure On-Demand Routing with Distributed Authentication for Trust-Based Ad Hoc Networks

Meng-Yen Hsieh[1,2] and Yueh-Min Huang[1]

[1] Department of Engineering Science, National Cheng-Kung University, Taiwan
{n9892111, huang}@mail.ncku.edu.tw
http://www.es.ncku.edu.tw/index.htm
[2] Department of Information Science,
Hisng-Kuo University of Management, Taiwan
tab.hsieh@mail.hku.edu.tw
http://www.hku.edu.tw/index.htm

Abstract. Due to node mobility, the ad hoc network topology is dynamical so that on-demand routing protocols are more fit than other routing protocols. Most secure on-demand routing protocols are designed that the destination or source is able to detect the attacks on routing paths after accepting routing requests or routing replies. In this paper, we present a secure on-demand source routing protocol without the assumption of a specific cryptographic system provides per-hop broadcast authentication in routing discovery phase and security in communication phase and takes effect on our trust-based ad hoc environment. Our hop by hop broadcast authentication provides forwarding routing packets with their trust levels for abstaining from unreliable or malicious nodes. Through security analysis and discussion, we characterize our mechanism and show that it is effectively and efficiently.

1 Introduction

According to the most secure routing protocols, control packets are able to be authenticated by Source or Destination. For battlefield applications, mobile nodes communicate each other in hostile environments so that we design a secure routing acting on unreliable ad hoc environments. A number of contributions are presented in this paper: First, we construct trust controls in the network so that routing messages are flooding to nodes with certain trust requirements. Second, without any assumption of cryptographic infrastructure, we applied few system asymmetric and symmetric keys for the security and privacy of the ad hoc routing. Third, in the trust-based network, we propose per-hop broadcast authentication during per forwarding.

In our scheme, system asymmetric keys are assigned to different trust levels. However, system private keys are divided into shares hold by ad hoc nodes. A node belongs to a trust level when its certificate signed by the certain private key. With the same level certificate, these nodes are in a common trust-level community. Then any two neighbors of them will share commitments of their one-way hash key chains each other. We also present a secure on-demand routing protocol (SODR) with distributed authentication including two phases, routing discovery phase and communication phase. The routing discovery can construct temporal session keys in each routing to

H. Jin, D. Reed, and W. Jiang (Eds.): NPC 2005, LNCS 3779, pp. 343–350, 2005.

protect data traffic since a key agreement scheme is applied into our routing discovery. Through session keys, end-to-end communications are encrypted and authenticated multiply. By using one-way hash key chain, routing packets are authenticated hop by hop. And, the SODR adopts one-way hash and message authentication code (MAC) to achieve the integrity of routing packets.

The remainder of this paper is organized as following. In section 2, related techniques in the SODR are described. And we give an overview of recent secure routing protocols. Section 3 describes our trust-based system design in ad hoc networks. Section 4 details the SODR with distributed authentication. In section 5, we give the analysis of SODR defending against attacks under various attack models. And we discuss related problems about one-hop broadcasting authentication and detection of un-trustable nodes. Finally section 6 offers concluding remarks.

2 Background

Ad hoc routing protocols have two categories. One is table-driven protocol. Another is on-demand protocol such as AODV[2] or DSR[1]. Due to network topology, on-demand routing methods are more fit. In AODV, attackers easily damage routing by compromising participants. Hence, the paper considers the DSR instead of the AODV.

Diffie-Hellman Key Exchange Protocol. By using the Diffie-Hellman (D.H.) key agreement protocol proposed in [3], two nodes generate their random private values Xa and Xb to drive their public values with two system parameters, so-called g and q. The q is a prime number and the g is an integer less than the q, with the property: for every number n between 1 and $p-1$ inclusive, there is a power x of g so that $Y = g^x$ mod q. Two nodes derive their public values using parameters g and q and their private values x, then exchange their public values. Since $k = (g^{Xb})^{Xa} = (g^{Xa})^{Xb}$, two nodes have a common secret key k.

One Way Trapdoor Function. [4]. A one-way function with a "trapdoor" is provided with a key that makes it easy to invert the function. A feasible approach of ad hoc networks in an on-demand routing is applied to an asymmetric cryptosystem or symmetric cryptosystem with a one-way trapdoor function. In an asymmetric cryptosystem, the encryption/verification function f^{-1} uses a public key(pk) such as $y = f^{-1}(pk,x)$, while the decryption/signing function f uses a private key(sk) such as $x = f(sk, y)$. In a symmetric cryptosystem, the one way function f is applied to both encryption and decryption with a common secret key(k) such as $y = f(k,x)$ and $x = f(k,y)$.

Secure Ad Hoc Routing. Most researches on the security design of routing protocol consider end-to-end authentication. Some papers [5,8] provide authentication for validating intermediate nodes. Another paper [6] considers privacy in routing discovery by hiding route information with encryption schemes or distributed route information over participant nodes. Recent papers use asymmetric cryptographies, for example [5,6]. And some papers [7,8,9] adopt symmetric cryptographies. A paper [8] uses TELSA key to achieve authentication.

Authentication routing for ad hoc networks (ARAN) proposed by [5] is a rigorous authentication protocol. Through the assumption of public key cryptosystem, it defeats malicious attacks with third parties and peers as modification or fabrication of routing messages or impersonation of valid nodes. By guaranteeing per-hop authentication achieving non-repudiation services with cryptographic certificates, the approach allows a victim selection of routes and denial–of–service attacks.

Features of the secure routing protocol (SRP) [9] are verifiable routing queries and replies, the binding of secure routing and network layer functionality, the partial acceptance of route error messages, a dual identifier in query or reply packets, and the regulation of the query propagation. SRP either rejects or prevents fabricated, compromised, or replayed route replies from the achievement of sending back the source with the only requirement of a priori a shared secret between any two communication nodes in place of any assumption regarding intermediate nodes or cryptosystem.

3 Trust-Based System Design

In this section, a trust-based infrastructure is designed without any specific cryptographic system. Three types of keys are used, as few system asymmetric keys for signature with trust levels, a system secret key for requesting a share, and one-way hash key chains for one-hop broadcasting authentication from a node to its neighbor nodes.

3.1 Trust Level Design

We generate few system public and private keys, so-called PK/SK, matching to the amount of trust levels. A trust level represents a certification signed with a system private key, and a matching system public key can verify the correctness of the certificate. System keys are divided into different trust levels according to the difficulty of obtaining system private keys and adopts a (t,n) threshold scheme. Each SK is divided into n shares and distributed over the network. Collecting t shares can return the key. System asymmetric keys with different trust levels have different t values.

Let q be a large prime and $GF(q)$ be a finite field. The system chooses a polynomial $f_i(x)$ of degree at most t-1, where t < n. Suppose that $f_i(x) = a_{i,t-1}x^{t-1}+...+a_{i,1}x +a_{i,0}$ mod q, where coefficients $a_{i,j} \varepsilon GF(q)$ are chosen at random for j = 1,...t-1. A system private key, SK_i, is decomposed to the shares $SSK_{i,j} = f_i(j)$ communicated to ad hoc nodes. Since each node enters the network, it holds a share of each system private key and holds a sequence of P elements $(SSK_{1,k}, ..., SSK_{P,k})$, where P is the number of trust levels. Asymmetric system keys have threshold values as $(t_1, ..., t_P)$, where $t_i \varepsilon Z^*$, $t_i < n$, and $t_{i-1} < t_i$. Besides a share of each SK, each node holds all PK for checking the validity of certificates from other nodes, as $(PK_1, ..., PK_P)$. A node belongs to the ith trust level since it has the certificate signed with the key, SK_i. For gaining the key, the node collects shares from other nodes up to the threshold value, t_i. For the following example, node u gets a share with the ith trust level from a neighbor node v.

u $\rightarrow$ *: REQ_{TLi}, $Nonce_u$, where REQ_{TLi} is a request for a SSK_i.

v$\rightarrow$ u: $E_{GK}(SSK_{i,u}, Nonce_u)$, where GK is the system secret key.

After enough collecting, it computes the private key $(SK_i =\Sigma^t_{j=1} SSK_{i,j}$ mod $q)$ to sign its certificate, so-called $CCert_{TL}$. An extended filed of a certificate records a trust level (TL) value. A $CCert_{TL}$ is used restrictedly in a period time such as (the expiration time (RET) – the issue time (ISST)) < Max_Used_Time (MUT). Certificates signed with different *SK* have different *MUT* value. Max_Used_Time of P kinds of certificates are $(MUT_1, MUT_2, ..., MUT_P)$, where $MUT_{i-1} < MUT_i$.

3.2 One-Hop Broadcast Authentication

For one-hop broadcasting authentication, our one-way hash key chain is different from TESLA or uTELSA. Each node generates a key hash chain of an appropriate length according to past change rate of neighbor nodes. By repeatedly computing with a hash function *hash*, the key chain values are: $<TK_0, ..., TK_N>$ since $TK_{i-1} = hash(TK_i)$, where the TK_0 is the commitment key. A node needs to announce its current trust level with its certificate ($CCert_{TL}$) by periodically broadcasting its HELLO message to neighbor nodes. The format of HELLO is $<HELLO, CCert_{TL}>$. If a node enters the network just now, a pure HELLO represents that the node is in trust level 0 and without any signed certificate. By listening for HELLO messages from neighbor nodes, a node gains their certificates and verifies their trust levels by corresponding *PK*. If they have the same TL certificate with it, the node encrypts with the *PK* to forwards a commitment to them. A encrypted message with PK is $<E_{PK}(TK_0, Nonce), CCert_{TL}>$.

Keys from a one-way key chain are used for one-hop broadcasting authentication per RREQ forwarding. Whenever a node floods a RREQ, it appends a MAC with the next key, TK_{next}, of its key chain since the key is disclosed in a reverse order of its key chain generation. The TK_{next} is disclosed immediately and appended to the RREQ since it is only effective in one-hop distance. The format of a RREQ from a node to neighbor nodes is $<RREQ', MAC(TK_{next}, RREQ'), TK_{next}>$. The MAC of a RREQ is authenticated by the instantaneous disclosed key since $(TK_0=hash(..hash(TK_{next})..))$.

4   Secure On-Demand Routing with Distributed Authentication

A routing discovery phase has two steps between source (Sour) and destination (Dest): the path discovery step and the path reverse step. In the discovery step, a routing request (RREQ') packet is addressed: <RREQ, Sour, Qid, Tdoor, NList, PVList, HChain, MList>. The node list (NList) represents intermediate nodes whose trust levels are same with Sour and Dest. The public values list (PVList) is a set of D.H. public values of intermediate nodes. The MList is a set of MAC values of intermediate nodes. The Hash chain value (HChain) is multiply hashing by per-hop intermediate node, and the field is equal to: $hash_i[...,[hash_1[a\ init\text{-}hash\ value]...]]$, where the intermediate nodes are from 1 to i. In the reverse step, a routing reply (RREP') is addressed: <RREP, Sour, Td_Proof, NList, PVList, MList, HAKList>. For adopting the trapdoor scheme, this paper assumes that each node shares an encryption key with each of its recipients to communicate with. Only a recipient is able to accept and decrypt a packet through its trapdoor, then gain a proof and a hiding public value of D.H.

A trapdoor (Tdoor) is constructed by Sour. According the description of trapdoor, a trapdoor is implemented with asymmetric key or symmetric key. Initially Sour just knows the certifiable public key PK_D of Dest. The Tdoor format in RREQ is: Tdoor = $[Dest, Tstamp, K_{S,D}, PWD]_{PK_D}$, PWD(Dest). The trapdoor is only opened by Dest and the random $K_{S,D}$ selected by Sour will be used for next route request as a shared symmetric key. The all later Tdoor format is: $[Dest, Tstamp, PWD]_{K_{S,D}}$, PWD(Dest). In

In the network, only Dest can see the destination tag Dest and conclude it is the intended destination. The random PWD is a secret during the discovery step. However it is be exposed during the reverse step. The proof of trapdoor format in RREP is: Td_proof = PWD, PWD(Dest'). By comparing PWD(Dest) = PWD(Dest'), any forwarding node can verify the proof of a trapdoor opening.

PATH DISCOVERY STEP (S$\rightarrow$A$\rightarrow$B$\rightarrow$D):
S: Tdoor = [Dest,Tstamp, $K_{S,D}$,PWD]$_{PK_D}$,PWD(Dest) or
      [Dest,Tstam,$K_{S,D}$,PWD]$_{K_{S,D}}$,PWD(Dest).
S: h0 = MAC_{PK_D}(RREQ, S, Qid, Tdoor, PWD(Dest), g^S) or
      $MAC_{K_{S,D}}$(RREQ, S, Qid, Tdoor, PWD(Dest), g^S).
S: RREQ' = <RREQ, S, Qid, Tdoor, PWD(Dest), g^S, h0>
S$\rightarrow$*: < RREQ', MAC(TK$_S$, RREQ'), TK$_S$>
A: Verify RREQ' by computing TK_0 = hash[hash...[TK$_S$]..]; Store PWD(Dest); Compute g^{s_A}
A: h$_A$=hash (h0, A, g^a); M$_A$=$MAC_{g^{s_A}}$(RREQ, S, Qid, Tdoor, A, g^s, g^a, h$_A$);
A: RREQ'=<RREQ, S, Qid, Tdoor, A, g^s, g^a, h1, M$_A$>
A$\rightarrow$*: <RREQ', MAC(TK$_A$, RREQ'), TK$_A$>
B: Verify RREQ' by computing TK_0 = hash[hash...[TK$_A$]..]; Store PWD(Dest); Compute g^{s_b}
B: h$_B$=Hash (h1, B, g^b); M$_B$=$MAC_{g^{s_b}}$(RREQ, S, Qid, Tdoor, A, B, g^s, g^a, g^b, h$_B$)
B: RREQ'=<RREQ,S,D,Qid,Seq,Tdoor,A,B,g^s,g^a,g^b,h$_B$,M$_A$,M$_B$>
B$\rightarrow$D: <RREQ', MAC(TK$_B$, RREQ'), TK$_B$>

Fig. 1. An example of a path discovery step

PATH REVERSE STEP: (D$\rightarrow$B$\rightarrow$A$\rightarrow$ S)
D: Td_Proof = PWD, PWD(Dest')
D: M$_D$ = $MAC_g^{S,D}$(RREP, S, Td_Proof, A, B, M$_A$, M$_B$)
D: RREP' = <RREP, S, Td_Proof, A, B, g^d, g^a, g^b, M$_A$, M$_B$, M$_D$, h(g^{da}), h(g^{db}), h(g^{sA})>.
D$\rightarrow$B: <RREP', MAC(TK$_D$, RREP'), TK$_D$>
B: Verify M$_B$, PWD(Dest'); Compute g^{db} and check h(g^{db}); Replace h(g^{db}) with h(g^{s_b})
B: RREP' = <RREP, S, Td_Proof, A, B, g^d, g^a, g^b, M$_A$, M$_B$, M$_D$, h(g^{sA}), h(g^{sb}), h(g^{sA})>.
B$\rightarrow$A: <RREP', MAC(TK$_D$, RREP'), TK$_B$>
A: Verify M$_A$, PWD(Dest'), Compute g^{dA} and check h(g^{dA}); Replace h(g^{dA}) with h(g^{sA})
A: RREP' = <RREP, S, Td_Proof, A, B, g^d, g^a, g^b, M$_A$, M$_B$, M$_D$, h(g^{sA}), h(g^{sb}), h(g^{sA})>.
A$\rightarrow$S: <RREP', MAC(TK$_A$, RREP'), TK$_A$>

Fig. 2. An example of a path reverse step

The example, as Fig. 1, describes our routing discovery phase, where S discoveries route to D (S$\rightarrow$A$\rightarrow$B$\rightarrow$D). Node A and B are intermediate nodes, participating the route. First, S sets an initial RREQ appended with its id, Query ID (Qid), Tdoor, a public value of S (g^S), and an initial-hash value (h0). At the first routing, h0 is constructed with public key of D. However, in the later routing, h0 is encrypted with a pairwise key shared between S and D. Since S creates a RREQ' for its one-hop broadcasting authentication in its trust level. A TK$_S$ is disclosed in an order reverse to the S key chain. If A, receiving the message can verify its authenticity based on the commitment or a recently disclosed TK key of S. Before forwarding a route request, A adds itself and related information to the NList, PVList, and MList fields of RREQ.

It replaces the hash chain field by hashing with Hash($h_{previous}$, A, g^A). A needs to generates a temporal key gs,a for this session with a D.H. public value g^A. The key $g^{s,a}$ mapping to the public value g^a is stored in its memory. After storing PWD(Dest) and appending a MAC to the MAC list, the A finally rebroadcasts the modified RREQ' to one-hop neighbor nodes. Like operations of the A, the B processes and discard/rebroadcast it. Finally, the RREQ' reaches the Dest D.

After accepting the RREQ, D opens the trapdoor to get a PWD and a symmetric key ($K_{S,D}$) and other information. The PWD is a proof of opening the trapdoor and the $K_{S,D}$ is for next communication session. D checks intermediate nodes by verifying the hash chain value of the RREQ. Then, D makes a set of temporal session keys, ($g^{d,a}$, $g^{d,b}$, $g^{s,d}$), which will be shared with intermediate nodes and S. When a reverse step starts, D makes a RREP consisting of some parts of the RREQ, a Td_proof, a MAC code M_D of the entire RREP. In addition, D insets its public value $g^{d,}$ and hashed session keys into the HAKList field of RREP, ($h(g^{d,a})$, $h(g^{d,b})$, $h(g^{s,d})$). In Fig. 2, we give the detail about a reverse path from D to S. Along a reverse routing path, a RREP' is also applied into broadcast key for one-hop authentication. When B receives the RREP', then check if the packet is from D with the current trust level. B checks PWD(Dest) = PWD(Dest') to know the trapdoor is opened. B gains a session key $g^{d,b}$ shared with D after checking the validity of $h(g^{d,b})$ and replaces $h(g^{d,b})$ with $h(g^{s,b})$. Then B rebroadcast the modified RREP'. All intermediate nodes forwarding the RREP' in the same trust level will gains session keys shared with S or D. Finally the RREP' reaches S. S generates session keys ($g^{s,a}$, $g^{s,b}$, $g^{s,d}$) shared with all intermediate node and D, then authenticates hashed session keys of the RREP'. And S verifies these codes of MList (M_A, M_B, M_D) to verify the correctness of each-hop forwarding.

$$S \rightarrow A \rightarrow B \rightarrow D: A, g^a, E_g{}^{s,a} (B, g^b, E_g{}^{s,b}(D, g^d, E_g{}^{s,d} (Msg)))$$
$$D \rightarrow B \rightarrow A \rightarrow S: B, g^b, E_g{}^{d,b}(A, g^a, E_g{}^{d,a} (S, g^s, E_g{}^{s,d} (Msg)))$$

Fig. 3. Communication phase between S and D

After finishing routing discovery phase, S or D shares session keys with all intermediate nodes so that multiply encryption and authentication are used for data transport between them. Fig. 3 is an example of communication of S and D. From S to D, S transmits messages with multi-layer encryption. A or B receiving the messages will strip one layer encryption with its session key corresponding to the D.H. public value.

5   Analysis and Discussion

5.1 Security Analysis

The SODR with distributed authentication can prevent external and internal adversary attacks. We give few scenarios to describe how our protocol is secure and authentic against active and passive attacks. Scenario1: a malicious node can not modify the route request RREQ since per-hash method guarantees the integrity of NList information and MAC codes of the MList of RREQ provide the integrity of per hop routing request during routing discovery phase. Scenario2: Since a trapdoor is designed by source, only destination can open it. When a proof of trapdoor is back to source, source knows RREQ has reached the target. The trapdoor is not been reused by adversary since timestamp is inside the trapdoor. Scenario3: When a malicious node without a certain trust level of source, it does not insert any packets to hurt the routing. The malicious node without certain Cert can not distribute its commitment to neighbor nodes. This scheme enhances the security, since a malicious node is difficult to participate in routing protocol. Scenario4: After receiving a RREQ, a node is able to verify the RREQ authenticity through confirming the disclosed key. It means the RREQ is passed by neighbor nodes owning certain trust level. Scenario5: Temporal session keys are to protect transferring messages such that the transport with multiply encryption proves to be resilient against path hijacking [6].

5.2 Challenge Scheme and a Problem of One-Hop Broadcasting Authentication

We assume four possible examples that a node can be challenged by neighbor nodes since it has misbehavior. In the first example, a node does not broadcast periodically HELLO messages with its certificate. In the second example, a node has been in the network for a long time, but it does not have a certificate in a reasonable trust level. In the third example, a node announces out-of-date certificates. Or a node steals and uses certificates of other nodes. In the fourth example, a node challenges the authenticity of other nodes with a certain probability. For solving four problems, two kinds of challenges are provided as the following. The first kind challenge is for a malicious node:

$$X \rightarrow M: C1, N_X, MAC(GK, C \mid N_X); M \rightarrow X: N_M, MAC(GK, C \mid N_X \mid N_M)$$

The second kind challenge is for a specific node holding a wrong certificate:

$$X \rightarrow M: C2, E_{PK_i}(N_X, CCert_X); M \rightarrow X: N_X, MAC(GK, N_X)$$

The one-way hash key chain for one-hop broadcast authentication does not demand loose time synchronization and delay key disclosure. A nod transmits the commitment to these nodes in a same trust level, encrypted with the matching system key. Due to the triangle inequality theorem, when a node floods a packet containing a message and a one-way hash key, its neighbor nodes will accepts the packet before a re-forwarded copy from a malicious node, as Fig. 4. The malicious node cannot reuse disclosed keys since these keys are effective in one-hop distance.

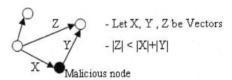

Fig. 4. The problem of one-hop broadcasting authentication

6 Conclusions

In this paper, a secure on-demand routing (SODR) is provided in trust-based ad hoc network. The SODR is with distributed authentication such as routing packets act on broadcasting authentication per flooding. Our design has these proprieties: (a) each node stores few system asymmetric keys and a system secret key. Temporal session keys are used for the confidentiality of end-to-end communication. (b) SODR provides the trapdoor method for end-to-end authentication since the trapdoor can be implemented with asymmetric or symmetric keys. (c) Through per-hop broadcasting authentication, SODR avoids that non-trusted nodes attend the routing communication. The control packets are forwarded only by these nodes with the same trust level. (d) SODR adopts per-hop hash and MAC schemes to achieve the routing integrity.

References

1. D. B. Johnson, etc.: The Dynamic Source Routing Protocol for Mobile Ad Hoc Networks (DSR). http://www.ietf.org/internet-drafts/draft-ietf-manet-dsr-09.txt, Apr. 2003.
2. C. E. Perkins and E. M. Royer: Ad hoc on-demand distance vector routing. In Proc. WMCSA, New Orleans, LA, Feb. 1999, pp. 90–100.
3. W. Diffie and M. Hellmann: New Directions in Cryptography. IEEE Transactions on Information Theory IT, vol. 22, no. 6, pp. 644–654, 1976.
4. A. C.-C. Yao.: Theory and Applications of Trapdoor Functions (Extended Abstract). In Symposium on Foundations of Computer Science (FOCS), pp. 80–91, 1982.
5. Sanzgiri, K., LaFlamme, D., Dahill, B., Levine, B.N., Shields, C.; Belding-Royer, E.M.: Authenticated routing for ad hoc networks. Selected Areas in Communications, IEEE Journal on Vol 23, March 2005 pp:598 – 610.
6. Boukerche, A., El-Khatib, K., Li Xu, Korba, L.: SDAR: a secure distributed anonymous routing protocol for wireless and mobile ad hoc networks. Local Computer Networks, 2004. 29th Annual IEEE International Conference on Nov. 2004 pp:618 - 624
7. Ting-Yao Jiang; Qing-Hua Li: A secure routing protocol for mobile ad-hoc networks. Machine Learning and Cybernetics, In Proc. of 2004 International Conference on Vol 5, Aug. 2004 pp:2825 – 2829.
8. YC Hu, A. Perrig and DB Johnson: Ariadne: A Secure On-Demand Routing Protocol for Ad hoc Networks. in Proc. of MobiCom 2002.
9. P. Papadimitratos and Z. J. Haas: Secure Routing for Mobile Ad hoc Networks. in Proc. of SCS Communication Networks and Distributed Systems Modeling and Simulation Conference, Jan. 2002.

Probabilistic Packet Filtering Model to Protect Web Server from DDoS Attacks*

Jung-Taek Seo[1], Cheol-Ho Lee[1], Jungtae Kim[2],
Taeshik Shon[3], and Jongsub Moon[3]

[1] National Security Research Institute,
KT 463-1, Jeonmin-dong, Yuseong-gu, Daejeon,
305-811, Republic of Korea
{seojt, chlee}@etri.re.kr
[2] Graduate School of Information and Communication,
Ajou University, Republic of Korea
coolpeace@ajou.ac.kr
[3] CIST, KOREA University,
1-Ga, Anam-dong, Sungbuk-Gu, Seoul, Republic of Korea
{743zh2k, jsmoon}@korea.ac.kr

Abstract. We present a probabilistic packet filtering (PPF) mechanism to defend the Web server against Distributed Denial-of-Service (DDoS) attacks. To distinguish abnormal traffics from normal ones, we use Traffic Rate Analysis (TRA). If the TRA mechanism detects DDoS attacks, the proposed model probabilistically filters the packets related to the attacks. The simulation results demonstrate that it is useful to early detect DDoS attacks and effective to protect the Web servers from DDoS attacks.

1 Introduction

These days, Web environments are very vulnerable Distributed Denial-of-Service (DDoS) attacks [1], [2]. In order to cope with the threat, there have been many researches on the defense mechanisms including several approaches based on real-time traffic analysis technique [3], [4], [5]. However, the previous mechanisms have some drawbacks such as overhead for managing IP address and lack of commonness. In this paper, we propose Probabilistic Packet Filtering (PPF) model to deal successfully with the flaws of the previous works. The proposed model distinguishes abnormal traffics from normal ones using Traffic Rate Analysis (TRA) method [6], [7]. When it detects DDoS attack, it probabilistically filters suspicious packets. Experiment results shows that the proposed model is useful to early detect DDoS attacks and it is effective to protect Web servers against DDoS.

---

* This work was supported by the Ministry of Information Communication, Korea, under the Information Technology Research Center Support Program supervised by the IITA.

H. Jin, D. Reed, and W. Jiang (Eds.): NPC 2005, LNCS 3779 , pp. 351–354, 2005.

2 The Proposed Probabilistic Packet Filtering Model

In a normal situation, network traffic rate has specific characteristics. For instance, SYN and FIN are in the ratio of 1:1 and TCP and UDP traffic are in the ratio of 9:1. However, in an abnormal situation (e.g., SYN flooding, UDP flooding), these ratios are broken. Using this fact, the proposed model distinguishes a normal situation and abnormal situation, and drop attack packet probabilistically.

To analyze web traffic, we use the TRA method that proposed in the earlier study [6], [7]. It examines the occurrence rate of a specific type of packets within the stream of monitored network traffic, and computes TCP flag rate and Protocol rate. The TCP flag rate means the ratio of the number of a specific TCP flag to the total number of TCP packets. The protocol rate means the ratio of specific protocol (e.g. TCP, UDP, and ICMP) packets to total amount of IP protocol packets. TCP flag rate and protocol rate is defined in the equation (1) and (2), respectively. In the equation, 'td' is the time interval used to calculate the value. The direction of network traffic is expressed as 'i' (inbound) and 'o' (outbound).

$$R_{td}[F\,i\,|\,o] = \frac{\sum flag\,(F)\ in\ a\,TCP\ header}{\sum TCP\ packets} \tag{1}$$

$$R_{td}[[TCP|UDP|ICMP]\,i\,|\,o] = \frac{\sum [TCP|UDP|ICMP]packets}{\sum IP\ packets} \tag{2}$$

Packet filtering mechanism of the proposed model is similar to the Random Early Detection (RED) algorithm [8]. The RED algorithm behaves according to the queue size of entire packets. Thus, it doesn't discriminate attack packet from normal packet. Thus, most legitimate packet is dropped with attack packet during DDoS attack. On the other hand, the proposed model acts according to the occurrence rate of a specific type of packets (i.e., TCP flag rate and Protocol rate of TRA method).

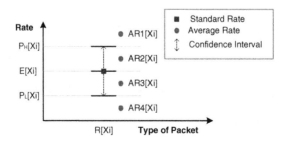

Fig. 1. Proposed PPF model; if the average occurrence rate of a type of packet X is $E[Xi]$ in normal environment, we have confidence interval from $P_L[Xi]$ to $P_H[Xi]$

Fig. 1 describes the PPF model proposed in this paper. Let the currently analyzed network traffic rate by the TRA as Current Rate (*CR*), average traffic rate from the initial time to the current time as Average Rate (*AR*), and network traffic rate of normal traffic as Standard Rate (*SR*). Current *AR* is calculated using an exponentially weighted average of previous *CR* values. If the previous *CR* values are non zero, current *AR* is defined by equation (3). Otherwise, current *AR* is defined by equation (4). The weight, w_q, determines how rapidly *AR* changes in response to changes in actual current rate. Flyod et al. recommend a quite small w_q to prevent the algorithm from reacting to short bursts of congestion [8]. However, the proposed algorithm adopts large w_q (e.g., 0.5) since bursts of traffic are very serious threat during DDoS attack.

$$AR_{cur} = (1 - w_q) \times AR_{prev} + CR \times w_q \tag{3}$$

where AR_{cur} is Current Average Rate and AR_{prev} is Previous Average Rate

$$AR_{cur} = (1 - w_q)^m \times AR_{prev} \tag{4}$$

where *m* is the amount of time that is TRA value was zero

In the proposed model, if average rate of a specific type of packet *AR* is less than lower bound of confidence interval P_L (e.g., AR_4), the incoming packet is serviced. On the other hand, if *AR* is greater than or equal to upper bound of confidence interval P_H (e.g., $AR1$), the incoming packet is automatically discarded. Between P_L and P_H is denoted by the critical region. In this region, PPF assigns a probability of discard to an incoming packet that defends on the factor; the closer *AR* to P_H, the higher probability of discarding. The confidence interval (P_L to P_H) and the probability of discard (P_d) are defined by equation (5) and (6), respectively. In the equation (5), the proposed mechanism used 95% confidence level according to our preliminary test results.

$$E - 1.96 \times SD \leq R \leq E + 1.96 \times SD$$
$$P_L \leq R \leq P_H \tag{5}$$

$$P_d = \frac{AR - P_L}{P_H - P_L} . \tag{6}$$

3   Experimental Results

In order to evaluate the effectiveness of the proposed model, we construct synthetic network and build attack model against the Web server using DDoS attack tools such as *TFN2K*. In the experiments, the normal Web service traffic flows during 60 seconds and the attacks using *TFN2K* are done between 20th second and 40th second.

Table 1 shows the experimental results of the proposed DDoS defense model. In the experiment, most of DDoS attack packets are dropped by PPF model with extremely low false positives. The most of attack cases the false positive rate is zero except for the case of SYN flooding attack. During the DDoS attacks, the *AR* values excessively exceed the traffic rate of the normal situation. Moreover, UDP packet rate and ICMP packet rate are almost zero. It means that the normal web traffic is scarcely dropped since it rarely contains these packets. There is 0.57% false-positive rate since

Table. 1 Performance of the proposed defense mechanism

Attack \ Packet	Received Packets		Dropped Packets		Drop Rate (%)		Overall
	normal	attack	normal	attack	normal	attack	
No attack	9,187	0	0	0	0%	0%	100%
SYN flooding	9,028	76,698	52	74,740	0.57%	97.45%	96.87%
UDP flooding	8,302	142,436	0	142,436	0%	100%	100%
ICMP flooding	8,545	63,674	0	63,674	0%	100%	100%

some legitimated SYN packets are generated while average $R[Si]$ is higher than standard $R[Si]$ in SYN flooding attacks. Nevertheless, almost all the attacking packets are dropped by our defending mechanism.

4 Conclusion and the Future Work

In this paper, we propose the Probabilistic Packet Filtering (PPF) model to protect Web servers from DDoS attacks. Our PPF model has not only an idea of RED mechanism to Internet traffic control, but also a mechanism to drop suspicious packets based on 95% confidence level in accordance with an appropriate threshold. In the experiment, most of attacking packets are blocked by the proposed defending mechanism. In the future work, we will try to evaluate the proposed model in more various situations, and we apply the proposed model to other specific targets such as a variety of application servers and Internet worms.

References

1. Garber, L.: Denial-of-Service Attacks Rip the Internet, IEEE Computer, vol. 33(4), (2000) 12-17.
2. Houle, J.K., and Weaver, M.G.: Trends in Denial of Service Attack Technology, CERT Coordination Center, (2001).
3. Gil, T.M, and Poletto, M.: MULTOPS: a data-structure for bandwidth attack detection, In Proceedings of the 10th USENIX Security Symposium, (2001) 23-38.
4. Householder, A., Manion, A., Pesante. L., and Weaver. M.G.: Managing the Threat of Denial-of-Service Attacks, CERT Coordination Center, (2001).
5. Kargl, F., Maier, J., and Weber, M.: Protecting Web Servers from Distributed Denial of Service Attacks, In Proceedings of the 10th International Conference on World Wide Web, (2001) 514-524.
6. Lee, C., Choi, K., Jung, G., and Noh, S.: Characterizing DDoS Attacks with Traffic Rate Analysis, In Proceedings of IADIS International Conference on e-Society 2003, vol. 1, (2003) 81-88.
7. Seo, J., Lee, C., and Moon, J.: Defending DDoS Attacks Using Network Traffic Analysis and Probabilistic Packet Drop, In Proceedings of the Third International Conference on Grid and Cooperative Computing, (2004) 390-397.
8. Floyd, S., and Jacobson, V.: Random Early Detection (RED) gateway for Congestion Avoidance, IEEE/ACM Transactions on Networking, vol. 1, no. 4, (1993) 397-413.

An Identity Authentication Protocol for Acknowledgment in IEEE 802.15.4 Network

Joon Heo and Choong Seon Hong*

School of Electronics and Information, Kyung Hee University,
1 Seocheon, Giheung, Yongin, Gyeonggi, 449-701 Korea
{heojoon, cshong}@khu.ac.kr

Abstract. This paper proposes an identity authentication mechanism at the link layer for acknowledgment frame in IEEE 802.15.4 network. With the proposed mechanism there are only three bits for authentication, which can greatly reduce overhead. The encrypted bit stream for identity authentication will be transmitted to device by coordinator within association process. Statistical method indicates that our mechanism is successful in handling MAC layer attack.

1 Introduction

The IEEE 802.15.4 specification defines four frame types: beacon frames, data frames, acknowledgment frames, and control frames for the media access control layer. The specification does not support security for acknowledgment frames; other frame types can optionally support integrity protection and confidentiality protection for the frame's data field.The lack of a MAC covering acknowledgments allows an adversary to forge an acknowledgment for any frame. An adversary need only create the forged acknowledgment with the appropriate sequence number from the original frame; this is not hard, since this sequence number is sent in the clear[1][2]. In this paper, we propose a lightweight identity authentication at the link layer for acknowledgment frame in IEEE 802.15.4 network. With the proposed mechanism there are only three bits for authentication, which can greatly reduce overhead. Also encrypted n-bits stream for identity authentication will be transmitted by coordinator within association process.

2 Proposed Mechanism

Unlike traditional authentication mechanism, the proposed mechanism determines the legitimacy of a sender by continuously checking a series of acknowledgment frames transmitted by the sender. Ideally, since the attacker does not have the shared key, the probability for the attacker to guess continuously k times of three bits is as small as 8^{-k}.

---

* This work was supported by University ITRC Project of MIC. Dr. C.S.Hong is the corresponding author.

H. Jin, D. Reed, and W. Jiang (Eds.): NPC 2005, LNCS 3779, pp. 355–358, 2005.
© IFIP International Federation for Information Processing 2005

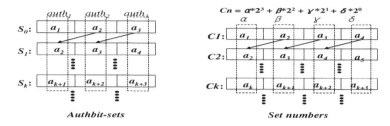

Fig. 1. *Authbit sets* and *Set numbers* generation mechanism

Fig. 2. The authentication chain of *Authbit sets*

2.1 *Authbit Set* and *Set Number* of Acknowledgments

If the coordinator determines acceptance of device, encrypted n-bits *Authbit* stream will be transmitted to device by coordinator within association process. Key management between coordinator and devices may be provided by higher layer, but are out of scope of this paper. And then, the coordinator and the device create *Authbit sets* and *Set numbers* as shown in Figure 1. Finally, the *Authbit set* and the *Set number* will be used making the same chain for authentication of acknowledgment between the coordinator and the device as shown in Figure 2.

2.2 Synchronization and Fault Tolerance Using the *Set Pointer*

Conceptually, both the coordinator and the device have a pointer pointing to the *Authbit set* for the next outgoing acknowledgment frame. Ideally, both the coordinator and the device will have their pointer pointing at exactly the same *Authbit set* and advance synchronously. Initially, the coordinator and the device pointers are synchronized. The device sends each acknowledgment frame with three additional bits and bits value is equal to the values of the *Set pointer* (P_n).

Algorithm : synchronization and fault tolerance

// Coordinator receive acknowledgment frame with *Authbit set* $\{S_{cm}\}_{device}$
      if $\{S_{cm}\}_{device} == \{S_{cm}\}_{coordinator}$ then
      P_m++
      else if $\{S_{cm}\}_{device} \neq \{S_{cm}\}_{coordinator}$ then
      $P_m = P_{m\text{-}k}$
      Coordinator $\rightarrow$ Device: Frame{failed, retransmission from $S_{cm\text{-}k}$}

Fig. 3. Pseudo code of synchronization algorithm

When the coordinator receives a frame successfully, the coordinator checks the bits value of the acknowledgment frame. The synchronization and fault tolerance of *Set pointer* explained above can partially be described with the following Figure 3.

3   Statistical Method and Implementation in LR-WPAN

The main objective of this authentication mechanism is to determine whether the sending device is an attacker or not. We have analyzed the proposed authentication mechanism and have devised a method to find out the authenticity of a device as a probability value. If the device's *Authbit set* doesn't match the coordinator's *Authbit set*, this means there are two possibilities either (a) there are no synchronization between the coordinator and the device *Set pointer* or (b) the sending device is an illegitimate device. In an error-prone wireless network, acknowledgment frames are 'frequently' lost due to wireless error. We use a statistical method to determine the authenticity of a device. We devise a statistical method to determine the probability of a station being an attacker. Let the number of acknowledgment frames from P_1 to P_n be n, let the number of synchronization done by device and coordinator be s, and let the acknowledgment frame loss rate be r, where r $(0 \leq r \leq 1)$. We have the following theorem[3][4].

[Theorem]
For a sending device D, assume the a priori probability of device D to be an attacker is $\frac{1}{8}$, i.e., $P(D=attacker) = \frac{1}{8}$ and $P(D=legitimate) = \frac{7}{8}$, the probability of this device D being an attacker one when the number of synchronization is s, $P(D=attacker \mid n, s)$, is given by

$$P(D = attacker|n, s) = \frac{2^{-n}}{2^{-n} + 7 * r^s (1 - r)^{n-s}} \qquad (1)$$

Also, we describe how to implement the proposed mechanism with the existing IEEE 802.15.4 protocol. Although an extra bit is needed in our proposed mechanism, we can use reserved bits in the frame without violating the IEEE

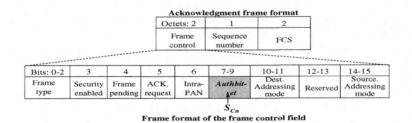

Acknowledgment frame format

Octets: 2	1	2
Frame control	Sequence number	FCS

Bits: 0-2	3	4	5	6	7-9	10-11	12-13	14-15
Frame type	Security enabled	Frame pending	ACK. request	Intra-PAN	*Authbit-set*	Dest. Addressing mode	Reserved	Source. Addressing mode

S_{Cn}

Frame format of the frame control field

Fig. 4. Frame format in the IEEE 802.15.4 Standard

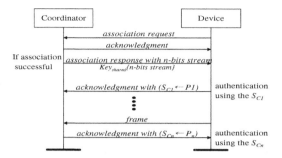

Fig. 5. Frame sequence chart with *Authbit set* chain

802.15.4 MAC frame format. This means the proposed mechanism does not modify the frame structure and is compatible with legacy devices which do not use the authentication mechanism. Figure 4 shows the common acknowledgment frame and frame control field of IEEE 802.15.4 protocol. We have used three bits reserved field of frame control field to authenticate of acknowledgment frame between coordinator and device. Figure 5 shows a frame sequence chart between coordinator and device by using the *Authbit set* chain to authenticate each other.

4   Conclusion

In this paper, a lightweight identity authentication protocol for acknowledgment frame in IEEE 802.15.4 network has been presented. The proposed mechanism inserts identity authentication bits from an acknowledgment frame known only to the two communicating stations. With the proposed mechanism there are only three bits for identity authentication, which can greatly reduce overhead and thus preserves the scarce wireless bandwidth resource.

References

1. "Wireless Medium Access Control and Physical Layer Specification for Low-Rate Wireless Personal Area Networks", IEEE Standard, 802.15.4-2003, May 2003.
2. N. Sastry, D. Wagner, "Security Consideration for IEEE 802.15.4 Networks", WiSe'04, Proceeding, pp.32-42, 2004.
3. Henric Johnson, Arne Nilsson, Judy Fu, S.Felix Wu, Albert Chen and He Huang, "SOLA: A One-bit Identity Authentication Protocol for Access Control in IEEE 802.11", In Proceedings of IEEE GLOBECOM 2002.
4. Haoli Wang, Aravind Velayuthan, Yong Guan, "A Lightweight Authentication Protocol for Access Control in IEEE 802.11", In Proceedings of IEEE GLOBECOM 2003.

A Design of the Digital Content Distribution System Based on the Public Key and the Hierarchical Web Caching Structure

Yun Ji Na[1], Ko Il Seok[2], and Gun Heui Han[3]

[1] Department of Internet Software, Honam University, Gwangju, Korea
yjna@honam.ac.kr
[2] Dept. of Information & Communications Engineering,
Chungbuk Provincial University of Science & Technology, Chungbuk, Korea
isko@ctech.ac.kr
[3] School of Information Communication,
Cheonan University, 115 Anseo-dong, Chonan, 330-704, S. Korea
hankh@cheonan.ac.kr

Abstract. The illegal distribution of duplicated contents on the Web is causing digital content providers great economic loss. Therefore, Information security is becoming a more important factor in distribution of digital contents. In this study, we designed a digital contents distribution system based on the public key techniques in hierarchical web caching structures. The superior performance of the proposed system has been proven in the experimental tests. The results of experiment show that the supposed system improved the security of DC without decreasing process speed and improved user convenience.

1 Introduction

Security problems occur because the Internet is a transmission medium that does not consider security problem. Moreover, as the most server systems are exposed to threats of illegal invasion and data destruction, threats of hacking or cracking become worse. Therefore, security techniques for the protection of server systems and digital contents are required for the safe distribution of digital contents. Distribution of contents duplicated illegally in the Internet is causing great economic loss to the digital contents providers. Therefore, a study for security and efficient distribution of digital contents is required [1,2,3].

Generally, for the safe distribution of digital contents, plaintext is transmitted through an encryption process to convert the data into cipher text. On this process, the size of encrypted digital contents is grows, it causes a transmission delay as network traffic increases and increase response delay. Thus, we consider user convenience, execution speed and security in the design of a digital content distribution system.

In this study, we designed a secure and efficient digital contents distribution system based on a public key in a hierarchical web caching structure. We use web caching technology [4] to decreasing of network delay, and use the RSA encryption / decryption technique to improve security and efficiency. Experimental tests verified

H. Jin, D. Reed, and W. Jiang (Eds.): NPC 2005, LNCS 3779, pp. 359–362, 2005.

performance superiority of the proposed system. The experiment results show that the proposed system has improved the safety of the DC while not decreasing the process speed.

2   System Design

Figure1 shows the configuration of the system. SPSM(Secure Proxy Server Manager) is an administrator managing a proxy server of the DCUG. DC means Digital Contents and DCP means Digital Contents Provider, DCUG means Digital Contents User Group.

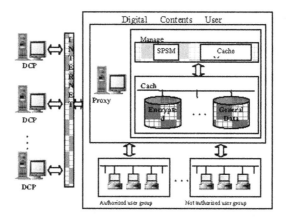

Fig. 1. System structure

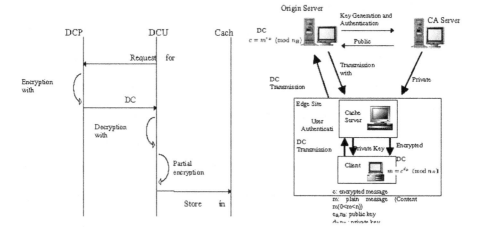

Fig. 2. DC transmission   **Fig. 3.** Authentication procedure

2.1 DC Transmission and Authentication

Figure 2 is a procedure transmitting the DC from the DCP to the DCUG. The DCP server encrypts the DC, which includes the public key. By using a private key, the DCUG decrypts the DC transmitted from the DCP and makes the original public key and plaintext. 10% of these decrypted contents with a public key is partially encrypted and saved in the cache of the DCUG. These contents are decrypted with a personal key in the user browser. The proposed system has system side security and process side security for the secure execution of contents. System side security can be attained through the security of the proxy server. It also has process side security by approved user certification on a system (the DCUG manager) and certification of private key value on the execution time (user browser). If a permitted user of the DCUG cannot find the desired contents in the cache list, the DCUG must transmit the contents from the corresponding DCP server. The DCUG and the DCP server must receive a certification statement to CA (Certificate Authority) server before exchanging encryption data. Figure 3 shows Authentication procedure for the system.

2.2 DC Transmission from DCUG

If an approved user of the DCUG requests contents, the DCUG manager transmits the partially encrypted DC in the encrypted contents cache scope to a user. A user decrypts the transmitted DC and a player in the personal Browser executes this DC. Figure 4 is a procedure to transmit contents from the DCUG to the DC.

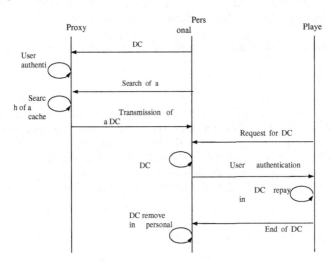

Fig. 4. DC transmission and replay

When DC transmission is requested, User certification is performed in the system. Then the DC is searched in a cache list. And when the cache is accessed, pertinent contents are transmitted. And DC decryption is performed in a personal Browser after transmission is completed. A user certification procedure is performed with a key value, and DC is replayed. Finally, DC is deleted from a user area after replay is completed.

3 Comparison to Other Systems

We compared the proposed system with SecuMAX and Digicap, which are the existing popular commercial systems to verify the superiority of the proposed system. Table 1 shows the comparison of the security level between two commercialized systems and the proposed system.

Table 1. DC security: proposed system vs. Existing Commercialized system

System \ Items	SecuMAX	Digicap	Proposed system
Authentication method	Personal encryption key	Token	Public key method
Security on contents illegality currency	×	×	○
Hierarchical Approach	×	×	○
Web Caching	×	×	○
User browser	○	○	○

In most commercialized systems, a user's personal interface is supported for security and user convenience. Table 1 shows that a commercialized systems' DC security level is decreased for the improvement of processing speed. It is difficult to improve process speed and DC security level at the same time only through encryption and personal interface technique. The two commercialized systems work better than the proposed system when web caching is not applied. But the proposed system works better for security and performs faster when web caching is applied.

4 Conclusion

The proposed system decreases the delay factor caused by network traffic by using web caching and uses a hierarchical structure encryption / decryption technique in order to improve the security level of the DC. The experiment results show that the proposed system has improved the safety of the DC while not decreasing the process speed. The proposed system could be used for an ISP (Internet Service Provider) that distributes mass multimedia digital contents like online education, web movies, and web music contents

References

1. R. Iannella, "Digital Rights Management Architecture," *D-Lib Magazine, Vol. 7, No.6*, June, 2001.
2. Spctral Lines, "Talking About Digital Copyright," *IEEE Spectrum, Vol.38 Issue;6, pp.9*, June 2001.
3. Thorwkrth N. J., Horvatic P., Weis R., Jian zhap, "Security methods for MP3 music delivery," Signals, Systems and Computers, *Conference Record of the Thirty-Fourth Asilomar Conference on, Vol.2, pp.1831-1835, 2000*.
4. G. Barish, K. Obraczka, World Wide Web Caching: Trends and Techniques. *IEEE Communications, Internet Technology Series, May 2000*.

Cluster-Aware Cache for Network Attached Storage[*]

Bin Cai, Changsheng Xie, and Qiang Cao

National Storage System Laboratory, Department of Computer Science,
Huazhong University of Science and Technology, Postfach 430074,
Wuhan, P.R. China
hust_caibin@sohu.com

Abstract. Decentralized, cooperative and large-scale distributed storage systems that consist of a cluster of storage nodes attached with local disks can deliver high resource utilization, high availability and easy scalability. This paper describes the design and prototype implementation of a novel Cluster-Aware Cache (CAC) algorithm that shares memories between nodes in cluster to construct an efficient and cooperative cache-to-disk accesses policy. The difference between our scheme and previous studies is that processes on different node can access the same page concurrently. Furthermore, CAC algorithm is also well suited to heterogeneous clusters where one or more nodes may have larger amounts of memory than the others. The performance measurements with a Web server on our system show dramatic performance improvements with increasing number of nodes.

1 Introduction

Large-scale distributed storage systems that consist of a cluster of storage nodes with local disks have become a cost-effective solution for wide range of applications, ranging form enterprise-class storage backend, HPC (High-Performance Computing) to data mining and Internet services. Such systems can be realized at little or no extra cost, can offer an inherently scalable aggregate I/O bandwidth, and can take advantage of existing cluster installations through double-use or upgrade of older hardware. Although the parallelism offered by the numerous disks in a cluster can alleviate the I/O bandwidth problem, it does not really address the latency issue which is largely limited by seek and rotational costs. Caching data blocks in memory is a well known way of reducing I/O latencies, provided we can achieve good hit ratio.

In this paper, we describe the design of a storage cluster using inexpensive PCs equipped with local disk. In our system, large files are stored in a scalable fashion by striping the data across multiple nodes to obtain high aggregate bandwidth. In order to solve the disks latency issue, we present the design and prototype implementation of a novel Cluster-Aware Cache (CAC) scheme, which changes the cache hierarchy of traditional distributed system (client cache, server cache, server disk) by letting one node cache misses to be checked against other node caches before the local storage

---

[*] This research is supported by National 973 Great Research Project of P.R. China under the grant No. 2004CB318200 and National Natural Science Foundation under grant No. 60273037 and No. 60303031.

H. Jin, D. Reed, and W. Jiang (Eds.): NPC 2005, LNCS 3779, pp. 363–370, 2005.

devices. Thus, the working set can grow beyond the local memory limit while applications read latency can be alleviated tremendously because remote caches were accessed faster over high-speed network than the disk even if it is local.

The remainder of the article is organized as follows: In section2, we describe the related work about cooperative caching scheme. In section3, we introduce the architecture of our storage cluster system, and detail the CAC scheme in section 4. The experimental results are evaluated at section 5. The conclusion comes at section 6.

2   Related Work

Using regular nodes as storage nodes has previously been suggested in the Slice [1,2] and OPIOM [3] projects, but where they primarily focus on using dedicated storage nodes, we examine the possibilities for distributing the load across all nodes in a cluster. The Network Block Device (NBD) [4] and GNBD/VIA [5] also provide network access to a remote block device, but the architectures are neither modular nor extensible. The xFS [6,7] introduced the notion of cooperative caching. Other I/O buffer cache management schemes exist on global memory management and cooperative caching [8] by extending the use of a shared distributed buffering mechanism to the I/O devices themselves. PACA [9] is another cooperative file system cache. It attempts to avoid replication and the associated consistency mechanisms by allowing only one cached block copy in the entire cluster-wide cache. That is possible since PACA uses a *memory copy* mechanism (a sort of Remote DMA) to send the data from the cache to the user memory. However, every data access has to go through this *memory copy* mechanism which is clearly much slower than accessing a local block copy. Other low level approaches to remote I/O include Swarm [10] and Network-Attached Secure Disks (NASDs) [11]. Swarm offers the storage abstraction of a *striped log* while NASDs provide an object-oriented interface.

3   System Architecture

In this section, we describe the main components of NAS storage cluster system and how they work together. We first provide an overview of the architecture, and then we cover the CAC algorithm in more detail.

The physical layout of such storage cluster is shown in figure 1. To provide an interface of a single virtual cluster server, each cluster is assigned with a multicast IP address. All participating cluster members joint in this multicast group, whose IP address is known to each other. The main advantage of NAS approach is that internally the design can seamlessly integrate major storage components to work closely together. All members in this system work collaboratively to construct a storage system with a unified storage space.

Each of the storage device members in the cluster runs a program, called daemon. Daemon communicates with each other and provides some functions, including transferring file data, transferring control message, and performing statistical information. When a node needs to get file at other node, the daemon finds the file firstly, and then gets the file from remote node. Daemon checks usage of the CAC at a fixed interval in order to provide reasonable cache replacement policy. When a node's residual cache capacity is less than the threshold value, the daemon will move some blocks from its local cache to the remote cache in order to balance the load.

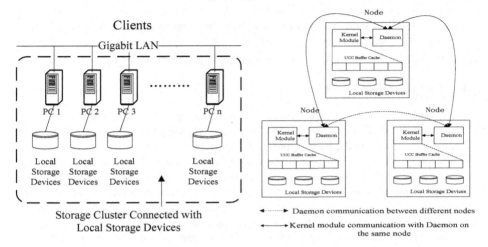

Fig. 1. Architecture of NAS Storage Cluster

Fig. 2. Daemon and CAC Kernel Module

Each of the storage device members in the cluster also has a kernel module. It divides the node's total memory into two parts: one is the node's local cache; the remainder memory at each node therefore makes of the CAC cache spaces. The typical setup and possible scenarios are shown in figure 2.

CAC hides the distributed nature of the cluster node's caches by offering the local hosts an interface to a global unified buffer cache. Similar to GMS [8], CAC uses a high-level abstraction (disk blocks) to deal with remote resources and cooperative cache algorithms to jointly manage the cluster caches. It rely on the low communication latencies of powerful interconnects to minimize block access times.

4   Implementation of CAC Scheme

Each node has a local cache to cater to the individual process requests at that node; and upon a miss goes to a shared cooperative cache running on one or more nodes of the cluster which can possible satisfy requests that come from different nodes.

4.1   Local Cache

We opted to implement the local cache within the Linux kernel that can be shared across all the processes running on that node. Only when the request misses in this cache (either all or some of the request cannot be satisfied locally), is an external request initiated out of that node to the cooperative cache. This cache is implemented using open hashing with second chance LRU replacement. There is a dirty list, a free list, and a buffer hash to chain used blocks for faster retrieval and access. The hashing function takes as parameters the inode number of the file and the block number to index the buffer hash table. There are two kernel threads called *flusher* and *harvester* in the implementation. Writes are normally non-blocking (except the *sync write* explained later), and the flusher periodically propagates dirty blocks to the cooperative cache. The harvester is invoked whenever the number of blocks in the free list falls below a low water mark, upon which it frees up blocks till the free list exceeds a high water mark. A block size of 4K bytes is used in our implementation. Note that such a kernel implementation automatically allows multiple applications/processes to share this local cache, thus making more effective use of physical memory.

4.2 Global Unified Cache

The cooperative cache, as explained earlier, adds one more level to the storage hierarchy before the disk at one node to be accessed, and we go over it in the following discussion, explaining the base algorithm in our implementation.

Currently, we use a separate cooperative cache for each file. If there is little file sharing across applications, or even across parallel processes of the same application, then the requests would automatically distribute the load more evenly with this approach. Since we would also like to be able to perform inter-application optimizations based on sharing patterns, we have opted to share the cooperative cache across applications. This can help one application benefit from the data brought in earlier by another from the cache. This feature is one key difference between our system and GMS [8] where the global cache is intended for optimizations within the processes of a single application. Similar to the local cache implementation, we implement the cooperative cache within the Linux kernel.

The internal data structures and activities of the cooperative cache are more or less similar with those for the local cache that were described earlier. One could designate such global caches on different nodes, particularly on those nodes with larger physical memory (DRAM). Consequently, this architecture is also well suited to heterogeneous clusters where one or more nodes may have larger amounts of memory than the others. The base algorithm of CAC is described in following pseudo-code:

```
Application issues file request;
if (file is at local cache){
  give the file to application;
  return;
}else{
  if (file is at remote cache){
repeat-remote:
    use Daemons Communication to fetch the file;
    if ( the file is hot){
repeat-local:
      if (local cache has space){
        add the file to local cache;
        give the file to application;
        return;
      }else{
        give the file to application;
        return;
      }
```

```
  }else{
     give the file to application;
     return;
  }
}else{
  if (file is at local storage devices){
     goto repeat-local;
  }else{
     if (file is at remote storage devices){
        goto repeat-remote;
     }else{
        can not find the file;
        return error;
     }
  }
}
}
```

4.3 Daemon Communication

Each node runs a user-level daemon program for the purpose of transferring file data, transferring control message, and performing statistical information. TCP/IP sockets are being explicitly used for sending messages to it from the individual local caches regardless of which application process is making a call. The convenience and flexibility of a user-level implementation has led us to implement the daemon running on each node of our cluster serving requests to a specific file running on a cluster node, to which explicit requests are sent by the local caches, and is shared by different applications.

When a node needs to get file at other node, the daemon finds the file firstly, and then gets the file from remote node. Daemon checks usage of the CAC at a fixed interval in order to provide reasonable cache replacement policy. When a node's residual cache capacity is less than the threshold value, the daemon will move some blocks from its local cache to the remote cache in order to balance the load. The process of communication between daemon and CAC is presented as following pseudo-code:

```
wakeup (Daemons Communication);
if (available CAC cache size < threshold_ CAC _size){
  discard some blocks;    // replacement policy
  sleep;
}else{
  if (available local cache size < thresh-
old_local_size){
     find the node with more available cache space;
     migrate the blocks to that node;
     sleep;
  }else{
     sleep;
  }
}
```

5 Experimental Results

In this section, we present an evaluation of the performance of the CAC prototype. The performance goal of CAC is to have a performance close to that of local cache and to have a small overhead on the nodes hosting the disks.

For the purpose of our experiments, we constructed a small cluster with five equivalent Pentium4/2GHz PCs with 256MB DRAM running Linux operating system with the version of the 2.4 kernel. Each PC was equipped with a single Gigabit network card as well as a single 160G IDE hard disk to provide storage space. No special kernel optimizations were done to optimize I/O or inter-process communications. One node was dedicated to servicing HTTP requests and the other four nodes were available to service data storage. Each node was running a daemon and a CAC kernel module, and shared 128MB RAM to consist of cooperative cache, therefore, the cooperative cache cache capacity is 640MB. Each client was a Windows PC running the WebBench [12] suite of e-commerce tests. WebBench is a benchmark program that measures the performance of Web servers using PC clients. In our test, the file set was 1.5GB and was placed on the disk of Web server initially, and we used 10 clients running WebBench to generate 1000 WebBench-client requests to Web server simultaneously. The experiments were done according to the request and cache hit ratio, irrespectively.

A comparison between remote disk, local disk, remote cache, and local cache in terms of the number of request operations is presented in figure 3. Notice that Web server's performance upgrades fast with the increasing number of the node. Large parts of requests hitting in Web server's local cache improves the I/O performance of Web server dramatically. Similar comparison in terms of request bytes is presented in figure 5.

A comparison between cache hit ratios in terms of the number of request operations is presented in figure 4. Notice that I/O in Web server's local disk degrades fast

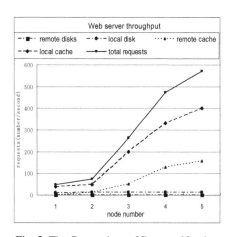

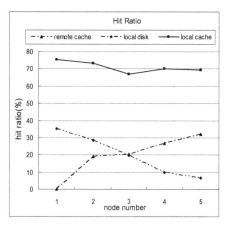

Fig. 3. The Comparison of Request Number   **Fig. 4** The Comparison of Hit Ratio

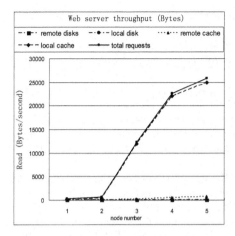

Fig. 5. The Comparison of Request Bytes

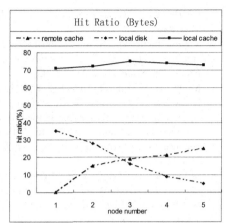

Fig. 6. The Comparison of Hit Ratio

with the increasing number of the node, large parts of requests hitting in Web server's local cache or remote cache improves the Web server's I/O performance. Similar comparison in terms of request bytes is presented in figure 6.

6 Conclusion

By leveraging the high-speed communication afforded by the cluster interconnect such as Fast/Gigabit Ethernet, large files can be stored in a scalable fashion by striping the data across multiple nodes; by distributing the disks across a sufficient number of cluster nodes, high aggregate bandwidth can be easily obtained with current hardware. In order to solve the disks latency issue, we present the design and prototype implementation of a novel cluster caching scheme, which changes the cache hierarchy of traditional distributed system (client cache, server cache, server disk) by letting one node cache misses to be checked against other node caches before the local storage devices. Thus, the working set can grow beyond the local memory limit while applications read latency can be alleviated tremendously because remote caches were accessed faster over high-speed network than the disk even if it is local. Performance measurements of such a system are encouraging, showing that the I/O performance of Web server improves fast with the increasing number of node.

References

1. D.C.Anderson, J.Chase, and A.Vadat, "Interposed request routing for scalable network storage", *Proceedings of the 4th Symposium on Operating Systems Design and Implementation*, October 2000.
2. J.Chase, D.Anderson, A.Gallatin, A.Lebeck, and K.Yocum, "Network I/O with trapeze" *Proceedings of 1999 Hot Interconnects Symposium*, August 1999.
3. P.Geoffray, "OPIOM: Off-processor I/O with myrinet", *Proceedings of the first ACM/IEEE International Symposium on Cluster Computing and Grid*, May 2001.

4. P.T.Breuer, A.M.Lopez, and A.G.Ares, "The network block device", *Linux Journal*, (73), May 2000.

5. K.Kim, J.Kim. and S.Jung, "BNBD/VIA: A network block device over virtual interface architecture on Linux", *Proceedings of the 16ᵗʰ International Parallel and Distributed Processing Symposium*, April 2002.

6. M.Dahlin, R.Yang, T.Anderson, and D.Patterson, "Cooperative Caching: Using remote client m emory to improve file system performance", *Proceedings of first Symposium on Operating Systems Design and Implementation*, November 1994.

7. T.Anderson, M.Dahlin, J.M.Neefe, D.Patterson, D.Rosseli, and R.Y.Wang, "Serverless network file systems", *Proceedings of the 15ᵗʰ Symposium on Operating System Principles*, December 1995.

8. M.I.Feeley, W.E.Morgan, F.H.Pighin, A.R.Karlin, and H.M.Levy, "Implementing global memory management in a workstation cluster", *Proceedings of the 15ᵗʰ ACM Symposium on Operating Systems Principles*, pp. 201-212, December 1995.

9. T.Cortes, S.Girona, and L.Labatra, "PACA: A distributed file system cache for parallel machines. Performance under Unix-like workload", *Technical Report UPC-DAC-RR-95/20 or UPC-CEPBA-RR-95/13*, Department d'Arquitectura de Computadors, Universitat Politecnica de Catalunya, 1995.

10. J.H.Hartman, I.Murdock, and T.Spalink, "The Swarm scalable storage system", *Proceedings of the 19ᵗʰ IEEE International Conference on Distributed Computing Systems (ICDCS 99)*, June 1999.

11. G.A.Gibson, D.F.Nagle, K.Amiri, F.W.Chang, H.Gobioff, E.Riedel, D.Rochberg, and J.Zelenka, "File systems for network-attached secure disks", *Technical Report CMU-CS-97-118*, School of Computer Science, Carnegie Mellon University, Pittsburgh, PA 15213-3890, July 1997.

12. http://www.veritest.com/benchmarks/webbench/

Design and Implementation of a SAN Agent for Windows NT Architecture*

Ran Meng, Jiwu Shu, and Wei Xue

Department of Computer Science and Technology,
Tsinghua University, 100084 Beijing, China
mengran@tsinghua.org.cn
http://www.cs.tsinghua.edu.cn

Abstract. In an out-of-band SAN virtualization system, the virtualization appliance maintains metadata, and the agents inside the kernel of servers use that data to supply virtual storage devices and to perform the mapping of I/O address. A design of an out-of-band SAN virtualization system based on Windows NT volume manager driver, and its underlining technologies were presented in this paper. It shows that, in general our system is able to supply large volume and high bandwidth virtual storage devices for applications, and it can be used as a basic environment to manage the SAN centrally. The system performance was investigated in comparison with a plain SAN under FAT32 and NTFS, using different data block sizes and access patterns. The results reveal that the overhead induced by our approach is much low. Under FAT32, the performance characteristics of the 3-striped virtual volume follow a typical strip distribution strategy and the bandwidth is 1.20 3.71 times greater than general volume. Furthermore, under NTFS, the bandwidth of the 3-striped virtual volume is an average of 4.10 (max 4.82) times greater than general volume with the random read access test. Hence it can be concluded that our virtualization approach could make use of the storage resources in SAN more effectively.

1 Introduction

According to the definition given by the Storage Network Industry Association (SNIA) [11], storage virtualization is "an abstraction of storage that separates the host view from the storage system implementation." Another more detailed definition of virtualization from Robert Frances Group is "Those architectures and products designed to emulate a physical device where the characteristics of the emulated device are mapped over another physical device" [1]. Virtualization provides many benefits to the SAN system, including:

* The work described in this paper was supported by the National Natural Science Foundation of China under Grant No.60473101, the National Key Basic Research and Development 973 Program of China under Grant No. 2004AA111120 and the National High-Tech Research and Development 863 Plan of China under Grant No. 2004AA111120.

H. Jin, D. Reed, and W. Jiang (Eds.): NPC 2005, LNCS 3779, pp. 371–378, 2005.

- The manpower needed to administer the SAN system is significantly reduced [1],
- The capacity of the virtual storage device is not limited by a single disk or a single RAID system [2],
- The virtualization can dramatically improve the utilization of storage resources [2].

The virtualization techniques inside a SAN system can be classified as two types in terms of their control path: in-band and out-of-band [3] [11]. In an in-band system the virtualization appliance is in the data path and virtualization functions such as address mapping are accomplished by the same component that performs reading and writing. In an out-of-band system the implementation related to the virtualization is not in the data path. Nowadays, there are already some SAN virtualization solutions, such as HP OpenView Storage Operations Manager [8]. In these solutions the storage management tasks ship with an integrated HBA (Host Bus Adapter). Therefore they are low-level implementations and some special HBAs and corresponding drivers and/or firmware are required.

This paper presents a design of an out-of-band SAN virtualization system based on the Windows NT volume manager. In this design we implement an agent to perform virtualization tasks at the Windows NT volume manager level; thus only standard HBAs are required. Additionally in our system there is a virtualization server centrally managing the storage resources. In section 3 the design of the virtualization agent based on the Windows NT volume manager are presented, and the key techniques we used are described. Furthermore we investigate the performance of our system compared with a plain SAN under FAT32 and NTFS with different data block sizes and access patterns and focus on the analysis of the virtual volume using stripe distribution strategy.

2   The Virtualization Server

In our design the virtualization server consists of five cooperative components: management module, interface module, communication module, device-monitor module and device-agent module. Here it is incumbent on the management module to maintain the virtualization metadata, to prompt and harmonize other components and the virtualization agents running on the application servers, and then to achieve the virtualization of the storage resources of the entire SAN system. The virtualization metadata is stored in a specific location in multiple devices in the storage pool. Each device has a complete copy and backs up the metadata for others.

3   Design and Implementation of the Virtualization Agent on Windows Platform

The virtualization agent running on Windows application servers is comprised of the kernel module and the communication module. The former performs virtualization functions, for example, creating virtual volumes, translating the I/O

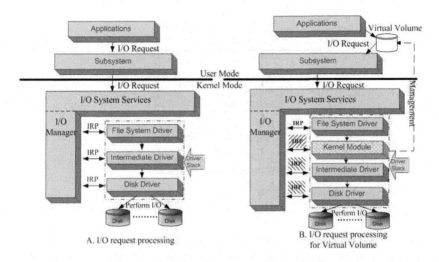

A. I/O request processing   B. I/O request processing for Virtual Volume

Fig. 1. Windows NT I/O driver stack model. The (*I/O Manager*) of the Windows NT operating system handles the flow of data to and from peripheral devices. It exports an (*I/O system services*) whose user-mode protected subsystem supplies a programming. (*Applications*) use that interface to manipulate the devices such as send I/O requests to them, so that the (*I/O Manager*) can intercept all those requests.

address from virtual volumes to physical devices, etc. The latter communicates with the virtualization server and assists the kernel module to accomplish the virtualization tasks. In this section, we first introduce the driver model of storage devices in the Windows NT architecture. Then the design and implementation of the Windows virtualization agent will be discussed.

3.1 The Windows NT Disk Driver Model

As shown is Figure 1, The I/O Manager provides a consistent interface for all kernel-mode drivers (including the lowest drivers, intermediate drivers and file system drivers (FSD)). All I/O requests sent to these drivers are represented as I/O request packets (IRPs). These drivers are called as driver stack in terms of the processing of IRPs. The driver (usually the FSD) that is situated on the top of the driver stack will process IRPs first, and then passes them to the next driver via the I/O Manager. [10] [12]

3.2 The Virtualization Agent

The communication module of our agent is a user-mode network program that uses TCP/IP over the Ethernet to talk with the virtualization server. It receives the metadata and instructions from the virtualization server, orders the kernel module to perform virtualization tasks and sends the results or other information back. The kernel module is represented as a volume manager driver inside the Windows kernel. Its functions include:

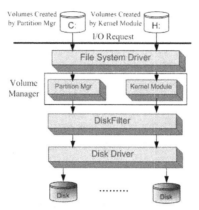

Fig. 2. The relation between the virtual volumes and the Windows system volumes and the relation between the (*kernel module*) and the (*Volume Manager*) are illustrated. The (*Disk Filter*) is an upper filter driver that hides the physical storage devices from accesses other than from the kernel module.

- Providing the virtual volumes for the applications in user mode, and maintaining and managing them,
- Distributing the data of virtual volumes between physical devices and mapping the I/O requests to them,
- Recording some statistics of virtual volumes and sending them to the virtualization server for further analysis.

Now we discuss the design of the communication module and the kernel module.

IRP Processing in Kernel Module. As viewed from the perspective of applications and file systems, the virtual volumes are the same as other volumes that are created by the Windows Disk Manager, so that they can access these volumes in the same way. As an example, the IRP representing a read request from an application to the virtual volume is viewed as a request to read a specific range of data on the virtual volume when it has been processed by the FSD. So the kernel module suspends the original IRP first, and then creates one or more IRPs to read the corresponding data from physical devices according to the distribution strategy. When those IRPs are completed by the disk driver and popped to the kernel module, the original IRP will be filled with the data they read and will be completed by the kernel module.

Distribution Strategy and Metadata Management. At the present time the kernel mode supports linear and strip distribution strategy. In linear strategy, data is continuously distributed on one or more physical devices. The strip strategy repeatedly places data among multiple devices according to a specific chunk size. In this way the reads and writes are done in parallel on the devices and the performance will improve.

In our design the metadata is centrally managed and distributively applied. While creating the virtual volumes the metadata containing distribution information is sent to the kernel module by the management module on the virtualization server. The kernel module stores this metadata in a kernel memory area that is associated with the volume device object. This metadata is a shared portion of all virtualization information and assists the kernel module in performing address mapping. If some settings are changed, updated metadata will be sent to the kernel module, which may perform some tasks such as data migration.

4   Results and Analysis

In this section we will give the experimental performance results of the virtual volumes on Windows servers in our out-of-band SAN system. The test system consisted of an application server for which the OS was Windows 2003 Server Enterprise Edition, a specialized virtualization server and a Fiber Channel (FC) disk array. These components were connected through an FC network. The configuration of the application server and the FC disks are listed in Table 1 and 2. We investigated the performance under FAT32 and NTFS separately. The test tool we used was the IOMeter [14].

4.1   Results Under FAT32

We compared the performance of our virtualization implementation to a plain SAN system. For this our test cases include:

- LV0: A virtual volume with 3 stripes and a chunk size of 64KB,
- LV1: A virtual volume using the continuous distribution strategy,
- PV0: A Windows system volume.

Table 1. The configuration of the application server

Processor	Intel®Xeon 2.4GHz × 2
Memory	1G
OS	Windows 2003 Server
FC HBA	Emulex LP982(2Gb/s)

Table 2. The parameter of the FC disks

Series	Seagate Cheetah 10K
Capacity	147G
Speed	10000 RPM
Cache Size	8M
Max Bandwidth	105MB/S

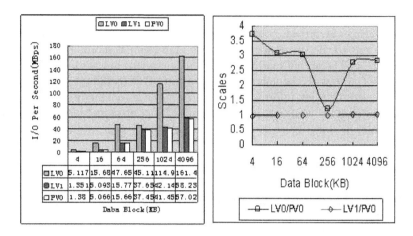

Fig. 3. Comparisons of the random read under FAT32

The file system was FAT32 and the capacity was 10G for all the volumes. We tested their I/O bandwidth with 4 access patterns: sequential read, sequential write, random read and random write. The results showed that the contrastive characteristics of the three volumes were familiar for these four patterns. We can safely draw some conclusions from the results.

- The bandwidth of LV1 was almost the same as that of PV0. This indicates that the overhead induced by the kernel module is quite low in the linear strategy,
- LV0 showed performance characteristics typical of strip data distribution. It gained an average 3.09 (max 3.71) times bandwidth greater than PV0 when the data block size was considerably less or greater than the product of the chunk size and the number of stripes (64KB * 3 in this case). When the data block size was comparable to 64KB * 3, LV0 showed a bandwidth similar to PV0,
- The ratio of LV0 and PV0 decreased in the endmost part of the curve. This may have resulted from the excessive amount of concurrent IRPs.

4.2   Results Under NTFS

The NTFS performance has been optimized in many aspects [10] [13], with the result that most Windows application servers format their volumes with NTFS. We repeated those tests described above for NTFS. Other parameters of LV0, LV1 and PV0 were the same but their file systems were changed to NTFS. The results showed that:

- The performance of LV1 and PV0 was quite similar; it showed that the overhead involved by the kernel module was fairly low,
- LV0 showed an analogical strip performance characteristics in the sequential and random write patterns,

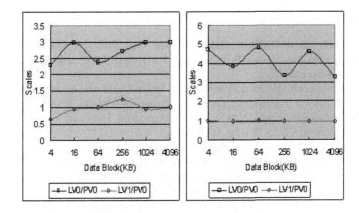

Fig. 4. Comparisons of the sequential read (*left one*) and random read (*right one*) under NTFS

- LV0 showed a much better performance in the sequential and random read patterns. LV0 gained an average 2.73 (max 2.99) times bandwidth compared to PV0 in the sequential read pattern, and an average 4.10 (max 4.82) times in the random read pattern.

Under the NTFS the virtual volume gained much higher bandwidth than the general volumes in read accesses irrespective of the data block size. This shows that our virtualization approach utilizes the SAN storage resource more effectively, especially with the NTFS.

5   Conclusions

A design of an out-of-band SAN virtualization system based on Windows NT volume manager driver, and its underlining technologies were presented in this paper. Virtual volumes can be provided to the applications and end users by the virtualization agent implemented as a Windows volume manager driver with a virtualization server. The agent maps the I/O accesses to the virtual volumes to physical devices and separates the physical devices from the application servers. Because the virtualizations are done at the volume manager level, only standard HBAs and corresponding drivers are required.

Generally our system is able to supply large volume and high bandwidth virtual storage devices for applications, and it can be used as a basic environment to manage SAN.

The system performance was investigated in comparison with a plain SAN under NTFS with different data block sizes and access patterns. The results showed that the utilization of the SAN storage resource could be increased significantly with our virtualization approach, particularly with the strip distribution strategy and the NTFS.

References

1. Charles Milligan, Sid Selkirk. Online Storage Virtualization: The key to managing the data explosion, Proceedings of the 35th Hawaii International Conference on System Sciences 2002.
2. Andre Brinkmann, Michael Heidebuer. V:Drive-Costs and Benefits of an Out-of-Band Storage Virtualization System, In Proceedings of the 12th NASA Goddard, 21st IEEE Conference on Mass Storage Systems and Technologies (MSST), College Park, Maryland, USA, 13 - 16 April 2004.
3. J.S.Glider, C.F.Fuente, W.J.Scales.The Software Architecture of a SAN Storage Control System. IBM SYSTEMS Journal VOL 42, NO 2, 2003.
4. Andre Brinkmann, Kay Salzwedel, Christian Scheideler. Compact, Adaptive Placement Schemes for NonUniform Distribution Requirements, Proceedings of the fourteenth annual ACM symposium on Parallel algorithms and architectures, Winnipeg, Manitoba, Canada, 2002.
5. Ismail Ari, Melanie Gottwals, Dick Henze, SANBoost: Automated SAN-Level Caching in Storage Area Networks, 13th IEEE International Conference on Autonomic Computing (ICAC'04).
6. Han Deok Lee, Young Jin Nam. Regulating I/O Performance of Shared Storage with a Control Theoretical Approach. Proceedings of the 21st IEEE Mass Storage Systems Symposium/12th NASA Goddard Conference on Mass Storage Systems and Technologies (MSST2004), April 2004.
7. Robert Gramacy, Manfred Warmuth, Scott Brandt and Ismail Ari, Adaptive Caching By Refetching, 2002 Neural Information Processing Systems (NIPS'02).
8. http://h18006.www1.hp.com/products/storage/software/som/index.html,   HP Open View Storage Operations Manager.
9. M. Farley. Building storage area networks McGraw-Hill, 2000
10. Microsoft Development Network, http://msdn.microsoft.com/.
11. Storage Networking Industry Association, http://www.snia.org/.
12. William J. Bolosky, Scott Corbin, David Goebel, and John R. Douceur, Microsoft Research Abstract, Single Instance Storage in Windows 2000, August 2000.
13. L. Chung, Windows 2000 Disk IO Performance, MS-TR-2000-55, June
14. IoMeter Project, http://sourceforge.net/projects/iometer/

MagicStore: A New Out-of-Band Virtualization System in SAN Environments*

Guangyan Zhang, Jiwu Shu, Wei Xue, and Weimin Zheng

Department of Computer Science and Technology,
Tsinghua University, 100084 Beijing, China
zhang-gy04@mails.tsinghua.edu.cn
http://www.cs.tsinghua.edu.cn

Abstract. In this paper, MagicStore, a new out-of-band virtualization system designed for SAN environments is proposed. Online multiplication of the components in a striped volume can help enhance both the I/O performance and storage capacity of a system, but it requires online redistribution of the data on the volume. MagicStore employs a new mapping management solution based on a sliding window to support the online data redistribution without loss of scalability. Furthermore, some virtualization transactions, such as online resizing, require modification of the virtualization metadata, which results in the challenge of keeping the persistent consistency of metadata. MagicStore, by using a combination of ordered writes, REDO logging and log integrity checking, can survive across panics and power failures robustly. In order to support log integrity checking effectively, MagicStore also uses a new log format.

1 Introduction

Storage virtualization [1] can enhance the overall quality of service in storage area networks because it enables the competence of a logical volume to go beyond the limit of single physical storage devices. For example, the online resizing and reconfiguration of logical volumes ensure business continuity. The disk utilization rate can also be increased from only 50% up to 80% through the centralized and more flexible administration of virtualization software [2].

However, an issue facing storage virtualization is the likelihood that it will put an inordinate strain on existing hosts. This concern has led to two schemes for offloading some of the work associated with virtualization: in-band and out-of-band virtualization. The in-band device, which is placed inside the data stream, could itself become a performance bottleneck. Conversely, out-of-band virtualization may provide better scalability because its main function device resides outside the data stream and does not touch the actual data.

In this paper, we propose a new out-of-band virtualization system working in SAN environments called MagicStore. It employs a new mapping management

* This research was supported by the National High-Tech Research and Development Plan of China under Grant No. 2004AA111120 and the National Grand Fundamental Research 973 Program of China under Grant No. 2004CB318205.

H. Jin, D. Reed, and W. Jiang (Eds.): NPC 2005, LNCS 3779, pp. 379–386, 2005.

solution based on a sliding window. When the data redistribution is not needed, our solution is equal to the mapping function. A sliding window is introduced when the data needs to be redistributed. The solution not only supports online data redistribution but also occupies a small amount of memory space.

Moreover, MagicStore uses a combination of ordered writes, REDO logging and log integrity checking to obtain high persistency. Ordered writes keep the sliding window and physical Extents consistent. REDO logging ensures that the multiple writes to metadata blocks in single virtualization transactions are atomic. And a new log format enables MagicStore to detect whether writing to the log is complete.

The remainder of this paper is organized as follows. Section 2 gives an overview of the MagicStore system. In Section 3, we propose a new mapping management solution based on a sliding window. The strategies for persistent consistency are presented in Section 4. In Section 5, we evaluate the I/O performance of MagicStore through the representative experiments. We conclude with related works and a summary.

2   Overview of the MagicStore System

MagicStore is made up of the manager and the agent software on each host (Figure 1). The manager knows the states of physical devices and manages logical volumes. Instructed by the manager, the agent virtualizes logical volume devices and does the address mapping from the logical address space to the physical address space. Each agent is connected to the manager via TCP/IP.

The manager consists of two cooperative modules: the metadata manager and the SAN monitor. The metadata manager organizes virtualization metadata using a simple 3-layered model separating physical volumes, volume groups and logical volumes [3]. Logical volumes may be allocated to hosts with access permissions. Information about the state of the SAN is collected by the SAN

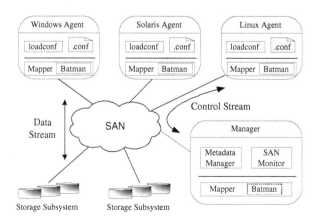

Fig. 1. Architecture of the MagicStore system

Monitor. In addition, the manager enables the applications on itself to access any logical volume by loading the agent on the corresponding platform.

The agent consists of the mapper in the kernel space and the loadconf utility and a configuration file in the user space. The mapper is a light-weight driver residing between the file system driver and the disk driver. When the mapper is loaded, it creates the batman, a kernel thread which receives virtualization instructions from the manager and executes them. The mapper maps the I/O requests sent to logical volumes to the corresponding physical volumes. The loadconf utility is used to ask the mapper to reload the configuration information from the configuration file.

The mapping mode for each logical volume can be alternated between the buffer mode and the non-buffer mode. The former can eliminate the overhead of the network communications for sending frequent mapping requests to the manager. The latter is convenient for online updating of the mapping information.

3 Mapping Management Based on a Sliding Window

To enhance the I/O performance and storage capacity of a system, users often have a reasonable need for increasing the number of components in a striped volume online. It is necessary for the data on the striped volume to be redistributed across the old and new volume components.

The address mapping can be expressed through the mapping function [3,4,5] and the mapping table [1,6] traditionally. The mapping table makes it possible to handle the data redistribution and normal I/O operations at the same time because it can keep track of the movement of data. However, the mapping table occupies a very large space. The transfer and storage of a large amount of mapping information puts tremendous pressure on both the network and the memory, and further impairs the scalability of the whole system.

In contrast to the mapping table, the mapping function which only stores its own function eliminates the transfer and storage of a large amount of mapping information. In this technique, unfortunately, the I/O operation occurring during the data redistribution can not find the correct location of relevant data because the data can exist on the original or new location.

We propose a new solution for managing mapping information. The key idea behind the solution is to introduce the concept of a sliding window into the mapping function. When the data redistribution is not needed, our solution is equal to the mapping function. A sliding window is introduced when the data needs to be redistributed.

Figure 2 illustrates how the metadata is updated when the components in a striped volume are multiplied from 2 to 3. The sliding window is a quite small mapping table which describes the mapping information of a continuous segment of the striped volume. At any time, only data within the range of the sliding window is redistributed. The normal I/O requests to the logical address before the sliding window are mapped through the original function; those sent to the address after the sliding window are mapped through the new function, and

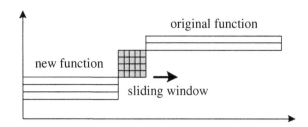

Fig. 2. The components in a striped volume are multiplied from 2 to 3

those to the address in the range of the sliding window are mapped through the sliding window. After all the data in the sliding window are moved, the window slides ahead by one window width. The data redistribution of the whole volume is completed when the sliding window reaches the end of the original striped volume. From then on, the address mapping of the whole volume is done through the new mapping function.

Introducing the concept of a sliding window enables online redistribution of the data on logical volumes. Additionally, the fact that the size of the sliding window is small and independent of the size of the logical volume contributes to the high performance and scalability of the whole system.

4   Strategies for Persistent Consistency

To enable the out-of-band virtualization system to survive across panics and power failures, virtualization metadata has to be both available and consistent when the system reboots. When the mapping information of a logical volume is modified, the manager asks the mapper to switch the mapping mode of the logical volume to the non-buffer mode. Thus, only the metadata consistency on the manager side has to be ensured.

Whenever online multiplication of the components in a striped volume occurs, we have to keep the sliding window and physical Extents consistent. This consistency can be achieved by the method of ordered writes. The physical Extent is first copied to the new location and then the map block is written to the disk. Even if the power fails in between, just an extent copy is wasted and the consistency is not destroyed. The opposite order is problematic.

Another issue of persistent consistency is that some virtualization transactions write multiple metadata blocks. MagicStore, by using REDO logging, ensures that the multiple writes to metadata blocks in single virtualization transactions are atomic. In this case, intentions are logged first and the metadata updates can be done. In case of a crash, when the manager comes up, it scans through and replays the log. Thus the metadata remains consistent.

A new issue that REDO logging brings is that, in case of a power crash while writing to the log, we must be able to detect that writing to the log is not complete. We propose a new log format, with which MagicStore can detect whether writing to the log is complete by checking the log integrity.

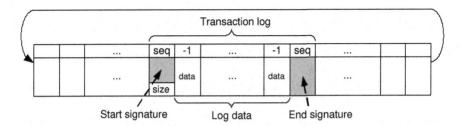

Fig. 3. The new design of the log format

Our new design of the log format is shown in Figure 3. It uses two special signatures to label the beginning and end of the log respectively. The sequence number fields of the start and end signatures store the sequence number of the transaction log, while that of the log data is set to the invalid sequence number value -1. The size of the whole log is recorded at the end of the start signature. This design eliminates the need for scanning through the whole transaction log to find the end signature because the size of the log has been introduced. In addition, there is no possibility of mistaking the old metadata or end signature for the current end signature since the values in their sequence number fields are different.

5 Experiments

The manager was implemented in the user space on the Linux platform. The agent software were implemented on the Windows, Solaris and Linux platforms. In this section, we compare the performance of the linear, striped and mirrored volumes managed by MagicStore with that of the plain volumes managed by the original operating systems.

5.1 Experimental Setup

The Solaris agent was installed on a two-way 300 MHz UltraSPARC-IIi machine with 256 MB of memory and an Emulex LP9802 HBA card running SunOS Release 5.10 Version. Each other subsystem of MagicStore was installed on a two-way 2.4 GHz Intel Xeon machine with 1 GB of memory and an Emulex LP982 HBA card running Linux kernel v.2.4.16 of RedHat 9 distribution or Windows Server 2003. The file systems used were NTFS, UFS and EXT2 respectively. Via a Brocade Silk Worm 3800 fibre channel switch, these machines were connected with an FC disk array controlling five 146 GB Seagate Cheetah 10K disks.

We configured IOmeter[7] to generate the representative workloads, and all of them consisted of 20% writes and 80% reads since Vogels found that 79% of accesses to files were read only [8]. All workloads used random addresses with transfer request size doubled from 8 KB to 4096 KB.

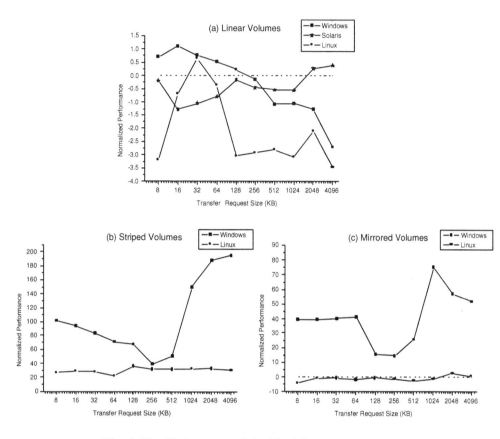

Fig. 4. The Performance of the MagicStore system

5.2   Results

We first measured the I/O throughput (MB/s) of each logical volume x managed by MagicStore with different transfer request sizes. According to the following equation, we got its corresponding normalized performance, where Thrput(plain) denotes the I/O throughput of the plain volume, which resides on the same platform with x, with the same transfer request size.

$$Norm\_Perf_x = \frac{Thrput_x - Thrput_{plain}}{Thrput_{plain}} * 100. \tag{1}$$

Figure 4 shows a plot of the normalized performance of logical volumes versus the transfer request size. The minimum, maximum and average normalized performances of linear volumes were respectively, -2.70, 1.10 and -0.29 on the Windows platform, -1.27, 0.39 and -0.43 on the Solaris platform, -3.46, 0.64 and -2.10 on the Linux platform.

All the striped volumes in the experiments were constructed of four FC disks with a stripe width of 64 KB. The minimum, maximum and average normalized performances of striped volumes were respectively 39.16, 194.81 and 103.89 on the Windows platform, 21.94, 36.21 and 30.03 on the Linux platform.

In the experiments, all the mirrored volumes were constructed of two components. Writes to mirrored volumes were initiated concurrently and reads were alternated between the copies. The minimum, maximum and average normalized performances of mirrored volumes were respectively, 14.47, 75.25 and 40.11 on the Windows platform, -4.16, 2.46 and -0.98 on the Linux platform.

6   Related Works

In recent years, considerable attention has been paid to the storage virtualization systems for SAN environments. Some of them, such as the Pool Driver [4], CLVM[5] and the SANtopia volume manager[1], employ symmetric architecture. This means that they only apply to clusters running a single operating system.

There are also some systems which use asymmetric architecture. However, they all have some limitations. For example, OpenView[9] only applies to the specified HBA card and driver because its agent is implemented on the HBA driver. When the SANfs-VM[6] or V:drive[2] is used, only Linux can be run on the hosts.

Among all the above systems, only the SANtopia volume manager supports online multiplication of the components in a striped volume. Unfortunately, the mapping management using a mapping table restricts its scalability and makes it inadequate for SAN environments with a large amount of storage. Jose and Toni proposed an algorithm for increasing the capacity of RAID5 [10], which has an easily controlled overhead. A similarity between the algorithm and our solution is that the new disks are gradually available to serve requests during the multiplication process.

Reference [11] presents a log format for detecting whether writing to the log is complete. However, it has no capability to tell log data blocks from the transaction epilogue block belonging to the same transaction log by their transaction ids and offsets. Furthermore, without introducing the size of the log, this solution makes it necessary to scan through the whole transaction log to find the transaction epilogue. If some data block of the transaction log exactly matches the current transaction epilogue, a checking mistake will appear.

7   Conclusions

MagicStore employs a new mapping management solution based on a sliding window. This solution enables it to support online multiplication of the components in a striped volume. Furthermore, it contributes to MagicStore's high scalability since it occupies a very small space. By employing a combination of ordered writes, REDO logging and log integrity checking, MagicStore can survive across panics and power failures robustly. Moreover, a new log format effectively supports log integrity checking. In the representative experiments, MagicStore demonstrated its ability to provide high performance.

References

1. Chang-Soo Kim, Gyoung-Bae Kim, Bum-Joo Shin. Volume Management in SAN Environ-ment. In: Proceedings of the 8th International Conference on Parallel and Distributed Sys-tems, ICPADS 2001. 2001. pages 500-505.
2. A. Brinkmann, M. Heidebuer, F. Meyer auf der Heide, et al. V:Drive - Costs and Benefits of an Out-of-Band Storage Virtualization System. In: Proceedings of the 12th NASA God-dard, 21st IEEE Conference on Mass Storage Systems and Technologies (MSST), pages 153-157, College Park, Maryland, USA, 13-16 Apr. 2004.
3. David Teigland, Heinz Mauelshagen. Volume Managers in Linux. In: Proceedings of the 2001 USENIX Annual Technical Conference, pages 185-198, June 2001.
4. David Teignald. The Pool Driver: A Volume Driver for SANs, In Partial of Fulfill-ment of the Requirements for the Degree of Master of Science, Oct 1999.
5. Heinz Mauelshagen. Linux Cluster Logical Volume Manager, In: Proceedings of the 11th International Linux System Technology Conference. Erlangen, Germany. Sept. 2004.
6. Seung-Ho Lim, Joo Young Hwang, Kyung Ho Kim, et al. Resource Volume Man-agement for Shared File System in SAN Environment. In: Proceedings of the 16th International Con-ference on Parallel and Distributed Computing Systems (PDCS), 2003.
7. Intel Corporation, Iometer, July, 2004. http://www.iometer.org.
8. W. Vogels. File system usage in Windows NT 4.0. In Proceedings of the 17th ACM Sympo-sium on Operating Systems Principles, pages. 93-109, Dec. 1999.
9. Hewlett-Packard Development Company. HP OpenView Storage Operations Manager v1.2. Sept. 2004. http://h18006.www1.hp.com/products/quickspecs/11778_div/11778_div.html.
10. Jose Luis Gonzalez and Toni Cortes. Increasing the capacity of RAID5 by online gradual assimilation. International Workshop on Storage Network Architecture and Parallel I/Os. Antibes Juan-les-pins, France, September 30, 2004
11. Suresh B Siddha, K Gopinath. A Persistent Snapshot Device Driver for Linux. In: Proceed-ings of 5th Annual Linux Showcase & Conference, 2001.

A Content Delivery Accelerator in Data-Intensive Servers

Joon-Woo Cho, Hyun-Jin Choi, Seung-Ho Lim, and Kyu-Ho Park

Computer Engineering Research Laboratory, EECS,
Korea Advanced Institute of Science and Technology
{jwc, hjchoi, shlim}@core.kaist.ac.kr, kpark@ee.kaist.ac.kr

Abstract. The standard OS and server platform hardware have not been optimized for applications that transfer large multimedia files, resulting in poor server I/O performance. One source of the problem is that several redundant copies are introduces when the data is transferred from disks to a Network Interface Card. To solve the problem of redundant copies, we propose a Contents Delivery Accelerator that accelerates large file transfers by eliminating the redundant copies from disks to the NIC. To eliminate the redundant copies, the CDA introduces a new function, called a logical direct link, which provides the shortest path from the disks to the NIC. By using the shortest path, we can completely eliminate the redundant copies, thereby improving the I/O performance of server. The CDA architecture is a combined hardware-software approach. Thus, it comprises CDA hardware and a modified Linux kernel. We implemented the current version of the CDA on a Linux 2.4.18 kernel and an IXP1200 evaluation board. In the experiment, we compared the logical-direct path with a redundant path. For the transfer of data from disks to the NIC, our experimental results show that the average transfer latency of a direct path is as much as 30 percent less than a redundant path.

1 Introduction

Internet web servers deal with an enormous amount of multimedia data. This work is highly time-consuming and can increase the response time of the server. Consequently, clients that connect to the server might not get multimedia data in time. When a multimedia server operates a general-purpose operating system (OS) such as Unix and Linux, the multimedia data is often too large to be handled effectively because those systems have not been optimized for multimedia data.

There are two critical problems in conventional Web-servers that handle streaming multimedia data. The first problem is that there are many redundant data copies between the disks and the network interface card (NIC). These redundant copies are due to the long data path and the modern OS architecture that splits the OS space and the application space. Figure 1 shows the data flow of this programming model. First, the CPU initiates the disk controller to get

H. Jin, D. Reed, and W. Jiang (Eds.): NPC 2005, LNCS 3779, pp. 387–395, 2005.

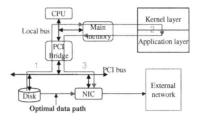

Fig. 1. Data-transfer path in general-purpose system

the data fragment that we wish to send. The data fragment is delivered to the main memory from the disks. The data in the main memory is then delivered to the NIC. During this path, redundant copying occurs between the disks and the NIC. Moreover, there is another redundant copy of the data, though it is not shown in figure 1. The data delivered from the disk is located in the kernel-space memory. The server application program then copies the data into the user-space memory region. A similar operation is required at the downside data path from the memory to the NIC. All these wasteful data flows are repeated until all the data is delivered [1]. If a server working set is small, the problem we just described is not critical because the operating system manages the buffer cache so that data can be located in the cache area in advance and these data can be directly delivered from the memory to the NIC rather than from the disks. However, if the server working set is large, especially a multimedia streaming server, these problems are critical.

Another problem is the TCP processing time. The processing of the TCP/IP protocol is difficult. Consequently, if the CPU of a Web server processes the TCP by itself, the CPU wastes many CPU clocks, and the response of the server therefore becomes slow. In a gigabit network, the problem is exacerbated [6]. Many researchers and companies therefore suggest various TCP offloading techniques to reduce the CPU overhead for processing the TCP packet. A well-known technique is to import TCP accelerating hardware such as a TCP offloading card [2][3]. However, to support these mechanisms, a new interface is required between the server application and the TCP offloading engine. This is critical problem for the system compatibility.

To solve these problems which are described above, we now propose a new architecture, which uses additional assisitant hardware Contents Delivery Accelerator. When the CDA is inserted into a PCI slot, it functions and interacts with the CPU to resolve the problems mentioned above. First, the CDA can make a direct path between the disks and the NIC, and between the memory and the NIC. By using this direct path, the CDA can eliminate the redundant copy and transfer large amounts of multimedia data without interfacing with the host CPU. Second, the CDA can manage the data cache for the hot data or frequently accessed data. As a result, Servers can improve their throughput and reduce the response time. Third, the CDA can offload the TCP job from the host. The CDA relieves the host from that heavy work so that the host can reduce the CPU overhead for the TCP packet processing and use the CPU for other purposes. In our approach, the more important thing is that the CDA does not harm Linux compatibility, obviating the need to modify current applications. The CDA has this ability because we kept the Linux system call interface when we modified the source codes of the host Linux kernel.

The organization of this paper is as follows. The next section covers related works. In Section 3, we describe the architecture of the CDA, while in Section 4 we discuss how we implemented the CDA. In Section 5, we show how the CDA performs. Finally, in Section 6, we make a comparison and offer our conclusions.

2 Related Works

There have been several works on eliminating the copy overhead and processing overhead of data intensive servers. The general approach to solving the redundant copy overhead involves optimizing the OS. To solve this problem, which is caused by a layered approach, general OSs introduce an 'mmap' and 'sendfile' system call. These system calls prevent one redundant copy between the OS and the application program so that the server can use its resources more effectively [7][8]. The sendfile system call is used in the Apache Web server to deliver requested data. Because this interface is only operated in the kernel-space region and sends data directly using the kernel copy operation according to the Apache document, the sendfile call enables Apache to deliver static content faster and with lower CPU utilization [5]. Alternatively, to enhance the data transfer and to increase the memory and cache efficiency, some OSs such as I/O Lite [11] unify the buffer of many subsystems in the OS to reduce the redundant copies between the subsystems. Moreover, someone has made an I/O-specific OS such as Hi-Tactix [12].

By using the approach of existing software, we can eliminate the problem of redundant copy in the main memory. However, the problem of producing redundant copies outside the main memory still exists. With the help of improvements to existing hardware techniques, many I/O-specific types of hardware have been introduced to solve the problem of redundant copy. The Xiran [3] offers I/O-specific hardware with a disk interface and a network interface. The two interfaces are connected to each other by a direct path that sends data without producing a redundant copy. However, to use this direct path, a new application was made by SDK provided by the Xiran company. As a result, this method has no software compatibility.

3 CDA Architecture

We suggest CDA architecture that uses the auxiliary hardware shown in figure 2. This architecture is similar to existing system architecture so that it can maintain its interface and compatibility. The purpose of the CDA is to improve the I/O performance of the server by eliminating the redundant copy problem and achieving zero copies between the disk and the NIC. To do this, the CDA

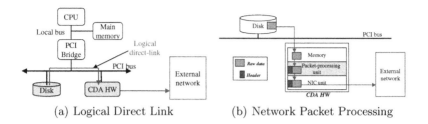

(a) Logical Direct Link   (b) Network Packet Processing

Fig. 2. Proposed CDA Architecture

provides two functions: the logical direct link and network packet processing. To provide these functions, the CDA is composed of CDA hardware and a modified Linux kernel. The prototype of the CDA hardware is a kind of intelligent NIC. It has many units. To use the CDA hardware in the Linux system, we modified the Linux kernel, version 2.4.18. Specifically, we implemented a device driver for the CDA hardware and modified the system call, the memory management and the file system.

The logical direct link provides a zero-copy path between a disk and the CDA hardware. This link can be made up through the address that redirects them from the main memory of the host to the CDA memory region. Through this link, we can directly copy the data from a disk, as shown in figure 2(a). By using this, we can eliminate the redundant copy that occurs outside the main memory.

The copied data from a disk to the CDA hardware through the logical direct link is raw data. This means that the data packets have no processing header for the TCP or IP. As a result, data cannot be sent to an outside network. To send that data, the raw data stored in the CDA memory must be processed to get the network header shown in figure 2(b). The header is then packetized with the raw data. After these operations, the network packet made at this packet is sent to an outside network through the NIC unit similarly to an Ethernet card.

4   Implementation

We made the prototype of the CDA using Intel's IXP1200 evaluation board [14]. The evaluation board has architecture that is similar to our proposed hardware. By using this board, we checked the validity of the CDA architecture and, accordingly, the OS that we modified to fit with the CDA prototype. Because the IXP evaluation board has no packet processing unit, it cannot convert raw data into a network packet at the sending time. To solve this problem, we used a virtual packet-processing method, as shown in figure 3(a). Before storing new raw data, the CDA preprocesses the data to get the network header for the raw data and it stores them together on the disk. At the transfer time, the CDA gets the network header and the raw data from a disk. By using this method, the CDA can send data without packet processing at the transfer time [13]. However, this method only supports the UDP because the TCP does dynamic processing; for

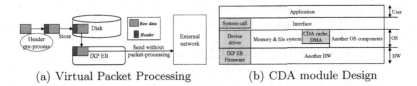

(a) Virtual Packet Processing   (b) CDA module Design

Fig. 3. Virtual Packet Processing and CDA module Design

example, controlling the fragments and flow during the transfer. In implementing the CDA mechanism, we considered conserving at the design stage Linux's I/O mechanisms such as page caching, reading ahead, and DMA, especially for fast file I/O operations [1]. If the CDA could not maintain these mechanisms, the I/O performance would be impaired. As a result, the CDA maintains these mechanisms to achieve a good I/O performance for general cases and for large cases. Figure 3(b) shows the CDA modules in the Linux OS. The inserted modules are the device driver of the IXP evaluation board, the CDA cache, the DMA, the firmware of the IXP evaluation board and the modified system call. We elaborate the implementation of the CDA module in detail.

Device Driver. To copy data from a disk to the memory of CDA hardware, a kernel is required to directly access the memory of CDA hardware. The role of the device driver, therefore, is to make a logical direct path that maps the hardware components such as the memory and registers into the kernel space. To do this function, Linux offers the following functions: *pci_read_config_dword* and *ioremap_no_cache*. A pseudo-code for using these functions is as follows:

```
pci_read_config_dword(&val);
bus address=val&MASK;
virtual address=ioremap_nocache(bus address);
```

After this operation has been completed, the kernel can transparently access and use components of the IXP evaluation board through the virtual address variable.

System Call. To send data to an outside network, we modified the sendfile system call provided by Linux. This system call is suitable for the CDA because it can explicitly send a file on a disk outside the network. In some cases, however, applications use this system call to quickly copy data from a disk to the memory of the host computer. We therefore modified this call to ensure it could be applied to both cases without destroying the interface of the system call. First, we chose one disk from among the many disks in the system to be the CDA's own disk. In that disk, we stored a file to be sent to an outside network. We also modified the sendfile system call itself. When a file is called by the modified sendfile call, the OS first checks where the requested file is located. If the file is not in the CDA's own disk, the OS calls the original function *do_generic_file_read* to copy the requested file to the memory of the host computer. Otherwise, the OS calls the modified function *cda_do_generic_file_read* to directly copy the requested file from the CDA's own disk to the memory of the CDA hardware.

CDA Cache. With the help of the CDA cache, the data stored in the CDA hardware memory can be reused without having to access the disk. The CDA cache can therefore increase the overall I/O performance of the CDA. In this section, we describe in detail how we implemented the CDA cache. The CDA cache is based on the Linux page cache mechanism. Because the page cache uses a hash algorithm for a fast search, the CDA cache uses the same algorithm. When a file is requested by the sendfile call, the CDA first searches for the requested data at the cache table in the CDA hardware. If there is no descriptor at the cache table, the CDA calls the *descriptor_alloc* function. This function allocates a new descriptor for that file and inserts it into the cache table by calling the *add_to_cache_table* function. After this operation, the OS reads the requested file from the disk and copies it into the memory of the CDA hardware. Finally, the OS accesses the requested file at the memory of the CDA hardware. How the CDA cache operates when data is cached in the memory of the IXP evaluation board is described below. When the sendfile call requests data, the CDA also searches for the requested data in the cache table of the CDA. In this case, the CDA uses a page descriptor to confirm the existence of data in the memory of the evaluation board. The CDA can therefore use data in the memory of the evaluation board without having to access the disk.

DMA Operation. To transfer data quickly, Linux uses a DMA mechanism to copy data between the memory and the I/O device. With DMA, the host CPU can do other tasks and significantly reduce the bus transactions when transferring large amounts of data. The DMA controller does the DMA operation with the aid of the bus address. The kernel, however, orders data to be copied from the I/O device to the memory through a virtual address. A translation function is therefore required to convert the virtual address to the bus address. When the OS orders a file to be copied from the disk to the memory, it sends a virtual address of the IXP memory to the DMA controller. The address translation function in the DMA module intercepts a virtual address and converts it into a bus address. It then sends the converted address to the DMA controller. Finally, the DMA controller uses the bus address for the copy operation.

5 Experimental Results

The logical direct link offers a zero-copy mechanism between a disk and a network interface. Using this mechanism, the amount of data on a PCI and a local bus can be reduced to half. If we can measure how much the bus is used, we can easily estimate the performance. However, there is no software tool or equipment for measuring how much the bus is used. We used the CDA system to compare how long it takes to transfer data between the logical direct path and the redundant path in a conventional system. For the experiment, we connected two computers via an Ethernet LAN.

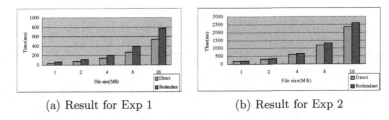

(a) Result for Exp 1   (b) Result for Exp 2

Fig. 4. Experimental Results for the data transfer using CDA

First, to determine the benefit of a direct path, we measured the data transfer-time in the two types of system architecture, which compares the direct path from a disk to the memory of the CDA hardware and the redundant path that uses the system memory. We generated synthetic workloads that performed several file transfer iterations. The workload applications generated file transfer requests from the disk to the NIC, which models the file send mechanism in multimedia servers. The variation in the size of the requested files ranged from 1 MB to 16 MB. Figure 4(a) shows the result of this experiment. For all file sizes, the processing time was, on average, 30 percent less for the direct path than for the redundant path. Moreover, the files were transferred more efficiently for the direct path than for the conventional system. As the file size increases, the transfer time is more significantly reduced than in the conventional method. This result means that the direct path is more suitable for transferring the large files of multimedia streaming servers. Next, we measured the total data transfer-time from a disk to another computer by comparing direct path and redundant path. In this experiment, we used the client-server model and we measured the overall performance of the system with respect to data-intensive servers such as multimedia systems. The workload of the experiment was the same as in the first experiment. The files we used ranged in size from 1 MB to 16 MB. Figure 4(b) shows the result of this experiment. For all file sizes, the copy time at the direct path was, on average, 10 percent less than at the redundant path. The performance of this experiment was worse than the previous experiment because of the IXP evaluation board, which makes a prototype of the CDA hardware. Because the network system in the IXP evaluation board formed a bottleneck, this experiment showed less improvement than the previous experiment. In the next experiment, we therefore present an analytical model that performs better without the effect of a network system.

Because existing CDA hardware (which includes the IXP evaluation board) has many limitations, the results of previous experiment are disappointing. Consequently, in this section, we use an analytical model to predict the overall performance of the CDA. We used the following variables to predict the performance:

1. T_{dm}, the duration of copying data from a disk to the memory of an IXP evaluation board
2. T_{mn}, the duration of sending data from the memory of an IXP evaluation board to an outside network
3. T_{total}, the total transfer time from a disk to an outside network. For analysis

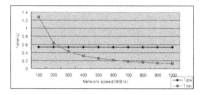

Fig. 5. Result of Experimental Model

of the model, we used the results of a 16 MB file. At this size, the bandwidth of
the disk shows that 29 MB of data per second can be stably transferred from a
disk to the memory of an IXP evaluation board. Unlike existing hardware, our
hardware can support concurrent I/O activity. Only the larger absolute value
between T_{dm} and T_{mn} affects T_{total}. In this case, one operation can proceed
without waiting for another task to be completed, thereby ensuring that one
task's operation time masks another task's operation time. Figure 5 shows the
results of this prediction. When the speed of network hardware is greater than
300 Mbps, T_{dm} is larger than T_{mn}, indicating that only T_{dm} has any effect. Accordingly, when we use a disk that shows a speed of 29 MB/s when the speed of
the network hardware is greater than 300 Mbps, T_{total} is 0.54 s.

6   Conclusion

We propose the design and implementation of fast I/O architecture called the
CDA to solve the problem of redundant copies between the disk and the NIC. The
CDA comprises CDA hardware, which is a substitute for the NIC, and a modified
Linux kernel, which provides the CDA functions for the CDA hardware. Because
existing versions do not have their own CDA hardware, we made a prototype
of the CDA architecture using the Intel IXP1200 evaluation board, which has
similar functions. With these two components, the CDA provides a logical direct
link that can do zero copies between the disk and the NIC. Using this function,
data can be copied directly from a disk to the CDA hardware so that the server
can improve I/O efficiency when sending a large file. Furthermore, to achieve
I/O efficiency in general, as well as for large files, we considered using the fast
I/O mechanisms of Linux such as page caching, reading ahead, and DMA. In our
experiments, we verified that the CDA can transfer data faster than a general
OS and regular hardware.

To take full advantage of the CDA, we need to use a fast network device such
as a gigabit Ethernet process or a simple network process. On the other hand,
because existing CDA hardware has no packet-processing unit, the existing CDA
uses virtual packet processing to store packets rather than raw data in the disk.
However, this method does not support the TCP. At present, only the UDP can
be used. Many Internet applications use the TCP to guarantee the reliability of
data transfers. For quick processing of the TCP, the packet processing unit must
be added [9][10].

References

1. Daniel P. Bovet, and Marco Cesati, Understating the Linux Kernel, OReilly, 2001.
2. Alacritech, Inc. Delivering High-Performance Stroage Networking, white paper, 2001.
3. Xiran, A Division of SimpleTech Inc, http://www.xiran.com
4. Soam Acharya and Brian Smith, "MiddleMan: A Video Caching Proxy Server", *10th International workshop on Network and Operating Systems support for digital audio and video*, 2000.
5. Apache web document, http://httpd.apache.org/docs-2.0/misc/perf-tuning.html.
6. Evangelos P. Markatos, "Speeding up TCP/IP: Faster Processors are not Enough", *21st IEEE International Performance, Computing, and Communication Conference*, 2001.
7. Dragan Stancevic, "Zero Copy I: User-Mode Perspective", *Linux Journal*, 2003.
8. W. Richard Stevens, Advanced Programming in the UNIX Environment, Addison-Wesley, 1992
9. Evangelos P. Markatos, "Speeding up TCP/IP: Faster Processors are not Enough", *21st IEEE International Performance, Computing, and Communication Conference*, 2001.
10. Eric Yeh, Herman Chao, Venu Mannem, Joe Gervais and Bradley Booth, Introduction to TCP/IP Offload Engine (TOE) Version 1.0, 10 gigabit ethernet alliance.
11. V.S. Pai, P. Druschel, and W. Zwaenepoel, "it IO-Lite : A unified I/O buffering and caching system", *The 3rd USENIX Symposium on Operating Systems Design and Implementation*, New Orleans, USA, 1999
12. Damien Le Moal, Tadashi Takeuchi, Tadaki Bandoh. "Cost-Effective Streaming Server Implementation Using Hi-Tactix"", *ACM Multimedia 2002*, pp. 382-391.
13. Halvorsen, P., Plagemann, T., Goebel, V. "Network Level Framing in INSTANCE", *Proceedings of the 6th International Workshop on Multimedia Information Systems 2000 (MIS 2000)*, Chicago, IL, USA, October 2000, pp. 82-91.
14. Intel IXP1200 Network processor Hardware Reference Manual, Intel document 278303-008, Aug. 2001.

A Systematic Scheme to Resolve QoS Dissatisfaction for Storage Cluster

Young Jin Nam[1] and Chanik Park[2]

[1] School of Computer and Information Technology,
Daegu University,
Kyungbuk, Republic of Korea
yjnam@daegu.ac.kr
[2] Department of Computer Science and Engineering/PIRL,
Pohang University of Science and Technology,
Kyungbuk, Republic of Korea
cipark@postech.ac.kr

Abstract. This paper addresses the types of QoS dissatisfaction caused by imbalance of the initial I/O workload pattern and storage performance across multiple storage servers in a storage cluster. It next proposes a systematic scheme to resolve the QoS problem that periodically monitors the QoS satisfaction level, analyzes the causes of the QoS problem, and performs data migration based on the analysis result. Finally, it verifies the effectiveness of the proposed scheme under a simulation environment under the different types of QoS dissatisfaction.

1 Introduction

A storage cluster typically consists of storage clients, virtual disks, and storage servers attached to a high-speed SAN. Each storage client distributes and accesses its data across multiple storage servers through a storage virtualization layer called a virtual disk. Storage clients represent various types of I/O applications that demand an underlying storage service, such as traditional file systems, cluster/SAN file systems, database applications, etc. Virtual disks, each of which is assigned to at least one storage client, represent logical volumes that map user data onto physically dispersed storage servers. Storage servers represent SAN-attached disk arrays or JBODs (Just Bunch of Disks). It mainly processes I/O requests arrived from virtual disks in a certain manner.

Large-scale storage systems like a storage cluster increase the chances that storage clients (or virtual disks) share the same storage server. Each storage client may require a different storage service, called storage Quality of Service (QoS); that is, each storage client requires receiving a guaranteed storage service, independently of the status of the I/O services in other storage clients. Unfortunately, the storage itself does not contain any feature of providing the storage QoS. Embedding QoS feature into a storage system needs to define storage QoS specifications [1], design a storage server to meet a given storage QoS specifications (requirements) [2,3], and enforce the storage QoS requirements for

H. Jin, D. Reed, and W. Jiang (Eds.): NPC 2005, LNCS 3779, pp. 396–404, 2005.

each I/O request from different virtual disks (storage clients) [4]. Huang in [2] has proposed a QoS architecture called StoneHenge for a storage cluster that assures given QoS requirements of I/O performance.

The initial I/O workload patterns and storage performance that have been used for designing virtual disks are subject to change due to numerous reasons [7]. This implies that a virtual disk may not meet its QoS requirement due to the changes in the initial storage design information. In the case of a single storage server, the types of the changes include the increased I/O traffic and the degraded storage performance. The changes are typically resolved by redesigning the virtual disk with the changed information. The previous automatic storage design tools of Minerva [1] and Hippodrome [3] employed an iterative design loop to resolve QoS dissatisfaction on a single storage server. In the case of the storage cluster, the design tools need to be combined with the virtual disk mapping schemes proposed in StoneHenge [2].

Under a storage cluster, extra types of changes exist that are related to imbalance of the initial I/O workload and storage performance across storage servers that comprise a virtual disk. The imbalance of the initial I/O workloads is closely related to the variations of I/O traffic intensity across the storage servers within a virtual disk. Investigating an actual I/O workload gathered from `cello` [5] during 04/18–04/21 revealed that the storage system might experience QoS deterioration during 04/19–04/20 with the striped mapping and during the entire days with the linear mapping, assuming that the I/O requests are initially distributed over the storage servers in a uniform manner. Next, the imbalance of the storage performance can occur due to many reasons, such as loss of internal disks within a storage server, application re-installation or copy/remove operations, changes in I/O traffic of competing virtual disks that share the same storage server, etc.

2   The Proposed Scheme

The proposed scheme consists of a (storage) cluster-wide QoS monitor, a data migration planner, and data migration agents. Let us start by defining a QoS requirement.

QoS Requirement. The QoS requirement from a virtual disk i (briefly VD_i), denoted by Q_i can be represented as $Q_i = (SZ_i, IOPS_i^{targ}, RT_i^{targ})$, where SZ_i represents an average I/O request size, $IOPS_i^{targ}$ represents a target IOPS, and RT_i^{targ} represents a target response time. Under a storage cluster environment, multiple storage servers should assure a given QoS requirement of Q_i from a virtual disk in a cooperative manner. If each storage server of a virtual disk is designed to guarantee the given QoS requirement, the virtual disk can meet the given QoS requirement with an extremely high probability. However, this design approach suffers from an excessive use of storage resources. A better design approach demands to have greater knowledge of I/O workload patterns and storage performance over the virtual disk.As a result, it divides the servicing of the tar-

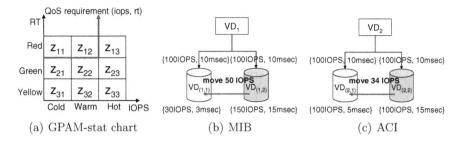

(a) GPAM-stat chart   (b) MIB   (c) ACI

Fig. 1. The GPAM-state chart, and the examples of the minimal IOPS balancing(MIB) and the actual current IOPS normalized to the actual storage performance(ACI)

get IOPS into each storage server, thereby reducing the storage resources in use. Note, however, that the given target response time should remain unchanged at each storage server. Assuming that VD_i with Q_i distributes its data across N homogeneous storage servers, the given QoS requirement at each storage N storage servers, the given QoS requirement at each storage server j denoted by $Q_{(i,j)}$ is written as $Q_{(i,j)} = (SZ_{(i,j)}, IOPS_{(i,j)}^{targ}, RT_{(i,j)}^{targ})$, where $1 \leq j \leq N$. In addition, $SZ_{(i,j)}$, $IOPS_{(i,j)}^{targ}$, and $RT_{(i,j)}^{targ})$ should meet the following relationships: $SZ_{(i,j)} = SZ_i$, $IOPS_{(i,j)}^{targ} \leq IOPS_i^{targ}$, $IOPS_i^{targ} \leq \sum_{j=1}^{N} IOPS_{(i,j)}^{targ}$, and $RT_{(i,j)}^{targ} = RT_i^{targ}$. In case that perfectly balanced I/O workloads are issued to the storage servers within a virtual disk, we can minimize the usage of the storage resources for VD_i [2], where $IOPS_i^{targ} = \sum_{j=1}^{N} IOPS_{(i,j)}^{targ}$.

The Cluster-Wide QoS Monitor. The cluster-wide QoS monitor (briefly QoS monitor) inspects the level of QoS satisfaction for each virtual disk and determines its state via a hierarchical QoS monitoring tree. The monitoring process is performed on a chunk of contiguous blocks at each storage server called BPAM. The BPAM stands for a base unit for performance monitoring and migration. The number of blocks under the control of each BPAM (shortly BPAM size) should not be too small to cause maintenance overhead and should not be too large to make it difficult to identify the cause of QoS dissatisfaction problem. Each BPAM includes the information of a virtual disk ID, a storage server ID, a start block address, a BPAM size, I/O requests per second (IOPS), response times (RT), and the target RT miss ratio (QoS requirement). The QoS monitor summarizes all the BPAMs of the same sub-virtual disk into the GPAM(Group of BPAMs) structure. Recall that a virtual disk consists of a set of sub-virtual disks.

A GPAM state can be classified into one of the nine combinations of the RT state and the IOPS state called GPAM-state chart, as shown in Figure 1(a). The RT states and IOPS states can be defined as follows. To begin, denote with $GPAM_{(i,j)}$ the j-th GPAM of VD_i. The QoS requirement of $GPAM_{(i,j)}$ is represented by $Q_{(i,j)} = (SZ_{(i,j)}^{targ}, IOPS_{(i,j)}^{targ}, RT_{(i,j)}^{targ})$. Three RT states exist in the

GPAM that include red, green, and yellow. The state of red represents that the current target RT miss ratio $> \mathcal{MR}_H$, green represents that $\mathcal{MR}_L <$ the current target RT miss ratio $\leq \mathcal{MR}_H$, and yellow represents that the current target RT miss ratio $\leq \mathcal{MR}_L$. The parameters of $\mathcal{MR}_H$ and $\mathcal{MR}_L$ can be configured, such that $0 \leq \mathcal{MR}_L \leq \mathcal{MR}_H \leq 1.0$. In addition, three IOPS states exist in the GPAM that include cold, warm, and hot. The state of cold means that $0 \leq IOPS_{(i,j)}^{cur} \leq \alpha_c IOPS_{(i,j)}^{targ}$, warm means that $\alpha_c IOPS_{(i,j)}^{targ} < IOPS_{(i,j)}^{cur} \leq IOPS_{(i,j)}^{targ}$, and hot means that $IOPS_{(i,j)}^{cur} > IOPS_{(i,j)}^{targ}$. The parameter of α_c can be configured in the range of $(0, 1.0)$ depending on the current administration policy. Denote each cell (or combination) by an indexed zone z_{ij}, where i and j respectively represent a RT state and a IOPS state. In addition, we define $\mathcal{Z}_i^{NE}$ and $\mathcal{Z}_i^{E}$ as a set of non-empty zones and a set of empty zones for VD_i, respectively.

A virtual disk state can be determined based on the distribution of the GPAM states upon the GPAM-state chart. A virtual disk has more than one GPAM states, as it distributes data over multiple storage servers. Let us define three virtual disk states depending on whether a virtual disk satisfies a given QoS requirement and whether its storage resources are under-provisioned. The well_designed VD state represents that the virtual disk meets the given QoS requirement well with sufficient storage resources. The imp_designed VD state represents that the virtual disk does not guarantee the given QoS requirement even though it has sufficient storage resources. This undesirable VD state is attributed mainly by imbalance of the I/O workload pattern and storage performance with respect to their initial configurations. Finally, the und_designed VD state represents that the virtual disk does not guarantee the given QoS requirement because storage resources are provisioned insufficiently to the virtual disk. To resolve this QoS dissatisfaction, the virtual disk needs to allocate more storage resources if allowed. Next, the relationships between the virtual disk states and the distribution of the GPAM states can be given as follows: the well_designed VD includes $\{z_{11}, z_{12}, z_{13}\} \subset \mathcal{Z}_i^E$, or $\{z_{11}, z_{12}, z_{31}\} \subset \mathcal{Z}_i^E$ AND $\{z_{13}\} \subset \mathcal{Z}_i^{NE}$, the imp_designed VD includes $\{z_{11}, z_{12}\} \subset \mathcal{Z}_i^E$ AND $\{z_{13}, z_{31}\} \subset \mathcal{Z}_i^{NE}$, $\{z_{11}, z_{32(33)}\} \subset \mathcal{Z}_i^{NE}$, or $\{z_{12}, z_{32(33)}\} \subset \mathcal{Z}_i^{NE}$, and the und_designed VD includes $\{z_{11}\} \subset \mathcal{Z}_i^{NE}$ AND $\{z_{32}, z_{33}\} \subset \mathcal{Z}_i^E$, or $\{z_{12}\} \subset \mathcal{Z}_i^{NE}$ AND $\{z_{32}, z_{33}\} \subset \mathcal{Z}_i^E$. The well_designed state of VD_i represents the condition that the current target RT miss ratio is not greater than its higher bound of $\mathcal{MR}_\mathcal{H}$ for each $G(i,j)$ with $IOPS_{(i,j)}^{cur} \leq IOPS(i,j)^{targ}$. The imp_designed state represents one of the following three conditions. The first condition is that a GPAM has a higher target RT miss ratio than $\mathcal{MR}_\mathcal{H}$ with a higher average IOPS than its target IOPS, while another GPAM has a lower target RT miss ratio than $\mathcal{MR}_\mathcal{L}$ with a lower average IOPS. It occurs if the initial I/O workload pattern becomes unbalanced, where I/O requests from the virtual disk are no longer distributed over its storage servers according to its target IOPS. The second and third conditions correspond to the situation where a GPAM has a higher target RT miss ratio than $\mathcal{MR}_\mathcal{H}$ even with a lower IOPS, while another GPAM has a lower target RT miss ratio than $\mathcal{MR}_\mathcal{L}$ with a target or even higher

IOPS. These cases occur when the initial performance of the storage servers becomes unbalanced. The und_designed state corresponds to the condition where no GPAM exists with a lower target RT miss ratio with a target or higher IOPS, whereas a GPAM has a higher target RT miss ratio with a lower IOPS. Thus, the data migration for this state occurs only when the virtual disk is allowed to use extra storage resources for future extension.

The Data Migration Planner. Previous research mainly stressed the problem of scheduling each migration from its original location to its new one to minimize the total migration time [7]. Little research exist to create an efficient data migration plan, for example, to maximize the number of clients that can be served by the parallel disks or to automatically improve storage I/O performance [8]. However, no such previous research has directly addressed and handled the QoS dissatisfaction problem under a storage cluster.

Let us start by defining a few notations. Denote with $GPAM_{(i,j)}$ the j-th GPAM for VD_i, where $1 \leq j \leq N$. Denote with $BPAM_{(i,j,k)}$ the k-th BPAM for $GPAM_{i,j}$. Denote with $IOPS^{cur}_{(i,j,k)}$ the current IOPS for $BPAM_{(i,j,k)}$. Denote with $IOPS^{targ}_{(i,j)}$ and $IOPS^{cur}_{(i,j)}$ respectively the target IOPS for $GPAM_{(i,j)}$ and the current IOPS for $GPAM_{(i,j)}$, *i.e.*, the weighted-average IOPS of all $IOPS^{cur}_{(i,j,k)}$. Assume that VD_i distributes its data across N storage servers. Denote with $VD_{(i,j)}$ the j-th sub-virtual disk of VD_i. Planning an optimal data migration is infeasible in practice, because future I/O access patterns are not foreseeable. Thus, it leads us to devise a heuristic algorithm based on past cluster-wide QoS monitoring information. Our proposed data migration planner operates based on the two key ideas, the "minimal IOPS balancing(MIB)" and the "actual current IOPS normalized to the actual storage performance(ACI)." Figure 1(b) shows an example for the MIB, where VD_1 with $Q_1 = (200\text{IOPS}, 10\text{msec})$ is initially mapped onto the two homogeneous storage servers, $VD_{(1,1)}$ with $Q_{(1,1)} = (100\text{IOPS}, 10\text{msec})$ and $VD_{(1,2)}$ with $Q_{(1,2)} = (100\text{IOPS}, 10\text{msec})$.

The QoS monitor detects $GPAM_{(1,1)} = (30\text{IOPS}, 3\text{msec})$ with no target RT miss ratio and $GPAM_{(1,2)} = (150\text{IOPS}, 15\text{msec})$ with 0.5 target RT miss ratio, where $\mathcal{MR}_H = 0.3$. Next, it determines that the $GPAM_{(1,1)}$ state is in z_{31} and the $GPAM_{(1,2)}$ state is in z_{13} and concludes that VD_1 is in the imp_designed state. Finally, according to the MIB, data blocks (BPAMs) equivalent to 50 IOPS of $VD_{(1,2)}$ migrates to $VD_{(1,1)}$, instead of 70 IOPS. Notice that the MIB minimally balances the IOPS across the storage servers to resolve the current QoS dissatisfaction. Figure 1(c) shows an example of the ACI, where VD_2 is configured exactly the same as VD_1. The QoS monitor detects that $GPAM_{(2,1)} = (100\text{IOPS}, 5\text{msec})$ with zero target RT miss ratio and $GPAM_{(2,2)} = (100\text{IOPS}, 15\text{msec})$ with 0.3 target RT miss ratio. The QoS monitor determines that the VD_2 is in the imp_designed state due to changes in the underlying storage performance. The actual target IOPS denoted by $I\hat{O}PS^{targ}_{(i,j)}$ for $VD_{(i,j)}$ can be computed from its target IOPS as follows:

$$I\hat{O}PS^{targ}_{(i,j)} = IOPS^{targ}_{(i,j)}(RT^{targ}_{(i,j)}/RT^{cur}_{(i,j)}). \tag{1}$$

Then, the actual target IOPS and RT for the storage servers become (200IOPS, 10msec) and (66IOPS, 10msec), respectively. Based on these, $VD_{(2,2)}$ migrates 34 IOPS to $VD_{(2,1)}$. For a given P IOPS to migrate from $VD_{(i,j)}$ to $VD_{(i,k)}$, we choose the first M BPAMs with the highest average IOPS, such that the sum of their average IOPS is equal to P IOPS. This design approach works well when the I/O workload pattern has a high spatial locality. Otherwise, more than one data migration is likely to occur by detecting an unbalanced condition repeatedly.

The imp_designed state can be caused by the changes in either the initial I/O workload pattern or the initial storage performance. The imp_designed state with the changed initial I/O workload pattern corresponds to one of two cases for the improperly-designed virtual disk VD_i, where $\{z_{11}, z_{12}\} \subset \mathcal{Z}_i^E$ and $\{z_{13}, z_{31(32)}\} \subset \mathcal{Z}_i^{NE}$. For this, the minimal amount of IOPS migrates from z_{13} to $z_{31(32)}$, resultingly the actual current IOPS of GPAM in z_{13} does not exceed its target IOPS. The imp_designed state with the changed initial storage performance corresponds to the following distribution of the GPAM states, where $\{z_{11}, z_{32(33)}\} \subset \mathcal{Z}_i^{NE}$ or $\{z_{12}, z_{32(33)}\} \subset \mathcal{Z}_i^{NE}$. We can compute an actual target IOPS based on the the observed RT and IOPS from Equation (1) that can meet the given target RT for VD_i. Next, we transform the observed IOPS into its actual current IOPS denoted by $\hat{IOPS}_{(i,j)}^{cur}$ on the basis of the actual target IOPS as follows:

$$\hat{IOPS}_{(i,j)}^{cur} = IOPS_{(i,j)}^{targ} + (IOPS_{(i,j)}^{cur} - \hat{IOPS}_{(i,j)}^{targ}). \qquad (2)$$

The migration planner first computes an actual target IOPS for each storage server, according to Equation (1). The migration planner calculates the actual current IOPS at each GPAM, according to Equation (2). To sum, a minimal amount of IOPS needs to be moved from z_{11} (or z_{12}) to z_{32} and z_{33}, so that the actual current IOPS of the GPAM in z_{11} (or z_{12}) does not exceed its target IOPS.

The under-designed virtual disk is mainly attributed to the lack of storage resources to meet the given QoS requirement for the virtual disk. This virtual disk state has a distribution of GPAM states that is similar to that of the second case of improperly-designed virtual disks; that is, $\{z_{11}\} \subset \mathcal{Z}_i^{NE}$ and $\{z_{32}, z_{33}\} \subset \mathcal{Z}_i^E$, or $\{z_{12}\} \subset \mathcal{Z}_i^{NE}$ and $\{z_{32}, z_{33}\} \subset \mathcal{Z}_i^E$. While z_{11} or z_{12} has a GPAM, no GPAMs exist that will process a part of I/O requests for GPAMs in z_{11} or z_{12}. As a result, we need to migrate the IOPS in z_{11} or z_{12} to a new storage server that can be additionally used by the virtual disk. Unless the extra storage server is available, no migration plan will be made. Instead, static virtual disk reconfiguration will deal with this problem. Hereafter, we assume that at least a single new storage server is available to each virtual disk. Given multiple extra storage servers, we need to decide which storage server will be used for the virtual disk. The proposed scheme selects a storage server, where the ratio of the current IOPS to the target IOPS is the lowest among others. More detailed descriptions for each algorithm can be found in [4].

Data Migration Agents and Operational Parameters. A data migration plan is
sent to the associated QoS servers to initiate actual data migration among the
storage servers. Then, a data migration agent at each storage sever is in charge
of executing the data migration plan. The proposed scheme can be configured
by a set of policy-based operational parameters that include a QoS monitoring
interval (T_I), QoS satisfaction level for each sub-virtual disk, $VD_{(i,j)}$ $(\mathcal{MR}_H)$,
sensitivity for determining a virtual disk state (T_m, U_m), BPAM size $(|BPAM|)$,
and marginal storage capacity ratio(MSR). Given (T_m, U_m), for example, a
virtual disk can be determined as an improperly-designed VD state only if the
QoS monitor detects the improperly-designed VD state U_m times over past I_m
monitoring intervals, *i.e.,* an observation time window of $T_m = I_m T_I$ seconds.
Configuring $MSR = 100\%$ implies that each sub-virtual disk reserves 100% of
its storage capacity for data migration.

3   Performance Evaluations

Performance evaluations have been conducted on a storage simulator that consists of an I/O workload generator, a set of virtual disks (storage clients), a
set of storage servers. The operational parameters are configured as $T_I = 5$sec,
$\mathcal{MR}_H = 0.3$, $\mathcal{MR}_L = 0.1$, $\alpha_c = 0.3$, $U_m = 1$, $T_m = 5$, $|BPAM| = 2048$blocks,
and $MSR = 100\%$. The two performance metrics include the average response
time and the target RT miss ratio for the I/O workload from each virtual disk.
In our simulation, two virtual disks of VD_1 and VD_2 are mapped onto the storage cluster of SS_1 and SS_2, implying that each storage server is shared by the
two virtual disks. The QoS the requirements of the virtual disks are Q_1=(4KB,
90IOPS, 70msec) and Q_2=(4KB, 90IOPS, 100msec). Thus, the QoS requirements of $VD_{(i,j)}$ for VD_1 and VD_2 are are defined as follows: $Q_{(1,1)}$= (4KB,
45 IOPS, 70msec), $Q_{(1,2)}$= (4KB, 45 IOPS, 70msec), $Q_{(2,1)}$= (4KB, 45 IOPS,
100msec), and $Q_{(2,2)}$= (4KB, 45 IOPS, 100msec). Our simulation employs four
different types of QoS dissatisfaction that include WS_1^{impl}, WS_2^{impl}, WS_1^{imp2},
and WS_1^{und}. The types of WS_1^{impl} and WS_2^{impl} represent that the most of
I/O requests from VD_2 are issued to the SS_2; that is, WS_1^{impl} and WS_2^{impl}
respectively send 100% and 90% of all the I/O requests of the VD_2 to SS_2.
In the case of WS_1^{imp2}, the performance of SS_2 decreases, because seek times
and rotational delays for processing I/O requests from VD_1 and VD_2 become
higher. Our simulator emulates storage performance degradation by adjusting
the equations and parameters to compute a seek time and a rotational delay
as follows: the long and short seek times of VD_2 are respectively changed to
$9.0 + 0.008d$ and $4.24 + 0.4sqrt(d)$ from the initial equations [6] of $8.0 + 0.008d$
and $3.24 + 0.4sqrt(d)$, and the average rotational delay is from 2.99msec to
4.28msec. In the case of WS_1^{und}, it is assumed that the VD_1 is initially mapped
onto SS_1 and SS_2, and the VD_2 is initially mapped onto SS_2 and SS_3. Then,
the response times of I/O requests at SS_3 will obviously become higher than its
target response time with a high target RT miss ratio. By contrast, the target
RT miss ratio at SS_2 remains slightly high, because the heavier I/O workload

Table 1. Result of RT variations of VD_1 and VD_2 with the four different types of QoS dissatisfaction: WS_1^{imp1}, WS_2^{imp1}, WS_1^{imp2}, and WS_1^{und}

		Avg. IOPS (IOPS)		Avg. resp. time (msec)		Target resp. time miss ratio		# of mig. BPAMs	T_{settle} (sec)
		no-mig	prop	no-mig	prop	no-mig	prop		
WS_1^{imp1}	VD_1	85.9	88.7	53.7	23.8	0.25	0.01	14	74.2
	VD_2	74.3	87.6	227	31.3	0.94	0.03	28	311.8
WS_2^{imp1}	VD_1	87.0	88.2	43.5	23.1	0.16	0.00	6	126.4
	VD_2	80.4	87.5	128	37.7	0.59	0.02	14	72.4
WS_1^{imp2}	VD_1	85.9	87.6	56.5	38.0	0.25	0.06	12	636.5
	VD_2	85.7	86.9	57.0	37.5	0.11	0.00	13	26.3
WS_1^{und}	VD_1	122.8	121.9	25.6	31.2	0.01	0.03	n/a	n/a
	VD_2	81.6	86.9	104.7	40.4	0.43	0.02	37	631.7

is given to SS_2 from VD_1. As a result, it needs to migrate an amount of data blocks to a new storage server that is allowed for extra use. In our experiment, the data migration planner will send data blocks from SS_3 to SS_1. Assuming that the extra storage resource for VD_2 is equivalent to the storage resource allocated to $VD_{(2,1)}$, the newly allocated storage server is configured with the same QoS requirement as in the other storage servers for the virtual disk. Table 1 summarizes the results of the experiments for the four types of QoS dissatisfaction. We add extra performance metrics of the number of migrated BPAMs and T_{settle}, where T_{settle} represents the elapsed time to complete data migration. In WS_1^{imp1}, the proposed scheme(prop) can guarantee the given QoS requirements with almost 100% for VD_1 and VD_2 even in the presence of the unbalanced I/O workload pattern by migrating 14 BPAMs of VD_1 and 28 BPAMs of VD_2 from SS_2 to SS_1. While the settling time (T_{settle}) of VD_2 is observed to be 311.8 seconds, the QoS dissatisfaction problem is actually resolved in about 34.2 seconds. By contrast, VD_2 violates its target response time mostly without data migration(no-mig), and VD_1 has also a high target RT miss ratio. We have a similar result in WS_2^{imp1}. However, notice that the number of the migrated BPAMs is slightly smaller, compared with WS_1^{imp1}. In WS_1^{imp2}, 12 BPAMs of VD_1 and 13 BPAMs of VD_2 migrate from SS_2 to SS_1 by the migration planner and agents. In WS_1^{und}, the target RT miss ratio of VD_2 decreases to 0.02 from 0.43 by migrating 37 BPAMs for VD_2 among different storage servers.

4   Concluding Remarks

This paper addressed the types of QoS dissatisfaction caused by the imbalance of the initial I/O workload pattern and storage performance under a storage cluster environment and the proposed a systematic scheme to resolve the problem. The proposed scheme introduced a base unit of storage called BPAM for efficient performance monitoring and data migration processes. The proposed scheme detects any problem of QoS dissatisfaction for each virtual disk and then identifies the cause of the problem in a systematic manner. Subsequently, it resolves the problem by minimally balancing actual current IOPS normalized to the actual storage performance across multiple storage servers within a virtual disk. For this, the proposed scheme provides a cluster-wide QoS monitoring scheme for each virtual disk, a data migration planner to change improperly-designed and under-designed virtual disks into well-designed ones, and data migration agents at storage servers to perform actual data migration between storage servers. The simulation results conducted in our storage cluster simulator revealed that the proposed data migration scheme can effectively handle any QoS dissatisfaction in the presence of various changes in the initial I/O workload pattern and storage performance. In future, we need to devise a more intelligent data migration planner that concurrently takes into account the status of data migration in the other virtual disks.

Acknowledgments

This research was supported by the Daegu University Research Grant, No 20050346. The authors would like to thank the Ministry of Education of Korea for its support towards the Elec. and Computer Eng. Division at POSTECH through the BK21 program. This research has also been supported in part by HY-SDR IT Research Center, in part by the grant number R01-2003-000-10739-0 from the basic research program of the Korea Science and Engineering Foundation, in part by the regional technology innovation program of the Korea Institute of Industrial Technology Evaluation and Planning, and in part by the next generation PC program of the Korea ETRI.

References

1. G. Alvarez, *et al.*, "Minerva: An automated resource provisioning tool for large-scale storage systems," *ACM Transactions on Computer Systems*, vol. 19, pp. 483–518, November 2001.
2. L. Huang, "Stonehenge: A high performance virtualized network storage cluster with QoS guarantees," Tech. Rep., SUNY at Stony Brook, January 2002.
3. E. Anderson, M. Hobbs, K. Keeton, S. Spence, M. Uysal, and A. Veitch, "Hippodrome: Running rings around storage administration," in *Proceedings of Conference on File and Storage Technologies*, January 2002.
4. Y. Nam, *Dynamic Storage QoS Control for Storage Cluster and RAID Performance Enhancement Techniques.* Ph.D Dissertation, POSTECH, February 2004.
5. C. Ruemmler and J. Wilkes, "Unix disk access patters," in *Proceedings of Winter USENIX*, pp. 405–420, January 1993.
6. C. Ruemmler and J. Wilkes, "An introduction to disk drive modeling," *IEEE Computer*, vol. 27, pp. 17–29, March 1994.
7. Y. Kim, "Data migration to minimize the average completion time," in *Proceedings of the 14th Annual ACM-SIAM Symposium on Discrete Algorithms*, 2003.
8. F. Hidrobo and T. Cortes, "Automatic storage system based on automatic learning," in *Proceedings of the International Conference on High-Performance Computing*, 2004.

Secure Anonymous Communication with Conditional Traceability

Zhaofeng Ma [1,2], Xibin Zhao[1,2], Guo Zhi[1,2], Gu Ming[2], and Jiaguang Sun [2]

[1] Department of Computer Science and Technology, Tsinghua University
[2] School of Software, Tsinghua University
100084 Beijing, China
{mzf, zxb, guozhi, guming, sunjiaguang}@tsinghua.edu.cn

Abstract. A new anonymous secure communication protocol with conditional traceability is proposed to provide personal anonymity and privacy protection, in which a secure mapping function is introduced to provide anonymity and personal information protection, when necessary, only authority principal part can act as arbitrator for communication validation. The proposed protocol has 3 advantages: 1) mutual communication; 2) anonymity of communication. 3) conditional traceability.

1 Introduction

Information exchange and sharing are the basic target for communication network including traditional connection-oriented computer network and modern wireless, in which with the commercial development security became an important and permanent issue were concerned much more, especially in E-business, electronic cash, electronic election applications in real life. For the history reason that current IP-address-based computer network communication and wireless communication are designed initially for their communication and data exchange, which involved communication content, communication address(such as destination and source IP address in computer communication, SIM, ME,TMSI et al.), message header, control information, which are close related to user identity or the location and topology of user's network, content-based behavior analysis, usage pattern mining can be employed to deduce user's habit, preference easily. For the reason of fairness, privacy and legislation, user anonymity becomes another important issues in security-related subjects.

In this paper, a generic and secure anonymous communication protocol was proposed both for user privacy of computer-oriented communication and for wireless phone communication, the protocol is conditional traceable under the control of independent authoritative institute(IAI). Comparing with current approaches, the advantage of our protocol is it is full privacy protection during the anonymous communication, even the administrator can not recover user's privacy information, while when necessary to recover the user's identity its must work under the legislation authority, while the system are efficient and effective for normal communication.

H. Jin, D. Reed, and W. Jiang (Eds.): NPC 2005, LNCS 3779, pp. 405–408, 2005.

2 Related Work

Concern over user privacy is constantly mounting as the role of the communication network.In 1983, Chaum D. proposed untraceable electronic mail[1], then in 1988, he proposed unconditional sender and recipient untraceability approach for privacy protection[2]. Kesdogan D, proposed Location management strategies in mobile communication systems for privacy protection[3]. Reed M proosed onion routing as anonymous access method[4]. In fact, blind signature, fair blind signature, group signature, group blind signature, zero-knowledge proof, undiable protocol, fairly good exchange protocol, secret sharing, verifiable secret sharing are the most popular technologies that can be employed to enhance privacy and anonymity[5-8]. Current methods for privacy protection are mainly concerned on special applications, the approaches are limited in practice.

The entire behavior of a user may be considered private. In mobile environments we can identify four types of sensitive user information: (1)identity;(2)message contents; (3)location (especially in million communication); (4)actions (content of navigation). The level of protection of this information may also vary depending on the trust the user has in various parts of the system, which can be classified as: (1)level-0: no privacy; (1) level-1: hiding information from external attackers;(3) level-2: hiding identity from foreign networks; (4)level-3: hiding the relationship between the user and the home network; (5)level-4: hiding identities of home and foreign networks;(6) level-5: hiding user behaviour from home authority. Personal identification includes: (1) Legal name; (2) Locatability;(3)Traceable pseudonymity or pseudo-anonymity;(4) Untraceable pseudonymity;(5) Pattern knowledge; (6)Social categorization;(7) Symbols of eligibility/non-eligibility. There are 4 types anonymous communications on the Internet: (1) Traceable anonymous communication;(2)Untraceable anonymous communication; (3) Traceable pseudonymous communication;(4) Untraceable pseudonymity.

3 Secure Anonymity with Conditional Traceability

The infrastructure of current communication network is de factor traceable network, which can be easily trace with the aid of special tools, such as IP-tracer tool, Hardware-based location discovery in GPRS system. Thus in this paper we contribute to conditional traceable anonymity in general communication system.

(I) System Preliminary

Param	Expression
IAI	Independent Authoritative Institute
U	End User
CSC	Commercial Service Center
E_k	Encryption with Symetric Key k
D_k	Decryption with Symetric Key k
E_{Apk}	Encryption with Public Key pk ownered by A
D_{Ask}	Decryption with Secret Key sk ownered by A

Sig	Signature of Message given
Ver	Verification of Sig given
H	Secure Hash function

(II) Privacy-Enable Initialization

Step1. Independent Authoritative Institute IAI authorizes to Commercial Service Center CSC the privacy-related but anonymous ID AID:

$$AID = E_{CSCPK}(RID)$$

where $RID = \begin{cases} IP_{addr} \parallel MAC_{addr} \parallel HID_{mchn} & , \; if \; Cmpt \; net; \\ UID \parallel Ph_{No} \parallel ISMI & , \; if \; Mobl \; net. \end{cases}$

Together, IAI creates secret key $K_{sk_{IAI}}$ for transactional communication session content signature, where Hash function H (.) may be employed fro anonymity.

Step2. IAI releases AID to CSC in communication in secure channel:

IAI->CSC: $AID' = E_{k_{IAI,CSC}}(AID)$

(III) Privacy-Enable Communication

Step3. CSC secretly gets AID' from IAI, then decrypt the AID' to recover the AID:

CSC -> IAI: AID'= $D_{k_{IAI,CSC}}(AID')$

Step4. Each end user Ui, Uj communication in a common secret way:

$U_i > U_j$: C= $E_{k_{i,j}}(M)$, and $U_j -> U_i$: M= $D_{k_{i,j}}(C)$

Step5. Under control of CSC, creates transactional session signature between U_i and U_j under the signature key:

$$S_{Content} = < AID_i \parallel AID_j \parallel T_{start} \parallel T_{end} \parallel S_{Type} >, < S_{Content}, Sig_{SK_{IAI}}(S_{Content}) >$$

where $S_{content}$ stands for session content, Sig. is the signature of the session content $S_{content}$.

(IV) Conditional Trace for Illegitimate Communication Intervention

Step6. When necessary to intervene to validate the historical transaction session content, IAI acts as arbiter to resolve the dispute CSC sends the signature of session between U_i and U_j to IAI:

CSC -> IAI: $E_{k'_{IAI,CSC}}(S_{Content}, Sig_{SK_{IAI}}(S_{Content}))$

Step7. IAI decrypts the message from CSC:

IAI ->CSC : $D_{k'_{IAI,CSC}}(E_{k'_{IAI,CSC}}(S_{Content}, Sig_{SK_{IAI}}(S_{Content})))$

Step8. IAI verifies the historical session transaction that recorded in $S_{content}$:

$$\text{bverRslt=} Ver_{PK_{IAI}} (Sig_{SK_{IAI}} (S_{Content}))$$

If bVerRslt=TRUE, it manifests the session trace is unassailable, then IAI open the session content and decide what ever happened during the session. Otherwise IAI disregards the request from CSC.

In fact, in step8, IAI has some optional ways to solve the dispute by pre-record mechanism to record the session message of what happened. By the way, conditional traceability can use escrowed encryption system (ESS) and threshold cryptography system to enhance privacy protection.

4 Conclusion

With fast development of Internet and mobile and wireless computing technologies such as GSM, CDMA, privacy-enhancement became an important issue in personal communication system (PCs). The approach proposed in this paper is a raw and roase discuss for controllable anonymous communication with privacy-enable application, efficient and effective approaches are to be studied in future, the art of how to ensure fairly good privacy-enable communication but can trace latent attacks legislatively is a trade off between privacy and security issues.

References

1. David Chaum: Untraceable Electronic Mail, Return Addresses, and Digital Pseudonyms. Communications of the ACM, (1981)84-88
2. David Chaum: The Dining Cryptographers Problem: Unconditional sender and recipient untraceability. Journal of Cryptology, (1988) 65–75
3. Kesdogan D, Federrath H, Jerichow A, Ffitzmann A.: Location management strategies increasing privacy in mobile communication systems. IFIP 12th International Information Security Conference. (1996):39-48
4. Reed M G, Syverson P F , Goldschlag D M: Anonymous connections and onion routing. IEEE Journal on Selected Areas in Communication Special Issue on Copyright and Privacy Protection, (1998)482-494
5. Sholmi Dolev and Rafail Ostrovsky. Xor-Trees for Efficient Anonymous Multicast Receiption. Advances in Cryptography – CRYPTO'97, 1997
6. Michael K. Reiter and Aviel D. Rubin. Crowds :Anonymity for Web Transactions. ACM Transactions on Information and System Security, (1998)66–92
7. Clay Shields and Brian Neil Levine. A protocol for anonymous communication over the Internet. In Proceedings of the 7th ACM Conference on Computer and Communications Security, (2000) 33–42
8. Wang C J, Leung H F:Anonymity and security in continuous double auctions for Internet retails market[A]. Proceedings of the 37th Annual International Conference on Hawaii System Sciences (CD/ROM)(2004) 5-8

Real-Time Video over Programmable Networked Devices

Tien Pham Van

International Graduate School of Dynamic Intelligent Systems,
University of Paderborn, 33102 Paderborn, Germany
vantien@uni-paderborn.de

Abstract. In this paper, we introduce a novel architecture for programmable
network nodes that work with a large number of real-time video streams. We
first discuss challenges in transmission of video streams over bandwidth-limited
networks, followed by the active approach as an advance for streaming real-
time video. In our model, each programmable node makes admission decision
for video frames based on evaluating their potential value. Frames "bid" their
expected distortion price and the node chooses the best ones first until resource
is fully utilized. Analysis of complexity and overhead shows clear benefit of
our framework. Simulation experiments demonstrate its consistent outperformance in comparison to lagrangian-based Rate-Distortion Optimized schemes.

1 Introduction

Though various compression techniques have been introduced, networks can still not
fully accommodate traffic generated by distributed streaming applications. During
congestion, discarding packets is unavoidable, playback process at receiver will consequently suffer additional distortion. Video compression techniques exploit temporal
redundancy, thus frames are not equally important with respect to reconstruction
process. For example in MPEG4 standard, B frame cannot be decoded without adjacent P frames, likewise P frame must refer to the previous one, all subsequent frames
of a GoP (Group of Picture) are considered useless if its I frame is lost.

On enhancing signal quality, several approaches have been proposed. First, modifications of retransmission [1][2] have been made, in which packets are selectively
retransmitted in case of loss. This strategy is suitable for non real-time video only due
to significant delay and load caused. A proxy selectively caching important video
frames may shorten retransmission path [3]. Note however that once congestion occurs at multiple hops, packets may be discarded before reaching the proxy itself. On
the track of active network architecture [11], [7] proposes a frame semantics based
policy where B frames are dropped first, followed by Ps. This approach improves
distortion in a low complexity, but it does not consider difference in size and associated distortion among frames of the same type, thus it is far suboptimal.

Another promising approach is Rate-Distortion Optimized scheme [4][5][6], or
RaDiO for short, where transmission policy is formed by minimizing a rate-distortion
lagrangian function. [6] attempted to bring the model to ordinary active nodes by
simplifying frame patterns. Despite variety of proposals have been made, complexity

H. Jin, D. Reed, and W. Jiang (Eds.): NPC 2005, LNCS 3779, pp. 409–416, 2005.

still remains challenging. Heavy complexity obviously hinders the network from accommodating large number of streams. Too much computation forced for optimization may cause excessive processing delay.

Our strategy aims at optimality under IP-based infrastructure with low complexity and overhead. It targets at ordinary active routers and any other type of existing programmable nodes that work concurrently with large number of streams, e.g. proxies/firewalls, WLAN routers, and wireless base stations. In the rest of this paper, we first formulate the problem of optimization in the next section, and then frame-bidding strategy is presented. Next, buffer management is described in section 3. Section 4 discusses implementation aspects and evaluates complexity. Simulation experiments are presented in section 5, showing outperformance with respect to average PSNR and complexity.

2 Frame-Bidding Approach

We consider a generic programmable node that needs to forward a set of frames from multiple streams. Decisions on which frame to send, which to drop, and when, will form a *transmission policy*. Each frame is associated with a distortion, which the total distortion at the receiver is reduced if it correctly arrives (hereafter called *distortion reduction*). When overflow occurs, a processor controlling the output interface reconsiders all the frames buffered to find an interim optimal policy. After that, if congestion occurs, the policy is updated with more packets rejected. This tactic lightens effects of prolonged congestion on optimality in a smooth way, and regulates computation load over time. Section 5 shows that a stable playback quality is observed.

2.1 Formulation of the Problem

Let's consider a programmable node that works with M video streams that are allocated a buffer capacity B. Within a period T, accumulated size of accepted frames must always satisfy the following constraint:

$$\sum_A S_{mni} \leq B + W(T) \tag{1}$$

where A is the set of accepted frames, forming a transmission policy π, S_{mni} denotes the total size of frame ith of GoP n of stream m (hereafter referred to as frame mni, or i); and W represents the maximum amount of data that can be dequeued from the buffer within period T:

$$W(T) = \int_0^T C(t)dt \tag{2}$$

where $C(t)$ is the bandwidth reserved for all the streams at time t. An optimal policy should maximize total distortion reduction that frames of A account for:

$$\pi^* = \arg\max_\pi \left(\sum_A D_{mni} \right) \tag{3}$$

where D_{mn} stands for total reduction pertaining to frame *mni*. Due to inter-frame dependency and irregularness of frame arrivals, any online algorithm can give approximate solutions only.

When a frame k arrives and buffer lacks space, some frame(s) must be dropped. Let's denote A_{max} as the set of frames if all remaining frames of the current GoPs are accepted, A_a as the set of currently buffered frames, and J as that of frames to drop. The problem for period T ending when all frames of the current GoPs arrive can be formulated as follows:

$$\left\{ \begin{array}{l} \dfrac{B + W(T)}{\displaystyle\sum_{(mni) \in A_{max}} D_{mni} \;-\; \sum_{(mnj) \in J} D_{mnj}} \;\Rightarrow\; \min \\[3em] \displaystyle\sum_{(mni) \in A_a \cup k} S_{mni} \;-\; \sum_{(mnj) \in J^a} S_{mnj} \;\leq\; B(t) \end{array} \right. \tag{4,5}$$

where $J^a \subset J$, containing currently available frames only. Imagine, in exchange for a reduction pertaining to frame *mni*, the node must spend a space equal to its frame size. So *price* per distortion unit can be estimated as (6):

$$p_{mni} = \frac{S_{mni}}{D_{mni}} \tag{6}$$

At best, the buffer and idle bandwidth are fully utilized so that (1) becomes an equality, and the left-side of (4) expresses the average price for all accepted frames. Approximately, the node gains highest total distortion reduction if it rejects the most "expensive" frames, and keeps the buffer full. Because of frame dependency, each frame should be associated with *expected distortion price*:

$$p^e{}_{mni} = \frac{\displaystyle\sum_{j \in G_i} S_j}{\displaystyle\sum_{j \in G_i} D_j} \tag{7}$$

where set G_i contains i and its dependent frames, excluding those already discarded.

2.2 Bidding Mechanism

Algorithm to locate dropping pattern is illustrated by pseudo code in fig. 1. Whenever the buffer lacks space to accept a new packet of frame k, the interface processor looks back to content of the buffer, calculates expected prices. A list of tag indicating each frame expected price $p^e{}_{mni}$ together with total size $\sum_{j \in G_i} S_j$ is created. The processor picks out tags with highest price first, records accumulated size, until total size of remaining frames is less than the buffer size, i.e., constraint (5) is satisfied. During the process, if k is hit the loop ends immediately, frame k is rejected, and content of buffer is kept intact. Once a frame is subjected to drop, its dependent frames must be too.

```
Frame (k) arrives;
free_buffer_space   =   B -  ∑  S m n i   ;
                              A a

IF (free_buffer_space >= S m n k ) admit (k)
ELSE
{
      Calculate  p ᵉ for available frames and k;
      Create a list of tag for A a ∪ k , called tag_list;
      drop_set  =  Φ /* empty */;
      free_buffer_space = 0;
      buffer_occupance =  S m n k +  ∑  S m n i ;
                                      A a

      while (buffer_occupance > B)
      {
            drop_set = drop_set ∪  pick(tag_list,
                                          highest_ p ᵉ );

            IF (pick(tag_list, highest_ p ᵉ ) == frame k)
               BREAK;
            tag_list  =  tag_list \ highest_ p ᵉ ;
            buffer_occupance =
                      total_size(remain_frames);
      }
      IF (k ∈ drop_set)
      {
            drop_set  =  Φ ;
            Drop frame k ;
      }
      Drop all frames in drop_set;
}
```

Fig. 1. Pseudo code for frame-bidding

3 Buffer Management

In real-time video communication, frames with end-to-end delay exceeding a predefined threshold (typically $500ms$) are considered unacceptable [9]. Thus, buffer should be properly maintained for higher efficiency. Given that a stream m is encoded at frame rate R_m, with GoP length of L_m^{GoP}, the number of frames in buffer at any time should be limited at $\frac{R_m}{2}$ and the number of GoP must satisfy:

$$N_m \leq \left\lceil \frac{R_m}{2 L_m^{GoP}} \right\rceil \tag{8}$$

Specifically, at each frame arrival time, if not both of the above conditions are satisfied, then earliest arriving frames should be deleted to reserve space for the new one. If (8) does not hold, the head GoP in buffer should be completely destroyed.

4 Implementation and Complexity

To ease computation, a logical list is maintained for each stream. Optimization process accesses the list rather than physical packets in buffer. As indicated in fig. 2, packets are first validated at a *GoP Checkpoint*, and then their video header is read and stored in the respective list. When a packet is sent out, the respective list is signaled to update. While queuing, packets may be displaced by new lower price one.

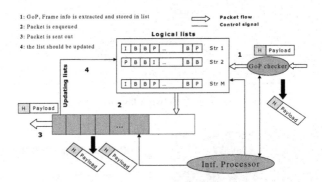

Fig. 2. Logical lists are maintained for streams

What the processor does when overflow occurs is calculating expected price for available frames to form a list of tag. Thus, overall complexity is $O(N)$, where N is the number of frames currently available. Practically, delay exceeding $500ms$ is unacceptable, average frame rate is less than 30 frames/s, so the maximum number of buffered frames pertaining to each stream is less than 15. Thus, the worst-case complexity can be expressed as $O(15 \times M)$, which is much lighter than that of *lagrangian* approach [6], where the complexity is exponentially proportional to M. Like *lagrangian* RaDiOs, correlation with previous GoP can be made to predict the statistics of frames that have not arrived [8]. Video header added to each frame is just to indicate its semantics, total size and distortion. Total number of added bytes is less than 3 per packet.

5 Simulation Experiments

We implement OPNET-based simulation experiments with real-life video streams provided from [10]. Network layout is shown in fig. 3, composed of 10 programmable routers. The four simulated MPEG4 CIF streams are *Akiyo, Container, Hall*, and *Tempete*, connecting Server1, Sever2, Sever3, and Server4 to fix_rx_1, fix_rx_2, mobile_node_0, and fix_rx_3, respectively. Encoded PSNRs are 38.93dB, 33.96dB, 35.35dB, and 26.04dB, respectively. Nominal bit rate of each streams is approximately 200Kbps. Additionally, a real-life trace-based FTP data flow is used to cause further congestion. Each original MPEG4 episode has 300 frames, but is repeated to have 6000 frames in total. Simulation experiments were conducted in both our proposed strategy and *lagrangian* RaDiO.

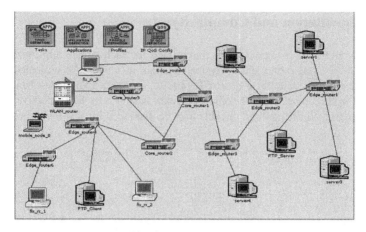

Fig. 3. Network layout

a) fr-bidding   b) lagrangian RaDiO

Fig. 4. A sample frame in two strategies

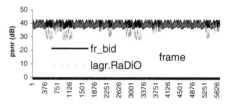

Fig. 5. A stable PSNR is observed in our case

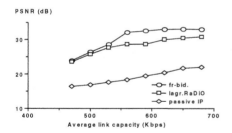

Fig. 6. PSNR vs. average link capacity

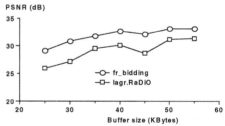

Fig. 7. PSNR vs. buffer size

5.1 Distortion

A sample of reconstructed video is shown in fig. 4. One can easily notice better perception quality in our strategy. PSNR of *Akiyo* is illustrated in fig. 5 as a sample, showing stable quality in our strategy.

First, we fixed buffer size at 40Kbytes and changed capacity of links so that the network experiences from severe to mild congestion. As indicated in fig. 6, PSNR in our strategy is consistently improved, up to 3.89dB. If all routers are passive, quality of reconstruction video is almost unacceptable. When congestion is not too severe, as buffer size increases, the improvement is clearly noticed (fig. 7). The reason is that our strategy admits more important packets whereas the buffer *lagrangian* RaDiO may unnecessarily reject

5.2 Delay

We tuned both buffer size B and average link capacity C, and collected delay statistics. Though queues tend to be longer in our strategy, no major difference between the two cases is observed (only several *ms*), as indicated in fig. 8. Packets in *lagrangian* RaDiO are dropped as soon as buffer fullness is greater than a threshold (B_{min}). Two different thresholds are separately simulated, as B_{min} is reduced from 75% of total reserved capacity B to 66%, delay slightly decreases.

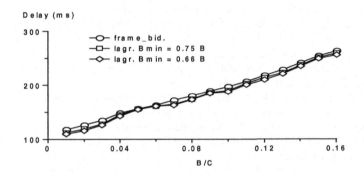

Fig. 8. Delay vs. ratio of buffer size and link capacity

5.3 Run-Time and Complexity

OPNET is discrete event-driven simulator, so run-time duration does reflect algorithmic complexity. In our approach, run-time length is approximately 20% shorter than *lagrangian*-based RaDiO. In a large network scenario with 8 video streams, simulations of *lagrangian* RaDiO hang halfway with 8 nested loops at each router to scan all possible dropping patterns [6]. In contrast, the simulations in our framework ran smoothly.

6 Conclusion

Toward enhancing transmission of real-time video, we have proposed a frame-bidding approach, taking complexity and overhead into account. Simulation experiments clearly demonstrate outperformance of our framework, regarding signal quality and computation complexity. The approach is especially suitable for real-time and interactive multimedia communication since neither retransmission nor acknowledgement is needed. Remarkably, complexity in our model is linearly proportional to number of streams, which is feasible for nodes that work with large number of streams.

In the next effort, we will consider whether cooperation between active routers further enhances end-to-end transmission performance. We also foresee the ability of integrating our model into path-diversity scenarios to extend aggregated bandwidth. At present, we implement the framework on a testbed composed of several Linux PC-based routers, with WLAN connections to end-users.

References

1. G. B. Akar, N. Akar, E. Gurses, "Selective Frame Discarding for Video Streaming in TCP/IP Networks," Packet Video, 2003.
2. Argyriou, A.   Madisetti, V., "Streaming H.264/AVC video over the Internet," IEEE Consumer Communications and Networking Conference, 2004.
3. I. Bouazizi, "Size-Distortion Optimized Proxy Caching for Robust Transmission of MPEG-4 Video," In LNCS 2899, Proceedings International Workshop on Multimedia Interactive Protocols and Systems, November 18-21, 2003.
4. E. Masala, H. Yang, K. Rose and J. C. De Martin, "Rate-Distortion Optimized Slicing, Packetization and Coding for Error Resilient Video Transmission," Proceedings of IEEE Data Compression Conference, 2004.
5. P. A. Chou and Z. Miao, "Rate-distortion optimized streaming of packetized media", IEEE Trans. Multimedia, 2001, submitted.
6. W. Tu, W. Kellerer, and E. Steinbach, "Rate-Distortion Optimized Video Frame Dropping on Active Network Nodes," Packet Video Workshop, 2004.
7. G. Ravindra, N. Balakrishnan, K. R. Ramakrishnan, "Active Router Approach for Selective Packet Discard of Streamed MPEG Video under Low Bandwidth Conditions," Proc. ICME 2000, 2000.
8. Z. He and S. K. Mitra, "A Unified Rate-Distortion Analysis Framework for Transform Coding," IEEE Transactions on Circuits and Systems for Video Technology, VOL. 11, NO. 12, December 2001.
9. X. Meng, H. Yang and S. Lu, "Application-oriented Multimedia Scheduling over Lossy Wireless Networks," IEEE ICCCN 2002, October 2002.
10. J. Klaue, "YUV CIF video sequences", http://www.tkn.tu-berlin.de/research/evalvid/
11. Y. Bai and M. Robert Ito, "QoS Control for Video and Audio Communication in Conventional and Active Networks: Approaches and Comparison," IEEE Communications Surveys & Tutorials, Vol.6, No.1, 2004.

A New Raid-Disk Placement Method
for Interactive Media Server
with an Accurate Bit Count Control

Yo-Won Jeong, Seung-Ho Lim, and Kyu-Ho Park

Computer Engineering Research Laboratory,
Korea Advanced Institute of Science and Technology,
Daejon 373-1, Republic of Korea
{ywjeong, shlim, kpark}@core.kaist.ac.kr

Abstract. In this paper, we propose a RAID-disk placement algorithm of coded video data and an efficient disk prefetching method to increase the number of clients who can be serviced interactive operations in the media server. Our placement policy is incorporated with a special bit count control method that is based on repeated tuning of quantization parameters to adjust the actual bit count to the target bit count. The encoder using this method can generate coded frames whose sizes are synchronized with the RAID *stripe size*, so that when various fast-forward levels are accessed we can reduce the seek and rotational latency and enhance the disk throughput.

1 Introduction

On-demand interactivity means that users can freely interact with the media server because video streams have extremely large data size, the high data retrieval bandwidth is required to support the interactivity to many users.

Generally, disk array technology is employed in multimedia server to provide the high disk bandwidth and satisfy real-time IO requirements [3][4][6]. In the disk array, disk striping is done by dividing the video data into blocks and storing these blocks into different disks. While storing these blocks into different disks, the proper placement algorithm should be considered in disk array to efficiently support the retrieval of such streams at different interactivity. X. Huang [3] studied the rate staggering method for scalable video in a disk array based video server. This method can reduce the buffer space and achieve better load balancing, but their allocation method did not consider the precise disk stirpe management and scalable encoding technique so that rate staggering method hardly apply to the real disk array. Shenoy [6] used the disk array to support the interactive operations in multi-resolution video. They present an encoding technique combined with placement algorithm to efficiently support interactive scan operation. Their variable-size block placement can reduce additional disk requests, but its management is very difficult in disk array.

In this paper, we propose an efficient placement algorithm to support the interactivity in media server, and develope the adaptive prefetching algorithm considering the interactive operation. We have set up real interactive media server using SCSI disk array and linux operating system. Our placement policy is incorporated with an special

H. Jin, D. Reed, and W. Jiang (Eds.): NPC 2005, LNCS 3779, pp. 417–424, 2005.

bitcount control method, called *Fine Tuning of Tail Amount*, that repeatedly tunes quantization parameters to adjust the actual bit counts of video frames to the given target bit counts. The encoder using this method can generate coded frames whose sizes are synchronized with the RAID *stripe size*, so that when various fast-forward levels are accessed we can reduce the seek and rotational latency and enhance the disk throughput of each disk in the RAID system.

The rest of the paper is organized as follows. In Section 2, we present the efficient placement algorithm and the adaptive prefetching algorithm. The proposed encoding technique is presented in Section 3. In Section 4, we present performance results of our placement algorithm and encoding technique.

2   Efficient Placement for Interactive Operation

2.1   Placement Policy on Disk Array

In general, MPEG video stream consists of GOP (Group of Picture)s, and each GOP is represented as a sequence of I-, P- and B-frames. For example, if a GOP structure is {IBBPBBPBB}, the next-level fast-forward scan could be {IPPIPP..} which is not include any B-frames, and the next one is {II..} without any P-frames, and so on. Each sub-sequence for each fast-forward level accessed during a round is required to retrieve together from disks so that more client's real-time playbacks are guaranteed.

When server employs disk array to store the video streams, the server interleaves the storage of each video stream among disks in the array. The amount of data interleaved on a single disk, denoted as *stripe size*, is fixed when the disk array is configured. In that environment, to minimize the seek and rotational latency incurred by the requests, the same types of frame accessed during a round are in the same disks, and the different types of frame are stored in adjacent disks. However, the video streams made from conventional encoder do not have fixed frame size which is opposite to the fixed *stripe size*. It causes the additional disk requests at different fast-forward levels because frames are spread over more disks. Therefore, the special encoding technique is required to apply our placement policy. We will describe it in next section. Using this special encoder, we can make the size of coded each I-, P- and B-frame is twice, same

Disk No.	1	2	3	4	5	6	7
Video i	I	I	BB	P	BB	P	BB
	I	I	BB	P	BB	P	BB
	I	I	BB	P	BB	P	BB
	I	I	BB	P	BB	P	BB
Video j	P	BB	I	I	BB	P	BB
	P	BB	I	I	BB	P	BB
	P	BB	I	I	BB	P	BB
	P	BB	I	I	BB	P	BB

Fig. 1. Proposed Placement Algorithm for Interactive Media Server on Disk Array. Let the GOP structure be {IBBPBBPBB}.

and half as the *stripe size*. Then, the GOP is stored as each I-, P- and B-frame consumes two, one, half stripes on disk array, and the next GOP is stored in next stripe level on disk array, and so on, as shown in Figure 1. At normal playback, the server should be retrieved from all disk array with evenly distributed number of frames. For K-level fast-forward, the server can skip every K-th disk to play out the video streams because the required frames to play fast-forward are separated beyond the disk boundaries. Notice that we can change the starting disk of the next video content for the load balancing of disk requests as shown in Figure 1.

2.2   Stream Classification

If streams stored by the above placement policy like Figure 1 have same frame rate, they have *same bitrate* because all stripe sizes of the RAID system are fixed. However, because many tpyes of streams, having big picture size, small picture size, high quality or low quality, can be stored in one RAID system, the limitation of same bitrate of all steams is a serious weak point in our placement policy. To relieve this limitation, we purpose the stream classification as follows;

 - Class A, the class of streams having high bitrate: Each I-, P- and B-frame consumes four, two and one consecutive stripes respectively. We set the ratio of bit count of I-, P- and B-frame is 4:2:1 because this ratio generally obtains best video quality [2].
 - Class B, the class of streams having middle bitrate: Each I-, P- and B-frame consumes two, one and half consecutive stripes respectively. The ratio of bit count of I-, P- and B-frame is also 4:2:1. Therefore, the bitrate of this stream is $half$ of the stream of Class A.
 - Class C, the class of streams having low bitrate: One I-frame consumes one stripe, but P-frames and B-frames cannot be synchronized with the stripe size. The ratio of bit count of I-, P- and B-frame cannot be same as other class. In this case, we cannot have gain for the fast-forward operation that I- and P-frames are scaned, but we still have gain for the fast-forward that only I-frames are accessed.

The placement of each frame in the RAID system is shown in Figure 2. In the stream of Class C, all I-frames consumes one stripe. For this, the sum total of sizes of P- and B-frames in one GOP is a multiple of the stripe size as shown in Figure 2-(c). the ratio of bit count of P- and B-frame has to be closest to 2:1. Therefore, To get the target bit counts of P- and B-frame, first, solve Equation (1) and (2), and select integer values closet to above solution satisfying Equation (2).

$$N_P C_P + N_B C_B = nS \qquad , n \text{ is apositive integer} \qquad (1)$$

$$C_P / C_B = 2 \qquad (2)$$

Where N_P and N_B are the numbers of P- and B-frames in one GOP, and C_P and C_B are the target bit counts of P- and B-frames. S is the stripe size.

In Figure 2-(c), The GOP structure alternates {IBBPBBPBBPBB} and {IBBPBBPBB}. In the {IBBPBBPBBPBB} case, Equation (1) can be expressed as

$$3C_P + 8C_B = 4S . \qquad (3)$$

Disk No.	(a) One Stripe		Disk No.	(b) One Stripe		Disk No.	(c) One Stripe	
1	I	I	1	I	I	1	I	I
2	I	I	2	I	I	2	BBP	BBP
3	I	I	3	BB	BB	3	PBBP	PBBP
4	I	I	4	P	P	4	PBBP	PBBP
5	B	B	5	BB	BB	5	PBB	PBB
6	B	B	6	P	P	6	I	I
7	P	P	7	BB	BB	7	BBP	BBP
8	P	P	8	P	P	8	PBBP	PBBP
9	B	B	9	BB	BB	9	PBB	PBB
10	B	B ...	10	I	I ...	10	I	I ...
11	P	P	11	I	I	11	BBP	BBP
12	P	P	12	BB	BB	12	PBBP	PBBP
13	B	B	13	P	P	13	PBBP	PBBP
14	B	B	14	BB	BB	14	PBB	PBB
15	P	P	15	P	P	15	I	I
16	P	P	16	BB	BB	16	BBP	BBP
17	B	B	17	P	P	17	PBBP	PBBP
18	B	B	18	BB	BB	18	PBB	PBB
⋮	⋮		⋮	⋮		⋮	⋮	
(a)			(b)			(c)		

Fig. 2. The position of each frame of a stream: (a) Class A; the GOP structure is {IBBPBBPBBPBB}. (b) Class B; the GOP structure is {IBBPBBPBBPBB}. (c) Class C; the GOP structure is {IBBPBBPBBPBB} or {IBBPBBPBB}.

If we set stripe size S to be 32KBytes, the solution of Equation (3) and Equation (2) is

$$C'_P = 128/7 \text{ KBytes} \ , C'_B = 64/7 \text{ KBytes} . \tag{4}$$

Therefore, The target bit counts of P- and B-frame, which are the integer values closest to Equation (4) and satisfying Equation (3) are

$$C_P = 18728 \text{ Bytes} \ , C_B = 9361 \text{ Bytes} . \tag{5}$$

Note that the ratio of bit count of I-, P- and B-frame is 4:2.29:1.14. By the same way, in the {IBBPBBPBB} case, The target bit counts of P- and B-frame are

$$C_P = 19662 \text{ Bytes} \ , C_B = 9830 \text{ Bytes} . \tag{6}$$

The ratio of bit count of I-, P- and B-frame is 4:2.4:1.2. In both cases, The bit count ratios of frames do not large deviate from the ratio of Class A or B.

2.3   Per-Disk Prefetching Method

In general system, when the server retrieves data from disks, consecutive frames are retrieved ahead with the currently requested frames to increase disk throughput. We call these frames are prefetch frames or requests. Because the prefetching requests incur more data transfer and buffer space, it is important that proper amount of frames are retrieved. The conventional prefetching requests are generated across disk array, as shown in Figure 3-(a) because file system only know about the logically continuous allocation of video files. It causes prefetching requests make unnecessary data (B-frames) retrieval for fast-forward plays and would be overhead.

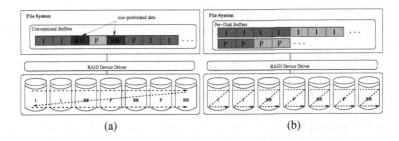

Fig. 3. Per-Disk Prefetching and Buffer Management; An example of Class B stream and X2 fast-forward operation. The light gray and dark gray represents well-prefetched data mis-prefetched data, respectively.: (a) Conventional prefetching requests, (b) Proposed per-disk prefetching requests.

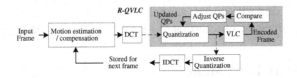

Fig. 4. The conceptual procedure of the R-QVLC scheme

We propose the generation of prefetching requests for per disk, as shown in Figure 3-(b). When current request are retreived from one disk, our file system generates the prefetching requests to retrieve more data from the *same disk not other disks*. We call this method *per-disk prefetching method*. Because our placement policy separates the other frame types to other disks, the per-disk prefetching requests do not generate any unnecessary requests. Note that the per-disk prefetching method can be appliable to other class streams.

3   Accurate Bit Count Control

In order to establish our placement policy, bit counts of all frames can be accurately controlled. However, conventional bit count control schemes cannot satisfy this requirement because of rate-distortion modeling errors and buffer controls for enhancing the subjective video quality [5]. We propose a method that exactly fixes each bit count of coded frames into given target bit count.

3.1   Fine Tuning of Tail Amount

Our bit count control method does not modify the process of the conventional encoding but work as a post-processing process after every one frame is encoded. If the actual bit count of the coded frame is not equal to the target bit count, we pause the encoding process and start to adjust quantization parameter (QP)s of macroblock (MB)s. Figure 4 shows the conceptual procedure of proposed bit count control scheme. We will call this scheme repeated-quantization and variable length coding (R-QVLC). If the actual bit count is lower (or higher) than the target bit count, we increase (or decrease) QPs of appropriate MBs, and carry out QVLC in these MBs, and repeat this process. Detailed algorithm is called *fine tuning of tail amount (FTTA)*. There are three stages, rate-decreasing stage, rate-increasing stage and fine-tuning stage. If actual bit count or AB is bigger than the target bit count or TB, we start the rate-decreasing stage, otherwise, the rate-increasing stage.

In the rate-decreasing stage, we increase some QPs by 1 and perform the QVLC. After that, if AB is still bigger, we increase the number of adjusted MBs or BN by *twice* for making AB approach to TB more fast. We repeat this process until AB becomes equal to or small than TB.

In the rate-increasing stage, the process is similar to the rate-decreasing stage except that QPs decrease by 1 instead of increase. In this stage, if AB becomes bigger than TB, we translate the fine-tuning stage.

In the fine-tuning stage, we restore QPs to previous values and, at this time, decrease BN by *half* for fixing AB into TB. After that, we goto the rate-increasing stage.

Note that the direction of adjusting MB is the reverse of encoding direction.

4   Performance Evaluation

To evaluate our proposed methods we have developed the prototype interactive media server with real disk array storage system and prototype MPEG-2 encoder in Linux operating system. We implement a system for only Class B streams, but these results can be applied to other class.

First, we describe about the FTTA method. We use the MPEG-2 codec provided by the MPEG Simulation Group [2]. Encoding system consists of Pentium 4 3GHz CPU and 1GB main memory. We use 'Mobile' and 'Susie' sequences with 100 frames. The frame size and rate are 720x480 pixels and 30 frames/s respectively. When we encode a source stream, we set the GOP structure to {IBBPBBPBB} and bitrate to 6Mbps. The default rate control method provided by the MPEG-2 codec is used as the conventional rate control. When we apply the FTTA, we set the target bitcounts of I-, P-, and B-frame to 512, 256 and 128Kbits for making constant bitrate of 6Mbps.

Figure 5 shows the encoding results for the two test sequences. *All* the generated bit counts by the proposed method are *equal* to the target bit counts. Average PSNRs and encoding time are summarized in Table 1. We can see that average PSNR is degraded by the FTTA (0.37 dB for 'Mobile' and 0.03 dB for 'Susie') because the FTTA

Table 1. The Average PSNR and Encoding Time

Test sequence	Rate Control Method	Avg. PSNR(dB)	Encoding Time(s)
Mobile	Conventional	27.50	116.6
	FTTA	27.13	140.1
Susie	Conventional	42.41	127.6
	FTTA	42.38	158.9

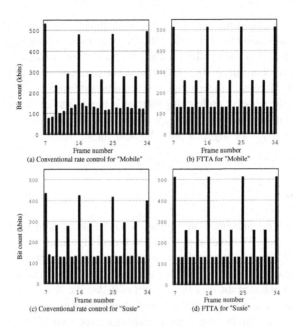

(a) Conventional rate control for "Mobile"

(b) FTTA for "Mobile"

(c) Conventional rate control for "Susie"

(d) FTTA for "Susie"

Fig. 5. The generated bit count of each frame

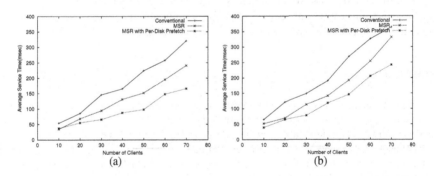

Fig. 6. Average Service Time for mixed fast-forward level: (a) X1 : X2 : X4 = 50 : 30 : 20, (b) X1 : X2 : X4 = 70 : 20 : 10

tries to fix bit count into target bit count without considering the rate-distortion characteristics. However, this PSNR degradation shown in Table 1 is acceptable. In Table 1, encoding time increases by the FTTA because the FTTA is post-processing process after a conventional encoding process. These additional processing times are cost for accurate bit count control. Next, we have evaluated the placement policy and per-disk prefetching method. The evaluation environment is as follows. The server system consists of 2.4GHz intel Pentium 4 CPU, 512MB main memory and disk array with seven SCSI disks, model ST318304FC. The stripe size is set to be 32KB. Each client accessing the randomly selected video stream retrieves the frame-sequence with at a normal playback of 30 frames/s. The performance metric is average service time for one round playback duration as the number of clients increases. We have experimented with mixed fast-forward levels by varying the ratio between fast-forward levels. As shown in Figure 6-(a) and 6-(b), as the number of users increases, our placement policy, denoted as MSR (Media Synchronized RAID), gives better performance because of reducing the disk requests. Moreover, the average service time retrieved from disk in our placement policy with the per-disk prefetching method is much smaller than others which use conventional prefetching method. This is because per-disk prefetching method retrieves the current frame-sequence together with the near future frame-sequence in same disk request.

5   Conclusion

In this paper, we have presented an interactive media sever with media synchronized RAID storage system. We have proposed a placement algorithm and per-disk prefetching method to effectively support the interactive operation in media server. By doing this, when various fast-forward levels are accessed, we can reduce the seek and rotational latency and enhance the disk throughput of disks. We also propose a stream classification scheme for applying our placement algorithm into various types of streams. Our placement policy can be implemented with the proposed FTTA encoder. Though this encoder spends more time on encoding and yields small quality degradation, it can generate the coded video stream which is *synchronized* with the RAID stripe size, so that we can significantly enhance the disk throughput and the average service time for each client connection as shown in our experimental results.

References

1. S. Lim, Y. Jeong, K. Park. Interactive Media Server with Media Synchronized RAID Storage System. *In Proceedings of ACM NOSSDAV 2005*, June 2005
2. Mpeg software simulation group: encoder/decoder. Version 1.1a, 1996.
3. X. Huang, C. Lin, and M. Chen. Design and performance study of rate staggering storage for scalable video in a disk-array-based video server. *In IEEE Transaction on Consumer Electronics*, 50(4):1119–1129, Nov 2004.
4. R. Katz, G. Gibson, and D. Patterson. Disk system architectures for high performance computing. *In Proceedings of the IEEE*, 77:1842–1858, Feb 1989.
5. J. Kwon and J. Kim. Adaptive video coding rate control for better perceived picture quality. *Proc. of APCC2003*, Sep 2003.
6. P. Shenoy and H. M. Vin. Efficient support for interactive operations in multi-resolution video servers. *ACM Multimedia Systems*, 7(3), 1999.

A New Region of Interest Image Coding for Narrowband Network: Partial Bitplane Alternating Shift

Li-Bao Zhang

College of Information Science and Technology of Beijing Normal University,
Beijing 100875, China
Libaozhang@163.com

Abstract. Regions Of Interest (ROI) image coding is one of the most significant features in JPEG2000. It allows ROIs of the image are of higher importance than background (BG). In this paper, a new and efficient scaling-based
method so-called Partial Bitplane Alternating Shift (PBAShift) is described.
The new algorithm firstly shifts up partial most significant bitplanes of ROI.
Then, the most significant bitplanes of BG coefficients and general significant
bitplanes of ROI coefficients are shifted up by bitplanes alternating scaling
method. The least significant bitplanes of ROI and BG coefficients are obtained
in the original position. The PBAShift method, in addition to supporting efficient single ROI coding, can flexibly code multiple ROIs with degrees of interest in an image. The experiments on remote sensing images show the presented
method supports ROI coding of both arbitrary shape and arbitrary scaling without shape coding. Additionally, it can handle complexity multiple ROIs of arbitrary shapes efficiently.

1 Introduction

The functionality of ROI is important in applications where certain parts of the image
are of higher importance than others. In such a case, these ROIs need to be encoded at
higher quality than the background. During the transmission of the image, these regions need to be transmitted first or at a higher priority, as for example in the case of
progressive transmission. JPEG 2000 standard in [1] and [2] not only supports ROI
coding firstly, but defines two coding algorithms that are called Maxshift (maximum
shift) method in part 1 and the general scaling-based method in part 2 along with the
syntax of a compressed codestream. In these methods, a region of interest of the image can have a better quality than the rest at any decoding bit-rate. In other words, this
implies a non-uniform distribution of the quality inside the image.

Although the Maxshift method is simple and efficient, two disadvantages are inevitable. First, this method requires decoding of all ROI coefficients before accessing
bit-planes of the background and uses large shifting values that significantly increase
the number of total bit-planes to encode. Second, it is difficult that this method handles multiple ROIs of any shapes.

In this paper, we present a new ROI coding scheme called PBAShift that not only
retains advantages, but also alleviates the drawbacks of both ROI coding methods in

H. Jin, D. Reed, and W. Jiang (Eds.): NPC 2005, LNCS 3779, pp. 425–432, 2005.

JPEG2000. Three main strategies are used to improving the ROI coding efficiency. Firstly, the presented method shifts up partial most significant bitplanes of ROI, which can ensure that the most important bitplanes of ROI coefficients are coded and transmitted. Secondly, the most significant bitplanes of BG coefficients and general significant bitplanes of ROI coefficients are shifted up by bitplanes alternating scaling method, which enables the flexible adjustment of compression quality in ROI and BG. Finally, the least significant bitplanes of ROI and BG coefficients are obtained in the original position.

The new method is based on the embedded block coding with optimized truncation (EBCOT) scheme. It reduces the priority of the less important region or background of an image, allowing the user to quickly view the ROI with higher quality without receiving the entire image. Thus, it substantially saves the transmission time, storage space, and computational cost of image compression. Simulation results show that the new method can combine the advantages of the two standard methods of JPEG2000 and efficiently compress multiple ROIs according to different degrees of interest without any shape information.

2 The ROI Coding in JPEG2000

In the part one and part two of JPEG2000, two kinds of ROI coding methods are included in the standard: the Maxshift method and the general scaling based method. As illustrated in Fig. 1(b) and Fig. 1(c), these two methods place ROI associated bits in the higher bitplanes by downshifting the bits of BG coefficients from Most Significant Bitplane (MSB) to Least Significant Bitplane (LSB) [3], [4], so that ROI coefficients can be coded firstly in the embedded bitplane coding [4], [5]. In figure 1(a), no ROI code and no scales. In figure 1(b), the general scaling-based method is shows and the scaling value is 5. In figure 1(c), the Maxshift method is shows and the scaling value is 10.

The general scaling-based method has two major drawbacks. First, it needs to encode and transmit the shape information of the ROIs. This rapidly increases the complexity of encoder and decoder implementations. Second, if arbitrary ROI sharps are desired, then shape coding will consume a large number of bits, which significantly decreases the overall coding efficiency. To solve above problems, a new effective solution-Maxshift method was proposed for JPEG 2000. The Maxshift method is a particular case of the general scaling-based method when the scaling value is so large that there is no overlapping between BG and ROI bitplanes, i.e., so the scaling value, s, must satisfy (1):

$$s \geq \max(M_b) \qquad (2)$$

Where M_b is the nominal maximum number of magnitude bitplanes in subband b. Fig. 1(c) shows the bitplane shift in Maxshift method. All significant bits associated with the ROI after scaling will be in higher bitplanes than all the significant bits associated with the background. Therefore, ROI shape is implicit for the decoder in this method, and arbitrarily shaped ROI coding can be supported.

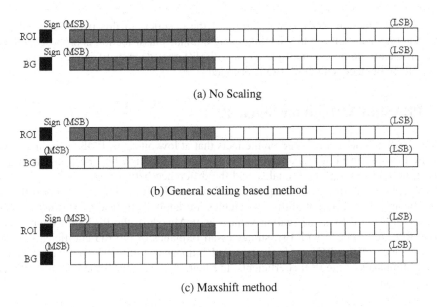

(a) No Scaling

(b) General scaling based method

(c) Maxshift method

Fig. 1. Two basic Scaling method of ROI in JPEG2000

3   Disadvantages of the ROI Coding in JPEG2000

Although the Maxshift method is simple, three limitations of this method are inevitable. First, it does not have the flexibility for an arbitrary scaling value to define the relative importance of the ROI and the BG wavelet coefficients as in the general scaling-based method. Second, this method requires decoding of all ROI coefficients before accessing bit-planes of the background and uses large shifting values that significantly increase the number of total bit-planes to encode. Finally, when there are multiple ROIs in the same image, any ROI cannot have its own scaling value, and therefore different priority during encoding and transmission of the image.

Because of the limitations of two standard ROI coding algorithms, some improved methods for ROI coding were proposed. A new method was proposed in [4] with low scaling values to take advantages of two standard methods. It is implemented by removing all the overlapping bitplanes between ROI and BG coefficients, which relatively modified the quantization steps of coefficients. However, the method brought the reduction of final ROI and BG qualities. A bitplane-by-bitplane shift (BbBShift) method was proposed in [6] by shifting the bitplanes on a bitplane-by-bitplane basis instead of shifting them all at once in Maxshift method. Although it supports arbitrarily shaped ROI coding without coding shapes, it is difficult for the BbBShift method to code multiple ROIs with different priority during encoding and transmission. The partial significant bitplanes shift (PSBShift) method proposed by [7] shifts part of the most significant of ROI coefficients instead of shifting the whole bitplanes as the standard methods do. But the PSBShift method needs the same scaling values for every ROI for multiple ROIs coding. Additionally, this method cannot fully decode ROIs coefficients before all BG coefficients are decoded because some residual significant bitplanes of ROIs is not shifted at the encoder. In this paper, a novel and flexible bitplanes shift coding method using bitplane classification is proposed, which can efficiently compress multiple ROIs with different degrees of interest and ensure all ROIs to be decoded before BG is decoded.

4 PBAShift Method for Single ROI

The PBAShift method is based on the facts that at low bit rates, ROIs in an image are desired to sustain higher quality than BG, while at the high bit rates, both ROI and BG can be coded with high quality and the difference between them is not very noticeable. So we divide the all bitplanes of ROIs and BG into three parts. For different significant parts, different shifting strategies are applied. Instead of shifting the bitplanes all at once by same scaling value s as in Maxshift, the PBAShift method can code ROI in an image with two strategies-all bitplanes of the BG coefficients below all bitplanes of the ROI coefficients or all bitplanes of the BG coefficients below partial bitplanes of the ROI coefficients. In Figure 2, we compare the PSBhift with the new method.

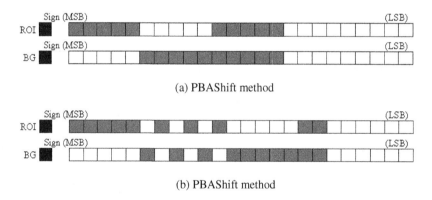

(a) PBAShift method

(b) PBAShift method

Fig. 2. Comparison of the PSBShift method and the PBAShift method for single ROI

We firstly define the parameters of PBAShift method as following,

1) s_1 -The most significant bitplane number of the ROI coefficients.

2) s_2 -The least significant bitplane number of the ROI coefficients.

3) s_3 -The most significant bitplane number of the BG coefficients, which is also the general significant bitplane number of the ROI coefficients.

4) s_4 -The least significant bitplane number of the BG coefficients.

In this paper, we index the bottom bitplane as bitplane 1, the next to bottom as bitplane 2, and so on. At the encoder, the bitplane shift scheme is as following,

A)   For any bitplane b of an ROI coefficient,

    a)   If $b \leq s_2$, no shift and encoding directly.

    b)   If $s_2 < b \leq s_2 + s_3$, shift b up to bitplane $s_4 + 2(b - s_2) - 1$.

    c)   If $s_2 + s_3 < b \leq s_1 + s_2 + s_3$, shift b up to bitplane $b + s_4 + s_3 - s_2$.

B)   For any bitplane b of an BG coefficient,

    a)   If $b \leq s_4$, no shift and encoding directly.

    b)   If $b > s_4$, shift b up to bitplane $s_4 + 2(b - s_4)$.

At the decoder, for any given non-zero wavelet coefficient, the first step is to identify whether it is a bitplane of the ROI coefficient or the BG coefficient. The ROI decoding algorithm is presented as following,

A)   If $b > s_4 + 2s_3$, then $b \in ROI$, shift b down to bitplane $b + s_2 - s_3 - s_4$.

B)   If $b = s_4 + 2i - 1, i = 1,2,3,\cdots,s_3$, Then $b \in ROI$, shift b down to bitplane $(b - s_4 + 1)/2 + s_2$.

C)   If $b = s_4 + 2i, i = 1,2,3,\cdots,s_3$, Then $b \in BG$, shift b down to bitplane $(b - s_4)/2 + s_4$.

If the wavelet coefficient's MSB belongs to bitplanes of ROI, then it must be is an ROI coefficient. Otherwise, it is a BG coefficient. The bitplanes are then shifted back to their original levels by the decoding algorithm.

5 PBAShift Method for Multiple ROIs

In JPEG2000, both the Maxshift method and the general scaling based method can support the multiple ROI coding. However, each method has itself the drawbacks. The main drawback of Maxshift method is that the coefficient bitplanes of all ROIs must be scaled with the same values, which does not have the flexibility to allow for an arbitrary scaling value to define the relative importance of the ROIs and BG wavelet coefficients, and cannot code ROIs according to different degrees of interest. Additionally, in Maxshift method, all bitplanes of the BG coefficients cannot be decoded until the all bitplanes of all ROIs are decoded.

The general scaling based method can offer the multiple ROIs coding with different degrees of interest, but it has three major drawbacks. Firstly, it needs to encode the shape information of ROIs. This shape information significantly increases the complexity of encoder/decoder when the number of the ROIs increases. Secondly, when arbitrary ROI shapes are desired, the shape coding of the ROIs will consume a large number of bits, which reduces the overall coding efficiency. The current standard in JPEG2000 attempts to avoid this problem and only defines rectangle or ellipse shaped ROIs because they can be coded with a small number of bits. Finally, it is not convenient to deal with different wavelet subbands according to different degrees of interest, which is sometimes is very important to code and transmit for objectors.

In this paper, we propose a new and flexible multiple ROI coding method-PBAShift. The presented method not only can support arbitrary ROIs shape without shape coding, but also allows arbitrary scaling value between the ROIs and BG, which enables the flexible adjustment of compression quality in ROIs and BG according to different degrees of interest. The scheme of the PBAShift method for multiple ROI coding is illustrated in Fig. 3. The encoding and decoding method for multiple ROIs are similar to that for single ROI. However, three points must be noticed. Firstly, if s_2 of each ROI is different, we choose the minimum one to compute the shifting-back value of ROI bitplanes. Secondly, s_1 of each ROI must is equal. Thirdly, s_3 is equal to the most significant BG bitplane number, which is also equal to the maximum value of the general bitplane numbers of all ROIs. At low bit rates, different bitplanes are decoded with different degrees of ROI interest. At mediate bit rates, the most significant BG bitplanes and general significant ROI bitplanes can be decoded. At high bit rates, both ROIs and BG can be coded with high quality and difference between them is not very noticeable.

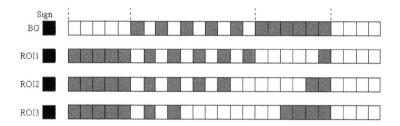

Fig. 3. The PBAShift method for multiple ROIs

6 Experimental Results

In Fig. 4, two reconstructed 512×512 remote sensing images-*San Diego Shelter Island* are given. They are coded with single ROI using PBAShift. In wavelet transform, we adopt (5,3) integer wavelet filters. The original bitplane number is 8. We define $s_1 = 4$, $s_2 = 1$, $s_3 = 3$, and $s_4 = 5$.

In Fig. 5, two figures give multiple ROI coding results for 512×512 *Fishing Boat* image at low bit rates and mediate bit rates. The people, the latter boat and the former boat are respectively defined as ROI-1, ROI-2 and ROI-3 in *Fishing Boat* image. The priority order of these ROIs is ROI-1>ROI-2>ROI-3. We hope that the ROI-1 has the best quality at low bit rates. The up-shifted numbers should be chosen as $s_{ROI-1}>s_{ROI-2}>s_{ROI-3}$, e.g., $s_{ROI-1}=6$, $s_{ROI-2}=5$, $s_{ROI-3}=4$. The scaling value stored in the codestream is $s= \max(s_{ROI-1}, s_{ROI-2}, s_{ROI-3})$. The reconstructed quality (PSNR) of three ROIs is shown in Fig. 6. From Fig. 5, it can be found that at low bit rates (e.g., bpp<1.0), all ROIs have the higher quality than BG. ROI-1 has the highest quality among three.

Fig. 4. The *San Diego Shelter Island* image with single ROI: 0.25 bpp (left), 1.0 bpp(right)

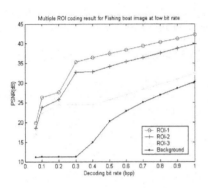
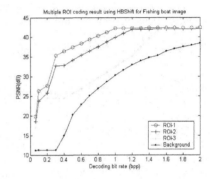

(a) Coding bit rates from 0.1 to 1.0 bpp   (b) Coding bit rates from 0.1 to 2.0 bpp

Fig. 5. Multiple ROI coding results for *Fishing boat* at low bit rates (a) and mediate bit rates (b)

(a) Original image   (b) 0.4 bpp   (c) 0.8 bpp   (d) 1.6 bpp

Fig. 6. The reconstructed *Fishing boat* image with three ROIs: ROI-1 is people, ROI-2 is the latter boat and ROI-3 is the former boat

ROIs. When the bit rates increases, the BG quality increases to some degree quickly. This is because the up-shifted numbers in the GSRB of ROI-2, ROI-3 are not large enough. Hence, the PBAShift method can support multiple ROI coding in a certain range of bit rates, which depends on the number of up-shifted bitplanes for each ROI.

7 Conclusions

In this paper, a new ROI coding method so-called PBAShift is proposed. It has three primary advantages for ROI coding. Firstly, the new method can support arbitrary ROI shapes without coding shape information, which ensures the low complexity for coding ROIs in real-world applications. Secondly, the whole scaling values of all bitplanes are fewer than Maxshift method. Thirdly, the PBAShift can control flexibly the quality between the ROIs and BG by adjusting scaling values. Finally, the new method can support multiple ROI coding with different degrees of interest. We expect this idea is valuable for future research in ROI image coding and its applications.

References

1. ISO/IEC, ISO/IEC 15444-1, Information technology JPEG 2000 image coding system-Part 1: Core coding system. http://www.jpeg.org (2003).
2. ISO/IEC JTC 1/SC 29/WC 1 (ITU-Y SC8) JPEG 2000 Part Final Committee Draft Version 1.0, (2000), December.
3. A. Skodras, C. A. Christopoulos and T. Ebrahimi, The JPEG 2000 still image compression standard, Vol. 9, IEEE Signal Processing Magazine, (2001), 36-58.
4. C. Christopoulos, J. Askelf and M. Larsson, Efficient methods for encoding regions of interest in the upcoming JPEG 2000 still image coding standard, Vol. 7, IEEE Signal Processing Letters, (2000), (9), 247-249.
5. R. Grosbois, D. S. Cruz and T. Ebrahimi, New approach to JPEG 2000 compliant region of interest coding, Proc. Of the SPIE 46th Annual Meeting, Applications of Digital Image Processing, San Diego, Vol. XXIV, CA, August, (2002).
6. Z. Wang and A. C. Bovik, Bitplane-by-Bitplane shift (BbBShift)-a suggestion for JPEG 2000 region of interest image coding, IEEE Signal Processing Letters, (2002), 9(5): 321-324.
7. L. Liu and G. Fan, A new JPEG 2000 Region of interest image coding method: Partial Significant bitpanes shift, IEEE Signal Processing Letters, (2003), 10(4): 35-38.
8. Zhang Li-bao and Wang, Ke. Research on Regions Of Interest Coding Based on Compensation Scheme. Third International Symposium of Multispectral Image Processing and Pattern Recognition. Proc. SPIE. Vol. 5286. (2003), 931-934.
9. C. A. Christopoulos, A. Skodras and T. Ebrahimi, "The JPEG2000 still image coding system: An overview", IEEE Transaction Consumer Electronics, (2000), 46(4):1103-1127

Using Route Probing to Derive Link Traffic Load with Edge-Based Measurements

Guofeng Zhao, Tang Hong, Zhang Yi, and Shangyu Gu

Chongqing University of Post and Telecommunication, Chongqing, China, 400065
zhaoguof@cqupt.edu.cn

Abstract. Obtaining traffic load on internal links of the network is crucial for network management and control. Though collecting can be available on each link, such as applying traditional SNMP scheme, the approach would be expensive because it may cause heavy processing load and sharply degrade the throughput of the core routers in high-speed IP backbone. Then monitoring merely at the edge and estimating traffic in the core provides a good alternative way for overcoming such functionality limitations. In this paper, we explore a scheme on deriving internal link load of network with edge-based measurements. Contrast to collecting routing data from core routers that costs much, we propose a route probing method based on hash sampling techniques and IP Measurement protocol between node-pairs. Based on statistical theory, we prove that our approach is effective and present the algorithm. Performance simulation results show the potential of our approach.

1 Introduction

Knowing the volume of traffic on each internal link is beneficial for network management and control. Basically, there exist three kinds of approaches based on passive measurement [1] that may observe link load traffic. In traditional IP-based networks, traffic is derived by per-link approach such that using simple network management protocol (SNMP) and remote monitoring (RMON) [2] mechanism. But this approach has the disadvantage that it will cause heavy processing load and sharply degrade the throughput of the core routers in high-speed IP backbone. So monitoring at ingress nodes and computing the link traffic load from these measurements provides another way to overcome such functionality limitations. With this notion, A.Feldmann et al. propose a flow-based measurement approach that traffic flows are measured only at the ingress and routing configuration are collected from routers [3]. But the approach has some handicaps: (1) difficult to measure each flow at the edge of backbone network since there may be simultaneously ten thousands of flows. (2) collected data sets are enormous and computation is time-consuming. (3) need of acquiring routing configuration from core routers costs great. Then the third type of traffic measurement is brought forward as direct observation. Trajectory sampling [4] is a method that provides an estimator of the path matrix using packet sampling technology. It doesn't need to know anything about network topology and routing information. It involves sampling packets that traverse each link within the network and regards the set of sampled packets as a representative of the overall traffic. However, selecting the exact hash sampling function to meet real world is too hard.

H. Jin, D. Reed, and W. Jiang (Eds.): NPC 2005, LNCS 3779, pp. 433–440, 2005.

The main contribution of this work is to develop a scheme that link traffic load on each link of a measurement domain will be estimated with edge-based measurements and route probing results. We apply node-pair based measurements at ingress nodes without enabling measurements in the core of the network. In order to know how the traffic is routed, routing matrix is constructed with route probing that using hash-based packet sampling and applying IP measurement protocol (IPMP) [5] to transmit path information. Based on statistical theory, we prove that our approach is feasible. Further, we propose an algorithm for link traffic computation.

2 Our Model for Link Traffic Measurement

In our model, we measure traffic at edge routers and transmit measurement data to a server named NCU(Network Collector Unit) where have traffic computation periodically as shown in Figure 1.

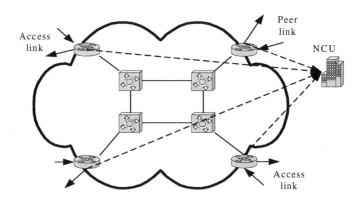

Fig. 1. Our model for link traffic measurement

At edge nodes, we measure aggregate traffic on node pairs. Edge routers send and receive IPMP-based route probing packets and extract path information from those packets. Such path information is collected by NCU to construct routing matrix.

Definition 1. Assume a direct graph $D = (V, E)$, $|V|=n$, $|E|=m$. Name $Y = (y_1, y_2, \cdots, y_i, \cdots, y_m)$ link traffic vector, where y_i denotes traffic on link e_i. Let $X = (x_1, x_2, \cdots, x_j, \cdots, x_L)$ be SD(Source-destination) measurement vector, where x_j denotes measured traffic on path over j^{th} SD pair and L denotes number of SD pairs within an interval T.

Definition 2. Let A be a routing likelihood matrix with scale $m \times L$. For link e_i and j^{th} SD pair, a_{ij} denotes the likelihood of traffic on j^{th} SD pair traverse over link e_i.

Then according to the following equation, we can obtain vector Y.

$$Y^T = AX^T \tag{1}$$

Obviously, edge node-pair based measurement can obtain vector X easily. Then the main problem is that routing likelihood matrix A should be constructed before link traffic can be derived from equation (1).

3 Route Probing

The intention of route probing rests on the idea that routers process probing packets in the same way as other packets. Based on IPMP, path can be recorded in the probing packet when it traverses the network. So relation between links and routes over SD pairs will be inferred from probing packets sent and received.

The IP Measurement Protocol (IPMP) is based on packet-probes. It supports forward and reverse path measurements of a single packet. The protocol has been designed so measurement packets can be processed with approximately the same level of computation as needed for IP packet forwarding. IPMP is implemented in AMP measurement system [6] developed by National Laboratory of Applied Networks Research.

3.1 Route Probing Based on Hash Sampling

In this section, first we give two theorems for route probing scheme. Secondly, we present a framework for hash-based probing system.

Theorem 1. For routing likelihood matrix A, with random and independent route probing, element a_{ij} has standard deviation

$$\sigma = \frac{\sqrt{n_{ij}(n_j - n_{ij})}}{n_j} \tag{2}$$

where n_j denotes probing packets sent over j^{th} SD pair and n_{ij} denotes probing packets traveled through the link e_i.

Proof. Since route probing packets are sent out to their destination in random and independent way and processed in the same way as common packets on routers. Path records can be extracted from these probing packets, so accurate routing information in the network can be revealed after enough probing.

Suppose within measurement period T, source node s has sent n_j number of probing packets over j^{th} SD pair. On link e_i, we obtain n_{ij} number of probing packets traveled through the link.

Then the routing likelihood of link e_i on paths over j^{th} SD pair is given by

$$\alpha_{ij} = \frac{n_{ij}}{n_j} \tag{3}$$

With large enough number of probing, obviously, a_{ij} has a Bernoulli distribution. So its standard deviation has

$$\sigma = \sqrt{\frac{\alpha_{ij}(1 - \alpha_{ij})}{n_j}} = \frac{\sqrt{n_{ij}(n_j - n_{ij})}}{n_j} \tag{4}$$

Thus give the proof of Theorem 1.

At each edge node, route probing is performed periodically as shown in Fig.2. Sampled packets are constructed as probing packets based on IPMP and sent out to destination.

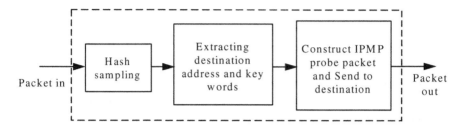

Fig. 2. Framework for route probing at edge router

When probing system receives a packet, it extracts specific bits from the packet to make a key including the packet's destination IP address. Then the key is matched to a predefined key mask. If they do not match, the packet is not chosen for sampling. If the packet is selected for sampling, a new IPMP request packet will be constructed as a probe packet using the sampled packet's destination IP address as its destination address. Then the new packet is sent out to its destination as a common IP packet in the network.

Definition 3. For a packet x, $\phi(x)$ denotes the key that made up of specific bits extracted from x and $\phi(m)$ the mask.

Hash-based sampling satisfies

$$h(\phi(x)) = \begin{cases} 1 & if\ \phi(x) = \phi(m) \\ 0 & otherwise \end{cases} \tag{5}$$

When $h(\phi(x)) = 1$, the packet is selected for sampling and a probe packet will be constructed. The length of mask bits determines sampling probability. Suppose a mask length m, there exist $M = 2^m$ different values for sampling and $p = 1/M$ is the probability of sampling a packet. Selecting adequate value of m may obtain the expected sampling results. We make $m = 1024$ for performance simulations in section 4.

Theorem 2. For any link e_i, within a measurement period T, with random and independent route probing, the relation between measurement error and route probing packet sampling probability p satisfies

$$\sigma_i \le \frac{1}{2\sqrt{n \cdot p}} + \frac{n \cdot p}{n_i} \tag{6}$$

where n denotes all traffic(packets) traveled over *network* and n_i denotes traffic(packets) traveled through the link e_i.

Proof. Within a measurement period T, with random and independent route probing, measurement error on link e_i contains two parts, one for influence of probing packets on background traffic denotes σ_{back} and the other for route probing error σ_{prob}.

So, measurement error sums that

$$\sigma = \sigma_{back} + \sigma_{prob} \tag{7}$$

i. Suppose n_c number of packets are inserted into network for route probing, then packet sampling probability p satisfies

$$p = \frac{n_c}{n} \tag{8}$$

For link e_i, the maximum of measurement error is

$$\max \sigma^i_{back} = \frac{n_c}{n_i} = \frac{n \cdot p}{n_i} \tag{9}$$

ii. For route probing error, from equation (4) we have

$$\sigma^i_{prob} = \sqrt{\frac{c}{n_c}} = \sqrt{\frac{c}{n \cdot p}} \tag{10}$$

where $c = \alpha_i (1 - \alpha_i)$. Then we have

$$\max(c) = \frac{1}{4}, \quad 0 \le \alpha_i \le 1 \tag{11}$$

So the following inequality satisfies

$$\sigma^i_{prob} \le \frac{1}{2\sqrt{n \cdot p}} \tag{12}$$

Then with equation (7), equation (9) and equation (12), we obtain equation (6).
Thus give the proof of Theorem 2.

3.2 Algorithm

Now we present the algorithm for link load computation.

Step 1. To initialize link traffic vector and routing likelihood matrix, let Y=0 and A=0.

Step 2. To compute routing likelihood matrix based on route probing scheme, we obtain the likelihood of a_{ij} is n_{ij}/n_j.

Step 3. To derive load on link e_i, we have

$$y_i = \sum_{j=1}^{L} \alpha_{ij} \cdot x_j \tag{13}$$

where y_i denotes traffic load on link e_i, x_j denotes measured traffic on path over j^{th} SD pair and L denotes number of SD pairs within an interval T.

Step 4. Repeat step 3 to compute traffic load on other links.
End.

The computation for routing likelihood matrix in step 2 of the algorithm is $O(mL)$. The maximum number of SD pairs has $\max(L) = n(n-1)$. Then we conclude the computation complexity of the algorithm is $O(mn^2)$ (m denotes links and n denotes nodes of network).

4 Performance Simulations

The main goal behind the simulation is to evaluate the performances of our model. The topology of simulation is shown in Fig.3. It includes five core routers and four access subnets as ingress.

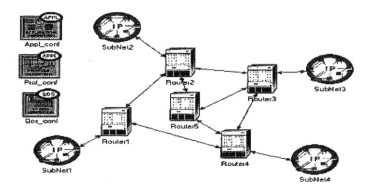

Fig. 3. Topology of simulation network

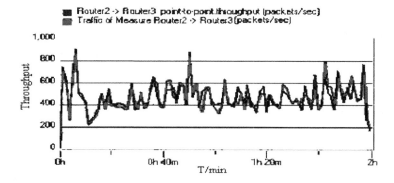

Fig. 4. Throughput on link Router2 to Router3 measured by our approach and per-link approach simultaneously when the link works in light-load situation for two hours

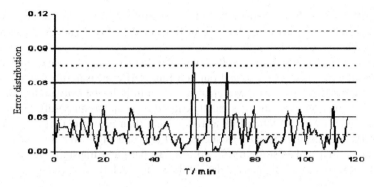

Fig. 5. Error distribution between our approach and per-link approach when the link works in light-load situation

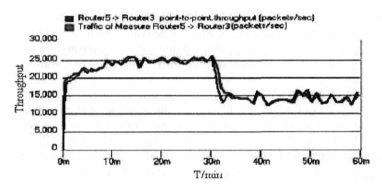

Fig. 6. Throughput on link Router2 to Router3 measured by our approach and per-link approach simultaneously when the link works in heavy-load situation for two hours

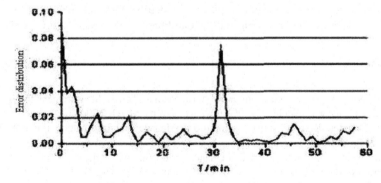

Fig. 7. Error distribution between our approach and per-link approach when the link works in heavy-load situation

For paper limitation, we just show simulation results of traffic on link Router2 to Router3. In the following figures, title including text as Traffic of Measure denotes throughput measured by our approach and title including text as point-to-point throughput denotes throughput measured by per-link approach. We show simulation results that the link works respectively in light-load as Fig.4 and Fig.5 shown, and heavy-load as Fig.6 and Fig.7 shown.

Investigating on simulation results concludes that: (1) results have little discrepancy between per-link approach and ours on link traffic measurement. It implies that our approach is effective. (2) lower error is shown in light-load situation compared to heavy-load situation. We think it's mostly caused by route probing traffic because that makes a higher overhead when link traffic is light than heavy. (3) error will increase when traffic decreasing abruptly as shown in Fig.6 and Fig.7. We think it caused by route change that makes some traffic go to other path and transmit over this link no more. But our route probing has a delay on detecting such routing change.

5 Conclusion

The work is to explore a new edge-based link load traffic measurement problem and results several contributions: (1) a model for deriving link load when measurement performing only at edge without enabling in the core. (2) a scheme for route probing based on Hash based packet sampling and IPMP context. (3) an algorithm for deriving link traffic load.

Compared with the SNMP scheme, our approach causes few overhead in the core because measurement is only at the edge of the network. With flow-based method, since node-pair measurement involves aggregate flows, our scheme produces less computation. Moreover, our scheme can probe route at the edge while need not extract routing data from the core routers. And with direct observation, our approach doesn't require label buffers and sampling operations in the core.

Acknowledgement

This work is supported by Chunhui project funded by Ministry of Education, Nature Science Foundation of Chongqing and Special Fund on 4G-research of CQUPT.

References

1. Matthias Grossglauser and Jennifer Rexford, Passive Traffic Measurement for IP Operations, http://www.research.att.com/ ~jrex/papers/sfi.ps, March 2,2003
2. S. Waldbusser. Remote Network Monitoring Management Information Base, IETF RFC 2819, May 2000
3. Feldmann A, et al. Deriving traffic demands for operational IP networks: methodology and experience. Proceedings of ACM SIGCOMM'2000, 2000. 257-270.
4. N.G.Duffield et al. Trajectory Sampling for Direct Traffic Observation, ACM Computer Communication Review, vol.30, NO.4, Oct. 2000.
5. A. McGregor and M. Luckie. IP Measurement Protocol (IPMP), IETF draft: draft-mcgregor-ipmp-04.txt, Feb.2004.
6. A.J.McGregor, and H.W.Braun. Balancing cost and utility in active monitoring: The AMP example, In Proceedings of INET2000, 2000.

Scheduling Multicast Traffic in a Combined Input Separate Output Queued Switch[*]

Ximing Hu, Xingming Zhang, Binqiang Wang, and Zhengrong Zhao

National Digital Switching System Engineering &Technological R&D Center,
NO. 783 P.O.Box 1001, 450002, Zhengzhou, Henan, P.R. China
{ximinghu, zhengrong_zhao}@gmail.com

Abstract. Although several promising multicast solutions have been proposed till now; however, the support of multicasting still remains notoriously difficult for switches or routers in networks because of the traffic expansion due to multicast replication. In this paper, we propose to use a Combined Input Separate Output Queued Switch (CISOQ for short) to achieve high performance when loaded with multicast traffic. By giving novel definitions for the waiting time and the queue occupancy of multicast cells, we extend the use of oldest cell first (OCF) and longest queue first (LQF) algorithms from the unicast-only traffic load to the multicast traffic load. Furthermore, we show that 100% throughput can be obtained by a CISOQ switch when it is scheduled by OCF and LQF without speedup or by any maximal matching algorithms, just used in the unicast-only traffic load before, with a speedup of 2. The only assumptions on the multicast traffic pattern are that it is *multicast-admissible* and *SLLN* and that it does not *oversubscribe* any inputs or outputs. As far as we know, this result is the first theoretical analysis of multicast traffic arrival process till now.

1 Introduction

Nowadays, multicast-dependent services, such as multiparty telephony, video-conferencing, distributed data processing and work-group applications, are expected to share a significant portion of network applications, and ineluctably, will generate tremendous amount of multicast traffic in networks. Along with the development of next-generation network (NGN), multicasting will definitely becomes an important feature for any future switching systems designed for working in NGN.

For routers or switches in networks, the traffic expansion due to multicast replication will degrade their switching performances which are achieved in the case of unicast-only load. In order to support multicast traffic with much less or no performance degradation under heavy multicast traffic load, several promising solutions [1] have been proposed. General speaking, these proposals can be classified into four kinds according to the means of multicast duplication: the first kind is that multicast cells are replicated at input ports before they are imported into VOQ so that the individual duplications are switched through the fabric as unicast cells [2]; the second alternative is to take advantage of the resource in switch fabrics to achieve multicast replication

---

[*] This work is supported by the National High-Tech Research and Development Program of China (863 Program) under grant number 2004AA103130.

H. Jin, D. Reed, and W. Jiang (Eds.): NPC 2005, LNCS 3779 pp. 441–448, 2005.

[3], [4]; the third kind is a hybrid replication scheme, where part of the replication occurs in the input ports and part occurs in the fabric [5]; the fourth kind is to use additional switching paths that allow the parallel transfer of multicast cells to their destinations (e.g., Multicast-enable Protocol Agnostic Forwarding Engine in [6]).

However forcible these theoretical multicast solutions may be, they have not made much difference to the way switches or routers are built due to their notoriously un-practical implementation complexities, which has been thoroughly discussed by F. M. Chiussi and A. Fraopncini (Refer to [1] for details.) In fact, most switches and routers are still put up on the assumptions that multicast traffic constitutes a relatively small part of the total traffic, and that the distribution of multicast destinations is rather benign [1]. Intuitively, the resulting multicast performance is far from satisfaction.

In order to find a more tractable and practical switch architecture for supporting multicast traffic, we propose a new Combined Input Separate Output Queued switch (CISOQ) in this paper. The scope of our discussion is restricted to the standalone switch fabric based on bufferless crossbar. But all the results presented qualitatively apply to highly distributed switching architectures (e.g., MSM fabric arrangement in [7]). The remaining parts of this paper are organized as follows. Section 2 presents the architecture of a $N \times N$ CISOQ. Section 3 describes the graph model of the cell scheduling problem for CISOQ, and extends the OCF and LQF in [8] from the uni-cast-only traffic load to the multicast load. In Section 4, both simulation results and theoretic analyses are provided to evaluate the multicast performance of CISOQ when it is scheduled by OCF and LQF and maximal matching algorithms. Finally, in Sec-tion 5, we offer some concluding remarks and topics for future studies.

2   A CISOQ Switch

Consider the $N \times N$ CISOQ [1] in Fig. 1, connecting N inputs to N outputs. At the be-ginning of time slot n, either zero or one cell (unicast cell or multicast cell) arrives at input $i (1 \le i \le N)$. Each unicast cell $A_{i,j}^{U}(n)$ $(1 \le i \le N, 1 \le j \le N)$ contains both an uni-cast identifier and an unicasting-destination identifier that indicates which Unicast Output Port UOP_j $(1 \le j \le N)$ it is destined for. When $A_{i,j}^{U}(n)$ destined for UOP_j ar-rives at input i, it is immediately placed in the queue $Q_{i,j}^{U}$. Correspondingly, each multicast cell $A_{i,N+1}^{M}(n)$ $(1 \le i \le N)$ contains both a multicast identifier and a multicast-ing-destination identifier that indicates its set of destined Multicast Output Ports $\{MOP_j : 1 \le j \le N\}$. When $A_{i,N+1}^{M}(n)$ arrives at input i, it is directly placed in the queue $Q_{i,N+1}^{M}$ no matter what multicasting-destination identifier is. This input queuing scheme overcomes the HOL blocking of unicast cells in the same way as the VOQ scheme presented in [8]. In each time slot, each arbiter in every input $i (1 \le i \le N)$ selects no cell or one cell from the HOL of either $Q_{i,j}^{U}$ or $Q_{i,N+1}^{M}$ according to the deci-

---

[1]   Without loss of generality, we assume that a CISOQ switch is fixed-size cell based. And, time is divided into time slots, equaling to the transmission time of one cell.

sion made by the central scheduler. Then, an Indication Signal is produced in accord with the unicast identifier or multicast identifier of the selected cell in order to control the selected unicast cell or multicast cell to be forwarded into either the Unicast Input Port UIP_i ($1 \leq i \leq N$) or the Multicast Input Port MIP.

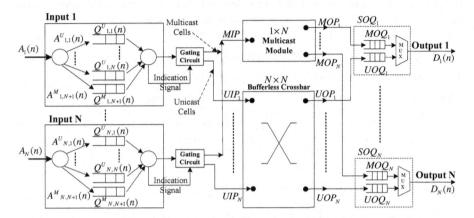

Fig. 1. Architecture of a $N \times N$ CISOQ switch

The $N \times N$ bufferless crossbar is responsible for the proper transfer of $A_{i,j}^U(n)$ from UIP_i to UOP_j. In a parallel manner, $A_{i,N+1}^M(n)$ is duplicated and multicasted from MIP to $\{MOP_j : 1 \leq j \leq N\}$ by a $1 \times N$ multicast module. The output queue architecture for output j ($1 \leq j \leq N$) is divided into two separate parts where $A_{i,j}^U(n)$ from UOP_j is placed into Unicast Output Queue UOQ_j and duplication of $A_{i,N+1}^M(n)$ from MOP_j is placed into Multicast Output Queue MOQ_j. The separation between UOQ_j and MOQ_j may be logical or physical. We call the resulting architecture as Separate Output Queue SOQ_j in this paper. Clearly, an output mechanism is needed in SOQ_j to regulate the access to the output line.

The approach about how to design and implement multicast modules is available and simple. Please refer to [13] for details. There is no need for us to repeat it again.

As shown in Fig. 1, by means of redundant multicast module to realize multicast replication, CISOQ brings along with it the advantages that there is neither explosion in the number of VOQ nor in the number of backpressure entities compared with the scenario where multicast replication occurs in the switch fabric. There are no needs to increase the speed of the VOQ or the speed of the switch fabric by a factor of N compared with the case where multicast replication occurs before VOQ. So, what can be concluded from a practical viewpoint is that the architecture of CISOQ is highly scalable and suitable to be deployed in the switches or routers with gigantic capacities. Furthermore, Section 4 will show that the multicast performance of CISOQ is remarkably well too, even under heavy multicast load.

3 Multicast Scheduling Algorithms for CISOQ

3.1 Graph Model for the Scheduling Problem

In each time slot, the cell scheduling problem on the $N \times N$ CISOQ can be modeled as finding maximum weight matching (Clearly, a maximum size matching is just a special case of the maximum weight matching with all edges associated with weight 1.) on bipartite graph $G = (V, E)$, where $V = V_I \cup V_O$, the set of inputs $V_I = \{i : 1 \le i \le N\}$, $V_O = \{UOP_j : 1 \le j \le N\} \cup \{MIP\}$, $|V_I| = N$ and $|V_O| = (N + 1)$, $E = \{$edges between vertices of V_I and $V_O \}$. Concretely, an edge between i and UOQ_j, associated with weight $w_{i,j}^U(n)$, represents the connection request of the unicast cell at the HOL of $Q_{i,j}^U$. An edge between i and MIP, associated with weight $w_{i,N+1}^M(n)$, represents the request of the multicast cell at the HOL of $Q_{i,N+1}^M$.

3.2 Maximum Weight Matching

In [8], two maximum weight matching algorithms: oldest cell first (OCF) and longest queue first (LQF) have been discussed just under the condition of unicast-only load. In this paper, we extend the use of OCF and LQF from the unicast-only load to the multicast load by giving novel *Definition 1* for the waiting time of the multicast cells in $Q_{i,N+1}^M$ and *Definition 2* for the queue occupancy $L_{i,N+1}^M(n)$ of $Q_{i,N+1}^M$.

Definition 1: At time slot n , the waiting time $W_{i,N+1,l}^M(n)$ of M_l in $Q_{i,N+1}^M$ $(1 \le i \le N)$ equals $\lceil \beta_l((n - s_l)m_l) \rceil$, where $M_l (0 \le l \le L)$ denotes the lth multicast cell in $Q_{i,N+1}^M$, M_1 is the cell which arrives $Q_{i,N+1}^M$ just at time slot n , M_L is the cell at the HOL of $Q_{i,N+1}^M$, and let $M_0, m_0 = 0$ when there is no cell in $Q_{i,N+1}^M$, $m_l (2 \le m_l \le N)$ is the number of destined Multicast Output Ports of M_l, $s_l (1 \le s_l \le n)$ is the time when M_l arrived at input i, $\beta_l (\frac{1}{m_l} \le \beta_l \le 1)$ is a QoS coefficient for multicast traffic.

Consider the situation when there is a $N \times N$ CISOQ scheduled by OCF and M_l is queuing in $Q_{i,N+1}^M$. Suppose M_l need to be multicasted to m_l output ports which means m_l duplications of M_l need to be transmitted. If M_l has waited in $Q_{i,N+1}^M$ for $(n - s_l)$ slots, it has the same effect that every duplication has been waited for $(n - s_l)$ slots too. So, the total waiting time of these m_l duplications equals $((n - s_l)m_l)$. While, in the same input i, if the cell arrived at slot s_l was an unicast cell U_l instead of M_l, the waiting time of U_l would equal $(n - s_l)$. In order to prevent the waiting time of M_l increase too faster than U_l, which may leads to heavy throughput degradation of unicast traffic, $\left((n-s_l)m_l\right)$ ought to be multiplied by a coefficient $\beta_l\,(\frac{1}{m_l}\le\beta_l\le1)$. As β_l decreases, the throughput of multicast traffic will be reduced. Specially, if $\beta_l=\frac{1}{m_l}$, M_l would just be viewed as an unicast one by OCF. Finally, in this paper, we just consider OCF algorithm for which the weight $w_{i,N+1}^M(n)$ and $w_{i,j}^U(n)$ is integer-valued, and $w_{i,N+1}^M(n)$ equals the waiting time $W^M{}_{i,N+1,L}(n)$ of M_l; in the same time, $w_{i,j}^U(n)$ equals the waiting time $W^U{}_{i,j}(n)$ of the unicast cell at the HOL of $Q_{i,j}^U$.

By means of the QoS coefficient, the provision of multicast cells' QoS can be controlled, which will be proven by simulation results in Section 4.

When the CISOQ is scheduled by LQF instead of OCF, a parallel definition of the queue occupancy $L_{i,N+1}^M(n)$ $(1\le i\le N)$ of $Q_{i,N+1}^M$ can be given.

Definition 2: At slot n, the queue occupancy $L_{i,N+1}^M(n)$ $(1\le i\le N)$ of $Q_{i,N+1}^M$ equals $\left\lceil\sum_{l=0}^L(\gamma_l m_l)\right\rceil$, where $m_l\,(2\le m_l\le N)$ is the number of destined Multicast Output Ports of M_l, let $M_l\,(0\le l\le L)$ denotes the lth multicast cell in $Q_{i,N+1}^M$, M_1 is the cell which arrives $Q_{i,N+1}^M$ just at slot n, M_L is the cell at the HOL of $Q_{i,N+1}^M$, and let $M_0,m_0=0$ when there is no cell in $Q_{i,N+1}^M$, $\gamma_l\,(\frac{1}{m_l}\le\gamma_l\le1)$ is a QoS coefficient for multicast traffic.

3.3 Maximal Matching

For practical use, a maximal matching algorithm is a better option than a maximum weight matching algorithm since it is easier to be implemented and possible to avoid unfairness. As can be concluded from the discuss of the graph mode for the scheduling problem on the CISOQ, iterative maximal size matching scheduling algorithms (e.g., PIM [9], iSLIP [10], DRR [11] etc) used in unicast-only load before can also be used to the case of multicast load by the CISOQ in order to find a maximal matching.

4 Performance Analyses of CISOQ

In this section, we adopt the conceptions in [12], and furthermore, we extend the definitions and results of [12] from the unicast-only load to the multicast case.

4.1 An *Efficient* CISOQ

Considering the fluid model of the CISOQ shown in Fig. 1, We define $A_{i,N+1}^M(n)$ as the number of multicast cells that has arrived at $Q_{i,N+1}^M$ and $A_{i,j}^U(n)$ as the number of unicast cells that has arrived at $Q_{i,j}^U$ up to time slot n. We assume the multicast and unicast arrival processes $\{A_{i,N+1}^M(\cdot), A_{i,j}^U(\cdot), i, j = 1, \cdots, N\}$ satisfy a strong law of large numbers (*SLLN*), as proposed in [12]: with probability one,

$$\lim_{n \to \infty} \frac{A_{i,N+1}^M(n)}{n} = \lambda_{i,N+1}^M, i = 1, \cdots, N, \lim_{n \to \infty} \frac{A_{i,j}^U(n)}{n} = \lambda_{i,j}^U, i, j = 1, \cdots, N. \tag{1}$$

Where $\lambda_{i,N+1}^M$ is called the multicast arrival rate at $Q_{i,N+1}^M$ and $\lambda_{i,j}^U$ is called the unicast arrival rate at $Q_{i,j}^U$. In the following definition, we extend the notion that no inputs or outputs are oversubscribed from unicast-only load to the case of multicast traffic.

Definition 3: When loaded with multicast traffic, no inputs or outputs are said to be *oversubscribed* if

$$\forall i, \lambda_{i,N+1}^M + \sum_{j=1}^N \lambda_{i,j}^U \le 1, i = 1, \cdots, N, \forall j, \sum_{i=1}^N \lambda_{i,j}^U \le 1, j = 1, \cdots, N. \tag{2}$$

Definition 4: The multicast traffic is said to be *multicast-admissible*, if

$$\sum_{i=1}^N \lambda_{i,N+1}^M \le 1. \tag{3}$$

Definition 5: When loaded with multicast traffic, a switch operating under a matching algorithm is said to be *rate stable* if, with probability one,

$$\lim_{n \to \infty} \frac{D_{i,N+1}^M(n)}{n} = \lambda_{i,N+1}^M, i = 1, \cdots, N, \lim_{n \to \infty} \frac{D_{i,j}^U(n)}{n} = \lambda_{i,j}^U, i, j = 1, \cdots, N. \tag{4}$$

where $D_{i,N+1}^M(n)$ is the number of multicast cells departed from $Q_{i,N+1}^M$ and $D_{i,j}^U(n)$ is the number of multicast cells departed from $Q_{i,j}^U$ up to time slot n.

Definition 6: When loaded with multicast traffic, a switch is said to be *efficient* if there at least exist one scheduling algorithm which can make this switch *rate stable* for any arrival processes satisfying (1), (2) and (3).

Theorem 1: When loaded with multicast traffic, CISOQ is *efficient* when it is scheduled by LQF or OCF, as long as the speedup $s \ge 1$.

Theorem 2: When loaded with multicast traffic, CISOQ is *efficient* when it is scheduled by any maximal weight matching algorithm, as long as the speedup $s \ge 2$.
Proof: Let $\lambda(n)$ be the rate matrix of the input traffic at time slot n:

$$\lambda(n) = [\lambda_{i,j}^U(n) \quad \lambda_{i,N+1}^M(n)], i, j = 1, \cdots, N. \tag{5}$$

From *Def. 3,4*, we know λ is a class of doubly sub-stochastic non-square $N \times (N+1)$ matrices. While in the unicast-only case, λ just change into square $N \times N$ ones as in [12], and,

$$\lambda(n) = [\lambda_{i,j}^{U}(n)], \ i, j = 1, \cdots, N. \tag{6}$$

So, the proofs of *Theorem 1,2* of [12], which are carried out in the unicast-only case, can be used to prove *Theorem 1,2* of this paper as long as the definitions of both fluid model and notations used in [12] are improved from square $N \times N$ matrices to non-square $N \times (N+1)$ ones by the same way as λ above. We omit the details here.

An *efficient* CISOQ can keep each output link 100% busy. From the long-run fraction of time viewpoint, an *efficient* CISOQ can achieve 100% throughput, if it has infinite buffer capacities. However, for practical use, a CISOQ with finite buffer capacities can approach *efficient* by means of an elaborate queuing discipline which is closely tied with CISOQ architecture and will be the topic of our forthcoming paper.

4.2 Simulation Result

The simulation is carried out in a 32×32 CISOQ scheduled by OCF, which is loaded with both multicast and unicast traffic. The multicast destinations of multicast cells are uniformly distributed, but the total number of destined Multicast Output Ports of every multicast cell is fixed. Let $\lceil \beta_3 m_3 \rceil > \lceil \beta_2 m_2 \rceil > \lceil \beta_1 m_1 \rceil = 1$. While with the ratio of multicast load increasing from 0.1 to 1, the performance of CISOQ turns worse more slowly as the value of $\lceil \beta \cdot m \rceil$ increases, as shown in Fig. 2.

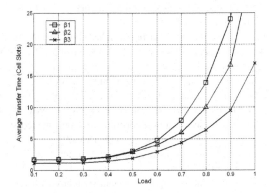

Fig. 2. Simulation result of a 32×32 CISOQ

5 Conclusion

In this paper, we have presented the Combined Input Separate Output Queued (CISOQ) switch, which is a new switch fabric configuration achieving 100% throughout as long as the multicast traffic load satisfies the assumption that it is *multicast-admissible* and *SLLN* and that there is no inputs or outputs to be *oversubscribed*. And, we are not aware of any analytical studies of multicast traffic arrival processes prior to this work. Obviously, the assumption applies to very general multicast traffic, so the results intrinsically have high practical significance.

Indeed, the provision of QoS guarantees for unicast and multicast traffic mainly depends on two key factors: one is the scheduling algorithm that arbitrates the transfer of cells prepared at the HOL of each input port across the switch fabric; the other is the queuing discipline that is responsible to prepare cells according to certain requirements of QoS within each VOQ and resolve the conflicts occurring among HOLs of all VOQs in each input port. Till now, in this paper, we have just concentrated on the scheduling algorithm pertaining to CISOQ. The queuing discipline which is closely tied with CISOQ will be the topic of our forthcoming paper.

References

1. F. M. Chiussi and A. Francini, "Scalable Electronic Packet Switches," IEEE J. Select. Areas Commun., Vol. 21, No. 4, (May 2003) 486–500
2. Chen X., Lambadaris I., Hayes J., "A general unified model for performance analysis of multicast switching," in Proc. IEEE GLOBECOM'92, New York, Vol. 3, (1992) 1498–502
3. W. Chen, Y. Chang, "A high performance cell scheduling algorithm in broadband multicast switching systems," in Proc. IEEE GLOBECOM'97, New York, Vol. 1, (1997) 170–4
4. B. Prabhakar, N. McKeown, R. Ahuja, "Multicast scheduling for input queued switches," IEEE J. Select. Areas in Commun., Vol. 15, No. 5, (June 1997) 855–66
5. M. Ajmone Marsan, F. M. Chiussi, A. Francini, et al, "Compression of multicast labels in large input-queued IP routers," IEEE J. Select. Areas Commun. Vol. 21, (2003) 21-30
6. M. Song, J. Song and H. LI, "Improved Multicast Traffic Scheduling Scheme in the Packet-Switching Systems," Journal of China Universities of Posts and Telecommunications, Vol. 11, (Sep. 2004) 1–7
7. F. M. Chiussi and A. Francini, "A Distributed Scheduling Architecture for Scalable Packet Switches," IEEE J. Select. Areas Commun., Vol. 18, No. 12, (Dec. 2000) 2665–2683
8. N. Mckeown, A. Mekkittikul, V.Anantharam and J. Walrand, "Achieving 100% Throughput in an Input-Queued Switch," IEEE Trans. Commun., Vol.47, (Aug. 1999) 1260–1267
9. T. Anderson, S. Owicki, J. Saxie, and C. Thacker, "High speed switch scheduling for local area networks", ACM Trans. Comput. Syst., Vol. 11, No. 4, (Nov. 1993) 319–352
10. N. McKeown, "The iSLIP scheduling algorithm for input-queued switches", IEEE/ACM Trans. on Networking, Vol. 7, No. 2, (April 1999) 188–201
11. J. Chao, "Saturn: a terabit packet switch using dual round-robin", IEEE Communication. Magazine .December, (2000) 78–84
12. J. Dai and B. Prabhakar, "The throughput of data switches with and without speedup", in Proc. of IEEE INFOCOM'2000, (May 2000) 556–564
13. Gua, Ming-Huang and Ruay-Shiung Chang, "Multicast ATM switches: survey and performance evaluation," Computer Communication Review, Vol. 28, No 2, (1998) 98–131

A QoS-Based Scheduling Mechanism for Overlay Aggregate Traffics

Yunbo Wu[1,2], Zhishu Li[1], Zhihua Chen[3], Yunhai Wu[4], Li Wang[1], and Tun Lu[1]

[1] School of Computer Science, Sichuan University,24 southern section1,
1st Ringroad, ChengDu, China
(ybwutm,tm_001,tm_002,ths_01)@tom.com
[2] Ningbo Fashion Institute, Ningbo, China
[3] Kunming Meteorological Administration, west of XiHua Park, Kunming, China
khzitm@tom
[4] Yunnan Design Institute of Water Conservancy and Hydroelectric Power, Kunming, China
juan01_tom@tom.com

Abstract. This paper presents a control mechanism in SON(Service Overlay Network) architecture to provide delay guarantees of different aggregate traffics over IP network. In addition to the bandwidth provision problem of aggregate-traffic in service overlay network, queuing delay in the service gateway is another critical QoS parameter, and diverse multimedia flows have different delay requirements. To assure the delay requirements of aggregate flows in service overlay network, we present a simple but effective adaptable control mechanism, which consists of two-queues with exhausitive service in cyclic order and characterizes the abilities to ensure delay requirements of various aggregate flows according to their burstiness. Moreover, Associated performance is analyzed by the Markov chain and probability generation function, and simulations validate this analysis.

1 Introduction

With the explosive of growth of the Internet and multimedia applications, the need for QoS guarantees is becoming more and more ubiquitous in the networks of future. Moreover, Everything over IP has been regarded as a preferred solution of next-generation Internet, then IPQoS emerges paramount importance in multimedia delivery. In order to achieve IP QoS, several new significant architectures such as IntServ, DiffServ, and MPLS have been proposed by IETF in last few years. However, these and other proposals for Internet QoS, have two key requirements: first, they require all routers along a path to implement QoS mechanisms for scheduling and buffer management, and second, they require the right incentives for Internet Service Providers (ISPs) to enable these functions. Unfortunately, these demands have often turned out to be difficult to meet. Internet QoS remains to be an open issue till now.

On the other hand, the Internet has evolved to become a commercial infrastructure of service delivery. Many value-added and content delivery services are developed via overlay networks rather than IP-layer, such as content delivery overlays [1], p2p

H. Jin, D. Reed, and W. Jiang (Eds.): NPC 2005, LNCS 3779, pp. 449–452, 2005.

file sharing overlays [2]. Besides, Ref. [3,4] discussed service overlay networks and service composition, while Ref. [5] studied service grid. SON architecture provides more effective and efficient solution in QoS guarantee. Relying on the bilateral SLAs the SON can deliver end-to-end QoS sensitive services to its users via appropriate provisioning and service-specific resource management. The underlying network domains can aggregate traffic based on the SONs they belong to and perform traffic and QoS control accordingly based on the corresponding SLAs.

In this paper, we'll deploy a control mechanism in SON architecture to provide delay guarantees of different aggregate traffic in service overlay networks. Considering that different types of multimedia traffics characterize various burstiness, our control model consists of two asymmetric queues with exhaustive service in a cyclic order. The model function independently in the service gateway of SON and has the ability of providing lower waiting delay to the flows with higher burstiness without any priority pre-assigning. Furthermore, we adopt an ingenious but efficient method to deal with this asymmetric polling system, and obtain exact average waiting time formula. Simultaneously, associated simulation verifications are presented.

The rest of the paper is organized as follows: in section 2 we describe our control model and make some analysis of this model, in section 3 we address our concluding remarks.

2 Model Evaluation

Our model consists of two queues with exhaustive service in a cyclic order. Considering that different types of multimedia traffics characterize various burstiness, we may classify multimedia traffics in to two queues according to burstiness, viz. one queue with larger burstiness and another with smaller ones. When server visits a queue in turn, not only all the packets already waiting in the queue will be served, but also comprise packets arriving during the service intervals. After completing the service of one queue, the server will move to the succeeding queue and incur a switching-over time, then start to serve the queue in the same way. There are three independent random processes relating to each queue separately, i.e., the packets arriving, servicing upon a queue, and switching-over from one queue to another. Considering difference between two traffics, parameters associated with these random processes are generally not the same. Namely, this queuing model is asymmetric queuing system. In terms of QoS requirements many metrics are concerned, such as delay, delay jitter and packet loss. Our work will focus on the performance of delay of multimedia resources, which incurred during networking node. In our analysis, we condition the discrete system and infinite capacity in each queue. Then Related joint generating functions are defined as follows:

$$G_1(z_1, z_2) = R_2(A_1(z_1)A_2(z_2)) G_2(z_1, B_2(A_1(z_1)F_2(A_1(z_1)))) \tag{1}$$

$$G_2(z_1, z_2) = R_1(A_1(z_1)A_2(z_2)) G_1(B_1(A_2(z_2)F_1(A_2(z_2))), z_2) \tag{2}$$

From equations (1)-(2), mean packet waiting time in queue Qi can be obtained as following:

$$\overline{w_i} = \frac{g_i(i,i)}{2\lambda_i g_i(i)} + \frac{\left(2\rho_i^2 + \rho_i - 1\right)A_i''(1)}{2\lambda_i^2\left(1 - \rho_i^2\right)} + \frac{\lambda_i B_i''(1)}{2\left(1 - \rho_i\right)}, \quad i = 1, 2. \tag{3}$$

Moreover, we'll present some numerical results of packet average waiting time in each queue according to Equations (3) (Refer to Fig.1 and Fig.2). Where w_{1s}, w_{2s} represent the simulation value of w_1, w_2, respectively.

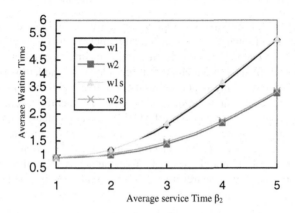

Fig. 1. Average waiting time versue average service time ($\gamma_1 = \gamma_2 = 1, \lambda_1 = \lambda_2 = 0.1, \beta_1 = 1$)

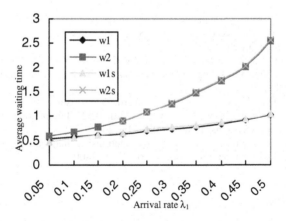

Fig. 2. Average waiting time versus average arrival rate ($\gamma_1 = \gamma_2 = 1, \beta_1 = \beta_2 = 1, \lambda_2 = 0.01$)

Fig.1 shows that the queue with larger value of β has lower mean waiting time than the other one. The reason is that service related to the queue has been intensified. While Fig.2 depicts that the average waiting time related to having higher arrival rate is always smaller than the other related to having lower arrival rate. Moreover, in both cases the waiting time increases as λ_1 raising, just for the reason that the load of system increases also. In addition, simulation results show good agreement with the analytical results.

3 Conclusions

From the discussions above-mentioned, we can draw the following conclusions: our scheduling model can provide lower waiting delay to the resource with higher burstiness without any priority pre-assigning. Meanwhile changing the value of β can influence the waiting delay, which implies that the length of information packet can affect waiting delay. These will benefit multimedia applications delivery over IP networks.

QoS provision for multimedia application delivery in Internet is a crucial and complex issue. Traditional IP QoS mechanisms, such as the ones offered by Interserv and Diffserv, have encountered more difficulties in implementation and deployment in current Internet. Instead, the method that provides value-added with QoS guarantee based on overlay networking is getting more attractive and to be a promising solution in Internet multimedia applications. Our control machinery can be embedded independently in the service gateway of SONs as a supplement, it can provide delay guarantee to various traffics with different burstiness. This combination architecture may implement all-around end-to-end QoS guarantees. To extend our research, we will further our control model to satisfy QoS demands of multi-types multimedia traffics, and continue our research on the end-to-end QoS issue of various overlay networks.

References

1. S. Ratnasamy, P. Francis, M. Handley, R. Karp, and S. Shenker. CAN: A scalable content-addressable network. In Proceedings of ACM Sigcomm, August 2001.
2. Gnutella. http://gnutella.wego.com/.
3. L. Subramanian, I. Stoica, H. Balakrishnan, and R. H. Katz. OverQoS: Offering QoS using Overlays. Proc. of First Workshop on Hop Topics in Networks (HotNets-I), Princeton, New Jersey, October 2002.
4. X. Gu, K. Nahrstedt, R. N. Chang, and C. Ward: "QoS-assured service composition in managed service overlay networks," in the 23rd IEEE International Conference on Distributed Computing Systems (ICDCS2003), May 2003.
5. Gill Waters, John Crawford, Sei Guan Lim: Optimising multicast structures for grid computing. Computer Communications 27 (2004) 1389–1400

Energy Conservation by Peer-to-Peer Relaying in Quasi-Ad Hoc Networks*

Andrew Ka-Ho Leung and Yu-Kwong Kwok**

Department of Electrical and Electronic Engineering,
The University of Hong Kong, Pokfulam Road, Hong Kong
ykwok@hku.hk

Abstract. Thanks to the highly popular dual channel capabilities (e.g., GSM plus Bluetooth) in modern handheld personal communication devices, an integrated cellular and ad hoc peer-to-peer network (i.e., a *quasi-ad hoc* wireless network) has already been widely reckoned as a readily practicable and attractive mobile computing environment. In this paper, we propose a co-operative relaying scheme, called *eeRelay*, for such a quasi-ad hoc network, to extend the life-time of low energy level users significantly. More importantly, the energy efficiency of the whole network is also remarkably increased.

1 Introduction

The problem of short service life of most 3G handsets serves as an alarming alert that *energy efficiency* is a crucial factor in making a ubiquitous wireless communication system a successful story [7]. In view of the fact that contemporary battery technology cannot solve the service life problem, in our study we find that "relaying" can be one promising strategy in addressing the issue.

Nowadays hand-held wireless communication devices are commonly equipped with more than one wireless interface and are capable of communicating both with the base station and directly with other users in ad hoc manner. Thus, we believe that an interesting kind of ubiquitous wireless networks in future is *quasi-ad hoc* in nature where communication links can be classified into two modes: (1) one-to-one communication among peers (e.g., a user shares files with another user directly using WLAN or data packets transmitted from one measurement node to another one) and (2) many-to-one communication from some nodes to the "sink" (e.g., mobile phone users access the base station in the uplink). We treat two modes of communication linkage differently (see Figure 1(a)).

We propose a new collaborative energy management scheme, called *eeRelay*, for such a quasi-ad hoc network to increase the energy efficiency. We adapt the transmission power of mobile terminals to reduce the energy used. This is done by using another nearby higher energy level user as a relay.

The remainder of this paper is organized as follows. In Section 2, we provide some background information on relaying systems and describe our approach to

---

* This research was supported by a grant from the Research Grants Council of the HKSAR under project number HKU 7157/04E.
** Corresponding author.

H. Jin, D. Reed, and W. Jiang (Eds.): NPC 2005, LNCS 3779, pp. 453–460, 2005.

increasing the energy efficiency by relaying actions. In Section 3, we present our simulation results. Finally, in Section 4 we discuss the benefit of our protocol by taking incentives into consideration.

2   Related Work and Proposed Approach

Relaying have been proposed in the literature [3], [5] and [9]. However, nearly all of these proposed relaying schemes do not explore the possibility of **co-operation in energy domain**. For this reason, we look at the relaying problem in another perspective in this paper. Specifically, we define who should be the relaying node so that the relaying process could be more energy efficient. We use the concept of "helpers" to replace the traditional simple concept of "relays".

2.1   Design of the Proposed eeRelay Protocol

We use cellular mobile network as an application example of quasi-ad hoc network to describe our *energy efficient relaying* protocol, namely *eeRelay*. When a low energy level user needs to set up a connection to the base station (BS). The BS dynamically select an energy efficient relay (helper) to relay the traffic for the low energy users. The BS is assumed to have location information of all users.[1] In our design, a user is categorized as a "Helper" in Helper Set **H** if: (1) its energy level is high enough; and (2) it is physically situated in the "Helper's Region **D**" with respect to a low energy level user.

Mathematically, for a set of users $n_1, \ldots, n_n \in \mathbf{N}$, a user $n_i \in \mathbf{H}$ if $E(n_i) \geq \gamma$ and $n_i \in \mathbf{D}$ where $E(n_i)$ denotes the energy level of a user $n_i, m \leq n, \mathbf{H} \subset \mathbf{N}$.

D is named as "Helpers' Region", and is defined as follows. It makes sure that, for a user to be qualified as a "Helper", it needs to be situated in certain geographical position such that the relationship $P_{u \to h} + P_{h \to BS} < P_{u \to BS}$ is satisfied. This ensures that the relaying action will not only reduce u's energy consumption *but* will also be an energy efficient one even when we focus on the total energy used.

We assume a path loss propagation model with path loss exponent β, i.e.,

$$P_{A \to B} = k d_{A \to B}^{\beta} \tag{1}$$

where $P_{A \to B}$ is the required transmit power between point A and B and $d_{A \to B}$ is the distance between them. In general, β is an integral value ranges from two to four in urban areas. In our analysis we set it as four which is a value commonly used in the literature [8]. Finally, k is a constant. [2]

---

[1] The location information can be obtained by using GPS on mobile devices or techniques such as time-difference triangulation performed by three or more nearby base stations.

[2] Please note that the value of k could be different for communication links for *BS–mobile terminal* or *mobile terminal–mobile terminal*. But here we used one fixed value of k as an approximation. Our simulations use more realistic path loss model to show that this approximation is justified for the purpose of defining the Helper's Region.

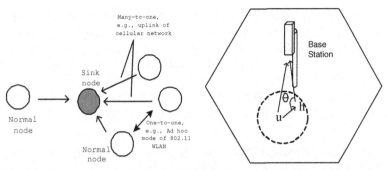

(a) A quasi-ad hoc network   (b) Using a high energy "helper" to relay data for a low energy source

Fig. 1. eeRelay

Now let us consider Figure 1(b) in which h acts as a relay of u to communicate with the BS. Our goal is to find out under what circumstances would $P_{u \to h} + P_{h \to BS} < P_{u \to BS}$ so that we can select a user (helper candidate) situated in such a position that its relaying action will not only reduce u's energy consumption *but* will also be an energy efficient one even when we focus on the total energy used.

According to our path loss model, to achieve this goal, we need:

$$d_{u \to BS}{}^4 > d_{u \to h}{}^4 + d_{h \to BS}{}^4 \qquad (2)$$

By cosine law, we have:

$$d_{u \to BS}{}^2 = d_{u \to h}{}^2 + d_{h \to BS}{}^2 - 2d_{u \to h}d_{h \to BS}cos\theta \qquad (3)$$

Substitute Equation (3) into Equation (2), we have:

$$\Rightarrow \frac{2(d_{u \to h}{}^2 + d_{h \to BS}{}^2)cos\theta}{d_{u \to h}d_{h \to BS}} - 2cos^2\theta < 1 \qquad (4)$$

A Helper's Region with respect to the position of the lower energy user[3] is plotted in Figure 2(f) (shaded area) and is found to be "ellipse-like".

2.2 Implementation

Phase I—Helper Request. At first, when a low power user u wants to make a connection, it triggers the helper request process. It transmits, with extremely low power (say, 0.1W or less), a "helper searching packet" to ask for any user *nearby* which could be a helper candidate according to the definition in Section 2.1 (see the condition specified by Equation (1)). Any nearby user which

---

[3] In this paper the term "user" is used interchangeably with the term "UE" (User Terminal) used in conventional 3G UMTS-WCDMA system.

receives this packet checks its energy level and see if it could be a helper candidate. If it fulfills the requirement of condition (1), it sends an "helper access packet" to BS *on behalf of u*, containing its own ID and *u*'s ID *after* a random back off period so as to minimize the probability of all ACKs from different helper candidates colliding with each other. *u* keeps a timer for "helper searching timeout". It re-sends a helper request packet if there is no reply from any nearby neighbor. If *u* still fails in finding a helper after several attempts it will connect to BS on its own.

Phase II—Base Station Acknowledgment and Relay Set Up. Upon receiving the access packet from the helper candidate, the BS checks whether this helper candidate is inside the helper's region and confirms that the candidate's energy makes it eligible for helping *u*. BS collects helper access packets from all the helper candidates and form a *helper set* $\mathbf{H_u}$ for *u*. BS then selects one eligible helper candidate *h* from $\mathbf{H_u}$ and acknowledges both *u* and *h* by sending an "BS-ACK packet" to them. After both *u* and the helper candidate *h* have received the BS-ACK, they do a handshaking with each other and connection from *u* to BS through *h* can be started.

Phase IV—Helper Maintenance and Tear Down. The helper set $\mathbf{H_u}$ formed before is still useful after a helper *h* has been selected for *u* already. This is because both *u* and *h* are moving, there can be a case that *h* is moving out of the "Helper's Region" of *u* suddenly, or *h* is moved to other cell, then a *helper handoff* is needed, so the BS asks the helper to update its position and *u*'s position periodically during the connection (*h* can get *u*'s GPS position information easily by asking *u* to add it into the data packet periodically). Both *u* and *h* tear down the connection after *u* terminates the call.

3   Performance Results

3.1   Simulation Platform

Now we study the performance of eeRelay using simulations. In our simulations, 50 UEs are scattered randomly in an 800 m × 800 m area initially and they are allowed to move freely according to the mobility model mentioned above. In this paper we consider a single cell case with no inter-cell handoff. We focus on our scheme and perform "helper handoff" only. The transmit power is selected when connection between BS and UE is established. We also assume that there is no collision in all ACK or BS-ACK transmissions. Each simulation is run for 50,000 seconds.

The wireless devices are assumed to have three possible modes of operation: Transmit, Receive and Idle. The energy consumption ratio of the three modes is set as 1 : 0.6 : 0.5, as indicated by the experimental measurements done by Feeney and Nilsson [4]. The energy consumption on a node is modeled as

$$P_{\mathrm{Tx}}T_{\mathrm{Tx}} + P_{\mathrm{Rx}}T_{\mathrm{Rx}} + P_{\mathrm{IDLE}}T_{\mathrm{IDLE}}$$

where the first three P terms represent power consumption in Transmit, Receive and Idle modes, respectively, the T terms represent corresponding time durations that the mobile devices are in different modes.

Our scheme applies to the uplink of an integrated cellular and ad hoc network. To simulate this environment, we obtain reference system parameter values from the link budget for the uplink of a typical UMTS-WCDMA 3G system. The maximum transmit power of mobile node is 0.25W (24 dBm) and the receiver Sensitivity for 384 kbps data service at BER = 10^{-3} is –109.2 dBm [6]: [4] Using the *Okumura-Hata Model* [6] we can estimate the transmission range of BS and mobile devices. We assume that the calls arrive according to a Poisson distribution where the call arrival times and the inter-arrival times between calls are mutually independent. Our mobility model assumes UEs' velocities follow a Gaussian distribution with mean = 3 km/hr, (i.e., 0.83 m/s) and variance = 0.54.

3.2   Simulation Results

First we consider the amount of energy used for control purpose (e.g., transmission or reception of helper search packets, helper access packets, BS-ACK packets, relaying set up and torn down). As shown in Figure 2(e), the total amount of energy consumed for control purpose is below 0.2% of total energy of each node. As eeRelay is running, more calls are set up and tear down. After a *transient period* of around 5,000 seconds, the percentage of total energy consumed for control purpose falls and finally attains an approximately constant value.

Performance Metrics. We consider two performance metrics, the first one is for low energy level users defined according to Section 2.1. We define the performance metric as "Percentage life extension of u_k":

$$\frac{\text{life of } u_k \text{ with helper scheme - life of } u_k \text{ without helper scheme}}{\text{life of } u_k \text{ without helper scheme}} \times 100 \qquad (5)$$

where $u_k \in \mathbf{U}, k \leq n$. Here, "life" is defined as the total duration of time that a UE operates until it exhausts its battery. From this metric we define the average percentage life extension of low energy level users as:

$$\frac{\sum_k \quad \text{Percentage life extension of } u_k}{k} \qquad (6)$$

A similar metric, which sums and averages over all users is defined as a measure for the overall energy efficiency for the whole network, namely "Percentage life extension of all users".

---

[4] "UE" and "Node B" are the terminology used in UMTS-WCDMA specification for Mobile Users and Base Station. We follow this convention and use each pair of them interchangeably in this paper.

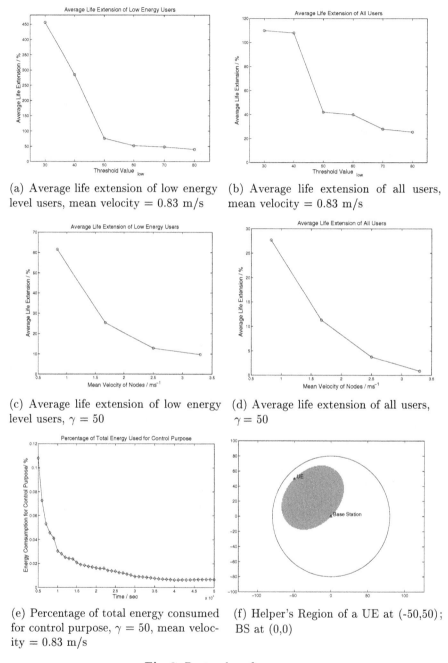

(a) Average life extension of low energy level users, mean velocity = 0.83 m/s

(b) Average life extension of all users, mean velocity = 0.83 m/s

(c) Average life extension of low energy level users, $\gamma = 50$

(d) Average life extension of all users, $\gamma = 50$

(e) Percentage of total energy consumed for control purpose, $\gamma = 50$, mean velocity = 0.83 m/s

(f) Helper's Region of a UE at (-50,50); BS at (0,0)

Fig. 2. Protocol performance

Effect of Threshold γ. For a mean velocity of users = 0.83 m/s, $\epsilon = 0.5$, the performance metrics we defined are plotted in Figure 2(a) and 2(b). We find that our scheme yields significant average life extension on the low energy users u_k, ranging from 456% to 40% for γ ranging from 30 to 80, depending on the threshold value γ (i.e., the definition of "low energy level user"). If the threshold is set to be very low (e.g., 30), then the average life extension for those low energy level users u_k is very significant (over 400%). We believe that this is due to the contribution from a large number of helpers (e.g., 38 helpers out of 50 users for $\gamma = 30$ in the example we plot). But the tradeoff is the number of users that can be classified as "low energy level user" is small and thus the ratio of users who can gain benefit is small (12 low energy level users out of 50 users). A more fair scheme is to define the value of γ as half of the maximum value of energy levels, the number of u and h would then be half-half, assume that the energy levels of all UEs are uniformly distributed. This "half-half" case yields an average life extension of around 76%. The simulation results also show increases in life extension averaged over all users, representing a system-wide energy efficiency. The life extension ranges from around 110% to around 28% (see Figure 2(b)). To conclude, we see a tradeoff between the average gains by each of the low energy level user ($u_k, k \leq n$) and the total number of low energy level users who could gain (k).

Effect of Mobility of Users. For $\gamma = 50$ (the numbers of low energy level users and helpers are half-half), the performance metrics we defined are plotted against mean velocity of users in Figures 2(c) and 2(d).

From our simulation results, we find that the gain through the use of our scheme is sensitive to the mobility of users. Consider Figures 2(c) and 2(d) that when the mean velocity of users increases from 0.83 m/s (3 km/hour) to 2.5 m/s (12 km/hour), the average life extension of low energy level users decreases from around 61.6% to around 9.7% while the life extension averaged over all users also decreases from 27.6% to around 0.8% as the mobility increases from 0.83 m/s to 2.5 m/s. This shows that our scheme is more suitable for low mobility users (e.g., pedestrians or people walking around in a shopping mall).

4 Incentives

Our scheme can be considered as "beneficial" on two aspects: (i) energy consumption of the whole network is reduced; and (ii) energy consumption of low energy level users is also reduced. Since helpers are asked to "share" their energy among those who need, this causes extra energy consumption on them, you may ask: **Are those helpers in fact "losers" in our protocol? The answer is no** and the reasons are: (1) when every node is running eeRelay protocol, it guarantees that whenever any node is in low energy state, high energy level users in its helper's region would help it by relaying its traffic, this provides incentive for any node to act as a helper when it is in high energy state since other nodes would help it in return when its energy level falls below the threshold; (2) In application like P2P file sharing, extending the life of low energy level users means more nodes could contribute to the P2P community. These arguments justify as to why we need to help those who are at low energy levels.

5 Conclusions

We have presented a new energy sharing scheme. With our theoretical analysis and simulations, we also demonstrate the increased overall energy efficiency. We believe that the key point to extend the service life of mobile user terminals is the co-operation between users.

References

1. P. Agrawal, "Energy efficient protocols for wireless systems," *Proc. IEEE PIMRC 1998*, vol. 2, pp. 564–569, Sept. 1998.
2. BitTorrent, http://bitconjurer.org/BitTorrent/, 2004.
3. S. Doshi, S. Bhandare and T. X Brown, "An On-demand minimum energy routing protocol for a wireless ad hoc network," *ACM SIGMOBILE Mobile Computing and Communications Review*, vol. 6, no. 2, pp 50–66, July 2002.
4. L. M. Feeney and M. Nilsson, "Investigating the energy consumption of a wireless network interface in an ad hoc networking environment," *Proc. IEEE INFOCOM 2001*, vol. 3, pp. 1548–1557, Apr. 2001.
5. T. J. Harrold and A. R. Nix, "Intelligent relaying for future personal communication systems," *Proc. IEE Colloquium on Capacity and Range Enhancement Techniques for the Third Generation Mobile Comm. and Beyond (Ref. No. 2000/003)*, Feb. 2000.
6. H. Holma and A. Toskala, *WCDMA for UMTS: radio access for third generation mobile communications*, John Wiley & Sons, 2002.
7. C. Panasik, "Getting the most from 3G: battery life is key," available from http://www.findarticles.com/p/articles/mi_m0MLY/is_9_3/ai_108331198, 2004.
8. T. S. Rappaport, *Wireless communication, principle and practice*, Prentice Hall, 1996.
9. H. Wu, C. Qiao, S. De and O. Tonguz, "Integrated cellular and ad hoc relaying systems: iCAR," *IEEE Journal on Selected Areas in Comm.*, vol. 19, no. 10, pp. 2105–2115, Oct. 2001.

Developing Energy-Efficient Topologies and Routing for Wireless Sensor Networks

Hui Tian, Hong Shen, and Teruo Matsuzawa

Graduate School of Information Science,
Japan Advanced Institute of Science and Technology,
hui_t@jaist.ac.jp

Abstract. The performance of wireless sensor networks (WSNs) is greatly influenced by their topology. WSNs with patterned topologies can efficiently save energy and achieve long networking lifetime. In this paper, we discuss different patterned topologies for constructing WSNs which can provide the required coverage area and the connectivity of all sensor nodes. We compare different performance measures among all patterned topologies, and find that WSNs in strip-based topology can provide the greatest coverage area with the same number of sensor nodes as used for WSNs in other patterned topologies. Strip-based topology also consumes least energy in the routing protocol of flooding. We show that triangle-based topology can provide the highest reliability among all patterned topologies. We also propose several routing protocols for WSNs in patterned topologies, which are based on different parameters when selecting next-hop neighbor. Our protocols require only local information and work in a simple and effective way to achieve energy efficiency.

Keywords: Wireless sensor networks, topology, routing, energy efficient.

1 Introduction

Due to the wide applications of WSNs and inherent limitations of sensor nodes on power and memory, study on energy-efficient topologies and routing becomes increasingly important for WSNs, especially in the scenarios of emergency treatment, disaster rescue and so on. All issues in WSNs are related to one fundamental and important issue, that is how to keep connected coverage in a WSN with as less power consumption in routing as possible.

The connected-coverage problem is to achieve two goals when deploying sensor nodes: coverage and connectivity [4]. Coverage is to ensure that the entire physical space of interest is within the sensing range of at least one of the active sensors. Connectivity is to ensure that all the sensor nodes can communicate with the base station by either single-hop or multi-hop path. The connected-coverage problem in WSNs can easily be solved if the number of sensor nodes and energy-constraint needn't to be concerned. However, it is not possible to construct a connected-coverage WSN without energy and economy concerns in

H. Jin, D. Reed, and W. Jiang (Eds.): NPC 2005, LNCS 3779, pp. 461–469, 2005.

practice. Energy-constraint, instead, is extremely stringent in WSNs. There-fore, it is significant to study on constructing a connected-coverage WSN while consuming as least energy as possible so as to maximize the networking life-time.

Networking lifetime is defined as the time internal from the start to the time that the WSN can provide satisfactory performance on sensing and transmission. It is directly affected by power consumption in the procedure of sensing, com-munication and data processing. Since all the sensor nodes are battery-powered, it is paramount to develop efficient methods to save energy. The existing work to save energy can be classified into two categories. One is turning off or changing some nodes to sleep mode as proposed in [3,4,10]. The other is minimizing sens-ing range and transmission range while keeping connected coverage as proposed in [5,8].

We address the issue of keeping connected coverage with power efficiency from the topology point of view in the paper. It is unlike existing studies in either connectivity and coverage problems, or in energy-efficiency routing proto-col. WSNs in patterned topologies are assured to provide longer network lifetime than randomly deployed WSNs if both use the same number of sensor nodes. We call these patterned topologies energy efficient topologies. They have many significant applications. For example, node placement in patterned topologies can efficiently save energy and achieve long networking lifetime in some scenar-ios where priori node deployment for WSNs are possible. Such scenarios exist in many applications such as danger alarm and vehicle tracking as we have dis-cussed in [11]. Thus study on energy efficiency topologies can guide to construct WSNs with potentially more energy saving and longer lifetime. It is also worth noting that patterned topologies can also instruct to choose duty-on nodes to keep connected coverage in a WSN and put all other sensor nodes in sleep-ing mode so as to avoid redundant overlapping area, save energy, and thus prolong the networking lifetime [4]. Therefore, in this paper, we study differ-ent patterned topologies for WSNs and compare their performance on different measures.

We also propose several routing protocols for WSNs with patterned topolo-gies and compare their performance by simulation. This work provides a supple-ment to [4] which only address how to save energy by choosing duty-on sensor nodes based on patterned topologies. The routing protocols proposed in this paper requires only local information, which is different from DSAP in [9]. Our routing protocols can achieves energy efficiency and perform in a simple and effective way.

The rest of the paper is organized as follows. In section 2 we present the model of connected-coverage WSNs and highlight the important parameters that affect the performance of WSNs. Section 3 compares different topology patterns and their affections on performance of WSNs. Section 4 proposes several routing protocols and compare their performance by simulation. Section 5 gives the concluding remarks.

2   Modelling Connected-Coverage WSNs

A connected-coverage WSN is defined as a wireless sensor network that can guarantee coverage of all the required region and connectivity among all sensor nodes in the WSN. We assume the region of interest to be 2-dimensional. Assume the area of the region to be A. There are N sensor nodes and one base station placed in the region. Each sensor node deployed in the region can sense any event within the disk with radius r_s centered at the sensor node. Each sensor node can communicate with other sensor nodes whose Euclidean distance between them is no more than r_t, that is, nodes s_1 and s_2 can communicate with each other if their Euclidean distance $Ed(s_1, s_2) \leq r_t$. Otherwise, they cannot. The sensing radius of a sensor node can be either equal or unequal to its communication radius in the WSN.

The sensing ability of each sensor node diminishes as distance increases. In [6], the sensing ability at point y of sensor node s_i is assumed to be inversely proportional to $Ed(s_i, y)^k$ where k is a sensor technology-dependent parameter. This characteristic of sensor nodes introduces an important parameter, we call it sensing strength factor d_{mm}, stating how well region A is covered and sensed. If we define $min_i Ed(s_i, y)$ as the distance of point y to its closest sensor node, $y \in A$, then all points in A have a distance at most $max_{y \in A} min_i Ed(s_i, y)$. We use d_{mm} to denote this distance:

$$d_{mm} = max_{y \in A} min_i Ed(s_i, y).$$

Thus d_{mm} is the maximum distance from any point to its closest sensor node. Usually a WSN is required to be deployed with a particular sensing strength factor equal to d_{mm} so that distance from any point to its closest sensor node is no more than d_{mm} to ensure coverage and sensing strength. The less d_{mm} is, the better each point is sensed in the WSN. In [2] and [7], similar parameters can be found, but they were proposed for other applications.

The power consumption is another important parameter to measure how much energy different topology patterns can save for WSNs. Since each sensor node usually includes a sensing unit, a processing unit, a transceiver unit and a power unit as modelled in [1], power consumption can be divided into three domains: sensing, communication, and data processing. Of the three domains, we are only concerned with the maximum energy spent by a sensor node in data communication. This involves both power consumed in data transmission, denoted by P_t, and in data reception, denoted by P_r. That is, the power consumed by a sensor node is $P_s = P_t + P_r$.

3   Patterned Topologies for Connected-Coverage WSNs

As we have discussed in in [11], sensor nodes can be placed in hexagon, square, and triangle-based topologies. In [4] strip-based topology has also been proposed to place nodes to construct a connected-coverage topology for WSNs. We will discuss all these topology patterns in this section and compare the performance of WSNs in different patterns. The case that the sensing range of a sensor node equals to its transmission range is discussed in the comparison part.

3.1 WSNs with Hexagon-Based Topology

In hexagon-based WSNs, each sensor node has three neighbor nodes located uniquely around the node. Connecting all sensor nodes to their neighbor nodes obtains the minimum unit in the shape of hexagon. Thus the WSN in this topology pattern is called the hexagon-based WSN. The distances of the node to its neighbor nodes are all set to r_t so that direct communication is available between the node and its neighbor nodes, and each neighbor provides maximal additional sensing area [11]. Figure 1 specifies a WSN with hexagon-based topology. To compare it with other WSNs with different topologies, we place the same number of sensor nodes (25) for all WSNs. We assume node 06 to be the aggregation node which plays the role of aggregating the sensed information in the WSN and reporting to the base station.

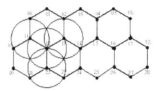

Fig. 1. A WSN with hexagon-based topology

3.2 WSNs with Square-Based Topology

In square-based WSNs, each sensor node has four neighbor nodes located uniquely around the node. Connecting all sensor nodes to their neighbor nodes obtains the minimum unit in the shape of square. Thus the WSN in this topology pattern is called the square-based WSN. The distances of the node to its neighbor nodes are set to r_t. A WSN composed of 25 sensor nodes is given in Figure 2. Node 04 is assumed to be the aggregation node.

3.3 WSNs with Triangle-Based Topology

In triangle-based WSNs, each sensor node has six neighbor nodes located uniquely around the node. Connecting all sensor nodes to their neighbor nodes obtains the minimum unit in shape of triangle. Thus the WSN in this topology pattern is called the triangle-based WSN. Same as above, the distances of the node to its neighbor nodes are set to r_t. Figure 3 is a triangle-based WSN with 25 sensor nodes deployed. Node 04 is assumed to be the aggregation node.

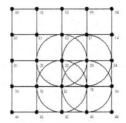

Fig. 2. A WSN with square-based topology

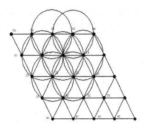

Fig. 3. A WSN with triangle-based topology

In WSNs with triangle-based topology, we find that every point within the area is covered by at least two sensor nodes. We call the reliability provided by such kind of node placement 2-reliability. A 2-reliability WSN can maintain its connected-coverage for any single sensor node failure. When every point is covered by at least k sensor nodes, the sensor network is called k-reliability. The WSNs with other patterned topologies are 1-reliability as discussed in [11].

3.4 WSNs with Strip-Based Topology

To keep the connectivity of two sensor nodes, their distance should be no more than r_t. To maximize the coverage area sensed by the same number of sensor nodes, [4] proposes a strip-based topology as in Figure 4.

The strip-based WSN in Figure 4 clearly shows that sensor nodes 40, 41 and 42 connect 4 self-connected strips $00 - 05$, $10 - 14$, $20 - 25$ and $30 - 34$. By this way of node placement, these sensor nodes construct a connected WSN with strip-based topology. The total number of sensor nodes is 25 as before. We assume node 05 to be the aggregation node.

3.5 Performance Comparison

Given the same number of sensor nodes, we compare the above four types of patterned topologies on coverage area, sensing strength factor, reliability and energy consumption. We assume $r_t = r_s = r$ in all WSNs. For coverage area

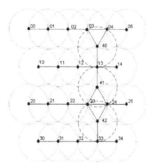

Fig. 4. A WSN with strip-based topology

Topology pattern	Coverage area by 25 sensor nodes A	Sensing strength factor d_{mm}	Reliability	Energy consumption by flooding Ps
Hexagon-based topology	$32.48\ r^2$	r	1	$24P_t+60P_r$
Square-based topology	$25\ r^2$	$0.71\ r$	1	$24P_t+78P_r$
Triangle-based topology	$21.65\ r^2$	$0.58\ r$	2	$24P_t+110P_r$
Strip-based topology	$46.65\ r^2$	r	1	$24P_t+53P_r$

Fig. 5. Performance comparison among WSNs with different patterned topologies

comparison, we do not consider the marginal places covered by edge sensor nodes because the marginal area exists only in a few places and occupies a negligible portion of the whole coverage area of the WSN which often includes a huge number of sensor nodes. For energy consumption comparison, we fix the destination to be the aggregation node as designated above. The source is fixed to be a node with distance $4r$ from the destination. In this case, the less the energy is consumed, the better the node placement pattern is. The table in Figure 5 gives the results of these performances comparison.

From the table in Figure 5, we can see that strip-based topology provides maximal connected-coverage with the same number of sensor nodes and consumes least energy by the routing protocol of flooding. WSNs in triangle-based topology provide the best reliability and the best sensing strength while trading off total coverage area and energy consumption. These conclusions hold when comparison is performed in general cases of large-scale WSNs.

4   Routing Protocols in Patterned WSNs

We propose several routing protocols in this section. Different from Directional Source-Aware Protocol (DSAP) [9] where each node must have the knowledge

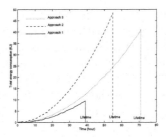

Fig. 6. Energy consumption and lifetime comparison among three approaches

of global information of topology, our routing protocols only require local information.

We define a routing selection function $f(h, s)$ for a sensor node to choose neighbor nodes when routing the message back to the aggregation node. The function is determined by the hop count value h of neighbor nodes and stream unit s which has been sent by neighbor nodes. Here we assume the stream sent by a sensor node can be measured by stream unit, thus s means how many units have been sent by the sensor node. We denote the battery life of sensor node i by b_i.

We propose three approaches to route back the message for different aims. All of them are based on the routing selection function $f(h, s) = \alpha h + \beta s$.

1. Maximize the total energy saving for WSNs, i.e., $B = \sum_i b_i$: This can be obtained by minimizing first the hop count value h when choosing next-hop neighbor and then minimize s. In this case, $\alpha = 1$, and $\beta = \sigma$, where σ is a small number which approximates to 0.

2. Maximize the minimal energy maintained by all sensor nodes, i.e., $min_i b_i$: This can be obtained by minimizing first the stream units s of next-hop neighbor and then h. In this case, $\alpha = \sigma$, and $\beta = 1$.

3. Maximize both the total energy and minimal energy of all sensor nodes: This can be obtained by minimizing both h and s. In this case, $\alpha = \beta = 1$.

We name the protocols as routing selection function-based protocols. It works as follows:

1. Distance identification: The aggregation node floods the discovery message in the WSN with a determined TTL value. Each sensor node records its distance from the aggregation node by hop count. If a sensor node receives several broadcast messages, it records the least value of hop count.

2. Data collection: When a sensor node senses any abnormal event and needs to report the event, it chooses a neighbor with minimized $f(h, s)$ to route back the message.

To compare the performance of our protocols, we simulate the square-based WSN with the routing protocol for simplicity. We use OPNET as the simulation environment. We assume the networking lifetime is from the start to the time that any node exhausts its power in the WSN since one node failure results in an unconnected coverage for WSNs with square-based topology.

From Figure 6, we can see that Approach 1 provides least network lifetime. Approach 2 gets a longer lifetime than approach 1 and, however, trades off much more energy consumption by choosing a longer path to the aggregation node in the WSN. Approach 3 can provide the longest lifetime, which is almost as twice as that provided by Approach 1 because it tries to find a shorter path and a next-hop neighbor with more energy in every step.

5   Conclusion

We discussed different patterned topologies for WSNs in this paper. It is found that strip-based topology provides the maximal connected coverage and consumes the least energy by flooding protocol, whereas triangle-based topology reaches the best coverage performance with a higher reliability and greater sensing strength. In WSNs with patterned topology, we proposed several routing protocols which achieve different goals. The simulation showed that the networking lifetime is maximized by selecting routing based on both hop count and stream unit of next-hop neighbor. Thus, patterned WSNs equipped with their protocols provide great promises and guarantees their potential applications to meet different needs. Our routing protocols may also be extended to WSNs without regular topologies, which will be explored in our future study.

Acknowledgement

This research is conducted as a program for the "21st Century COE Program" by Ministry of Education, Culture, Sports, Science and Technology.

References

1. I.F. Akyildiz and W. Su, Y. Sankarasubramaniam and E. Cayirci, Wireless Sensor Networks: A Survey, Computer Networks, Vol. 38(4), pp.393–422, 2002.
2. Edoardo S. Biagioni and Galen Sasaki, Wireless Sensor Placement For Reliable and Efficient Data Collection, Proc. of the 36th Hawaii International Conference on System Sciences (HICSS), 2003.
3. Alberto Cerpa and Deborah Estrin, ASCENT: Adaptive Self-Configuring sEnsor Networks Topologies, Proc. of INFOCOM, 2002.
4. Koushik Kar and Suman Banerjee, Node Placement for Connected Coverage in Sensor Networks, Proc. of WiOpt, 2003.
5. Martin Kubisch and Holger Karl and Adam Wolisz and Lizhi Charlie Zhong andJan Rabaey, Distributed Algorithms for Transmission Power Control in Wireless Sensor Networks, Proc. of IEEE Wireless Communicationsand Networking Conference (WCNC), 2003.
6. Xiang-Yang Li and Peng-Jun Wan and Ophir Frieder, Coverage in Wireless Ad-hoc Sensor Networks, Proc. of IEEE ICC, 2002.

7. Seapahn Meguerdichian and Farinaz Koushanfar and Miodrag Potkonjak and Mani B. Srivastava, Coverage Problems in Wireless Ad-hoc Sensor Networks, Proc. of IEEE INFOCOM, 2001.
8. Jianping Pan and Y. Thomas Hou and Lin Cai and Yi Shi and Sherman X. Shen, Topology Control for Wireless Sensor Networks, Proc. of MobiCom, 2003.
9. Ayad Salhieh and Jennifer Weinmann and Manish Kochhal and Loren Schwiebert, Power Efficient Topologies for Wireless Sensor Networks, Proc. of Int'l Conf. on Parrallel Processing, 2001.
10. Di Tian and Nicolas D. Georgannas, A Coverage-Preserving Node Scheduling Scheme for Large Wireless Sensor Networks, Proc. of ACM Int'l Workshop on Wireless Sensor Networks and Applications(WSNA), 2002.
11. Hui Tian and Hong Shen, An optimal coverage scheme for wireless sensor network, Proc. of 2005 IEEE International Conference on Networks (ICN'05), Reunion Island, France, April 2005, pp. 722-730.

The Efficient Transmission Scheme in Wireless Crypto Communication

Jinkeun Hong[1] and Kihong Kim[2]

[1] Division of Information and Communication, Cheonan University,
115 Anse-dong, Cheonan-si, Chungnam 330-740, South Korea
jkhong@cheonan.ac.kr
[2] Graduate School of Information Security, Korea University,
1, 5-Ka, Anam-dong, Sungbuk-ku, Seoul 136-701, South Korea
hong0612@hanmir.com

Abstract. An efficient interleaving algorithm is applied to reduce the loss of ciphered information when a cipher system transmits over a wireless fading channel environment. As such, a new scheme for deciding the interleaving depth over a wireless environment is described. Simulations confirm that the proposed effective algorithm with a variable interleaving depth produces a better performance over a fading channel than a static depth algorithm with a fixed interleaving depth. Experimental results showed that the BER performance of the proposed efficient interleaving scheme was higher than that of the fixed interleaving depth scheme. Of particular note is that the dynamic allocation algorithm (DAA) reduces degraded error bits by up to 51.5%, compared with static allocation algorithm (SAA) of depth 48 in 224MHz.

1 Introduction

Aviation industries are undergoing a major paradigm shift in the introduction of new network technologies [1, 2, 3]. Tactical information LINK22 is a NATO term for a message standard that includes an anti-jam, secure data system with standard waveforms and messages used for exchanging tactical information between different military platforms, thereby providing a common communications network to a large community of airborne, surface, and even subsurface or space elements [4, 5, 6, 7, 8]. In previous studies about tactical networks, performance of high rate LINK22 operation obtained by using quadrature amplitude modulation presented by R. Le Fever, et al. [4], and B. White [5] presented layered communication architecture for the global grid, while B. F. Donal [6] introduced digital messaging on the Comanche helicopter, the area of tactical data links, air traffic management, and software programmable radios has been researched by B. E. White [7]. As the coordination concept of ADS-B civil network and tactical networks becomes more widespread, the necessity of security for these networks is of increasing importance [8, 9, 10].

However, in order to solve security issues in secure tactical networks, the efficiency and transmission performance of security services must be taken into

H. Jin, D. Reed, and W. Jiang (Eds.): NPC 2005, LNCS 3779, pp. 470–477, 2005.

account. From the point of view of aeronautical environmental characteristics, research on optimizing the security considerations of tactical network services, such as low bandwidth, limited consumed power energy and memory processing capacity, and cryptography restrictions is important issue. A cipher system using a link-by-link encryption technique is generally used for security. Except for error propagation, the security level is reflected by the period, common immunity, and linear complexity and since these properties are easy to implement in terms of hardware and do not create any communication channel delays, a cipher system is usually applied to wireless communications. However, when enciphered data is transmitted on a wireless channel, poor communication channel environments, multi-path fading, and interference result in a burst of errors at the decipher output. The fading received at the mobile unit is caused by multi-path reflections of the transmitted encrypted information by local scatters, such as forests, buildings, and other human-built structures, or natural obstacles such as forests surrounding a mobile unit [11, 12, 13]. Interleaving is one practical solution for combating burst errors, where a poor encryption communication channel resulting from a burst of errors can be enhanced using an interleaving scheme, and the transmission performance over a wireless channel and radio communication channel has already been evaluated when using an interleaving method in [14, 15, 16, 17]. About the area of interleaving research, X. Gui, et al. [14] proposed a novel chip interleaving in DS SS system, and the subject of multiple access over fading multi-path channels employing chip interleaving code division direct sequence spread spectrum has researched by Y. N. Link, et al. [15], the research of required interleaving depth in Rayleigh fading channels has been proposed by I. C. King, et al. [16]. And also, in terms of transmission performance, the performance considerations for secure tactical networks, such as mobility, bandwidth, and BER, are very important. This paper presents a cipher system for security in LINK22, plus an effective interleaving scheme is applied to the ciphered information to enhance the transmission performance over a fading channel.

Section 2 reviews the nature of a fading channel and provides statistical expressions for burst error sequences, then section 3 outlines the cipher system with synchronization information. Thereafter, interleaving scheme based on a variable depth of interleaving using a non fixed interleaving depth allocation algorithm is explained and simulation results presented in section 4. Finally, section 5 summarizes the results of this study.

2   Characteristics of Wireless Mobile Environment

Wireless fading channel modeling is used to perform a statistical analysis based on defining the relational functions, such as the probability density function (PDF), cumulative probability distribution (CPD), level crossing rate (LCR), average duration of fades (ADF), and bit error rate (BER). The mean burst length is derived from the defined relational functions and experiments are used to consider the interleaving depth based on the mean burst length.

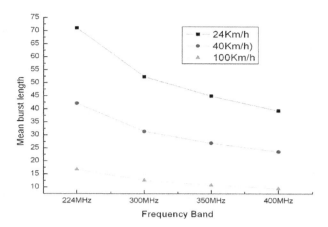

Fig. 1. Mean burst length for variation of power in tactical data link environment

In the above equation ρ is the C/N ratio and K is the power ratio of the direct wave and reflected waves. The equation of $CPD(F(L))$ for Rician fading is used as follows :

$$BER(\rho, K) = \frac{1 + K}{2(\rho + 1 + K)} exp(\frac{-K\rho}{\rho + 1 + K}) \tag{1}$$

In a Rician fading channel, the symbol error rate (SER) is applied in Eq. (1).

$$SER(\rho, K) = 1 - (1 - BER)^8 \tag{2}$$

It can be derived mean burst length as in Fig. 1 [11,12,13]. Where frequency range is from 224MHz to 400MHz, the variation of power deviations is down to -25dB, and the velocity of mobile device is 24Km/h.

3   Secure Wireless Cipher System

This paper presents a secure cipher system. Plus, interleaving scheme is also applied to the ciphered information to enhance the transmission performance over a fading channel. To provide robust encrypted communication, the transmitter and receiver are both synchronized using a synchronization pattern. If the received synchronization pattern is detected normally, the error-corrected coded session key bit-stream is received and the ciphered data is deciphered. The LINK22 system consists of the data link processor (DLP) for presentation layer, the system network controller (SNC) for transport and network layer, link level COMSEC (LLC) and signal processing controller for data link. The service of SPC in data link supports point to point link oriented. The data rate of SPC are 16Kbps in fixed frequency mode of UHF. The Reed-Solomon code scheme(such as RS(90,66), RS(90,75), according to the number of message per slot) is applied signal processing controller (SPC) of data link layer.

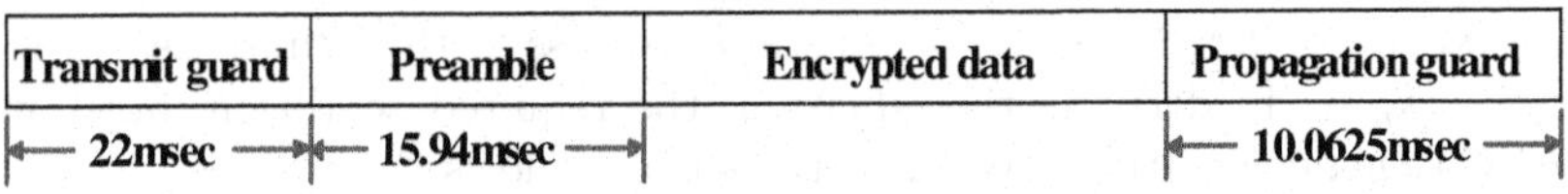

Transmit guard	Preamble	Encrypted data	Propagation guard
←— 22msec —→	←— 15.94msec —→		←— 10.0625msec —→

Fig. 2. TDMA time slot architecture of LINK22 tactical data link

The key-stream generator was designed considering the security level [18,19], i.e. the linear complexity, randomness, common immunity, period, and composition of a nonlinear function. In Fig. 2, the transmit guard part is assigned during 22msec, the preamble is 15.94msec, and propagation guard is 10.0625msec The propagation/guard interval is the time period that allows for the propagation of the signal to the maximum range and time required for the NUs to prepare for the transmissions in the next time slot. In encrypted region, the allowed latency time of maximum encryption and decrytion is between 12.1msec and 15.8msec. The encrypted date rate in link layer COMSEC of LINK22 is between 4.8Kbps and 115.2Kbps.

4   Performance of DAA and Experimental Results

When ciphered information is transmitted over a Rician fading channel in which the received signal level is time variant, some of the ciphered information is lost due to burst errors, resulting a loss of the synchronization pattern and error in the session key in a period of synchronization. Interleaving is an effective way of randomizing burst errors, plus, burst errors can not be corrected without the application of interleaving and deinterleaving. The function of the received power (nL) at $K = 0$ can be expressed as follows :

$$
\begin{pmatrix} n_{L_0} \\ \vdots \\ n_{L_{n-1}} \end{pmatrix} = \begin{pmatrix} L_0 e^{-L_0} \\ \vdots \\ L_{n-1} e^{-L_{n-1}} \end{pmatrix}
\tag{3}
$$

The ADF, $t(L)$ can be expressed as follows :

$$
\begin{pmatrix} t(L_0) \\ \vdots \\ t(L_{n-1}) \end{pmatrix} = \begin{pmatrix} \frac{F(L_0)}{n_0} \\ \vdots \\ \frac{F(L_{n-1})}{n_0} \end{pmatrix}
\tag{4}
$$

Therefore, the relationship between the mean burst length (mbl), the transmission rate (B), and the average duration of fades $(t(L))$ can be expressed as follows :

$$
\begin{pmatrix} mbl_0 \\ \vdots \\ mbl_{n-1} \end{pmatrix} = \begin{pmatrix} B \times t(L_0) \\ \vdots \\ B \times t(L_{n-1}) \end{pmatrix}
\tag{5}
$$

Let $k_n, n = 0, 1, 2, \cdots$, be a constant process with a finite set of states $k_0, k_1, \cdots, k_{n-1}$. In deriving the equation, the required condition under which the FEC scheme can still correct all errors is as follows :

$$\begin{pmatrix} k_0 \\ \vdots \\ k_{n-1} \end{pmatrix} = \begin{pmatrix} mbl_0 \\ \vdots \\ mbl_{n-1} \end{pmatrix} \times \begin{pmatrix} d_0 \\ \vdots \\ d_{n-1} \end{pmatrix} \qquad (6)$$

These interleaving schemes were evaluated in a simulation environment where the wireless channel is a Rician fading channel, the date rate was 16Kbps, the frame size is 14.4Kbits, the communication access time was 60minutes, the SER was 7.9×10^{-4}, the data rate of LLC was between 4.8Kbps and 115.2Kbps, the moving velocity was 24Km/h, and the carrier frequency applied was from 244MHz to 400MHz. The performance of the DAA and SAA interleaving depth algorithms was then evaluated though simulations. Since the structure of interleaving basically depends on the interleaving depth (d), four types of DAA structure were used: $depth(d) \times span(S) = 4 \times 1200, 8 \times 1200, 12 \times 1200, 24 \times 1200, 48 \times 1200, 96 \times 1200$. When the depth is 12, the delay time is consumed about 1sec. As the depth increase, the delayed time increase. But as transmission rate of SPC is fixed and date rate of LLC increase, the delayed time decrease. However, it is difficult to adapt the depth of interleaving in a variational fading channel, plus, the required depth should be sufficient to handle the resulting errors in the SAA. Therefore, to adapt the depth of interleaving in the variational fading channel, the flexible DAA method was applied.

In condition of No RS coding and RS(120,75) coding with SER of 7.9×10^{-4} channel, the resulting performance of the SAA is shown in Fig. 3 and Fig. 4, respectively. When the transmission rate was 16Kbps, the date rate of LLC was 14.4Kbps, the SER was 7.9×10^{-4}, the iteration was 48, the depth of the SAA

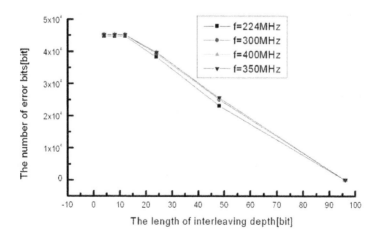

Fig. 3. Error bits relative to depth of SAA (SER : 7.9×10^{-4}, No RS coding)

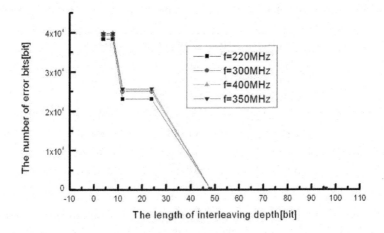

Fig. 4. Error bits relative to depth of SAA (SER : 7.9×10^{-4}, RS(120,75))

was 24, as shown in Fig. 3, the error bits of the deciphered data without RS coding were degraded 17% at a SAA depth of 8. In condition of transmission condition with RS(120,75) coding, the depth of the SAA was 24, the error bits of the deciphered were degraded 65% at a SAA depth of 8. Of particular note is that the RS(120, 75) coding reduces degraded error bits by up to 65.9%, compared with No RS coding at SAA depth of 24 in 224MHz environment. When the depth of the DAA was 12, 24, 48, 96, as shown in Table 1, the performance of the DAA block interleaving was better than that of the others. The corrected symbol rate in the DAA applied is higher than that of the other types ($depth = 4, 8, 12, 24, 48, 96$).

At a SAA depth of 24, the corrected symbol rate was corrected 14.5%, 48.5% at a SAA depth of 48, 100% at a SAA depth of 96, in severe channel without RS coding of 224MHz environment. Meanwhile, Table 2 presents a comparison of DAA and SAA with 55 iterations. When the delayed time when using DAA was about 3,095sec, however, the delayed time by the SAA depth of 24 was about 1,738sec, the SAA depth of 48 was 3,476sec, the SAA depth of 96 was 6,952sec. Therefore, when increasing the depth, the corrected symbol rate and delayed time were enhanced. With regard to the delayed time and corrected symbol rate, the performance of the proposed method was superior to that of

Table 1. Comparison of delayed time relative to depth of SAA

Trans. rate (Kbps)		Depth=4	Depth=8	Depth=12	Depth=24	Depth=48	Depth=96
SPC=16	LLC=14.4	0.25sec	0.5sec	1sec	2sec	4sec	8sec
	LLC=28.8	0.125sec	0.25sec	0.5sec	1sec	2sec	4sec
	LLC=57.6	0.0625sec	0.125sec	0.25sec	0.5sec	1sec	2sec
	LLC=115.2	0.03125sec	0.0625sec	0.125sec	0.25sec	0.5sec	1sec

Table 2. Comparison of DAA and SAA with 55 iterations (SER : 7.9×10^{-4}, 28.8Kbps)

Depth	Corrected Symbol Rate	Delay
DAA	100%	3,095sec
Depth = 4	1.0%	217sec
Depth = 8	2.3%	434sec
Depth = 12	5.4%	8,695sec
Depth = 24	14.5%	1,738sec
Depth = 48	48.5%	3,476sec
Depth = 96	100%	6,952sec

SAA when applied to allow the delayed time of DAA. Consequently, the results of the transmission performance when using the DAA and SAA confirmed that the performance of the proposed DAA method was better for the case of signal recovery in an erasure channel.

5   Conclusions

This paper examines a cipher system for security in tactical network, plus an interleaving scheme is applied to the ciphered information to enhance the transmission performance over a fading channel. As such, a frame of ciphered information is lost if the synchronization pattern and session key for the frame are lost. Therefore, applying an interleaving method to reduce the frame loss and thereby enhance the transmission performance would seem to be an effective option that can be evaluated using the non fixed interleaving depth scheme. A cipher system was proposed using an effective interleaving scheme for the interleaving depth to enhance the transmission performance of the ciphered information.

Experimental results showed that the SER performance of the proposed efficient interleaving scheme was higher than that of the fixed interleaving depth scheme. Of particular note is that the DAA reduces degraded error bits by up to 51.5%, compared with SAA of depth 48 in 224MHz.

References

1. T. Mulkerin. Free Flight Is in the Future : Large-Scale Controller Pilot Data Link Communications Emulation Testbed. *IEEE Aerospace and Electronic Systems Magazine*, 2003.
2. R. T. Oishi. Future Applications and the Aeronautical Telecommunication Network. *IEEE Aerospace Conference*, 2001.
3. EUROCONTROL. Feasibility Study for Civil Aviation Data Link for ADS-B Based on MIDS/LINK 16. *TRS/157/02*, 2000.
4. R. Le Fever and R. C. Harper. Performance of High Rate LINK22 Operation Obtained by Quadrature Amplitude Modulation (QAM). *IEEE Milcom'01*, 2001.

5. B. E. White. Layered Communication Architecture for the Global Grid. *IEEE Milcom'01*, 2001.
6. B. F. Donald. Digital Messaging on the Comanche Helicopter. *DASC'00*, 2000.
7. B. E. White. Tactical Data Links, Air Traffic Management, and Software Programmable Radios. *DASC'99*, 1999.
8. H. J. Beker and F. C. Piper. *Cipher Systems : The Protection of Communicstions*, Northwood Books, Londos, 1982.
9. Bruce Schneier. *Applied Cryptography*, 2nd ed., John Wiley and Sons Inc., 1996.
10. A. R. Rainer. Analysis and Design of Stream Ciphers. *Springer-Verlag*, 1986.
11. W. C. Y. Lee *Mobile Cellular Telecommunications : Analog and Digital Systems*, 2nd ed., McGraw-Hill, 1996.
12. C. Y. William. *Mobile Communications Engineering*, McGraw-Hill, 1982.
13. C. Y. William. *Mobile Communications Design Fundamentals*, John Willey & Sons, 1993.
14. X. Gui and T. S. Ng. A novel Chip Interleaving DS SS System. *IEEE Trans. Veh. Technol.*, Vol.49, No.1, pp.21-27, 2000.
15. Y. N. Link and D. W. Lin. Multiple Access Over Fading Multi-Path Channels Employing Chip Interleaving Code Division Direct Sequence Spread Spectrum. *IEICE Trans. Commun.*, 2001.
16. I. C. King and C-I C. Justin. Required Interleaving Depth in Rayleigh Fading Channels. *Globecom'96*, 1996.
17. S. J. L. et al. Effective Interleaving Method in Wireless ATM Networks. *ICT'97*, 1997.
18. M. Kimberley. Comparison of Two Statistical Tests for Key-Stream Sequences. *Electronics Letters*, Vol.23, No.8, pp.365-366, 1987.
19. M. G. Helen. Statistical Analysis of Symmetric Ciphers *Thesis submitted in accordance with the regulations for Degree of Doctor of Philosophy, Queensland University of Technology*, 1986.

Constructing k-Connected k-Cover Set in Wireless Sensor Networks Based on Self-pruning*

Jie Jiang, Minghua Han, Guofu Wu, and Wenhua Dou

School of Computer Science,
National University of Defense Technology,
410073, Changsha, China
jiangjie@nudt.edu.cn

Abstract. Density control is a promising approach to conserving system energy and extending lifetime of wireless sensor networks. Most of previous work in this field has focused on selecting a minimal subset of active sensor nodes for high efficiency while guaranteeing only 1-coverage (or plus 1-connectivity of the network). In this paper, we address the issue of constructing a k-connected k-cover set of a wireless sensor network for fault tolerance and balance efficiency. We propose a distributed, localized algorithm based on self-pruning for selecting active sensor nodes to form a k-connected k-cover set for the target region. The performance of the proposed algorithm is evaluated through numerical experiments.

1 Introduction

Because of advances in micro-sensors, wireless networking and embedded processing, wireless sensor networks (WSN) are becoming increasingly available for commercial and military applications, such as environmental monitoring, chemical attack detection, and battlefield surveillance, etc [1,2,3].

Energy is the most precious resource in wireless sensor networks due to the following factors. First, the sensor nodes are usually supported by batteries with limited capacity due to the extremely small dimensions. Second, it is usually hard to replace or recharge the batteries after deployment, either because the number of sensor nodes is very large or the deployment environment is hostile and dangerous (e.g. remote desert or battlefield). But on the other hand, the sensor networks are usually expected to operate several months or years once deployed. Therefore reducing energy consumption and extending network lifetime is one of the most critical challenges in the design of wireless sensor networks.

One promising approach to reducing energy consumption is density control, which only keeps a subset of sensors active and puts other sensors into low-powered sleep status. Most of previous researches on density control focus on

---

* This work is supported by the National Natural Science Foundation of China under grant number 90104001.

H. Jin, D. Reed, and W. Jiang (Eds.): NPC 2005, LNCS 3779, pp. 478–486, 2005.

only sensing coverage [4,5,6,7,8,12]. If a sensor node's sensing area is completely included by its neighbors' sensing coverage, it is redundant and can be turned off safely. These papers don't consider the impact of coverage-scheduling on network connectivity. Some other researches [9,10,11] consider the coverage and connectivity requirement at the same time. That is, every point in the target region must be covered by at least one active sensor and the communication graph induced by active sensors must be connected. But only 1-coverage and 1-vertex connectivity can be guaranteed.

The k-coverage and k-connectivity properties are desirable in some critical applications. k-coverage and k-connectivity can enhance the robustness and fault-tolerance of the sensor network. Even if $k-1$ sensor nodes fail due to accidental damage or energy depletion, the target region is still completely covered and the communication network is still connected. Therefore the network can survive the failure of at most $k-1$ sensor nodes. And the k-coverage can improve the sensing accuracy. As the sensing function is often interfered with by noise signals, the sensing accuracy can be improved when each point is covered at least by k sensor nodes.When different sensor nodes report the sensed data back to the sink along different routes, the loss of event can be avoided. And in localization applications, the location of a target will be more accurate when it is detected by many sensors from different bearings. Also the k-connectivity can provide more routing flexibility, which is helpful to realize the load balancing of data traffic among sensor nodes.

The major contributions of this paper are as follows. First, we propose a general framework based on self-pruning to construct a k-connected k-cover set. The degree of coverage and connectivity can be flexibly specified in this framework according to application requirements and different algorithms that detect k-connectivity or k-coverage redundancy in a distributed, localized manner can be integrated into the proposed framework. Second, we propose a distributed, localized algorithm to detect whether a sensor node is k-coverage redundant based on order-k Voronoi diagram.

The rest of this paper is organized as follows. The problem addressed in this paper is formulated in section 2. And a general framework and distributed, localized algorithms are proposed in section 3. We present the experimental results in section 4 and end with conclusion remarks in section 5.

2   Problem Formulation

A point p is covered by a sensor node s_i if the distance between p and s_i is not larger than R_s, i.e., $d(s_i, p) \leq R_s$. A point p is k-covered if it is covered by k distinct active sensor nodes. An area R is completely k-covered by a sensor network if every point in R is k-covered by sensor nodes in the networks. Using omni-direction antenna, a sensor node s_i's communication range is a circle centered at s_i with radius R_c. Sensor nodes within s_i's communication rage are called s_i's communication neighbors, which s_i can directly communicate with.

Definition 1. *(communication graph/path) Given a sensor network consisting of a set of sensor nodes, $S = \{s_1, s_2, \ldots, s_n\}$, the communication graph of the sensor network $G_c = (V_c, E_c)$ is an undirected graph, where $V_c = S$ and $e_{ij} = (s_i, s_j) \in E_c$ if $d(s_i, s_j) \leq R_c$. We say that the communication graph G_c is induced by S. A communication subgraph induced by a subset of sensor nodes $S' \subseteq S$ is the subgraph of G_c which only involves sensor nodes in S'. A communication path in the communication graph is a sequence of sensors where any two sequential sensors are communication neighbors. A communication graph G_c is connected if there is a communication path between any two vertices of G_c.*

Definition 2. *(k-connected k-cover set) Consider a sensor network consisting of a set of sensor nodes $S = \{s_1, s_2, \ldots, s_n\}$ deployed in a target region R. A subset of sensors $S' \subseteq S$ is said to be a k-connected k-cover set for R if:*

(1) R is completely k-covered by S', that is, every point in R is covered by at least k distinct sensor nodes in S'.
(2) The communication graph induced by S' is k-vertex connected.

Minimal k-Connected k-Cover Set (MKCC) Problem: Given a sensor network consisting of a set of sensor nodes S deployed in a target region R, where S is a k-connected k-cover set for R when all sensor nodes are active. The minimal k-Connected k-Cover Set problem is to find a k-connected k-cover subset $S' \subseteq S$ with the minimal cardinality.

The **MKCC** problem is $\mathcal{NP}$-hard as it is a generalization of the minimal 1-connected 1-coverage problem, which is already known to be $\mathcal{NP}$-hard [9].

3   Distributed and Localized Algorithm Based on Self-pruning

3.1   Basic Framework

The distributed, localized self-pruning algorithm is based on the following idea. A sensor node s_i can be safely turned off if its removal will not destroy the k-coverage and k-connectivity properties of the network. That is, the remaining sensor nodes after removing s_i from the sensor network still form a k-connected k-cover set for the target region. Sensor node s_i is not needed for k-connectivity if every pair of its one-hop neighbors has k alternate replacement communication paths not involving s_i. And sensor node s_i is not needed for k-coverage if each point in its coverage area is covered by at least k other sensors. When a sensor node satisfies both the above two conditions simultaneously, its removal will still preserve the k-connectivity and k-coverage characteristics of the sensor network. When several nodes rely on each other to satisfy the above two conditions, node priorities are used to resolve the cyclic dependency. And to limit the communication overhead in a reasonable level, each node makes its own decision based on neighborhood information only within l communication hops, where l is a small integer (about 2 or 3). Although the partial neighborhood information may generate incomplete communication graph and incorrect Voronoi diagram and thus cause more sensors than optimal to be active, the properties of k-connectivity and k-coverage are still guaranteed.

In this framework, the required connectivity degree and coverage level can be specified separately and arbitrarily according to application requirements. And also any algorithm for detecting k-connectivity redundancy and k-coverage redundancy in a distributed and localized manner can be integrated into this framework.

3.2   Algorithm Description

A. k-Connectivity Redundant Condition

A sensor node s_i is not needed for preserving the k-connectivity property of the sensor network S if it is k-connectivity redundant. We denote the set of remaining sensors after removing s_i from S by $S\backslash s_i$.

Definition 3. *(k-connectivity redundant)   A sensor node s_i is k-connectivity redundant if the communication graph induced by $S\backslash s_i$ is still k-connected.*

k-**Connectivity Redundant Condition:** A sensor node s_i is k-connectivity redundant if for any two one-hop neighbors s_n and s_m of s_i, there are k node disjoint replacement paths connecting s_n and s_m via several intermediate nodes in $N_l(i)$ (if any) with lower priority than s_i, where $N_l(i)$ is node s_i's l-hop communication neighbors.

The node priority can be any combination of the remaining energy, node id, and random numbers. The only requirement is that the priority should be able to set up a total order among all sensor nodes so as to resolve the cyclic dependent relationship among neighbors. In paper [13], Wu et al. use a similar condition to construct a k-CDS for MANET.

B. k-Coverage Redundant Condition

A sensor node s_i is not needed for preserving the k-coverage property of the target region if it is k-coverage redundant.

Definition 4. *(k-coverage redundant) A sensor node s_i is k-coverage redundant if the target region is still completely k-covered by $S\backslash s_i$.*

The k-coverage redundancy of sensor node s_i is detected by utilizing the order-k Voronoi diagram.

Definition 5. *(order-k Voronoi diagram [14])   Given a set of distinct generator sites $P = \{p_1, p_2, \ldots, p_n\}$ in the 2D plane $\mathbb{R}^2$. The order-k Voronoi region associated with a subset $P_i^k = \{p_{i1}, p_{i2}, \ldots, p_{ik}\} \subset P$ is defined as:*

$$V\left(P_i^k\right) = \left\{ q \in \mathbb{R}^2 \mid \max_{p_h}\left\{ d\left(q, p_h\right) \mid p_h \in P_i^k\right\} \leq \min_{p_j}\left\{ d\left(q, p_j\right) \mid p_j \in P\backslash P_i^k\right\}\right\}.$$

The set of order-k Voronoi regions, $V^{(k)} = \left\{ V_1^{(k)}, V_2^{(k)}, \ldots\right\}$, is called the order-$k$ Voronoi diagram of $\mathbb{R}^2$ generated by P.

Fig.1 is an example of order-3 Voronoi diagram with 20 random generator sites. Sensor node s_i can calculate the order-k Voronoi diagram of the

   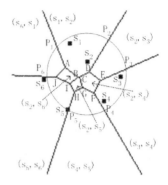

Fig. 1. Order-3 Voronoi Diagram with 20   **Fig. 2.** Neighbor order-2 Voronoi diagram
random sites

target region by taking its l-hop neighbors $N_l(i)$ as generator sites. We use $NOVD(l,k,i)$ to denote the resultant Voronoi diagram, $NOVV(l,k,i)$ to denote a Voronoi vertex of $NOVD(l,k,i)$, and $NOVIP(l,k,i)$ to denote an intersection point between an edge of the $NOVD(l,k,i)$ and the circumcircle of s_i's sensing disk. In Fig.2, suppose the circle represents sensor node s_7's (which is not shown in this figure) sensing area and assume its the 2-hop neighbor set is $N_2(7) = \{s_1, s_2, s_3, s_4, s_5, s_6\}$. Taking $N_2(7)$ as Voronoi sites, we can construct the neighbor order-2 Voronoi diagram $NOVD(2,2,7)$. Each Voronoi polygon is associated with a pair of sensor nodes (shown in bracket) and $NOVV(2,2,7) = \{A, B, C, D, E, F, G, H, I, J\}$ and $NOVIP(2,2,7) = \{P_1, P_2, P_3, P_4, P_5, P_6\}$.

Theorem 1. *A sensor node s_i is k-coverage redundant if and only if every $NOVV(l,k,i)$ vertex and every $NOVIP(l,k,i)$ point, which lies in s_i's sensing disk, is covered by all of the k corresponding Voronoi sites (sensor nodes in $N_l(i)$).*

Proof. (1) necessary condition. If sensor node s_i is k-coverage redundant, all $NOVV(l,k,i)$ vertices and $NOVIP(l,k,i)$ points in S_i are k-covered by other nodes. According to the definition of order-k Voronoi diagram, each of these points must be covered by its k closest sites, i.e., the corresponding nodes associated with the Voronoi polygon.

(2) sufficient condition. Sensor node s_i's sensing disk S_i is divided into several subareas by $NOVD(l,k,i)$. There are two types of subareas. One is the closed convex polygon involving only $NOVV(l,k,i)$ vertices. The other is a convex area involving not only $NOVV(l,k,i)$ vertices, but also $NOVIP(l,k,i)$ points.

Case 1. Consider the subarea involving only $NOVV(l,k,i)$ vertices. If all these $NOVV(l,k,i)$ vertices are covered by the k associated Voronoi sites, according to the convexity of the Voronoi region and sensor node's sensing area, the subarea formed by these $NOVV(l,k,i)$ vertices is covered k sensor nodes in $N_l(i)$.

Case 2. Consider the subarea of the second type. In this case, the boundary of the convex subarea includes an arc segment of s_i's coverage circumcircle C_i. Let's take Fig.3 as an example. Points VIP_1 and VIP_2 are the intersection points between C_i (solid circle) and two Voronoi edges. To cover these two $NOVIP\,(l,k,i)$ points, sensor node s_j must lie in the intersection area between circles C_1 and C_2 (dotted circle), where $C_1\,(C_2)$ is centered at $VIP_1\,(VIP_2)$ with radius R_s. For every point p on the arc segment between VIP_1 and VIP_2 (counterclockwise), $d\,(s_j,p) \le R_s$. If all other $NOVV\,(l,k,i)$ vertices (e.g., A, B, and C) of this convex region are also covered by s_j, every point in this convex region will be covered by s_j. Similar to case 1, if all $NOVV\,(l,k,i)$ vertices and $NOVIP\,(l,k,i)$ points of the convex region are covered by each of the associated k closest sensor nodes, this convex subarea is surely k-covered even without s_i, which means that s_i is k-coverage redundant in this case.   ■

To avoid that two neighboring sensor nodes turn off simultaneously thus leaves blind points in the target region, node priority is also used to prevent the cyclic dependent relationship as the k-connectivity redundant condition does.

k-Coverage Redundant Condition:
A sensor node s_i is k-coverage redundant if every $NOVV\,(l,k,i)$ vertex and every $NOVIP\,(l,k,i)$ point, which lies in s_i's sensing disk, is covered by the corresponding associated Voronoi sites (sensors) in $N_l\,(i)$ with lower priorities than s_i.

Fig.4 illustrates the k-coverage redundant condition on the basis of Fig.2. The shadowed circle is sensor node s_7's coverage area. If we take node id as node priority, node s_7 has the highest priority among its 2-hop neighbors. And we can see that, when P_6, J, I, H, P_5 points are covered by both s_5 and s_6, P_5, H, G, F, P_4 are covered by both s_4 and s_5, P_4, F, E, P_3 are covered by both s_3 and s_4, P_3, E, D, P_2 are covered by both s_2 and s_3, P_2, D, C, B, A, P_1 are covered by both s_1 and s_2, P_1, A, J, P_6 are covered by both s_1 and s_6, A, B, I, J are covered by both s_2 and s_6, B, C, G, H, I are covered by both s_2 and s_5, D, C, G, F, E are covered by both s_2 and s_4, then s_7 is 2-coverage redundant. If a sensor node meets both the above two redundant conditions, it is safe to put

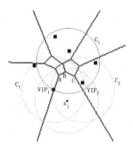

Fig. 3. Proof of Case 2

Fig. 4. Example of k-coverage redundant condition $(k = 2)$

the sensor node into low-powered sleep status immediately. Finally, all sensor nodes that don't satisfy the above two conditions remain active and form the k-connected k-cover set for the target region.

It has been shown that when $R_c \geq 2R_s$ the complete coverage of the target region implies connectivity of the network [11]. Further, it can be easily proved that the k-coverage implies k-connectivity if $R_c \geq 2R_s$. So in the case of $R_c \geq 2R_s$, the k-coverage redundant condition alone can construct a k-connected k-cover set for the target area.

4 Performance Evaluation

The target region is an area of 40×40 unit square. The sensing model and wireless communication model are presented in section 2. In our experiments, neighbor hop number l is 2 and node id is used as node priority. All results shown here are the average values over 50 runs.

Fig.5 shows how the size of KCC (number of active sensor nodes) constructed by the proposed self-pruning algorithm varies with the network size (deployed node number) when k is set to 1, 2 and 3 separately. We can see that the size of KCC is much smaller than that of the original network. Therefore the proposed algorithm can decrease the number of active sensor nodes and hence reduce the total energy consumption effectively, which is helpful to prolong the network lifetime. In both figures the size of KCC increases with the network size under all settings of k. We also notice that when $R_c = 2R_s$ the size of KCC is smaller than the corresponding size when $R_c = R_s$.

Fig.6 shows how the size of 2-connected 2-cover set varies with R_s when R_c is fixed to 10 units. We see that under different network size (150 and 250), the number of active sensor nodes decreases with the increase of R_s. In Fig.7, we compare the performance of the proposed self-pruning algorithm with the distributed version of the Greedy algorithm in [9] under different network size when $k = 1$ and $R_c = R_s = 10$. Although the Greedy algorithm can result in a

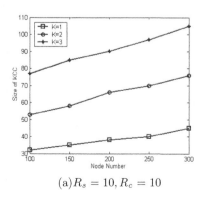
(a)$R_s = 10, R_c = 10$

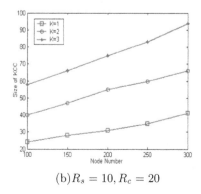
(b)$R_s = 10, R_c = 20$

Fig. 5. Size of KCC vs. network size

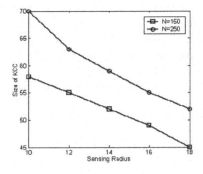

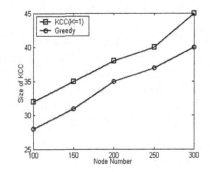

Fig. 6. Size of KCC vs.R_s (k = 2, R_c = 10)

Fig. 7. Self-pruning (k = 1, R_s = R_c = 10) vs. Greedy

Table 1.

Node Number	Original VCD	Origianl CD	KCC VCD	KCC CD	Success Ratio
100	3	4	2	2	100%
150	5	4	3	2	100%
200	9	5	3	2	100%
250	10	5	4	2	100%
300	10	6	4	2	100%

slightly smaller active sensor node set, it must maintain global state information during its executing process and therefore it is prone to message loss. On the contrary, the proposed self-pruning algorithm only needs local neighborhood infomation and hence is more robust to message loss.

Table 1 shows the variation of the network Vertex Connectivity Degree (VCD) and the Coverage Degree (CD) before and after applying the self-pruning algorithm. The original vertex connectivity degree is computed when all sensor nodes are active using the max-flow min-cut algorithm. The coverage degree d means that each sensor node can cover its associated Voronoi vertices in the order-d Voronoi diagram while can't cover all of its Voronoi vertices in the order-$(d+1)$ Voronoi diagram. We consider the comparison when $k = 2, R_c = R_s = 10$. From Table 1 we can see that both the vertex connectivity degree and the coverage degree are reduced but still satisfy the specified requirement ($k = 2$). The success ratio is 100% under different network size.

5   Conclusions

In this paper we address the issue of constructing a minimal k-connected k-cover set (KCC) for a target region and propose a general framework for this problem. Different algorithms for detecting k-connectivity and k-coverage redundancy in a localized manner can be integrated into the self-pruning framework.

And different connectivity and coverage requirements can be specified flexibly in our framework. We also propose a novel, distributed and localized algorithm to detect k-coverage redundancy of a sensor node based on order-k Voronoi diagram. Experimental results show that the proposed self-pruning algorithm can construct the k-connected k-cover set reliably and reduce the number of active sensor nodes whilst maintaining the k-connectivity and k-coverage properties of the original network, which is helpful to reduce system energy consumption and prolong the network lifespan.

References

1. A. Mainwaring, J. Polastre, R. Szewczyk, and D. Culler. Wireless Sensor Networks for Habitat Monitoring. In Pro. of WSNA'02, Atlanta, USA, September, 2002.
2. J. Elson and D. Estrin. Sensor Networks: A Bridge to the Physical World. Wireless Sensor Networks, Kluwer, 2004.
3. I. F. Akyildiz, W. Su, Y. Sankarasubramaniam, and E. Cayirci. Wireless Sensor Networks: A Survey. Computer Networks (Elsevier) Journal,pp.393-422, 2004.
4. B. Carbunar, A. Grama, J. Vitek, and O. Carbunar. Coverage Preserving Redundancy Elimination in Sensor Networks. In Proc. of SECON 2004, Santa Clara, CA, USA, 2004.
5. F. Ye, G. Zhong, S. Lu, and L. Zhang. Peas: A Robust Energy Conserving Protocol for Long-Lived Sensor Networks. In Proc. of ICDCS'03, 2003
6. H. Chen, H. Wu, and N. Tzeng. Grid-Based Approach for Working Node Selection in Wireless Sensor Networks. In Proc. of IEEE ICC'04, Paris, France, 2004.
7. S. Slijepcevic and M. Potkonjak. Power Efficient Organization of Wireless Sensor Networks. In Proc. of IEEE ICC'01, Helsinki, Finland, 2001
8. T. Yan, T. He, and J. Stankovic. Differentiated Surveillance Service for Sensor Networks. In Proc. of SenSys'03, Los Angels, CA, USA, 2003.
9. H. Gupta, S. R. Das, and Q. Gu. Connected Sensor Cover: Self-Organization of Sensor Networks for Efficient Query Execution. In Proc. of MobiHoc'03, Annapolis, Maryland, USA, 2003.
10. X. Wang, G. Xing et al. Integrated Coverage and Connectivity Configuration in Wireless Sensor Networks. In Proc. of SenSys'03, Los Angeles, CA, 2003.
11. H. Zhang and J. C. Hou. Maintaining Sensing Coverage and Connectivity in Large Sensor Networks. In Proc. of NSF International Workshop on Theoretical and Algorithmic Aspects of Sensors, Ad Hoc Wireless, and Peer-to-Peer Networks, 2004.
12. D.Tian and N.D.Georganas. A Coverage-Preserving Node Scheduling Scheme for Large Wireless Sensor Networt. In Proc. of WSNA'02, Atlanta, Geogia, USA, 2002.
13. F. Dai and J. Wu. On Constructing K-Connected K-Dominating Set in Wireless Networks. In Proc. of IEEE IPDPS, 2005.
14. A. Okabe, B. Boots, K. Sugihara, and S. N. Chiu. Spatial Tessellations: Concepts and Applications of Voronoi Diagram. John Wiley & Sons Press,1999.

GCMPR: Gateway-Centric Multi-path Routing for Internet Connectivity of Wireless Mobile Ad Hoc Network

Yongqiang Liu, Wei Yan, and Yafei Dai

Computer Networks and Distributed Systems Laboratory, Peking University,
Room 1716, Science Building No.1, Peking University, Beijing, China
{lyq, yanwei, dyf}@net.pku.edu.cn

Abstract. Connecting Mobile Ad Hoc Network (MANET) to the Internet will extend Internet into a new territory by making web service available "anytime, anywhere". However, many simulations and practical experiments have shown that when communication is between mobile nodes in MANET and fixed nodes on Internet, the bandwidth is asymmetrical and the available throughput is greatly limited. In this paper, we present a gateway-centric multi-path routing protocol (GCMPR), which ensures every mobile node has a set of link-disjoint and loop-free paths to gateway. The novel routing algorithm over multiple paths can provide higher aggregate bandwidth and improve the end-to-end delay. Simulations for comparing performance between GCMPR and other connectivity methods show that GCMPR achieves 40% throughput enhancement and remarkable improvement for the end-to-end delay. Furthermore, GCMPR can be easily applied to other scenarios in MANET when some hosts provide special service and are visited frequently.

1 Introduction

Mobile ad-hoc communication [1] has been one of the most active research areas in the past decade. For many applications in the mobile environment, it is much desired that a self-organizing ad hoc network is somehow connected to the world-wide Internet. We refer to such connecting networks as wireless hybrid networks. Usually, a MANET node with Internet access can operate as a *gateway* and provide Internet access to other nodes in the MANET.

There have been some researches on connectivity for MANET, such as node addressing[2], gateway discovery[3] and routing algorithms[4-5]. The performance evaluations of wireless hybrid networks [6,7] have shown that the communication bandwidth between MANET nodes and Internet nodes is asymmetrical. As illustrated in Fig.1-(a), the end-to-end throughput is actually determined by the bandwidth between MANET nodes and the gateway. The aim of our work is to develop a multi-path routing protocol for providing higher aggregate bandwidth to gateway and improve the performance of the wireless hybrid network.

H. Jin, D. Reed, and W. Jiang (Eds.): NPC 2005, LNCS 3779, pp. 487–494, 2005.

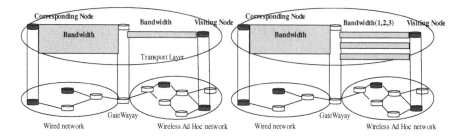

Fig. 1. Bandwidth illustration over wireless hybrid network

Some multi-path routing approaches have been proposed, such as TORA[8],SMR[9], AOMDV[10], and AODVM[11]. But none of them can be directly applied to the wireless hybrid network, because these protocols require the destination node to be in MANET. To solve this problem, we present a Gateway-Centric Multi-Path Routing (GCMPR) protocol. As illustrated in Fig.1-(b), GCMPR is a hybrid routing protocol. The gateway pushes proactively its link-disjoint routing entries into the routing tables of the rest of the nodes in MANET. The communications among MANET nodes still use single path routing on-demand.

The advantages of GCMPR can be summarized as follows:

1. When there is a large percentage of traffic between MANET nodes and Internet nodes traversing the gateway, GCMPR can greatly improve the end-to-end throughput compared to the single path routing approach.

2. When there are many nodes need to establish multi-path routing to the gateway, GCMPR requires fewer additional control messages than other multi-path routing protocols, therefore, lower overhead in MANET.

3. In other routing approaches, only the source node has multi-path information to the destination. The intermediate nodes in GCMPR also keep multi-path information to the gateway. Therefore, GCMPR is more effective in recovering the broken path.

The remainder of this paper is organized as follows. Session 2 describes the protocol mechanism in detail. Performance evaluation by simulation is presented in Section 3 and concluding remarks are given in Section 4.

2   Gateway-Centric Multi-path Routing in Hybrid Network

2.1   Protocol Overview

The GCMPR is a distributed *message-based* routing scheme. As illustrated in Fig.2, the basic idea of message-based routing is that a gateway information message is generated by the gateway and sent to its neighbors. The neighbors add their own information into the message and forward it to the downstream nodes. Analyzing the messages coming from different neighbors, the MANAT node can form multiple link-disjoint paths to the gateway. The main steps of GCMPR are as follows:

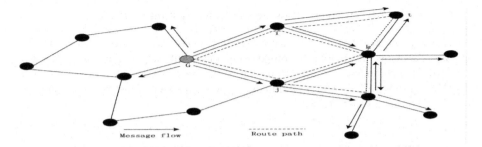

Fig. 2. An example of setting up multiple paths to the gateway with GCMPR

1. Gateway broadcasts periodically a gateway advertisement (GWADV) message throughout the ad hoc network.

2. When the GWADV message is received from its neighbors, a node makes a decision based on its states. These states include following scenarios: 1) whether the GWADV can provide the information for it to find another link-disjoint path to the gateway. 2) whether the message should be forwarded to its downstream nodes. To achieve these two goals, each MANET node uses a variant *PID* to identify each path to the gateway. The *PID* is defined as follows:

$$PID = < next\_hop, first\_hop > \tag{1}$$

where the *next_hop* is the IP address of the upstream neighbor along the path and *first_hop* is the IP address of the first hop just before the gateway. For the path1 (t->k->j->G) in Fig2, from the view of node t, $PID_1 = < k, j >$

We define that

$$PID_i == PID_j \Leftrightarrow (next\_hop_i == next\_hop_j) \vee (first\_hop_i == first\_hop_j) \tag{2}$$

$$PID_i \neq PID_j \Leftrightarrow (next\_hop_i \neq next\_hop_j) \wedge (first\_hop_i \neq first\_hop_j) \tag{3}$$

By comparing the *PID*s in the GWADV messages, GCMPR can guarantee that the paths to the gateway are link-disjoint and loop-free. This is accomplished by applying GWADV forwarding rule to each intermediate node. Details and proof of the forwarding rule will be discussed in following sessions.

3. In order to reduce the overhead in the ad hoc network, only useful GWADV messages which can create a new link-disjoint path or shorter path to downstream nodes are modified and forwarded by the receiving node.

4. When a node detects its next hop in the path out of its range, it performs a micro repair to find an alternative path to the gateway and the cost of this repair is very low.

5. If a mobile node (S) wants to communicate with another node (D), S estimates the location of D (whether D is in MANET or on Internet) by broadcasting a network-wide RREQ and waiting for corresponding RREP. In GCMPR, RREQ is extended to contain additional information for forming reverse multi-path routing to the source.

2.2   Gateway Advertisement Message and Gateway Routing Table

A gateway can advertise its presence by sending a GWADV message. The GWADV message contains information for propagating a new link-disjoint path to the gateway for downstream nodes. The general format of this message is shown in Fig.3, where ADVERTISEMENT ID (ADV_ID) is the sequence number of the message and lager ADV_ID means fresher message.

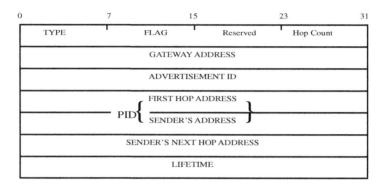

Fig. 3. Format of Gateway Advertisement Message

As introduced in section1, in GCMPR, each MANET node only establishes multi-path routing to the gateway and keeps single path routing among MANET nodes. An additional gateway routing table (called gw_rtable) is designed to record path information to the gateway. The structure of the gw_rtable and the relationship between the two routing tables are illustrated in Fig.4.

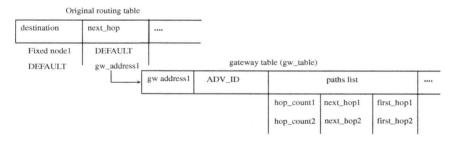

Fig. 4. The structure of gw_rtable and the relationship between the two routing tables

2.3   GWADV Forwarding Rule

As mentioned in section 2.1, GCMPR uses GWADV forwarding rule to form multiple loop-free paths to the gateway. Moreover, the rule can reduce additional routing overhead and prevent downstream nodes from receiving wrong *PID* information. The detailed GWADV forwarding rule is shown in Fig.7.

Intermediate node i receives a GWADV from neighbor j, assume that i already has n paths to gateway G
(PATH$_{i1}$, PATH$_{i2}$,... PATH$_{in}$), node i does as follows:

1.0 forward_flag = false

   IF (GWADV$_j$::sender's next hop == i)   /*prevent route loop*/

   1.1 DROP(GWADV$_j$);

2.0 IF (GWADV$_j$::ADV_ID>ADV_ID$_i$)   /*fresher advertisement*/

   2.1 delete PATH$_{i1}$, PATH$_{i2}$,... PATH$_{in}$

   2.2 ADV_ID$_i$ = GWADV$_j$::ADV_ID

   2.3 insert (G, j, GWADV$_j$::first hop , GWADV$_j$::hop_count+1) into gw_rtable

   2.4 forward_flag=true

   2.5 insert (ADV::sender's addr, ADV::sender's next hop) into neighbor table

3.0 IF ($\forall$ k ∈ {1...n} PATH$_{ik}$::next_hop ≠ ADV::sender's addr and PATH$_{ik}$::first_hop ≠ ADV::first_hop) /*a new dis

   joint route*/

   3.1 insert (G, j, GWADV$_j$::first hop , GWADV$_j$::hop_count+1) into gw_rtable

   3.2 forward_flag=true

   3.3 insert (ADV::sender's addr, ADV::sender's next hop) into neighbor table

4.0IF ($\exists$ k ∈ {1...n} PATH$_{ik}$::next_hop==ADV::sender's addr and

   PATH$_{ik}$::first_hop==ADV::first_hop and GWADV$_j$::hop_count+1< PATH$_{ik}$:: hop_count)

   4.1 update (GWADV$_j$::hop_count+1) PATH$_{ik}$

   4.2 forward_flag=true

   4.3 update (ADV::sender's addr, ADV::sender's next hop) in neighbor table

5.0 IF (forward_flag==true)

   /*rebroadcast the GWADV*/

   5.1 IF(j is gateway) GWADV$_i$::first hop = i;

   5.2 GWADV$_i$::send's next hop = j

   5.3 GWADV$_i$::send's addr = i

   5.4 copy other fields from GWADV$_i$

   5.5 broadcast (GWADV$_i$)

6.0 ELSE drop(GWADV$_j$)

Fig. 5. GCMPR GWADV forwarding rule

3   Performance Evaluation

3.1 Simulation Environment

The simulations were done with ns2 [12]. All of the simulations were run in an ad hoc
network consisting of 50 nodes uniformly spreading in an 1000x1000 meter area.
Nodes are equipped with an IEEE 802.11 radio network interface, operating at 1Mbps
with 250m transmission range. Nodes move according to the Random Waypoint mobility model, at uniformly distributed speed between 0 and 15m/s.The traffic pattern
consists of several CBR/UDP connections between randomly chosen source and two
fixed nodes in wired network. The sending interval at the source is 20ms and packet
size is 80 bytes.

In [11], the AODV protocol is modified to implement solutions to the wireless hybrid network by adding node addressing and the gateway discovery methods. We

refer to the modified AODV as AODV+. There are two gateway discovery mechanisms In [11], the AODV protocol is modified to implement solutions to the wireless
hybrid network by adding node addressing and the gateway discovery methods. We
refer to the modified AODV as AODV+. There are two gateway discovery mechanisms in AODV+: reactive gateway discovery and proactive gateway discovery. In
the simulation, four protocols are measured. They are AODV+ with reactive gateway
discovery (called reactive AODV+), AODV+ with proactive gateway discovery (proactive AODV+), AODV incorporating GCMPR without micro repair (GCMPR) and
AODV+GCMPR with micro repair (GCMPR with micro repair). We use salvage
mode as multi-path selection scheme [10] and the gateway broadcasts an advertisement in every 5 seconds.

Three important metrics of protocol performance are evaluated:

Packet Throughput: This is the product of the size of the packet and the number of
packets received by destination in a unit time. Data packets can be dropped in the
network either at the source or at intermediate nodes for node mobility and wireless
channel collision.

End-to-End Delay of Data Packets: This includes all possible delays caused by
buffering during route discovery, queuing delay at the interface, retransmission delays
at the MAC, propagation time and transfer time.

Routing Control Messages Overhead: Routing control messages include gateway
discovery advertisement, request and reply. The metric is the ratio of the number of
control message to the total data packets received by the destination.

3.2   Simulation Results

Fig.6, 7 and 8 show the results with varying mean node speeds. Fig 6 compares the
packet throughput performance of four protocols. The throughput of all protocols
decreases with increase of mean node-speed, because nodes will drop packets if they
have no routes to forward when topology changes. GCMPR always drops fewer packets than other protocols and the throughput improvement is up to about 40%. This is
because of the availability of alternative paths to forward the packets when one path
fails. The GCMPR with micro repair outperforms other protocols because of its rapid
route recovery at intermediate nodes.

Fig.7 shows the end-to-end delay of four protocols. As expected, the delay increases with mean node-speed grows. This is because of the increase in the number of
route failures and the consequent packet cache. GCMPR with micro repair improves
the delay almost by a factor of two. So the improvement of packet end-to-end delay is
more significant than that of the throughput.

In Fig.8, it can be seen that GCMPR has more control overhead (average about
20%), because it uses additional GWADV messages to form multiple paths to the gateway. With the increasing mobility, reactive AODV+ has to send more route discovery
requests to discover the path to the gateway and therefore higher overhead.

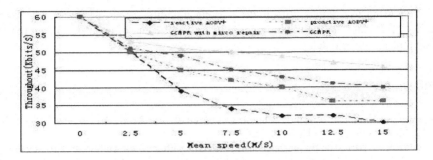

Fig. 6. Throughput with varying mobility

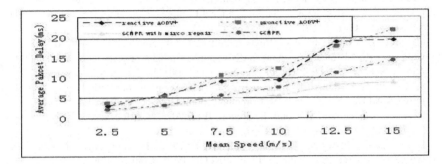

Fig. 7. End-to-end Delay with varying mobility

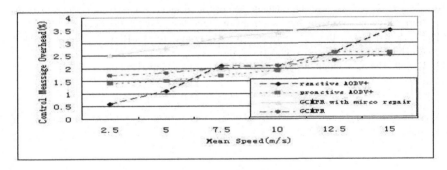

Fig. 8. Routing overhead with varying mobility

4 Conclusions

Routing protocols with multi-path capability can improve the bandwidth between the gateway and mobile nodes in MANET, because it can effectively deal with mobility-induced route failures. In this paper, we have proposed a gateway-centric multi-path protocol (GCMPR) which ensures that each mobile node has a set of link-disjoint and loop-free paths to the gateway. Another feature of GCMPR is the micro repair with minimal additional overhead. We have studied the performance of GCMPR relative to

AODV+ using ns-2 simulations under varying mobility scenarios. The results show that GCMPR can improve the throughput by up to 40% and offers a significant reduction in the end-to-end delay.

Reference

1. Alex Ali Hamidian: A Study of Internet Connectivity for Mobile Ad Hoc Networks in NS 2. Master's thesis, Lund Sweden (2003)
2. Jönsson U, Alriksson F,Larsson T: MIPMANET- Mobile IP for Mobile Ad Hoc Networks. In Proceedings of the Workshop on Mobile Ad Hoc Networking and Computing (Mobi-Hoc), Boston, USA (2000)
3. Xi J.; Bettstetter C: Wireless Multihop Internet Access: Gateway Discovery, Routing and Addressing. In Proceedings of the International Conference on Third Generation Wireless and Beyond (3Gwireless'02), San Francisco, USA(2002)
4. Perkins C: IP Mobility for IPv4, Revised. draft-ietf-mobileip-rfc2002-bis-08.txt(2001)
5. Wakikawa R., Malinen J., Perkins C., Nilsson A: Global Connectivity for IPv6 Mobile Ad Hoc Networks, IETF Internet Draft, November 2001.Work in progress.
6. S. Xu and T. Saadawi: Does the IEEE 802.11 MAC protocol Work Well in Multihop Wireless Ad Hoc Networks. IEEE Communication Magazine, Volume 39(2001) 130-137.
7. G. Anastasi, E. Borgia, M. Conti, E. Gregori: IEEE 802.11Ad Hoc Networks: Performance Measurement. IIT Internal Report(2003)
8. V.D. Park and M.S. Corson: A Highly Adaptive Distributed Routing Algorithm for Mobile Wireless Net-works. Proceedings of IEEE INFOCOM'97 Conf (1997)
9. Lee, S.-J., Gerla, M: Split Multipath Routing with Maximally Disjoint Paths in Ad Hoc Networks. IEEE International Conference on Communications, Vol. 10 (2001)
10. Marina, M.K., Das, S.R.: On-demand Multipath Distance Vector Routing in Ad Hoc Networks. Proceedings of the International Conference for Network Protocols (2001)
11. Ye, Z., Krishnamurthy, S.V., Tripathi, S.K.: A Framework for Reliable Routing in Mobile Ad Hoc Networks. IEEE INFOCOM (2003)
12. K. Fall: The ns Manual. http://www.isi.edu/ ns/nsdocumentation.htm(2002)

A Semantic and Adaptive Context Model for Ubiquitous Computing

Yunting Tang[1] and Qing Wu[2]

[1] Ningbo Institute of Technology, Zhejiang University,
Ningbo, Zhejiang, China 315001
tyt@nit.net.cn
[2] College of Computer Science, Zhejiang University,
Hangzhou, Zhejiang, China 310027
wwwsin@cs.zju.edu.cn

Abstract. Ubiquitous computing pursues naturalness and harmony. We think that semantic and adaptation are two important aspects. This paper presents a semantic and adaptive context model for ubiquitous computing. We emphasize the fusion of semantic information and context model in smart vehicle space to support ubiquitous computing. In our work, we use a web ontology language to model ontologies of context including the common essential ontology and the application domain-specific ontology. In addition, we present an application scenario in smart vehicle space. Also, we propose a prototype system of our model.

1 Introduction

A new computing model is coming into our life, which we called "ubiquitous computing" [1]. Environment, people, and smart devices are three elements of this novel computing model. In order to relate with each other harmoniously and naturally, we should synthesize multifarious techniques. As a result, ubiquitous computing integrates many research areas including software architecture, middleware platform, languages design, distributed systems, artificial intelligence, vision recognition, user interfaces, and biological authentication. Recently, many related academic research efforts and commercial reality are made for ubiquitous computing. As a whole, they focus on active and smart spaces such as intelligent home, easy meeting-room, and smart museum. In the smart spaces, in terms of changes of the people, environment and devices, this computing model automatically and continuously self-adjusts according to pre-defined strategies to new states in order to provide better cooperation and communication between entities. Achievement of this attractive goal poses a large number of new challenges for software architecture and middleware technology. The traditional computing models are no longer suitable [2]. Therefore, a novel middleware architecture is needed to support ubiquitous computing. We consider the keystone to be adaptation, which we use a semantic context model to realize. Context-aware mechanisms provide an infrastructure for adaptation. Since there are many different run-time environments, in order to achieve greatly improved cooperation,

H. Jin, D. Reed, and W. Jiang (Eds.): NPC 2005, LNCS 3779, pp. 495–502, 2005.

they should understand and communicate with each other better than they do today. Thus we define common essential ontology for smart space. On the other hand, to deal with the specific application domains, we first find problem domains, and then build ontology of specific domains. Moreover, according to the context complexity, we deal with context according to hierarchy and priority. Emphatically, we argue that "semantic view" for context is the key enabler of smart space.

Vehicles have merged into our daily life, playing an important role. Because we need more comfort, facility and safety in vehicles, we select vehicle space as a representative scene of ubiquitous computing. In this paper, we propose a semantic context model integrating semantic web technology and ontology language for self-adaptation. Our work is related to other pervasive and context aware computing research such as CoBrA [3], Context Toolkit [4], One.World [5], TOTA [6]. Compared with the previous systems, our design focuses are twofold. Firstly we focus on smart vehicle space; secondly we emphasize the semantic view of a context-aware middleware model in smart vehicle space and we propose a semantic context model. Because context-driven and person-centric are the characteristics of ubiquitous computing, we consider the semantic context model is very important. We have defined the common essential ontology and application domain-specific ontology in smart vehicle space.

The structure of the paper is as follows. Section 2 presents the the semantic and adaptive context framework, which comprises smart vehicle space overview, semantic view for context and the formal specification of our context model. Section 3 introduces an application domain-based ontology in smart vehicle space. Next, section 4 presents an application scenario in smart vehicle space and a prototype system of our model. Finally, section 5 summarizes the discussion.

2   Semantic and Adaptive Context Framework

As Tim Berners-Lee [7] described, semantic web is an extension of the current web where information is given well-defined meaning, better enabling computers and people to cooperate better. Below, we present smart vehicle space and semantic view for context. In addition, we propose a semantic and adaptive context model.

2.1   Smart Vehicle Space

Smart vehicle space is an essential research field of smart spaces. Using security authentication, image processing and pattern recognition technology, in terms of relationships between people, vehicle and environments, the grade of security and comfort is greatly improved.

Smart vehicle space has four parts, which is defined as SVS=(CA, CR, AC, CP), where CA is a context acquisition system; CR is a context repository reasoning system; AC is an auto controlling system and CP is a centralized processing system. CA is defined as CA=(($\triangle$statpe,$\triangle$statdv,$\triangle$staten), (sen, cam, soundrec)). CA comprises sensors, cameras and sound receivers, which aims at sensing the status change of people, devices and environments in the vehicle. CR is defined as CR=(context, ontology, domain, inference), and uses correlative contexts and application domain-based ontologies to make the manipulating strategy for adaptation. AC is defined as AC=(ste, com, ent, nav, sec), which includes steering, communication, entertainment, navigation and security subsystem. Particularly, CP is the kernel of smart vehicle space, which controls above third parts co-operating effectively and adaptively. We define CP as CP=f(CA, CR, AC), where f is a control function.

2.2 Semantic View for Context

Context [8] is any information that can be used to characterize the situation of an entity. An entity may be a person, place, or object that is considered relevant to the interaction between a user and an application, including the user and application themselves. Commonly used contexts consist of location, identity, time, temperature and activity. We consider specific objects in environments are all context. The semantic information of context is essential for dealing with complex tasks in ubiquitous computing environments.

Context-aware is an ability to sense and use different context. Any application that takes advantage of context is a context-aware application. Context-aware computing is the ability of computing devices to detect, interpret and respond to the change of environment and system. The W3C organization has specified a language OWL that is based on DAML and OIL for semantic web, which is more expressive than RDF and RDF-S. Because context is so complicated and hard to understand and use, we have introduced semantic web technology into the context framework in smart space. We share common vocabularies and use OWL as our standard syntax to present information and inference. In this way, we model the different context hierarchies more effectively and adaptively.

2.3 Semantic and Adaptive Context Model

In this part, we give a detailed formal specification for the semantic and adaptive context model, including three definitions and one algorithm.

Definition 1 Context Model. Context model CON=(S, P, V) is a 3-tuple, where S=$\{s_1, s_2, ..., s_n\}$ is a set of context semantic information; P=$\{p_1, p_2, ..., p_n\}$ is a set of attributes of S; and V=$\{v1, v_2, ..., v_n\}$ is set of values of S.

Definition 2 Semantic Context Model. Semantic Context model MSC=(K, T, S) is a 3-tuple, where K is context-driven kernel including basic context services; T is a set of context base and process tools; T is defined as T=(B, O), where B=(SB, TB) is a set of context bases comprising context shared base and transcendent base; O=(SR, CF) is a set of context tools such as smart reasoning and context fusion algorithm. S, defined as S=$(St_{pe}, St_{en}, St_{de})$, is a set of states of people, environments and smart devices.

Definition 3 Semantic and Adaptive Context-Aware Processing Model.
Semantic and adaptive context-aware processing model SACM=(O, A, S, G, N,
T), where O is the application domain-based ontology; A is a process of context acquisition, which aims to gain raw data from sensors and transform it to
ontology entities or attributes. The data they export are of different type and
structure, which is abstracted so that it can be used by an application; S is
a process of context storage, which stores the acquired context in a repository
for access when necessary; G is a process of context aggregation, which integrates correlative context for a specific entity; N is a process of context analysis,
which infers current status of entities or the intention of users; T is a process
of context-aware actions. We specify appropriate action rules for a number of
context scenarios. At run-time, whenever the system state matches a particular
scenario, the associated action will be automatically executed according to pre-
defined strategies. Emphatically, T process is not serial and static, because of
the execution of actions will cause the system to enter a new state, so bringing
the system to a new context scenario. In addition, there may be multiple processes in progress interacting with each other. As a result, T is a stochastic and
recursive process.

Algorithm SAC. To elaborate the semantic and adaptive context process, we
present the SAC algorithm.

*Algorithm SAC(msc, sacm, $\triangle con$): According to semantic of the context-aware
tasks, it implements the adaptive context process.*

```
Input:
  Semantic context set msc (a subset of MSC);
  Semantic and adaptive context-aware processing sacm (a subset of
  SACM);
  A set of change of context ccon;
Output:
  A new semantic context set msc' (a subset of MSC);
Begin
  Decompose ccon into several basic atom-context sets (atcs);
  Foreach atc in atcs do
    Do sacm.a according to sacm.o, msc.s;
    Do sacm.s, sacm.g, sacm.n according to msc.b.sb and msc.b.tb
    Until sacm.t;
    Update(msc.b.sb);
    Update(msc.b.tb);
  Endfor
End.
```

3   Application Domain-Based Ontology

An ontology [9] is an agreement about shared conceptualization, which includes
conceptual frameworks for modelling application domain knowledge, content-

specific protocols for communication among interacting agents, and agreements about the representation of specific domain theories. Ontology has such characteristics as definitions of representational vocabulary, a well-defined syntax, an easily understood semantics, efficient reasoning supports, sufficient expressive capabilities, and convenience of expressions. We understand ontology at two different levels. (a) It is a vocabulary, which uses appropriate terms to describe entities and relationships between entities. (b) It is a knowledge base for a specific domain. In our view, ontology describes domain knowledge in a general way and provides consistent understanding of one application domain.

3.1   Common Ontology

For smart spaces, we have built some common essential ontology EO=(SS, PL, TI, PI, DC, SP), where SS is a set of smart space characteristics, which describes names, types, important locations and devices; PL is a set of physical location of person and devices; TL is a set of time, presenting the period of time or instant time; PI is a set of person identities, on which the system confirms one person different to others; DC is a set of devices characteristics, including names, types and attributes; SP is a set of security and privacy policy, denoting a person's capabilities.

3.2   Specific Ontology

Because smart vehicle space is a specific environment, we examine its characteristics from the view of context. (a) Space -inside vehicle- is relatively confined. The devices inside the vehicle may have limited capabilities and be fixed to the vehicle. Also, the space for user to move is restricted. (b) Though environments -outside of vehicle- continually change, we need not consider the whole range of dynamics, just those can influence our system.

The above characteristics determine the definitions of context in smart vehicle space. We use the idea of ontology to describe the context information. The context in smart vehicle space is defined as CONsvs=(VC, EC, DC), where VC is a set of vehicle context, concerning the statuses and attributes of devices inside the vehicle, such as air-condition, wiper, light, engine, ABS, and seat; EC is a set of environment context, comprising the environmental elements which may influence driving, such as weather, road status, fingerposts, and signal lamps; DC is a set of driver context, including (a) the status of a driver, such as the suitability and ability to driving; (b) physiological parameters, such as alcohol levels and pupil diameter.

We have used Protégé [10] tool to build context and create instances in smart vehicle space. Protégé is an ontology editor tool, providing a GUI for the user to create and manage the ontology architecture. Using Protégé, we export files in OWL format for inference. Figure 1 shows the ontology of smart vehicle space.

3.3   Ontology Usage

We have developed an ontology repository and defined three base classes, which represent the context inside the smart vehicle, the outside environment of the

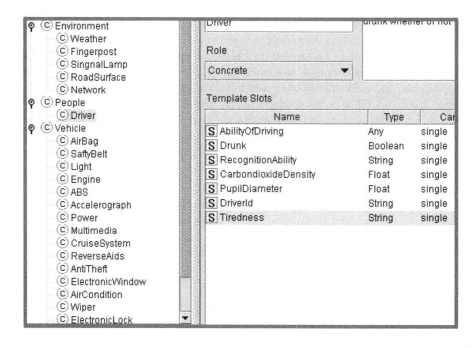

Fig. 1. Ontology Built in Protégé

vehicle, and the driver respectively. In order to be able to rely on the knowledge base, we filter the context scenario and specify fixed conditions(context) that trigger specific actions. Once the system meets the condition we have defined, the context reasoning system will be triggered and will perform the associated actions.

The context scenarios that we are interested in comprise three parts. We define IS=(SD, OI, DR), where SD is a set of security driving, including the scenario of driving at high speed in case of emergency; OI is a set of influences of outside environment, such as the vehicle can follow the signpost and turn to the right , or the ABS will engage in the case of loss of traction; DR is a set of the driver status. Importantly, we specify several driver conditions. Each one corresponds to different physiologic parameters. According to different danger level, system takes various actions. For example, if the driver is unable to continue driving when the danger level is high, the system will force a controlled stop and call for help. If the condition is not very serious, the system may simply park at the nearest convenient location. As a result, in terms of the ontology, the system can deal with different problems adaptively.

4   One Scenario

To demonstrate the application of the semantic and adaptive context model, we present the following scenario. It is time for Mr. Wu to go to work. He approaches his vehicle and puts his palm on the lock authentication machine. Next, his fingerprint information is sent to the in-vehicle computer that receives the data, analyzes them, confirms him as a legal driver, and then orders the door to open. After the door opens, he gets into the vehicle, sits down, and puts his ID card on the ID machine. At the same time, a sensor measures his weight and a camera records his appearance. These data are sent to the in-vehicle computer, which recognizes his identity. If allowed, the system sends a welcome command to the audio device in the entertainment system. A voice "Welcome, Mr. Wu" comes from the speaker. At the same time, the in-vehicle computer orders the entertainment system to play his favourite music and the climate system to adjust the air quality according to his preferences. Mr. Wu inputs his destination into the in-vehicle computer. The optimal router and some alternative routers are given. He selects the optimal one and the in-vehicle computer accepts his selection. He may say: "start". His command is received by voice sensor and sends it to the in-vehicle computer. Then the in-vehicle computer sends a command to the control system and the motor starts. The vehicle monitoring system detects the vehicle's status is good, and reports the status to the in-vehicle computer. If the control system detects water in the road, it will send a message to the in-vehicle computer. Therefore, Mr. Wu is warned to pay attention to the road condition and the control system sets the vehicle parameters to avoid skids. On arrival at the destination, the in-vehicle computer stops the motor and opens the door. Mr. Wu gets out. The in-vehicle computer orders the door to close after his departure is detected by the lock sensor.

According to the above scenario, we have developed a prototype system for smart vehicle space based on the semantic and adaptive context model. Figure 2 shows one screen shot of the system. According to our context model, we

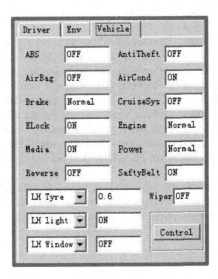

Fig. 2. A Screen Shot of the Prototype System

have defined an ontology related to smart vehicle space. With this prototype system, we can capture the required information about drivers, environments and vehicles. The system adapts to different conditions automatically.

5   Conclusions

In this paper, we have proposed a semantic and adaptive context model for smart vehicle space to explore ubiquitous computing. We focus on synchronization and adaptability aspects of semantic context, using OWL to build an ontology of smart vehicle space. Further, we argue that it is crucial to focus on the ontology-based context-aware aspect of interaction and communication. Moreover, from a practical point of view, we give a scenario in smart vehicle space and present a prototype system of our context model.

References

1. Weiser M: The Computer for the 21st Century. Scientific American, pp.94-100 (1991)
2. Anand Tripathi: Next-Generation Middleware Systems Challenges Designing. Communications of the ACM, 45(6), pp. 39-42 (2002)
3. Harry Chen, Tim Finin and Anupam Joshi: A Context Broker for Building Smart Meeting Rooms. American Association for Artificail Intelligence (2004)
4. Daniel Salber, Anind K. Dey and Gregory D. Abowd: The Context Toolkit : Aiding the Development of Context-Enabled Applications. Proceedings of CHI'99. ACM Press (1999)
5. Robert Grimm, Janet Davis, Eric Lemar, Adam MacBeth, Steven Swanson, Thomas Anderson, Brian Bershad, Gaetano Borriello, Steven Gribble, and David Wetherall: System support for pervasive applications. ACM Transactions on Computer Systems, 22(4), pp. 421-486 (2004)
6. Marco Mamei and Franco Zambonelli: Programming Pervasive and Mobile Computing Applications with the TOTA Middleware. In proceedings of the 2nd IEEE International Conference on Pervasive Computing and Communications, (2004)
7. Tim Berners-Lee and Mark Fischetti: Weaving the web: The original design and ultimate destiny of the world wide web by its inventor. (2001)
8. Anind K. Dey: Providing Architectural Support for Building Context-Aware Applications. PhD thesis, Georgia Institute of Technology (2000)
9. B. Chandrasekaran, John. R Josephson, and Richard V. Benjamins: What Are Ontologies, and Why do We Need Them? IEEE Transactions on Intelligent Systems, pp. 20C26 (1999)
10. Natalya, F. N., Michael, S., Stefan, D., Monica, C., Ray, W. F., Mark, A. M. : Creating Semantic Web Contents with Protege-2000. IEEE Intelligent Systems, Vol. 16, No. 2. IEEE Computer Society, pp. 60-71 (2001)

Research of Survival-Time-Based Dynamic Adaptive Replica Allocation Algorithm in Mobile Ad Hoc Networks[*]

Yijie Wang and Kan Yang

National Laboratory for Parallel and Distributed Processing, Institute of Computer,
National University of Defense Technology, Changsha, China, 410073
wwyyjj1971@vip.sina.com

Abstract. Power conservation and extending survival time are critical issues in mobile ad hoc networks, as the nodes are powered by battery only. In this paper, according to the mobility of nodes, the survival-time-based adaptive replica allocation algorithm is proposed. In the survival-time-based dynamic adaptive replica allocation algorithm, based on the locality of data access, the replica allocation scheme is adjusted regularly in order to reduce the power consumption, and thus extend the survival time of network. The relation between mobility models and efficiency of survival-time-based dynamic adaptive replica allocation algorithm is studied. The results of performance evaluation show that the survival-time-based dynamic adaptive replica allocation algorithm can reduce the total power consumption of network greatly and extend the survival time of network evidently.

1 Introduction

The mobile ad hoc networks [1] (MANET) consist of a collection of wireless nodes without a fixed infrastructure. In addition to the issues associated with a mobile network, the power consumption and mobility of the server(s) must also be considered in a MANET. While data replication is very effective for improving the data availability, mobile nodes generally have poor resources and it is impossible for mobile nodes to have replicas of all data items in the network.

At present, several algorithms are proposed for replica allocation in mobile ad hoc networks. Most of the existing algorithms are focused on the data availability during the network division, the power consumption of nodes is not considered sufficiently. The algorithms SAF[2], DAFN[3] and DCG[4] are proposed by Takahiro Hara in Osaka University. In these three algorithms, the access frequency from mobile nodes to each data item and the status of the network connection are taken into account to improve the data availability during the network division. The collection of global information of data access frequency will bring about vast communication cost, especially while the network topology changes frequently. The algorithm [5] proposed by Karen H. Wang in

[*] This work is supported by the National Grand Fundamental Research 973 Program of China (No.2002CB312105), A Foundation for the Author of National Excellent Doctoral Dissertation of PR China (No.200141), and the National Natural Science Foundation of China (No.69903011, No.69933030).

H. Jin, D. Reed, and W. Jiang (Eds.): NPC 2005, LNCS 3779, pp. 503–510, 2005.

Toronto University, the algorithm [6] proposed by Jiun Long Huang in National Taiwan University and the algorithm [7] proposed by Kai Chen in Illinois University are all aimed at the group mobility model, and the replica allocation is decided by the prediction of network division.

In this paper, in view of the power consumption and survival time of nodes, a survival-time-based dynamic adaptive replica allocation algorithm (STDARA) is proposed. Section 2 states the problem and our motivation. Section 3 describes the survival-time-based dynamic adaptive replica allocation algorithm. Section 4 presents the results of performance evaluation. Section 5 provides a summary of our research work.

2 Model and Statement of the Problem

2.1 Power Control

Definition 1. Relay Region
The relay region of a node r for a node s is defined as

$$R(s,r) = \{x | P(s,r) + P(r,x) < P(s,x)\}.$$

$P(s,x)$ is the power incurred if node s directly transmits signal to node x, and $P(s,r) + P(r,x)$ is the power incurred if node s uses the node r as the relay node for transmission from s to node x.

Definition 2. Enclosure Region
The enclosure region of a node s is defined as

$$E(s) = \bigcap_{r \in T(s)} E(s,r)$$

The region $E(s,r)$ is called the enclosure region of node s by node r, it is the complement of region $R(s,r)$. $T(s)$ is the set of nodes lying within the transmission range of node s.

Definition 3. Neighbors
The neighbors of a node s is defined as

$$N(s) = \{y | y \in T(s), y \in E(s)\}$$

The nodes that lie in the enclosure region of s is called the neighbors of s, and they are the only nodes to which s will maintain communication links for power-efficient transmission.

2.2 Data Access

Definition 4. Read-Write Pattern
The read-write pattern for an object O is the number of data access requests (read and write) to O generated by each node in a time interval t.

As the replica allocation is adjusted dynamically according to data access requests, the number of data access requests is weighted in view of the residual power of nodes.

Definition 5. Weighted Number of Read-Write Requests

The weighted number of read requests on object O received by u in the time interval t is

$$read_E(u) = \sum_{i \in N_{receive}(u)} \left(read(i) \times \frac{E_{residual}(i)}{E_{init}(i)} \right)$$

$read(i)$ is the number of read requests on object O generated by node i in the time interval t. $E_{init}(i)$ is the initial power of node i. $E_{residual}(i)$ is the residual power of node i. $N_{receive}(u)$ is the set of nodes, from which the data access requests are transmitted to node u.

The weighted number of write requests on object O received by u in the time interval t is

$$write_E(u) = \sum_{i \in N_{receive}(u)} \left(write(i) \times \frac{E_{residual}(i)}{E_{init}(i)} \right)$$

$write(i)$ is the number of write requests on object O generated by node i in the time interval t.

2.3 Replica Allocation

Definition 6. Replica Allocation Scheme

The replica allocation scheme for an object O is the set of nodes at which O is replicated.

The power consumption of a single read request by node s is

$$P_{read}(s, O) = P(s, \ldots, r_v) = P(s, n_1) + \sum_{i=1}^{u-1} P(n_i, n_{i+1}) + P(n_u, r_v)$$.

r_v is the replica node of object O, which is chosen for read request. n_i (i = 1, 2, …, u) is the relay nodes between s and r_v.

The power consumption of a single write request by node s is

$$P_{write}(s, O) = P(s, \ldots, r_v) + \sum_{r_i \in r\_set(O)} P(r_v, \ldots, r_i)$$.

$r\_set(O)$ is the set of replica nodes of object O. $P(s, \ldots, r_v)$ is the power consumption of update operation on r_v, $\sum_{r_i \in r\_set(O)} P(r_v, \ldots, r_i)$ is the power consumption of update operations on other replica nodes in $r\_set(O)$.

The total power consumption of data access to object O in a time interval t is

$$POWER(O) = \sum_{s \in N} \left(\mathrm{Re}\,ad(s,O) \times P_{read}(s,O) + Write(s,O) \times P_{write}(s,O) \right)$$

$\mathrm{Re}\,ad(s,O)$ is the number of read requests to O in a time interval t, $Write(s,O)$ is the number of write requests to O in a time interval t.

The problem of finding an optimal replica allocation scheme has been proved to be NP-complete for different power consumption models. In this paper, based on the heuristic algorithm, a survival-time-based dynamic adaptive replica allocation algorithm is proposed to find a suboptimal replica allocation scheme.

3 Replica Allocation Considering Survival Time

STDARA is executed periodically and independently in each replica node, the execution cycle is set according to the change of network topology and read-write pattern.

STDARA includes expansion test, switch test and contraction test. The description of STDARA is as follows:

```
//for object O, m∈ r_set(O)
Calculate the neighbors of replica node rn, which is
denoted as N(rn).
for ( u∈N(m) , u∉r_set(O) )
{ // expansion test is done for each neighbor of m,
which is not replica node of object O
      if ( the expansion condition is satisfied )
      { // replica expansion
            r_set(O) = r_set(O) + {u} ;
            return;
      }
}
for ( u∈N(m) , u∉r_set(O) )
{ // expansion test is done for each neighbor of m,
which is not replica node of object O
      if ( the switch condition is satisfied )
      { // replica switch
            r_set(O) = r_set(O) - {m} + {u} ;
            return;
      }
}
for ( m )
{ // contraction test is done for m
      if ( the contraction condition is satisfied )
      { // replica contraction
            r_set(O) = r_set(O) - {m};
            return;
      }
}
```

There are two extreme situations for expansion test (Fig.1).

In Fig.1(a), each shortest path between u and replicas of object O will pass through m. In Fig.1(b), each shortest path between m and other replicas of object O will pass through u. The compromised expansion condition is as follows:

$$\Delta E = \sum_{r \in r\_set(O)} write_E(r) \times P(r,...,u) - (read_E(u) + write_E(u)) \times P(u,m) < 0 \qquad (1)$$

$write_E(r)$ is the weighted number of write requests on object O received by r in the time interval t, $read_E(u)$ is the weighted number of read requests on object O received by u in the time interval t.

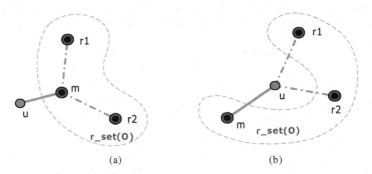

(a)   (b)

Fig. 1. Two extreme situations for expansion test and switch test

There are two extreme situations for switch test (Fig.1).

In Fig.1(a), each shortest path between u and replicas of object O will pass through m. In Fig.1(b), each shortest path between m and other replicas of object O will pass through u. The compromised switch condition is as follows:

$$\Delta E = (read_E(m) + write_E(m)) \times P(u,m) - (2 \times write_E(u) + read_E(u)) \times P(u,m) < 0 \qquad (2)$$

There are two extreme situations for contraction test (Fig.2).

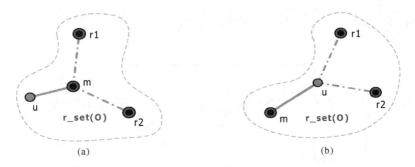

(a)   (b)

Fig. 2. Two extreme situations for contraction test

In Fig.2(a), each shortest path between u and other replicas of object O will pass through m. In Fig.2(b), each shortest path between m and other replicas of object O will pass through u. The compromised contraction condition is as follows:

$$\Delta E = \left(read_E(u) + write_E(u)\right) \times P(u,m) - \sum_{r \in r\_set(O)} write_E(r) \times P(r,...,u) < 0 \qquad (3)$$

4 Performance Evaluation

4.1 Influence of Mobility of Nodes on Efficiency of Survival-Time-Based Dynamic Adaptive Replica Allocation Algorithm

The parameters of test environment are shown in Table 1. We compare STDARA and algorithm ADR-G [8]. In ADR-G, the spanning tree is build to organize replicas. The mobility model of nodes is Random Waypoint Mobility Model [9].

Table 1. Parameters of test environment

parameter	default value
range of movement	1000m×1000m
number of mobile nodes	50
speed of migration	0m/s ~ 10m/s
direction of migration	0 ~ 2π
number of objects	1
interval of algorithm execution	10s
initial number of replica	5
ratio between reads and writes	5:1
initial node power	10×10^3 J
power consumption model	two-ray ground reflection Model (n=4)
antenna	Omni-directional Antenna

In Fig.3, the total mobile node power decreased gradually. Compared with ADR_G, the mean power consumption in STDARA is 35.7% less. In STDARA, the replica allocation scheme is adjusted according to power consumption, so the power consumption is reduced greatly, and the survival time of network is extended evidently.

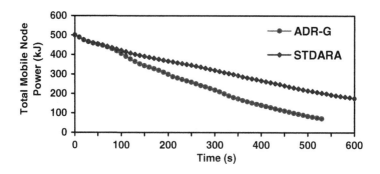

Fig. 3. Mobility of nodes

4.2   Relation Between Mobility Models and Efficiency of Survival-Time-Based Dynamic Adaptive Replica Allocation Algorithm

Three typical mobility models [9] are selected to investigate the relation between mobility models and efficiency of STDARA. Three mobility models are Random Waypoint Mobility Model, Random Gauss-Markov Mobility Model and Reference Point Group Mobility Model, which are denoted as RW, GM and RPG respectively. The parameters of test environment are shown in Table 1. We observe the influence of different mobility models with different speed of migration on efficiency of STDARA.

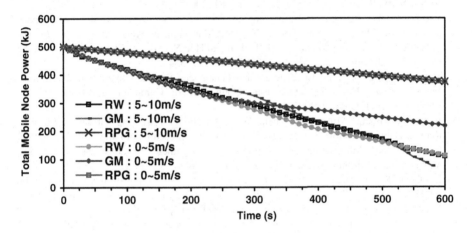

Fig. 4. Mobility models

In Random Waypoint Mobility Model (Fig.4), the power consumption difference between different speeds of migration is little. In Random Gauss-Markov Mobility Model (Fig.4), the speed of migration influences the power consumption obviously. The speed of migration is higher, network topology changed more frequently, if the replica allocation scheme is not adjusted in time, the power consumption will be increased more greatly. In Reference Point Group Mobility Model (Fig.4), only one group is selected, the relative movement between nodes is little, the network topology is relatively stable, thus the replica allocation scheme can be adjusted in time, so the power consumption will not increased greatly.

5   Conclusion

The power consumption and mobility of nodes are significant characteristic of mobile ad hoc network. In the survival-time-based dynamic adaptive replica allocation algorithm, according to the power consumption of nodes, the replica allocation scheme is adjusted regularly, the replicas are distributed evenly among all the nodes, thus extend the survival time of network. The results of performance evaluation show that the survival-time-based dynamic adaptive replica allocation algorithm can reduce the total power consumption of network greatly and extend the survival time of network evidently. The relation between mobility models and efficiency of survival-time-based dynamic adaptive replica allocation algorithm is studied.

References

1. Gruenwald, L., Javed, M., and Gu, M. Energy-Efficient Data Broadcasting in Mobile Ad-Hoc Networks. In Proc. International Database Engineering and Applications Symposium (IDEAS '02), July, 2002.
2. Takahiro Hara. Effective Replica Allocation in Ad hoc Networks for Improving Data Accessibility. Proceeding of IEEE Infocom 2001, 2001, 1568~1576
3. Takahiro Hara. Replica Allocation in Ad hoc Networks with Periodic Data Update. Proceedings of Int'l Conference on Mobile Data Management (MDM 2002), 2002, 79~86
4. Takahiro Hara. Replica Allocation Methods in Ad Hoc Networks with Data Update. Mobile Networks and Applications, MONET, 2003, 8(4):343~354
5. Karen H Wang, Baochun Li. Efficient and Guaranteed Service Coverage in Partitionable Mobile Ad-hoc Networks. IEEE Joint Conference of Computer and Communication Societies (INFOCOM'02), 2002, 1089~1098
6. Jiun-Long Huang, Ming-Syan Chen, Wen-Chih Peng. Exploring Group Mobility for Replica Data Allocation in a Mobile Environment, Proceedings of the 12th International Conference on Information and Knowledge Management, Database Session 3: Data Management in Mobile Environments, 2003, 161~168
7. Kai Chen, Klara Nahrstedt. An Integrated Data Lookup and Replication Scheme in Mobile Ad Hoc Networks. Proceedings of SPIE International Symposium on the Convergence of Information Technologies and Communications (ITCom 2001), 2001, 1~8
8. O Wolfson , S Jajodia , Y Huang . An Adaptive Data Replication Algorithm . ACM Transactions on Database System , 1997 , 22(4):255~314
9. T Camp , J Boleng , and V Davies . A Survey of Mobility Models for Ad Hoc Network Research . Wireless Communication & Mobile Computing (WCMC) , Special Issue on Mobile Ad Hoc Networking , 2002 , 2(5):483~502

Author Index

Lecture Notes in Computer Science

For information about Vols. 1–3685

please contact your bookseller or Springer

Vol. 3733: P. Yolum, T. Güngör, F. Gürgen, C. Özturan (Eds.), Computer and Information Sciences - ISCIS 2005. XXI, 973 pages. 2005.

Vol. 3731: F. Wang (Ed.), Formal Techniques for Networked and Distributed Systems - FORTE 2005. XII, 558 pages. 2005.

Vol. 3729: Y. Gil, E. Motta, R.V. Benjamins, M.A. Musen (Eds.), The Semantic Web – ISWC 2005. XXIII, 1073 pages. 2005.

Vol. 3728: V. Paliouras, J. Vounckx, D. Verkest (Eds.), Integrated Circuit and System Design. XV, 753 pages. 2005.

Vol. 3726: L.T. Yang, O.F. Rana, B. Di Martino, J.J. Dongarra (Eds.), High Performance Computing and Communcations. XXVI, 1116 pages. 2005.

Vol. 3725: D. Borrione, W. Paul (Eds.), Correct Hardware Design and Verification Methods. XII, 412 pages. 2005.

Vol. 3724: P. Fraigniaud (Ed.), Distributed Computing. XIV, 520 pages. 2005.

Vol. 3723: W. Zhao, S. Gong, X. Tang (Eds.), Analysis and Modelling of Faces and Gestures. XI, 4234 pages. 2005.

Vol. 3722: D. Van Hung, M. Wirsing (Eds.), Theoretical Aspects of Computing – ICTAC 2005. XIV, 614 pages. 2005.

Vol. 3721: A. Jorge, L. Torgo, P.B. Brazdil, R. Camacho, J. Gama (Eds.), Knowledge Discovery in Databases: PKDD 2005. XXIII, 719 pages. 2005. (Subseries LNAI).

Vol. 3720: J. Gama, R. Camacho, P.B. Brazdil, A. Jorge, L. Torgo (Eds.), Machine Learning: ECML 2005. XXIII, 769 pages. 2005. (Subseries LNAI).

Vol. 3719: M. Hobbs, A.M. Goscinski, W. Zhou (Eds.), Distributed and Parallel Computing. XI, 448 pages. 2005.

Vol. 3718: V.G. Ganzha, E.W. Mayr, E.V. Vorozhtsov (Eds.), Computer Algebra in Scientific Computing. XII, 502 pages. 2005.

Vol. 3717: B. Gramlich (Ed.), Frontiers of Combining Systems. X, 321 pages. 2005. (Subseries LNAI).

Vol. 3716: L. Delcambre, C. Kop, H.C. Mayr, J. Mylopoulos, Ó. Pastor (Eds.), Conceptual Modeling – ER 2005. XVI, 498 pages. 2005.

Vol. 3715: E. Dawson, S. Vaudenay (Eds.), Progress in Cryptology – Mycrypt 2005. XI, 329 pages. 2005.

Vol. 3714: J. H. Obbink, K. Pohl (Eds.), Software Product Lines. XIII, 235 pages. 2005.

Vol. 3713: L.C. Briand, C. Williams (Eds.), Model Driven Engineering Languages and Systems. XV, 722 pages. 2005.

Vol. 3712: R. Reussner, J. Mayer, J.A. Stafford, S. Overhage, S. Becker, P.J. Schroeder (Eds.), Quality of Software Architectures and Software Quality. XIII, 289 pages. 2005.

Vol. 3711: F. Kishino, Y. Kitamura, H. Kato, N. Nagata (Eds.), Entertainment Computing - ICEC 2005. XXIV, 540 pages. 2005.

Vol. 3710: M. Barni, I. Cox, T. Kalker, H.J. Kim (Eds.), Digital Watermarking. XII, 485 pages. 2005.

Vol. 3709: P. van Beek (Ed.), Principles and Practice of Constraint Programming - CP 2005. XX, 887 pages. 2005.

Vol. 3708: J. Blanc-Talon, W. Philips, D.C. Popescu, P. Scheunders (Eds.), Advanced Concepts for Intelligent Vision Systems. XXII, 725 pages. 2005.

Vol. 3707: D.A. Peled, Y.-K. Tsay (Eds.), Automated Technology for Verification and Analysis. XII, 506 pages. 2005.

Vol. 3706: H. Fuks, S. Lukosch, A.C. Salgado (Eds.), Groupware: Design, Implementation, and Use. XII, 378 pages. 2005.

Vol. 3704: M. De Gregorio, V. Di Maio, M. Frucci, C. Musio (Eds.), Brain, Vision, and Artificial Intelligence. XV, 556 pages. 2005.

Vol. 3703: F. Fages, S. Soliman (Eds.), Principles and Practice of Semantic Web Reasoning. VIII, 163 pages. 2005.

Vol. 3702: B. Beckert (Ed.), Automated Reasoning with Analytic Tableaux and Related Methods. XIII, 343 pages. 2005. (Subseries LNAI).

Vol. 3701: M. Coppo, E. Lodi, G. M. Pinna (Eds.), Theoretical Computer Science. XI, 411 pages. 2005.

Vol. 3700: J.F. Peters, A. Skowron (Eds.), Transactions on Rough Sets IV. X, 375 pages. 2005.

Vol. 3699: C.S. Calude, M.J. Dinneen, G. Păun, M. J. Pérez-Jiménez, G. Rozenberg (Eds.), Unconventional Computation. XI, 267 pages. 2005.

Vol. 3698: U. Furbach (Ed.), KI 2005: Advances in Artificial Intelligence. XIII, 409 pages. 2005. (Subseries LNAI).

Vol. 3697: W. Duch, J. Kacprzyk, E. Oja, S. Zadrożny (Eds.), Artificial Neural Networks: Formal Models and Their Applications – ICANN 2005, Part II. XXXII, 1045 pages. 2005.

Vol. 3696: W. Duch, J. Kacprzyk, E. Oja, S. Zadrożny (Eds.), Artificial Neural Networks: Biological Inspirations – ICANN 2005, Part I. XXXI, 703 pages. 2005.

Vol. 3695: M.R. Berthold, R.C. Glen, K. Diederichs, O. Kohlbacher, I. Fischer (Eds.), Computational Life Sciences. XI, 277 pages. 2005. (Subseries LNBI).

Vol. 3694: M. Malek, E. Nett, N. Suri (Eds.), Service Availability. VIII, 213 pages. 2005.

Vol. 3693: A.G. Cohn, D.M. Mark (Eds.), Spatial Information Theory. XII, 493 pages. 2005.

Vol. 3692: R. Casadio, G. Myers (Eds.), Algorithms in Bioinformatics. X, 436 pages. 2005. (Subseries LNBI).

Vol. 3691: A. Gagalowicz, W. Philips (Eds.), Computer Analysis of Images and Patterns. XIX, 865 pages. 2005.

Vol. 3690: M. Pěchouček, P. Petta, L.Z. Varga (Eds.), Multi-Agent Systems and Applications IV. XVII, 667 pages. 2005. (Subseries LNAI).

Vol. 3689: G.G. Lee, A. Yamada, H. Meng, S.H. Myaeng (Eds.), Information Retrieval Technology. XVII, 735 pages. 2005.

Vol. 3688: R. Winther, B.A. Gran, G. Dahll (Eds.), Computer Safety, Reliability, and Security. XI, 405 pages. 2005.

Vol. 3687: S. Singh, M. Singh, C. Apte, P. Perner (Eds.), Pattern Recognition and Image Analysis, Part II. XXV, 809 pages. 2005.

Vol. 3686: S. Singh, M. Singh, C. Apte, P. Perner (Eds.), Pattern Recognition and Data Mining, Part I. XXVI, 689 pages. 2005.